JEAN SIBELIUS

Jean Sibelius

Tomi Mäkelä

Translated by Steven Lindberg

THE BOYDELL PRESS

An authorised translation and licensed edition of
Jean Sibelius: Poesie in der Luft by Tomi Mäkelä

Geisteswissenschaften International —
Translation Funding for Humanities and Social Sciences from Germany.
A joint initiative of the Fritz Thyssen Foundation, the German Federal Foreign Office,
and the German Publishers & Booksellers Association.

Published 2011
The Boydell Press, Woodbridge

ISBN 978 1 84383 688 9

The Boydell Press is an imprint of Boydell & Brewer Ltd
PO Box 9, Woodbridge, Suffolk IP12 3DF, UK
and of Boydell & Brewer Inc.
668 Mount Hope Ave, Rochester, NY 14620, USA
website: www.boydellandbrewer.com

A catalogue record for this book is available from the British Library.

Papers used by Boydell & Brewer Ltd are natural, recyclable products
made from wood grown in sustainable forests.

FSC www.fsc.org MIX Paper from responsible sources FSC® C013604

Designed and typeset in Minion by
The Stingray Office, Chorlton-cum-Hardy, Manchester

Printed and bound in Great Britain by
CPI Group (UK) Ltd, Croydon CRO 4YY

Contents

Acknowledgements

Edward W. Clark of the UK Sibelius Society was the first to plead for the translation of a 'book written in German by a Finn'. Despite the humanist approach, aiming at the maximum of perspective even for compositions, some German critics celebrated *Jean Sibelius: Poesie in der Luft* as the best music book of 2007. This new English edition was made possible by the 'Geisteswissenschaft International' prize awarded by the Börsenverein des Deutschen Buchhandels, VG Wort, the Federal Foreign Office and the Fritz Thyssen Foundation in 2008.

Of the many commentators who through published reviews contributed to this new edition, at least Jan Brachmann, Andreas Dorschel, Daniel M. Grimley, Norbert Hornig, Hans-Klaus Jungheinrich, Michael Kube, Jürgen Ott, Wolfgang Sandner and Albrecht Thiemann deserve to be mentioned. The author thanks them all for their support. Special thanks go to Herbert Blomstedt, Leon Botstein, Philip Bullock, Andreas Briner, Wolfgang Dömling, Albrecht Dümling, Susanne Fontaine, Peter Franklin, Peter Kislinger, Max Paddison, Derek B. Scott, Timo Virtanen and Manfred Wagner for encouragement and substantial comments.

Even though several books on Sibelius have been published since 2007, and some difficult topics like his supposed affinity to Germany in the 1930s and 1940s have recently been widely discussed, very little needed updating. While revising details for the present edition, valuable help has been received from the translator Steven Lindberg and his research assistant Aimee Lind.

Berlin, May 2011, Tomi Mäkelä

List of Illustrations

Chronology

The Prehistory of Finnish Culture between East and West

1155 The first crusade to Finland was initiated in Uppsala, Sweden; cf. *Scènes historiques*, no. 2 (1899). During the twelfth and thirteenth centuries, Swedish fortresses were built in Åbo (Turku) and Viborg in southern Karelia (1293); cf. *Karelia* Suite, no. 1 (1893).

1266 Birger Jarl, King Valdemar's guardian since 1250, undertakes second crusade to Finland and subjugates Tavastland (Häme); Tavastland Fortress in Tavastehus (Hämeenlinna), where Sibelius was born in 1865, is built in the fourteenth century.

1323 Border between Sweden and Novgorod is established.

1346 Teutonic Knights settle in Reval (Tallinn); their influence is felt, even in Finland, until 1561.

1475 Olavinlinna (Olofsborg) Fortress built on an inland lake (now the site of a festival in Savonlinna).

1488 Printing of *Missale Aboensis* in Lübeck, for diocese, monastery and cathedral in Åbo.

1523 Reign of Gustav I (Gustav Vasa) of Sweden (including the modern-day Finland) begins.

1527 Protestant Reformation in Sweden.

1549 Michael Agricola publishes the first Finnish songbook: *Messu eli Herran Echtolinen.*

1556 Åbo becomes ducal residence; cf. *Scènes historiques*, no. 3 (1899).

1616 Finnish edition of *Piae cantiones* published (begun in 1582).

1640 Founding of university in Åbo.

1642 Finnish translation of the Bible published.

1649 *Linguae finnicae brevis institutio* published.

1721 Sweden loses parts of Finland to Russian in Nordic War; cf. *Scènes historiques*, no. 5 (1899). Population of Finland *c.*390,000 (today over 5 million).

1731 First orchestral concerts in Stockholm with participation of professional musicians.

1807 Napoleon I and Alexander I establish their respective areas of interest. In 1809, following the Finnish War, a minor theatre in the wars between the French-Russian and Swedish-British alliances, Finland becomes a Grand Duchy of Russia. Sweden loses its position as a great power. In Porvoo (Borgå) Alexander I promises the Finnish estates that he will respect the independence of the Grand Duchy ('placé desormais au rang des nations'). In Finland, his speech is interpreted as a basic law; in St Petersburg, as a declaration of intent. In 1827/8, the old capital, Åbo, burns down. Helsingfors (Helsinki) becomes the new capital, designed by Carl Engel according to the principles of his teacher Friedrich Schinkel, Berlin's most prominent architect.

1830 Uprising in Poland against Russia. Birth of Karl Goldmark, Sibelius' teacher in Vienna (d. 1915).

1831 Founding of Suomalaisen Kirjallisuuden Seura (Finnish Literary Society).

1834 Births of Albert Becker, Sibelius' teacher in Berlin (d. 1899), and Aleksis Kivi (Stenvall, d. 1872), early master of Finnish prose.

1835 Fredrik Pacius (1809–1891), a student of Louis Spohr and Moritz Hauptmann from Hamburg and the 'father of Finnish music', becomes director of music at the University of Helsinki. Sibelius will say he lacks the 'Finnish tone'. Elias Lönnrot publishes the *Kalevala*. The first edition contains 12,078 lines; the second edition (1849), 22,795; and the shortened version for schools (1862), 9,732.

1838 Death of Bernhard Henrik Crusell (b. 1775), composer and clarinettist, the first musician from Finland to achieve international success.

1846 Birth of Martin Wegelius (d. 1906), founder of the Music Institute in Helsinki (1882) and Sibelius' first composition teacher.

1847 Birth of Robert Fuchs (d. 1927), Sibelius' composition teacher in Vienna in 1890/1.

1848 Flora's Day is celebrated in Helsinki on 13 May. The idea of 'Finland' is expressed, and the future national anthem, *Vårt land* (1846, music by Pacius, text by Zachris Topelius), is performed. The ballads of Runeberg's *Fänrik Ståhls sägner* are published.

1849 Birth of August Strindberg (d. 1912), author of *Svanevit*; cf. Sibelius' incidental music in op. 54.

1851 The World's Fair in London celebrates the industrial aesthetic. In reaction, a concept of art (with regional hue) evolves that will influence world's fairs after 1889.

1852 Pacius' opera *The Hunt of King Charles* (text by Topelius) premiered. Birth of Hermann Czillag (aka Csillag-Stern), Sibelius' Hungarian violin teacher in Helsinki (d. *c.*1927 in Vienna).

1854 Eduard Hanslick's *Vom Musikalisch-Schönen* published in Vienna.

1855 The Crimean War reaches Finland's southern coast. In order to attack St Petersburg, the Western alliance has to pass Helsinki's island fortress, Sveaborg (Suomenlinna).

1856 Saimaa Canal built between Baltic Sea and inland lakes. Births of Russian composer Sergey Taneyev (d. 1915); Finnish conductor and composer Robert Kajanus, Sibelius' mentor (d. 1933); and Norwegian composer Christian Sinding (d. 1941).

1857 First dissertation written in Finnish defended at the University of Helsinki. Liszt composes the cantata-symphony *Faust* (cf. Sibelius' *Kullervo* of 1892, Vítežslav Novák's *Storm* of 1910). Births of Heinrich (Harry) Berté, *Singspiel* composer (*Das Dreimäderlhaus*, 1916), student of Fuchs and friend of Sibelius in Vienna in 1890/91 (d. 1924); Edward Elgar (d. 1934); Jenö Hubay (d. 1937); and Ruggiero Leoncavallo (d. 1919). Death of Michael Glinka (b. 1804).

1858 Births of Giacomo Puccini (d. 1924) and Eugène-Auguste Ysaÿe (d. 1931).

1859 Birth of Knut Hamsun (Knut Pedersen), Norwegian author and acquaintance of Sibelius (d. 1952). Death of Louis Spohr (b. 1784).

1860 Robert W. Ekman paints *Ilmatar*, a romantic vision from the *Kalevala*; cf. Sibelius' *Luonnotar*. Aleksis Kivi's *Kullervo* published. Filip von Schantz (1835–1865) composes first music based on *Kullervo*, a theatre-overture, cf. Kajanus' *Kullervo* in 1880 and Sibelius' in 1892. Births of Hugo Wolf (d. 1903); Isaac Albéniz (d. 1909); Ignacy Paderewski (d. 1941); Emil von Reznicek (d. 1945); and Gustav Mahler (d. 1911), who, like Sibelius, studied with Fuchs in Vienna (many study harmony and counterpoint with him, but Sibelius studied 'advanced composition' privately).

1861 Births of Juhani Aho (Brofeldt, d. 1921), a writer and around 1891 Sibelius' rival in love for Aino Järnefelt; Rudolf Steiner (d. 1925); Rabindranath Tagore (d. 1941); M. Enrico Bossi (d. 1925), Italian composer and friend of Sibelius; Anton Arensky (d. 1906); and Ludwig Thuille (d. 1907). Death of Bądarzewska (b. 1834), whose piano piece *La Prière d'une vierge* Sibelius will consider superior to Anton Rubinstein's Piano Trio in 1891.

1862 Railway between Helsinki and Hämeenlinna completed. Founding of *Helsingfors Dagblad* (now *Hufvudstadtsbladet*). Births of Claude Debussy (d. 1918); Arthur Schnitzler (d. 1931); Frederick Delius (d. 1934); conductor Walter Damrosch (d. 1950); and Gustav Klimt (d. 1918).

1863 Second Polish uprising fails, and Poland loses its independence. In Finland the emperor introduces liberalisation measures: Finnish recognised as language of administration, which was immediately implemented by Sibelius' future father-in-law, Governor Alexander Järnefelt. Births of Linda Sibelius, the composer's sister (d. 1932); Adolf Paul (d. 1943), author and friend of Sibelius; Gabriel Pierné (d. 1937); Felix Weingartner (d. 1942); Edvard Munch (d. 1944); Pietro Mascagni (d. 1945); and Alexander Siloti (d. 1945). Death of Jacob Grimm (b. 1785), who had influenced Lönnrot (*Kalevala*).

1864 Edvard Grieg (1843–1907) composes his Symphony in C major. Ludwig II becomes King of Bavaria. Founding of First International in London. Births of Eugen d'Albert (d. 1932); Johan Halvorsen (d. 1935); Richard Strauss (d. 1949); Guy Ropartz (d. 1955); and Alexander Gretchaninov (d. 1956). Death of Giacomo Meyerbeer (b. 1791).

The Young Artist

1865 Edward Whymper climbs the Matterhorn. Premiere of Wagner's *Tristan und Isolde* in Munich. Finland introduces currency independent of the rouble (placed on gold standard in 1878). Birth on 8 December of Johan (Jean, cf. 1886 entry) Christian Julius Sibelius in Hämeenlinna (Finnish calendar has been Gregorian since 1753). Births of Albéric Magnard (d. 1914); Théophyle Ysaÿe (d. 1918); Carl Nielsen (d. 1931); Paul Dukas (d. 1935); Alexander Glazunov (d. 1936), composer of *Finnish Fantasy* (1910); August Ferdinand Ringvall (d. 1941), Sibelius' musician friend in Hämeenlinna; Friedrich Lienhard (d. 1929), precursor of the *Heimatkunst* movement; and Rudyard Kipling (d. 1936).

1866 Austro-Prussian War. Premiere of Smetana's *The Bartered Bride*. Births of Vasily Kalinnikov (d. 1901), whose First Symphony resembles Sibelius' style; Ferruccio Busoni (d. 1924); Erik Satie (d. 1925); Wassily Kandinsky (d. 1944); and Georg Alfred Schumann

(d. 1952), Bruch's successor at the master class in composition of the Akademie der Künste in Berlin in 1913.

1867 Austria-Hungary dual monarchy established. Modest Mussorgsky composes *A Night on Bald Mountain*. Premiere of Verdi's *Don Carlos*. Births of Enrique Granados (d. 1916); Wilhelm Peterson-Berger (d. 1942); Charles Koechlin (d. 1950); and Arturo Toscanini (d. 1957). Death of Charles Baudelaire (b. 1821).

1868 Joseph Joachim (1831–1907) becomes director of a new conservatory in Berlin. Famine and epidemics in Finland. Death of Christian Sibelius (b. 1821), Jean Sibelius' father. Births of Scott Joplin (d. 1917); Max von Schillings (d. 1933); and Heinrich Schenker (d. 1935). Death of Gioacchino Rossini (b. 1792).

1869 Hofoper am Ring in Vienna built and inaugurated in late May with Mozart's *Don Giovanni*. Mily Balakirev (1837–1910) composes piano fantasy *Islamey*. Births of Christian Sibelius (d. 1922), the composer's brother; Siegfried Wagner (d. 1930); Willy Burmester (d. 1933), intended soloist for the premiere of Sibelius' Violin Concerto; Hans Pfitzner (d. 1949); and composer and conductor Armas Järnefelt (d. 1958), Sibelius' brother-in-law. Deaths of Hector Berlioz (b. 1803) and Louis Moreau Gottschalk (b. 1829).

1870 Opening of railway line between Helsinki and St Petersburg. Kivi's *Seven Brothers* (1866) published. Wiener Musikverein built. Haussmann completes modernisation of Paris. Births of Franz (Ferenc) Lehár (d. 1948); Florent Schmitt (d. 1958); Vítežslav Novák, a composer in Prague (d. 1949), who, like Sibelius, was considered as a successor to Fuchs in Vienna in 1912; Louis Vierne (d. 1937); Oscar Straus (d. 1954); and Alfred Hill (d. 1960), composer of *Celtic Symphony* (unpublished).

1871 End of Franco-Prussian War; founding of German Reich and coronation of William I as emperor. Founding of Société Nationale de la Musique in Paris. Birth on 10 August of Aino (Aina) Järnefelt (Sibelius from June 1892) (d. 1969). Births of Wilhelm Stenhammar (d. 1927), Swedish composer and pianist, and Alexander von Zemlinsky (d. 1942), another student of Fuchs.

1872 Sibelius begins school and piano lessons. Finnish National Theatre in Helsinki founded. Max Liebermann paints *Women Plucking Geese*. Births of Alexander Scriabin (d. 1915); Paul Juon (d. 1940), Sibelius specialist at Robert Lienau's publishing house; Ralph Vaughan Williams (d. 1958); and Fritz Kreisler (d. 1962).

1873 Premiere of Bruckner's Third Symphony; in 1891 Sibelius admires the second version. Schopenhauer's complete works and Nietzsche's *Geburt der Tragödie* published. Births of Max Reger (d. 1916); Sergey Rachmaninoff (d. 1943); and Nikolai N. Cherepnin (d. 1945).

1874 Smetana composes *The Moldau*; Saint-Saëns, *Danse macabre*. Premiere of Mussorgsky's *Boris Godunov* (second version). Swiss Swedenborg-Vereinigung founded (in Germany not until 1922; in contrast, the English Swedenborg Society was established in London in 1810). Births of Gustav Holst (d. 1934); Franz Schmidt (d. 1939); Arnold Schoenberg (d. 1951); Sergei Koussewitzky (d. 1951), whose future wife, Natalia (née Ushkov), spent her summers as a child near Sibelius' house, Ainola.

1875 Premiere of Bizet's *Carmen* and Goldmark's *The Queen of Sheba*. Ludwig Bussler's *Harmonielehre in Aufgaben* published; Wegelius teaches Sibelius using Bussler's method

(*Praktische musikalische Kompositionslehre* I–III; 1878–80). Births of Ida Ekman (d. 1942), the muse of Sibelius' Lieder; Mikalojus Konstantinas Čiurlionis (d. 1911); Donald Francis Tovey (d. 1940); and Reynaldo Hahn (d. 1947).

1876 Opening of Bayreuth Festival. Grieg composes music for Ibsen's *Peer Gynt*. Sibelius attends Finnish-language high school in Hämeenlinna. Birth of Aino Ackté (d. 1944); Manuel de Falla (d. 1946); and William Havergal Brian (d. 1972), composer of *Gothic Symphony* (1919/25).

1877 Russian-Turkish War. Publication of Joseph-Arthur Comte de Gobineau's *La Renaissance*, which Sibelius was able to translate at sight when a student. Death of Johan Ludvig Runeberg (b. 1804), the poet Sibelius set most frequently.

1879 Alliance between the German Reich and Austria-Hungary. Anti-Semitism receives official support. Conflict between advocates of Wagner and Brahms intensifies. Albert Neisser isolates the pathogen of gonorrhoea (gonococcus); Sibelius will later boast of having suffered from it. Births of John Ireland (d. 1962) and Cyril Scott (d. 1970).

1880 Mahler completes *Das klagende Lied*. Kajanus composes *Kullervo's Death*. Böcklin paints *The Isle of the Dead*. Socio-critical newspaper *Valvoja* founded in Helsinki. Czech language is granted a status equal to German in Bohemia and Moravia. Émile Zola's *Le Roman expérimental* published. The final instalments of *Nana* (1879/80) published in *Le Voltaire* and as a book. Twenty years later Sibelius will advise his wife to ignore this work, even though he had been inspired by *Thérèse Raquin* (1867) as a student. Philipp Spitta finishes his biography of Bach. Death of Jacques Offenbach (b. 1819).

1881 Debussy spends summer with Nadezhda von Meck in Moscow. Otto Lessmann (b. 1844) takes over as editor of *Allgemeine Musikzeitung*; in 1901 he will help Sibelius achieve his breakthrough in Germany. Birth of Béla Bartók (d. 1945). Assassination of Tsar Alexander II (b. 1818). Deaths of Modest Mussorgsky (b. 1839) and Henri Vieuxtemps (b. 1820).

1882 Premiere of Wagner's *Parsifal*. Sibelius learns the violin, reads Adolf Bernhard Marx and composes short pieces. Wegelius founds the Music Institute (today's Sibelius Academy) in Helsinki. Kajanus founds Orchestra Society in Helsinki (first concert on 3 October; name changes to Philharmonic Orchestra in 1895 and to Orchestra of the City of Helsinki in 1914). Births of Karol Szymanowski (d. 1937); Percy Grainger (d. 1961); Zoltán Kodály (d. 1967); and Igor Stravinsky (d. 1971).

1883 Opening of Metropolitan Opera in New York. Death of Richard Wagner (b. 1813).

1884 Mahler composes *Lieder eines fahrenden Gesellen*. First performance of a composition by Richard Strauss (Symphony in F minor) in the United States (New York). Premiere of Massenet's *Manon*. Huysmans's *À rebours* and Tolstoy's *What I Believe* published. Construction begins of Parliament in Berlin. Deaths of Bedřich Smetana (b. 1824) and Lönnrot (b. 1802).

1885 Nietzsche's *Also sprach Zarathustra* and Friedrich von Hausegger's *Die Musik als Ausdruck* published. Premiere of Johannes Brahms's Fourth Symphony and Johann Strauss's *Der Zigeunerbaron* in Vienna as well as Kajanus' *Aino* as part of a *Kalevala* celebration in Helsinki. Edelfelt paints portrait of Louis Pasteur. The Sibelius family (mother Maria and three young children) moves to Helsinki; Johan (1886 'Jean') studies law and music. Death of Victor Hugo (b. 1802).

1886 Suicide of Ludwig II of Bavaria (after being declared incapacitated). The Berne Convention on copyright is signed by Germany (but not by Russia, including modern-day Finland). Johan — now calling himself 'Jean' — begins to use the calling cards of his uncle Johan 'Jean' Sibelius and meets Adolf Paul. Death of Franz Liszt (b. 1811).

1887 Neutrality pact between Germany and Russia. Tensions between those countries strengthen the Finnish independence movement, whose leaders look to Germany. In 1894 Russia allies with France (against Austria-Hungary as well). *Münchener Beobachter* (known after the First World War as *Völkischer Beobachter*) begins publication; in 1923 the Sibelius connoisseur Alfred Rosenberg will become its editor-in-chief. Death of Alexander Borodin (b. 1833).

1888 William II becomes German emperor. Sibelius composes *Lovisa* Trio and meets Busoni, who has come to Helsinki for two years to teach piano, and Aino Järnefelt. The first composition Sibelius will publish, the song 'Serenad' (text: Runeberg) is written. Brahms abandons his plans for an opera; Satie composes *Gymnopédies*. Nietzsche's *Der Fall Wagner* published; work on *Der Antichrist* and *Ecce Homo*.

1889 Henri Bergson's *Essai sur les données immédiates de la conscience* published. The Eiffel Tower in Paris is completed for the World's Fair; Debussy hears Javanese gamelan performed there. Premiere of Franck's Symphony in D minor and original version of Mahler's *Titan* (early version of his First Symphony). Sibelius plays second violin in Schumann's Piano Quintet, op. 44 (Busoni at the piano). Wegelius introduces Busoni to Liszt's music; Busoni performs Liszt's *Don Juan* Fantasy. Premiere of Sibelius' String Quartet in A minor in Helsinki in May. In autumn begins private studies with Albert Becker in Berlin. Baron Heinrich von Herzogenberg (1843–1900) again takes over direction of a master class for composition in Berlin after a long period of illness. Birth of Adolf Hitler (d. 1945).

1890 Bismarck (the 'Iron Chancellor') dismissed; the Wilhelmine era begins. Strauss composes *Tod und Verklärung*. Founding of Socialist International; 1 May declared a holiday. Founding of Freie Bühne in Berlin, which will become important for Scandinavian Modernism. Premiere of Gerhart Hauptmann's drama *Vor Sonnenaufgang*. Paul's *En bok om en människa*, a literary portrait of Sibelius, published. In Berlin, Sibelius hears Kajanus' *Aino* (1885) and Richard Strauss's *Don Juan* (1889). Engaged to Aino and beginning in October studies in Vienna with Fuchs and Goldmark. (Metropolitan Vienna has 19 districts and 1,364,000 inhabitants. In 1900 there will be 1,727,073 inhabitants; in St Petersburg, there are 1,260,000 in 1897; Berlin already has 1,888,848 by then, with only 826,341 around 1871. The largest metropolis on the European continent around 1900 is Paris, with *c.*2,700,000 inhabitants; London already has 6,506,954 in 1901. In New York there are 3,437,202 in 1900. Helsinki did not reach 100,000 until around 1900, half of whom were Swedish-speakers.) Hermann Bahr's *Zur Kritik der Moderne* and Max Klinger's *Malerei und Zeichnung* published. Premiere of Mascagni's *Cavalleria rusticana* in Rome; Sibelius hears the opera in Vienna in 1891 and is, like Janáček, fascinated by it. Ibsen writes *Hedda Gabler*. Juhani Aho's *Yksin* (Alone) published as a declaration of love to Aino Järnefelt, Sibelius' later fiancée. Daily newspaper *Päivälehti* (today's *Helsingin Sanomat*) founded. Gallén (Gallen-Kallela) paints first version of his *Aino* triptych. Birth of Jacques Ibert (d. 1962). Deaths of César Franck (b. 1822) and Niels Gade (b. 1817); suicide of Crown Prince Rudolf von Habsburg.

Beginning of Independence

1891 Johann Strauss junior composes the waltz *Gross-Wien*. Publication of Felipe Pedrell's manifesto *Por nuestra música*, whose ideas will return in Sibelius' sample lecture in 1896. Wegelius published a Swedish-language history of Western music, in which he declared that 'the history of Finland's music must first occur before it can be written'. Sibelius seeks a position with the Vienna Philharmonic. Premieres of *Scène de ballet* and Overture in E major, orchestral works written in Vienna, with Kajanus conducting in Helsinki, repeated in the autumn under Sibelius (his conducting debut). Sibelius hears Larin Paraske singing *runos*. Wolf composes *Spanisches Liederbuch*. Huysmans's *Là-bas* published. Premiere of Arthur Sullivan's (1842–1900) opera *Ivanhoe* in London. Max Bruch (1838–1920) takes over the master class in composition at the Akademie der Künste in Berlin; Ernst Mielck (1877–99), among others, studies with him.

1892 Premiere of Sibelius' *Kullervo* (the third *Kullervo*-based composition after Schantz and Kajanus) in Helsinki. Sibelius weds Aino Järnefelt on 10 June. The couple honeymoon in Savo-Karelia. Sibelius visits folk musicians. Munch exhibits in Berlin; the exhibition is forced to close on grounds of moral indecency. Premiere of Leoncavallo's *Pagliacci*. Founding of the Munich Secession. German premiere of Tchaikovsky's *Eugen Onegin* under Mahler in Hamburg. Use of local language in religious instruction is prohibited in Poland. Death of Édouard Lalo (b. 1823).

1893 Premiere of first version of Sibelius' *En saga* (second version in 1902). Plans for an opera. Premiere of Dvořák's Ninth Symphony. Munch paints *The Scream*. Freie Künstlervereinigung founded in Berlin. Tolstoy's *The Kingdom of God Is Within You* published. Birth of Alfred Rosenberg in Reval (d. 1946). Deaths of Ferenc Erkel (b. 1810); Tchaikovsky (b. 1840), after completing his Sixth Symphony; and Charles Gounod (b. 1818).

1894 Coronation of Tsar Nicholas II. Dreyfus Affair begins in Paris. Founding of the Nietzsche Archive in Weimar. Complete edition of Palestrina concluded. Sibelius travels via Cologne and Mainz to the Bayreuth Festival and continues on to Munich and Venice. Conceives four orchestral *Lemminkäinen Legends*. Debussy composes *Prélude à L'Après-midi d'un faune* to Mallarmé's eclogue 'L'Après-midi d'un faune' (1876); Reznicek composes *Donna Diana*. Busoni settles in Berlin (after stays in Helsinki, Moscow and Boston). Death of Anton Grigorjevitš Rubinstein (b. 1829).

1895 Karl Marx's *Das Kapital* and Josef Breuer's *Studien über die Hysterie* published. Premiere of Mahler's Second Symphony in Berlin. The journal *Pan* published in Berlin (Symbolism and Jugendstil). Members of the eponymous artists' association include Dehmel, Liebermann, von Stuck, and Hartleben. Sibelius participates in the publication of A. A. Borenius' *Kalevala* (Lähteenkorva). First film showings in Berlin and Paris. In a joint exhibition with Munch, Gallen-Kallela shows *Symposium* (1894), which features Sibelius among others, at the Salon Ugo Baroccio (Berlin; Unter den Linden).

1896 The Grosse Berliner Gewerbeausstellung (Great Berlin trade exhibition) is held. The Wandervogel youth group is initiated in Berlin-Steglitz. Premiere of Puccini's *La Bohème*; Umberto Giordano's (1867–1948) *André Chenier*; Sibelius' *Jungfrun i tornet* and *Lemminkäinen Legends*; Alfred Jarry's *Ubu roi*; and Oscar Wilde's *Salomé*. Sibelius applies for position as director of music (official title is 'music teacher') at the University of Helsinki with a lecture on the influence of folk music on art music. Deaths of Alexander Järnefelt (b. 1833), Sibelius' father-in-law, general, governor and senator; Anton Bruckner (b. 1824); and Clara Schumann (b. 1819; née Wieck).

1897 Founding of Viennese Secession. Mahler becomes artistic director of the Wiener Hofoper. Decree of equality of Czech and German languages in Bohemia is proclaimed in Vienna. Gallen-Kallela completes his *Lemminkäinen* project with *Lemminkäisen äiti* (Lemminkäinen's mother). Sibelius visits Berlin and Italy. Dukas composes *L'apprenti sorcier*. Hugo Wolf becomes mentally ill. Deaths of Minna Canth (b. 1844) in Kuopio, socio-critical writer and friend of Aino's mother, and of Brahms (b. 1833).

1898 Climax of Dreyfus Affair: Zola's open letter 'J'accuse: Lettre au Président de la République' is published in the newspaper *L'Aurore* on 13 January and 300,000 copies are sold. Of the Nordic composers, Grieg responds strongly to these events. Founding of Berlin Secession. Strauss initiates the founding of the Genossenschaft deutscher Tonsetzer and is appointed Royal Prussian Director of Music in Berlin. Nikolay Bobrikov becomes Finland's governor-general and begins to place limits on the region's special status. Sibelius composes incidental music to Paul's *King Christian II* and negotiates with Breitkopf & Härtel in Leipzig. Gabriel Fauré (1845–1924) composes *Pelléas et Mélisande*. Death of Theodor Fontane (b. 1819).

1899 A Russian manifesto on restricting Finland's autonomy influences the mood in Finland. Sibelius composes the *War Song of Tyrtaeus*, literally 'Song of the Athenians', and *Scènes historiques* (the most famous of which is the final one, which became the tone poem *Finlandia* and derives from the choral hymn on Veikko Antero Koskenniemi's and Wäinö Sola's texts). Premiere of Sibelius' First Symphony in Helsinki in April. Schoenberg composes *Verklärte Nacht*, Debussy his *Nocturnes* and Elgar his *Enigma Variations*. Chamberlain's *Die Grundlagen des XIX. Jahrhunderts* and Tolstoy's *Resurrection* published. Karl Kraus founds the journal *Die Fackel* and Freud publishes *Die Traumdeutung* (*The Interpretation of Dreams*; the title-page has the date 1900). Eero Järnefelt paints *Autumn Landscape near Pielisjärvi* (Mount Koli) and Gallen-Kallela his *Kullervo's Curse*. Oskar Merikanto (1868–1924), also known as a Lied accompanist, organist and essayist, composes the first Finnish-language opera *Pohjan neiti*. His son Aarre (1893–1958) will later set different standards with his opera *Juha* (1922). Heinrich Wölfflin's *Die klassische Kunst* published, inspiring the reception of antiquity. August Bungert (1845–1915) in Berlin works on his tetralogy *Homerische Welt* (1898–1903). Death of Johann Strauss junior (b. 1825). The Golden Age of the operetta (Strauss, Suppé, Zeller and Millöcker die prior to 1900) transitions into the Silver Age (Oscar Straus, Lehár, et al.).

1900 Adolf Harnack's *Das Wesen des Christentums* contains 'conception of the Greek spirit on the foundation of the Gospel'. Lienhard's *Die Vorherrschaft Berlins* articulates the ideology of *Heimatkunst* ('homeland art'). Thomas Mann publishes *Buddenbrooks*.

First Peace Conference in The Hague (second in 1907). Premieres of Puccini's *Tosca* and Charpentier's *Louise*. Engelbert Humperdinck (1854–1921) appointed lecturer in composition in Berlin. Second version of Sibelius' First Symphony. Contact between Sibelius and Baron Axel Carpelan, then journey to Paris to the World's Fair with the Philharmonic Orchestra of Helsinki via Copenhagen, Berlin and Brussels. Russian Pavilion attracts attention with the Trans-Siberian Railway. The Métro is inaugurated in Paris. Graf von Zeppelin experiments with airship at Lake Constance. Sibelius family travels via Berlin to Italy (1901), where Sibelius reflects deeply on aesthetics, in part in relation to classical antiquity. Sibelius' orchestral works — including *The Swan of Tuonela* and *Finlandia* — are prepared for publication by Breitkopf & Härtel in Leipzig. Death of Friedrich Nietzsche (b. 1844).

The Turn

1901 Alberto Santos-Dumont flies from Saint-Cloud to the Eiffel Tower. Strauss appointed first chairman of the Allgemeiner Deutscher Musikverein in Heidelberg, where two *Lemminkäinen Legends* are performed as new works with Sibelius conducting. Prior to the performance works on *Pohjola's Daughter* and Second Symphony in Rapallo and Rome. On return journey visits Vienna; Prague, where he meets Dvořák (1841–1904) and Josef Suk (1874–1935); Dresden; and Berlin. Sibelius' first orchestral performance (*King Christian II* Suite) in the United States (Cincinnati) under Frank Van der Stucken. Two *Lemminkäinen Legends* are performed in Chicago under Theodore Thomas and in New York under Emil Paur. Sibelius ends teaching activity at Kajanus' orchestral school. Premiere of Debussy's *Nocturnes*. Rachmaninoff writes his Piano Concerto in C minor. Universal Edition founded. In Berlin, the Siegesallee project — also known as Emperor William's Doll Avenue — is completed: 'Art should contribute to having an educational effect on the people.' Birth of Edmund Rubbra (d. 1986), a British follower of Sibelius. Deaths of Giuseppe Verdi (b. 1813); Ludwig Bussler (b. 1838); and Arnold Böcklin (b. 1827). Death of Queen Victoria (b. 1819).

1902 Steiner takes over as director of the German section of the Theosophical Society. Klimt presents his *Beethoven Frieze*. Berlin inaugurates its Underground. Mahler composes his Fifth Symphony. Premier of Sibelius' Second Symphony in Helsinki. Sibelius conducts *En saga* as part of Busoni's 'rarities concert' in Berlin. Henry Wood and Felix Weingartner discover Sibelius. Premiere of Debussy's *Pelléas et Mélisande* in Paris. Strindberg writes the drama *Svanevit*, for which Sibelius will compose incidental music in 1908–9.

1903 Anstalt für musikalische Verwertungsrechte in Deutschland begins work. Sibelius composes the first version of his Violin Concerto and *Valse triste*, as part of the incidental music to Järnefelt's *Kuolema*. Premiere of Janáček's *Jenůfa* and d'Albert's *Tiefland*. First volume of Eino Leino's *Helkavirret* (Helka Songs; vol. 2 follows in 1916) and Otto Weininger's *Geschlecht und Charakter* published. Sibelius' house, Ainola, is conceived in Tuusula (Tusby) by Lars Sonck. Birth of Theodor W. Adorno (d. 1969). Death of Paul Gauguin (on a South Pacific island).

1904 Russo-Japanese War. Zemlinsky and Schoenberg found the Vereinigung schaffender

Tonkünstler (Society of creative musicians) in Vienna. First American performance of Mahler (Fourth Symphony) in New York under Damrosch. First American performance of a Sibelius symphony, Second Symphony under Van der Stucken in Chicago. Premiere of the Violin Concerto (first version) in Helsinki. Family moves into Ainola. Sibelius begins composing Third Symphony. Busoni composes Piano Concerto with final chorus. Death of Governor-General Bobrikov in Helsinki (assassinated by Eugen Schauman); in 1909 Sibelius will compose *In memoriam* for Schauman. Deaths of Eduard Hanslick (b. 1825) and Anton Chekhov (b. 1860).

1905 General strike in many Russian cities and in Helsinki as well. Fritz Schaudinn and Erich Hoffmann identify the pathogen for syphilis, Treponema pallidum; toxic remedies are available beginning in 1909. In Vienna in 1891, Sibelius claimed he had had an 'Eierstocks Entzündung' — a wordplay on the male (*Stock*, or 'stick', and even *Eier* or 'eggs', a slang word for 'testicles') versus female sex organs (correctly, *Eierstöcke*) — as well as 'two bouts of syphilis' and gonorrhoea several times. Sibelius conducts his Second Symphony in Busoni's concert series in Berlin and signs a contract with Robert Lienau. Premiere of Sibelius' music for *Pelléas et Mélisande* (text by Maeterlinck; translated by Bertel Gripenberg) and of Schoenberg's *Pelleas und Melisande*. Sibelius gives concerts in Liverpool. Makes acquaintance of Rosa Newmarch. Premiere of new version of Violin Concerto in Berlin under Strauss. Disbanding of Viennese Secession; founding of Die Brücke artists' association in Dresden. Picasso paints circus themes; Mata Hari dances in Paris. Sibelius visits Paris for a second time. Premieres of Strauss's *Salome* and Lehár's *Die lustige Witwe*. Novák — a leading figure in Czech Modernism, teacher of Hába (among others), and, like Suk, a master student of Dvořák's — composes the symphonic poem *Von ewiger Sehnsucht* (after Andersen), employing the symbols of the moon, the sea and a swan (desire, rising to unattainable ideals) and with parallels to, among other works, Strauss's *Also sprach Zarathustra* (1896). Premier of Debussy's *La Mer*. Births of Karl Amadeus Hartmann in Munich (d. 1963) and Eduard Tubin (d. 1982) in Kallaste (Estonia). Death of Finnish painter Albert Edelfelt (b. 1854). Sibelius composes *Ej med klagan* (text by Runeberg) for mixed choir in memory of Edelfelt.

1906 Hundred-and-fiftieth anniversary of Mozart's birth, a milestone in contemporary interest in Classicism in music (in Sibelius' case, the Third Symphony). Premiere of *Pohjola's Daughter*. Sibelius composes German Songs, op. 50 (Dehmel et al.). Newmarch's book on Sibelius published and translated into German. Death of Henrik Ibsen (b. 1828).

1907 Kokoschka's *Mörder, Hoffnung der Frauen* and Busoni's *Entwurf einer neuen Ästhetik der Tonkunst* published. Premieres of Schoenberg's First String Quartet and First Chamber Symphony in Vienna and Sibelius' Third Symphony in Helsinki. Mahler conducts Kajanus' orchestra and hears Sibelius' compositions in a series of popular concerts. The same year Mahler moves from Vienna to New York. Bossi also conducts in Finland. Sibelius visits Berlin, where Weingartner conducts the First Symphony.

1908 Picasso and Braque invent Analytic Cubism. Sibelius conducts the Third Symphony in London and conceives *Voces intimae*. Premiere of Schoenberg's Second String Quartet. Sibelius begins an extended period of abstinence following a throat operation. Wilhelm Bopp (1863–1931), founder of the Musikhochschule Mannheim, is appointed director of the Wiener Konservatorium der Musikfreunde and defends Schoenberg — 'despite his compositions' — and Neoclassical Modernism. In 1912 Bopp contacts Sibelius regarding a professorship in composition. Deaths of Nikolay Rimsky-Korsakov (b. 1844) and Pablo de Sarasate (b. 1844).

Masterpieces and Crises

1909 Marinetti's *Futurist Manifesto* published; Strauss's *Elektra* premiered. Sibelius travels to England, conducts *En saga* and *Finlandia* in London and visits Paris and St Petersburg. Meets Debussy in London and begins diary (entries until 1943/4). Meets Max Reger in Berlin. Term of contract with Lienau ends, and he begins working directly with Breitkopf & Härtel. Travels to Koli massif in North Karelia with Eero Järnefelt. First ideas for Fourth Symphony ('wanderer's ideas'). Olin Downes writes of the Second Symphony: 'a nation becomes articulate'. Niemann dedicates *Das Nordlandbuch* to Hugo Riemann and states: 'In Sibelius, Finnish art has found its most splendid expression of personality.'

1910 Passing of Halley's Comet. Kandinsky paints abstracts paintings. Oskar von Hase, proprietor of Breitkopf & Härtel, launches Anstalt für mechanisch-musikalische Rechte, a precursor of GEMA. Premieres of Debussy's *Iberia* and Novák's 'sea fantasy' *Storm* (text by Svatopluk Čech, 1869). Vaughan Williams composes his *Sea Symphony* and Busoni his *Fantasia contrappuntistica*. Premiere of Stravinsky's *Firebird* by Sergey Diaghilev's Ballets Russes in Paris and Sibelius' *Voces intimae* in Helsinki. Sibelius follows with *The Dryad* and a new version of *Origin of Fire* and sketches for a song on Poe's 'The Raven'. Sibelius' name appears for the last time in the list of instructors at the conservatory, having previously been listed from 1892 to 1900 and from 1907 as teacher of music theory and composition and from 1892 to 1894 of violin performance. Birth of Samuel Barber (d. 1981). Death of Leo Tolstoy (b. 1817).

1911 Schoenberg's *Harmonielehre* and Guido Adler's *Der Stil in der Musik* published. *Voces intimae* performed in Leipzig und Berlin in January by the Sevčik Quartet. Premiere of the Fourth Symphony in Helsinki. Remodelling in Ainola. Mahler falls ill in February and is unable to conduct a planned performance of Sibelius' Violin Concerto in New York. Premier of Strauss's *Der Rosenkavalier* in Dresden and Siegmund von Hausegger's (1872–1948) *Natursymphonie* in Zurich. Charles Villiers Stanford (1852–1924) composes Seventh Symphony, op. 124, and Piano Concerto, op. 126. Sibelius visits Berlin, Paris and Sweden. Death of Johan Svendsen (b. 1840), Kajanus' composition teacher.

1912 Sinking of *Titanic*. Apollinaire in Paris calls for the formation of an 'avant-garde'. Kandinsky and Marc found *Der blaue Reiter*. Hauptmann receives the Nobel Prize for Literature. Kandinsky's *Über das Geistige in der Kunst* and Nadler's *Literaturgeschichte der deutschen Stämme* published (4th vol. in 1928). Premieres of Schoenberg's *Pierrot lunaire* in Vienna and Mikalojus Konstantinas Čiurlionis's symphonic poem *Miške* (In the forest) in St Petersburg. Sibelius composes three Sonatinas for Piano. Declines to succeed Robert Fuchs at the Hochschule für Musik in Vienna. The Vienna Philharmonic refuses to perform Sibelius' Fourth Symphony, which had already been announced. (The work was not performed in Vienna until 1970 — by the Wiener Symphoniker.)

1913 Premieres of Stravinsky's *Le Sacre du printemps* and Schoenberg's *Gurre-Lieder*. Proust begins *À la recherche du temps perdu* (completed in 1927). Premieres of Sibelius' *The Bard* and *Luonnotar* by Aino Ackté (soprano) in Gloucester. Karl Muck conducts Fourth Symphony in Boston. Death of Felix Draeseke (b. 1835).

1914 Sibelius encounters Schoenberg's works in Berlin. Sibelius' only trip to United States (New York, Norfolk, Niagara); premiere of *The Oceanides* (first version). Strauss awarded honorary doctorate by Oxford and Sibelius by Yale. First World War begins during his return journey. First sketches for Fifth Symphony. Copyright expires on Wagner's works. The International Music Society in Paris, which will soon disband in the wake of the war, is dedicated to medieval music. Kafka writes *Der Prozess*. Reger dedicates his *Vaterländische Ouvertüre* to the army in the 'world war of the German spirit'.

1915 Sibelius ends his abstinence from alcohol. First version of Fifth Symphony completed. Griffith begins the trilogy *The Birth of a Nation* (1915), *The Fall of a Nation* (1916) and *Intolerance* (1916). The Swedish composer and critic Wilhelm Peterson-Berger composes his *Samenland* Symphony; Strauss finishes *Die Alpensymphonie* (sketches begun in 1900). Rosa Newmarch visits Finland — despite world war.

1916 Premiere of second version of Fifth Symphony. Sibelius composes *Humoresques* for Violin and Orchestra. Fourth Symphony heard in Berlin under Oskar Fried. Prokofiev composes *Symphonie classique*; Holst, *The Planets*; Respighi, *Le fontane di Roma*; and Bloch (1880–1959), *Schelomo: Hebraic Rhapsody* for Cello and Orchestra. Social Democratic Party wins majority in Finnish parliament.

Cultural Changes

1917 Revolution in Russia begins in March. United States enters First World War. Declaration of Finnish independence on 6 December. Sibelius works on third version of Fifth Symphony and two other symphonies. Finland's independence recognised by Lenin on 31 December (by the United Kingdom and the United States in 1919). Finland retains the borders of the Grand Duchy until 1945 and thus has more area than it did in 1809. Premiere of Pfitzner's *Palestrina*. Apollinaire publishes *Les Mamelles de Tirésias, drame surréaliste*.

1918 Oswald Spengler's *Der Untergang des Abendlandes* and Heinrich Mann's *Der Untertan* published. Premiere of Stravinsky's *Histoire du soldat*. 'Fraternal and independence war' in Finland. Premiere of Sibelius' *March of the Finnish Jaeger Battalion*. General Carl Gustav Mannerheim, who had been educated in Russia, is named commander-in-chief of the paramilitary troops in Finland. German soldiers land on the southern coast, led by Count von der Goltz. Prince Friedrich Karl von Hessen is chosen as king. First World War ends on 11 November with the Armistice at Compiègne. Collapse of German empire results in the constitutional plans in Finland being altered in favour of a republic. Electricity comes to Ainola. Deaths of Guillaume Apollinaire (b. 1880) and Toivo Kuula (b. 1883), a student of Sibelius.

1919 On 17 July, the republication constitution of Finland is confirmed. Prohibition comes into effect in Finland and the United States (in Finland until 1931 and in the USA until 1933). Pfitzner publishes *Die neue Ästhetik der musikalischen Impotenz*, a significant step in the direction of extreme positions that marks a contribution to splitting the conservative and moderate versions of Modernism. Premiere of Sibelius' Fifth Symphony (final version). In response to advanced hair loss, Sibelius shaves his head and has himself photographed thus for the first time in Copenhagen in June. Deaths of Axel Carpelan (b. 1858), a baron and supporter of Sibelius, and Hugo Riemann (b. 1849), who had paved the way for Busoni to come to Finland.

1920 Founding of National Socialist Party in Munich; Dada fair in Berlin. Hamsun, author of *Markens grøde* of 1917 (translated as *Growth of the Soil* in 1920), among other works, receives the Nobel Prize for Literature. Sibelius turns down the first chair of composition at the Eastman School of Music (USA). Schreker, professor in Vienna since 1912, is appointed rector there. Busoni takes over a master class at the Akademie der Künste in Berlin. Strindberg's *Sokrates Welthistorie* published. Paavo Nurmi's Olympic victories begin, continuing in 1924 and 1928. The young republic has a 'genuinely Finnish' hero.

1921 Hitler becomes chairman of National Socialist Party. Sibelius becomes foreign member of the Akademie der Künste in Berlin. He visits Berlin, the United Kingdom and Norway. Premiere of Janáček's *Káťa Kabanová*. Howard Hanson (1896–1981) composes his 'Nordic' Symphony. Founding of Donaueschinger Kammermusiktage. Nordic Music Days held in Helsinki (for the first time in Finland) under direction of Kajanus. Death of Camille Saint-Saëns (b. 1835).

1922 Mussolini marches on Rome; Stalin becomes general secretary of the Communist Party of the Soviet Union. Founding of International Society for Contemporary Music (ISCM). Sibelius meets Wilhelm Kempff junior in Helsinki. In the same year, Sibelius becomes a Freemason.

1923 Attempted putsch by the National Socialist Party. The exhibition *Neue Sachlichkeit* held in Mannheim. Alfredo Casella and Gian Francesco Malipiero found Corporazione delle Nuove Musiche. Schoenberg announces his new method of twelve-tone composition. Premiere of Sibelius' Sixth Symphony in Helsinki. Sibelius visits Berlin and Rome and vacations on Capri. Otto Taubmann (1859–1929), who had been commissioned by Breitkopf & Härtel to arrange a number of Sibelius' orchestral works for piano, becomes senator of the Akademie der Künste. Zemlinsky composes his *Lyric Symphony*.

1924 André Breton publishes the first Surrealist Manifesto. Premiere of Sibelius' Seventh Symphony in Stockholm. Alban Berg composes his Chamber Concerto. Mann's *Zauberberg* (translated as *Magic Mountain*) published. Death of Lenin (b. 1870).

1925 Sibelius composes music for Shakespeare's *The Tempest*. His artist's pension is increased to the equivalent of 25,000 euros per year. Schoenberg is appointed professor at the Akademie der Künste in Berlin. Aaron Copland (1900–1990), who attacked American imitators of Sibelius, composes *Music for the Theatre*.

1926 Kandinsky publishes *Punkt und Linie zur Fläche* (translated as *Point and Line to Plane*). In Rome and on Capri, Sibelius completes *Tapiola*, which comes across like an emblem of Kandinsky's title, which had been commissioned by Damrosch and the New York Symphony Society. (He also visits Berlin on this trip.) The Social Democratic majority in Finland contributes to political polarisation. Yrjö Kilpinen (1892–1959) composes *Tunturilauluja* (Fjäll songs). Sibelius has a new sauna built at Ainola. Death of Finnish author Eino Leino (b. 1878).

The Artist Withdraws

1927 Passage of new copyright law saves Sibelius' finances; Finland joins the Berne Convention on copyright in 1928. Composes ritual music for Freemasons. The first volume of Hamsun's *Landstrykere* (Wayfarers) trilogy published; Sibelius purchases a copy. Downes visits Finland and Sibelius Paris.

1928 Premiere of staged version of Stravinsky's *Oedipus Rex* in Berlin; Sibelius does not attend. Uuno Klami (1900–1961) composes *Merikuvia* and *3 Bf* (supposedly uninfluenced by Ravel). Anniversary edition of Tolstoy's works published. Birth of Ronald Stevenson, who after 1948 will take an interest in Sibelius' compositions. Death of Leos Janáček (b. 1854).

1929 Sibelius composes Five Sketches for Piano, op. 114. Death of Elisabeth Järnefelt (née Clodt von Jürgensburg 1839), Sibelius' mother-in-law.

1930 Alfred Rosenberg becomes editor of *Nationalsozialistische Monatshefte*. Sibelius purchases a radio. Milhaud composes *Christophe Colombe* and Heitor Villa-Lobos (1887–1959) *Bachianas brasileiras* for cellos. Cecil Gray visits Finland. Koussewitzky commissions from Stravinsky (as he has earlier from Sibelius) a work for the anniversary of his orchestra — though Sibelius probably never learned of this.

1931 Sibelius takes what will be his last trip abroad — to Berlin. Sibelius promises Koussewitzky he will finish the Eighth Symphony for Boston. Edgard Varèse composes *Ionisation*. Deaths of Gallen-Kallela (b. 1865) and Vincent d'Indy (b. 1851).

1932 Beginning of armed uprising of the radical right-wing Lapua movement in Finland, with which Aino Sibelius sympathizes. The Sibelius Society in the United Kingdom produces records with Kajanus (from 1930 on). Death of author Arvid Järnefelt (b. 1861), Sibelius' brother-in-law.

1933 Hitler becomes Chancellor of the Reich; Strauss takes over the Reichsmusikkammer. The largest wave of exiles from Germany begins (Schoenberg and Brecht). In Finland, the extreme right-wing Patriotic People's Movement forms. GEMA becomes STAGMA (then GEMA again from 1947). The existence of a fair copy of parts (23-page score) of Eighth Symphony is documented. Death of Henri Duparc (b. 1848).

1934 Goebbels gives a speech against atonal music and the compositions of Hindemith, and Furtwängler resigns his position as vice-president of the Reichsmusikkammer. Foreign stage names are prohibited in Germany. Kilpinen signs the founding document of the Ständiger Rat für die internationale Zusammenarbeit der Komponisten (Permanent Council for the International Cooperation of Composers, a Nazi counterweight to the ISCM) in Wiesbaden. Strauss becomes founding president; Sibelius, Albert Roussel and Adriano Lualdi are vice-presidents. Sibelius' work on the Eighth Symphony stagnates. Hindemith composes the opera *Mathis der Maler*. Hartmann writes pacifist opera *Des Simplicius Simplicissimus Jugend* (second version in 1955). Birth of Peter Maxwell Davies, whose three symphonies were inspired by Mahler and Sibelius. Death of Franz Schreker (b. 1878).

1935 According to a survey of the listeners to a large radio station in the United States, Sibelius is the most famous contemporary composer. Strauss is dismissed as president of the Reichsmusikkammer. Performance of the third movement of *Kullervo* on the occasion of a joint anniversary of Sibelius and the *Kalevala*. Sibelius receives the silver Goethe Medal from Goebbels. Sibelius performs publicly in Helsinki for the last time. Bartók composes *Music for Strings, Percussion and Celesta* and Hindemith his viola concerto *Der Schwanendreher*. Deaths of Alban Berg (b. 1885) and Max Liebermann (b. 1847).

1936 Berlin–Rome Axis is established. Schoenberg composes his Violin Concerto and Samuel Barber his *Adagio for Strings*. Gottfried von Einem (1918–1996) dedicates his *Adagio for Large Orchestra* to Sibelius. Deaths of Maxim Gorky (b. 1868), who met Sibelius in 1905, and Ottorino Respighi (b. 1879). Outbreak of Spanish Civil War.

1937 *Degenerate Art* exhibition in Munich. Adorno's 'Fussnote über Sibelius und Hamsun' published as contribution to Leo Löwenthal's Hamsun debate in *Die Zeitschrift für Sozialforschung*. Orff composes *Carmina burana* and Picasso paints *Guernica*. Deaths of Eero Järnefelt (b. 1863); Albert Roussel (b. 1869), vice-president, along with Sibelius, of the Ständiger Rat für Internationale Zusammenarbeit der Komponisten; Maurice Ravel (b. 1875); and Finnish composer Erkki Melartin (b. 1875).

1938 *Degenerate Art* exhibition in Düsseldorf. 'Kristallnacht' on 9 November. Adorno publishes his 'Glosse über Sibelius' in exile. Santeri Levas begins working as Sibelius' secretary.

1939 Sibelius conducts for the last time: *Andante festivo* with the Radio Orchestra in Helsinki in a live broadcast on the occasion of the World's Fair in New York. Outbreak of Second World War on 1 September when the Germans march into Poland. On 30 November the Soviet Union attacks Finland, and the 'Winter War' begins. Ermanno Wolf-Ferrari (1876–1949), a member of the Ständiger Rat für internationale Zusammenarbeit der Komponisten, becomes director of the Mozarteum in Salzburg.

1940 End of the 'Winter War' in March: 'Interim peace' until June 1941. Roosevelt abandons neutrality. Bartók completes the *Mikrokosmos* cycle for piano. Toivo Haapanen's *Suomen säveltaide* (History of music in Finland) published. Death of Fini Henriques (b. 1876), a friend of Sibelius when he studied in Berlin. Koskenniemi publishes poem on the *Finlandia Hymn* ('Oi; Suomi; katso; Sinun päiväs koittaa'; previously there had been texts by Finne in 1907 and by Sola in 1938).

1941 War between Germany and the Soviet Union; 'Continuation War' in Finland with assistance from the German Army. Messiaen composes *Quatuor pour la fin du temps*; Krenek, *Lamentatio Jeremiae Prophetae*; and Shostakovich, 'Leningrad' Symphony. Rosenberg becomes Minister of the Reich for the eastern regions. Hitler and Mussolini declare war on the United States. The first dissertation on Sibelius, Eino Roiha's *Die Symphonien von Jean Sibelius*, published.

1942 Founding of Sibelius-Gesellschaft and many concerts in Germany, some conducted by

Furtwängler. Sibelius addresses Berlin audience by radio. Schoenberg composes *Ode to Napoleon.* Stefan Zweig completes *Die Welt von gestern* (translated as *The World of Yesterday*). Deaths of Ernest Pingoud (b. 1888) and Erwin Schulhoff (b. 1894).

1943 Ernst Tanzberger receives a doctorate in Jena for a thesis on Sibelius' symphonic poems. Tubin composes *Sinfonia lirica.* Vaughan Williams completes first version of Fifth Symphony, which is dedicated to Sibelius. Death of Walter von Konow (b. 1866), art historian, who even as a student was fascinated by Sibelius, though the feeling was not mutual.

1944 Of Finland's *c.*4 million inhabitants, 65,000 die in the war, 158,000 are injured and 432,000 are refugees. Finland has to pay high reparations for its participation in the world war, which it continues to do over the years, in contrast to the others also punished thus, in order to demonstrate its economic credibility. Thanks to refugees from Karelia, cultural centres are formed, for example, the Viipurin Musiikkiopisto (Music Institute of Vyborg) in Lahti. Michael Tippett (1905–98) composes *A Child of Our Time* and Copland his *Appalachian Spring.*

The End

1945 Atomic bombs explode over Hiroshima and Nagasaki. Nuremberg trials begin. Sibelius' eightieth birthday celebration reinforces Finnish national emotions. A short film about him is shot in Ainola. Destruction of Eighth Symphony (date uncertain, perhaps in 1943). Deaths of Anton Webern (b. 1883) and Väinö Raitio (b. 1891).

1946 Britten composes *The Young Person's Guide to the Orchestra*; Boulez, his First Piano Sonata. The International Summer Course takes place in Darmstadt for the first time. Schoenberg suffers a 'death' (asthma and heart stoppage) and composes his String Trio, op. 45. Sibelius writes Freemasons' music.

1947 Mann publishes *Doktor Faustus.* Birth of John Adams, who in 1985 will compose the three-part orchestral work *Harmonielehre*, inspired by Sibelius. Deaths of Alfredo Casella (b. 1883) and Leevi Madetoja (b. 1887), Sibelius' most important student.

1948 Berlin Airlift. Sibelius orchestrates his melodrama *Ett ensamt skidspår* (The lonely ski trail) of 1925.

1949 The famous portrait photographs of Sibelius by Yousuf Karsh are produced. Birth of Manfred Trojahn, composer and Sibelius connoisseur. Death of Maurice Maeterlinck (b. 1862).

1950 Schoenberg composes his last works.

1951 First Sibelius Week takes place in Helsinki. Premiere of Stravinsky's *The Rake's Progress.* Shostakovich composes *Twenty-Four Preludes and Fugues* and Charles Ives his *Universe Symphony* (begun in 1911). The artist's pension Sibelius receives is increased to the equivalent of 31,000 euros annually. Thus the republic, weakened in the war, lays claim to possession of Sibelius' work (cf. Downes in 1909: 'a nation becomes articulate'). Deaths of Carl Gustaf Emil Mannerheim (b. 1867) and Selim Palmgren (b. 1878).

1952 Helsinki is modernised to host the Summer Olympics. Miss Universe Armi Kuusela becomes a popular idol in Finland. Birth of Wolfgang Rihm, composer and Sibelius connoisseur. Death of Rued Langgaard (b. 1893), composer of sixteen programmatic symphonies.

1953 Electronic music (at WDR in Cologne) and *musique concrète* (at Radio France in Paris) are developed. Deaths of Sergey Prokofiev (b. 1891); Emmerich Kálmán (b. 1882); Arnold Bax, British composer and Sibelian (b. 1883); and Walter Niemann (b. 1876), who wrote about Sibelius.

1954 Premiere of first two acts of Schoenberg's *Moses und Aron*. Boulez composes *Le Marteau sans maître*. Two *Lemminkäinen Legends* published. Deaths of Wilhelm Furtwängler (b. 1886) and Charles Ives (b. 1874).

1955 Herbert von Karajan becomes principal conductor of the Berlin Philharmonic Orchestra. In Finland the pacifist-realist film *The Unknown Soldier* (based on Väinö Linna's novel) is shown with Sibelius' *Finlandia*, among other works, on the soundtrack. In reaction to a French survey in which Sibelius is considered the best composer, René Leibowitz (1913–1972) claims rather that he is 'le plus mauvais compositeur du monde'. Deaths of Thomas Mann (b. 1875); Ilmari Hannikainen (b. 1892); and George Enescu (b. 1881).

1956 Urho K. Kekkonen elected president. As a journalist in 1948, he had opposed composer Yrjö Kilpinen being named a member of the Finnish Academy. Erik Tawaststjerna (1916–93), pianist and biographer, visits Ainola. Nono composes *Il canto sospeso*. Deaths of Gustave Charpentier (b. 1860); Gottfried Benn (b. 1886), whose Sibelius poem *Valse Triste* (1936) is a document of his own ideological transformation; and Bert Brecht (b. 1898), whose exile took him to Finland.

1957 Jean Sibelius dies on the evening of 20 September 1957. The Finnish population's spontaneous participation in his funeral ten days later surpasses all artists' funerals in history. Premieres of Hindemith's *Harmonie der Welt*; Stravinsky's *Agon*; and Leonard Bernstein's *West Side Story*. Stockhausen composes *Gruppen* and John Cage (1912–92) his Concerto for Piano and Orchestra. Deaths of Othmar Schoeck (b. 1886) and Erich Wolfgang Korngold (b. 1897).

'Does he know anything about music?'

'He talks a music-lover's patter, but his information is shallow. You'll probably find him raising ecstatic eyes to heaven at the name of Beethoven and shuddering piously if someone should be so indiscreet as to mention Ethelbert Nevin.'

'Would he know the difference' — Mark consulted his notebook — 'between "Finlandia" by Si-bee-lee-us and "Toccata and Fugue" by Johann Sebastian Bach?'

'Anyone who can't distinguish between Sibelius and Bach, my dear fellow, is fit for treason, stratagem and spoils.'

'I'm a cluck when it comes to music. Duke Ellington's my soup.' He offered a sheet from his notebook. 'This is what Carpenter told me they were playing on Friday night. He didn't bother to check on the program. This is what they played.'

I drew a sharp breath.

'It shoots his alibi as full of holes as a mosquito net.'

— Mark McPherson and Waldo Lydecker
in Vera Caspary's *Laura* (1942)

ZACHARIAS WERNER [...] Unfortunately, my musical education is not very advanced. If anything, the melancholic majesty of the likes of Jean Sibelius from the Baltic region has appealed to me most.

BEATE Me-lan-cholic majesty? ... Si-be-lius? Please show Mr Werner the door. That name has just been pronounced in our house without disgust. That was the famous tiny step too far that is followed by the certain plunge into the abyss. [...]

ZACHARIAS WERNER Just forget it. I can easily make it right again. [...] I take Sibelius back without hesitation. What's the point? I don't understand anything about music.

— Botho Strauss, *Der Narr und seine Frau heute abend in 'Pancomedia'* (2001)

Preface

It may seem surprising to find a quotation from Botho Strauss's Viennese satire *Der Narr und seine Frau heute abend in 'Pancomedia'* as an epigraph to a monograph on Jean Sibelius,[1] and perhaps even more so an excerpt from the book on which a Hollywood classic of the 1940s, Otto Preminger's *Laura*, was based. In Vera Caspary's psychological thriller *Laura* (1942, p. 46), the source for the film noir of 1944, both Sibelius and Johann Sebastian Bach are part of the capital erudition of a New Yorker, while the uneducated character knows only Duke Ellington. Moreover, the snob rejects Ethelbert Woodbridge Nevin of Boston, who made it on to a ten-cent United States postage stamp in 1940. In Preminger's film, the corresponding scene is more embarrassing for Sibelius. It is said that a concert programme by the New York Philharmonic with Brahms und Beethoven was changed at the last moment and 'nothing but Sibelius' was performed. Who could miss the irony?

The idea present in Strauss's satire — that Sibelius, an artist 'from the Baltic region' with 'melancholic majesty', is the easily digestible diet of an unsophisticated person — will no doubt seem inappropriate to connoisseurs and lovers of his music. Some will suspect that the Botho Strauss reference is a recent example of Theodor W. Adorno's pernicious influence on post-war literature in German. Others will be outraged by the image of the life of the educated bourgeoisie that Strauss offers in his satire. Perhaps there are also readers who find the dialogue between the detective Mark McPherson and the famous writer Waldo Lydecker amusing and when faced with Strauss's satire simply lean back casually and think about what the author really wants to say and why he needs Sibelius to say it.

The same questions come up with Adorno, whose critique of Sibelius has been a concern for generations of Sibelius scholars: champions of Sibelius will ask themselves what distinguishes Adorno's oft-cited malice towards Sibelius from his appreciative words for the 'extra-territorial' music of Gustav Mahler, Franz Schreker, Leoš Janáček and Béla Bartók, and why he was not prepared in Sibelius' case to reflect as

[1] Strauss 2001, pp. 79–80. See above, the second epigraph of this preface. The characters are the 'Scriabin sisters', Anja and Beate; the composer Elmar Kitz; and the publisher Zacharias Werner — whose name is an allusion to Friedrich Ludwig Zacharias Werner, a dramatist born in Königsberg (1768–1823) who belonged to Goethe's circle.

subtly on the *Naturzusammenhang* (identity with nature) of the arts as he did in his essays on Wagner.[1]

The real problem for the publisher Zacharias Werner in Strauss's text is that he is uninformed. Werner cannot stand up to the rhetorically skilled but equally uninformed 'Scriabin sisters', Anja and Beate. Aggressive anti-intellectualism — an inedible fruit of the 'fear of knowledge' articulated so elegantly by John Keats, because knowledge is said to hamper aesthetic experience[2] — is not a useful alternative for the naive philistine. Out of lazy habit, he regrets his ignorance rather than standing up for what he likes.

Sibelius may not be the only twentieth-century artist whose popularity has hampered his acceptance by critical intellectuals, but in his case the disparity of popularity and enlightenment, or mythology and contemporaneity, is striking. That goes a long way towards explaining why he has become a plaything for impertinent writers. Because the dramatist Strauss owes no loyalty to Sibelius scholars, who have recently demonstrated analytically the composer's technical refinement, he can employ untenable clichés at the expense of another artist to construct a scene, confident the audience will be amused.

For the few Sibelius connoisseurs in the audience at Strauss's *Pancomedia*, it is all the more bitter to see how few of the others recognize how badly distorted Beate's and Zacharias Werner's images of Sibelius are. Understanding Sibelius' creative processes and intentions is beyond most fans of contemporary Viennese theatre, but prejudices about him are not. One has to be well informed on the matter in question to appreciate the difference between gentle satire on the one side and cynical criticism on the other. Thus Botho Strauss's intention of exposing the behaviour of Beate and Zacharias Werner to be ridiculous by showing how they deal with Sibelius cannot help but fail, since many audience members will associate Sibelius with a lack of education and with the 'Baltic region' without recognising the absurdity of this characterisation.

For decades now, Jean Sibelius has been one of the most frequently performed of those composers who represent the mysterious, always fascinating *fin de siècle* and also the heterogeneous decades of early Modernism. Moreover, Sibelius is one of the very few composers of that era from the Nordic countries whose name is still generally known even outside the music academies. But those who suppose that northern Europe, from Glasgow to Moscow, played a peripheral role in the late phase of Modernism should recall the influence held around 1900 by Grieg, Strindberg, Ibsen, Hamsun, Gogol, Swedenborg, Kierkegaard, Tolstoy and Munch — and Sibelius as well. Several of them receded to the background somewhat in the wake of the later avant-gardes, and only in recent years have they begun to be fully appreciated again.

[1] See Adorno 1985, pp. 35–6; Adorno 1991, p. 137; and chapter 5.2 in the present volume.

[2] See Wind 1985, p. 47.

But now the reconstruction of the cultural history of the modern North has begun,[1] and few artists will profit more from it than Sibelius. Above all, he will benefit from the increasingly tolerant approach to Modernism after the Second World War. This makes it easier to appreciate his contribution.

Only those who know both Swedish and Finnish will have access to everything that Sibelius did, said and thought, including his love letters and his top-secret diary. An even greater limitation than the fact that several publishers in different countries (with no clear centre of gravity) were responsible for disseminating Sibelius' work, is the fact that the original language of most of the essential sources (diaries, letters, notes) is Swedish, which has lessened his presence in that gallery of Western heritage known as 'the canon'. The more we know about an artist, the easier it is to make him interesting again and again. Although it is not difficult to acquire a rudimentary knowledge of Swedish and some Finnish, a moderate level is scarcely sufficient for historical texts and correspondence. Not without reason, Reinhold Brinkmann of Harvard University did not wish to supervise research on Sibelius unless the student was competent in Finnish. On a television programme with Brinkmann, Wolfgang Rihm, a composer with a well-known affinity to Sibelius' scores, reminded him how essential Swedish is for studying Sibelius, but perhaps that does not represent a comparable hurdle.[2]

Only with the assistance of a third party, which would be unusual in the profession, can an author who does not know Finnish or at least Swedish risk a study of Sibelius. The consequences are many, and the linguistic problem has perhaps done more to harm to Sibelius than the occasional verdicts of misguided or irritable critics. The technical difficulties of mastering Sibelius as a subject of study have frustrated academic reception over the years and has left room for prejudices spawned of embarrassment. At the same time, the immense popularity of Sibelius has created a huge market for books on Sibelius.

No matter how general its intended audience, the language problem is also connected to a practical difficulty that every Sibelius book has to confront. It is not easy to choose a specific version or translation of the titles of the works taken, directly or indirectly, from the *Kalevala*. Proper names of (mostly mythological) individual figures (Kullervo, Lemminkäinen, Tiera, Kyllikki, Tapio) and titles other than *Kalevala* (*The Bard*, *En saga*, *The Oceanides*, etc.) may seem unambiguous, but it can be useful to know, for example, that the Finnish word *lempi* means 'love', and that the name Lemminkäinen, the hero of op. 22, is derived from it — hence 'Don Juan of the North'. That does not, however, make it a good idea to refer to the *Lemminkänen Legends* as 'Legends of a Lover'. *The Swan of Tuonela* (*Tuonelan joutsen*), the most popular of the four *Lemminkäinen Legends*, and the Modernist *Tapiola* show how tricky title translations can be. Whereas Finns know that *tuonela* means 'the underworld', and Tapiola

[1] More recently, see Adams, Hoelscher and Till 2001; Davidson 2005; and Grimley 2006.

[2] Brinkmann and Rihm 2001, p. 141.

is the court of the forest god Tapio, the title *The Swan of Tuonela* has confused others. Another bilingual title, *Pohjolas Tochter* (Pohjola's Daughter), was proposed in German by the Berlin publisher Robert Lienau, so that a literal translation ('The Daughter of the North') is hardly justified — and neither is the Finnish version, *Pohjolan tytär*. It does help to know that 'Pohjola' means the North and also that it is a location in the *Kalevala*. In some cases, translation is unproblematic: *Night Ride and Sunrise*, for which Sibelius used the equivalent German title, *Nächtlicher Ritt und Sonnenaufgang*, rather than the Finnish, *Öinen ratsastus ja auringonnousu*.

There are plenty of similar issues with the songs, for which original titles are preferred in the present volume, since there are often competing translations. In general, details such as title, opus number, date are based on Fabian Dahlström's 2003 catalogue of Sibelius' works (unless otherwise indicated). The established English titles are used wherever possible. The main rule is not to translate mythological names (mostly Finnish) and titles with an essential relation to a poem (mostly Swedish). The secondary rule is to respect the fact that some titles are established in English literature and the recording industry, for example, *Kuolema* and *Rakastava*. The beautiful title *Kuolema*, which simply means 'death' in Finnish, makes it clear that sometimes the original title is even weaker in the minds of those who understand it. For anyone not familiar with Finnish, *Kuolema* is a mystical title, and that is the right attitude for listening to, say, *Valse triste*, the most prominent part of the original incidental music for *Kuolema*. Where an English title is possible without loss, it will be used here. The original titles are given in a list of Sibelius' works in the appendix.

In recent years, interpretation of Sibelius has increasingly become the domain of conductors and soloists from Finland. Even apart from the fact that the audiences in many places expect to hear Sibelius from a Finnish conductor, Finnish musicians have indeed been able to help the world rediscover the composer, thanks to a special knowledge they have acquired from their friendly interactions with Finnish scholars and even from their own work in the archives. In contrast to the refined, sometimes brilliant fostering of Sibelius in the years immediately after the war by Herbert von Karajan and Sir Colin Davis, among others (worthy successors to Wilhelm Furtwängler, Bruno Walter, Arturo Toscanini and Serge Koussevitzky), today's conductors have been imaginative in their thoughts about tempi and accentuate 'pedal points' above which 'the thematic material floats, as it were'.[1] On the basis of studies of the sketches, a new Sibelius is being heard, most likely more closely related to the intended version than some of the intuitive efforts in the interim. The authenticity that distinguishes the old recordings by Robert Kajanus is possible once again.

Detailed knowledge of the manuscripts — which Jussi Jalas, a conductor who was Sibelius' stepson, grew up with and which Paavo Berglund, a passionate, self-critical

[1] Sakari Oramo, in Maidt-Zinke 2002, p. 14.

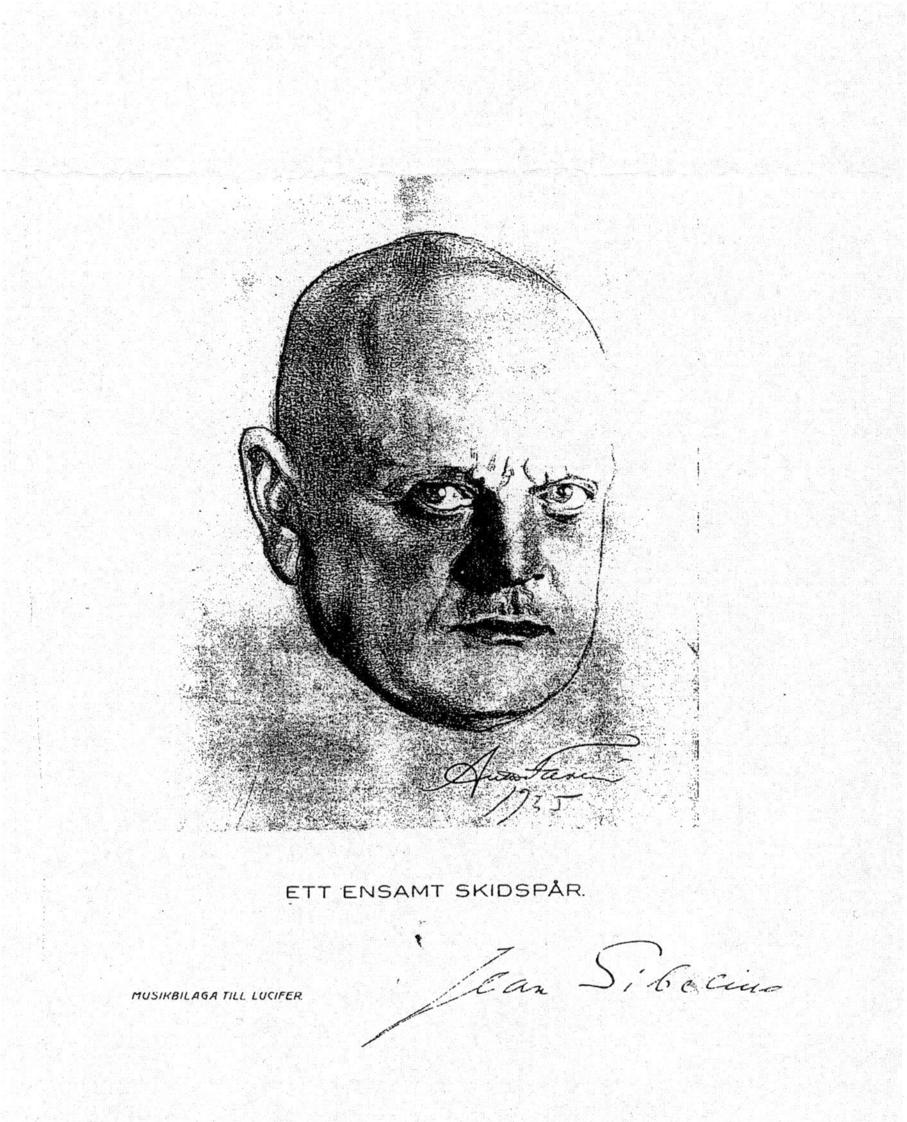

FIG. 1. Antti Favén, cover of the musical supplement for *Lucifer: Jultidningen utgifven af Finlands svenska publicistförbund*, December 1925. This drawing, signed by the composer, shows Sibelius' characteristic features: intense eyes, large ears and a skull like a monolith. *Ett ensamt skidspår* (The Lonely Ski Trail, 1925), the work included, is a melodramatic miniature of ninety measures based on a poem by Bertel Gripenberg from the collection *Aftnar i Tavastland* (Evenings in Häme, 1911). It illustrates scenes from the region where Sibelius spent his childhood and youth.

spirit, acquired — is a prerequisite for the practical artistic interpretation of his music, which will not be revealed to a connoisseur with a one-sided training in the Classical and Romantic tradition, especially given that the scores and orchestral materials have errors. The days are over when masterly orchestral interpretations could be achieved with cheap pocket scores (Karajan could pull it off). The same can be said of Finnish pianists such as Erik T. Tawaststjerna, Eero Heinonen, Folke Gräsbeck and recently Henri Sigfridsson. Wilhelm Kempff and Glenn Gould were prominent early advocates of Sibelius, but more recent artists have achieved a very different intensity in their approach to Sibelius' style thanks to their own historical and philological work. But perhaps the best proof of the immense power of Sibelius' music is that Finnish conductors with similar training and similar experiences of Nordic lifestyle do not produce similar interpretations. In addition to those already mentioned, conductors like Okko Kamu, Sakari Oramo, Esa-Pekka Salonen, Jukka-Pekka Saraste, Leif Segerstam, Osmo Vänskä and many others have astonishingly different accents when they speak the language of Sibelius, which, to paraphrase Haydn's famous reply to Mozart before leaving for London in 1790, 'all the world understands'.

However, if Sibelius interpretation, for academic reasons, has increasingly become a privilege of Finnish artists, that might be misunderstood as evidence supporting the cliché that it is necessary to know 'the North' and its nature in order to play, sing or even learn to love Sibelius. This is a fallacy, and a major issue tackled in the present volume. It is not only the availability, for more than a decade now, of high-quality scores in the *Complete Works* edition that is a necessary precondition for making Sibelius suitable to a future Arturo Toscanini or Leonidas Kavakos, but also proper attitudes (for example, underlining the Southernness of Sibelius' mentality). Substantial assistance to that end is provided by such publications as Fabian Dahlström's thematic-bibliographical catalogue (published in German in 2003) as well as editions of selected correspondence by Dahlström and SuviSirkku Talas. It is easy to get lost in the huge masses of material, but printed collections of important parts help them to survive.

This book was written under favourable circumstances in many respects. The Suomen Kulttuurirahasto (Finnish Cultural Foundation) and Max-Peter Hirmer in Munich financed travel to archives and the purchase of materials; the staff of the archives in Finland and Germany helped make my study of the sources extraordinarily efficient. The support of many colleagues and friends was irreplaceable, especially that of Gitta Henning, research assistant to the Sibelius biographer and interpreter Erik Tawaststjerna. Her trust enabled me to assess for the first time Tawaststjerna's private collection and many an obscure document for the readers of this book.

The circle of individuals whose conversations have contributed to this project of many years is large. Ludwig Finscher, editor of *Die Musik in Geschichte und Gegenwart*, one of the world's most extensive encyclopaedias on music, encouraged me by unexpectedly confessing at a crucial moment that he was a Sibelian and offering cogent arguments for the value of Sibelius' symphonies. One of the very first people to have a scholarly discussion with the author about Sibelius and also about current trends in musicology was James Hepokoski, whose monograph on the Fifth Symphony was not yet finished when we met in 1990. Arnold Whittall reminded the author of the justifications for the Modernist position in 1992, in the context of collaborating on organising a conference on nationalism, with his then still critical (but later thoroughly revised) stance. Hence the premise of this book is not unbounded admiration but rather a desire to understand the critics as well and the problems they have with Sibelius, and to learn from the provocative questions they ask.

I am especially grateful to Manuela Schwartz for her support and for conversations about Richard Wagner and Sibelius' French contemporaries as well as about the cultural politics of those regions of Europe that were (like Finland) under heavy German influence in the 1930s and early 1940s. The willingness of our children Meri and Lennart, both of whom were born during the project, to listen to the supposedly 'harsh' sound of Sibelius at the beginning of their lives was also encouraging. In the meanwhile, it would appear this did not ruin them musically. They are some of the reasons that Sibelius, the father of six girls, fascinates the author not only as an artist but also as a man, and that he now realizes that with this book, *horribile dictu*, his lifelong interpretation of the composer has only begun.

Jean Sibelius' Family

Maternal Grandparents[a]

Katarina Juliana née Haartman 1812–1892 | Gabriel Borg 1797–1855

Jean Sibelius' Parents

Christian Gustaf Sibelius 1821–1868 | Maria Charlotta née Borg 1841–1897

Maria and Christian Sibelius' Children

Linda Sibelius 1863–1932
Johan Christian Julius (*Jean*) Sibelius 1865–1957
Christian Sibelius 1869–1922

Paternal Grandparents

Katarina Fredrika née Åkerberg 1792–1897 | Johan Sibelius 1785–1844

Aino Järnefelt's Parents

August *Alexander* Järnefelt 1833–1896 | Elisabeth née Clodt von Jürgensburg 1839–1929

Elisabeth and Alexander Järnefelt's Children

Kasper Järnefelt 1859–1941
Arvid Järnefelt 1861–1932
Erik (*Eero*) Järnefelt 1863–1937
Ellida (*Liida*) Järnefelt 1865–1885
Ellen (*Elli*) Järnefelt 1867–1901
Armas Järnefelt 1869–1958
Aina (*Aino*) Järnefelt 1871–1969
Hilja Järnefelt 1873–1879

Daughters, Sons-in-law, and Grandchildren of Jean and Aino Sibelius

Eva 1893–1978 × Arvi Paloheimo 1888–1940
- Marjatta Kirves (née Paloheimo) 1915–
- Martti Paloheimo 1917–1987
- Janne Paloheimo 1922–1989

Ruth 1894–1976 × Jussi Snellman 1879–1969
- Erkki Virkkunen (Snellman)[b] 1917–
- Laura Enckell (née Snellman) 1919–

Kirsti 1898–1900

Katarina 1903–1984 × Eero Ilves 1887–1953
- Merike Ilves 1925–
- Jan Ilves 1927–

Margaretha 1908–1988 × Jussi Jalas (Blomstedt)[c] 1908–1985
Risto Jalas 1929–1956
Pauli Blomstedt 1937–1941
Tapio Jalas 1941–1993
Satu Risito 1943–
Aino Porra 1946–
Heidi 1911–1982 × Aulis Blomstedt 1906–1979
Juhana Blomstedt 1937–2010
Petri Blomstedt 1941–1998
Anssi Blomstedt 1945–
Severi Blomstedt 1946–

Other Relatives[d]

Sibbe and Åkerberg Families

Evelina Sibelius 1832–1893 (aunt)
Pehr Sibelius 1819–1890 (uncle)
Johan Matias Fredrik (*Jean*) Sibelius 1818–1864 (uncle), ship's captain
Mathias Åkerberg 1750–1831, physician
Juho (*Johan*) Sibbe 1759–1820, Lapinjärvi
Elias Unonius 1732–1802, businessman in Loviisa
Matti (*Matts*) Martinpoika/Mårtensson 1721–1782, Lapinjärvi
Martti Pekkala ca. 1680–1742, Artjärvi
Matts Sjögård 1702–38, Lapinjärvi
Anders Åkerberg 18th cent., councillor in Ystad, Sweden
Gustav Sibbe 17th/18th cent., Lapinjärvi
Pietari Ruuth d. 1670, businessman in Wiborg
Petter Unonius 17th cent., businessman in Gevle, Sweden
Olaus Unonius 17th cent., professor in Uppsala
Per Snifs, Ratsmann in Gevle, Sweden
Heikki Simonpoika Pekkala 17th cent. in Artjärvi
Ernest Henriksson Sibbe 17th cent.
Lauri Laurinpoika Lassila 17th cent. in Artjärvi
Jakob Dannenberg 17th cent., businessman in Wiborg

Borg and Haartman Families

Anna Juliana Borg 1850–1909 (aunt)
Tekla Borg 1839–1912 (aunt)
Gustaf Haartman 1786–1845, civil servant
Gabriel Borg 1758–1824, CP
Jakob Chydenius 1732–1809, CP
Henrik Justander 1676–1749, CP
Jakob Haartman 1677–1729, CP
Johan Utter d. 1722, CP
Simon Tolpo 1652–1711, professor of theology in Turku
Johannes Amnorinus d. 1691/92, CP
Carolus Prochman 1628–1691, CP
Johan Carlander d. 1680, CP
Gabriel Gottleben d. 1673, councillor in Pori
Gabriel Gammal d. 1664, CP
Bertil Ruuth 1594–ca. 1650, Amtmann in Vöyri
Johan Welinus 17th cent., CP
Elias Enckell 17th cent., CP
Jakob Flachsenius 17th cent., provost
Erik Justander 17th cent., professor of poetry in Turku
Johannes Wanaeus 17th cent., CP
Karl Bildstein 17th cent., factory owner in Fagervik
Kristoffer Floor 17th cent., equestrian
Benedictus Caroli 17th cent., CP
Martin Florinus 17th cent., CP
Sven Mellenius, 17th cent. deputy mayor in Uusikaupunki

Notes

[a] The primary source for this list is Dahlström 2005, pp. 526–8. As unambiguous as the Swedish version of his name, Johan, chosen in March 1886, may have been, the young artist claimed the right to create a supra-regional identity by calling himself Jean. Nevertheless, the attempts to 'correct' the artist's name have been numerous. Some congenial recipients of his music find the name Jan more suitable, Johannes and Giovanni have also been used. 'Jan' resembles the nickname that was used by his family: 'Janne', which is derived from his first given name, Johan, and was common in the region. JS had two additional given names. Until the publication of the annotated letters from his youth (Goss 1997), scholars wrote Johan Julius Christian (see Salmenhaara 1984, p. 19 and passim). The correct name is Johan Christian Julius, with his father's name second.

[b] 'Virkkunen' is the Finnish version of the Swedish name 'Snellman'.

[c] The conductor Jussi Jalas was originally 'Blomstedt'. Several of his children retained that Swedish name.

[d] The primary sources for this list are Marvia 1955 and Salmenhaara 1984, pp. 430–1. The selection aims to give a sense of the professions and whereabouts of JS's ancestors, so the maternal lines have been left out. If no profession is indicated, they were landowners or famers. The abbreviation CP stands for Chief Pastor (head pastor of a larger Protestant parish).

It is — it appears — impossible for me to offer a completely exact, objective, credible picture of myself. My mixed race, Swedish and Finnish, stands in the way![1]

1 INSIGHTS

1.1 SIBELIUS THE 'NEGLECTED'

The Mystery of His Generation

'YOUR MUSIC and the unique nimbus around it are deeply rooted in the soil of your people, illustrious maestro, and are surrounded by its mysticism. That is why this music is so close and open to us Slavs as well.'[2] The 29-year-old Croatian composer Boris Papandopulo, Yugoslavia's delegate to the Ständiger Rat für die internationale Zusammenarbeit der Komponisten (Permanent Council for the International Cooperation of Composers), wrote this to Sibelius, the vice-president of the council, whom he called the 'master of the Finnish saga in the magical world of music'. The vice-presidency of the council — founded in 1934 under the leadership of Richard Strauss, to provide a regionalist counterweight to the International Society for Contemporary Music (ISCM) — was shared by Sibelius, Albert Roussel and Adriano Lualdi. The 'backward-directed' nature of this organisation, initiated by 'Nazi music politicians', was made unsparingly clear by Theodor W. Adorno soon after the Second World War.[3] This brings us to the heart of why Sibelius is one of the most famous but also most enigmatic musicians of the twentieth century.

How can one explain the 'nimbus' and 'mysticism' that Papandopulo felt had a special appeal to the Slavs? By contrast, in 1936 the Boston-based writer and journalist Lucien Price asked why the music of Sibelius 'speaks so powerfully to us North Americans' and concluded: 'It is the North speaking in tone poetry to men of the North.'[4] Why, if these things are true, did both Slavs and North Americans — two groups to which Sibelius by no means belonged — find him so appealing? Was Sibelius already in the 1930s, as he would be later during the Cold War, one of the common denominators of East and West? How important to Sibelius himself were regional factors,

[1] Diary, 11 September 1911; in National Archive of Finland, Helsinki: 'Jean Sibelius Collection', 'Erik Tawaststjerna Collection' (hereafter: National Archive) Boxes 37–8, and Dahlström 2005, 93. Hereafter, references to the diary will be by date alone.

[2] National Library of Finland (former University of Helsinki Library, Department of Special Collections and Rare Books), Helsinki: Collection 206 (Sibelius Papers), 'Sibelius Sketches' and scores in Sibelius' possession (hereafter National Library Coll.) 206: 28; Boris Papandopulo to JS, 1 December 1935 from Split.

[3] Adorno 1976, p. 185.

[4] Price 1936, p. 271.

the 'soil of his people', their 'mysticism', a heartfelt relationship to the landscape and nature of his native land? Do similar categories apply to him as to Siegmund von Hausegger, whose *Natursymphonie* (1911) was, according to a contemporary review by Rudolf Birgfeld, based on 'man's relationship to nature', and whose theme of nature is 'encircled by mysterious organ chords in the depths'? Is such similarity even possible given that Sibelius explicitly conceived his Fourth Symphony as a 'protest' against the gigantism and 'circus' of such contemporaries as Hausegger? The New York-based German critic and pianist August Spanuth reacted to Hausegger's piece, and to Rudolf Birgfeld's review, in a damning review headed: 'Musikalischer Mammutismus'. According to a diary entry for 13 March 1912, Sibelius read the issue of *Signale für die musikalische Welt* in which it appeared and was familiar with this sort of discourse.[1]

Is it right to listen to Sibelius much as one would listen to Hans Pfitzner's symphonic cantata *Von deutscher Seele* (Of the German soul; 1921), especially its first section, 'Mensch und Natur' (Man and nature)? How close is his work to Richard Strauss's *Alpensymphonie* (1915; which Strauss also called *Der Antichrist*), in particular to the powerful sounds of the beginning, of night and dawn? Or to the symphonic poems *Miške* (In the forest; 1901) and *Jura* (The sea; 1907) by Mikalojus Konstantinas Čiurlionis of Lithuania, who dreamed of a unity of man and nature and managed, despite successfully avoiding folkloristic elements, to achieve a national sound by means of synaesthesia? Or to Alexander Glazunov's *The Forest*, a fantasy in C sharp minor for orchestra (1887), and *The Sea*, a fantasy in E major for orchestra (1889)? What does it mean when Sibelius calls *Tapiola* his 'forest' and *The Oceanides* his 'sea symphony'? We know that Glazunov tried to occupy the territory of Finnishness in music with his *Finnish Fantasy* (1912) and *Finnish Sketches* (1914; dedicated to the Finnish conductor Robert Kajanus), and that Sibelius hardly missed an opportunity to feel bad about his Russian colleague even though (or precisely because) he himself dealt with the issue of calling symphonic works 'fantasies'. The necessity to read between the lines is exemplified by this diary note of 18 January 1915: 'Jag är ej rigtigt frisk. I dag afton Glazunov-konsert i Helsingfors.' (I am not really fresh. Glazunov concert in Helsinki this evening.)

Is there even an essential (rather than stylistic) connection to Charles Ives's fragmentary *Universe Symphony* (1911/16) and to Concord Transcendentalism? Or should Sibelius (or at least the reception of his music) rather be explained with a view to the community of the 'Antichrist' that Friedrich Nietzsche outlined in 1888 in the 'Hyperborean' spirit of antiquity: 'Let us face ourselves. We are Hyperboreans; we know very well how far off we live. "Neither by land nor by sea will you find the way to the Hyperboreans" – Pindar already knew this about us. Beyond the north, ice, and death – *our* life, *our* happiness ... [...] Rather live in the ice than among modern

[1] See Birgfeld 1912, p. 107; see also JS to Rosa Newmarch, 2 May 1911, quoted in translation in Newmarch 1939, p. 24. Original (in German) in National Archive Box 121.

virtues and other south winds!'[1] Does Sibelius symbolise the 'experience from out of the seven solitudes' that Nietzsche longed for? Or does his work perhaps even establish a musical parallel to Néstor Martín Fernández de la Torre's pictorial *tipismo* and *regionalismo*?[2] Like Akseli Gallen-Kallela in Finland, Néstor contributed to the evolution of the folkloric art of the Canary Islands in the early twentieth century. In his art and in his design, he tried to record, in a contemporary way, regional myths and the substance of nature. His paintings mark the southern tip of European Symbolism. Is Sibelius the tone poet of the North, as Néstor is the designer of the South? If so, is this 'North' identical with the Republic of Finland or rather a dream that could coincide with any nation? Is *Finlandia* patriotic at all, in the twentieth-century sense, or rather a poem of the 'North' and of the 'Nordic' attitude in the spirit of the poet Johan Ludvig Runeberg, who idealised 'Finland' around 1850 but by his terms 'North' and 'Finland' intended ethical values rather than an ethnic and geopolitical identity?[3] Is Sibelius' music perhaps even 'Nordic' without being 'Finnish'?

We can dig even deeper. Did what C. G. Jung called 'extroverted' creativity truly dominate Sibelius' work in a 'Nordic' form,[4] or was his music the result of the most magnificent period of a Central and Western European spirit that surrounded this composer, who inclined towards the bohemian? Or did rather the special mixture of the small-town environment of his childhood and his own most original ideas play a crucial role in the creation of such tone poems as *The Bard*, *Luonnotar* (Goddess of nature and the spheres) and *Tapiola* (Realm of the forest god Tapio); in the symphonies, which the composer also called 'fantasies', 'declarations of faith' and 'prayers'; and in songs such as 'Höstkväll' (Autumn night), 'Jubal' and 'Kaiutar' (The echo nymph)? Like 'Kaiutar', *The Oceanides* raises the question of how important models from classical antiquity were for Sibelius. After all, the composer moved in the 'neo-Hellenist' *Euterpe* circle in Helsinki,[5] and he had learned Greek and Latin in high school in Hämeenlinna. Was he, the man who had his orchestra imitate the singing of the choir of Oceanids – to paraphrase Nietzsche's vision[6] – the embodiment of 'the artistic power of all nature', the 'highest gratification of primordial unity', which reveals itself 'in these paroxysms of intoxication'? Or were his symphonies – after Nietzsche had, as a critic of our 'exhausted culture', analysed Wagner's supposed failure – rather inhabited by the mystical sound of a 'reawakened tragic music'?[7]

As we start to round up the secrets of Sibelius, one question leads to another. Was

[1] Nietzsche 1976a, p. 569. On the significance of this myth for the swan symbolism in the second *Lemminkäinen Legend*, *The Swan of Tuonela*, see Oksala 2004, p. 45.

[2] See Almeida Cabrera 1993.

[3] See Klinge 2004, pp. 11 ff.

[4] See Jacobi [1940] 1978, p. 33. On JS and Jung, see Mosig 2003.

[5] On the 'neo-Hellenists', see Riikonen 2000. *Euterpe* was a Swedish-language journal.

[6] On the Oceanids and art (though not specifically JS), see Nietzsche 1967, p. 57. JS composed the tone poem *The Oceanides*, op. 73, for the Norfolk Festival.

[7] Nietzsche 1967, pp. 37 and 123.

Sibelius in any way seeking the traces of the artistic expression of the *Naturzusammenhang* (identity with nature)[1] for which people had been searching for generations? Was he a *primus inter pares* or unique? Did he suffer under the provincialism of his origins, or did the delay of his confrontation with Modernism instead help him, since he learned the craft of his profession only after his personality had already developed? Did the tensions in the history of genre and composition after Hector Berlioz and Franz Liszt put him too in the position of desiring something original? Or did he rather, thanks to the 'highly developed awareness of dissonance' that was either innate to him or part of his Finnish nature, write the 'most dissonant music [...] ever composed'?[2] Perhaps Wolfgang Rihm meant here the same thing Herbert von Karajan did when he characterised the Fourth Symphony as 'one of the very few symphonies that ends in complete disaster'.[3]

Such questions make palpable how deeply Sibelius' art, for all its originality, was anchored in his time, not just in his homeland. Such questions distract from the well-worn clichés that have led to the monumental, classicising, de-sexualising ('Apollonising'), and 'de-urbanisation' of his art — supported by an image disseminated in photographs portraying him as a rock-solid man with a shaven head, which underscores his mature masculinity: a symbol of 'the North' and the granite remains of a high mountain range from time immemorial. The vitality of his expression,[4] which has more to do with the South than with the North,[5] is in fact not limited to the works whose themes reveal it through sexuality (*Scène de ballet, Kullervo, The Wood Nymph, Lemminkäinen, Kyllikki*). Nor should the South only be sought where the programme calls for it, as in *Belshazzar's Feast*. For example, the 'influence' of Giovanni Pierluigi da Palestrina can be heard in the Sixth Symphony.[6] The pastoral and Dionysian vitality of that symphony in particular — which Sibelius himself called 'wild and passionate in character. Sombre with pastoral contrasts'[7] — are brought to bear despite the predominance of Dorian scales and occasionally ornate imitations.

Nevertheless, Palestrina also has been used as a role model for the 'Nordic' style.

[1] See Adorno 1991, p. 137 (orig. pub. in German in the *Zeitschrift für Sozialforschung* in 1939).

[2] Brinkmann and Rihm 2001, pp. 90–91.

[3] Osborne 1998, p. 108.

[4] On this concept and its significance for the artist around 1900, see Martens 1971.

[5] See, most recently, Downes 2004 on structural properties (sequences of notes, combinations of chords) in JS' music that can (as *topoi*) be labelled erotic.

[6] On Palestrina, whom JS did indeed study in Rome in 1901, at least superficially, see the detailed studies by Tawaststjerna: Erik W. Tawaststjerna 1996, p. 69, and Erik W. Tawaststjerna 1997a, pp. 144 ff., 155 and 188 ('texture with Palestrina-like quality'), 191 ('Palestrina-like polyphonic structure'), and Erik W. Tawaststjerna 1997b, p. 281 (the Sixth Symphony 'gives evidence of having steeped himself in Palestrina'). Even in the case of the piano piece *The Village Church*, op. 103, no. 1, from the collection *Five Characteristic Impressions* (1923–4), Tawaststjerna writes of his 'free Palestrina style' (Erik W. Tawaststjerna 1997a, p. 186). All of this presumably reflects the author's interests as well as those of the composer.

[7] JS to Axel Carpelan, 20 May 1918, in Dahlström 2010, p. 423.

The artful, modal polyphony of the Renaissance has been regarded by some as 'Netherlandish' ever since Raphael G. Kiesewetter, despite being criticised by Manfred Bukofzer and Hugo Riemann, who favoured England and Italy as its origin. It was a central aspect of the defence of Palestrina during the nineteenth century that his art could be ranked with the profound Middle Ages rather than with the superficiality and egocentrism of the Renaissance.[1]

Even the Danish philosopher Søren Kierkegaard's category of 'repetition',[2] Carl Ludwig Freiherr von Reichenbach's theory of energy, Henry van de Velde's vision of the energetic 'line' and Henri Bergson's 'élan vital' as a timely intensification of the 'nature', 'landscape', pantheism, and 'vital force' of music deserve careful consideration with regard to the 'life-giving' force of Sibelius' music,[3] as do Theodor W. Adorno's complex remarks on Wagner and nature.[4] Admittedly, Sibelius' letters and diary entries tend to be critical of all philosophy and contain no references to his having read these or other contemporaries. This passage in a letter by Sibelius in Vienna to his fiancé, Aino Järnefelt, from 18 December 1890, is strikingly self-analytical: 'You will surely find it strange that I have become a philosopher. But I am not a philosopher, nor will I become one, for it is the most difficult thing there is and surely not within my reach.'[5] However, only when the intellectual culture of Modernism, including academic philosophy, is permitted to supplement traditional musical analysis can Sibelius be taken seriously as a Modernist. Only then is the danger avoided that he gets branded for ideological reasons as a Nordic eccentric and national composer or reduced by New Criticism to the scores.

Also relevant to the analysis of his creativity is the role played by multilingualism in his life, with his Swedish-language origins often in open conflict with his Finnish-language socialisation in school and ultimately in his 1892 marriage to Finnish-orientated Aino Järnefelt, who (despite her Swedish-German-Russian origins) was actively pro-Finnish in cultural politics. Of equally complex significance is the curriculum of the high school he attended, which conformed to an educational ideal that was almost unique at the time because of its emphasis on the Finnish language. The high school in Hämeenlinna was founded in 1873. It was originally planned for Helsinki but was moved to the provinces in response to protests from establishment circles. Within a few years of its founding, it became famous even beyond the region for pursuing the curriculum in Finnish on an ambitious level. The first Finnish-

[1] For example, in August Wilhelm Ambros, *Geschichte der Musik*, vol. 4 (Leipzig: Leuckart, 1878). See Gülke 1961, cols. 1461–2, and Ellis 2000, pp. 180–1. Palestrina is associated with Sibelius in Alex Ross, 'Apparition from the Woods: The Loneliness of Jean Sibelius', in Ross 2007, pp. 235–83.

[2] Cf. the concept of 'rotation' in Hepokoski 1993, 62 ff., and chapter 4.1 in the present volume.

[3] 'Life-giving' is a quotation from Marquery Stoddard to JS, 11 January 1938 (National Library Coll. 206: 37). On similar issues in Munch, see Asendorf 2003, pp. 83–90; Hoerschelmann 2003, p. 11. On Munch and JS, see chapter 2.2 in the present volume.

[4] See Adorno 1991, p. 137, and chapter 5.2 in the present volume.

[5] National Archive Box 95.

language high school, founded in Jyväskylä in 1858, never achieved such popularity.[1] The classes in Hämeenlinna included classical subjects (Greek, Latin), modern languages (French, German, Russian) and regional culture (*Kalevala* and *Kanteletar*, and the Finnish language in general). The language of his musical education was German, which Sibelius had been learning since he was fourteen.[2] Later he could read Swedish, Finnish, German, French and English as well as Latin and Greek, but he spoke only Swedish, Finnish, German, French and a little bit of Russian. His violin teachers in Helsinki, Hermann Czillag and Mitrofan Vasiliev, probably spoke exclusively German with their students. The influence of this multilingualism and cultural diversity on his art might be one of the most interesting questions for future Sibelius research.

Moreover, anyone who wishes to deconstruct his 'mystery' must understand what nationalism meant to him. The 'Finnish' nature of his music is by no means undisputed. The painter Akseli Gallen-Kallela, who was the same age as Sibelius, recognised the problem as early as 1898, and his position was also that of Sibelius: 'Neither I nor anyone else can create a "Finnish style". Art is supposed to be the expression of individuality and not, as the textbooks would have it, a good example of the dominant taste of my country. Moreover, my taste is anything but the "taste of my country".'[3]

More convincing in any case than a post-Herderian *Volksseele* (soul of the people) or 'taste of my country', is the influence of fellow students, colleagues, teachers and idols. Nevertheless, it will not suffice to explain Sibelius' mystery in terms of conversations in Gallen-Kallela's 'symposium' in 1890s Helsinki (in particular those with the conductor and composer Robert Kajanus) or even earlier in Vienna, with Karl Goldmark and other musicians, for example. Nor can his regular studies with Martin Wegelius in Helsinki, Albert Becker in Berlin and Robert Fuchs in Vienna be seen as crucial to his development. No teacher, acquaintance or friend played an essential role. Although Sibelius was not self-taught, his special synaesthetic talent – which enabled him to hear the 'sound' of dark, ripe fields of rye before the harvest and to understand the swans, geese and cranes flying south in proud formations over his house as messengers from another world – probably provides more insight into his creativity than does the influence of his teachers and possible role models.

Whatever his mystery may have been, one thing is certain: one has to know it to understand his music. Traces of truth await the attentive observer not only in his finished compositions but also in his diary, letters and sketches for compositions, but they are easily misunderstood unless one makes the effort to read all the hints without being prejudiced by the stereotypes that have become common in the specialist literature since 1906, when Rosa Newmarch's lecture on Sibelius at the Music Club in London in 1905 was published in English and German.[4] His letters and diary entries

[1] See Klinge 1997, pp. 256 ff.

[2] JS to Evelina, 11 October 1879, in Goss 1997, p. 46.

[3] Gallen-Kallela to Louis Sparre, 26 December 1898; quoted in Gallen-Kallela-Sirén 2002, p. 49.

[4] Newmarch 1906.

are fragments of ideas and moody statements, full of allusions. Often they contain traces of an informal engagement with the leading thinkers of his era. It is quite obvious that Sibelius was neither an isolated 'apparition from the woods' nor the truly Nordic personification of Heinrich Heine's 'spruce tree' that dreams of being a palm.[1]

Taking into consideration his position in the context of the history of ideas is the first condition for the objectivity necessary to address his art. His creative work is too 'auratic' – in Walter Benjamin's sense – to belong to 'history' and to ensure the objectivity of delicate 'traces'.[2] Excellent sound documents quickly enable us to negate what Gustav Mahler permitted himself in a letter to his wife in 1907: an assessment of the oeuvre as a whole on the basis of such peripheral early works as *Spring Song* for orchestra, also known as *La tristesse du printemps* (The sadness of spring), and *Valse triste*, taken from its original dramatic context – both of which were heard in a *concert populaire* conducted by Kajanus.[3] Only someone who knows neither Sibelius' individual orientation nor the history of Finnish culture, but has nevertheless heard of the *Kalevala*, would be tempted to equate the tone poem *The Bard* with the old singer and magician Väinämöinen, even though the short piece is a personal and, in its musical gesture, also lyrical portrait of a poet without time or place, inspired by the eponymous poem by Johan Ludwig Runeberg.[4] A hero from the *Kalevala* like Kullervo can in turn be considered a typically mythological figure, even though he has also been depicted naturalistically by Aleksis Kivi, Armas Launis and Aulis Sallinen as a rake with an unhappy childhood.

To sum up, any attempt to shed some light on the 'twilight zone', to paraphrase Eric J. Hobsbawm,[5] is far more difficult in the case of Sibelius than in that of many composers about whom much less has been written, because many authors on Sibelius have been concerned with attack or defence rather than sober analysis and interpretation with an open mind. Today, however, it is possible to strive for a value-neutral assessment, as Sibelius is no longer quite such a political football.

[1] An expression most prominently employed by Alex Ross in his essay 'Apparition from the Woods', Ross 2007. See also JS to Busoni, 22 November 1921, Stiftung Preussischer Kulturbesitz, Staatsbibliothek zu Berlin (hereafter Staatsbibliothek Berlin), Mus. ep. J. Sibelius 6. The *Dance Intermezzo*, op. 45, no. 2 (1907) was originally (in 1904) titled 'Scène. Motto: A spruce ... dreams of a palm (Heine)' on Heine's 'Fichtenbaum'. See chapter 6 in the present volume.

[2] Benjamin 1999, p. 447 (M16a,4): 'The trace is appearance of a nearness, however far removed the thing that left it behind may be. The aura is appearance of a distance, however close the thing that calls it forth. In the trace, we gain possession of the thing; in the aura, it takes possession of us.'

[3] Gustav Mahler to Alma Mahler, 30 October 1907, in La Grange and Weiss 2004, pp. 240–41.

[4] The distance between the Väinämöinen and the idea of a Scandinavian bard was not always so great, as is clear from an illustration of a Viking bard in the *Minnesblad* of Nordiska Museet in Stockholm, ed. Artur Hazelius (1888); reprinted in Andersson 2001, p. 16. For a recent interpretation of Runeberg's poem, see Oksala 2004, pp. 56–9.

[5] Hobsbawm 1987, p. 3.

Fig. 2. Väinö Blomstedt, *Episode from the Kalevala* (1897). Kullervo is depicted as an ill-behaved, aggressive youth planning his revenge, shortly before he kills Ilmarinen's cows (see the *Kalevala*, Runo 34:95 ff.). Compared to Gallen-Kallela's paintings, Blomstedt's is more informative but also less mythological. In 1898 this painting was included in an exhibition of Russian and Finnish artists by Sergei Diaghilev in St Petersburg, which would lead to the founding of the journal *Mir Iskusstva*.

'A Kind of Prometheus'

Sibelius' individuality evolved during the heyday of culture in the North. Albert Edelfelt, the Finnish painter of prominent French and other contemporaries (Louis Pasteur in 1885, for example), characterised it in a letter from Paris to his mother on 3 April 1890: 'The younger generation is more brutal but more genuine. It does not lie to itself as much. I do not wish to assert that is therefore less idealistic than the party-and-punchbowl idealists of my era.'[1] Edelfelt saw himself as a representative of a transitional period between Finland's national poet Runeberg around 1850 and the 'younger generation' to which Sibelius belonged.

Even those we think of today, and not just in Finland, as mythical shining lights were his contemporaries. It was typical of them that they affirmed and defended their own status institutionally. The Akademie der Künste (Academy of the arts) in Berlin

[1] Quoted in Kortelainen 2001, p. 666.

named Sibelius a corresponding member in 1921, under Max Liebermann's presidency. The head of the section was Friedrich E. Koch, who on 21 July 1921 reported to Sibelius in detail about the latter's appointment on March 21. The determining reason was the 'authenticity' of his music. Unfortunately, Koch, an ultraconservative composer, did not refrain from indicating that his own enthusiasm for Sibelius was based on ethnic reasons.[1] The National Society of Music in New York had already made Sibelius an honorary member in 1913, even before he visited the United States, thus honouring him as one of the seven greatest composers in the world,[2] and the reasons for it were probably similar to Koch's. The Regia Accademia di Santa Cecilia in Rome named 'Giovanni' Sibelius to its Comitato internazionale d'onore in 1916,[3] which for Sibelius was a particularly bright spot during the war years. He noted in his diary on 8 February 1917: 'Received the appointment [...] today. The name Roma has always had a strange attraction for me.' Other members included Guido Adler, Arrigo Boito, Max Bruch, Claude Debussy, Théodore Dubois, Edward Elgar, Alexander Glazunov, Karl Goldmark, Engelbert Humperdinck, Vincent d'Indy, Semen Kruglikov, Alexander Mackenzie, Jules Massenet, Ignacy Paderewski, Felip Pedrell, Giacomo Puccini, Max Reger, Camille Saint-Saëns, Alexander Scriabin, Charles Villiers Stanford, Richard Strauss and Edgar Tinel. In part because of this kind of 'accademia', the generation of the late nineteenth century was in a position to maintain for several decades the historical pendulum swing between becoming established and losing power. As a matter of fact, a new age has not really begun even today, and hence the major representatives of this generation are still just as much a presence as they were around 1900.[4] Anyone who speaks of 'the shadow of Jean Sibelius' in this context is overlooking the fact that a shadow is cast not just by Sibelius but by his entire generation.[5]

The high price for continued public relevance – especially when concentrated on a few works, as in Sibelius' case – is the impossibility of forming a genuine 'aura'[6] and focussing on genuinely major works (as in Beethoven's case) that could save authors from constant questioning of their true and timeless (or, to paraphrase Walter Benjamin again, traceless) greatness. Only rarely does Sibelius' generation benefit from the honour of the auratic patina of the past. Beyond that, their positions of predominance provoke the strongest criticism from anti-conservatives. Moreover, their status has been coupled with that of the West in general, since they embody its most recent

[1] See National Library Coll. 206: 20. Liebermann himself signed the document of the appointment; Archiv der Akademie der Künste Berlin, Dok. J.-Nr. 438.

[2] See Diary, 16 November 1913.

[3] See the official list from December 1916 in National Archive Box 16. JS was appointed on 24 December 1916.

[4] Hobsbawm 1987, pp. 3–4, calculates that scientists, artists and politicians active between 1880 and 1914 or adult in 1914 make up roughly half of the entries in *The Dictionary of Modern Thought* (1977). Those born after 1914 account for 23 per cent and those born between 1900 and 1914, 17 per cent.

[5] Englund 1977.

[6] Benjamin 1999, p. 447 (M16a,4).

heyday. As long as Western civilisation asserts itself, the representatives of the final phase of thoroughly convinced Eurocentrism will probably not lose their position.

As to the role it played in Western culture in the twentieth century, this generation can be divided into two age groups: those who were not yet forty-five in 1917, and those who, like Sibelius, were no longer at the forefront in terms of influence on world events around 1917. The popularisation of extreme, ill-fated political positions was above all a contribution of the younger group. Many of the exceptional figures belonged to the generation of the 1880s and 1890s (Stalin was born in 1879, Mussolini in 1883, Hitler in 1889, Franco in 1892, Mao Zedong in 1893, Goebbels in 1897), whereas several of the heroes of free Europe were often older (Churchill was born in 1874, Adenauer in 1876; in Finland, Paasikivi in 1870, Mannerheim in 1876). This generation as a whole no doubt shares responsibility for some of the century's tragedies, but it also deserves credit for a lot of good. It is, admittedly, difficult to defend some of its members from the accusation of having participated directly or indirectly in a chain of events that ultimately led to catastrophes. Strategies for such a defence based on a biographical close reading have yet to be developed and are an important issue in this work.

The fact is that widespread doubts about the moral integrity of this generation still detract from the fascination for the mysteries of the Sibelian world of sounds. If artists like Sibelius are associated with National Socialism or simply with late Wilhelminian and Victorian thinking, aesthetic aversions are likely consequences for demanding Modernist audiences. However, as apostles of the end of the world and a radically utopian, by no means affirmative closeness to nature, many of them — not just Nietzsche but also Sibelius — have offered substantial critiques of Western civilisation, provoking reflection on whether the modern age in Europe does perhaps represent one long misguided path, whose correction is possible only with the help of nature itself and is hence correspondingly global and universal. Whether or not Sibelius' mystery is also one of the mysteries of his generation, the cultural and artistic events of his intellectual environment were so extreme that it would be hopeless to understand the essence of his artistry without taking into account the era in which he lived, as one of many remarkable individuals.

Works considered the 'bread and butter' of an impoverished artist are a heavy burden on Sibelius' historical greatness.[1] Moreover, some minor works are disproportionately popular. His oeuvre is aesthetically heterogeneous; even the separate major areas within it do not support one another optimally — as they do in Beethoven, for example, where the symphonies are 'interpreted', so to speak, by the piano sonatas, concertos and string quartets. The British composer and Sibelian Arnold Bax suspected that a performance of a selection of Sibelius' songs in London in 1909 hindered the dissemination of the orchestral masterpieces in Great Britain: 'I believe that this lamentable affair was a serious setback to the acceptance in England of Sibelius'

[1] Markku Hartikainen has documented his income, expenses and debts; see www.sibelius.fi.

best works, and delayed the recognition of the grandeur of the later symphonies for several years.'[1]

The antiquated debate over Sibelius' historical 'greatness' – which recalls Jacob Burckhardt's and Nietzsche's thinking and is typical of his time – was initiated by his friends. Their task was to reject the questions the German composer and critic Walter Niemann raised regarding the relationship of the composer to his milieu. Universal greatness should triumph over supposed connection to a native land.[2] Another relationship, that of greatness and ability, was juxtaposed with that. Even Richard Strauss is said to have confessed: 'I can do more, but Sibelius is greater than I am.'[3] (Jussi Jalas, Sibelius' stepson, spoke to an American journalist who had visited Strauss and noted this sentence. It is difficult to judge whether it is authentic.) But the universally 'Nordic', or even universal greatness in general, does not justify weaker compositions. Reception is crucial: Beethoven's weaker pieces have been almost entirely forgotten, and his greatness has endured – despite the occasional interference of critical historians who point to profane aspects of his nature – since the middle of the nineteenth century, thanks in large part to influential authors who have always directed attention to the essential and classical. By contrast, Sibelius' lesser works have always been more famous than his major works. It is certainly possible to define greatness in such a way that a small number of compositions suffice for that distinction. That is the path the English critic Guy Rickards chose when answering the question 'Was Sibelius then a "great" composer, or merely one who could at times achieve great things?'[4]

The whole debate among Sibelius scholars over whether individual works, or even artists, are weak or 'minor', all too popular or sadly forgotten, is a problem of their own making. In the twentieth century in general, artistic quality was by no means defined in terms of how well the formal framework was rounded off or even in terms of the cyclical quality or rigour of an oeuvre as a whole. Quality now allows for isolated experiments that prepare the way for something else or belong to the compositional process like inevitable detours, as part of the development of a specific idea. Even when an artist distinguishes between 'bread and butter' and great art – in a private memorandum Sibelius wrote of 'composing on two levels'[5] – and indeed sends some pieces to his current publisher or even others only in order to feed the family, it has to be asked whether the very question does not perhaps reflect an idea of historical greatness from around 1900 that is no longer entirely up-to-date. The aesthetic dignity of a fragment that for a few decades now has enabled composers to define works of art as 'in progress' was, unfortunately, not something familiar to Sibelius. Even if

[1] Bax 1943, pp. 61–2.

[2] On Niemann and JS in greater detail, see chapter 5.2–3 in the present volume.

[3] Quoted in Jalas 1981, p. 62.

[4] Rickards 1997, p. 205.

[5] Diary, 17 September 1914; see also JS to Aino, 22 March 1901; National Archive Boxes 95–6. Unless otherwise indicated, the letters to Aino cited are in this collection. For the entire correspondence, see also the commentated editions edited by SuviSirkku Talas (2001, 2003, 2007).

many artists of his generation experienced their work as a process – or even, like Stravinsky much later, preferred composing as a process to the finished works[1] – they were not able to elevate this to an official aesthetic. Stravinsky was the first to do so when he deduced the essence of art from the craft.[2]

Consequently, it remains the task of a critic either to reject greatness as a concept or not to base judgements of artistic greatness on apparently finished, more or less authentically authorised and printed works. He should rather view an artist's creative work as a process of production whose success depends not on the perfection of what is published (to the extent that can be measured at all) but rather on the overall weight of the oeuvre and its aesthetic or intellectual (perhaps even ideological) goals. Thus the individual work recedes to the background and the artist's personality, method and 'the act of composition itself (and the genius who performs it)'[3] become foregrounded. The original, finished text's claim to 'aura' is seen in perspective with the creative oeuvre in all its details. This in no way results in the demystification of works of art, since the aura of creation surrounds the individual compositions as well. This position is in keeping with Nils-Eric Ringbom's summary of Sibelius' work: 'The symphonies represent the synthesis, all the other works, however, separate elements of those spiritual impulses that together form the criterion of symphonic art.'[4]

Greatness is already emphasised in Rosa Newmarch's 1906 brochure on Sibelius: 'The nearer I approached to the work of Sibelius the larger it loomed, until its limitations seemed to recede into an unknown past and stretch into an unconjectured future.'[5] In this view, Sibelius' genius begins in the 'fierce protest', 'throwing to the four winds all the *pacta convecta* of its art, and eventually settle[s] down in dignity and contentment within its own self-adopted limits of expression. [...] With the advance of years, he has shown an increasing respect for the requirements of conventional form, without, however, becoming conventional in the contemptible sense of the word.'[6]

The Finnish author and composer Erkki Salmenhaara, who introduced his Sibelius book in 1984 by raising the question of his 'supra-historical greatness' and ended it with his 'universality', postulated historical distance as a distinctive feature: something that constitutes a composer's oeuvre whether, after a century of being appreciated by others, it remains a 'document of its epoch' or is 'liberated from its era and becomes an enduring cultural legacy'. It is the latter that the author, apparently influenced by Walter Benjamin's distinction between 'aura' and 'trace', would like

[1] Danuser 1991, p. 54, which quotes Paul Sacher's speech from 1984, complemented by documentary films on Stravinsky in the collections of the Paul Sacher-Stiftung.

[2] Stravinsky 1947.

[3] Eggebrecht 1975, pp. 228 ff., and Riethmüller 1988, p. 19.

[4] Ringbom 1954, p. 81.

[5] Newmarch 1906, p. 3.

[6] Ibid., p. 11.

FIG. 3. Ilya Repin, *Finland's Great Men* (*Suomen suurmiehiä*, 1922, detail). This detail from Repin's monumental painting shows Sibelius working during a banquet. Eino Leino is reciting (Sibelius, on the left edge of the painting, is writing and not listening, which is in keeping with the relationship between the two); opposite him stands Robert Kajanus; the architect Eliel Saarinen is sitting in the foreground, with the painter Gallen-Kallela next to him. Sibelius is still depicted with hair, though he shaved his after 1919.

to call 'greatness'.[1] In his view, Sibelius possessed 'such an inner universality, that it can continue to fascinate listeners and scholars'; in his conclusion, Salmenhaara observes that only superhuman and incomparable geniuses such as Bach, Mozart and Beethoven have come closer to the absolute.[2] Sibelius is not one of them, as he sees it, but he nevertheless belongs to the 'universal classics' and continues the tradition of Beethoven, Bruckner and Brahms, since what matters are the motifs and the organic form that grows out of melodic cells.[3] But doesn't this argument, an attempt to defend Sibelius against critics who claim his work lacks architecture, also limit Sibelius' significance? Why should it be so important to establish his reputation first and foremost as an architect? It must be said that the nature of Sibelius' reception has always been specific to a region. Salmenhaara's sketch is valid in Finland. And beyond this limitation, a century is too short a span to assess the true historical greatness of a complex artist. So the question of greatness should be left unanswered.

Erik Tawaststjerna, an even more prominent Finnish author, asked Sibelius which twentieth-century composers were, in his view, the 'greatest'. Sibelius is said to have

[1] Salmenhaara 1984, p. 8.

[2] Ibid., p. 428.

[3] For example, see Diary, 9 March 1913.

answered, after thorough consideration: 'Richard Strauss, Bartók and Shostakovich'.[1] Interestingly enough, he was prepared to give the question thought. Not one of these three artists is an unrecognised great composer who – to paraphrase Cecil Gray's introductory reflections on Sibelius' greatness – was 'a kind of Prometheus, bound to the rock of public indifference and neglect' who had to endure the criticism of the envious.[2] Not even Béla Bartók is an unrecognised genius of the sort Gray makes Sibelius out to be. All three of them achieved a unique synthesis of progressive and easily accessible elements. Ultimately, even Gray concedes that lack of recognition is not an absolutely necessary condition of historical greatness. He collects arguments against Sibelius' harshest critics (such as Adorno), who see the function of 'stars' and 'fetishes' within the market economy as a symptom of a connection to the ephemerality of the present – an analysis that also misses the point of Sibelius' essence as an artist. Gray demonstrates how even the reception of Bach and Beethoven functioned in an alternation of recognition and forgetting, but he overlooks the fact that the history of art in the early twentieth century represents a new context from the perspective of critics, in which popularity was no longer compatible with true authenticity (Adorno's 'Wahrhaftigkeit'). Gray's strategy for defence is therefore doomed to failure.

As is demonstrated above all by the attempt to define Sibelius not as a 'star' but, rather, to stick to Adorno's category, an 'extra-territorial' figure, one of the composers (like Bartók, Leoš Janáček and Mahler as well as Franz Schreker) who transcend any regionalism and cultural criticism and are thus truly great,[3] the main problem when assessing Sibelius in the context of his era is that he never established a method, a compositional technique or even a theory.[4] Already as a student, perhaps disillusioned by Martin Wegelius' teaching in Helsinki or by Albert Becker in Berlin, Sibelius insisted on that – at least if one credits the portrait in *En bok om en människa* (A book about a man) by Adolf Paul (alias Georg Wiedersheim). In that work from 1891, Silén, an alias for Sibelius as a student in Berlin, observes: 'Everything the teachers tell you is humbug! At least in my case, they taught me nothing but their methods! [...] And every teacher has a method! If you show me a teacher whose method is not to have one, then I'll go to him! Otherwise I'll make more progress without any teaching.'[5]

Sibelius' concept of the work of art ('das Kunstwerk') was, moreover, so well established that he produced no contribution to the evolution of compositional techniques but only many individual compositions. In the context of a century in which works slowly became documents of a technique or an idea, and methods become the key criterion of a progressive artist,[6] that might seem old-fashioned. It detracts from his

[1] Erik W. Tawaststjerna 1997a, pp. 7–8; n.d.

[2] Cecil Gray 1931, p. 3.

[3] On Adorno, see chapter 5.2 in the present volume.

[4] Cecil Gray 1931, pp. 8–9. Jalas noted, however, that JS 'developed a specific technique' for each of his symphonies; note from 17 July 1943; quoted in Sirén 1999, p. 40.

[5] Paul 1891, p. 206.

[6] See Dahlhaus 1983, pp. 149–50.

greatness in the eyes of those who fail to recognise his inability to record his ideas in the form of textbooks, a consequence of the situation in which he lived. It was also related to his rejection of the authority of all teachers. Right up to the end, he tried to refine his art rather than ceasing at a convenient moment to write down the state of affairs as a technique, standard and method. That is precisely why his music sounds so 'auratic' and intangible. Whereas many of his contemporaries fabricated refined 'cocktails' with their technique (and in many cases even left behind fancy recipes), to borrow a sarcastically inclined expression from Sibelius, he served 'pure cold water'.[1] This is a valuable metaphor.

'No composer of our time has suffered more neglect than has Jan Sibelius, the Finnish Master', wrote a friend of Sibelius' in 1930,[2] even though his music's continued presence in concerts and on the radio annoyed others. But quantity does not always equal quality. And quantity is an invitation to misreading by those who envy. The fact that Sibelius is one of the most commonly misunderstood composers of his time lies partly in the antagonisms of his life and work, several of which were determined by his historical context. For critics insufficiently initiated in both the subtleties of Finnish history and the work of Sibelius as a whole, compositions such as *Finlandia*, *The Breaking of Ice on the Oulu River*, *War Song of Tyrtaeus* and *March of the Finnish Jaeger Battalion* are enough to make him a politicising, nationalist populist with fascistoid tendencies, whereas others — on the basis of *Tapiola*, the Fourth Symphony and the Ernst Josephson songs of Opus 57 — reject him as a 'Cubist' and Expressionist producer of anarchistic horror.[3] Still others cannot accept that Sibelius made repeated reference, at least in his titles, to a mythological use of regional folk poetry in Elias Lönnrot's *Kalevala*. By contrast, others find fault with him because he was not consistent in his connection to nature and homeland but rather enjoyed life in international metropolises and in hotels in Helsinki where he worked and, for example, did not seek out local (northern) luxuries but instead preferred the finest available (whether it was tobacco, drinks or shoes) from London, Paris and Berlin. All of these points of criticism, some of which contradict one another, are based on misunderstandings of a multifaceted individual who is difficult to grasp. Anyone who wishes to understand Sibelius has to be prepared to grapple with a complex era, a little-known region and an unwieldy biography. It is not sufficient to evoke his greatness.

[1] Cecil Gray 1931, p. 11. According to Furuhjelm 1916b, these metaphors were used by JS.

[2] Anonymous, 'Why No Sibelius?' *Musical America*, 10 January 1930.

[3] Such thinking was typical of, for example, Karl Flodin (founder of the journal *Euterpe*) as well as Henry Krehbiel and William J. Henderson. See Erik W. Tawaststjerna 1992, p. 92, and Erik W. Tawaststjerna 1994, p. 310, as well as chapters 2.2 and 3.5 in the present volume.

FIG. 4. F. Liewendahl, *J. L. Runeberg*, 1841, lithograph based on C. P. Mazer's painting of 1837.

In the Conflict of Languages and Peoples

In addition to the alienation of his generation and the sociocultural upheaval prior to the independence of 1918, there were also regional explanations why Sibelius' antagonism detracts from his accessibility even for Finns today: his multilingualism and his multicultural descent, both of which make him a very typical example of a regional constellation in Finland but also a challenge to cultural politics that are still vivid. The two most important languages in the country, Swedish and Finnish, divided it into camps well into the twentieth century, and indeed they still exist today. They represent a structure more powerful than any *realpolitik*. When the Finnish historian Matti Klinge advocated in his study of Johan Ludvig Runeberg the thesis that Runeberg's rural and moral idealism – his conservative nationalism shaped by antiquity – was the foundation for the identity of the 'Finnish nation' and that Runeberg not only 'invented' Finnish identity but was also able to convince the 'Finnish people' that they existed as such,[1] he was oversimplifying the reality of the late nineteenth century. Just how far Runeberg was from respecting the Finnish-speaking population (and there were many who felt that) is clear from a letter to Jacob Grot from 21 April 1839, in which the 'national poet' proudly described himself as a son of colonised Swedes and portrayed in clear words his intellectual distance from the Finns who lived in the centre of the country.[2] At the very least, one should not underestimate the role of younger generations, and of Sibelius himself, as the first true inventors of Finnish identity, even if in many cases they started out from Runeberg's oeuvre. For example, in 1892 Albert Edelfelt was the first to produce an effective, autonomous depiction of the Runeberg poem 'Björneborgarnas marsch' (March of the Björneborgers; 1860), which shows the Swedish and Finnish soldiers (with distinct physiognomy) as a unified front, led by a young man with Teutonic (Viking) features. This painting made the poem really famous and gave Finland an identity. The orchestral versions of the traditional *Björneborgarnas marsch* by Filip von Schantz (*c.* 1860), Sibelius (1892/1900) and Kajanus (1904) helped link the Western European quadrille to expressions of supporting the state and cultural identity, and since 1918 it has been used as the Finnish Army's celebratory march.

The conflict over a national language was a touchy issue for Finnish nationalism of the late nineteenth century, for more so than elsewhere in Europe the 'imagined order' of nations[3] lacked a solid linguistic or ethnic basis. Based on the assumption that national identity could only be a question of internal and external (and personal and social) perspective, Finland's unusual situation becomes evident. Giving the 'imagined order' political specificity presumed a complex equilibrium of forces achieved only slowly – and in any case long after the country had established itself internationally as a modern nation with its own culture. The Finnish 'linguistic and cultural community' could not easily emerge 'from the world of passive existence as peoples',[4] as was typical of the post-war nationalism of 1918, because it had never been one. Under these circumstances, everyone was aware of the role of language and cultural community in establishing identity, precisely because no such unity existed. The remarkable achievement of the artists influenced by Runeberg was overcoming these hurdles. The Finnish nation could have been defined geopolitically as a nation within the Grand Duchy of Finland (Runeberg wished to do no more than that) without regarding its linguistic communities as divided sub-nations, if one were prepared to dispense with membership in a given ethnic group as the criterion for a nation. The outstanding solution was a 'national culture' that transcended the ethnic and linguistic realities. That is why Germany's very similar history as a highly complex 'nation'

[1] Klinge 2004, pp. 403 ff.

[2] Runeberg 1879, p. 223.

[3] 'Gedachte Ordnung', a term coined by Emerich Francis (1957, pp. 100 ff.) that was taken up by M. Rainer Lepsius ([1990] 1993, p. 193); see Koselleck 1992, pp. 149 ff.

[4] Karl Renner, *Selbstbestimmungsrecht der Nationen* (1918), quoted in Hobsbawm 1990, p. 121.

('imagined' in a highly utopian manner already in the early eighteenth century) was a model for many Finnish idealists of the nineteenth century.

When the prestigious Suomalaisen Kirjallisuuden Seura (Finnish literary society) was founded in 1831,[1] the idea of a Finnish linguistic community and culture was the political agenda of a group of largely Swedish-speaking members of the educated middle classes in an autonomous Grand Duchy that belonged to Russia. Although Sibelius attended a Finnish-language high school in Hämeenlinna, only much later – inspired by a feeling of being different that peaked in Vienna in 1891, in a cosmopolitan and metropolitan community – did he become familiar with the artistic possibilities of the unique (Finnish) language of his homeland. This was a huge source of material and modernity. Yet when composing his Lieder, Sibelius avoided the work of the writer Eino Leino (Lönnbohm), who for good reason is the Finnish-language poet most often set to music, albeit not solely because of language.[2] The two artists knew each other well and did not like each other, but what was probably the most intense fight between them, on 16 February 1920, was also about questions of cultural belonging and origins. Sibelius did not want to accept that he, like Leino, was supposedly a 'son of farmers'. Leino, by contrast, was proud of his peasant origins. The reason for this touchiness was a public debate over genealogy, sparked by the music historian Otto Andersson, who had emphasised somewhat one-sidedly that Sibelius' family was from the Swedish-speaking coastal region, known for its fishermen and farmers. As early as 1915 there is a diary entry that reads: 'Otto Andersson has dug up my "ancestors", making me feel sick. As if I were dead.'[3]

By contrast, in 1920 the eccentric author Eeli (Eliel) Granit-Iloniemi believed he had shown that Sibelius' great-great-grandfather, Matts Mårtensson (Martinpoika), had spoken Finnish. In his diary on 9 February 1920, Sibelius criticised his son-in-law Arvi Paloheimo, who had financed the pro-Finnish genealogy. Sibelius directly associated Walter Niemann's comments with the efforts of these Finnish-speaking Finns (including his son-in-law) to establish 'their' Sibelius. As early as 2 February, Sibelius had addressed in his diary the problem of origins, which into the 1940s would not leave him in peace. But the line of his argumentation changed according to the spirit of the era. At a time when many Finns already considered him all too elitist and cosmopolitan, the concept of the 'genuinely Finnish' that concerned the likes of the industrialist Paloheimo represented a marvellous opportunity for the Finnish-speaking population to establish their identity finally. In the young republic, it was not enough that Sibelius had acted in a pro-Finnish manner in the crucial phase of the preparations for political independence; he was also supposed to be as ethnically 'Finnish' as possible. Sibelius was outraged. In 1913, prior to the first public debate on

[1] On the history of this important society, see Sulkunen 2004.

[2] See Erik W. Tawaststjerna 1997a, pp. 30–31.

[3] Diary for December 1915 (undated, before 18 December). See also 2 February 1916, 20 August 1919, 20 January 1920 and 20 September 1943.

his genealogy, he had still described his mixed heritage freely: 'Certainly my name is a Latinisation of the Swedish name Sibbe, but nevertheless I am convinced there was mixing with Finns.'[1] But after Granit-Iloniemi brought to light the 'purely Finnish' and peasant origins of one branch of his family, Sibelius despaired. On 19 August 1918, he wrote in his diary, full of spite: 'And I am so an aristocrat — despite my humble origins.' As a member of a genealogical society, he followed with increasing sensitivity the debates over his origins.[2]

On 9 August 1943, in a very different time, he wrote in his diary: 'Origins don't interest me.' Then too he was thinking of himself and attacked the 'genealogists'.[3] Just one month later, on 6 September, however, he was writing about anti-Semitism: 'I can no longer consider this primitive way of thinking — anti-Semitism, etc. — proper at my age.' This sentence has perplexed many: what could he have meant here by 'no longer'? Similarly explosive-sounding is a formulation in his diary for 19 September: 'In certain countries such as Germany, "Aryan paragraphs" are necessary to get rid of talents. In another case, "puhdasrotuisuus" [racial purity] does not prevail.' Only a familiarity with his particular form of irony can point the way to the only plausible reading of this: he was of the view that without race laws the 'pure-blooded' 'talents' could not prevail against other, much greater, albeit less 'pure-blooded', genuine artists. After all, he too was ranked with the supposedly 'impure', which was by no means irrelevant to either the German copyright society Staatlich genehmigte Gesellschaft zur Verwertung musikalischer Urheberrechte (STAGMA) or the initiators of the homage paid to Sibelius under the National Socialists. The hasty note from September 1943 cannot, in any case, be read as a sign that he admired the German law.

Just one day later, however, he asked the laconic question: 'How could you, Jean Sibelius, have taken these "Aryan paragraphs" seriously?' On 22 September 1935, he wrote: 'These racial laws are humbug. After all, I am an artist, and certainly it was too my advantage to profit from the good sides of various peoples.' He knew that his mixed origin was his strength, even when such thinking was not fashionable in an age influenced by eugenics, even in Finland and especially regarding the Swedish-speaking elite to which he belonged.

A bilingual, culturally diverse nation that took no notice of ethnicities was the goal of Finland's leading nationalist liberals around 1850 — an idea Sibelius personified. The strong position of Swedish had been called into question since the 1860s, however, by pro-Finnish measures, and the foundations of nationalism were politically constrained. Russia, too, had an interest in weakening the Swedish element. The reforms strengthened the position of the pro-Finnish activists (the Fennoman movement), who later became the biggest supporters of the independence movement of 1917, but they also contributed to polarisation and hence to weakening the overall

[1] National Library Coll. 206: 61: outline of letter from JS to Gunnar Hauch, 20 April 1913.

[2] See also Erik W. Tawaststjerna 1997a, pp. 16 ff.

[3] See also Diary, 16 September 1943.

cultural potential — and to dividing the elite. The Finnish language gave the Grand Duchy a distinctly more Eastern tinge than it had had with Swedish. It was not just in the western provinces of Russia, including St Petersburg, where the demarcation between East and West began but on the Finnish peninsula, which is further east than most of Poland.

The founding of Svenska Litteratursällskapet i Finland (Society of Swedish Literature in Finland) in 1885 contributed to slowing the purely Finnish utopias and the enthusiasm for the *Kalevala* by offering a counterforce: the poet Runeberg.[1] The artistic products of the *Kalevala* cult, which the Suomalaisen Kirjallisuuden Seura had been administrating since 1831, had not seemed original enough by 1880 — before Kajanus, Sibelius and Gallen-Kallela remodelled them — to demonstrate the power of the collection to establish a culture. It would be only a few years, however, before it became necessary to found Svenska Litteratursällskapet as a bulwark for the region's old Scandinavian tradition.

In the 1880s, when Sibelius was studying in Helsinki, a constellation of cultural policies was forming that, while it allowed for alternatives, espoused the cause to establish a common basis for belonging to the Finnish nation. The reformed constitutional order of the Grand Duchy in 1869 provided for the representation of the 'people of Finland', rather than the old estates, by the parliament, whereas sovereignty was still in the hands of corporations of 'residents'.[2] It was not just progress with cultural policy but also famines and epidemics — which, after all, caused the death of Sibelius' father in 1868 — that drew attention to 'the people'. The unprecedented flowering of the arts during this period is, however, sometimes seen as an 'independent phenomenon' from political events.[3] By contrast, Harold J. Johnson has asserted (simplistically and provocatively — that is, with his characteristic straightforwardness, keenly criticised in Finland) that the trends of the time 'made' Sibelius an international figure he could not have become twenty years earlier.[4] Certainly, the identity of the new national culture was as contradictory as it was stimulating, because ideas about which paths would lead to the future were widely divergent. There was fertile soil for artistic innovations in particular, especially since artists all over Europe were searching for new material and significance.

The role of the arts within the culture as a whole during the 1890s can be summed up by reference to the apparent significance of the mythological machine *sampo* in the *Kalevala*: for this generation, the *sampo* (perhaps a reflection of the multifunctional windmills introduced by Daniel Thunberg during construction on the Sveaborg fortress near Helsinki in the 1750s) was no longer a magical device made by the smith Ilmarinen,[5] but rather the original composition of the nation, 'the most wonderful

[1] See also Salmenhaara 1996b, pp. 40–41.

[2] See Klinge 1997, pp. 227–8.

[3] Ibid., p. 357.

[4] Johnson 1959, p. 3.

[5] See Salminen 2001, p. 166.

idea of a Finnish national poet, the great heroic dead of the Finnish spirit.'[1] The happiness that the *sampo* brought to the people was thus the founding idea of the new nation. This is, at least, the Finnish writer Juhani Aho's Symbolist interpretation. In the literature on the *Kalevala*, there are other, less complex interpretations of the *sampo*: an instrument, an image of God, a ship, a sun, a witch's drum, a money machine and so on. The idea of 'forging' works of art derives from this historical context. According to Aho, however, the 'forging' of the *sampo* in the *Kalevala* is 'nothing other than the symbolic depiction of artistic work in general'. Sibelius did not compose anything on the subject of the *sampo*, but he had planned to, as Armas Otto Väisänen related in 1921: 'The most fascinating thing about the *sampo* is that one never knows what the *sampo* is. The whole story of the forging of the *sampo* has to be performed pianissimo in the music ... as if from a great distance. Everything has to be conceived symphonically, by the way. The composition should not seem literary. The poem [*runo*] is just the point of departure.'[2]

Sibelius ended up at the centre of this radical action. Its context was, on the one hand, the national predicament in the face of the threat of Russian pan-Slavism and, on the other hand, the utopian nonchalance of the educated classes in the prosperous Grand Duchy. Sibelius was surrounded by excited academics who believed in the glorious future of the Finnish North (and Nordic Finland) and in the local solution to the global problems of Western civilisation. The 'light' of the new civilisation was to come from the North, not from the Orient. Armas Järnefelt, who would become a famous conductor and his brother-in-law, studied with Sibelius at Wegelius' music institute. Hence Sibelius had early contact with an old (German-Russian-Swedish) aristocratic family whose significance in the early days of cultural liberation can scarcely be overestimated. The Järnefelt family showed Sibelius the path to emotional independence from the conservative Swedish-language 'culture' that had surrounded him since childhood. Despite the resistance of her husband (general, senator and governor), whose office and character aligned him with the more moderate resistance, Elisabeth Järnefelt (née Clodt von Jürgensburg), the mother of Aino (Aina), Armas, Eero (Erik) and Arvid, maintained contact with the politically progressive, socialist writer Minna Canth in Kuopio. Elisabeth Järnefelt and Minna Canth were two mother-figures for the radical movement in the arts. When her husband was away, Elisabeth hosted a salon in Helsinki (especially from 1881 to 1884), and at the time it was the centre for the intellectuals around Lauri Kivekäs then known as 'the left' and later as the Päivälehti or Nuori Suomi Group (Juhani Aho, Arvid Järnefelt, Juhana Henrik Erkko, Eero Erkko, Kasimir Leino, Eero Järnefelt, Akseli Gallen-Kallela, Pekka Halonen, Louis Sparre, Robert Kajanus, Oskar Merikanto and others), today's *Helsingin Sanomat*. The artists — many of whom would later live in Tuusula, near

[1] See Konttinen 2001, p. 15.

[2] 'Jean Sibelius vaikutelmistaan', in *Kalevalaseuran vuosikirja* 1, 1921; quoted in Salmenhaara 1985, pp. 85–6.

Ainola, and were living in an apartment house in Ullanlinna in 1892, an urban district in the southern part of Helsinki – were already friends at this time.[1]

In the 1920s, the Freemasons joined the palette of liberal worldviews and groups with which Sibelius can be associated through formal membership. It is interesting to note that he planned to write a choral piece, *Har du mod?* (Do you have courage?), op. 31, no. 2 (to a text by Josef J. Wecksell), in the 'Freemasons' style', 'like a march – alla marcia', according to a diary entry on 10 July 1912, long before the first lodge was founded in Finland. Lodges had been prohibited in Finland (and throughout Russia) in 1822. Nothing is known about secret lodges after that, though they probably existed.

In the new cultural constellation, Armas and Aino Järnefelt's parents, who spoke other languages better, nevertheless consciously chose the Finnish language. They supported the national 'awakening', not the reconstruction of the Swedish empire. In contrast to Norway, Poland, and even Hungary, the Finnish awakening (the *Kalevala* notwithstanding) did not have a revanchist goal of liberating an ancient culture from foreign rule but rather sought to found a new one. There was no royal family; anyone could join the new aristocracy. The nation to be awakened was in mythological (not historical) slumber.

This enlightened and liberal circle received strong impetus from Germany.[2] Given the German Reich's aggressive policies towards Russia, which made the career of the revolutionary Vladimir Ilyich Lenin possible, the Finnish independence movement could count on active support from Berlin, which alarmed the tsarist government.[3] By contrast, Western (mostly Anglophile or Francophile) intellectual inclinations were widespread among Swedish-leaning contemporaries, perhaps as a late influence of eighteenth-century loyalism.[4] Many leading industrialists, in turn, believed that remaining within the Russian Empire (in contrast to important parts of Finland, Russia was still far off from a modern economy) was a prerequisite for further industrialisation, which is why the radical nationalists did not immediately receive their full support.[5]

The artists around Sibelius profited from the intellectual inspiration – at least partly decoupled from materialist efforts by patriotic supporters – that made it possible to play a role in the first period of national innovation in helping shape a culture that, as a result of a distinctive idea and external threats, evolved, at least theoretically, as a whole. Finnish nationalism lent this phase an energetic profile directed at a tangible goal and offered the new society a task, in contrast to the widespread hopelessness elsewhere (particularly in Poland and the south-eastern Baltic countries).

[1] See, for example, Erik [Eero] to Aino, 20 November 1890, in Talas 2000, p. 75. See also, more recently, Konttinen 2001, pp. 9 ff. and 22 ff.; and Salmenhaara 1984, pp. 81–2.

[2] Klinge 1997, pp. 281, 284.

[3] See ibid., pp. 326 ff.

[4] Pacius' *Kung Karls Jakt* (1852) symbolises this position; see Mäkelä 2002a, pp. 52 ff.

[5] Klinge 1997, p. 494.

The heterogeneous basis of the prospective nation ensured, until independence was achieved in 1918 (and even afterwards), the necessary cosmopolitanism and diversity, which represented in turn, despite the fact that the unity was only theoretical, fertile ground for the artistic and cultural flowering that took place around 1900. Artists in particular were able to use the power of their works to awaken the slumbering and utopian nationalism of Finland as a unity.

Sibelius himself never inclined towards ideological enthusiasm or political activism; only his works did, and only in the hands of others. Later he accepted all national and other honours, if only out of politeness – much like he composed music for national and local events now and again. But more than most other artists of his generation – in Finland and elsewhere, such as Strauss, Puccini, Shostakovich and others – he kept his distance from the political avant-garde as much as possible during this period. His former student and later colleague Leevi Madetoja has written of a visit to Sibelius in December 1935, during which first a painter called, and then some minister of state in Ainola, to ask whether one or another Finnish-German, Finnish-Italian etc., society could make him an honorary member. Sibelius allegedly said: 'Human friendliness is so effusive that you have to try to be polite to everyone, even when that is exhausting. But I leave alone anything that smells even slightly of politics. I think I can say that the only idea to which I have remained faithful all my life is my hatred of all political intrigues. Or rather: my indifference. Such things do not interest me.'[1] Consequently, his contribution to the cause of radical patriotism took the form of only minor works or semantically ambiguous ones. Further, he was especially emphatic in his rejection of the socialism that evolved after the revolution. This justifies his reputation as politically conservative. Although he dined with the radical Russian writer Maxim Gorky in 1905, still under the shadow of the great general strike, he wrote in December 1917: 'The anarchy is increasing. My unhappy country.'[2]

Sibelius learned to know and love Finland during the 1870s and 1880s as divided, not only linguistically and ethnically but also historically, culturally and regionally. The core of his family was tied not to life in Helsinki but to the southern Finnish provinces (Hämeenlinna, Loviisa, Turku and Lappjärvi). In Hämeenlinna, he was confronted both with the Russian military government and with the young culture of nationalist education. Then in the salons there were the Swedish-educated middle classes. Even as a child, he was accustomed to the cultural complexity of Finland. He did not experience a nationalist or idealist revelation at school, but with the Järnefelt family he could at least stand on the foundations the model high school in Hämeenlinna had given him. As the child of Swedish-speaking parents from well-educated families with only minimal ethnic mixing but also the graduate of a Finnish-language high school, he perhaps represented for the Järnefelts the perfect example of the new

[1] See Madetoja, 'Järvenpäässä käymässä', *Musiikkitieto* (December 1935); quoted in Salmenhaara 1987, pp. 95–6.

[2] Diary, 18 December 1917.

Finland that was to be 'awakened'. They recognised his talent even before the world premiere of *Kullervo* in 1892. In any case, his love for their only daughter and sister, Aino, was clearly regarded favourably. The young couple was predestined to found the nation. Financial concerns and class consciousness played no role. The Finnish ideal was to create a new aristocracy of the mind, and Sibelius would be one of its founding members, no matter what his ancestry or expected family income was. On the contrary, it had been the custom for generations in Elisabeth Järnefelt's family – the Clodt von Jürgensburgs, who could trace their history back to the Romans (the family of Claudius) – never to speak or even be proud of the achievements of their ancestors. Sibelius was born to forge the *sampo*, or at least to set it to music, and that was more than enough.

The couple's decision in favour of one of Finland's two languages was therefore all the more important. This explains her older brother Eero's anxious question to Aino: 'In which language do you discuss and write?'[1] The question expresses his concern that his dear sister might have been lost to a Swedish-speaking youth. Aino and Jean used both languages in turn, sometimes in a rather wild mix. He wrote to her in Swedish from Vienna on 26 October 1890: 'Write to me in Finnish; it is as if I were listening to Finnish melodies.' He could hardly have expressed it in a more charming way. He wanted to use Swedish himself, so as not to need 'five minutes for every word'.[2] In December 1890 he wrote in Swedish: 'I am reading the *Kalevala* diligently and already I understand Finnish much better.'[3] From 1894 onwards, Sibelius often wrote in (more or less proper) Finnish or composed his letters in his anarchic mix – for example: 'Tänään Fred. Borgin luona är jag på middag.'[4] ('Today I'm at Fred. Borg's at noon.') The first four words are Finnish; the last four, Swedish. Even more chaotic is a combination from 20 July 1900: 'mitt språkeni', a Swedish phrase ('my language') with a Finnish genitive ending (*-ni*).

Nevertheless, Swedish remained Sibelius' primary language until the end of his life, increasingly so even in his correspondence with the mainly Finnish-speaking Aino, especially since she also often wrote in Swedish. The diary is clearly dominated by Swedish: around 90,000 words, including a mixture of Danish and Norwegian expressions, followed by German (352 words, often in sayings), Latin (271), French (227), Finnish (only 61), English (17) and Italian (11), and four Russian words in Cyrillic.[5] His contact with the elitist Swedish-language *Euterpe* circle from 1902 suggests that his orientation towards Swedish only increased after 1900.

[1] On this, see Aino's correspondence with her family in Talas 2000, p. 74, such as Eero (Erik) to Aino, 10 November 1890. According to family tradition, the name 'Eero' was modelled on Kivi's *Seven Brothers* (Eero is the name of the youngest and cleverest of the seven brothers). JS always used his given Swedish name, Erik.

[2] JS to Aino, 18 October 1890.

[3] JS to Aino, 26 December 1890.

[4] JS to Aino, 9 December 1904.

[5] See Dahlström 2003b.

On 18 November 1890 he wrote to Aino: 'Naturally you remain a Fennoman: Aino Järnefelt does not change her spots, right? It will be amusing to see whether we will quarrel one day.' No quarrel on cultural politics is documented, but the question alone shows his own orientation. It was about more than belonging to a political party or having ties to a region. Around 1890 Sibelius clearly belonged to the Swedish-speaking faction, which was emphatically represented by his musical mentor, Wegelius. But when his mentor showed no sympathy for the Finnish *Kullervo* project in 1892 (based on the *Kalevala*), the young artist was outraged: 'The whole Swedish theatre crowd, these imported Stockholmers, disgust me.'[1] If only because of *Kullervo*, he sympathised more with the Fennoman front (and with Aino). The phrase 'these imported Stockholmers' was by no means accurate given the Finnish origins of most Swedish-speaking Finns, but it suited the occasion at hand. It was also about problems and intrigues in the Swedish-language theatre in Helsinki. Sibelius was not himself affected by it, but he adopted the Fennoman position of the Järnefelts. In 1892, moreover, his grandmother Katarina Juliana Borg died, and she represented the Swedish-language education of his childhood.

When he wrote in his diary on 27 April 1912: 'How I love the Finnish people! How close they are to my heart!' he was not including himself among those 'people'.[2] The 'Finnish people' were for him — as for nearly all cultural idealists and romantics — an object, not part of himself. Just how explosive the question of an individual's origins could be is illustrated by the sober directness of his friend Georg von Wendt on 20 January 1920. He alluded to the 'latest research' by Granit-Iloniemi that had shown that Sibelius' great-great-grandfather spoke Finnish. This resulted in a Finnish 'genetic makeup' of '1/32'. Because Wendt himself was a Swedish-speaking Finn, and also defined himself as a faithful physician, he wrote: 'As long as I can hold a pen and am allowed [to write prescriptions], the other thirty-one parts of your genetic makeup will not lack medicine.'[3] Wendt's later letters to the composer show that he helped obtained vitamins (C and A) for Sibelius and also, during the Second World War, arranged for the family's food rations to be increased — and occasionally also arranged for prohibited drinks. Wendt was not just a good physician to Sibelius but also (as an active member of the parliament's international committees) a direct connection to world events, as demonstrated by a letter from 21 April 1945 in which he analysed the proximity of Sibelius' birthday to the conference of the Allied forces in San Francisco with an eye to a propaganda strategy (including Sibelius' contribution) that could benefit Finland.[4]

The letters from Wendt offer insights into the atmosphere of Sibelius' environment. On 31 December 1943 Wendt described his experiences as a visitor in Germany

[1] JS to Aino, 5 February 1892.

[2] Tawaststjerna remarked on this (Erik W. Tawaststjerna 1994, p. 173).

[3] National Library Coll. 206: 41; Georg von Wendt to JS, 30 January 1920.

[4] National Library Coll. 206: 41.

and defended the conservatives, who formed a unified front with the National Socialists only after the Allied aerial attacks (the 'terror bombing'). Until then, he wrote, the National Conservatives had been the 'fiercest opponents' of the Nazi government. From a Finnish perspective, Germany seemed divided until 1942 and, as Wendt wrote with respect to the population, incapable of seeing an 'enemy' on the Western side of the front. That changed.

With the founding of the state in 1918, the Hessian prince and landgrave Friedrich Karl was to become King of Finland, which had seemed logical in view of the existing constitution and role of the German Reich in the run-up to the Grand Duchy separating from Russia (especially with a German royal house at its head). Sibelius too supported the idea, particularly because he did not believe his countrymen, and most especially not the 'Finns', were capable of founding a new nation on their own.[1] However, he also found the line of his publisher, Breitkopf & Härtel, too aggressive: it published a 1917 edition of his *March of the Finnish Jaeger Battalion* — 'Tief ist unser Stich, unbesiegbar unser Hass' (Our stab is deep, our hate invincible) — with an essay on German–Finnish friendship, the Hohenzollern coat of arms and a foreword critical of the Triple Entente. Sibelius demanded the edition be destroyed at his own cost (telegram to Breitkopf & Härtel: 'Because the preface must be changed, please destroy the *Jaeger* edition');[2] presumably he was most concerned about the expression 'the lies of the Entente' in the foreword.[3] But hostility towards Germany was also foreign to him; what mattered to him was the ability to make fine distinctions in a complex situation (as he was always accustomed to doing in Finland). In another note from 25 May 1918, right after the short but bloody civil war which ended with the bourgeoisie backed by German military intervention on the winning side, he wrote: 'I cannot describe the feeling with which I shook the hands of the German heroes. You only experience something like that once.' He and most of his friends belonged to a tradition that touched on nationalism, the homeland movement, fascism (but not National Socialism) and idealism as well as groups around writers such as Runeberg, Tolstoy, Strindberg and Swedenborg; musicians such as Wagner; philosophers such as Nietzsche and Johan Vilhelm Snellman; and Finnish politicians such as Carl Gustav Mannerheim and Per Svinhufvud, but that tradition was not identical with any of these positions.

But caution is called for even in relation to the national idealism of the most general kind in Sibelius' work. Mario Licho asked about his stance in 1929. Licho was working on a study of nationalism in music and asked Sibelius, among other things, about the use of folksongs in his own music and that of Kajanus. His thanks to Sibelius reflect indirectly the subtlety of the composer's reply:

> I wish to thank you sincerely for the explanations in your last letter, which

[1] Diary entries from 1918.

[2] In National Archive Box 42.

[3] National Archive: Copy of note from 20 November 1918, in the Tawaststjerna Collection.

seem extremely valuable to me. With your determined refusal to be classified as a national composer, you confirm for me my own view of music. To illustrate this issue, I would like to inform you that I am in the possession of two letters from Alfredo Casella in which he emphasises in particular that he until now has done everything to be considered an Italian national composer and that he used Italian folk music in his works whenever possible. He went so far as to observe that he was of the view that modern composers *should* be national and (in his case) propagate fascism in their music. If I understood you correctly, you reject all propaganda in music, and by doing so you support the basis for my book (which, by the way, will be published in New York next year): namely, that propaganda of any ideas whatsoever devalues music. I thank you sincerely once again for your interest and the valuable information.[1]

It was precisely in their 'idealism' that the song composer Yrjö Kilpinen believed (in vain, it may be said) that he had something in common with Sibelius. As late as 8 December 1945 he congratulated Sibelius in the 'idealistic spirit',[2] yearning for a fraternity in their worldviews that surely did not exist — certainly not in the years when Kilpinen was very eager to please the Reich administration in Berlin. Sibelius, unlike Kilpinen, was not a member of any Finnish organisation preparing the nation for the post-war years under Reich supervision (such as Suomen Valtakunnan Liitto, the Finnish Reich Union).[3]

Tawaststjerna claims to have discovered in Sibelius an enduring enthusiasm for the Baroque philosopher Emanuel Swedenborg.[4] Sibelius must have heard of Swedenborg, who was a fashionable author for the Strindbergian Modernists, in Berlin around 1889. When Martin Lamm's *Swedenborg* was published in Stockholm in 1915, he bought it. At the time he was writing his Fifth Symphony, he would presumably have been just as fascinated by Swedenborg's intuition, imagination and spiritual divinity as he was by the unreal visions of Swedenborg's worldview. As careful as one needs to be with indirect quotations of this kind in the literature on Sibelius, it is therefore quite conceivable that Sibelius (who was familiar with classical antiquity, including Pythagoras) said at least something like this: 'There may or may not be life on other planets. But one thing is certain: there is music there — as there is everywhere.'[5]

[1] National Library Coll. 206: 22; Licho to JS, 24 February 1939 from Paris. No publication by Licho on this topic could be identified.

[2] National Library Coll. 206: 19.

[3] For an author who aims to show much more intimacy between JS and the Nazis, see Timothy L. Jackson 2010.

[4] Erik W. Tawaststjerna 1997b, pp. 75–6. These formulations give the impression that Tawaststjerna was quoting JS, but the extensive passages on the subject reflect above all his own enthusiasm — as in the above citations relating to Palestrina.

[5] JS quoted in Ronka 1948, p. 46. Ronka was an orchestral musician, composer and conductor of Finnish ancestry who was born in Minnesota. In his description of himself (ibid., appendix), Ronka claims that he 'studied interpretation' with JS from 1936 to 1938, which is unlikely. Ronka may have consulted JS in Ainola a few times.

> 'Odi profanum volgus et arceo' [I hate the vulgar crowd and keep it at bay]. [...] The more Sibelius in his art turns his back on the noise of the world and withdraws further into himself, the more sensitive and delicate his artistry becomes.[1]

1.2 The Avant-Garde's Alternatives

When Did the Twentieth Century Begin?

As a subject of the Russian emperor (the functional title *tsar* did not apply in the autonomous Grand Duchy of Finland), Sibelius continued to serve feudalism's most powerful stronghold until the age of fifty-two, and his mentality retained traces of that cultural sphere even later. Long after the Finnish senate declared independence on 6 December 1917, and after the establishment of the republic in international and domestic policy, the spirit of the huge Eurasian empire of the north-east was omnipresent – palpable in Helsinki in the architecture and the presence of immigrants – to say nothing of its customs and traditions. Even today, the silhouette of the city is marked by the juxtaposition of the Protestant cathedral radiating bright colours and the Russian Orthodox cathedral of red brick and gold. The representatives of the Russian state (the senate, the university) assert themselves alongside the market squares and national cultural sites. This aesthetic contrast is outdone by the neoclassical Protestant churches and the colourfully decorated Orthodox cathedrals in St Petersburg, but in Helsinki the two cathedrals can be viewed simultaneously and with equal aesthetic presence in prominent locations.

Numerous Russian families had lived in the Grand Duchy of Finland prior to the revolution, or at least spent summer in a villa on a lake in Finland, far from Russia's social conflicts, in particular the legendary Ushkovs in Syväranta, just a few kilometres from Sibelius' home, Ainola. Konstantin Kapitanovich Ushkov was one of the richest men in Russia, usually described in the sources as a tea merchant but sometimes as a railway magnate. Before the revolution, Sergey Rachmaninoff, Feodor Shalyapin and Serge Koussevitzky, among others, visited Ushkov and his wife, Theresa Valentinova, in Finland. Later, the Ushkovs' daughter, Natalia, married the conductor Sergei Koussevitzky, a friend of Sibelius' and later famous for his work in Boston. Astonishingly, the artists who visited the Ushkovs until 1916 went unnoticed by the Finnish artistic colony. Unfortunately, the splendid villa Syväranta no longer stands today. Despite more than a century of Russian government in Finland (1809–

[1] JS' student Leevi Madetoja described this opening line of the first of the Roman Odes (Horace, *Odes* 3.1.1) as the motto for everything JS composed in his final years; see 'Jean Sibeliuksen taiteilijanuran yleiset piirteet', in *Helsingin Sanomat*, 8 December 1915; quoted in Salmenhaara 1987, p. 86.

FIG. 5. Panorama from the tower of the Saint Nicholas Church in Helsinki (known since 1917 as Suurkirkko or the 'Great Church', or simply as the Protestant cathedral), facing south-east (photo: Signe Brander 1909). The photograph shows the neoclassical building of the Senate (lower left); Alexander Street, the southern harbour on the right, and on the left the Katajanokka landing stage with trade ships (international harbour); in the background are the fortress island Suomenlinna (originally Sveaborg, established after 1748) and smaller islands with fishermen's huts. Kaivopuisto Park is in the background on the right. Outside this picture on the right is the main building of Helsinki University and, next to the church, the university library with its large Sibelius collection. The national archive, which has an equally extensive and interesting Sibelius collection, is located behind the church.

1917), Russian culture never achieved an importance comparable to Swedish culture — whose history began with the medieval Vikings, after all — but it lent an unmistakable touch to the culture of the capital around 1900 (and later as well).

The idea of an independent Finnish nation united idealist intellectuals and increasingly conservatives, too. After nationalist dreams were realised in 1917, the domestic situation grew unexpectedly complicated, even far beyond the initial crisis of the civil war ('war of independence') in 1918. Although royalist nostalgia was foreign to Sibelius, everyday life under the national republic was just as uncongenial to him. His spiritual roots lay in the culture of the Grand Duchy founded by Alexander I Pavlovich in 1809, with its pronounced internationality and its romanticising transcendentalism. Many nineteenth-century visions of utopian nationalism could not be absorbed by the twentieth-century reality. Moreover, especially after the civil war of 1918, which divided for generations a nation that had not really even begun to exist, there was no connecting, guiding idea, and certain disadvantages of national democracy and of independence became obvious when dealing with everyday problems. That also explains the oppositional stance of Aino Sibelius in the years when 'the people' were not voting 'nationalist' but rather social democratic, when Bolshevism was not yet a thing of the past, and the fascists were trying to push through their own order. In Finland, too, the new National Conservatives (formerly the most radical patriots) sympathised with the fascists for lack of an alternative. Although they had been among those who initiated the reforms that only the Russian revolution made possible, they could scarcely identify with all the consequences.

The idea of an extended century, so important to the profile of Sibelius' generation, took the form in music of a unity of Classicism (the main style) and Romanticism (a secondary style), of a great 'epoch' (politically in Europe as a whole from 1789 to 1914, in music from Christoph Willibald Gluck's Parisian version of *Alceste* to Igor Stravinsky's *Le Sacre du printemps*, and in Finland from the founding of Åbo Musikaliska Sällskapet [Turku musical society] in 1790 and the first version of Sibelius' Fifth Symphony). At the same time, as the first culmination of the new Modernism, it prepared the way for the twentieth century. The question whether the dividing line should more plausibly be dated to 1914 or rather 1918, which is certainly critical in the pan-European context, is almost irrelevant in the case of Finland. The historical turning point of the declaration of independence (politically and culturally) and the actual recognition of the republic by Lenin at the turn of the year 1918 now seem compelling as the date for the founding of the nation, whereas the beginning of the First World War and even the war in general can hardly be said to have shaped the region. Sibelius' diary reflects this: whereas the Senate's declaration of independence is not mentioned there, in January 1918 (undated but prior to January 7) he wrote at length on 'Finland, a free country'. Finland became free in 1918, but the process started long before 1917.

Sibelius did not reflect on this huge political change in his art. Or perhaps it should be seen as a reaction to these events that only ten years later he had already written his last great works. That argument is not convincing, however, especially since he also worked on big projects later, and he sketched his Eighth Symphony – his *opus ultimum* in the tradition of 'Eighths' from Bruckner to Shostakovich, in some respects even of Mahler – at the age of seventy-five. In that sense Gray was correct when he wrote:

> Sibelius is probably the only composer of the older generation whose new works are still capable of arousing our liveliest curiosity and our most sanguine expectations. It would certainly be impossible to hope for any sudden revelation of unsuspected potentialities on the part of Strauss or Elgar, for example, but Sibelius, one feels, might do anything. Alone in his generation, almost alone at the present time even, he does not give the impression of being, temporarily, at least, played out.[1]

[1] Cecil Gray 1926, pp. 336–7, and Cecil Gray 1927, pp. 483–4.

Granted, after 1926 Sibelius no longer expressed himself adequately in great, published works of art but rather primarily in fragments. He had already undergone a major stylistic turn around 1905, during an exciting time, in both politics and art, when the great realist painter Max Liebermann in Berlin was confronted with the new form of Expressionist Modernism of Wassily Kandinsky and others, and Arnold Schoenberg was developing atonality in Vienna. In Finland, the funeral of the national painter of the first generation, Albert Edelfelt, on 24 August 1905, represented an art-historical dividing line. Sibelius composed the solemn choral work *Ej med klagan* (Not with grief; text by Runeberg) for the occasion.

Sibelius had experienced the Secessionist turn around 1890. At that time, the focus of his interests shifted quickly from conventional string quartets to modern orchestral works (*Scène de ballet* in 1891 and *Kullervo* in 1892). Around 1890, art in Europe was reformed from immanent needs, without parallel social upheavals (comparable to those of 1905 and later). Publicly, this took the form of young painters leaving the royal and imperial academies in Munich, Berlin and Vienna after 1892, and even earlier, though unnoticed by the international press, by a national exhibition in Helsinki in October 1891: Suomen Taiteilijain näyttely (Exhibition of Finland's artists).[1] In Helsinki, the 'academy' was Suomen Taideyhdistys (Finland's art society). In addition to Akseli Gallen-Kallela, Sibelius' friends Eero Järnefelt and Albert Edelfelt (both from the ranks of the Suomen Taideyhdistys that was founded in 1846) belonged to the Fennoman Secessionists. Young Finnish artists had organised an alternative exhibition as early as 1882, inspired by the exchange of ideas at the meeting of Nordic artists in 1881 and provoked by squabbles over the Finnish presence in the Pan-Russian Art Exhibition in Moscow in 1882. The earliest conflict of this kind that resulted in a secession took place in Denmark in 1882. Whereas both in 1905 and 1914, social aspects should be emphasised (even Edelfelt's death was less significant than the general strike), for artists like Sibelius the new century really began in the early 1890s. He was one of the oldest composers of the long twentieth century. It is only because of his birth year, 1865, that the relevant encyclopaedias include him in the nineteenth century, as they make 1870 the dividing birth date.[2]

In the history of music, too, the idea of the unique progressiveness of the reforms of 1910–20 was by no means a foregone conclusion. Already by 1890, a solid foundation had been established for a stylistic pluralism without role models, and it was expanded by historical tendencies and a heightened interest in earlier music (in the form both of new editions and arrangements) and ethnomusicology. This turn differed from the avant-garde after 1910 mainly because it placed less value on a revolutionary self-image. Although the modern was perhaps not as clearly articulated as it was after 1910 — only then did treatises and polemics become *de rigueur* among musicians as well — the exhilaration of the reforms of 1880–90 was so profound aesthetically that even those aged around thirty felt 'young'. There was an obligation to

[1] See Konttinen 2001, pp. 51 ff.

[2] See Finscher 2004, pp. 152–3.

break with what was pre-established, both programmatically and technically. Both critics and the representatives of the academies and of late-Romantic realism of 1890 quickly registered this as an unacceptable rebellion — albeit in the framework of what was, in retrospect, a still moderate codex of values not yet violated by the revolutions. It has since become common to derive even the radical quality of the later Modernists of the second decade of the twentieth century — apart from peripheral exceptions such as Futurism — from earlier forms, even when that conclusion contradicts the writings of the artists in question. Anyone today (a Sibelius scholar or anyone else) who starts out from the premises of Postmodernism and views history retrospectively can scarcely avoid treating the change of the years around 1890 as the main dividing line between epochs.

When Sibelius completed his first orchestral compositions, *Scène de ballet* and *Kullervo*, in 1891–2, a modern diversity of styles gathered pace in Europe, the ruthless egocentrism of Don Juan and the freedom from all traditions. With an eye to Richard Strauss, one could indeed speak of the period from 1890 onwards as the age of Don Juan, which would be plausible not only in terms of the reception of Richard Dehmel and of *Don Giovanni* but also the use of the Lemminkäinen *topos* (*Kalevala*) in Sibelius' work. Around 1894, the Norwegian Modernist Edvard Munch spoke of the 'age of Carmen' and emphasised the emancipation of women,[1] which is not necessarily a contradiction.

Whereas the long nineteenth century nevertheless lasted at least until 1914 and inspired important masterpieces even later, long after 1890, the twentieth century began with the actual or virtual departure of young artists from the academies and with an exemplary lack of respect for the educational authority of their elders. In general, the younger generation was intolerant of any signs of a standardised aesthetic. Hence the 'twilight zone'[2] — in Hobsbawm's phrase — that surrounded Sibelius' generation is both an appropriate name for the period of transition to the avant-garde proper and a term for the first genuine avant-garde. However, to put into perspective the historical position of the generation that followed poses a real challenge. The theorists around Schoenberg, Stravinsky and others, for whom an intellectual streak was otherwise characteristic, were, of course, unable to do so either, since it would have meant putting their own historical achievement in perspective. But today it should at last be possible.

Hobsbawm emphasises how 'we certainly start with the assumption of our own time, place and situation, including the propensity to shape the past in our terms, to see what it has sharpened our eye to discern and only what our perspective allows us to recognize'.[3] Starting from this idea, the problems posed for historians of music by

[1] See Müller-Westermann 2003, p. 71. On the *topos* of femininity, see chapter 2.2 in the present volume.

[2] Hobsbawm 1987, p. 5.

[3] Ibid., p. 4.

FIG. 6. Theatre esplanade in Helsinki, seen in winter (photo: K. E. Stålberg, *c.* 1895). This photograph shows the boulevard between the market square at the harbour and the Swedish Theatre; appearing in the background are the monument to the poet J. L. Runeberg and carriages in the centre. Note the temporary cross-country skiing trail produced after a heavy snowfall.

the personal and social dependence of the present age on the achievements of this transitional period (and the challenge of any effort to study them) are obvious. This implies not only that every generation is obliged to write 'history' itself and to assess the beginning and end of important processes but also that every generation, if not every later-born individual, is in a position to see things that were invisible to those living at the time. Since historical eyewitnesses are involved in the things on which they are supposed to report, their presence at the scene of the crime undermines their claim to unimpeachable objectivity. So the first witness cannot be the best witness.[1] Objectivity with regard to the overlapping of centuries, for instance, can only be expected to increase substantially after the long twentieth century has come to an end once and for all. That is when the 'twilight' ends.

[1] Jalas admitted this in JS' presence; see Jalas 1981, p. 54.

The Third Path: Barber, Busoni, von Einem and Stevenson

For several of his contemporaries, Sibelius was the hero of a different path, one that exposed the unreflected tradition of the not-yet-post-Romantics and the systematic renewal through dodecaphony. For the British composer and pianist Ronald Stevenson, as late as 1948, Sibelius and Busoni were 'the only great signposts pointing the way to true art'[1] against the 'thorns of modern experimentalism, which all too often is an end in itself'. Stevenson, a convinced Marxist and pacifist, had been imprisoned for conscientious objection and asked Sibelius for support. In 1938 the 28-year-old Samuel Barber sent his famous *Adagio for Strings* and *Essay for Orchestra* for Sibelius to look at and wrote: 'Your music means so much to us who are trying once more to compose, after the years of post-war experimentation into which we were born – your example as an artist is so beautiful and encouraging.'[2]

Sibelius liked to read such things. He reacted extraordinarily amiably to the dedication with which Frederick Hunt of Woodstock, New York, honoured him on 4 September 1934. Hunt wrote on his new string quartet: 'It is still the Hebrew from Russia and Poland who labels himself "American Composer", and in doing so reflects little credit upon either himself or America. Up to the present time, and probably it will be true for some years to come, the musical culture of our country is seriously biased by a conglomerate of European tastes and prejudices.'[3] Sibelius noted in his draft letter of 12 August 1935: 'especially your quartet [is] a very interesting one. It is well and poetically written. I want also to tell you that my sincere opinion is that the genuinely American musical ~~al art~~ will prove to have a great future.' Sibelius did not repeat Hunt's anti-Semitic sideswipes. Despite Louis Moreau Gottschalk, Charles Ives, Henry Cowell and Edgard Varèse, whom Sibelius had already met at Busoni's home in Berlin prior to the war, his prediction was a bold one, and perhaps primarily gallantry. Although it cannot always be assumed that Sibelius wrote such notes himself, as a rule they were cleared with him. It must be assumed that his English correspondence was a task for the entire family (his wife, Aino, and their eldest daughter, Eva, in particular) until Santeri Levas was hired as his part-time secretary in 1938.

The Anglo-American enthusiasm for Sibelius, which extends on the highest level from Ralph Vaughan Williams to John Adams and Peter Maxwell Davies, makes it easy to overlook Continental Europeans such as the German-Austrian composer Gottfried von Einem. While still a senior in high school, he wrote to Sibelius on 30 March 1936 to request an autograph for his copy of Sibelius' Violin Concerto. Six months later, after hearing the Second Symphony in London, he wanted to dedicate a piece to Sibelius. Around 1935, his diary records only his detailed reception of Gus-

[1] National Library Coll. 206: 37; Stevenson to JS, 25 October 1948. On Stevenson's own career, see, for example, MacDonald 1997.

[2] National Library Coll. 206: 2; Samuel Barber to JS, 16 December 1938, from New York.

[3] National Library Coll. 206: 16. Hunt wrote to JS from Rochester on 3 October 1939.

tav Mahler. The name Sibelius first appears on 17 September 1936, as the dedicatee of a new work (*Adagio*): 'And worked on Sibelius piece.'[1] In 1936, Sibelius had already supplanted the Jewish-Austrian Mahler. A few weeks earlier, von Einem noted: 'Read Hitler, Goethe, Horace then polished the piece [*Adagio*].' On 23 September 1936, he called his Sibelius piece 'blessed', but on 3 October he recognised that adjustments were urgently necessary. On 7 November, he sent his *Adagio* to Finland.

On 27 November he received Sibelius' reply. The waves of ecstasy pounded in his young chest: 'Eternity – Sibelius – life – divinity – nobility' he wrote in his diary. On 2 December, von Einem expressed his enthusiasm for the Second Symphony: 'Gloomy, austere, hard = 1st movement [...] Forest, gloomy Finnish winter = 3rd movement. A wonderful human being this genius.' In late December he was occupied both with the Norwegian Knut Hamsun's ultramodern narrative style in *The Ring Is Closed* (orig. 1936) and the instrumentation of his *Adagio*. In February 1937 he was eagerly awaiting a 'Sibelius concert' in Berlin, but on 25 February he did not in fact attend it. In March he purchased a recording of *Finlandia*. From the luxurious Hotel Adlon in Berlin, where he later lived for a year, he sent Sibelius a friendly request for a recommendation, with which he hoped to win over Wilhelm Furtwängler. This time Sibelius' reply was negative: 'Please do not send me scores as I am travelling [...]. I never write recommendations. Yours, Sibelius.'[2] Von Einem was very disappointed. Neither Sibelius' departure nor his systematic refusal to write recommendations was accurate. Von Einem's *Adagio für grosses Orchester*, whose piano score was 'Dedicated to Professor Jean Sibelius with respect and admiration' and dated 16 October 1936, is found in Sibelius' collection of scores in Helsinki, along with Stevenson's *Choral Prelude* for piano (1948). Another piece in the same archival collection is titled 'Symphonic Phantasy: Sun of the Sleepless' (Lord Byron) in B flat minor (1948); the composer is unknown but the paper on which it is written was made in the United States.[3]

As Albrecht Riethmüller has shown using the example of Ferruccio Busoni, for the first 'Leskovite' (a term for the young men around Busoni and his Newfoundland dog, Lesko, who included Sibelius in Helsinki),[4] 'the new dawn of twentieth-century music did not point forwards in a straight line but was Janus-faced'. Riethmüller emphasised an aspect that was important for Busoni but is evident only in Sibelius' early work, and even there only as an idea – namely, that 'the will to innovation retains a powerful retrospective quality'.[5] In Sibelius' work, the retrospective was connected only indirectly with the archaism of the *Kalevala*, free of Central European historicism. Closer to Sibelius' ideas of art is the Danish composer Carl Nielsen's note from 1913: 'We would have to ensure we get away from keys and yet still seem convincing

[1] Diary in the von Einem papers in the archives of the Gesellschaft der Musikfreunde, Vienna.

[2] National Library Coll. 206: 10.

[3] National Archive Box 57; a copy exists in von Einem's papers.

[4] See Erik W. Tawaststjerna 1976, pp. 45–6. Busoni's *Geharnischte Suite* is a musical portrait of the 'Leskovites'.

[5] Riethmüller 1988, p. 7.

FIG. 7. Gottfried von Einem, *Adagio für grosses Orchester* (piano score). This composition ('Calm, solemn [. . .] very warm in expression!') was dedicated by an eighteen-year-old Gottfried von Einem to Sibelius in 1936 ('with respect and admiration'), who immediately accepted the dedication and sent a signed copy to the young composer.

diatonically. That is the point, and in that I feel a striving for freedom in me.'[1] The parallels between Nielsen and Sibelius have hardly been studied at all,[2] while it is a cliché of the reception of Modernism to reflect on the nature of Sibelius' modernity in terms of Busoni's work. The Danish church historian Jørgen I. Jensen has in the meanwhile called attention to a streak in Nielsen that deviates from Busoni, and what he writes applies without qualification to Sibelius as well:

> Under no circumstances, however, did he wish to write in the old style; it is as if he felt a challenge to bring together extremely different impulses and inspirations in one and the same work. His intention was, in a chaotic world in which every personal, artistic and social foothold is slipping, to allow immense forces into his music but not simply to depict them but find a meaning – musically: a form – that can pass something on despite everything. [...] He wants to say 'Yes!' despite everything.[3]

Busoni was connected to Helsinki not only by his activity as a piano teacher but also by his marriage to the daughter of the Swedish sculptor Carl A. Sjöstrand, who was active in Helsinki. According to Sibelius, he met Busoni daily in 1888–9, even though Busoni was a foreign piano teacher in a senior position and he was studying the violin.[4] Busoni confirmed friendships with the 'pupil Sibelius' as well as with Adolf Paul and the Järnefelts.[5] Sibelius did not think highly of Busoni as a composer, as he noted in his diary on 3 November 1910: 'Why must this great artist of the piano compose?' He respected him all the more as a pianist. On 22 January 1905, he wrote to Kajanus from Berlin: Busoni played 'like an angel'.[6] Not even as a conductor could Busoni maintain his position in Sibelius' eyes. 'He is not an especially good conductor', he wrote to his Berlin publisher Robert Lienau on 21 December 1907.[7] On 11 January 1913, he wrote with concern in his diary that Busoni wanted to conduct the Fourth Symphony in Berlin on 25 January: 'Am extremely unhappy about that, because the piece is at the beginning and he is no conductor. He cannot conduct this work. Oh dear!' Their friendship survived the decades anyway. Henry Wood wrote of their legendary meeting in London as late as February 1921: 'I could generally manage Busoni when I had him to myself, but my heart was always in my mouth if he met Sibelius. I never knew where they would get to. [...] They were like a couple of irresponsible schoolboys.'[8]

It seems obvious to compare Sibelius to Busoni. Thus Stevenson described these

[1] Jensen 1996, p. 393.
[2] See Simpson [1952] 1986.
[3] Jensen 1996, p. 394.
[4] Ekman 1946, pp. 60 ff., and Erik W. Tawaststjerna 1976, p. 45.
[5] Busoni to Hans Huber, 29 April 1918; quoted in Erik W. Tawaststjerna 1976, p. 45.
[6] Erik W. Tawaststjerna 1986, p. 25.
[7] Quoted ibid., p. 102.
[8] Wood 1938, pp. 141–2; quoted in Erik W. Tawaststjerna 1997b, p. 200.

two musicians — in a letter to Sibelius on 25 October 1948,[1] which is revealing about both Stevenson's life and the early history of Busoni's British reception — as exceptions in the age of 'modern experimentalism'.[2] Tawaststjerna suspects that Busoni had been discussing his new ideas on *Junge Klassizität* (young classicism) with Sibelius since 1905 and notes that Busoni's ideas of depth in seemingly cheerful music were relevant for Sibelius, too, around 1905.[3] One of Busoni's examples of 'cheerful depth' was Mozart's *Don Giovanni* and especially its 'champagne aria'. Sibelius had been already encountered that opera in autumn 1890 and in 1891. Both in Berlin and in Vienna he attended current productions of *Don Giovanni* immediately on arrival. In spring 1889, he had heard Busoni perform Liszt's *Réminiscences de Don Juan* in Helsinki. In 1905, moreover, Sibelius was interested in the neoclassical realist Edelfelt. But he distanced himself from Gallen-Kallela, whom Edelfelt had also criticised as 'dark' and demonic.[4] It is possible to read the Hellenistic depth of *Junge Klassizität* as a reaction against the melancholy of the *fin de siècle*, the sensuousness of grand late Romanticism with ideological depths and Symbolism. It is highly probable that Busoni was one of the colleagues who aroused Sibelius' interest in universal classicism.

Busoni and Sibelius are both victims of the Modernist idea of development and progress — as opposed to organic change and contrast — as the driving forces of European history. Comparing them can help us to analyse an alternative modern approach typical of its day. Both loved to experiment but were at the same time in a position to avert both radical and reactionary tendencies. Albeit not with the power of Busoni's theoretical treatises, Sibelius' music also compels us to reflect critically on the multidimensional nature of the present. It is easy to overlook this, as is clear from the German musicologist and composer Hans Heinz Stuckenschmidt's reply to Erik Tawaststjerna on 3 September 1969. Tawaststjerna had asked why Stuckenschmidt had not mentioned Sibelius in his book *Schöpfer der Neuen Musik* (The creators of new music; 1958), whereas the entire first chapter was devoted to Busoni: 'My answer is: Because the whole book is written with an eye to phenomena that shaped the future, composers who inspired a school. And I don't see that quality in Sibelius. That does not change anything about his absolute importance and singularity. As a creative power, he is doubtless superior to Busoni, but Busoni led to the founding of a school and thus had to be a major figure in my book.'[5] His reply is unconvincing, though it

[1] In a later, undated letter, Stevenson asked JS for material assistance with the design of his book on Busoni; National Library Coll. 206: 37.

[2] National Library Coll. 206: 37, Stevenson to JS, 25 October 1948. According to a formal note, JS answered this letter, in which Stevenson also asked his opinion of a piano piece he had dedicated to Aino, on 5 December 1948. Stevenson thanked JS for a reply from 16 January 1948, so apparently the reply of 5 December 1948 was undated, and Stevenson did not receive it until January. Stevenson wrote the first letter in Peeblesshire, Scotland, and the second from 1948 in Blackburn, Lancashire.

[3] Erik W. Tawaststjerna 1986, p. 26.

[4] Ibid., p. 36.

[5] National Archive: Original in the Tawaststjerna collection.

is true that Sibelius was not active in shaping the future as a teacher of master classes — or anything else comparable to Busoni's activity at the academy and elsewhere, for example, in Helsinki in the 1890s — and did not write an aesthetic 'sketch' with important innovations that could be compared to Busoni's publications, particularly *Entwurf einer neuen Aesthetik der Tonkunst* of 1907 (translated as *Sketch of a New Esthetic of Music* in 1911).

In the literature on Sibelius, the idea of a multilateral Modernism traditionally provides the foundation for defending the composer against the mainstream avant-garde. His heterogeneous oeuvre was schooled in multilayered, historically polylinear thinking and in the acceptance of the current synchronicity of the historically non-synchronous. For example, Constant Lambert's *Music Ho! A Study of Music in Decline* did not intensify into an attack on the 'official revolution' of Schoenberg, who 'escaped from an academic set of rules only to be shackled by his own set of rules' and founded a school in the traditional sense.[1] Following a complex dialectical debate that does not seem at all incorrigibly anti-Modernist, Lambert formulated the sentence: 'In Sibelius, however, we have the first great composer since Beethoven [...].' Though often cited in this form (as a fragment), his idea does not end where it generally ends when cited in the literature on Sibelius but instead continues: 'whose mind thinks naturally in terms of symphonic form'. Lambert wrote this after observing that around 1910 the symphony was already considered a worn-out 'horse bus'.[2] Moreover, Lambert regarded Sibelius' particular genius as deriving from the rare combination of Beethoven's symphonic writing and the timbres of the 'Impressionist' revolution. In his view, the prerequisite for an approach to Beethoven as a model that had promise for the future was Sibelius' supposed distance from the Romantic and the so-called New German ('Neudeutsche') movement (Liszt, Wagner). To put it another way, Lambert believed that Sibelius had absorbed Romantic practice not uncritically, so that he could begin his own creativity in a very unconstrained way at the roots of Beethoven's symphonic writing. Lambert saw the contemporaneous and the genuinely classical, the timeless and natural quality of Sibelius' symphonic writing as lacking both Romantic and realistic veils as well as any neoclassical self-consciousness in the wake of either Schoenberg or Stravinsky.

After a detailed study of Sibelius' orchestral works, Lambert's final chapter is titled 'Sibelius and the Music of the Future'. He numbered the Fourth and Seventh Symphonies among the 'most astonishing creative efforts of our time'. He considered Sibelius the answer to many of the questions of the aesthetics of music he had posed in his lifetime.[3] He wrote that 'since the death of Debussy, Sibelius and Schoenberg are the most significant figures in European music', but he found Sibelius to be 'the more complete artist of the two'. The difficulty of imitating Sibelius' style, which is notable

[1] Lambert 1934, p. 288.
[2] Ibid., p. 318.
[3] Ibid., pp. 326–7.

especially when considering the criterion of establishing a school, is not, in Lambert's view, one of the drawbacks of Sibelius' work but rather its exemplary characteristic in comparison to that of Schoenberg. This thought contains both the paradoxical and the fruitful aspect of the idea of shaping the future: not inventions and experiments but artistic qualities, the expression of true life experience ('spiritual experience of a lifetime' rather than 'external mannerisms'), make the 'future' possible. For Lambert, then, it is not just Sibelius' music as it sounds that is exemplary but also, and especially, his 'solitary figure', setting off on his own paths.[1] Writing in 1934, and thus not having to argue specifically with Adorno's still unpublished 'gloss' on Sibelius of 1938, much less with a colleague like Stuckenschmidt, Lambert observed from his own point of enquiry that in the twentieth century it could not be the artist's task to be a troublemaker but rather to search for new forms of spiritual affirmation as a way to approach the world (especially since, from a postmodern perspective, regardless of one's political stripe, thoroughly structured, totalitarian states represent the culmination of 'modern', superficially rational civilisation). The artist's task was not to reject the world critically (as Adorno would have expected him to do) but to establish open contact to the genuine 'world' as such.

Technical studies of composition and the extension of the range of legitimate aspects of musical analysis have made it increasingly difficult for critics to attack Sibelius for a supposed lack of knowledge of developments in Central Europe or as a spoilsport of Modernism, much less to ignore him as a marginal phenomenon (and a 'Nordic' one at that). Whereas Busoni certainly earned his undeniably special place in the history of Modernism as a performer, theorist and unique 'mentor of modern music'[2] – being active right up to his death as the teacher of such radical avant-gardists as Edgard Varèse and Kurt Weill, who strove to achieve a different kind of Modernism, and even, in the broadest sense, Stuckenschmidt[3] – Sibelius appears to stand outside of the history of musical education. Within the paradigm of monolinear progress, it is legitimate to ignore Busoni's work as a composer for that reason and instead to concentrate on his nonconformist writings and students, whereas Sibelius cannot be overlooked in concert life but had nothing to offer other than his music. He operated on the principle – since claimed by Riethmüller for Busoni as well – that the *telos* of his creation shapes the composition,[4] without any restriction. His conducting of his own work was 'effective' but by no means as technically perfect as the baton work of Mahler or Strauss. His instrumental prowess could not be compared to that of Debussy or Reger. His theoretical fragments were similarly modest. For both

[1] Ibid., p. 331.

[2] Riethmüller 1988, p. 12.

[3] See Stuckenschmidt 1979, pp. 44 ff.

[4] Riethmüller 1988, p. 7.

Sibelius and Busoni, however, 'the act of completing was just as important as the thing completed'.[1]

The creative work of Busoni and Sibelius followed a process whose stages demonstrated that each had his own relationship to late eighteenth-century classicism. In each case, the early work has 'strong signs of a lack of independence and of borrowing'. For both, their penchant for modern classicism after 1900 also represented maturity. The classicistic aspect of Sibelius' work, which does not completely preclude elements of Romanticism (Ringbom wrote: 'He is neither a pronounced romanticist nor a classicist. He is both, and yet he is neither the one nor the other'[2]), was influenced by his own violin playing. Later Sibelius pursued his path along the edge of tonality and seemingly historicising modality (the *tonus ecclesiasticus*): organic, less consciously constructed but nevertheless intently reflecting on the relevance of what has already been completed and what remains to be completed. Both artists tried, each in his own way, to work in a synthesising way and to combine their original experiences with artistic qualities of lasting value. Both were also concerned with the question whether 'what has been completed stood and still stands in the correct or incorrect relationship to the incredible will, the unprecedented tension and strain and the distant and elevated objective'.[3] In Sibelius' work, the utopian will is thus less obvious, since his oeuvre lacks a clearly articulated 'sketch of a new aesthetic'. Yet this makes his objective all the more prominent in his compositions.

Both artists chose the martyr's path: Busoni by abandoning his natural calling as a concert pianist and instead trying to develop as a composer and conductor laboriously working against the resistance of the 'material' and tradition; Sibelius by giving up his calling as a composer of pleasing salon music and pursuing pseudo-religious goals, without being able to fully realise his own new art music, his *opus ultimum maximum*. Hence his unfinished Eighth Symphony shared the fate of the other great utopian works of that era – from William Havergal Brian's *Fantastic Symphony* and Busoni's fragmentary opera *Doktor Faust* to Schoenberg's *Die Jakobsleiter* and *Moses und Aron*. Busoni concretised his utopia in the concept of 'Young' – that is, not yet fully mature and established but rather youthful – Classicism,[4] whereas Sibelius managed only suggestions on the theme of classicism. No one today can know how close the Eighth Symphony came to being the ultimate work of art before the score was destroyed.[5] Busoni and Sibelius shared a 'distrust of everything conventional'[6] and an eclectic openness to the old-fashioned styles and forms.

[1] Ibid., p. 11.

[2] See Ringbom 1954, p. 79. According to Ringbom, JS ended his 'romantic period' with his Second Symphony.

[3] Wassermann 1928, p. 4; quoted in Riethmüller 1988, p. 13.

[4] Riethmüller 1988, p. 28.

[5] Josephson 2004 argues that JS' Eighth Symphony can be reconstructed based on sketches he has identified.

[6] Riethmüller 1988, p. 29.

Fig. 8. Ronald Stevenson, *Choral Prelude for Jean Sibelius* (known as no. 2 of the *Three Lyric Pieces* for piano). This interesting composition, which the British composer dedicated to Sibelius in October 1948, documents Stevenson's interest in Sibelius. The piece has 206 bars. An addition to the tempo indication is revealing: 'velato e visionario'.

Busoni's influence on Sibelius' turn from Wagner to Liszt is solidly documented, as is the reference to the discovery of Debussy around 1905.[1] Thus in Busoni's case Sibelius admitted more influences than ever regarding contacts with colleagues or concrete sources. Unfortunately, most of the conversations in Berlin – much less those among the Leskovites in Helsinki or in London in 1921 – cannot be reconstructed. The significance of Busoni's influence on Sibelius was probably matched only by that of his violin teachers and of Kajanus, who placed his orchestra in Helsinki 'completely at the service of my art – partly by placing it at my disposal whenever I wanted to try out the effects of certain tonal combinations, or wished to hear how my scores really sounded'.[2] The influence of these artists was doubtless more important than the influence of his harmony and composition teachers and mentors, including his occasional conversations with the illustrious Viennese composer of romantic opera Karl Goldmark.

Nevertheless, Nils-Eric Ringbom's assertion – freely based on Lambert – that Sibelius occupies 'a unique position in the music of our time' is right. The Danish critic Gunnar Hauch's view, which Ringbom also made his own, seems counterproductive: 'that Sibelius was *the* great personality in an arid period'.[3] People speak of desperate times when they feel threatened. Given his success, Sibelius had no need for such formulas, especially as he never used the 'silence of Ainola' – inasmuch as his work was not interrupted by his large family, his friends and the Foreign Ministry – solely to listen to performances of his symphonies on the radio but also to work on his art.

'Spiritual Energy' as Model

Busoni and Sibelius shared the idea of 'pure music' – which is also what Sibelius meant by saying he offered 'pure cold water' rather than 'cocktails'[4] – despite the constant striving to achieve utopia that is manifested in various 'declarations of faith' and 'prayers' (symphonies). For Busoni, pure music was a synonym for Young Classicism. It included both instrumental and vocal genres. Unlike Paul Valéry's 'poésie pure', it remained open to metaphysics. This opening also provided Sibelius with the basis for his metaphor of 'water'. Revealingly, he characterised Busoni's relationship to nature and perception of the environment (especially the outdoors) as follows: 'In the early stages of our friendship [said Sibelius] he could never get over how much I had gained through my contact with nature. Later he understood me better, although with his very pronounced intellectual, reflective attitude he could never surrender himself

[1] See chapter 3.5 in the present volume.

[2] Quoted in Ringbom 1954, p. 38.

[3] Ibid., p. 3.

[4] Cecil Gray 1931, p. 11. According to Furuhjelm 1916b, these metaphors were used by JS. On Busoni, see Riethmüller 1988, pp. 29 and 182 ff.

directly to nature's impressions.'[1] What Sibelius associated with nature was indeed completely incomprehensible and incredible for many. Paul Bekker wrote: 'We know that nature is nothing other than the eternally growing, eternally renewing in ourselves. We believe we want to grasp and hold this nature.'[2] Thus he too revealed how little idea he had of the subject under discussion and how faithfully he followed the Hegelian manner. Bekker was, however, right in his criticism of the racist tendencies in that era's ideology of nature and ethnicity.

The American cellist Marquery Stoddard, who was convinced she had understood Sibelius' art and who had worked with one of Sibelius' favourite conductors, Werner Janssen, tried in 1938 to win him over to the idea of a cello concerto with an aphoristic concatenation of technical and aesthetic concepts: 'What is it I ask you that makes your Music so Life giving?? Is it because of the wide distribution of parts? or your underlying base in everything that gives it that tremendous power of the elements????'[3] The desire to derive the 'tremendous power of the elements' and the ability to 'give life' from the instrumentation and harmony and counterpoint was characteristic of this NBC Symphony Orchestra cellist and teacher at the Nature Music School of California. She wanted not just to sense but also understand Sibelius' 'Life giving' function, the 'pure water'.

Sibelius' elemental effect on many composers and music lovers is linked not only to the scores and the soulful creative force palpable in his works but also to his image as an artist. Salmenhaara writes at the beginning of his Sibelius biography that further studies were motivated not only by the 'spiritual energy of his masterpieces' but also by Sibelius' particular 'creative activity'.[4] Even earlier, Karl Ekman wrote an introduction to 'the artist's life and personality' – explicitly leaving out the compositions, which had already been the subject of 'excellent studies'.[5] Ekman certainly considered the Scottish music critic Cecil Gray's *Sibelius* of 1931 to be one of these, in which fewer than fifty of some two hundred pages are devoted to aesthetic premises and explanations of his biography and cultural history.

The conflict between construction and destruction typical of that entire era, breaking the boundaries of hermetic composition and making an artist's creativity in general the object of reception, was particularly flagrant in the case of Sibelius. His emphatically imaginative way of working – far from the idea of a skilled artisan filling his orders in a functional workshop – becomes evident not least from his dependence on 'moods' (*stämming* in Swedish, a favourite topic in his early letters to Aino, for example on 28 July 1894), walks and the weather, and not so much on desk, pencil, piano and paper. In that sense, his personality and music are rightly associated with nature and naturalness, the elements and the universe, even though many

1 Quoted in Ringbom 1954, p. 15.

2 Bekker, 'Die "Rückkehr zur Natur"' (1920), in Bekker 1921, p. 336.

3 National Library Coll. 206: 37; Stoddard to JS, 11 January 1938.

4 Salmenhaara 1984, p. 8.

5 Ekman 1946, p. xiii.

compositions were written in smoke-filled hotel rooms – where there were 'moods' as well, after all. Even Salmenhaara underscored this by placing the early string duo *Waterdrops* (1881?) at the beginning of his argument because of its programme based on nature and the obvious attempt to use the violin and violoncello to capture natural sounds.[1] Whether or not this piece is correctly dated, it is an early document of the subjective importance of the parameters of sound and gesture.

Wendy Hall observed that Sibelius, as a 'Finn', had a 'primeval relationship to nature'.[2] Hall's richly illustrated essay 'Sibelius and the Finnish Landscape' (1950) is a perfect example of the creation of analogies between music and nature – rarely so concretely verbalised – possibly inspired by Robert Schumann's 'landscapes in sound' and 'Naturwahrheit', or 'truth of nature' (though not abandoning a 'poetic view').[3] Writing on Sibelius, Hall emphasised nature as an 'elemental force against which man must struggle constantly'. Her thesis is that every landscape finds expression in an artistic form. She hears the gentle curves of the English countryside in poetry and sees France's light in painting. She suspected that the symphony is the only form adequate to the northern landscape and saw Sibelius' music as its 'true utterance'. Hall saw the following relationships between Sibelius and a selection of photographs of Finland:

1 the main theme of the First Symphony: Wäinö Aaltonen's bust of Sibelius ('characteristic power and depth');
2 the oboe theme from the Scherzo of the Second Symphony (Lento e suave): an aerial photograph of Lake Saimaa ('Island-dotted, stretches in its wide silence beyond vision', 'enchantment and serenity');
3 a fortissimo theme with its counterpart in a flowing movement of eighth-notes from the Second Symphony: the rapids of Imatra (with hydroelectric power systems in the background);
4 another aerial photograph of Lake Saimaa, with two Nordmann firs in the foreground: the first motif of the Violin Concerto ('From the heights above Saimaa the distance shimmers gently beyond motionless trees');
5 the Tempo di minuetto theme of the *Karelia* Suite: a peasant with a small *kantele* (a traditional Finnish string instrument) on his knees;
6 the massively orchestrated Adagio in 3/2 from the first movement of the Fourth Symphony: remains of trees on Mount Koli ('Wind-gnarled trees and granite boulders at Koli');
7 the Tempo Largo of the Fourth Symphony: birches in winter ('The stark wintry nakedness of the birch forest in the snow brings to mind the solitary

[1] Salmenhaara 1984, pp. 11–12.

[2] Hall 1950 (cited here from the reprint). For more details and illustrations, see Mäkelä 2010, pp. 344–50.

[3] Cf. Schumann's review of William Sterndale Bennett in Schumann 1914, pp. 246–7.

and strained mood of the Fourth Symphony, with its lonely notes and unyielding form');
8 the Alla marcia theme from the *Karelia* Suite: a boy and his horse.

Such visual analogies are by no means solely an unhealthy product of misguided amateurism. The British composer Arthur Bliss suddenly thought of Sibelius when flying to Moscow over Helsinki in April 1956: 'Flying over Finland with its network of lakes, its forests, its mists and snows, was like experiencing a Sibelius tone poem.'[1] Unfortunately, we do not know which tone poems Bliss knew.

Such associations with nature have accumulated over the history of Sibelius' reception; they make it almost impossible to grasp the core of the composer's personality. The first to choose this focus was Paul, who in his novel *En bok om en människa* (A book about a man) has Silén, alias Sibelius, himself say that art 'cannot constitute mathematical puzzles [...]. Rather, it has to be nature – more like the nature that has produced both of them [science and art].'[2] The 25-year-old postulated nature as the opposite pole to mathematics (representing technology, civilisation and reason), which shows just how experience-based – explicitly not philosophical – his understanding of the theme was. To be sure, the categories of nature and naturalness have taken on lives of their own as keywords in the secondary literature – for example, when Sibelius' interest in Bruckner is explained by noting that Bruckner's 'feeling for nature and religiosity' corresponds to Sibelius' 'pantheistic outlook'.[3] On the one hand, this distracts from the melodic and harmonic subtleties in Bruckner that captivated the young Sibelius. On the other, it presumes that the complex of nature and a feeling for nature does not necessitate a distinction – never mind that the composer's relationship to myth and pantheism is anything but a demonstrated fact, to say nothing of his supposed pantheism ever having been considered with a critical eye to the sources.

In a letter to the maestro, the famous German dramaturge Hans Joachim Schaefer compared Sibelius, 'a Finnish landscape turned into sound', to Bruckner:

> This is not a question of technical issues but rather of spiritual attitude, of a humble relationship to nature and to the eternal in it and above it. It is a matter of the 'sanctification' your music experiences from this attitude. [...] Considering that, in an age that wants to write music according to theories, you always had the strength to express simply and without compromise what is essential to us as human beings, that you had the courage to stand up, even alone, to the tide of passing fashion, [there is] still much to be done in our

[1] Bliss [1989] 1991, p. 196.
[2] Paul 1891, p. 227.
[3] Erik W. Tawaststjerna 1991, p. 22.

country to ensure that your work meets with the response and understanding that it has in England, for example.[1]

In conclusion, Schaefer managed to compare Sibelius to Michael Tippett, supported by this reference to Bruckner.

The projection of feelings and ideas into nature, to paraphrase the philosopher Friedrich Theodor Vischer, is sometimes seen as Finnish pantheism, though this turns out to be a cliché. When Tawaststjerna speaks of Sibelius' 'pantheistic-mystic disposition', it is an effort to explain Sibelius' interest in Runeberg, the Swedish-language poet of the older, loyalist generation, though every educated Finn around 1880 had read him, and in Emanuel Swedenborg, who was fashionable in Central Europe.[2] The idea of equal value may also be connected to the fact that Finland's natural environment differs from that of western, central and southern Europe and is not characterised by gorges, massifs or storm tides. Nature in Finland represents for artists (including Sibelius) a space for thinking and feeling that is not spectacular but rather accessible. At the same time, it remains unruly in terms of its basic elements, since the water freezes, the sun shines in unbalanced proportions, and the stone can barely be modelled (there is a lot of granite in Finland, but hardly any limestone or sandstone). Nature did not give itself over to human beings as gentle farmland but neither did it threaten them; it presented itself as a wilful vis-à-vis. That is not an appropriate foundation for pantheism but rather for respect and love for and interest in the elements. Nature does not seem like a beautiful or sublime landscape, flora and fauna but rather as light, water and stone (earth), into which human beings too are organically integrated.

The central question is the extent to which his music can be associated with nature in the usual meaning of the word or rather with myth and mythology as alternative worlds, apart from trivial programmatic relationships such as those of the *Kalevala* tone poems, the portraits of artists of *En saga* and *The Bard* and the images of nature from antiquity of *The Oceanides* (ancient goddesses of fresh water, daughters of Poseidon, in the *Kalevala* Canto 1:110 ff.) and *The Dryad*, a tree nymph. He has another relationship with civilisation, which consists not only of his 'cultural environment' – namely, the Swedish language and the codex of bourgeois values – but also in the whole fabric of impulses he took not only from Viennese Classicism but also from salon Romanticism and such contemporaries as Wagner, Tchaikovsky and Bruckner. In Finland of the late nineteenth century, myth and mythology did not really represent an alternative world but are rather themselves one fruit of contemporary culture. In mythology, in keeping with the etymology of the word, elementary experiences are merely verbalised and understood in a way suitable to language. Only pre-linguistic, elementary nature as such is an alternative, as the first Romantics – and not least

[1] National Library Coll. 206: 33; Hans Joachim Schaefer to JS, 2 June 1954; cf. JS' reply on 10 June 1954, and Hans Joachim Schaefer to JS, 2 June 1953, and JS' reply on 2 July 1953.

[2] See Erik W. Tawaststjerna 1996, p. 148, and Erik W. Tawaststjerna 1976, p. 20.

Rousseau – recognised. In its most characteristic manifestations, it alone actively resists verbalisation and concretisation.

The conventional explanatory models for mythology, which see it as an attempt to subordinate nature and its forces to a system of thought, differ in their response to the question of the significance attributed to mythological raw material (prior to verbalisation) or to the omnipresence of mythical 'forces'. Even those who emphasise this last aspect always point to forms of society and community (to the cultural function of myth) in which the myth functions, thus making the individual's relationship to myth secondary.[1] Verbalisation does not, however, imply that myths should be seen as trivial fairy tales and legends. With regard to their religious dimension, they can certainly be intended as traditional knowledge, since 'the myth tells a sacred story'.[2] For Sibelius, poetic ideas and suggestions were more important than stories. His task was not to achieve a completely structured narrative in beautiful sounds but rather to give musical form to the poetic.

[1] For example, Malinowski 1962.

[2] Eliade 1962, p. 15.

The whole winter under summer's signs.
The poetry in nature makes one mad?
If I merely avoid going under,
I cannot live this wonderful rich life.
I have to stimulate myself.[1]

1.3 The Rights and Duties of the Interpreter

The True 'Picture of Life'

To illustrate the conflict between archived and personal memory of the years 1875 to 1914, of crucial importance to Sibelius' fate and to Finland's as well, Eric J. Hobsbawm introduced the idea of the 'history of the twilight zone' and the perplexing simultaneity of historical distance and proximity. Hobsbawm aptly describes the dilemma that confronts anyone interested in Sibelius as a composer of that era, which is of immense relevance to the present:

> It [the history of the twilight zone] is itself an incoherent, incompletely perceived image of the past, sometimes more shadowy, sometimes apparently precise, always transmitted by a mixture of learning and second-hand memory shaped by public and private tradition. For it is still part of us, but no longer quite within our personal reach. It forms something similar to those particoloured ancient maps filled with unreliable outlines and white spaces, framed by monsters and symbols. The monsters and symbols are magnified by the modern mass media, because the very fact that the twilight zone is important to us makes it central also to their preoccupation.[2]

Because Sibelius was already a focus of public attention around 1900, the public myths of the day before yesterday and the shadows of the twilight are especially complex in his case. At the same time, he is a monument to a national identity and to the mythical North that emerged in the 'twilight' of imperialism. Until the late 1950s, he was present as a living person, albeit seldom 'within our personal reach'. A few contemporaries who spoke to Sibelius are still alive today,[3] but their memories reach back at most to the composer's final years, which are generally encapsulated as the 'silence of Ainola' – elegantly, but not quite accurately, since he composed until shortly before his death in 1957. The historical contextualisation of his music requires that his mentality be analysed in the years prior to Finland's declaration of independence in 1917 (he turned fifty-two two days later) during the wave of Russification of

[1] Diary, 18 February 1925.

[2] Hobsbawm 1987, p. 5.

[3] A selection of such statements, as well as previously published anecdotes, is summarised in Sirén 2000.

the autonomous Grand Duchy under Emperor Nicholas II Alexandrovich as well as in the early 1920s (as opposed to the 1950s, when those alive now could still have met him). Only archives can help with that.

'More than any other, the Age of Empire cries out for demystification, just because we – and that includes the historians – are no longer in it, but we do not know how much of it is still in us.'[1] This warning also comprehensively applies to biographically orientated interpreters of Sibelius who take seriously their obligation as historians of culture and art.[2] In Finland in particular, his creative work and his personality still represent a force that contributes to a sense of national identity, and they represent serious hurdles to a scholarly interpretation trying to take all of the relevant themes into account in a balanced way, without a political agenda. On the other hand, it helps that nostalgic glorification of the 'belle époque' is rare in the Finnish context, because of the suppression of the Grand Duchy.

Among the 'monsters' of the European 'twilight' are ideological positions in art theory whose original form and intention eventually become difficult to identify because of later polarisation in the context of National Socialism, Socialist Realism and neo-conservatism. One example that shows how differently parliamentarian 'left' and 'right' were defined prior to 1905 is Sibelius' *Workers' March* of 1893 to Juhana Henrik Erkko's text. Tolstoy's writings and his idea of the 'people' are the prime context for the ideas behind this march. The translation of the original Finnish title *Työkansan marssi* that may seem more idiomatic from our present perspective, 'March of the workers' – which would correspond to the Finnish 'Työläisten marssi' – would be inappropriate, because the original word *työkansa* is a poetic term that is unusual today, whereas the Finnish word *työläinen* (a worker in the sense of modern union membership) derives from socialist vocabulary; there is also the neutral word *työntekijä* (employee). For Tolstoy and Erkko (and Sibelius as well) it was about the 'people', not about the unions. Moreover, Tolstoy and Erkko were in effect authors of Finnish independence, since without Tolstoy's idealisation of the uneducated people and without local talents such as Erkko, Finnish national identity would have lacked the critical mass of intellectualism that the formation of a political nation requires. These authors also helped to define the 'people' in such a way that it was not just the higher social strata that counted.

The influence of Tolstoy on Sibelius' brother-in-law, the great landscape and portrait painter Eero Järnefelt, was decisive. Järnefelt wrote in his diary about Tolstoy's aesthetic on 18 October 1898. A highly demanding conversation with the brilliant-minded Järnefelt would account for Sibelius' uncharacteristic use of Finnish in an undated critical remark on Tolstoy in a sketchbook and for his need to sketch out

[1] Hobsbawm 1987, p. 5.

[2] For recent considerations of problems of biography in musicology, see Schubert 1997 and Waczkat 2003.

his arguments.[1] Probably both men were responding to Tolstoy's *What Is Art?* (orig. pub. in Russian in 1897). The date of 1898 in Järnefelt's diary would also make sense for Sibelius' note.

Right at the start of his essays on Beethoven, which are still a model for grappling with complex biographical tasks in musicology such as those faced in the present study, Carl Dahlhaus distances himself, for good reasons, from the desire to sketch a fully formed 'image' of a composer based on hypotheses and evidence that reflect not only the availability of the material but also trivial premises.[2] There is, admittedly, a great deal more intimate archival material on Sibelius than on Beethoven, especially his diaries and draft letters in his own hand. The latter in particular constitute an important, authentic source for Sibelius. Moreover, with an eye to Dahlhaus's critique of the 'legitimacy or illegitimacy of the biographical method' in light of the 'nearness or remoteness of a work from classicist aesthetics', it may be noted that Sibelius, unlike Beethoven, did not compose anything that could be understood solely within the framework of a classicist aesthetic. This might make it easier to cope with the problems that Dahlhaus explored in relation to Beethoven.

The 'image' of a composer does not, however, necessarily imply that the musical oeuvre is seen as his or her 'life's work': 'as a work, that is, that expressed the substance of the life out of which it had proceeded' (Dahlhaus). Constructing a canon of major works that belongs to 'mythologizing' biography is avoidable. Yet the category of major works should not be abandoned in the present study, since Sibelius himself made that distinction. The important thing – and even Dahlhaus was asking for no more than this – is not to bracket out marginal cases, such as Sibelius' Third Symphony or Beethoven's Fourth. There is nothing problematic about paying more attention to certain works than to others, as long as one does not inappropriately claim the validity of powerful aesthetic premises on that basis. The 'image' of the artist may be the 'totality of an oeuvre to the totality of a life', as Dahlhaus puts it, but this additive totality does not have to be forced into the straitjacket of the futilely and exclusively whole. Organic or historical 'totality' is not all-embracing and definitive.

Another difference from the hurdles Beethoven poses for hermeneutics concerns the separation of the aesthetic and the biographical subject, which is not meaningful in Sibelius' case, contrary to Dahlhaus's doctrine. The private aspect is also more strikingly manifested in his case than it is for artists who write their diaries as public personalities. Sibelius treated his diary as the wastepaper basket of his soul.[3] The quotidian also shaped his aesthetic subject, which according to Dahlhaus is supposed to exist 'in this one work, this one aesthetic object, and nowhere else'. In Sibelius' case, it was reflected not in dedications and anecdotes – which for Dahlhaus represent

[1] National Library, Sibelius Sketches 1472b, fol. 40. For Järnefelt's diary, see Waenerberg 2004b, p. 299.

[2] Dahlhaus 1991, pp. vi and 1 ff.

[3] In addition to the diary proper from 1909 to 1943 (National Archive), one sketchbook contains diary-like notes from August 1896 to November 1900 (National Library: Sibelius Sketches 1472a).

particularly tricky examples for Beethoven as an empirical personality – but rather in his attitude towards life and his relationship to nature.

Although the conventional public image of Sibelius may be mythologising and anecdotal, there is plenty of authentic documentary evidence that can help to differentiate a psychological portrait of the composer from biographical derailments. Even reflections of his biography in his art – 'music as autobiography', as Constantin Floros has called it[1] – not just of his attitude of a person in nature can be discussed in relation to a number of occasions, such as events from his life as a student in *Scène de ballet* (1891) and motifs relating to Aino and Ruth in his sketches around 1920. His daughter Ruth became an actress under the name Ruth Snellman and played Ariel in the Finnish premiere of Shakespeare's *The Tempest* on 4 November 1927 with incidental music by Sibelius (op. 109). Even in his case, of course, the so-called aesthetic subject is not identical with the empirical person, but neither is there an obvious separation. The author Sibelius is, pace Roland Barthes's and Michel Foucault's formula, not yet 'dead', and his work is not influenced by the anti-semantics or anti-rhetoric of the post-war period. The 'inner biography' is a necessary category as we discuss Sibelius, but its presentation need not have speculative or novelistic features.

Unlike Beethoven scholarship, the debate over Sibelius is still dominated by one monumental summary: Erik Tawaststjerna's five-volume biography. Robert Layton's abridged English translation, published in three volumes in 1976, 1986 and 1997, without extensive discussions of the works, is also widely read. Tawaststjerna had since been published in full in Swedish, 1991–7, edited by his research assistant Gitta Henning (and in part by Fabian Dahlström). The Finnish edition is, apart from the fifth volume, a skilfully elaborated translation from Tawaststjerna's Swedish edited by Tuomas Anhava and Erkki Salmenhaara. Henning's version could be preferred as the most recent edition, especially as it was corrected in a number of places. The Finnish version and Layton's translation do, however, include valuable details that are, astonishingly, lacking in Henning, which makes a definitive decision for one edition impossible. There are a lot of major and minor problems with each of these editions. Most scholars use all of these editions in parallel – even in different printings, as the most recent one is not necessarily the best.

Tawaststjerna distanced himself from Dahlhaus's observation that the time of 'encyclopaedic' monumental biographies had irrevocably ended with the First World War. Tawaststjerna wrote about a composer's life and work at a time – from the 1960s to the 1980s – when hardly any other musicologist at an academic institution would have dared to do so, at least on the same scale. Tawaststjerna's position was from the outset messianic and marked by the myth of the chosen one. As early in 1912, Sibelius noted expectantly in his diary that 'sometime there will be a man who will help bring to light the achievements of my works'.[2] There was no doubt within Sibelius' family

[1] Cf. the subtitle of Constantin Floros's 1992 book on Alban Berg.

[2] Diary, 7 September 1912.

circle in the late 1950s that Tawaststjerna was that man.[1] That did not make his task easier. The relationship became strained in the wake of the first discussion of the publication of unpublished versions, in particular of the Fifth Symphony, for which Tawaststjerna argued vigorously. No matter whether his lifework is considered a relic of a past epoch or the rebirth of a practice mistakenly considered dead, it is striking how precisely Tawaststjerna's five volumes correspond to what Dahlhaus criticised methodologically in his work on Beethoven. Dahlhaus and Tawaststjerna met frequently during the years in which the Beethoven book and the fifth volume of the biography were being written. They had already met in the 1970s, when Dahlhaus published his position paper 'Wozu noch Biographie?' (Why biography now?).

When the first volume of Tawaststjerna's *Sibelius* had just been published in its first version, Otto Andersson, a Sibelius scholar of the first generation and founder of the Sibelius Museum in Turku, wrote to Tawaststjerna: 'I would never have been able to write Sibelius' biography as you have done. I had neither the time nor the ability to treat the enormous material as thoroughly as you. By the way, I would not have structured the work in a way similar to yours.'[2] Did Andersson envy the achievement of his younger colleague drawing on the 'enormous material' from the Sibelius family archive or were his words ironic? Andersson's problem was the active resistance of the composer. Was Andersson actually acknowledging that Tawaststjerna's approach suited the subject best? Tawaststjerna's project rendered years of Andersson's efforts worthless. Andersson quoted Sibelius wondering aloud: 'How will such [authors] be able to write about me who were not even born when Sibelius died?' This remark becomes ambiguous when Andersson criticises Tawaststjerna's negative profile of Wegelius and his sharp polarisation of Wegelius versus Kajanus in the first edition of the first volume. The criticism applies to Tawaststjerna, who was born in 1916, ten years after Wegelius died. Sibelius had asked Andersson for advice on how to prevent such 'scribbling'. It was typical of Sibelius to speak of himself in the third person, which also explains the vision of his own death. With regard to the conflict between Kajanus and Wegelius, Andersson cited Anna Tigerstedt, Sibelius' fellow student from Hämeenlinna and Helsinki, who had remarked that the legend stirred up by Tawaststjerna of the conflict between Wegelius and Kajanus in the 1880s in Helsinki did not imply that all Wegelius' students were prohibited from attending Kajanus' concerts. 'The tense relationship between Kajanus and Wegelius never assumed such dimensions.' This detail has consequences for the question of the repertoire the composer knew before he began writing his first great orchestral works and even before his year in Berlin with regard to assessing his originality.

Anyone who opens Andersson's *Jean Sibelius i Amerika*, for instance, will encounter a scholar who was able to circumscribe his theme and was in a position to offer

[1] See, for example, Jalas 1981, p. 60.

[2] National Archive: Tawaststjerna Collection: Andersson to JS, 11 January 1969. Andersson was working on a Sibelius project as early as 1912 (see Diary, 24 April 1912).

a sober, well-researched report. It included a vivid depiction of the popularity of specific composers in the United States of America between 1875 and 1950, statistics on performances and an illustration of the pyramid of popularity quoted from John H. Mueller's study *The American Symphony Orchestra*. Andersson's illustration of American editions of the *Valse triste* is also a valuable curiosity.

Letters, Sketches and Diaries as Source Materials

The many letters and diary entries Tawaststjerna was permitted to use for his biography are profitable to the competent reader in their aphoristic profundity but filled with hidden dangers for inexperienced readers. They never 'speak to' the reader as sources in Leopold von Ranke's sense. But neither do they emerge as eloquent prose. The diary was a 'jardin secret', as he wrote on 19 September 1914:[1] 'This diary must remain entirely unknown to everyone other than Aino and me – and perhaps one other person', as he had already decided on 13 September 1911. 'This diary cannot be shown to anyone. It is truly my faithful friend, and I will not tolerate any publication of it', he confirmed on 30 January 1920.

The correspondence from 1874 to 1957 is an even more challenging source, since 'letters from Sibelius' are not always authentic. In addition to autograph letters, there are typewritten letters that a family member or, after 1938, his secretary, Levas, presented for him to sign. All that is truly authentic about the latter are their concepts and outlines, as well as handwritten corrections in drafts presented to him. They do not, of course, have full value as 'correspondence', because they do not contain the final word selected in a moment of calm, and no direct replies to them exist. Consequently, one searches in vain for such documents in the great editions of the letters. They are all the more valuable in the context of a biographical close reading, however. Whereas some of the individual letters may seem isolated, the correspondence as a whole, including the letters to Sibelius, is a rich treasure, even of social history. Such an example is the collection of correspondence with foreign sympathisers, a neglected group of little relevance for the history of music but with touching references to *Finlandia* and *Valse triste* as his 'greatest masterpieces', but also the expression of honest willingness to help when even Sibelius was suffering from the consequences of the Second World War. Then there is the correspondence with fellow Freemasons throughout the world. Astonishingly, he or his assistants usually took a lot of time answering messages of congratulation and letters from admirers abroad.[2]

Conductors, musicians, journalists and publishers would ask about the Eighth Symphony or possible commissions such as solo concertos for cello or piano as well

[1] Diary, 19 September 1914.

[2] A typical example is Anne Svitak, who between 1947 and 1956 wrote numerous letters from Texas addressed to 'Jean Sibelius, Helsinki, Finland' and asked for autographs (National Library Coll. 206: 38). It appears that JS or Levas answered at least one letter.

as programmatic orchestral works on confessional poetry of their own or by others. The lack of restraint shown by many of these interested parties, especially from the Anglo-American world, who ordered sublime occasional works from Sibelius for their own texts, may be due to the biographies by friends such as Rosa Newmarch, Karl Ekman and Bengt de Törne, which represented him as a great Nordic spirit but also made him seem like a jovial Finnish man. By the same token, he rarely received insolent letters.

The value of the letters, diaries and personal statements of others for research on Sibelius is traditionally surpassed only by critiques of performances. One reason for the exceptional attention paid to these documents in Finland may be that nearly all historians of music in Finland were (or are) active reviewers. When we read scholarship on Sibelius, or books on Finnish music in general, music critics appear to be central characters in musical life, even though Sibelius said: 'Never pay any attention to what critics say. [...] Remember [...] a statue has never been set up in honour of a critic!'[1] In 1911 he wrote to his wife, who dutifully read the Finnish newspapers, which included translated reports from abroad: 'Why do you worry about reviews? We are no longer dependent on them. In isolation [in Ainola and Finland] such scribblings probably seem important.'[2] His distance from the written word notwithstanding, Sibelius by no means rigorously followed this guideline himself, as his reactions to the German composer and writer Walter Niemann, the Swedish critic and composer Wilhelm Peterson-Berger and even to the simultaneously feared and admired critic Evert Katila in Helsinki demonstrate. Adorno's 'Glosse über Sibelius' (Gloss on Sibelius; 1938) and 'Fussnote zu Sibelius und Hamsun' (Footnote on Sibelius and Hamsun; 1937) were apparently kept from Sibelius. Otherwise, he (or his friends and family) collected mentions in newspapers and even received such items from Finland's embassies.[3]

Sibelius supposedly said with regard to his statements that he felt 'caught up in a net of lies' from which he could not extricate himself. Given his unfailingly polite comments on inadequate performances, he alone was to blame for that situation. Thus numerous conductors possess a cordial letter from Ainola, even though Sibelius was obviously appalled by their interpretative achievements. His son-in-law, the conductor Jussi Jalas, reported how furious Sibelius was after a radio broadcast of his Fourth Symphony, because 'the conductor had obviously not studied the score at all'.[4] In its wake, he planned an 'instructive letter', but in fact he wrote a note of modest praise, of which the conductor, whom Jalas later met himself, was proud. Sibelius also wrote to his friend the conductor Georg Schnéevoigt about performance under Carl Schuricht in Wiesbaden in a tone he would never have used to Schuricht directly:

[1] Törne 1937, p. 27.

[2] National Archive Box 96: JS to Aino, 4 November 1911, from Paris.

[3] This material may be found in the National Archive and the National Library; for example, National Library Coll. 206: 76 ff. Adorno is discussed in detail in chapter 5.2 of the present volume.

[4] Jalas 1981, pp. 55–6.

'It is strange how foreign my music is to conductors as a rule. For example, recently in Wiesbaden, where Mr. Schuricht conducted my *Saga*, the violin concerto and the Second Symphony without understanding them or showing an interest in them and without success.'[1]

Tawaststjerna compares Sibelius' way of corresponding in general with 'Strindberg's spirit', whereas Sibelius himself limited the description 'Strindbergian style' to his correspondence with Adolf Paul. He did indeed consciously react to the style of the correspondent in question.[2] Sibelius mentions the letters to Paul, which were written in the style of his friend August Strindberg, because Paul wrote that way himself. Tawaststjerna generalises that characterisation and thus obscures the flexibility the composed showed with regard to the addressee. At times, the consideration Sibelius showed the recipient could be extreme. The Finnish composer Bengt de Törne reports that Sibelius asserted out of sympathy to a childless couple that he had no children either.[3] Equally striking is a draft letter to Steinway & Sons in New York. When the company wrote to him in German on 26 September 1929 about the 'effective and characteristic' *Finlandia* painting at company headquarters, he drafted a reply with an exact repetition that was highly provocative if conscious: 'I find the painting very effective and characteristic.'[4] Moreover, Sibelius regularly changed his positions, which were, in his own words, based on 'hetkellisyys' (momentariness).[5]

Newmarch was not exaggerating when she wrote: 'Sibelius was never a great letter writer, and one of our little jokes together was that there would be no ponderous tomes of Sibelius letters for anyone to edit after his departure.'[6] In comparison to many other composers of his day whose own words were a valuable instrument for their art as well (Busoni, Strauss, d'Indy, Debussy, Vaughan Williams, Schoenberg), Newmarch's remark is accurate: Sibelius' letters and other writings would not hold interest as independent texts. They are only helpful in a biographical context and as tools of interpretation.

His general spontaneity, together with his polite reserve when it came to publicly correcting misunderstandings, makes Sibelius the helpless victim of ideologically motivated interpreters. In the first part of the twentieth century, there were plenty of them in Europe. His naivety when dealing with the press is reflected in his lack of control when dealing with delicate subjects. Quite clearly he underestimated how

[1] Åbo Akademi University, The Sibelius Museum Archive, Turku: Collection of Press Clippings, General Collections of Correspondence and other Research Material (hereafter Åbo Akademi): JS to Georg Schneevoigt (draft letter from 8 October 1942).

[2] Erik W. Tawaststjerna 1991, p. 99. Cf. National Archive Box 41: Jussi Snellman's manuscript letter in Finnish of 25 December 1943, written on behalf of JS to the newspaper *Kaleva* in reply to an article by 'Tähystäjä' (a pseudonym).

[3] Törne 1937, p. 102.

[4] National Library Coll. 206: 50.

[5] Cf. Erik W. Tawaststjerna 1994, p. 143.

[6] Newmarch 1939, p. 47.

interested music journalists were in all his statements, since, although, as an artist in the media age, he was *per se* a public persona, he nevertheless believed in the private sphere. Sibelius felt that he was misunderstood not only by composer-writers such as Niemann but also and especially by the journalists and musicologists who confronted him. In an undated draft for a letter to the German-Danish author and friend Georg Boldemann, he openly discussed the problem of distorted and misunderstood verbal statements.[1] Harold E. Johnson, one of the greatest Sibelius scholars in the United States, experienced the same problem. It was his impression – which he formulated as an apology in his book – that Sibelius had either forgotten many facts or in general refused to contribute to the creation of an objective picture as a consequence of his distrust of notepads of any kind.[2]

Otto Andersson's final attempt, on 16 October 1951, to convince Sibelius to approve his book project, which had already progressed very far, reads like a biographer's nightmare: 'In the spring we spoke a great deal about the significance and necessity of historical material for a biographical work. [...] [The discussion revolved around] getting some of the correspondence in your possession. [...] You said that you could imagine going through the material and then letting me see it. [...] You said "Well, much of it contains such dangerous things."'[3] Sibelius expressed himself with similar clarity to Jalas with regard to his sketches: 'On my death, please remember that all my sketches are to be burnt. I don't want anyone going round gathering Sibelius' *letzte Gedanken* [final thoughts] and suchlike.'[4] Here he was thinking primarily of his Eighth Symphony. The letters in the archive, at least, do not contain any truly 'dangerous things' from today's perspective. Of course, individual letters may have been destroyed. But the ones we know contain so many titillating details that it seems improbable that someone would have destroyed others, even though Aino had at least planned to review them critically.

Sibelius' distrust of authors who insistently asked for facts and background to his work was elemental. He knew that history was not made up exclusively of facts but rather had to be narrated, and that any book, even the simplest chronicle, was also a document of its author. But the more ambiguous and incomplete the sources, the more authors have to invent in order to be able to offer their audience something that seems complete. Sibelius did not consider that.

'It is all approximate': Letters to Conductors

Sibelius' letters to conductors are the most important part of his correspondence. Only recently have Sibelius' letters to his brother-in-law and expert conductor Armas

[1] National Archive Box 34; draft letter.

[2] Johnson 1959, p. ix.

[3] Åbo Akademi. On this subject, see Dahlström 1998.

[4] Note by Jalas, 17 July 1943, quoted in Sirén 1999, p. 40. On Jalas's conversations with JS, see Jalas 1981 and Jalas 1988.

Järnefelt become public; they contain several precise details for the performance of *Pohjola's Daughter* and *Tapiola*.[1] *Pohjola's Daughter* in particular should be more expressive, more dramatic, in many passages slower (Sibelius used the expression 'à la Mahler'), and by no means should the main parts alone be accentuated.

One of the great maestros with whom Sibelius corresponded was the Hans Pfitzner student and pioneer of Modernism Otto Klemperer, who was preparing for the German premiere of the Seventh Symphony in Wiesbaden on 20 September 1926, and in that context he asked the composer several precise questions:

> It concerns your wonderful Seventh Symphony, whose music has delighted me so much that I am considering performing it in the symphony concert of the Staatskapelle here and in New York (where I will be in January and February). The concert in Wiesbaden is already on 20 September. [...] The quarter-note motion in the Adagio can presumably give way to a more flowing movement occasionally over the course of the introduction. On page 20 6/4 is presumably Allegro ordinario. Here, from the fourth measure, I do not understand precisely how the second violins and the violas are supposed to play! But surely staccato. Or portamento? [...] What tempo do you picture for the last measure on p. 36. Presumably quasi Allegro, and likewise the fifth measure on p. 46. The Presto on p. 64, seventh measure, is presumably very fast, decidedly faster than the Vivacissimo on p. 23.[2]

Peter Heyworth's view that Klemperer later acceded only to specific local 'demands' when he conducted it in Los Angeles, where Arnold Schoenberg, Bertolt Brecht and other German exiles were living,[3] does not fit the undertone of curiosity in 1926. For Klemperer, who immediately recognised the significance of the Seventh Symphony, this interest was certainly European in origin.

Issues of tempo were Sibelius' favourite subject, on which he made detailed statements in letters all his life.[4] He was unmistakably critical in a letter of 1 December 1931: 'Listened to my Belshazzar's Feast Suite on the radio today at 10:15 p.m. Royal Norwegian Orchestra under Fritz Gartz. It was embarrassing!! Wrong tempi, notes, entrances! The orchestra was presumably sightreading?'[5] In the context of wartime performances in Germany, a letter from his publisher, Breitkopf & Härtel, to the

[1] See Sirén 2004. The letter on *Pohjola's Daughter* is undated. Sirén presumes a date between 1906 and 1916. All these letters are in the JS collection of the National Archive in Helsinki. The details of the subject matter suggest *c.*1907.

[2] National Library Coll. 206: 20; Otto Klemperer to JS, 3 September 1926, from Wiesbaden.

[3] Heyworth 1996, p. 27.

[4] See also Legge (of the British Sibelius Society and HMV) in National Archive Box 23. In another letter to a 'friend' (National Archive Box 36; JS to an unknown recipient, 24 February 1911), there are numerous specific recommendations for conductors, not all concerning tempi. On this subject, see also the various loose drafts in National Archive Box 36.

[5] National Archive Box 36.

Reichsfunk Berlin on 3 June 1942, is important, since it comments on a letter from the composer of May 15:

> The elderly maestro replied to us as follows on this: 'The performance on the radio on 27 April was very unfortunate, especially on account of the incorrect tempi. For example, the "Night Ride" was two times too slow. In the Fourth Symphony, the second movement was more than half too slow, and in the finale [...] two times too slow [...] [In *The War Song of Tyrtaeus*] the tempo has changed a great deal over forty-three years. When I first performed the work, the quarter note = 100. That is the proper tempo. I hope that the recently founded Deutsche Sibelius-Gesellschaft can help gradually correct the tempi of my works.' We hope that The War Song of Tyrtaeus [literally 'Song of the people of Athens'], with its rousing music and its lyrics appropriate to the times, will still be heard quite frequently on the radio. In that case, we ask you to base it on the composer's metronome markings.[1]

Hence Sibelius even based practical and technical musical expectations on the founding of an association, the first German Sibelius society, under the Third Reich. A list of metronome marks was published by Breitkopf & Härtel in August 1942 under the title *Metronombezeichnungen zu seinen Symphonien*.

Hans Weissbach, who had first contacted Sibelius on 23 September 1934 concerning music he was to conduct (namely, the Second Symphony, which was to be played on 28 September on the Leipziger Rundfunk), wrote on 10 October 1937: 'I would like to get it to the point where something like an exemplary performance practice emanates from here, thereby catching up on a duty that has – I must confess – thus far been neglected in Germany.' He asked Sibelius for advice, and the composer, taken by the musician's extraordinary humility, responded. In the draft for his letter, he recommended already existing recordings that had had a similar motivation, those of the British Jean Sibelius Society and HMV:[2]

> The First and the Second by Kajanus are especially good; the Third and the Fifth not so successful. The Sixth by Schneevoigt is rather good and the Seventh by Koussevitzky is good too. [...] In any case, I will have the tempi on these records converted to metronome markings and have them sent to you. [...] To be honest, I very much dislike giving metronome indications, because ~~the so often~~ it is, as you know, so difficult to take down tempi. It is all approximate.

He went on to criticise Weissbach's choice of tempi in the *Lemminkäinen Legends*, whereas he felt the Fifth Symphony was 'excellently' played, with only the first movement and Scherzo played a little too slowly. A sketch for a telegram from 28 October

[1] Publishers' archive.

[2] National Library Coll. 206: 40 (correspondence with Weissbach).

1937 summarised these notes, and on 10 December 1937 Weissbach thanked him only for that. Apparently the detailed, critical letter was never sent.

On 21 May 1938 Weissbach reported that his Sibelius cycle was to be taken up again, following an interruption, and he asked Sibelius to assess the radio broadcasts. On 15 July 1938 he thanked Sibelius for a telegram after the performance of the Seventh Symphony and for criticisms of the tempi in the Sixth. He discussed some tempo markings, for instance, the Presto in 6/4 time in the Seventh (p. 23 of the score), which was presumably supposed to be Prestissimo. Weissbach suspected as much based on the list of metronome indications published by Edition Wilhelm Hansen. Julia A. Burt's Hansen edition has 'Vivacissimo'. Weissbach even drew attention to inadequate coordination of the notation of phrasing between the score and the orchestral parts and to the lack of indication of dynamics following pauses, and he asked which text should now be considered authoritative. He was also interested in the proper size for the orchestra (Sibelius had praised the sound of fifty musicians), and he regretted very much that the British records were unavailable in Germany in 1938. Later letters have not survived; and unfortunately we have no draft of Sibelius' reply.

Sibelius also wrote about tempi to one of his favourite conductors: the Danish-American-Jewish Werner Janssen. Janssen visited Sibelius in February 1933: 'You and Mr. Herberth Peyser are most warmly welcomed to Finland. *Tapiola* was recently performed here and killed by a too slow tempo. [...] it would be good if you could rescue *Tapiola*.'[1] Sibelius also said of Janssen to the Finnish-American journalist Paul Sjöblom in a draft letter: 'In the event in question I was entirely caught up by the power of my music. Jansen [*sic*] conducted the entire programme from memory and swept the orchestra along with him. I have not heard Tosc., Koussev., Stokowski and so on. Jansen is the only foreigner. He conducts from memory with his entire soul [...].'[2] It is easy to date this document to 1933, since Sibelius said to the New York critic Olin Downes that his right hand hurt him more and more. 'As you see, my hand hurts.' The reference to Arturo Toscanini, Sergei Koussevitzky and Leopold Stokowsky pertains to *Tapiola*. Downes was not impressed by the support of Sibelius and such Finnish critics as Uuno Klami and Heikki Klemetti – to say nothing of the enthusiastic reports on Janssen's conducting in Helsinki, which had also been published in New York and quoted Sibelius (for example, in the *New York Times* on 25 February 1934), but instead criticised Janssen's interpretation of *Tapiola* so cuttingly in November 1934 that Janssen had to retreat to Southern California. Enthusiasm died down in Finland as well after Downes's verdict. Notable too is Downes's insinuation that Janssen claimed a role in Sibelius' fame (*New York Times*, 19 November 1934).[3] It is possible that Downes in particular did not want to share his own role as the apostle of the Nordic maestro with the young foreign conductor.

[1] National Archive Box 34; undated draft.

[2] National Archive Box 35; undated.

[3] See Downes 1945, pp. 129–30.

The winding roads an interpreter of Sibelius must follow in search of valuable hints are documented by Giovanni di Bella's letter from Berlin on 6 June 1942; di Bella was the deputy director of the Berliner Gemeinschaft junger Musiker (Berlin Society for Young Musicians) and not active in Copenhagen until 1943:

> I myself have always been astonished by the handling of the tempi in your orchestral works that are often found in Germany especially. I often felt that the melancholic character was far too emphasised by such handling of tempi, at the expense of freshness and vitality. These circumstances probably also explain why the grace you mentioned in our telephone conversation cannot be felt properly.[1]

The image of Sibelius as a melancholy artist in Nordic isolation may have influenced the attitude of some of his interpreters and moved the handling of the tempi in the direction of heavy beats — at the expense of the grace, vitality and (perhaps 'Nordic') freshness that Janssen in turn understood. This has struck the conductor Neeme Järvi as well (in the context of the final movement of the Fourth Symphony): 'Who says that it has to get slower and slower? Certainly not the score.'[2] Even Colin Davis has defended the old position that Sibelius' music is precisely not 'frivolously attractive' and that its texture is 'often very low' (and hence 'old man's music').[3] Helmut Thierfelder conducted it too quickly, however (Thierfelder to Sibelius, 14 May 1943): '[I have] received your valuable remarks of May 7 [and must admit that I was] not pleasantly surprised by my far too rapid tempo of the second movement, even from the loudspeaker. The recording must have been made rather quickly.' And on 9 July 1943: '[I hope that] the radio station will give me another opportunity to repeat the second movement [...].'[4]

Making reference to Sibelius' remarks, Adrian Boult wrote of the Fifth Symphony on 27 April 1927: 'I will certainly remember what you say about the Second Movement, and will see that there is a little more andante next time.'[5] Following a performance of the Second Symphony, Sibelius wrote to Boult on 15 February 1938: 'Extremely satisfied with your masterful performance. The [second movement of the] Fifth Symphony is called in print "Andante mosso, quasi allegretto."' A letter from the pianist Alf Nestmann contains a provocative remark concerning the idea of correct basic tempo (Nestmann was improvising, on the radio as well, on themes by Sibelius):

> Many thanks for sending the theme, which offers incredible possibilities for variation. I hope that you had good reception and that various contrapuntal treatments reached your ear unhampered by disruptions. Mindful of your

[1] National Library Coll. 206: 9.
[2] See Kislinger 2002, 5.
[3] See Grimley 2004b, p. 231.
[4] National Library Coll. 206: 38.
[5] National Library Coll. 206: 5.

> warning to avoid rapid tempi, in keeping with Finland's feeling for music, I took pains to create a broadly flowing structure. I hope specifically that the double stretto with the theme in retrograde (in the bass) pleased you.[1]

Another valuable reference to Sibelius may be found in the director Hellmuth von Hase's letter to the headquarters of Sibelius' publisher, Breitkopf & Härtel: 'Dr Sibelius gave me the enclosed list of metronome indications [...]. Sibelius says "It changes every day [...]!" Please make the indications for the Third Symphony available to Lienau as well. But not Hansen; he has shown himself to be so tedious!'[2] Sibelius' conviction that a normative list was generally problematic[3] is clear from a draft letter: 'I do not want any ~~metronome in~~ metronome specifications, because they always inhibit a personal conception.'[4] This position is surprising given the severity of his judgements on wrong tempi.

The English musician John Harrison asked whether the cellos on page 48 of the Second Symphony should be played spiccato (as notated) or pizzicato, as in Kajanus' recording, to which Sibelius replied: 'My intention is that they should play spiccato as marked.'[5] This brief sentence may help to assess properly the value of the recordings under Kajanus as a prime source for the performance practice of Sibelius' music. There are also his detailed and intelligible notes for a reply to Armas Järnefelt, who in 1949 asked about the phrasing of the final movement of the Fifth Symphony. Sibelius grouped the sixteen notes in 2+2+3 beats (at the marking 'A').[6] Malcolm Sargent posed a question that has occupied many conductors and is not really answered in the documents, namely, the type of bells to be used in the Fourth Symphony: 'tubular bells or a glockenspiel, or have you a particular type in mind which is a Finnish speciality?'.[7] One answer – albeit one not quite as authentic as his remark on the spiccato cellos – may be found in Andersson's letter to the Swedish conductor Sixten Eckerberg of 21 May 1949: Andersson confirmed that Sibelius meant 'små klockar' (small bells) in the Fourth Symphony, and explicitly not large ones.[8] Andersson, who is a reliable reporter, gave his source as a conversation with Sibelius, but he neglected to explain what 'små klockar' could be, if not the profane glockenspiel (*klockspel* in Swedish).

[1] National Library Coll. 206: 27; Alf Nestmann to JS, 16 May 1930.

[2] Åbo Akademi (copy; original in Wiesbaden); Hellmuth von Hase to Breitkopf & Härtel, 11 August 1942. On JS' delicate relationship with his publishers, see Reinisch 2000, 175 ff.

[3] On 6 April 1914 he ordered a metronome; on 29 September, he paid the bill (see Diary).

[4] National Archive Box 36 (in German).

[5] National Library Coll. 206: 15; John Harrison to JS, 24 October 1937. This source for solving the serious problem of performance practice is not mentioned in vol. 1/3 (Fourth Symphony) of *Jean Sibelius Complete Works*.

[6] National Archive Box 21; Armas Järnefelt to JS, 3 August 1949, drafts sometimes on the verso or on an extra sheet.

[7] National Library Coll. 206: 33; Malcolm Sargent to JS, 31 October 1946, JS replied on 5 December 1946.

[8] National Archive: copy in the Tawaststjerna Collection.

Fantasised a great deal, without concentrating, and hence no results worth mentioning.[1]

My infinitely tragic fate! Is it really tragic? You old humorist!![2]

2 THE CREATOR IN HIS WORLD

2.1 'Clothes Off'

'Poeta laureatus (!)'

Jean-François Lyotard's insight that people in general are 'not masters of language and do not make use of it for their own goals, for example, communicating or expressing themselves' is by no means true only of Sibelius' generation, which, in reaction to a past with a literary bent, was dominated by a scepticism about words and even by doubts about the validity of all rational systems. Lyotard intends it critically when he says that people in general have 'no "identity" other than the one assigned to them by the situation created for them in the universe of phrases'.[3] Although this post-humanist critique of the state of alienated civilisation applies to someone as unusual as Sibelius in only a limited way if at all, the general interdependence of the formation of personality and the individuation of language – regardless of one's own talent or the culture in which one lives – could explain why creative individuals generally, and Sibelius especially, perceive conventional professionalisation as a threatening attempt to establish norms for communication rather than increasing individuality. Few professionals are capable of truly original statements, and fewer still are able to do so thanks to their training. The expressive and structural limitations inherent not only in the verbal but in all language-like systems are no doubt unacceptable to a creative individual in an era that defines art not as keeping to established principles but as original invention. Therein lies the heart of the conflict that emerged at the beginning of the twentieth century between self-confident originality and the progress that occurs in schools (including conservatories). An awareness of it can be extraordinarily helpful when investigating Sibelius' creative essence.

In contrast to Lyotard, the German philosopher Manfred Frank considers language a pragmatic medium, an instrument for grasping the world.[4] His theory explains Sibelius' high degree of competence in language, including musical language. Lyotard encouraged criticism of the repressive power of all traditions (and indirectly

1 Diary, 8 May 1910.

2 Ibid., undated entry (*c.* 25 February 1912).

3 Lyotard 1987, p. 44.

4 Frank 1988.

the teaching of composition as well). For him, free individuality is a prisoner of language, whereas Frank does not take the liberating quality of nature into account as a reference. Both theories, Lyotard's and Frank's, can be applied here to unveil some of Sibelius' most intimate secrets.

Sibelius is a classic example of an unconditional modern individualist confronting the imprisoning power of systems of language. His nonconformist critique of the craft applied even to artists he admired most: 'The wind is blowing outside. How infinitely richer is artless blowing than the poems of Goethe and other gentlemen.'[1] The statement reveals both the offhand disrespect with which he dismissed the creative achievements of other artists and his elemental approach to nature. The following day he noted: 'A poetry in nature that drives one crazy!'[2] He attributed meaning to 'artless blowing'. He often tried – as in the tone poem *Luonnotar*, for example – to mould the wind musically, not just to illustrate it by imitation. He wanted to liberate himself from the control of all languages – even musical languages – that restrain free thoughts and inhibit original expression. Grammar, vocabulary and idioms of all kinds were superficial and thus inadequate tools of expression for him; they made the playfully sparkling formulations in his letters and diaries as well as many brilliant musical works possible, but also made the unhampered flight of his true inspiration more difficult in its pragmatic manifestation in compositions.

Anyone who appreciates his lyrically concise manner can overlook some of the naivety that resulted from his inability to articulate himself adequately and intelligibly in a way that did justice to the complexity of things and his own visions. Glenda Dawn Goss recommends the early letters to anyone who wants to get to know the 'real' Sibelius: 'the disarming child who thanks his aunt for the stamp album and then asks her to remember to send more stamps'.[3] That collection of letters, published as *The Hämeenlinna Letters*, could sooner be said to document the long road he had to travel to liberate himself from the conventional scenery of his youth. While still in Vienna, writing to Aino on 21 March 1891, he wrote in a detached way and with irony about his past as 'a physician's son from Finland'. That was supposed to say everything.

But the region in which he grew up was in fact multicultural, multilingual and in many ways quite stimulating. Social life was organised either within the framework of an old tsarist empire or in the spirit of the Swedish superpower of the Baroque era. In parallel with that, a complex fabric of divergent cultural norms and efforts on the regional level had become established in Finland. It made it possible to overlook the advantages of a firmly established, cultivated language and its brilliant mastery. Even later, Sibelius retained his reserve towards rationally structured and systematic language as an instrument for explaining complex matters and solving problems of

[1] Diary, 17 February 1925.

[2] Diary, 18 February 1925.

[3] Goss 1997, p. 10. The reference is to a letter of 2 April 1877.

all kinds. He first encountered language as an elaborate collection of translatable and idiomatic game pieces, not as a chance to grasp the significance of important things. Analogously, he had no desire to develop a musical system, a set of rules or a technique; he experimented with the individual case. He used the vocabulary of symphonic music freely without forcing it into a grammar-dominated dogma.

He was, however, also aware of the dangers of his path. He confessed to his diary on 19 September 1914: 'Oh, if only I could work!! But my way of working, based as it is on inspiration, is not "bourgeois".' A remark on 27 February 1911 is symptomatic: 'Today I am working with my head, not with my "heart". That is, I am making a fair copy.' His art aimed for the irrational and achieved the most important thing: 'No dead, unnecessary notes. Every note must live.'[1]

In his critique of a rational worldview based on the word and his preference for synaesthetic holism, Sibelius was a child of his epoch but not a product of his time. Sensuousness, emotionality and holism were backed up by a worldview common at the time. This makes Sibelius into an embodiment of an attitude that for others was the result of a verbal engagement with the problem but for him was inevitable. At least since René Ghil's *Traité du verbe* (1886), an 'instrumentation verbale' which aims at holism is recognized in literature and postulated as the goal of synaesthetic art. It is not common to compare Sibelius with Ghil, but it helps to underline the importance of the Symbolist era – as opposed to nationalism and the regional 'awakening' – for the composer.

At the beginning of his career, Sibelius wrote: 'For my symphony I have moods but no musical expression for them';[2] by contrast, many contemporaries and especially the crucial forces of the next generation (above all Schoenberg and his students) purposefully developed compositional techniques. His pure musical expression and lack of a standardised framework threatened to become an insoluble problem, however, as the fate of Sibelius' Eighth Symphony demonstrates. He too proved unable to free himself of the standard medium of composers – the score that had to be written down as a text. His effort to achieve a special closeness to nature and harmony with the elements, rather than the manifestations of civilisation, remained utopian. When Ferruccio Busoni wrote that the 'function of the creative artist consists in making laws, not in following laws ready made. He who follows such laws, ceases to be a creator',[3] he could be sure Sibelius would agree. Both of them overlooked, however, that tradition consists not of laws but of habits, which are much harder to avoid than any violation of the rules.

In the earliest known portrait of Sibelius – a short essay called 'Ur vännen Jeans

[1] Reported by Leevi Madetoja, 'Jean Sibelius opettajana', *Aulos* (1925); quoted in Salmenhaara 1987, p. 93, and Erik W. Tawaststjerna 1976, p. 126.

[2] JS to Aino, 16 April 1891.

[3] Busoni 1911, p. 22.

skissbok' (From friend Jean's sketchbook), which dates to the period immediately before his year in Berlin (1889) – his friend Adolf Paul wrote:

> [He was] a starry-eyed dreamer, that is certain and true, an original who finds it somewhat more difficult to master the hurdles of daily life but who nevertheless truly exists and lives his fantasy life among us realists. You have surely seen him once or twice [...] a melody on his lips, a motif that occurred to him while observing the reflections of the sun in water, the sound of the fountains, the form of a beautiful girl, or in some way or another as inconceivable for him as it is for others. Every situation, every mood, no matter how insignificant, triggers a poem in him; for him, setting all of nature to music is a simple matter; in that respect, his inventiveness is as inexhaustible as it is original.[1]

As in his short novel *En bok om en människa* (A book about a man; 1891), Paul was not yet interested in extolling his friend – as he was later, when he chatted about Sibelius in a similarly familiar tone in the *Völkischer Beobachter* in the 1930s. From 1941 onwards, Paul displayed the 'Cross of Merit of the Order of the German Eagle', 'to be worn on a black, white and red ribbon', as he proudly reported.[2] Rather, Paul's early writings raise the suspicion that they seek to present an exaggeratedly fashionable and bohemian image. The young Sibelius could be a model for such a portrait, as demonstrated by Eero Järnefelt's 1892 sketch of Sibelius very early in the morning after a long evening. Walter von Konow, his friend from youth, preferred the image of a person with an anti-bourgeois imagination[3] – a person who dreams rather than reasons. Jussi Jalas, Sibelius' son-in-law, called the 'apocryphal' Paul a friend who was in a position to see Sibelius' 'innermost essence' – or at least better than his biographers could.[4] This is quite remarkable praise. Paul dared to offer an idealistic depiction that was ambitious as literature, imaginative, unhampered by logic, since by 'poem' he meant the (sub-medial) poetic quality beneath the artistic text.

The correspondence between Jean and Aino in the summer of 1894, after two years of marriage, is authentic and revealing. Of particular note is Jean's letter of 28 July, in part relating to the important question of the role Aino might have played in her husband's creative process.[5] Aino commented: 'I would like to say of your artistic side that it is, in my view, good as it is. I mean that your momentariness [*hetkellisyytesi*] is perhaps very fortunate for your art. Because a great moment can be more and more perfect than protracted reflections. [...] But as a person, your momentariness is perhaps the saddest thing in the world for me. But I have begun to believe that it is precisely what gives your music its verve, so it is easier to endure and to hold you

[1] *Åbo Tidning*, 7 June 1889.

[2] National Archive Box 25; Adolf Paul to JS, 15 February 1941.

[3] Ringbom 1954, pp. 6–7.

[4] Jalas 1981, p. 59.

[5] JS to Aino, 28 July 1894, from Munich.

in high esteem.'[1] Sibelius repeatedly came into conflict with the institutionalisation of social norms and educational content. After completing his school-leaving exams, he is said to have expressed his enthusiasm for the unintentionally delayed end of his life as a high school student (he had repeated a grade) by improvising his 'song of freedom' on the violin and saying: 'It is so wonderful that I no longer have to read; from now on, I will only make music.'[2] He generously admitted his weaknesses: 'One thing is certain: that I am able neither to speak nor write.'[3] This ironic self-criticism also makes clear how emphatically he meant 'able to'. For him, it meant more than achieving what he had learned in school. He still expressed scepticism about words several decades later: 'When I began my career, I made the irrevocable decision that I would only express myself in music. As you know, I have always done it that way.'[4] He wrote something similar to a music journal that had asked him for a contribution: 'An irrevocable decision to produce only music makes it impossible for me to comply with your request.'[5]

He never completed a written work more extensive than a long letter. The fragments of his efforts to write down his reflections on the subject of music reveal shadows of his intellectual environment. Neither his report of his trip to Karelia to conduct research in 1892 nor his sample presentation before the university's selection board in 1896 — a fragment whose similarity to Felip Pedrell's *Por nuestra música* of 1891 is striking[6] — is a finished text of any significant complexity. In the latter case, the board made that very criticism and ultimately chose his competitor, Robert Kajanus, as the university's new music director.[7] In comparison to the highly gifted organiser and rhetorician Kajanus, he was a 'starry-eyed dreamer'. Sibelius' remarks — on opera and drama, for example — were copied from standard works of the time; some of it was probably taken from remarks by friends, including even Kajanus and Busoni. His circles included well-versed representatives of the era whose conversation was on a par with the discourse in Berlin and Paris.

The contradictions in his responses to questions about his life and art theory are also primarily connected to his irony — heightened by the business-like impulse of the reporters. In general, irony is far too little appreciated as a factor in Sibelius' character; after all, '*irony*, *melancholy*, and *pessimism* are the chords of the moods of an emotional state that of necessity grows out of the permanent contradiction with reality, since reality proves to be stronger, impossible to influence, and inalterable,

1 Aino to JS, 4 August 1894.
2 Sirén 2000, p. 47: Ilmi Koponen was reporting on Eva Savonius.
3 JS to Aino, 10 December 1891.
4 National Archive Box 34; draft letter from JS to Georg Boldemann, 20 October 1943.
5 National Archive Box 36; draft letter from JS, 24 September 1932; the recipient is not indicated.
6 See Gallego 1985.
7 See Erik W. Tawaststjerna 1976, pp. 190 ff.

driving the artist to flee into unreality or resignation.'[1] Kajanus' son Kai characterised Sibelius' way of speaking in public as 'aphoristic like Nietzsche'.[2]

Conversation on important matters such as music (especially his own) was something he seems to have avoided just as he almost never wrote in detail about such subjects in his letters: 'not a word had been said about music during the whole day. [...] no musical subject was mentioned at luncheon'.[3] When Bengt de Törne asked him if he had favourite pieces among his own works, he said: 'Be sure I have [...] but nobody will ever know which!'[4] Nevertheless, Törne was able to report: 'there is no composition of his which he talks of so often as his Fourth Symphony'.

Sibelius was no asocial loner. From 1902 onwards, he belonged to the neo-Hellenist *Euterpe* circle (Karl Flodin, Bertel Gripenberg, Werner Söderhjelm and others), a circle of high-calibre intellectuals that also published an important journal (*Euterpe*). They were preceded in his life by the 'Leskovites' around Busoni (including Armas and Eero Järnefelt and Adolf Paul in 1888–9); the *Päivälehti* group around Juhani Aho, Eero Erkko and Pekka Halonen around 1890; and the 'symposium' in 1892–5 around Kajanus and Gallen-Kallela with such guests as the violinist Willy Burmester and pianist Alfred Reisenauer.[5] That was followed in 1922 by the New York-based Freemasons of the Suomi Lodge, though Sibelius rarely, if ever, participated in their events.[6] Several memoirs refer to a talkative Sibelius. At thirty-seven, he was even described as jovial, charming, sensitive, understanding and, though somewhat tired, mentally vital.[7] But he could also playact. 'You have to put on a mask. Otherwise it is unbearable being among people', he noted in Paris and deliberately acted gregariously.[8] The culture of his childhood — personified by his grandmother, Katarina Juliana Borg née Haartman — made this mask possible. Let's call it the Apollonian mask of the art of Albert Edelfelt, Johan Ludvig Runeberg and Zachris Topelius.

Although guests certainly disrupted his work, he could also be the perfect host, by no means a hermit turning people away: 'Coming to your home, the guest too falls into the proper mood and grows and rises to become close to what one strives for: release from the self and involvement in great humanity.'[9] Törne summed it up: 'It is impossible to imagine a more perfect host than Sibelius. He combines with the great kindliness and exquisite manners of a *grand seigneur* the fascinating talk and wide outlook of a great intellectual.'[10] His outward appearance radiated elegance and estab-

[1] See Hofstätter [1965] 1978, p. 58.

[2] *Suomen Kuvalehti*, 25 April 1986.

[3] Törne 1937, p. 45.

[4] Ibid., p. 101.

[5] See also Burmester 1926, p. 89.

[6] Sirén 2000, p. 420.

[7] Erik W. Tawaststjerna 1992, p. 199.

[8] Diary, 6 November 1911.

[9] National Library Coll. 206: 20, Matti Kivekäs to JS, 16 December 1914.

[10] Törne 1937, p. 43.

lishment. His manner of dress and his frequenting the finest tailors and shoemakers of Berlin at great expense impressed even his most exacting contemporaries.[1] In his memoirs, Franz Emil Sillanpää, winner of the Nobel Prize for Literature (1939), wrote of Sibelius: 'his appearance, down to the tips of his shoelaces, was always superbly elegant and furthermore quite individual, with nothing obviously imitative – at the time he used a kind of double collar whose front corners were not creased sharply but instead folded round.'[2] Sibelius' concern was not appearing fashionable but rather the inner effect. He even wore a suit when fishing in a small boat. He experienced the qualities even of temporary living spaces not only as welcome comfort but also as part of his identity. In that spirit, he remarked in Berlin (Diary, 28 April 1909): 'I find that I am living too simply. Expectations for living!'

To some, his appearances seemed staged. The most prominent Swedish music critic, Wilhelm Peterson-Berger, who was also the composer of the melancholic 'Same Ätnam (Lapland)' Third Symphony (1913–15) and hence possibly envious, found the appearance of 'Professor Sibelius' absurd in 1923: 'But instead she beheld a rather thickset, bald-headed gentleman, who behaved indeed like a man of the world but officially on the programme bears the title "Professor". Really, how can one do that when one is after all Jean Sibelius?'[3]

Sibelius could indeed be vain. One bit of evidence of this is a letter from 14 August 1900 to the conductor Georg Schnéevoigt: 'Dear Schneevoigt! Please send me Lazar's hair tonic. I am getting a bald spot.'[4] From photographs from this period it is possible to make out that his hair was no longer quite as full. Photographs from six years later and from as late as January 1919 reveal his effort to cover his bald spot by combing his hair back. In advance of the Nordic Music Days in Copenhagen in June 1919, he finally shaved his own head in the old Roman manner, thus laying the cornerstone for his image as an unshakably masculine and classicistic composer. The first photograph showing him without hair was taken in Denmark. Later his bald head became a monument to the nation and to the North, like a round granite rock off the Finnish coast, full of masculine sex appeal. This complete adaptation of his profile to the elements of the Finnish landscape is articulated by Wäinö Aaltonen's bust of Sibelius (1935), whose oversized base and rendering of Sibelius' head as part of an ancient granite rock is captivating.[5] A few years later, during the war, Aaltonen was a member – along with the Finnish-Swiss mathematician Rolf Nevanlinna, the composer Yrjö Kilpinen and the ophthalmic surgeon Mauno Vannas – of Suomen Valtakunnan Liitto, the spearhead of active contact between Finland and the National

[1] See Carl Stoeckel, 'Some Recollections of the Visit of Sibelius to America in 1914' (MS in Yale University Library); quoted in Erik W. Tawaststjerna 1986, pp. 269–70. JS spent extravagantly when shopping in Berlin and Paris (see ibid., p. 208).

[2] Sillanpää 1953, p. 221.

[3] Erik W. Tawaststjerna 1986, p. 228.

[4] Åbo Akademi.

[5] Both are illustrated in Levas 1992 (unnumbered).

Socialist dictatorship, which also claimed classicistic aesthetics for itself (albeit, like Mussolini, without justification).

According to oral tradition, his tendency towards existential amalgamation also corresponded with his relationship to Finland and his attitude to life. He supposedly said to Törne: 'Although I like seeing other countries and staying in foreign cities for a time, I must *live* in Finland. I could never abandon this country for good; that would finish me, and mean death to my art!'[1] Occasionally, as in August 1894, he said that he wanted 'to go abroad' because 'the fatherland no longer satisfies him',[2] but that was an exception (and may have referred to the limited scope for influence of his music in a small country). Not even a professorship at the Eastman School of Music in Rochester, which offered him quite respectable conditions as early as 1920 and an opportunity to become an American composer, could make him unfaithful to his country. He described his position in Finland to the incumbent rector Alf Klingenberg, who had been a fellow music student with Sibelius in Berlin in 1890, as 'poeta laureatus (!)'.[3] That included a fixed, though modest, artist's salary from the state. His ironic attitude towards his status is evident from the exclamation mark after the job title.

Another reason, perhaps more telling, for turning the position down was his relationship to teaching. He had neither the ambition nor the ability to teach regularly with a position at an institution. From 1892 to 1910, he had occasionally (at least on paper) taught harmony and counterpoint ('Tonsatz') and violin for as many as thirty hours a week at Martin Wegelius' and Robert Kajanus' music institutes in Helsinki.[4] Kajanus' School for Orchestral Music (founded in 1885) was integrated into Wegelius' Music Institute (founded in 1882) in 1914. This was the origin of today's Sibelius Academy. Teaching was a temporary necessity, which he often avoided, *de facto* with Wegelius' support.[5] In 1907–8, he had two advanced students, Toivo Kuula and Leevi Madetoja, but he promptly sent them abroad. He reportedly said to Törne, who probably studied with him as well: 'I don't know whether I am a good teacher or not; I think the better the composer, the worse the teacher.'[6] In his heart of hearts, he knew the answer to that question. Törne underscored this statement at a time when the polemic around Schoenberg and Sibelius had already begun, and Schoenberg was held up as a prominent teacher. Sibelius supposedly said to Leevi Madetoja when he began teaching him in 1907: 'I am a bad teacher.'[7] He wrote in his diary on 14 April 1921: 'I cannot teach others. That would be the greatest disappointment for the people in Rochester and for me as a composer. I cannot speak English adequately. Nor do I play

1 Törne 1937, p. 70.

2 JS to Aino, 17 August 1894.

3 National Library Coll. 206: 62; JS to Alf Klingenberg, 28 February 1920.

4 Karvonen 1957, pp. 276 and 288.

5 Madetoja, 'Jean Sibelius opettajana', *Aulos* (1925), quoted in Salmenhaara 1987, p. 92.

6 Törne 1937, p. 26; see also Erik W. Tawaststjerna 1997b, pp. 176, 188, 203 and 206–7.

7 Madetoja, 'Jean Sibelius opettajana', *Aulos* (1925), quoted in Salmenhaara 1987, p. 93.

the piano.' On 8 April 1921, he wrote to Klingenberg: 'I can conduct my compositions somewhat but as a teacher – impossible.'[1] He had no method that he wished to, or could, explain to others.

He had decided against taking a professorship in Vienna in 1912 for similar reasons. At the time, it was suggested in a nonbinding way that he could teach composition as the successor to his own teacher, Robert Fuchs. In her history of the Hochschule für Musik und darstellende Kunst, Lynne Heller reports on this dramatic search for a candidate – a well-known story because of its bearing on Arnold Schoenberg.[2] The episode was summed up as follows in the final report to the committee:

> so we soon had to admit that it would be impossible for secondary reasons to attract first-rank names like Max Reger or Richard Strauss. For a time we also considered summoning foreign candidates such as Dukas, Sibelius and Rachmaninoff; these combinations had to be stifled in turn, because apart from the greater or lesser inclination shown by those mentioned to accept any appointment, it did not seem sufficiently certain that they would be able to master our language of instruction.[3]

The files of the Hochschule show that Wilhelm Bopp, the rector of the conservatory, was Schoenberg's supporter and considered Fuchs's teaching to be behind the times, though he did not want the 'imperial and royal academy as such to gain a reputation for subscribing to the modern movement'. Sibelius seems to have been of a different view where Fuchs was concerned, since as late as 1911 he had sent Madetoja to study with him, after he had been unable to study with Vincent d'Indy in Paris in the academic year 1910–11, which Sibelius had also recommended. On 9 November 1911, Madetoja wrote from Vienna: 'Prof. Fuchs is very friendly towards me, and I immediately recognised that it is largely because of your recommendation.'[4]

In the end, Sibelius summed up his reasons for 'rejection' (Diary, 8 March 1912): 'Patriotism and love of my own independent work'. On 30 January, Bopp had asked Sibelius extensively and in detail – but not in the name of the academy – to think about the professorship:

> Prof. Grümmer, our esteemed musician and virtuoso, asked you whether you would perhaps be inclined to accept a professorship in composition at the imperial and royal academy. From your kind reply to Prof. Grümmer, I was pleased to see that you are not disinclined to accept an appointment in Vienna. I now repeat and state more precisely the request, though, as I must emphasise, in utterly unbinding form, because the requirements for such a position to become free must first be met. Hence I am asking you today whether you would

[1] National Library Coll. 206: 62; JS to Alf Klingenberg, 8 April 1921.

[2] See Lynne Heller 1994, pp. 72 ff.

[3] Ibid., pp. 87–8.

[4] National Archive Box 16.

agree to the propositions I could offer you in accordance with our salary scale — inclusion in state civil servants Class 8 and a salary of 6,410.00 crowns annually — and would be prepared to relocate to Vienna should the occasion arise.[1]

Initial contact had been made two weeks previously — and immediately circulated in the press in Finland. In his diary on 20 January 1912, Sibelius observed: 'The matter of the professorship in Vienna was published in *Nya Pressen*.' On 3 February he noted: 'A letter from Vienna from the director of the academy and proposal of professorship' — although the word 'proposal' did not mean a proposal in the name of the committee that he should fill the position. On 5 February he wrote: 'Wrote to the director, Wilhelm Bopp, Vienna'; and on 1 March, very revealingly: 'Rejected professorship in Vienna by telegraph. I cannot enslave myself again *pour l'honneur*.'[2]

On 17 January Sibelius was leaping to conclusions — conclusions that have become established in the secondary literature — when he wrote in his diary: 'Received appointment to professorship at the imperial and royal academy in Vienna. Am considering it a little.' There is, however, a world of difference between an appointment and an initial enquiry. In any case, Sibelius rejected it, saying he wanted to be free to compose.[3] He preferred to finance his artistically important projects and the life of his family with occasional compositions rather than with teaching. Only in 1896 did he try, more or less seriously, to obtain a position with a firm obligation to teach: the office of music director at the University of Helsinki.[4] His teaching for Kajanus and Wegelius and his occasional private lessons were marked by interruptions for overriding obligations and projects and cannot be compared to a permanent position.

From the perspective of 1952, one of his students, the composer Viljo Mikkola, reported from Turku: 'When I studied at the Music Institute in Helsinki at the end of the last century, I had the pleasure of being a student of the great composer Jean Sibelius, if only for a short time. But I learned a great deal in that short time. I learned that a young music student should study and analyse the works of great masters and expand his senses by listening to good music.'[5] This 'method' is not bad for composers already trained in the basics. Sibelius' idea of what a composition teacher was supposed to do before that (which is the most difficult part of the job) was influenced by his harmony and counterpoint teachers — Wegelius, Becker and Fuchs — which is why he did not believe in his own competence. Madetoja also wrote that Sibelius was the sort of teacher 'one does not find in conservatories' and from whom one did not so much obtain 'narrow professional details' as a 'general musical education'.[6] But Sibelius also knew Busoni (who led a successful master class in Berlin with such

[1] National Library Coll. 206: 5.

[2] See also JS to Axel Carpelan, 18 January 1912, quoted in Dahlström 2010, pp. 322–3.

[3] Diary, 8 March 1912.

[4] Erik W. Tawaststjerna 1976, pp. 190 ff.

[5] National Library Coll. 206: 25; 12 March 1952.

[6] Madetoja, 'Jean Sibelius opettajana', *Aulos* (1925), quoted in Salmenhaara 1987, pp. 92–3.

students as Kurt Weill and Edgard Varèse) and knew just how much education in method was required for independent, truly inspiring instruction.

Although the semi-urban culture of his childhood was shaped by ideals of education common at the time and by literary maxims, Sibelius was one of those composers whose core personality was dominated by intuitions and visions rather than literary formulations and logical and didactic constructs, which certainly limited his abilities to teach within the framework of a regular curriculum. Even as a youth, he read not only Runeberg's poetry but also August Strindberg,[1] then somewhat later Émile Zola and even Knut Hamsun. His favourite poet was, of all people, Horace, the great nature poet of antiquity, and his favourite reading matter ancient history. Newmarch quoted the statement: 'Homer and Horace had a significance in my development I cannot value highly enough.'[2] Around 1911, to the author of the text for 'Kaiutar', op. 72, no. 4, a friend from his youth, Larin-Kyösti (Kyösti Larson), he recommended literature in a philosophical undertone:

> Because I am a good deal older than you, and have been through a few things, I venture to offer you a bit of good advice. Try to remove yourself from time, studying the Divina Commedia, Milton and other old poets. By doing so, I can say with certainty, you will achieve a strange 'peace' and plasticity, both for your style and for your life. [...] Everything becomes poetry, and poetry with a form that is as confident as it is original. Believe me, good brother.[3]

This statement documents his original approach to literary texts. But nevertheless on 12 June 1925 Aino drew her brother Arvid's attention to the fact that her husband almost never read literature.[4] His essence was flooded by fantasies – not by a pronounced interest in the written word. Both ancient and Finnish myths and legends served him merely to suggest themes or titles for a subjectively conceived 'essence', especially in the tone poem *Tapiola*, in which 'everything becomes poetry'.[5] He was not a big reader.

However typical of his time this distance from the world and from a verbally determined worldview in favour of holism and an inter-medial understanding of the poetic core of things may have been, few artists took these things to their ultimate conclusions, and even fewer were predestined to do so. The Austrian poet and critic Hermann Bahr's *Zur Kritik der Moderne* (Towards a critique of modernity; 1890) and his argument for sensuality as well as his *Die Überwindung des Naturalismus* (The overcoming of naturalism; 1891) are early milestones in this trend, which is manifest in Sibelius' work and calls into question any dominance of rational perception and any preference for realistic memory over dreams, unconscious insights, intuition

1 See Erik W. Tawaststjerna 1976, p. 28, and Törne 1937, pp. 43–4.

2 Newmarch 1939, p. 9.

3 National Archive: copy in the Tawaststjerna Collection.

4 Talas 2000, p. 296.

5 Salmenhaara 1970, p. 20.

and the imagination. Henri Bergson expressed similar ideas in *Essai sur les données immédiates de la conscience* (1889) and *Matière et mémoire* (1896). This is the kind of reading we need in order to understand Sibelius.

The 'Dreamer of Nature'

In the late nineteenth century, Hämeenlinna was a centre of education and administration, surrounded by the aura of an ancient agrarian culture. The region radiated an archaic quality of life that had already moved the ancient inhabitants of the Finnish peninsula to establish one of the first-known settlements there, just a few kilometres from the house in which Sibelius was born. As a particularly sensitive child he was enchanted by nature. Very early on he would often lose his sense of the concrete and earned a reputation as a daydreamer.[1] In particular his grandmother, the widow of a Protestant provost, accused Finland's future national artist of a tendency to the irrational that was, as she explicitly stated, completely unknown in her own family. She was repressing the fact that her daughter Maria Charlotta, the composer's mother, was known for hypersensitivity, instability and chaotic dream visions, and Sibelius' aunt Tekla also seems to have been psychologically unstable: a 'hypochondriac who spent a disproportionate amount of time in bed'.[2]

Ilmi Koponen, a local teacher and friend of the family, praised Tekla in particular for her practical disposition. The pianist and later piano teacher Julia (or Juliana), by contrast, was said to have been the most talented of the provost's widow's three daughters.[3] The reports Koponen collected about how the composer's parents met are only plausible if Maria is not taken to be a hypersensitive woman.[4] Supposedly, Maria was chosen by a group of elderly men for the local physician Christian Sibelius, who had neither the time nor the energy to search himself. The future couple had not known each other previously. But perhaps Maria's alarming sensitivity could explain why her mother allowed her to marry a man twenty years her senior even before (which was crucial in traditional society) her eldest daughter was married. Tekla and Julia, whom Sibelius himself criticised, in a letter to Aino on 13 December 1890, as 'terribly frightened' ('pjåkig', an old-fashioned word for anxiously weepy in a pseudo-religious sense), never married. The later illness of Sibelius' sister, Linda, suggests a hereditary weakness, which would also explain many of his own characteristics without making them pathological. This reference to a concentration of psychological problems in the family, which Sibelius' grandmother did not wish to acknowledge, must of course be offset by the fact that nearly all the members of the Borg family had an academic edu-

1 On the memories of his contemporaries, see, for example, Koskimies 1990, pp. 10–11.

2 Salmenhaara 1984, 16. Cf. Goss 1997, p. 203.

3 'Sibelius-muistoja Hämeenlinnassa I–II', Suomen Historiallisen Seuran kokoelmat, National Archive; quoted in Sirén 2000, p. 18.

4 Sirén 2000, pp. 15 ff.

Fig. 9. Hämeenlinna's church before 1892 (interior and exterior). Prior to 1892 this church had a classicistic interior, with its altar in the centre. Much like the cathedral in Helsinki, this sacred building was round and extraordinarily simple.

cation and occupied prominent positions in education and government. Sensitivity (even neurological) often goes hand in hand with supreme talent.

The essential qualities for artistic activity, in particular sensitivity, are usually associated with the genes of his mother and the Borg family (especially) and also the Haartman side, especially as it was Maria's younger sister, Julia, who taught Sibelius to play the piano and thus was the first person who demonstrated to him the way to the realm of musically beautiful sounds. The sister of his equally musically refined father, Christian, Evelina Sibelius in Loviisa — for whom Sibelius named his first daughter, Eva, in 1893 — and her brother Pehr Sibelius in Turku were among the few who believed in his special talent and financially supported his professional training.[1]

In an anecdote from his year studying in Vienna around 1891, Sibelius said reflectively of his old instrument maker, who as an apprentice had tuned the elderly Beethoven's piano: 'And it was wonderful to look into those eyes, which had seen the master of the Ninth symphony.'[2] The significance Sibelius attributed to this fact is striking — as if he had seen Beethoven himself through the eyes of piano tuner. In Törne's report of his first encounter with him, Sibelius also appears as an augur:

> 'Now, since you have become my pupil, I must see into your mind, because I can't be expected to teach you something if I don't know you thoroughly. Look at me. No, not that way; straight into my eyes.' He suddenly grew silent, his face assuming a serious, almost severe expression, and as he sat motionless I felt his keen scrutiny right through my head. Presently there came words, pronounced quite slowly and in a low voice. He told me all about myself and my life. It was the clearest and most perspicacious psychological analysis I had ever heard.[3]

Other contemporaries found his gaze introverted.[4] Gallen-Kallela's painting *Jean Sibelius and the Imaginary Landscape*, also known as *Sibelius as the Composer of 'En saga'* (1894), confirms this impression. The portrait resembles the depiction of Sibelius in the scandalous canvas *Symposium*, whose final version was also painted in 1894. As in the early portrait by his brother-in-law Eero Järnefelt (1892), his eyes can be seen more clearly than in most photographs. In studio photographs the elegant man in Helsinki and Berlin had taken of himself before contemporary backdrops, his eyes stand out for their beauty. The introverted gaze could not be photographed.

The modern 'dichotomy between an aesthetic experience of nature and a scientific, technical understanding of nature' that Hermann Danuser made the basis for his analysis of the 'functions of nature' in Gustav Mahler can only be found to a limited extent in Sibelius.[5] For him, so-called nature was not a place of undisturbed work, recreation and a source or refreshing inspiration but rather an essential dimension of himself. Peter Franklin summarised the reactions to Niagara Falls of Mahler (in 1910) and Sibelius (in 1914): Mahler's 'articulate art is greater than inarticulate nature', and Sibelius' 'Of all that I had ever seen, this comes nearest to being a religious experience, nearer in fact than music.'[6] Immanuel Kant's proposition that all geniuses have a connection to nature is more clearly true of Sibelius (and perhaps only for him).[7] At least,

[1] See Erik W. Tawaststjerna 1976, pp. 5–6, and 30, and Goss 1997, pp. 16–17.

[2] Törne 1937, p. 47.

[3] Ibid., p. 26.

[4] Erik W. Tawaststjerna 1976, p. 54.

[5] Danuser 1991, p. 65.

[6] Franklin 2003, p. 356. Unfortunately, both quotations sound inauthentic.

[7] Kant, *Kritik der Urteilskraft* (*Critique of Judgement*), §46.

FIG. 10. Akseli Gallen-Kallela, *Jean Sibelius and the Imaginary Landscape*, also known as *Sibelius as the Composer of 'En saga'* (1894). Sibelius was not prepared to comply with Gallen-Kallela's wish that he write a few bars from *En saga* on the blank space in his own hand. Gallen-Kallela associated a colourful imaginary landscape with the composition, but he also emphasised its author's spiritual presence. In 1894 Gallen-Kallela can only have known the original version of 1892, which was premiered in 1893 under Robert Kajanus. *En saga* was revised in 1902 and was even heard in Berlin in Ferruccio Busoni's concert series.

the immediacy of the relationship between nature and the genius of artistic creativity that Kant presumed was heightened in his case. The same is true of the nature philosophy of art in the Romantic theory of the genius.[1] Thus in his case, nature did not so much influence compositional details, as Danuser detected in Mahler's case, as it did offer models for subliminal aesthetic principles and style beyond the design of concrete works of art, outside the triad of 'structure', 'form' and 'totality of the work'.[2]

Whereas in Mahler's work it is difficult to distinguish between the connection to nature and that to tradition, this separation is instructive in Sibelius' case. He had nothing of the vague relationship to nature of those Romantics who stared out of their reading rooms into forests as fresh as the dew, as they forced their subjective stirrings into brilliant texts while now and again consulting the writings of others. Nor was the conscious confrontation with 'nature in its pagan, mythical innocence', which knows nothing of 'the human being as someone seeking an adversary or

[1] Marquard 1968, pp. 375 ff.; quoted in Danuser 1991, p. 67.

[2] Danuser 1991, p. 69.

redemption',[1] something with any meaning for him. Sibelius' characteristic was a desire for an active experience of nature (not perception of nature) whose consequences were destructive and led to a superficial abandonment of the self, and which could not be limited by any common medium such as writing, images or sound. His friends called him a 'dreamer' and a poet of nature.[2] The source of his inspiration was nature in all its complex sensuality. This concept of nature had little to do with topographic landscape, renewal, or even, in the spirit of regional poets (representatives of the regionalist schools, *Heimatkunst* in German), the 'monuments' of the region.

Törne's depiction of Sibelius' essence, projected onto a big white swan in the blindingly clear autumn light of the North, seems authentic:

> On a cold day at the end of the autumn he went for a walk. The crimson of the setting sun was reflected in the wide surface of the lake outside his villa, and the calm mirror of water was framed by a border of thin, pale grey ice. A huge bird came flying from the north and alighted on the lake. It was a white swan, resting for a while on its long journey to southern climes. As the sun went down the transparent frame of ice gradually approached the solitary bird from either side. Sibelius watched the scene until nightfall. He then went home to compose one of his andantes.[3]

Regardless of the truth of this report from an unreliable witness (the book contains provocative opinions and a lot of 'inaccuracies'),[4] it is unsurpassed in its idyllic beauty. The elemental appearance of this is transformed by the effect of the basic elements of sun and water. The appearance of the swan thus corresponds to a regional reality, as it is found in southern Finland in summer, though not an everyday occurrence. More important than Finnish fauna, perhaps, is the ancient tale of Apollo travelling with a team of swans to the Hyperboreans, who lived beyond the North Wind.[5]

Both the elemental quality and the presence of the 'favourite animal of the art nouveau'[6] made Finnish artists receptive to the trends of Central and Western European Symbolism (Stéphane Mallarmé, Arnold Böcklin and so on). Sibelius was an extreme case, however. He noted in his diary on 24 April 1915: 'I'm always thinking about swans, and they add splendour to my life. Strange that almost nothing in the world, in art, literature or music, makes an impression on me quite like these swans & cranes & wild geese.' All these birds are integral components of the national symbolism (in Finland especially *Cygnus cygnus* rather than *Cygnus olor*), the desire for

[1] Hirsbrunner 1981, pp. 190–91. The author was reflecting on Mauclair 1909, pp. 53 ff.

[2] Ekman 1946, p. 20 ff.; Howitz 1967, pp. 78–83, turns Ekman's or von Konow's formulation into a quotation of JS.

[3] Törne 1937, p. 101.

[4] See National Archive Box 34: draft letter by JS, 14 February 1946; on Törne, see chapter 5.2 in the present volume.

[5] Nietzsche 1986, p. 569. See also Horace, *Odes* 2.20.9–16.

[6] Hofstätter [1965] 1978, pp. 207–8.

distant lands, humanistic goals and freedom of thought. Väinö Blomstedt's sketch for the poster for the Finnish exhibition in St Petersburg in 1898 is in this same spirit. It illustrates a peaceful lake landscape with spruces and pines, and a chain of wild geese floats in the sky.[1] Yet Sibelius even remembered his father as the man who showed him the image of a white swan.[2] Thus perhaps the bird became the symbol of the father. The standard symbolic qualities of specific kinds of birds were by no means crucial to his fascination for these free creatures. As a youth he conducted an orchestra of birds;[3] later he reported – freely adapted from Joseph von Eichendorff's *Life of a Good-for-Nothing* – how much he liked to take his violin on his summer hikes, 'so that whenever I felt inspired I could express it in music'.[4] From a large rock with a view over Lake Vanajavesi, 'I gave the birds endless concerts.' He often improvised before the open sea in Loviisa, for example. When one of his orchestral rehearsals, conducted by Bernardino Molinari, was interrupted by birdsong in Rome in 1923, Sibelius supposedly said: 'I am certain that the little singers understand my music!'[5]

His attitude towards nature resembled Émile Bernard's and Paul Gauguin's critique of Impressionism: the point of departure for his art was intuition, but then 'the painter should become engrossed meditatively in the object to be depicted and then create it anew from memory in the studio. [...] What the artist noticed of the object, because it seemed important to him, necessarily contains the essence of the event.'[6] Correspondingly, in Törne's story of the cold day at the lake, the result was not a programmatic symphony or an Impressionist tone poem but rather (as an 'essence') a small Andante.[7] A diary entry of 21 April 1915 that connects his Fifth Symphony to an experience of nature is programmatic:

> Just before ten-to-eleven saw sixteen swans. One of the greatest experiences in life. Oh God, what beauty: they circled over me for a long time. Disappeared into the hazy sun like a silver ribbon, which glittered from time to time. Their cries were of the same woodwind timbre as the cranes but without any tremolo. The swans are closer to trumpets, though there is an element of the sarussophone. A low suppressed memory of a small child's cry. Nature's mystery and life's melancholy. The Fifth Symphony's finale theme. [Music follows: the final theme in E flat major of the Fifth Symphony] The trumpet will bind it together.

[1] See illustration in Klinge 1997, p. 333.

[2] Erik W. Tawaststjerna 1976, p. 13 (here no mention of a swan, just 'animal pictures'), and Levas 1992, p. 25; see also Sirén 2000, p. 24 (with a white swan). Sirén also includes a similar childhood memory from Sibelius' sister Linda; see ibid, p. 25, quoting Linda Sibelius' memoirs in the National Archive.

[3] JS to Pehr, 10 July 1885, in Goss 1997, p. 72.

[4] Ringbom 1954, p. 10.

[5] Salmenhaara 1984, p. 383; first quoted in Törne, 'Sibeliuksen seurassa Roomassa', *Musiikkitieto* (December 1940), p. 20.

[6] Hofstätter 1972, p. 75.

[7] Törne 1937, p. 101; cf. note 26.

FIG. 11. Väinö Blomstedt, 'Kansanlaulu' (Folk song), in *Nuori Suomi* (1897). *Nuori Suomi* (Young Finland) was the arts supplement of *Päivälehti* (now known as *Helsingin Sanomat*). The first issue appeared in Christmas 1891. The term 'Young Finland' first emerged in the 1880s; the term became established as a cultural-political movement around the writer Minna Canth in the 1890s. The journal *Uusi Kuvalehti* appeared in this same cultural context. The *kantele* player in peasant clothing – the Finnish peasant was 'free' even under Russian rule – symbolises the creative power of the individual; the swan signifies freedom and the young nation's high ambitions for education.

> [...] This must now come to me which has so long resonated in the air. Have been transported today.

The end of this quotation has been assumed to indicate pantheism.[1] In his diary, at least, he expressed his dissatisfaction with *Le bréviaire d'un panthéïste et le pessimisme héroïque* by Henri Cazalis's alias, Jean Lahors (Diary, 17 December 1912): 'Typical that I am regarded this way.' This book was published in Paris in 1906. The pantheistic quality is also put into perspective by a note from 19 April 1916: 'Saw cranes. Heard again my voices'[2] and on the following day: '12 swans landed on the ice. Watched them with binoculars!!! – Saw 6 wild geese and an eagle. Ample day!! – Was on Puotinokka [in Lake Tuusula] with Heikki's [Järnefelt] binoculars and studied the life of swans. Strange, poetic!' In addition to the ornithology, the references to 'my voices' and 'poetic' are important. Sibelius was not listening to a lyrical voice but to the voices of the environment, which also were his. Even on 19 September 1957, the day before he

[1] Erik W. Tawaststjerna 1997b, p. 49.

[2] Diary, 19 April 1916: 'Såg tranor. Hörde åter mina låten!'; quoted in Erik W. Tawaststjerna 1997b, p. 86 (translation modified).

died, he reported to Aino that he saw cranes – 'the birds of my youth' – flying south, and one bird separated from the group and circled around him to honour him.[1] This scene, so piously cited in the secondary literature, is surely too mystical to be true (and very typical of Aino's manner of constructing Sibelius). But we can nevertheless learn all the more about its teller from this tale.

His art deco log cabin, Ainola, located not far from a clean lake, was surrounded by spruces and by land that was partly in its natural state and partly cultivated as a kitchen garden. He liked this landscape. Thus he noted in his diary on 5 November 1910: 'The day is magnificent – typically Finnish – with "snow on the branches of the trees". I leave it only when absolutely necessary.' On a beautiful summer's day in 1916 he supposedly said to Törne: 'Look at this scenery, I like it; it's so restful, the best possible *milieu* for my work; these vast peaceful fields going right down to the lake.'[2] This notion of a regional connection of a different kind is, however, put in context by other documents, such as this only apparently paradoxical sentence in a letter from Rome of 1901: 'I must go to solitude and beauty.'[3] The fact that he passionately enjoyed visiting cities such as Berlin and Paris shows that his relationship to rural surroundings varied, at least. The ideas he expressed to Aino from Munich on 12 August 1894 read like an artistic programme: 'How good it was that I got out of there [Finland]. That gives new blood. One finds oneself.' Towards the end of that journey, he wrote from Berlin on 2 September: 'I'm much more autonomous than I was when I departed. This has been a rather good lesson for me. If only I could realise my ideas in music now.'

Big cities were just as important to him as natural landscapes. In spring 1901, while working on the Second Symphony, he fled to Rome from his seriously ill daughter in the small-town idyll of Rapallo. Enthusiastic about the art and culture of the Eternal City, he wrote, with shockingly little sensitivity to the situation of his wife and daughters: 'I recognise what hell for me both Berlin and Rapallo were. Here I am working very hard and, I hope, writing well. And there are so many artistic distractions when my imagination is exhausted. I seem to need them, and also to be completely alone when I am working.'[4]

There are many such scenes in the sources: 'If I could find a place on Earth where I would have my peace and quiet to work. Now everything depends on me' (Diary, 1–2 January 1911); 'Getting settled in Helsinki' (3 January 1911); 'Fled to Hotel Fennia! […] Have to endure it here' (6 January 1911), and so on. In August one reason for wishing to flee was the fact that he wanted to sleep with the window open, which Aino could not do because of her rheumatism. And the children were too loud for him (on 17 August 1911). 'Hammering out themes for the symphony. Am like a tabula rasa, and have to be alone', in another entry (10 August 1914). Later, too, he supposedly wrote

[1] Erik W. Tawaststjerna 1997b, p. 331.

[2] Törne 1937, p. 42.

[3] National Library Coll. 206: 61; JS to Gunnar Hauch, 26 March 1926.

[4] National Archive Box 95 und 57; JS to Aino, 27 March 1901.

the Sixth Symphony at the luxurious Hotel Fennia in Helsinki, which had been built in 1899.[1]

On 4 April 1901 he wrote to Axel Carpelan from Rome: 'Here you get strange ideas about what the essence of music is.' The ancient metropolis – whose name alone 'always had a strange attraction for me' (Diary, 8 February 1917) – did indeed trigger a thoroughgoing change in style. The tendency to classicism that becomes evident by the Third Symphony at the latest correlated with other projects in a classicistic spirit from that period, such as August Bungert's tetralogy *Die Homerische Welt* (The Homeric world) of 1898–1903 and Adolf von Harnack's *Das Wesen des Christentums* (translated as *What Is Christianity?*) of 1900, with its 'conception of the Greek spirit on the foundation of the Gospel', to name just two other examples in the shadow of Heinrich Wölfflin's *Die klassische Kunst* (translated as *Classic Art*) of 1899. As early as 1897, shortly before beginning work on the First Symphony, he was spending time in Rome with the art historian Walter von Konow and visiting many museums. On that same journey, he had earlier been inspired by Raphael's *Santa Cecilia* in Dresden on 26 June, as he reported to Aino on 1 July. We can only assume that Sibelius meant Carlo Dolci's delightful *Cecilia*, since the Raphael is in Bologna. Moreover, Sibelius says Aino resembles Cecilia; in the case of the Raphael, that would not fit at all.

Sibelius travelled to Rome with von Konow again in 1926: 'He suddenly decided to do so on Wednesday, and everything could be arranged in a blazing hurry.'[2] They departed on Saturday, 20 March, and *Tapiola* was in his luggage as a project to work on. He also experienced Paris as an intimate environment. Several months after completing the Fourth Symphony, he wrote about the soothing anonymity of a large city: 'I have come here – to Paris – for a while. Here indeed is solitude! Give me either the loneliness of the Finnish forests or of a big city.'[3] He repeatedly mentioned Paris in particular as a preferred environment: '"I think Paris is an excellent place for working", he said. "It stimulates one's energy. I know it from my own experience."'[4]

Contemporaries who were aware of his long trip to Germany and Italy in 1901 were already speculating about the stylistic and mental changes to be expected. Mikko Slöör, Gallen-Kallela's brother-in-law, reported acquaintances in Helsinki who counted on Sibelius becoming cosmopolitan in Italy and others who suspected that, reinforced by his Finnish nature, he would react critically to cosmopolitanism.[5] Sibelius developed an original synthesis of cosmopolitanism and connection to his homeland. From Aino's perspective, his Finnish nature was the proper basis for understanding his music; she herself detested large cities and the chic. She compared

[1] Jalas 1981, p. 55.

[2] See Aino to Saimi Järnefelt, 22 March 1926, in Talas 2000, p. 307.

[3] Newmarch 1939, p. 25.

[4] Törne 1937, p. 64.

[5] National Library Coll. 206: 36; Mikko Slöör to JS, 13 April 1901.

Berlin, which Sibelius visited most frequently of all,[1] to the 'gates of hell',[2] and when her husband was working on *Voces intimae* in London, she flattered Rosa Newmarch: 'You are fond of music and nature, and I think that is the reason why you understand my husband so well.'[3] This shows how Aino worked to establish clichés, but at the cost of the ambiguity manifested not least in the role large cities played as sources of inspiration. Finally, the property around Ainola was characterised less by untamed nature than by its proximity to an old country road and the homes of other artists and in particular to those of Aho, Halonen and Järnefelt. Sibelius supposedly said to his biographer Karl Ekman: 'my art demanded a different environment. In Helsinki all melody died within me.'[4] The artist's home, Ainola, had nothing of the urban anonymity of Rome and Paris, but neither was the house located in the 'forest',[5] at most on the edge of a small patch of wood. With that as his base, Sibelius frequented chic restaurants and composed in his hotel room.

One motivation for Sibelius' trips was the lack of space in Ainola, which everyone senses who visits his home (now a museum). It must have been oppressive prior to the renovations of 1906. As early as 1910, they were considering a new house. In his diary for 17 May 1910, Sibelius wrote: 'Lars Sonck was here yesterday. Planned a new house.' This plan may have been initiated by Sonck, but Sibelius was not disinclined. Nevertheless, there are reports by visitors that describe the house as 'large',[6] perhaps because it better suited the myth of Sibelius than the idea of a cramped space. Moreover, in the 1930s the children were out of the house, or only visiting with their many children. Ainola initially lacked modern sanitary facilities. Sibelius was therefore all the more pleased when he encountered a bathroom in New York in 1914, fully enjoyed the comfort of a hotel bath in Rome in 1926 (at the centrally located Hotel Minerva, where he stayed regularly) and even as late as 1931 reported on a similar one in Berlin.[7] His daughters were schooled at home by their mother, and the servants often contributed to their vibrant life. Moreover, the idyll was frequently interrupted by public attention in him personally and there were often unannounced visitors. Birthdays and national holidays represented particular challenges, as did times of crisis for the Finnish Republic. At the time of the great jubilee of 1935, he wrote to Newmarch: 'my claims on quietude in order to compose have grown immense. As to tranquility, here I am in the very heart of it; I dwell in the very heart of solitude; but this autumn has been very odd: Interviews – often rather stupid – photographs, visitors, etc.'[8]

[1] See Gleissner 2002, p. 43, quoting Markku Hartikainen's studies.

[2] Aino to her mother, 12 December 1900, in Talas 2000, pp. 193–4.

[3] Newmarch 1939, p. 13. See also National Archive Box 121; Aino to Newmarch, 5 March 1909.

[4] Ekman 1946, p. 177.

[5] Newmarch 1939, p. 7: in his foreword, Bantock speaks of a 'forest home'. This description is, however, accurate for Gallen-Kallela's house in Ruovesi, which he left for Tarvaspää, near Helsinki.

[6] For example, Ronka 1948, p. 46.

[7] Erik W. Tawaststjerna 1997b, pp. 267 and 306.

[8] See JS to Newmarch of 1935, quoted in Newmarch 1939, p. 48.

FIG. 12. Sibelius in front of the sauna of Ainola. This old sauna, which stood until 1927, was conceived by Aino Sibelius in 1905. The famous residence (not pictured), located on slightly higher ground, was built in 1903–4 according to plans by Lars Sonck. From 1911 to 1935, there was extensive remodelling (including the façade). Electricity was added in 1919, running water only after the composer's death. The new sauna was built in 1928. Not far from the sauna – to the left outside the picture – is the present location of the composer's gravestone.

The composer's childhood is the key to his relationship to nature. According to his part-time secretary and biographer Santeri Levas, the elderly Sibelius recalled a landscape in Loviisa from his childhood: 'Then I lived in nature. Even today I remember some dense grass that grew high above my head, and how I felt that I was within the grass and that I had entirely grown up with it.'[1] Koskimies offered this striking formulation: 'Sibelius did not look at nature; he lived in nature and from nature.'[2] As a schoolboy, Sibelius was a good conservationist of birds, and later too he liked to go sailing, fishing and swimming for extended periods.[3] 'Had a magnificent swim!' reads his diary on 29 July 1910. In summer 1912, a lodge brother, the opera singer Wäinö Sola, gave him helpful hints about the most effective methods for fishing at Säikänkärki in Lake Päijänne,[4] and his diary he noted on 5 July 1912: 'In Kuhmoinen,

[1] Levas 1960b, p. 181; see Erik W. Tawaststjerna 1991, p. 103.

[2] Koskimies 1990, pp. 10 ff.

[3] Sirén 2000, p. 214, quoting Jonatan Reuter's report in *Hufvudstadsbladet* in 1902, which was strongly criticised in a letter from Aino to JS, 23 September 1902.

[4] See National Library Coll. 206: 36; see also Sola 1952, p. 170.

Uunasjärvi. Arrived here yesterday [with family]. The landscape has a lot of drama in its lines. Päijänne is like the sea.' He had completed his Sonatinas for Piano, op. 67, a few days earlier. At the age of thirteen, he injured his right elbow while mooring a rowboat, which hampered his preferred career as a violin virtuoso.[1] This accident may even have contributed to the trembling in his right hand he experienced later.

In contrast to artists like Gallen-Kallela, who moved to Helsinki as a schoolboy, Sibelius' relationship to nature lacked any timeless symbolism, ritualising[2] or mythologising. In Gallen-Kallela in particular, the ritual element is unmistakable, which makes it easier to understand in biographical terms his late work as the designer of state symbolism for the young republic. A collective spirit forged through repetition and specification — as opposed to individual and individualistic spontaneity — was, by contrast, foreign to Sibelius. The following sketch for a letter to the pianist and writer Walter Rummel can only be understood as irony: 'For your extremely friendly greeting under the sign of the great Väinämöinen, I thank you from the bottom of my heart and hope, great maestro, that your stay here in the land of the *Kalevala* will be pleasant.'[3] The elemental, not the ritual and mythological, dominated in him, as these would have signified dramatisation and verbalisation.[4] Such categories were not part of his constitution.

According to Levas, who was generally a reliable witness, he was in the habit of saying: 'No sooner do they [people without either imagination or a sense of beauty] see a stately tree than they consider whether or not it is good for building. [...] But they are the unluckiest of people, for they have lost what is most important.'[5] Sibelius himself was quite unlike that: he possessed an 'immense power of empathy'.[6] Even apart from the fact that in the North, much like in the mountains, the typical experience of nature — to say nothing of that of farmers and fishermen, of course — is perhaps not generally dominated by analytical observation of the landscape, that is, the study of flora and fauna,[7] and should instead be thought of as a subject-orientated diving into and immersing oneself in the elements, rather than object-orientated observation, Sibelius had an unusual talent for amalgamation in a culturally sophisticated environment. It was the granite of the Baltic Sea skerries, and explicitly not the panorama of the coastline, that he described as the source of important inspiration for his orchestral sound.[8] He allegedly said that while working on *Finlandia* he thought of the landscapes of his youth in Hämeenlinna,[9] but 'thinking' here most

1 Erik W. Tawaststjerna 1976, p. 21.
2 Hofstätter 1972, p. 49.
3 National Archive Box 35, n.d..; Rummel was staying at the Hotel Torni in Helsinki.
4 Braungart 1996, pp. 67–73, specifically on ritual and myth.
5 Levas 1960b, p. 48.
6 Ibid., p. 125 (translation modified).
7 JS showed an interest in biology at school as well; Erik W. Tawaststjerna 1976, p. 20.
8 Törne 1937, p. 97.
9 Koskimies 1990, p. 17, quoting Kurjensaari, *Jean Sibelius: Mestari ja maisema* (N.p.: n.n., 1965).

likely does not imply trivial tone painting but rather the immersion in the 'essence' of a region.

Sibelius did not glorify nature; rather, he experienced it in its elemental materiality. In Newmarch we read how he shrugged off the ordinary order of the elements and made it his habit to perceive synaesthetically the primal sound of nature and every environment in order to experience the elemental quality of its tonality: 'Sibelius had at that time a passion for trying to catch the pedal notes of natural forces. [...] he often seemed satisfied with the results of his rapt listening, when he caught the basic sounds of the forests or of the wind whistling over lakes and moorlands. To share Nature with him is a wonderful but silent experience.'[1] This same intensity is expressed in the following sentence: 'When stillness speaks, there are dreadful overtones.'[2] Or: '"In the country I have sometimes heard overtones from a rye field, as I dozed on the edge of the field", said my teacher.'[3] Some authors have interpreted such statements as evidence of pantheism. For example, Fritz Stege, an author from the Kampfbund für deutsche Kultur (Combat League for German Culture), did so in his effort to bring the Finnish closer to German readers:

> It is indispensable to an understanding of Finnish music that the listener empathise with the character of the landscape. It is nature that forms human beings and buoys them with their own wishes and emotions. The heroes and gods of the *Kalevala* are not dead; even today they wander through the endless forests and across the chains of lakes in Finland; they speak with the language of the wind, with the murmurs of the waves; they reveal themselves in the magic of the bright summer nights, recognisable only by the poet who captures the sound of their voices and records it with notes. That is how Jean Sibelius, the leading figure of Finnish music, became the musical 'magician of the North'.[4]

The authors of this German-Finnish publication included the composer Erkki Melartin with a series of contemporary aphorisms. Sibelius was not represented.

In another book from this dark period, *Finnische Gespräche* (Finnish conversations), Yrjö von Grönhagen introduced the reader to the customs and traditions of Finland, but also included a chapter on the history of Finnish music, in which Sibelius is mentioned only in passing: 'The song of the sagas and the melodies of ancient peoples come alive again most perfectly in the symphonic creations of our great master Jean Sibelius. His forebears were peasants in southern Finland. As with every true Finn, the source of the power of his being is nature. His connection to the myths of

[1] Newmarch 1939, p. 19.

[2] Erik W. Tawaststjerna 1986, p. 142. To be exact, the quoted entry in the diary of 15 August 1910 reads rather: 'Aftonstämningen underbar. Som alltid då stillheten talar: ett hemskt drag af evig stillhet och – lifsångest.' The metaphor of 'overtones' is only in the translation.

[3] Otto Kotilainen, quoted in Salmenhaara 1984, p. 98; see also Madetoja, 'Sibelius opettajana', *Aulos* (1925); quoted in Ringbom 1954, p. 55.

[4] Stege 1942, p. 144.

his people is heartfelt. […] In him, Finland has preserved Väinämöinen's *kantele* in altered form.'[1] Interpretations of this kind have led to the reinforcement of clichés, especially of the importance of mythology and discredited such inherently important, timeless categories as nature. Sibelius' pantheism was more abstract than Stege suspected, since he had been irreparably blinded by the pernicious ideology of National Socialism. The shadowy existence Sibelius has in such publications calls for analysis. In Walter Abendroth's *Deutsche Musik der Zeitwende* (German music at the turning point; 1943), for example, Sibelius is the only composer of symphonies still present around 1940 who is not even mentioned in passing. Examples of this kind have to be considered as we try to understand how famous Sibelius really was in Germany during that era.

Sibelius' statement of 20 July 1909 speaks volumes: 'This wonderful logic — let us call it God — that dominates the work of art is so compelling.'[2] He was not thinking of mythology but rather alluding to the idea that the harmony of music conveys a universal harmony of the spheres. Thus Ilmari Ronka could quote him saying: 'There may or may not be life on other planets. But one thing is certain: there is music there — as there is everywhere.'[3] Sibelius did not see himself as a medium of the divine but rather felt he was in a position to transform artistically the 'logic' of the world. Harmony had nothing to do with the *Kalevala* or other narrative myths and legends — but all the more so with the primal sound of nature. That which seems pantheistic in Sibelius is what Gallen-Kallela considered 'specific to us Finns':

> Anyone who lives and works a great deal outdoors in nature will ultimately achieve such a personal relationship to his environment that he may catch himself talking to the trees — just as one often hears a child chatting with the flowers in the field. Profound empathy with nature is specific to us Finns, as our folk poetry proves. We may have a particular penchant for personification, which is expressed so clearly in our more recent art poetry and novels.[4]

The elemental experience of nature marked the composer's behaviour even in childhood, without him having to reflect on it. He was, of course, still unaware of the contemporary worldview of concentrating on the 'essence' of one's surroundings. After all, he wrote to Aino on 18 December 1890: 'I am not a philosopher, nor will I become one, for it is the most difficult thing there is and surely not within my reach.' In his diary for 6 November 1910, he wrote just as clearly: 'That is art that you are making, ego — not science! God only knows, by the way, whether science

[1] Grönhagen 1951, pp. 98–9.

[2] JS to Axel Carpelan, 20 July 1909, in Dahlström 2010, pp. 245–6.

[3] JS quoted in Ronka 1948, p. 46. The particulars are from the 1930s. Ronka was an orchestral musician, composer and conductor of Finnish origin, born in Minnesota, who visited JS several times. In his c.v. he even indicated that he 'studied interpretation' with Sibelius from 1936 with 1938, which should probably be taken with a grain of salt.

[4] Gallen-Kallela, 1924, in *Kallela-kirja*, quoted in Gallen-Kallela-Sirén 2001, p. 159.

is not the antipode of art.' His understanding of nature did not presume academic conceptualisation or close reading of modern philosophers. The scientific approach to one's surroundings and striving for objectivity were also foreign to him.[1] Likewise, the 'sharing Nature' with Sibelius that Newmarch mentioned did not mean analytical conversations; rather, it was a 'silent experience'. She photographed him by a lake, 'gazing over still waters and lost in contemplation'.[2] A photograph from 1909, in which he is looking into the landscape near Mount Koli and Lake Pielinen, was interpreted by Tawaststjerna as his life passing for him in review, since he had just gone through a crisis and had spent part of his honeymoon on the other side of the lake in 1892.[3] Newmarch had the impression – and the published photograph makes this seem plausible – that Sibelius did not regard 'the view' as an object before him but rather as the essence of landscape, looking into its core and thereby becoming part of it. At the same time, he was able to reflect with open eyes on his projects and their sensory qualities without being able to verbalise this process later.[4] The totality of perception and his ability to mix fantasy and reality[5] should be taken into account as a tendency – perhaps a utopian one – when interpreting his music, especially since it motivates his search for contemporary, unusual forms for his musical syntax. All literary and logical formation was foreign to Sibelius; his abilities to grasp the world and its events through the senses accounted for the unique quality of his own 'nature' and formed the original basis for his way of making music.

Whereas Plato feared art from the perspective of society, we have 'another fear, which I believe was unknown to Plato – the fear that knowledge might harm the imagination, that the exercise of artistic faculties, both in the artist and in the spectator, might be weakened by the use of reason. This is a modern fear and, if I am not mistaken, unfamiliar before the Romantic period; but for more than a century and a half it has dominated our view of art with such force that we have come to look upon it as a basic truth.'[6]

'He has to be free'

His impulsive modernity in the age of Balzac, Dehmel and Zola was a burden on his relationship with his wife. The Anna of Juhani Aho's autobiographical novel *Yksin* (Alone) of 1890 is a literary portrayal of Aino (née Aina) Järnefelt. The author had long been interested in her. He described Aino in the weeks immediately preceding

[1] As a child, however, JS had the best collection of wild flowers and fauna in his class, and he collected butterflies; see Erik W. Tawaststjerna 1976, p. 20.

[2] Newmarch 1939, pp. 18 ff.

[3] Erik W. Tawaststjerna 1986, p. 130.

[4] See also Erik W. Tawaststjerna 1976, p. 46 (which quotes a remark about JS by Arvid Järnefelt, 1944).

[5] Rickards 1997, p. 19, described this as 'Attention Deficit Disorder'.

[6] Wind 1985, p. 47.

her engagement to Sibelius and, in his preface, as a young girl. The book is a declaration of love for her, with episodes interesting for cultural history such as its description of the effects of absinthe on the Parisian *demi-monde*.[1] For Wegelius, Aino was the 'prettiest girl in all Finland' around 1890.[2] Her worldview was influenced by her mother. Arvid Järnefelt's novels provide information about that as well: *Heräämiseni* (My awakening), a lyrical, realistic novel by a disciple of Leo Tolstoy, and *Veljekset* (The brothers), with a magnificent description of the Finnish psyche and of Helsinki in the late nineteenth century, which despite having just under 100,000 residents was a mixture of coastal fishing village and the capital of a lively grand duchy. Arvid Järnefelt also writes about his and Aino's mother, Elisabeth, and her literary, political salon in *Vanhempieni romaani* (The novel of my parents), which was published in three parts from 1928 to 1930. Aho mentioned Elisabeth frequently in *Yksin*.[3]

A foretaste of the problems to be expected and the not always productive conflict between his life as an artist and as head of a family — a conflict that escalated in Italy in 1901 — is found in a letter to his fiancée on 6 March 1892: 'Then look, the last thing he [the artist as husband] can be is a nice, pleasant, pipe-smoking "head of household". He has to be free and be able to continue the life of his imagination undisturbed, that is completely clear, isn't it? A marriage centred entirely on children is a terrible idea to me — there are other things one should think about when one is an artist.' When Aino later asked him why he had married at all, he wrote from Rome to Rapallo on 27 March 1901 and asked whether he had perhaps not understood her question: 'But if someone loves, and keeps his love pure, may he not then possess the object of his love[?]' Aino defined marriage as a 'great task of life', as she proudly told him on 20 December 1890, a year and a half before they married.[4] She also wrote to a woman friend before the wedding: 'I am always busy with my conscience and have made it my main goal to become a good wife, a genuine wife for the one I love and not try to turn him into a good husband.'[5] She knew what she was in for. Yet she was surprised. In early 1903 she wrote to Sibelius (in an undated letter): 'Remember that you are supposed to be a man, because you were born a man. But are you a man? No!' 'Man' is a moral category here.

The letters from 1894, when Sibelius was in southern Germany and Italy, are revealing. On 23 July he was sad because he considered himself too fat and hence physically unattractive, and he feared that Aino would not '— —' a fat man (the dashes indicate the unmentionable). After addressing the manners of the public, which ate 'sausage sandwiches during Tannhäuser's tale', and of his colleagues (especially Ruggiero Leoncavallo and his lover) in Bayreuth, he wrote on 24 July: 'Your image does not fade from my memory, and the last night — you remember — is like a junction

1 Aho 1890, pp. 120 ff.

2 See Erik W. Tawaststjerna 1976, p. 43.

3 See also Armas Järnefelt's remarks in Häkli 1955, and Järnefelt 1944, pp. 356 ff.

4 Aino to JS, 19 May 1892.

5 Aino to Maikki Pakarinen, 10 April 1892, in Talas 2000, p. 100.

in my life.' Four days later he believed that he was much too 'tuhma' (naughty). In such moments, he imagined Aino and himself in action: 'It is wonderful.' He proposed they write each other 'naughty' letters, but then immediately burn them. Aino responded hesitantly to these requests. Aino herself used the word 'tuhma' in her letters, and on 20 November 1900, for example, Sibelius greeted her in a letter from Amsterdam: 'I miss you, my naughty girl.' It is difficult today to imagine the vestal Aino as 'naughty.' However, she encouraged her husband — more out of generosity than with relish — to write 'naughty' letters, since she too was certainly a 'person of fantasy'.[1] At some point after 2 September 1894 he wrote these undated lines: 'I will have a lot to explain when I come. Whatever happens with me, I am always a man and that is the main thing.' Unfortunately, no report of his later explanation exists.

Whether Sibelius actually had syphilis as a student, as he had asserted in Berlin in 1889,[2] or some other infection (such as candidiasis), remains an open question, but at least there were none of the other usual (though not inevitable) consequences. He certainly had some troublesome ailments. Moreover, his emotional balance was shaken, especially in Vienna, by a *faux pas* that can no longer be identified. Following intense winter months in Berlin and an emotionally moving summer in Finland in 1890 — he got to know Aino better, and they were secretly engaged in late September, shortly before his departure — Sibelius plunged into the metropolis on the Danube. On 25 October 1890, immediately after his arrival, he wrote to Wegelius: 'This air is driving me crazy. My head is filled with waltzes, and they all remind me of Schubert's waltzes.'[3] In a letter to his mother he also noted: 'All of Vienna is ringing with waltzes and laughter.'[4] He admired the churches decorated for Christmas and the 'opera orchestra, which is twice as large as the one in Berlin'.[5] To his family's confidante, Werner Söderhjelm, he described the churches at Easter.[6] As expedient as these remarks may have been — as opposed to reports from fashionable establishments — dependent as he was on donations from others to finance his studies, they are credible. The biographer Karl Ekman, who was part of Sibelius' circle,[7] reported on Vienna in terms of a happy and 'intense' life in a cosmopolitan city and his 'faithful companions' there.[8] Because physical love is already a central subject of *Kullervo*, his first major work, as it is in *The Wood Nymph*, the *Lemminkäinen Legends* and the piano cycle *Kyllikki*, more precise details would be of interest even for interpreters.

Love is also programmatic in *Scène de ballet* (1891), written in Vienna. The hints of

[1] Aino to JS, 4 August 1894.

[2] National Library Coll. 206: 62; in JS to Adolf Paul, 19 February 1889.

[3] JS to Martin Wegelius, 25 October 1890.

[4] JS to his mother, 26 December 1890, in Goss 1997, pp. 119–20.

[5] National Library Coll. 206: 62; in JS to Adolf Paul, 9 December 1890.

[6] JS to Werner Söderhjelm, 28 March 1891, quoted in Erik W. Tawaststjerna 1991, p. 174.

[7] His mother, Ida (née Morduch, 1875–1942), was a famous singer and his father, Karl Ludvig Ekman (1869–1947), a respected pianist and conductor.

[8] Ekman 1946, pp. 92–105.

his first (and reliable) biographer, Erik Furuhjelm, were clear enough: *Scène de ballet* is 'entirely cosmopolitan', 'pure romanticism' and 'fantasy', which is perplexing, since this score (with castanets, etc.) has nothing to do with metropolitan romanticism. Nevertheless:

> He [Sibelius] is here, rarely enough, engrossed in illustrating the big city. It is the only example of this kind in his oeuvre; it represents a world he seldom touches on in his compositions. There is, however, no unconditional realism. *Scène de ballet* is rather pure romanticism; it vividly recalls a picture of a nocturnal intermezzo elevated to the level of fantasy. The composition is nevertheless an interesting bit of evidence concerning his personal life.[1]

One interesting possibility to link *Scène de ballet* to anti-naturalistic trends and to explain Furuhjelm's interpretation is to draw parallels to the Viennese literature of the period, in particular to Frank Wedekind's Vitalism and works such as *Frühlingserwachen* (translated as *Spring Awakening*) of 1891. There is, however, no evidence that Sibelius followed the latest trends consciously.

Much easier to prove and yet similarly spectacular is the autobiographical background. Furuhjelm also mentioned the world-famous singer Pauline Lucca, the 'nightingale of Vienna', in this same context, though without establishing a connection to the composition. In a letter from 4 May 1891, Sibelius wrote to Wegelius that *Scène de ballet* sprang 'from a bitter experience. [...] I have never wept as profusely as I did while writing this.' The authentic description he sent to Paul, from man to man, was strikingly prosaic: the work depicted 'whores dancing in a bordello'.[2] Certainly this dance could also be read in the context of Vitalism, in particular of Wedekind's *Erdgeist* (translated as *Earth Spirit*) of 1895 and *Die Büchse der Pandora* (translated as *Pandora's Box*) of 1903. Paul wrote his portrait of 1890 in the style of such confessions: 'For me, a woman is like a frivolous book',[3] says Paul's Silén alias Sibelius. The very name Silén could be a subtle insult: Silenus is a hybrid of horse and man associated with Dionysus — a satyr with a bushy tail. All those involved were aware of the name's antique etymology. Sibelius was of the view that Paul wanted to do him great harm privately and professionally (Sibelius to Aino, 7 March 1892), but he never questioned the accuracy of the depiction. Nietzsche elevated 'wise Silenus' to a central place when explaining the 'Dionysian' attitude — which is, incidentally, certainly relevant when explaining Sibelius — and the 'artist in both dreams and ecstasies'.[4] In Nietzsche's sense, then, the name Silenus is no insult but a reference to the young composer belonging to the world of the great Dionysus (with mythological roots in the East

[1] Furuhjelm 1916a, pp. 117–18.

[2] Erik W. Tawaststjerna 1976, p. 91 (the letter to Paul of 8 May 1892 is only hinted at there). See also Sirén 2000, p. 93. The subject became current again in 1894 when JS was planning an opera in which a student would fall in love with a dancer (see chapter 3.3 in the present volume).

[3] Paul 1891, pp. 193, 197–200.

[4] Nietzsche 1967, pp. 36 ff. and 38.

and in the 'orgiastic Sacaea').[1] Although Sibelius was visual, rather than literary, in orientation, Nietzsche's image of the Apollonian — despite the 'architectonics' of his music — suits him less well than Dionysian, or even that of the mythical role model, the 'artist in both dreams and ecstasies' of ancient tragedies.

Although Maikki Järnefelt-Pakarinen consoled Aino Järnefelt, who was already engaged to 'Silén', that the book was somewhat 'realistic, but not so bad', Aino was noticeably uneasy: 'There is so much about "genibarnet" [the genius child, i.e., Silén] that I don't like for that reason as well. [...] There is nothing bad; I have heard this sort of thing before [...]. I get so sad and have bad memories. Perhaps that is very girlish. Write Janne [Jean] whether that is bad.'[2] In any case, Aino, who was translating a great deal for *Päivälehti*, did not wish to translate Paul's book into Finnish.

This unsparingly anti-bourgeois piece of modern literature sketches a portrait of an absent-minded artist and confronts the general public with the lifestyle of the bohemian. At the same time, it is the earliest document of Sibelius' talent for determining the norms of everyday life for himself and for distancing himself by large steps from the grandmother's home of his childhood. In Vienna, he was known as 'le comte', conducting himself in the aristocratic manner. 'My father behaved that way as well', he wrote to Aino on 21 March 1891. He had 'the passions of a rich man but the income of a beggar', as Aino could read in an earlier letter of 12 March 1891. Only much later could Sibelius afford this lifestyle. As far as Paul is concerned, it should be noted that Sibelius provides this friend, of all people, with a naturalistic caricature 'in the Strindbergian style'. Sibelius' letter from Vienna to Kajanus should also be interpreted in that spirit: 'I have not only had gonorrhoea countless times but also two healthy cases of syphilis. Perhaps you are familiar with its consequences from acquaintances or "friends".'[3] This letter — medical boasting to an old acquaintance, here once again with clear traces of adapting himself to the world of the letter's recipient — dates from the same period as his sorrow over *Scène de ballet*. Nevertheless, the occasion for it must have been something more intimate — a relationship, probably in Lucca's circle — since only an experience that was neither quotidian nor frivolous could explain the 'weeping' of which Sibelius wrote to Wegelius in May (without any traces of this kind of adapting). In general, Sibelius was uninhibited when he wrote to Wegelius; he even reported on his 'inflammation of the ovaries', writing in German ('Eierstocks Entzündung'), which permits this wordplay on the male (*Stock*, or 'stick', and even *Eier* or 'eggs', a slang word for 'testicles') versus female sex organs (correctly, *Eierstöcke*) — and of the tumour in his stomach.[4] To Paul, by contrast, he wrote with enigmatic caution on 4 May 1891 about a successful 'kidney stone operation'.[5]

[1] Ibid., p. 36.

[2] Correspondence between Maikki Järnefelt-Pakarinen and Aino (27 December 1891) and Aino and JS (20 December 1891), in Talas 2000, pp. 96 ff.

[3] Åbo Akademi; JS to Robert Kajanus, 14 March 1891.

[4] JS to Martin Wegelius, 4 May 1891. He was treated by Dr Neumann in Dr Eder's clinic.

[5] Erik W. Tawaststjerna 1991, pp. 183–4.

His correspondence with Aino began only with his trip to Vienna on 18 October 1890. He wrote from Vienna again right away, on 26 October 1890, the day after his arrival. The journey was interrupted in Berlin, so that he arrived in Vienna too late to register for courses, which apparently he had not intended to do. Already on 30 November Sibelius reported that he was 'not thinking of other women, although Vienna is filled with beauties'. His insistent openness probably embarrassed Aino, but she knew enough to conceal that. On 21 December 1890 he told of a long evening at Ronacher's, and on 2 January 1891 he described his longing for affection. The following day, he mentioned an invitation to Pauline Lucca's. That was followed by letters that demonstrate how capably Sibelius could maintain contact with chic salons, and how much he enjoyed it. On 11 January he had to report on a crisis, caused by an unsuccessful rehearsal on 9 January in front of the leader of the orchestra Jakob Moritz Grün, the opera management and the opera orchestra. If his description were not so detailed, one might think that it was simply about a student standing in, thanks to Grün's help, for a top musician — a practice that was officially prohibited but was (and perhaps even is) in fact common. Sibelius was aware that Grün had a lot of influence on this (and on performances of works by young composers). Only at that point, when the possibility of joining the Viennese orchestra any time soon seemed unrealistic, did he stop playing the violin.

On 24 January he mentioned to Aino a young woman, the sister of a fellow student. She wanted him to 'forget his fiancée for a few hours'. He added the reflective, revealing thought: 'Vienna is a fine city, but one shouldn't be alone here.' On 3 February, after a long interruption, he wrote only a short letter, in which he reported on a new crisis. Only after several guarded letters did the big confession follow on 8 March: 'I am no longer pure.' Barely a week later he wrote to Kajanus about 'syphilis'. After an emotional phase of consolidation, the theme 'Viennese ladies' came up again, and on 17 March Sibelius was already doubting whether he still deserved his Aino at all, since: 'There are a great many worries, of the sort you may not learn about in a letter.' Moreover, he believed that he was fundamentally 'bad'. Finally, on 21 March, he wrote a letter explaining the not-to-be-ignored advantages of premarital sex for the future husband (but not wife), and just happened to continue the letter with a detailed report of an evening at Lucca's. On 28 March, he wrote again: 'We will speak about the worries I had when we are face to face. I would have a hundred things to tell but there are so many letters to answer.' One can imagine how Aino felt about that.

In early April, he wrote about his work on a 'symphony' with movements titled 'Dance Scene' and 'Ballet Scene'.[1] Not until 13 April did he report how he had turned down Lucca's invitation to her country home in Gmunden 'for certain reasons' (a young Finnish singer, Filip Forstén, was already her lover), thereby presumably removing Lucca as the source of his sorrow. He was 'crazy' about the older soprano,

[1] On 9 April 1891, the latter was finished, and it was premiered in Helsinki on 28 April by Kajanus.

as Wegelius was permitted to read, but the reason was her singing.[1] Aino received more details about Lucca on 23 April: 'She is not satisfied with one or two lovers. And now I have drawn the lot.' So Lucca remained a topical theme. This last date was, admittedly, too late to be relevant to the origins of the enigmatically expressive *Scène de ballet*, but the letter at least indicates what kind of world was influencing him. As late as May 25 he wrote: 'What I have done to you (and it is not trivial), I will try to make good again in that you will always be the centre of my life.' The above-cited letters of 1894 and 1901 show how difficult that would be. Further hints of missteps can be found in the few letters from his friends in Vienna. The solution to the riddle is the poetic programme of *Scène de ballet*. Later, however, such documents disappear.

Of the not very numerous friends in Vienna with whom Sibelius corresponded, the most important letters are from the conductor and composer Leo Held on 20 [29?] December 1891; Franz Georg Mücke on 23 December 1891; the famous violinist Alois Rosenberg, 19 May 1892; and the Slovakian (later American) violinist Ottakar Nováček (undated): 'Dear Sibelius, I congratulate you from the bottom of my heart on your splendid talent; your music is full of imagination, magnificent timbre – but occasionally I want to discuss a small "but" with you. Come see me sometime soon.' The letters also mention names such as Robert Sand, Ida Grünfeld, and Theodor Christoph as Viennese friends from the circle around Mücke and Held. One of his best friends was Carl Frühling, who wrote to Sibelius (on 16 June 1929, for example) from Vienna as a fellow student, composer and Freemason. One curious case is a letter from Christoph to Sibelius on 9 March 1935: 'You will probably no longer remember me, but I have not forgotten that we were both students of Prof. Robert Fuchs at the conservatory in Vienna [in fact Sibelius had not been]. That circumstance gives me reason to tell you that I will be performing your First Symphony on the 17th of this month with the Wiener Symphoniker in a radio concert at twelve noon, and it would give me great pleasure if you, honoured maestro, would listen to the performance.' This name occurs earlier in a letter from Rosenberg written in Spalato, Dalmatia, on 19 May 1892: 'T. Christoph performs in the military band in Vienna.' Sibelius mentioned Christoph in his letter to Aino of 22 November 1890: 'I have an acquaintance here now, a Christop[h]. He is a violinist.' Christoph was his first friend in Vienna. More significant as insight to his time studying in Vienna is Sibelius' sketch for a reply on the back of the letter. 'Dear Mr Christoph, When I read your charming letter, I could hear your voice. [...] Unfortunately, it was impossible for me to listen to your performance – Vienna was silent this time.' He wrote about Rosenberg in a letter to Held on 11 January 1891: 'The most talented [of the local artists] is Rosenberg, and he is a genuine friend of mine.' Held wrote, after addressing Sibelius with a blank exclamation point ('!' with no name or anything): 'For some time now I have intended, my dear friend – may I call you that? – to send you several stories from Vienna, but

[1] JS to Martin Wegelius, 9 April 1891, in which JS tells of the invitation.

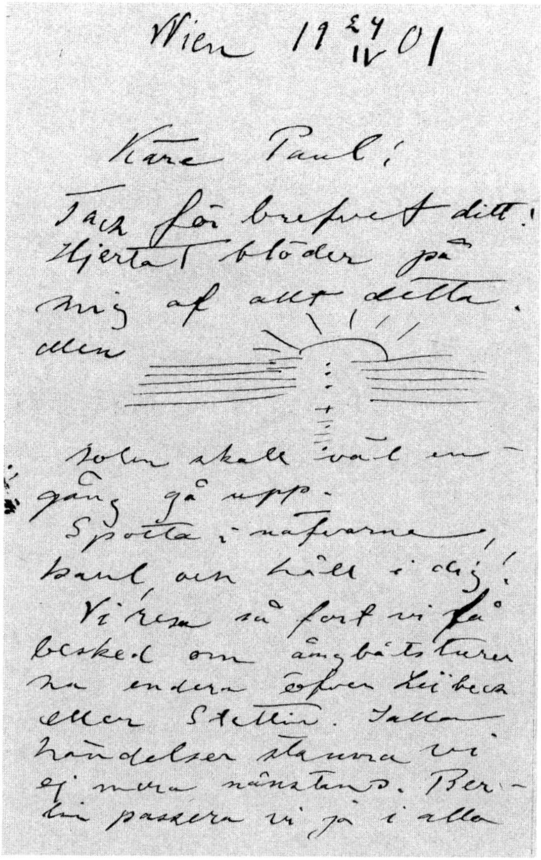

Wien 19 24/IV 01

Kära Paul!

Tack för brefvet ditt! Hjertat blöder på mig af allt detta. Men

Solen skall väl en gång gå upp.

Spotta i näfvarna, Paul, och håll i dig!

Vi resa så fort vi få besked om ångbåtsturerna endera öfver Lübeck eller Stettin. I alla händelser stanna vi ej mera nånstans. Berlin passera vi på i alla

FIG. 13. Sibelius' letter to 'Paul' (24 April 1901). The letter illustrates Sibelius' synesthetic inclination. The sunrise in C major follows painful thoughts, but unfortunately there are no more details. Sibelius wrote this letter to 'Paul' (likely Adolf Paul) from Vienna. His visits here were noticeably infrequent — alone or with Aino — after his intense year of study in 1890–91. Soon after returning home in May 1901, Sibelius travelled to Germany to conduct the *Lemminkäinen Legends* in Heidelberg in June.

(1) I did not have your address and (2) did not know whether you would remember your stay in Vienna.'[1]

As far as we know, Sibelius visited Vienna after that point only briefly — for example, in 1901 on a trip home from Italy by way of Prague and Dresden and in 1897 on the way to Italy. His correspondence with Aino reveals that he was still in Dresden on 26 June 1897, and on 27 June, after twelve hours on the night train, was visiting 'old places' in Vienna and was in the Prater that evening, but on 28 June was already sending a postcard from the railway station in Graz. In Vienna on 24 April 1901 he drafted a mysterious sketch to [Adolf?] 'Paul', with a drawing of a rising sun on staves and the

[1] All documents in National Library Coll. 206.

poetic message: 'my heart bleeds from all that. But the sun will presumably rise again one day.'[1] He wrote to his student Leevi Madetoja in 1911: 'The countless memories that tie me to this place are unforgettable for me. Certainly you will profit from this city, so rich in memories, in your work.'[2] As late as 1915, Madetoja confirmed that Sibelius had very positive memories of Vienna.[3] He also indicated that other Finnish composers spent pleasurable hours at Lucca's home.

When compared to the Overture in E major, also written in Vienna, the originality of *Scène de ballet* becomes clear. The themes of the overture, organised in the style of Finnish folk songs, seem more progressive. The overture is forward-looking, but at the same time old-fashioned, in terms of its classicistic manner and tonality, which is largely free of dissonances – its form is in essence that of a cautiously extended sonata movement with an intensely elaborated secondary folk theme in the minor – with a rhythmical gesture that reveals Sibelius' relationship to Antonín Dvořák, Emmanuel Chabrier and the Russian modernists. Imaginative modulations alternate with clichéd episodes, and the overall impression it leaves is modest. Sibelius himself wrote to Wegelius: 'But it very clearly has, I find, technical advantages.'[4] *Scène de ballet*, by contrast, was 'a sad, sad memory'. In the original Swedish he wrote: 'Det är något af "rus" och "lår" i den. Om Du hört den måste Du väl medgifva att jag tagit steget ut åtminstone. Jag har aldrig gråtit så mycket som då jag lagade den.' This sentence is tricky, since it means that the composition contains not only Nietzsche's 'Rausch' (ecstasy) but also 'thigh' ('lår'[5]) and that he 'got down to the tiniest detail'. It is not clear whether this should be taken literally.

The beginning is already characteristic: the imaginary scene starts without an introduction, on a subdominant 6/4 chord with an F sharp in the bass, accentuated by mixed winds and rather shallow in terms of functional harmony, but at the same time serving as a harmonic bridge between the Overture in E major and the ballet movement. This is followed first by individual themes in F sharp minor – the focus is initially on the woodwinds, especially cor anglais, oboe and bassoon, including a rhythmic theme with castanets, which do not, however, turn the piece into a frivolous dance scene. The tone is macabre, exotic and yearning, as is emphasised both by the rhythmic irregularities and the chromaticism – in the artful Fugato, for example. The castanets emphasise the Iberian atmosphere. When Sibelius was 'crazy' about Lucca, as he confessed in his 9 April 1891 letter to Wegelius, she had sung arias from Bizet's *Carmen* in a private setting and danced to it, probably with castanets. The alternation of expressive themes is too hectic to convey much pathos. Knowing that the

[1] National Library Coll. 206: 62.

[2] National Archive: copy in the Tawaststjerna Collection; JS to Madetoja, undated, postmarked 20 October 1911.

[3] Madetoja, 'Jean Sibeliuksen taiteilijanuran yleiset piirteet', *Helsingin Sanomat*, 8 December 1915, quoted in Salmenhaara 1987, p. 79.

[4] JS to Martin Wegelius, 4 May 1891.

[5] The handwriting is unclear, but neither 'lår' (box) nor even 'låt' (melody) would make sense.

composer is said to have wept bitterly while working on it explains the dramatic shattering of form and the expressive outbursts. All in all, *Scène de ballet* is an example of a technique that will also be important later: incompletely exploiting the available motivic material. Advocates of later modernism may criticise this as a lack of rigour, but it is nevertheless a legitimate means of style and expression typical of Sibelius. The simple but nonetheless extraordinarily effective initial gesture[1] is not repeated even once at first but instead only cited as a conclusion. Sibelius was operating here on the margins of the south-eastern Central European modernism of Alexander Zemlinsky, Franz Schreker and Antonín Novák, between Paul Dukas and Nikolay Rimsky-Korsakov. He distanced himself from that direction almost immediately, in favour of modern classicism. Stylistic reminiscences of *Scène de ballet* remain rare. One exception is the programmatically related scene 'A Spring in the Park' in the suite of occasional music for *Pelléas et Mélisande* (1904–5; no. 3, Prelude to the Second Act).

Another theme that comes up frequently in the literature on Sibelius, along with sexuality,[2] is his penchant for alcohol. Eyewitnesses are easy to find. Paul's portrait of the Berlin period, *En bok om en människa*, already includes indecorous scenes of this sort. For example, there is an entertaining passage in which Paul alias Hans and Sibelius alias Silén see an advertisement for 'champagne' (2 marks a bottle) in a shop window in Berlin: Silén wants to spend the last of his money for immediate personal enjoyment.[3] And the notary Felix Droysen from Halle an der Saale, a former law student in Munich, reminded Sibelius in a letter of 13 December 1940 of their time together in the Pension Suisse in Rapallo in 1901, especially evenings in a restaurant 'where we drank some vermouth together'.[4] The ironically reproachful remark of the Leipzig-based pianist Alf Nestmann on 13 May 1930 is equally striking: 'I am accustomed to playing strictly sober, and I have never violated this supreme commandment. It was not the nights spent on trains but rather your fabulously good whiskey, which I did not want to, could not, and was not permitted to turn down.'[5] Since such drinks were difficult to obtain in Finland during prohibition, Sibelius wrote to the authorities in question: 'Because my physician, Dr Elmgren, has ordered me to obtain alcohol privately, I kindly request your permission to purchase 10 litres of sherry.'[6] There are no details about the daily dose ordered by the doctor, the intended duration of this cure, the planned participation of third parties or the appropriate brand.

Around 1926–7, his diary entries are almost exclusively concerned with alcohol. In September 1926, when prohibition was already the law of the land, he wrote that

[1] These melodically accompanied chords are B^6 minor and F sharp minor, the upper part with B and A, and F sharp in the bass.

[2] See Kallberg 2003.

[3] Paul 1891, p. 218.

[4] National Library Coll. 206: 10.

[5] National Library Coll. 206: 27.

[6] National Library Coll. 206: 63, letter from JS, 22 January 1918.

he wanted to give up drinking but unfortunately it was 'fashionable'.[1] This sentence shows the effect that ill-considered regulation can have on people who have remained 'young' in their behaviour, as Sibelius described himself in this context. In Helsinki in 1915, Alexander Glazunov supposedly remarked of Sibelius' ostinato sequences that they were drunkard's music.[2] This shows that Glazunov adored Sibelius quite as much as Sibelius did Glazunov. One bit of evidence that he also purchased alcoholic drinks for his guests, who were of course rarely in a position to write such music, with or without ostinatos, is a shopping list on the same slip of paper as a sketch for a letter dated 4 February 1913: '2 bl. sherry, 4 bl. Madeira, 3 bl. Burgundy, brandy, 2 Rhenish (Liebfraumilch), 2 cognac, 2 whiskey.'[3]

To the Danish-German author Gunnar Hauch, who had asked about the Eighth Symphony, he replied with a reference to his trembling hand in 1934: 'It will come "in its time". As you can see from my handwriting, it is almost impossible for me to write. This letter is costing me an appalling effort.'[4] The last sentence of the letter in particular reveals a very unsteady hand. Other letters and drafts draw attention to this failing as well. After completing the third version of his Fifth Symphony, he confessed (Diary, 22 April 1919): 'My hands are shaking so much that I can barely write.' He was fifty-three years old and excited about completing the project. Later the problem grew worse, surely in part because of his consumption of alcohol. To a certain Herr Lehmann he wanted to write in German on 3 January 1937: 'Thanking you for your kind letter, I must tell you that I am writing notes very badly at the moment. Hence I ask you to wait.' And on 7 May 1945 he noted ideas for a letter to his colleague Dmitry Kabalevsky (in Finnish, apparently for a translation): 'As you can see, it is difficult for me, because of my hand, to write dedications.'[5] On the most important occasion of the final decade of his life, he let 'music director Lessing' know: 'because I do not know when I will and can complete it, and thus whether there will really be a ~~viiith~~ ixth Symphony'.[6] The correction in shaky handwriting shows that Sibelius changed the number of the symphonies and hence was already working on 'his Ninth'; in an early letter to Newmarch he had already described *Kullervo* as 'an independent symphony'.[7]

A draft letter to the English conductor and violinist Basil Cameron makes it clear that his symptoms were in part psychosomatic: 'I was in Germany for a few months to listen to music and fell ill. I was even in a clinic. Then I found a wonderful sherry and now I am healthy.'[8] Along with Hauch, Cameron was one of the few to whom he

[1] Diary, 12 September 1926.
[2] See Erik W. Tawaststjerna 1997b, p. 33.
[3] National Archive Box 36.
[4] National Library Coll. 206: 61; JS to Gunnar Hauch, 1 February 1934.
[5] See National Archive Box 35; sketches.
[6] National Archive Box 35, sketch.
[7] Newmarch 1939, p. 11.
[8] National Library Coll. 206: 61, draft letter, 5 July 1931.

at least wanted to reply about the state of the symphony, as this somewhat desperate draft letter shows:

> I very much regret speaking of my new symphony. The work is of ~~such [???] so I can rush myself~~. If it has to be finished for a certain ~~deadli~~ time, I get nervous. I cannot rush the work. It may be that ~~finished~~
>
> You and your friends are always welcome in my homeland. But if your journey depends on the symphony, ~~I ask~~ we must not ~~speak~~ or ~~write~~ correspond about it before September.[1]

His finances and the way he handled money likewise hold an undiminished fascination today. At present, it is all about the income of heirs and the oddities of the relevant copyright, which in Sibelius' case remains in effect until 2027. The often-mentioned state artist's pension that Sibelius received from 1898 onwards was not lavish, and the imbalance between his income and expenses remained problematic until around 1927. On 21 April 1909 he wrote to his wife, in a way that reflected his synaesthesia: 'Money matters are like going to the toilet for me: a necessary evil.' To his son-in-law he wrote that he was always being cheated because no one assisted him with practical matters,[2] though that can only apply to the first decades of his career. Later he had the good fortune to receive sufficient money from his performance rights and to have several sons-in-law who were well versed in legal and business matters.

The fourth popular subject is his melancholy. There is isolated evidence of this problem as well. Admittedly, even Sibelius' *Spring Song* (1894–5) was also called *La Tristesse du printemps*. It was typical of him for his emotions to run hot and cold: 'Mood up – in the Himalayas again.' 'Was in hell. A valley like never before.'[3] Generally, however, such utterances deserve only fleeting attention from a biographer searching for the 'true Sibelius' and his secrets. The inexperienced reader is misled by his laconic sentences, particularly when they are not cited in full. Sibelius wrote a letter to Axel Carpelan from Rome on 2 April 1901 in which he spoke of his 'tragic fate', without being in the least bit depressed: 'Ultimately, I believe that one does not suffer for nothing.'[4] His fatalism was situational. Beyond the level that goes with creativity in any case, he was neither melancholy nor depressive, though he was certainly highly sensitive. His absurd sense of humour should also be considered in this context. His diary entry on 10 January 1922 documents that quality: 'It becomes clearer and clearer. I will probably commit suicide. Then they should give everything a good cleaning. On the veranda?'

[1] National Library Coll. 206: 61; undated draft.

[2] Jalas 1981, p. 55.

[3] Diary, 3 and 8 November 1909.

[4] Dahlström 2010, p. 77.

Unfortunately, I now have 'painters' as neighbours.[1]

2.2 'The Sounds Glow'

Symposium as Portrait

The 'eternal feminine' and 'nature' preoccupied young and youthful artists during many a late-night round in the 1890s. Sibelius and his colleagues lived in the Schopenhauerian faith in the philosophical and political/ideological capacities of the arts and concerned themselves, unrestrained by a lack of proper academic training, with the philosophical question 'What is life?' Arthur Schopenhauer began his lecture 'On the Inner Nature of Art' with the sentence: 'Not merely philosophy but also the fine arts work at bottom towards the solution of the problem of existence.' Hence a Beethoven symphony could be 'a true and perfect picture of the world'.[2] In the nineteenth century, composers and philosophers became comrades-in-arms, so to speak.

The male circle that Akseli Gallen-Kallela depicted in his oil painting *Symposium* in 1894 was just one of many in decadent Europe. Although – or perhaps precisely because – such circles often speculated about the feminine, women were excluded, as by Plato. After all, even Nietzsche had not consulted women but rather Oedipus on this matter, since the murderer of his father and husband of his mother had been able to solve the 'riddle of nature – that Sphinx of two species' when he violated the 'most sacred natural orders'.[3] Consequently, in this view, a woman could not analyse the 'feminine'. In this tradition of thought, perceiving complex connections presumes distance, not an identity of essence between the subject and object. What is true of nature in general must also be true of the feminine.

Ola Hansson wrote about the debates of the Strindberg circle in Berlin from a Scandinavian perspective in the *Neue Freie Presse* of 26 August 1890, just a few weeks before Sibelius arrived: 'Grasping, describing and explaining such subspecies of Eva, from the trivial coquette to the grand Sphinx, vermin and enigma, dual human and cripple – all inaccessible to methodological research – is the task of the poet of the future.'[4] Edvard Munch, one of the members of the circle of artists that met at Gustav Türk's Weinhandel und Probierstube (Wine shop and tasting room) on Unter den Linden in Berlin, which they called Zum schwarzen Ferkel (At the black piglet), noted: 'I stood before the mystery of woman – I gazed into an unknown world – My curiosity was awakened – What did it mean – that look I did not know – That look came from a terribly strange – and marvelous world – what did that world consist of – ' and further: 'Woman, in all her diversity, is a mystery to a man.'[5]

[1] Diary, 10 September 1926.

[2] Schopenhauer 1977, pp. 176 and 235.

[3] Nietzsche 1967, p. 69.

[4] See Zeitler 1990, p. 167.

[5] Munich's manuscripts, quoted in Müller-Westermann 2003, pp. 67 and 69.

Stanisław Przybyszewski, another Strindbergian, began his *Totenmesse* (Requiem) of 1893, which was inspired more by the meetings of the Ferkel circle than any other work of art, with the sentence: 'In the beginning was gender.'[1] Sibelius' participation in the Berlin symposiums is not documented,[2] but the symposium in Helsinki was a worthy offshoot. Also it was one of Sibelius' best friends, Adolf Paul, to whom we owe one of the best accounts of the circle: *Aus der Chronik des 'Schwarzen Ferkels'* (From the chronicle of the Black Piglet) of 1922. As a composer, Sibelius took part in this 'Woman' project in his works *Scène de ballet*, *Kullervo*, *Lemminkäinen*, *The Wood Nymph*, *Kyllikki* and perhaps also in *En saga*. His incidental music *Kuolema* (Death; 1903) and *Pelléas et Mélisande* (1905) and his ballad for chorus and orchestra *The Captive Queen* (1906; the original title *Vapautettu kuningatar* is closer to 'liberated queen') and the symphonic fantasy *Pohjola's Daughter* (1906) are not so much about the feminine as about women from history and mythology. In *Luonnotar* (1913) and *The Oceanides* (1914), the feminine seems desexualised, and in later works (*The Tempest*, *Väinämöinen's Song*, *Tapiola*), the focus is on the masculine world. Since he considered active members of the Strindberg group his friends and visited Berlin in the years in question, Sibelius can be included in the Ferkel circle in the broadest sense.

As early as 1891, Sibelius reported on 'symposiums' his father, Christian, had with his old Latin teacher Johan Ludvig Runeberg. His father the physician supposedly advocated the thesis that 'woman' is childish and natural, while Runeberg said she should be 'like Hanna'.[3] He was referring not Otto Erich Hartleben's *Hanna Jagert*, but his own gentle and innocent character in a novel from 1836, a girl in the tradition of Johann Heinrich Voss's Luise and Goethe's Dorothea.[4] In the most famous monument to the genre of the symposium, that problem painting from Sibelius' innermost circle, Gallen-Kallela's *Symposium*, Sibelius is seated, pensive and absent, in the noctuenal meeting like the angel of Albrecht Dürer's *Melencolia I* (1514): he has sunk into impenetrable contemplation, or, as Gallen-Kallela soberly described him in Willy Burmester's presence: 'introspective'.[5] The painting can be read against Hermann Bahr's essay 'Die Rätsel der Liebe' (The mystery of love) in *Die Überwindung des Naturalismus* (1891) and Otto Weininger's *Geschlecht und Charakter* (translated as

[1] Quoted ibid., p. 69. Munch also painted the oil painting *Woman (Sphinx)* in 1894, he produced a lithograph with the same title in 1896. Illustrated ibid., pp. 70 and 72.

[2] On JS' relationship to Strindberg around 1890, see Erik W. Tawaststjerna 1976, p. 40. On Richard Dehmel, whose poetry JS set, Adolf Paul (cf. ibid., p. 229) and other Modernists around Strindberg, including Otto Julius Bierbaum, Busoni, Ibsen, Walter Leistikow, Bengt Lindfors, Julius Meier-Graefe, Sigbjörn Obstfeld, Emil Orlik, Stanisław Przybyszewski (who wrote an autograph dedication to Sibelius in a copy of his novel *Totenmesse* of 1893), Josef Sattler, Paul Scheerbart, Franz Skarbina, Fritz Thaulow, Jens Thiis, Gustav Vigeland, J. F. Willumsen and Anders Zorn, see Zeitler 1990, 156.

[3] JS to Aino, 10 February 1891.

[4] See Oksala 2004, p. 99.

[5] Akseli Gallen-Kallela to Adolf Paul, 26 December 1894, quoted in Gallen-Kallela-Sirén 2001, p. 189.

FIG. 14. Akseli Gallen-Kallela, *Symposium* (sketch, 1894).

Sex and Character; 1903) or with reference to Ola Hansson's essay in Przybyszewski's *Das Werk des Edvard Munch* (1894).

There is a great deal of talk about 'gender' in Hansson's work. Munch's sexuality, too, does not seem erotic or pornographic, but viewers are perplexed by his vividness – in particular because of the pictorial reduction to essential elements and the asexuality in paintings such as *The Scream* (first version 1893) – and by an involvement that eliminates distance.[1] For Tawaststjerna, the figure in *The Scream* is specifically a woman; for Munch, it was the 'self'.[2] According to the art historian Reinhold Heller,

[1] See Pevsner 1991, p. 88.

[2] Erik W. Tawaststjerna 1986, p. 177, and Zeitler 1990, p. 156, quoting Nergaard's interpretation of Munch's drawing.

the women in Munch's work are not 'physically present' but only 'visualised ideas',[1] but this very quality, as opposed to realism, involves the viewer in more than what is figuratively obvious. The figurative elements and the universal formal principles of Classicism, however, permit access; the interpretation is ultimately unambiguous, even in a Symbolist, idea-orientated painting like, for example, Munch's *Woman in Three Stages* (*c.* 1895), which differs markedly from version to version.

The earliest known colour sketch for *Symposium* shows on the left, cut off by the artist himself with a hunting knife,[2] a naked figure with hints of wings (barely visible), a sphinx or even a 'flayed female',[3] preoccupying the men in the painting: Sibelius gazes inwardly; Gallen-Kallela, excitedly; the fourth man, perhaps Oskar Merikanto, laughs exaltedly. On 28 April 1894, Gallen-Kallela wrote to Louis Sparre:[4] 'I have done away with Merikanto, that knucklehead, by putting him to sleep.' He wrote to Kajanus in May: 'You don't need to send the sketches to Merikanto, since I will paint the little devil sleeping, his head on the table. That way I avoid the parodistic element and the painting becomes more serious.' In the final version, Merikanto is unrecognisable. Only Kajanus raises his index finger. The final version shows Sibelius smoking, while Kajanus is once again all rhetorical seriousness, searching for words and holding out his right hand. Gallen-Kallela stands in the background, with the gaze of a connoisseur, while the fourth man has fallen asleep or has capitulated before a difficult philosophical task and placed his head on the table. Sibelius' unwillingness to hold forth is obvious.

The most important difference between the two versions of *Symposium*, a 'painting about a problem', as it is also often called, is that the female sphinx sitting flayed on the table in the first version later becomes an enigmatic figure, an angel with splendid wings (another quotation from Dürer's *Melencolia I*): a figure from another world whose appearance does not, however, frighten those present; it seems to stand with open wings in order to offer time to reflect. Unlike in Dürer, however, the angel is the object, not the subject, of the narrative. The symbolism of the first version (astral bodies, stars) is decimated in the second; the painting has become a study of a milieu. By contrast, Munch's *Woman* (*Sphinx*) (1894–6) is completely removed from the man's control. Munch was conscious of the change in the image of woman at the time: 'I have lived in a transitional period – in the middle of the emancipation of women. – Then it was the woman who seduced and tempted and deceived the man – the age of Carmen – In the transitional period, the man became the weaker sex.'[5] Gallen-

[1] Heller, 'The Iconography of Edvard Munch's Sphinx', *Art Forum* 9 (October 1970), p. 77, quoted in Gallen-Kallela-Sirén 2001, p. 217.

[2] On the destruction of the painting in reaction to the horror of a bourgeois woman, see Gallen-Kallela-Sirén 2001, p. 201.

[3] Erik W. Tawaststjerna 1976, p. 139, quoting Onni Okkonen. One might also think of Munch's oil painting *The Woman* (*Sphinx*) of 1894 here.

[4] Quoted in Gallen-Kallela-Sirén 2001, pp. 199–200.

[5] See Müller-Westermann 2003, p. 70; Munch's texts, Oslo, 27 February 1929.

Kallela had presumably not yet absorbed this change around 1894, since his men still observe the woman in the spirit of Don Juan: as an object. Sibelius, by contrast, wrote to Aino as early as 18 December 1890: 'This is the era of woman.' Only his continuation reveals the traditional nature of the idea that had initially sounded so promisingly modern: 'Nothing is as irresistible to men as a woman who thinks and feels.'

Symposium is still one of Gallen-Kallela's most often misunderstood paintings. The distinguished German-Swedish art historian Rudolf Zeitler has written: 'The painting is unsuccessful because it has three programmes that the artist was unable to unite. First, the painting is a group portrait [...]. Second, the wings of the sphinx are supposed to make it clear [...] why the men's ideas go in circles [...]. Third, Gallén painted a still life [...]. Only afterwards did he give the whole thing a deeper meaning, which we find unconvincing.'[1] Even today, the conventional reading of the painting concentrates on the bottles,[2] rather than seeing the painting as a ritual depiction of a Platonic symposium in the elegant Kämppi hotel restaurant in Helsinki and interpreting it as ecstasy in Nietzsche's sense.[3] Its value lies precisely in its multiple meanings, typical of Symbolism; its fissures reproduce an atmosphere in an immediate way. The painting smells of smoke and male skin after a long night. The bizarre quality of the contemporary studies of women that Hansson documented is also tangible. Only in the eyes of a Victorian society uninterested in the problem of woman does the atmosphere seem dubious.

In all the versions of *Symposium*, Sibelius is a silent guest unmoved by the cogitations of his colleagues. His access to the present was unlike that of Kajanus and Gallen-Kallela. According to Paul, Sibelius was 'the least able to form a thought in a rational, bourgeois way'.[4] He was the master of the nonverbal materiality of ideas and synaesthesia. This is emphasised by Karl Flodin, a music critic and founding editor of *Euterpe*, who knew Sibelius as well as Paul:

> His conversation overflowed with paradoxical statements and ideas without one being able to say how much was serious and how much merely played on the surface, like bubbles of combinations and passing baroque whimsies generated in his nimble brain. [...] His conversation soon stalled like a hare in a thicket. But right on its heels came the musical ideas like hunting dogs [...]. Before one knew it, Sibelius was juggling with colors and tones as though they were colored glass balls. He made the colors sound and the tones sparkle so

[1] Zeitler 1990, p. 124.

[2] Erik W. Tawaststjerna 1976, p. 162; Adolf Paul to Akseli Gallen-Kallela, n.d., also mentions the scandal on the presentation of the painting.

[3] According to Gallen-Kallela-Sirén 2001, pp. 204ff., however, it is a depiction of the miracle of Pentecost. This view is supported by a sketch that has wings on the naked woman of the earlier version. In order to refute the 'myth' of a sphinx, he quotes Adolf Paul, who claimed that he initially 'mistakenly' took the woman for a symbol of the 'female material' (ibid., p. 209).

[4] Paul 1891, p. 150.

> that A Major was blue and C Major red, F Major green and D Major yellow, more or less; and everything in the world had its melodic label, every voice of nature its ready coined motif, every emotional impulse its primordial harmony [...].[1]

Sibelius also spoke to Otto Andersson of fixed relationships between keys and colours. Unfortunately, Andersson did not publish them anywhere.[2] As a small child, Sibelius associated colours of carpets with sounds from the piano his Aunt Juliana played so magnificently.[3] Franz Emil Sillanpää recorded another of the composer's statements: 'Whenever I smell fresh bread, I think of my mother.'[4]

Because of his incidental music, which responds sensitively to the dramaturgy of the stage and of the text, the Finnish scholar Eija Kurki associated Sibelius directly with so-called Symbolism, since, after all, Sibelius, a Freemason, said: 'Anyone who can interpret symbols understands the secrets of the universe' and 'one gets further with the help of symbols than with reason'.[5] She qualifies this with the remark that Sibelius probably never studied the theories of 'true' Symbolism. His Symbolism was unreflected and was tied to his ability to indicate phenomena synaesthetically and in multiple dimensions, rather than verbalising them. Robert Donington's principle of Symbolism suits his music well: 'to say the least in order to communicate the most'.[6] Hence Sibelius was in a position to realise the synaesthetic basic principle of Symbolism, which is what distinguishes it both from the objectivity of Impressionism and from clinging to the possibilities of reflection in Realism and Naturalism.

The concept of Symbolism is, admittedly, controversial, especially in the English-speaking world and as it pertains to music. Even Carl Dahlhaus considered 'Symbolism' a 'makeshift coinage by Jean Moréas's (Manifesto of 1886) and preferred, unlike the Modernist music critic Paul Bekker, the generic term 'die Moderne' (modernity).[7] Dahlhaus may have wished for ideological reasons to replace the concept of Symbolism, which was associated with far-right movements – Moréas was a co-founder of the École romane, along with Charles Maurras of the Action Française – in order to protect Franz Schreker, whose music was the focus of the debate. As early as 1897, Symbolism and the expressive world of the German illustrator and sculptor Sascha Schneider were turned against Sibelius. Flodin equated the *Lemminkäinen Legends* with Schneider's 'images of horror'.[8] Sibelius and Schneider found themselves on a detour, setting out from Romanticism with the distant goal of a new kind of Classicism.

1 Ringbom 1954, pp. 17–18; in abridged form also in Erik W. Tawaststjerna 1976, p. 15.

2 Sirén 2000, p. 27, quoting Otto Andersson's notes.

3 Erik W. Tawaststjerna 1976, p. 15.

4 Sillanpää 1953, p. 222 (chapter on Eero Järnefelt's family).

5 Kurki 1997, p. 43; see also Levas 1992, p. 453.

6 Donington 1990, p. 152.

7 Dahlhaus 1978, p. 160. On the concept, see also Jarocinski 1976; Kolbus 2001; and Schneider 1982.

8 Erik W. Tawaststjerna 1992, p. 92.

Faced with criticism, Sibelius limited his remarks on the subject of Symbolism. Symbolist trends are, however, already found in a drawing from 1887: a hyper-romantic rarity with river, boat, forest and castle in the moonlight. The drawings in his sketches are more interesting.[1]

When Sibelius was asked about influences from paintings, he avoided the question, because he 'always was, strangely, closer to sculpture than to painting'.[2] On 2 September 1894 he wrote to his wife from Berlin: 'In comparison to Munich, everything is so inartistic here [in the Nationalgalerie]. All the paintings are battle scenes or name days for the empress. Old Greek sculptures are the only genuine works. I cling so to the sculptures that it really surprises me.' He perceived sculpture with all the senses. He touched statues with his hands, even in museums. In later diary entries he even uses the expression 'forge' (as well as 'hammer' or 'I am forging musical metal') to refer to composing.[3] In a letter to Axel Carpelan, this tendency became programmatic: 'As always, the sculptural is in the foreground of my music. Hence this forging on the ethical line, which preoccupies me totally.'[4] In a letter from Vienna in which he defined 'art' — by which he meant the symphony — and at the same time supposed he could never find 'success' — writing 'success' (*Erfolg*) in German — he described his inter-medial plans from childhood. These did not imply a 'total work of art' but rather represented a surreal variant — setting out from the idea of multimedia, which combines synaesthesia with Symbolism. He also articulated the problem of form and content: 'As a child I thought about founding an entirely new kind of art (it should be, I thought, half sculpture, half music). I began with sculpture, and that, as you know, turned into a fiasco. Nevertheless, I had this compulsion to create something in art. I became a musician.'[5]

Although sculpture meant even more to him than painting, and he was also interested in the spatial structure of architecture — above all the work of his friend Eliel Saarinen and the architect of Ainola, Lars Sonck[6] — painting was an important aspect of his milieu later in life, thanks to his neighbours Pekka Halonen and Eero Järnefelt as well as Gallen-Kallela. On 18 April 1911, he wrote in his diary about a meeting in Tuusula: 'Saw Halonen's painting today. A likeable artist, this Pekka! I find many analogies between painting and music in our time.' Unfortunately, he did not reflect on whether this affinity struck him because of a development in painting or one in music. On 10 September 1926 he met Järnefelt: 'I usually like symphonies for their lightness and purity. I have to break with "brother-in-law Erik" [Eero]. He — "an imitative artist." — They are perhaps "artists". Decorate walls and flattering models. Es-

[1] Illustrated in Johnson 1959, p. 15.

[2] Väisänen 1921, pp. 79 ff.

[3] Diary, 7 May ('hammer'), 15 August and 2 September 1910 ('forge'). On the concept in the context of the period, see Konttinen 2001, p. 15, and chapter 1.1 in the present volume.

[4] JS to Axel Carpelan, 20 May 1918, in Dahlström 2010, p. 423.

[5] JS to Aino, 18 December 1890.

[6] See Erik W. Tawaststjerna 1986, p. 18.

pecially their own. Unfortunately, I now have "painters" as neighbours.' (One thinks, perhaps, of Theodor W. Adorno and Hanns Eisler here, who remarked: 'Roughly speaking, all music, including the most "objective" and nonexpressive, belongs primarily to the sphere of subjective inwardness, whereas even the most spiritualized painting is heavily burdened with unresolved objectivity.'[1]) Sibelius suffered under his brother-in-law's superior rhetoric. In his diary he wrote on 21 October 1912: 'All the naivety in me which means so much to my soul, even if it has no inner logic, is gone [after taking a walk with Eero]. And yet I have to love this noble, fine friend. – And that is typical for us Finns: being "open".' And on 15 September 1912, he wrote: 'When I am together with Erik, I talk too much. Open myself and dabble in philosophy and imagination. That always leaves an uncomfortable feeling.'

On 10 February 1892, however, he wrote to Aino: 'I have spoken with Erik a great deal about life, etc. He is a very wise man.' Indeed, from Järnefelt, Halonen and others, he learned, *nolens volens*, about current trends in the fine arts – even though, according to an unreliable anecdote that is nevertheless frequently cited, Sibelius supposedly remarked: 'It is so difficult to mix with artists! You must choose business men to talk to, because artists only talk of money.'[2] Rosa Newmarch described how Sibelius led her through the galleries: 'I frequented the Exhibition of National Painters, installed in the Atheneum, with Sibelius as guide. It was an experience as illuminating and refreshing as a walk by his side through the characteristic scenery itself.'[3] It is unusual for a composer to wander through museums with a music writer and sympathetic interviewer. Sibelius sought the visual arts everywhere – even in Gothenburg, Sweden, where he saw an exhibition of work by the Symbolist Ernst Josephson, whose work had fascinated Sibelius even as a youth, and whose poem 'Svarta rosor' (Black roses) he set as a masterpiece of the art of the *Lied*.[4] He probably wished to communicate something about his own music to Newmarch in this museum visit. In Josephson's work, Sibelius must have been fascinated by the way its mixture of Classical and Impressionist tendencies unfolds in a Symbolist way. Zeitler suspected artistic connections between the distinguished Finnish painter Albert Edelfelt and Josephson.[5] Be that as it may, Edelfelt admired Josephson's portraits; Sibelius, his visions of nature.

'The Blood of All Nature': Hamsun, Munch and Böcklin

In the Scandinavian context, which around 1900 was spearheading the international avant-garde, with Kierkegaard, Ibsen, Strindberg, Munch, Josephson and Gallen-Kallela, the Norwegian writer Knut Hamsun, the penname of Knud Pedersen, played an important role as an interpreter of the irrational and as an inventor of modern

[1] Adorno and Eisler 1947, p. 71.
[2] Törne 1937, p. 94.
[3] Newmarch 1939, p. 22.
[4] Diary, 13 March 1915.
[5] Zeitler 1990, p. 80. On Classicism in Symbolism, see Linnebach 1991.

narrative techniques. Hamsun spent time in Helsinki in 1898–9, where he met Sibelius, on whom he made a 'powerful impression.'[1] The reason for Hamsun's interest in Helsinki, apart from a general enthusiasm for travel, was his close contact with Gallen-Kallela, whom he had met in Paris in 1893–4. The question how well Hamsun knew Sibelius has never been explored, even though he was compared to Sibelius in Adorno's harsh 'footnote' on Sibelius of 1937. Hamsun's biography reports of his stay in Helsinki only that he lived with his wife on Råholmen (Rajasaari) Island in west Helsinki. On 1 September 1899, Hamsun and his wife left Helsinki and travelled to Russia.[2] At the end of September he was in Constantinople and then in Copenhagen at the end of October. The journey took him across Russia and the Caucasus as far as the Caspian Sea, and from there he went to Constantinople, Bulgaria and Serbia.[3]

For Adorno in 'Fussnote zu Sibelius und Hamsun', Hamsun's aesthetic relevance to Sibelius was beyond question.[4] Adorno continued Leo Löwenthal's critical debate over Hamsun's ideology. In this view, the Nobel Prize-winner Hamsun was, on the evidence of *Markens grøde* (1917; translated as *Growth of the Soil* in 1920), a 'regional writer', whose stories involve experiences with local nature and reflect intimate knowledge of the milieu. The German literary scholar Martin Dreher has written of this view:

> The alleged 'Blood and Soil' romanticism of *Markens grøde*, which was greeted so emphatically in the Germany of the Third Reich in particular, is based on the same misunderstanding as the reticence towards Hamsun's oeuvre that was maintained at least during the first few years after the collapse of Hitler's Germany. Both assessments miss the substance of the book, which must be considered timeless and counted among the enduring works of world literature, if only for its sparse, austere, artfully reduced, often biblical-sounding language and its vivid, objectifying narrative style — despite all its tendentiousness and Hamsun's later dubious attitude towards National Socialism.[5]

Much of this applies to Sibelius as well. Hamsun's essay 'Aus dem unbewussten Seelenleben' (From the unconscious life of the soul) was published in 1890, and his book *Pan* (1894) addressed synaesthetic subject matter in the Symbolist spirit: 'This silence murmuring in my ears is the blood of all Nature seething; it is God weaving through the world and me.' Pan's world is shaped by holistic and synaesthetic perception, rather than realistic observations. The self is transported into a state of contemplation, liberated from the inhibitions of reflection, connected with ideas, ordered according to subjective standards with no prevalence granted the word. These ideas

1 Erik W. Tawaststjerna 1976, p. 218, quoting Ekman 1946.
2 Ferguson 1987, pp. 182 and 261.
3 Knut Hamsun to Albert Langen, 20 October 1899, in Næss and McFarlane 1998, p. 24.
4 Adorno 1986, p. 804. See also Wiggershaus 1988, p. 214.
5 Dreher 1986, p. 6049.

from one of the inventors of the modern narrative style and of inner monologue circle around essential aspects of Sibelius' mentality. Accordingly, such impressions are common in the literature on Sibelius.

Perhaps even as a reaction to Adorno's 'Fussnote', the question whether Hamsun and Sibelius had a chance to talk in Helsinki has been neglected in the research. After all, Hamsun's name is associated with the National Socialist ideology and thus hangs like the Sword of Damocles over him. Even Tawaststjerna presumes they had only fleeting contact, if any, and in 1899 'the object disappears from sight'.[1] In the summer of 1899, Sibelius wrote just one letter to Aino, on 26 July 1899, and it begins with the words: 'You are wondering where I am.' Tawaststjerna published without comment an illustration of a poem that Hamsun sent to Sibelius from Turkey via writer and publisher Wentzel Hagelstam.[2] These lines prove that their shared experiences must have gone beyond the fleeting, since Hamsun knew what drinking and gambling meant to Sibelius: 'Sibelius. / Du er i Musik, / i gylden Lyrik / en grønøjet Gud her paa Jorden. / I Dobbel og Drik / et I med Prik, / et Under, en Fan i al Norden. / Knut Hamsun, / Konstantinopel, 30 Septbr. 1899.' (You are in music / in golden poetry / a green-eyed god here on earth. / In gambling and drinking / you are a dotted i, / a miracle, a devil in all the North.)

The Swedish writer Ernst Malmberg's letters to Sibelius shed light on the circumstances under which Sibelius and Hamsun met. Malmberg, who also corresponded with Hamsun, recalled much later in a postcard (featuring Prince Eugen's *Det lugna vattnet* (The still water)) their 'delightful journey' to Helsinki. It led to the first, 'unforgettable' meeting of Sibelius, Hamsun and him, along with the author and graphic artist Albert Engström and Baron Calle Cederström. Cederström was also known in Sweden as the Flying Baron, because he organised the first flights in Sweden; he crashed, disappeared and presumably died somewhere off Åland Island on a flight to Finland.[3] Their meeting is also documented in Engström's letter to Sigrid Sparre of 4 August. A drawing by Engström in the Swedish journal *Strix* ('Åländska skärgårdens utseende efter vår genom-resa', or 'What Åland Archipelago looked like after we passed through it') gives a sense of the atmosphere on Cederström's yacht *Clary*: the sea behind the boat is full of empty champagne bottles.[4] The 'delightful journey' is also mentioned in Engström's *En brevbok* (A book of correspondence), in which he refers to Sibelius familiarly as 'Sibba'.[5] This 'Viking expedition' to Finland in July

[1] Tawaststjerna 1989, vol. 2, p. 155, and expressed somewhat more moderately in Tawaststjerna 1992, p. 122.

[2] Knut Hamsun to Wentzel Hagelstam, 21 September 1901(?), from Ostende, in Næss and McFarlane 1998, p. 50. Illustration of the original in the form of a poem from Hamsun to JS, ibid., unnumbered illustration facing p. 65. On JS' habits, see very clearly his letter to Aino on 10 February 1891.

[3] National Library Coll. 206: 24: postcard from Ernst Malmberg to JS, 31 December 1948.

[4] Engström 1953, pp. 70–71; for a portrait of JS (very serious), ibid., p. 75.

[5] Ibid., pp. 77, 129, 133–4, 136, 144–5, 153–4, 167, 170 and 248. See also Engström, *Åt Häcklefjäll*, pp. 24–5.

1899 (in a sailboat along the old eastern route of the Vikings) also included Carl von Knorring, who had only one leg, and Baron Anders Cederström, who was two years older. Malmberg joined them on Åland Island.[1] Knorring had been a navy officer and later chorus director and manager of the Svenska Teatern in Helsinki. The Cederströms were large-scale landowners from Ingarö, near Stockholm, and sponsors of the adventure: 'I have no more money, but Anders is taking care of it for me', wrote Engström on 23 July.[2]

Malmberg's salutations to Ainola from Paris are fascinating and at times informative. On 8 December 1956, he wrote: 'All of the participants in the emphatic symposium – apart from you, Knut Hamsun and me – are resting in various cemeteries'; and on 16 December 1953: 'All our merry comrades are gone – 92-year-old Knut Hamsun this past spring; he would have grown even older, if his compatriots had not treated him so harshly.' The reference is to the debate over Hamsun's sympathies with the Third Reich – an attitude shared by many in Sibelius' circle, even in Finland. Malmberg mentioned Sibelius' stay in the Pavillon Henri IV in St Germain-en-Laye during a trip to Paris in 1905–6 as well as various encounters in Stockholm. He repeatedly mentions the melody 'God's Prayer', which Sibelius had improvised in his presence and he had since discovered in the Third Symphony. For example, he wrote on 2 December 1915: 'It will be interesting to hear how "God's Prayer" sounds with the orchestra. And I will feel transported back to the Pavillon Henri IV in St Germain – and remember how it sounded there.'[3] 'God's Prayer' is probably a quotation from his own song 'Soi kiitokseksi Luojan' of 1897 (Resound in praise of God; or, We praise thee, our creator; Finnish church song, *Virsikirja* no. 462, cf. op. 23 no. 6a: refrain with a rising movement of seconds and a striking harmony) in the third movement, bars 115 ff.

Shortly after Sibelius had sailed with Armas Järnefelt and Yrjö Weijola in the region Virolahti, west of St Petersburg, in the summer of 1899, he was one of the 'Finns' who welcomed the 'Vikings' in Helsinki, along with Werner Söderhjelm, Albert Edelfelt, Wentzel Hagelstam and Johannes Hartman. For Malmberg, those days in Helsinki were a 'lifelong memory': 'In the summer of the romanticism that reigned in the years before the turn of the century, everything was so different, so that someone from the post-war period would have difficulty imagining the mentality of the time, and even we who lived in the midst of it observe the phenomena with alien eyes and marvel at how life was accepted with such playful lightness and how carefree exist-

1 Engström 1953, pp. 129 and 134 ff.

2 Quoted ibid., p. 123. On the friendship between Calle Cederström ('Calle på Brunn') and Engström and on Cederström's life as friend of artists, see Malmberg 1941, pp. 59 ff.

3 National Library Coll. 206: 24. When JS was in Paris with his wife in 1927, he revisited this place (see postcard from Aino to Elisabeth Järnefelt, 21 March 1927; collections of Järvenpää high school). On the history of the facilities and of tourism, see Rouzaud, Beaud and Brachet 1994.

ence could be.'[1] Such observations sum up the difficult of adequately assessing and completely understanding the art of this only seemingly recent past.

The Norwegian writer Sigurd Holl asked Sibelius for a contribution to a *Festschrift* for Hamsun's seventieth birthday,[2] but Sibelius declined – as he always did when asked for a written contribution. He had not forgotten Hamsun: in 1927 he purchased the first volume of the *Landstrykere* trilogy,[3] and in Oslo he spent boisterous hours with Hamsun on repeated occasions.[4] In Oslo, of all places, it became known that Sibelius was, like Hamsun, an artist who travelled frequently. The journal *Verdens Gang* published an interview in 1911 in which the journalist characterised Finns as 'a traveling people, a new form of the wandering Jews': 'You encounter them everywhere in Europe.' Sibelius reportedly said to the journalist: 'Yes, all Finns travel, and then they have money wired from home. Travelling is our only salvation; it keeps us alert.' Later he sent a letter of protest to the editor, denying he had made that statement – though it sounds authentic. It had caused a small domestic political crisis in Helsinki. Nearly everything written about Sibelius was translated and published – and in consequence carefully evaluated – in Helsinki. That was not always pleasant for Sibelius.

Of names from the Scandinavian ('Viking') context – which is generally rather underexposed in the Sibelius literature, perhaps because it does not suit well the image of Sibelius as Finland's nationalist Modernist – Munch's is one, unlike Hamsun's, that Tawaststjerna says 'comes to mind when one thinks of Sibelius' music', since 'like Strindberg in his plays and Munch in the irrational atmosphere of his paintings, Sibelius recorded in his *Valse triste* something of the angst typical of his age'.[5] Tawaststjerna also associated the Fourth Symphony with Munch's art: 'In visual terms, this music is connected, in my opinion, to Edvard Munch's visions of life and death as a mystery, with human angst and loneliness.' He also addressed the problem of the Dionysian and Apollonian in contemporary artists such as Oskar Kokoschka as well as the problem of the 'visual' and of 'visions'.[6] The author may have been thinking of Munch's *Death and the Maiden* (1893–4, various versions): a modern interpretation of the medieval dance of death, with the spermatic ornaments typical of Munch. Bold, but apt, is the arc he draws from the incidental music *Valse triste* to the Fourth Symphony. The comparison can help us to re-evaluate a masterpiece that has been unjustly trivialised. Munch's peculiar relationship to Classicism, Naturalism and Symbolism is an important model when considering Sibelius. In Munch's images of women, the viewer is confronted with a proximity of the life of the Other that contradicts Classicism. *Madonna* (1893–5) and *Loving Woman* (1894–5) embody

[1] Malmberg 1941, p. 64. Weijola and Järnefelt were there but Malmberg was not mentioned.

[2] National Library Coll. 206: 45; JS to Sigurd Holl, 3 June 1929, from Oslo, in Swedish.

[3] Erik W. Tawaststjerna 1997a, p. 268.

[4] Jalas 1981, p. 59.

[5] Erik W. Tawaststjerna 1997a, p. 299, and Erik W. Tawaststjerna 1976, p. 289.

[6] Erik W. Tawaststjerna 1994, p. 228; on Munch, see Tawaststjerna 1989, vol. 4, p. 352, but this daring passage is omitted in Tawaststjerna 1996 and in Layton's translation.

'devotion' and 'being overpowered';[1] at the same time, they involve the viewer in a way that is, at first glance, irreconcilable with the objectifying of the work and the classical distance from the work preferred by many lovers of art. In Berlin, as early as 1892, there was talk of 'Ibsen-like images of mood'.[2] The figures are depicted from an inner perspective outwards, but the contours consist of a line of several colours that prohibits any clear separation between figure and background and compels one to perceive the objects in a totalising, emphatically organic way. The classical principles of form are not obvious, as in Paul Cézanne's geometrically based configurations,[3] but they certainly exist in the background. They control the proportions of colours and planes. However, many did not see this. Munch's patrons even criticised his abandoning of draughtsmanship, colour and handling (emphatic modelling) 'for the sake of an impression or mood'.[4]

Munch himself responded to his critics, in the style of Sibelius, by alluding to the 'emotional expression' the artist experiences when looking at the object. Despite the immanent symmetry of his pictorial elements, he attacked conventional paintings of milieus or interiors. He wanted to see living, breathing and feeling, suffering and loving human beings. The audience should 'understand the sacredness and power of this moment' – at least as when he wrote the 'Saint-Cloud Manifesto' (1889). Or in Nikolaus Pevsner's words: 'Whatever he [Munch] paints, he makes us feel the inexhaustible power of Nature parturient.'[5] Munch painted the other in himself, not through and outside of himself as in an objectifying classicism. There is even an authentic note – in a chaotic Norwegian transcribed by Trygve Nergaard – about *The Scream* (1893): 'I stood there paralysed by fear – and I felt like a great, unending scream was going through *infinite nature*.'[6] He did not paint 'from nature'; he took 'from its kingdom'.[7] Nor did he depict sexuality elegantly; rather, it is integrated into the paintings and has its effect there as well, where only a woman, trees, water and the moonlight are actually recognisable.

Munch, who was familiar with Strindberg's proto-Surrealist ideas of 'automatic art', grasped the processes of nature as a component of art by exploiting the grain of the wood for figuration in his woodcuts and exposed his art to corrosion in open nature. Strindberg developed the idea of art as an imitation of the way creation works in nature.[8] By means of lines of force, depiction of aura and the design of the dissected surface of painting, energies are illustrated and 'life force' objectified – also in the

[1] Zeitler 1990, p. 19.

[2] Adolf Rosenberg in *Kunstchronik und Kunstmarkt* 4 (1892–3); quoted in Zeitler 1990, p. 152.

[3] Edward Clark was the first to compare JS to Cézanne. He divided JS' work into a 'figurative' phase (up to op. 56) and an 'abstract' one (Kurki 1997, 44, quoting Clark's 'Sibelius lecture in 1996').

[4] Zeitler 1990, p. 151.

[5] Munch 2001, p. 249; Pevsner 1991, p. 88.

[6] Zeitler 1990, p. 156.

[7] Munch, *Livsfrisens tilblivelse* (1928): 1; quoted in Buchhart 2003, p. 25.

[8] Ibid., pp. 25–6. On Strindberg, see Fechner-Smarsly 1998, pp. 31, 34, and 38.

spirit of Henri Bergson's 'élan vital' and Harry van de Velde's lines charged with energy (1902).[1] *The Scream* is about the frightening proximity to 'infinite nature', which can be perceived inter-medially. The fear itself, as a component of a feeling about life, is secondary; by contrast, the specific perception of nature, which Munch could only hint at in words, is important. The comparison to Sibelius is an obvious one, not least with an eye to the works mentioned by Tawaststjerna, but not because of a single category of expression: namely, 'angst'. Rather, the crucial thing is the suggestive, involving expressiveness that does not neglect the rules of Classicism, but neither does it make them visible as a figurative geometry. It gives rise to a Munchian lack of distance in the work's overall impression by means of well-chosen forms of musical intonation.

In an authentic note from 1892 on Arnold Böcklin, who was one of Munch's idols,[2] Sibelius remarked (without indicating the painting intended): 'The air is much too bright, the swans too white, the lake much too blue, etc.' In the same letter to Paul, he wrote that he had been 'contemplating' Böcklin.[3] From this same period dates a brief *Saga* for orchestra (the ur-form of the tone poem *En saga*), which he had just 'completed'. Two years later, he described Böcklin's *The Elysian Fields* with its luminous swans to the young painter Magnus Enckell.[4] This painting by Böcklin was also emphasised by Eero Järnefelt: 'His simple world of images sank in favour of sacred groves from antiquity, lyres, swans and temples. To the extent he moved away from the reality of his homeland and its people [and moved closer to Böcklin], his art lost its power "to move the soul."'[5] *The Elysian Fields* in particular is considered evidence of the painter's interest in romantic themes of water spirits and the world of nixes and water sprites,[6] with which Sibelius was familiar as a subject, especially thanks to its strong presence in Nordic poetry, which he even employed himself in compositions.[7]

When Sibelius distanced himself from hard-core Wagnerism, he began to be interested in Symbolism in painting and in the landscape of southern Finland. He spent the summer of 1895 in Vaania on Lake Vesijärvi,[8] on an old waterway between the medieval church Hollola and the governmental centre of Heinola. There are no spectacular natural monuments there, but there is 'all nature' not far from civilisation. That autumn he took note of the march of progress of the 'soul' in Finnish art (Magnus Enckell). A complex emotional world, fairy tales, religion, legends and myths,

[1] Asendorf 2003, pp. 85 ff. The author postulates a connection between Munch and Carl von Reichenbach's theory of energy. These references to contemporaneous concepts with an eye to JS are an important contribution to correcting the popular theory of pantheism.

[2] Munch in 1893, according to Benesch 1962, p. 345, quoted in Vaughan 2000, p. 80.

[3] National Library Coll. 206: 62; JS to Adolf Paul, 10 December 1892 (originals in the Kungliga biblioteket, Stockholm).

[4] Magnus Enckell to Yrjö Hirn, 28 October 1894 (National Library), quoted in Sarajas-Korte 1966, p. 134.

[5] See Waenerberg 2002, p. 218; see Zeitler 1990, p. 112.

[6] Linnebach 1991, pp. 45–6. The painting from 1877–8 illustrated there is considered lost.

[7] On songs and the theme of the water sprites/nixes ('näcken'), see chapter 4.3 in the present volume.

[8] Erik W. Tawaststjerna 1976, pp. 164 ff.

Far Eastern forms and dreams came together into a connection that conveyed meaning and had a fundamental tone specific to the region. In 1896, this attitude found its way into a brief manifesto: his lecture (fragment) 'Några synpunkter beträffande folkmusiken och dess inflytande på tonkonsten' (Several ideas concerning folk music and its influence on composition), in which Sibelius also mentions *Ars nova* and *Ars antiqua*.[1] He felt privileged that he had been able to develop independently, without being hampered by the latest techniques. Hence he felt in a position to compose in a lively and dynamic way on the basis of church modes, which others were trying in vain at the time.[2]

Accompanied by Armas Järnefelt, Sibelius had an opportunity in Munich in late summer 1894, immediately following Bayreuth, to see works by Böcklin, Franz von Stuck and Max Klinger. Aino summed it up for Saimi Järnefelt: 'He writes terribly enthusiastic letters, among other things about paintings in Munich.'[3] When he composed *Swan of Tuonela*, one of the *Lemminkäinen Legends*, he was able to relate it — in addition to Johann Gottfried Herder's poem 'Der sterbende Schwan' (The dying swan) — to the swan in Gallen-Kallela's *Lemminkäinen's Mother*, which in the sketch is still white and only later becomes grey,[4] though not especially luminous. There is a Finnish depiction of an extremely white swan by Ferdinand von Wright: *Två svanar i fjällsjö* (Two swans on a mountain lake; 1868). In the finished painting (1897), the swan of Tuonela is swimming in the shade. In Gallen-Kallela's *Lemminkäinen and the Maidens on the Island* of 1895 (cf. Sibelius' eponymous composition, op. 22, no. 1), the swan is red. Enckell painted black and blazingly white swans in his *Fantasia* of 1895, which was supposed to be a direct imitation of Böcklin's *Elysian Fields* — in fact, however, it more closely resembles William Degouve de Nuncques's *Le cygne noir* (1896). It is possible that Gallen-Kallela and Sibelius, and perhaps Enckell as well, discussed the colour of the swan, and that Sibelius even influenced the painter by critiquing the painter's palette. Tawaststjerna also suspected that Sibelius, whose *Swan of Tuonela* was associated with Böcklin's *Isle of the Dead* by a critic in Berlin in 1901, appreciated the German painter not only for his colours — despite the 'too white' swans of *The Elysian Fields* — but also for his ability to imagine himself in the 'mythical elements of nature'. Tawaststjerna risked speculating on a parallel between Böcklin's *Pine in the Alps* and the piano *The Spruce*, op. 75, no. 5 (1914–19).[5]

What fascinated Sibelius about Böcklin were not his themes but rather the multiple meanings, the Dionysian 'ecstasy' and the suggestive fantasy world, which had less to do with myths and concrete programmes than with surreal visions and dreams. Böcklin's world of symbols is indeed more ambivalent than the National Social-

[1] Sibelius [1896] 1980, pp. 86 ff.

[2] See also later in Diary, 26 January 1914.

[3] Aino to Saimi Järnefelt, 28 August 1894, in Talas 2000, p. 123.

[4] Illustrated in Gallen-Kallela-Sirén 2001, p. 247.

[5] Erik W. Tawaststjerna 1991, p. 247.

FIG. 15. Akseli Gallen-Kallela, *Lemminkäinen's Mother* (1897).

ists who admired him were able to recognise.[1] Sibelius' critique of Böcklin and his colours did not signify a rejection. The fact that Böcklin was mentioned at all, and even inspired Sibelius to 'contemplate' – and to admit doing so – is a sign of inner excitement as well as of ability to recognise intuitively that Symbolism, in contrast to Naturalism, 'which returns to the principle of mimesis', 'pushes the hostility of nature to the extreme' and does not exactly 'revive the symbol as the key to the book of nature'.[2] Every 'key to the book of nature' seemed suspect to him; for him, nature was not a book, not even an object, for which a 'key' exists.

The relationship of naturalism to nature – 'no longer as landscape but as milieu'[3] – was one Sibelius found sympathetic at times, but he was no naturalist in sound; the surreal content of his major works is too obvious for that. The philosophical rather than aesthetic foundation of Symbolism and its primarily literary quality were also hardly accessible to him. His aesthetic was that of a visionary, ecstatic,[4]

[1] On this specifically, see Beaucamp 2001a, p. 51.

[2] Jauss 1989, pp. 148–9.

[3] Brunetière, quoted ibid., p. 148.

[4] On the concept of 'ecstasy' in JS, see Erik W. Tawaststjerna 1991, p. 247, and on 'ecstasy' versus 'dream', see Nietzsche 1967, pp. 37 ff.

imagination-based synaesthete, not that of the concept-orientated idealist or that of the Impressionist, Realist or even Futurist. After all, Symbolism was a product of the mid-nineteenth century, which saw literature permeated with music as the crucial art for the formation of meaning. Consequently, 'the task of the Symbolist artists was in part to transform the dominant literary and terminological thinking into a visual clarity'.[1] True Symbolism – which existed more as an idea than in practice – in which 'things are expressed that are not primarily a concern of art but rather employ art as a means of expression', went too far for Sibelius, despite his possible sympathy for dividing the world into 'art' and 'non-art'. What he could find sympathetic about the Symbolist stance was its critique of the formalism of national art academies, of historicism, positivism and bourgeois ideas of morality – by contrast, nearly all of its ideology would have been problematic for him.[2] His own concern was what one of the leading specialists on Symbolism, Hans H. Hofstätter, has called the 'third type of synaesthesia': an 'art of forms that agitates the human soul simply through forms that resemble nothing familiar, depict nothing and symbolise nothing, and art that works by means of freely invented forms, just as music does with free sounds'.[3] The 'first type' of synaesthesia was allegory; the second, the indirect statement of romanticism; and the third, Wassily Kandinsky's abstraction.

There is no concrete evidence of encounters between Munch and Sibelius or even of Sibelius' reception of Munch's work. Their common friend Adolf Paul tried to help Munch, and he managed to persuade Akseli Gallen-Kallela to a joint opening in Berlin.[4] Gallen-Kallela was in Berlin in early 1895 when his *Symposium* was being exhibited at the Salon Fritz Gurlitt as part of the exhibition of the Freie Vereinigung of Munich. The joint exhibition of Gallen-Kallela and Munch opened at the Salon Ugo Baroccio on 3 March 1895.[5] Sibelius was not there; Gallen-Kallela later said it had been a mistake to exhibit with Munch, since their approaches were so different: 'Even so, the critics saw us as a team.'[6] The fact that Sibelius did not mention Munch anywhere tells us very little. He mentioned Böcklin only once in passing, even though he had studied his technique not only in Vienna but also in Berlin.[7] Munch's and Sibelius' development ran parallel in terms of the history of their style and reception. Stylistically, Munch is regarded as a follower of James McNeill Whistler (who had a solid family background in St Petersburg) and a late Impressionist, which is also said of Sibelius. The conservative Berlin critic Adolf Rosenberg found that the early reception of Munch saw formlessness, brutality, rawness and nastiness – all adjectives familiar from criticisms of Sibelius. Munch's art was considered scrawling, 'house painting',

[1] Hofstätter [1965] 1978, p. 17.

[2] Similarly in Russia: 'Symbolism is a worldview or would have to become a worldview'; on Russian Symbolism and the Symbolist debate of 1909–10, see Kluge 1997, p. 67.

[3] Hofstätter [1965] 1978, p. 145, quoting August Endell (after 1890).

[4] Adolf Paul to Akseli Gallen-Kallela, n.d. (April 1894), quoted in Tawaststjerna 1992, p. 41.

[5] Ilvas 1996, p. 16.

[6] See Okkonen 1961, p. 311.

[7] Erik W. Tawaststjerna 1991, pp. 246 ff.

'roughly executed' and 'random experiments with color.'[1] Only one reviewer of 1892 was in a position to find his way into the paintings, to get involved and to articulate their modernity: Theodor Wolff, the co-founder of the Freie Bühne and later editor-in-chief of the *Berliner Tageblatt*. What he characterised as liveliness and vitality was for others non-representationalism and the freedom of two-dimensional figures — that is, suggestive Symbolism in virtual space that tends to reality: 'I went to the rotunda to laugh. But by everything holy, I did not laugh. For among all the strange notions and purely horrific pieces, I believed I saw fine, extraordinarily delicate moods — in dark rooms filled with moonlight, on lonely paths, in silent Norwegian summer nights — I believed I heard quiet, melancholy, strange people. People who wandered somnambulating and silently around the round blocks on the beach and concealed profound pain in their breasts. And I did not laugh.'[2] Wolff positively assessed what Adolf Rosenberg criticised, and he found categories that help in our reading of Sibelius even today.

The 'New Renaissance': 'Fennoman Chiefs' and the Kalevala

The interest in the remote regions of Savo and Karelia, which had preserved their original character as the traditional borderline periphery between Scandinavia and Russia, between the West and East, did not arise from any regressive glorification of a culture but rather from a very contemporary search for unused symbols and new experiences. The actual unspoiled character of the region played a minimal role; its differentness, an essential one. It was about the roots of suitable ideas for the future. The 'experience of the impossibility of preserving the natural attitude towards life'[3] that was increasingly influencing the evolution of Central European Modernism (Rainer Maria Rilke, Franz Kafka) was behind it. That explains why Gallen-Kallela travelled to East Africa (to Kilimanjaro in Kenya) several years after his first trip to Karelia and after long stays in Paris: as an opportunity to explore a new world. Later, in the service of the republic, he designed symbols for the nation, after 1919 as General Carl Gustav Mannerheim's artistic aide-de-camp.[4] As early as 1894, the year he painted *Symposium*, he wrote: 'In little Finland a new renaissance must be created now — that is, new energy, new life, and a new world. We need that now in this age of miserable, melancholic decadence.'[5] There was no trace in Finland of the fashionable fear that the *fin de siècle* could soon become the *fin du monde*.[6]

[1] For 'house painting', see Adolf Rosenberg in *Kunstchronik und Kunstmarkt* 4 (1892–3); quoted in Zeitler 1990, p. 153. For Andreas Aubert in *Morgenbladet*, 9 November 1886, and N.N. in *Deutscher Reichs-Anzeiger und Königlich Preussischer Staats-Anzeiger*, 12 November 1892, see Buchhart 2003, 23, quoting reviews from 1886 and 1892.

[2] Zeitler 1990, p. 153.

[3] Jauss 1989, p. 243.

[4] See Gallen-Kallela-Sirén 2001, pp. 387 ff.

[5] Erik W. Tawaststjerna 1991, p. 234, according to Onni Okkonen.

[6] Jauss 1989, pp. 239–40.

The impression that Sibelius was dominated by the *Kalevala* as a text and a world of ideas and by Gallen-Kallela's visions of the *Kalevala* is deep-seated in Sibelius scholarship. Several Finnish authors of the early twentieth century are guilty of this simplification, which continues to influence writers. The connection to the *Kalevala* spoke for a Finnish, populist attitude at a time when national symbols and values were not yet abundant. Thanks to his occasional inspiration from the *Kalevala*, beginning with *Kullervo*, Sibelius became an artist of the people and his music became folk/art music. Moreover, the analogy between Sibelius and the *Kalevala* is the result of seeing Gallen-Kallela and the composer in parallel. In a review of the Second Symphony, Peterson-Berger observed in 1904: 'Gallén's Kalevala paintings are probably analogous to this music: one feels as if in a world where wan fairy-tale suns or powerful dusks glow.'[1] The remarkable thing here is the not entirely false assumption that Sibelius' symphonies are programmatic, especially in terms of their initial occasion. *De facto*, Peterson-Berger was not attributing to the finished work a programme in the manner of Liszt but rather speaking of the atmospheric effect evoked by gesture, harmony and rhythm. He was arguing for a semantic interpretation – independently of the composer's intention. He meant neither a musical programme that relates to specific paintings nor inspiration from the painter but rather a genuine analogy. This approach is legitimate. It is obvious that this relationship occurred to Peterson-Berger because both men not only advocated Finnish Modernism but had also evolved side by side, if not actually together. For that reason, in 1926 Sibelius argued against comparisons with Gallen-Kallela: 'My life and Gallén's took their course under the sign of the fatherland. I was [however] already someone else in 1896. But the critics and the public. [They are] Dumber than God is wise!'[2] Indeed, to use Gallen-Kallela's *Kullervo's Curse* (1899), say, as a model for a proper reading of Sibelius' *Kullervo* (1892) is as misleading as it is common, as will be shown below.

Only from the autumn of 1891 – immediately after completing the *Aino* triptych and at the time of the first exhibition of younger Finnish artists, a kind of secession in the year of the Secession in Munich – is there evidence for a friendship between Sibelius and Gallen-Kallela.[3] They also differed in character, since Gallen-Kallela tended towards everyday activism, politically as well. For example, Sibelius would never have written 'I am presumably not enough of an artist to separate myself entirely from political questions; rather, they occupy me the entire time when I am trying to forget everything else and dedicate myself to my art.'[4] Despite his position as 'poeta laureatus (!)', Sibelius kept himself as far from the tasks of *realpolitik* as was possible in that politically sensitive and differentiated era. He was a classic example of the type of the disengaged, romantic composer. Whereas Gallen-Kallela created his role as master of

[1] Erik W. Tawaststjerna 1992, p. 232.

[2] Diary, 10 September 1926.

[3] Erik W. Tawaststjerna 1976, p. 103.

[4] Akseli Gallen-Kallela to Karl Hedman, quoted in Gallen-Kallela-Sirén 2001, p. 402.

the symbolism of the young republic on his own initiative (and ended up designing symbols for military ranks), Sibelius limited his clear political effect to such secondary works as the *March of the Finnish Jaeger Battalion*, about a group of young soldiers trained by the German military in 1916, and the march of the Finnish Lapua fascists, *Karelia's Fate* of 1930. The rest is ambiguous romantic patriotism.

Nevertheless, both artists were already celebrated as a team in Paul's essay 'Zwei Fennonenhäuptlinge' (Two Fennoman chiefs).[1] For Paul, there were only two other truly great contemporaries: Strindberg and Munch. In 1895, after the symposium broke up and the painter moved to Paris, the connection between Sibelius and Gallen-Kallela was already growing looser, and there were only a few, brief opportunities for an intimate exchange of ideas. It was only possible in Berlin in the spring of 1898,[2] and in the early summer of 1899 in Jyväskylä and Ruovesi.[3] Finally, in 1906 they dined together at Eero Järnefelt's house, next to Ainola, in honour of Maxim Gorki. For Gorki, who was a wanted man at the time, Sibelius, the poet Eino Leino and of course Gallen-Kallela, his patron, were the 'fathers' of everything Finnish.[4] His student Madetoja wrote in 1915: 'Sibelius created the "Finnish style".'[5]

Around 1909, at the same time but independently of one another, Sibelius and Gallen-Kallela experienced a profound crisis. Gallen-Kallela was reacting to 'decadence'; he was dissatisfied with the 'deliberate distortion of visually experienced reality' of Henri Matisse, Pablo Picasso and Georges Braque. His own Modernism was anchored in Realism,[6] which is why he was compelled to expand his experiences in the real world in order to make progress as an artist, and so travelled to Kenya. By contrast, Sibelius, who was also searching for origins in times of modern superficiality, went with Eero Järnefelt to Koli in northern Karelia.[7] In 1899 Järnefelt recorded his interpretation of Lake Pielisjärvi, near Koli, as a panorama painting, which as a festive motif for telegrams helped to define the national sense of landscape. The point now was to set off on common paths together. If the legend that Järnefelt 'gave' Sibelius a 'programme' for his Fourth Symphony on Koli is valid,[8] it was a late Impressionist one — much like Järnefelt's own landscape of 1909. If one compares the symphony with Järnefelt's later painting of Koli, the aesthetic distance between the two artists is, however, clear. The panorama of 1899 is closer in its effect to the Fourth

[1] Paul 1914, pp. 114–15.

[2] Erik W. Tawaststjerna 1976, p. 202.

[3] Ibid., p. 218.

[4] Erik W. Tawaststjerna 1986, p. 47.

[5] Quoted in Salmenhaara 1987, p. 81.

[6] Gallen-Kallela-Sirén 2001, pp. 348–9.

[7] Erik W. Tawaststjerna 1986, p. 130.

[8] Ibid., p. 171, quoting 'Bis' (Wasenius) in *Hufvudstadtsbladet*, 8 April 1911. See also Diary, 27 September – 3 October 1909: 'Plans. "La montagne."' See also Axel Carpelan to JS, 27 December 1909, in Dahlström 2010, p. 262, for passages from a 'mountain' project and 'wanderer's thoughts', which JS had improvised for Carpelan, mentioning a symphony in that context.

Symphony (1911), which Sibelius did, after all, dedicate to Järnefelt.[1] Järnefelt commented on a performance with the words 'deep' and 'rich with life'.[2] Several of his paintings of Koli could be characterised with those very words, and yet they would hardly work as programmatic illustrations of the symphony.

When Gallen-Kallela included a portrait of Sibelius in his watercolour *Sibelius as the Composer of 'En saga'* of 1894, also known as *Jean Sibelius and an Imaginary Landscape*, then asked the composer to complete the work, which consisted of three isolated planes held together by passe-partout, by adding a handwritten theme from the composition, Sibelius dismissed the idea.[3] The work remained a fragment.[4] It ended up in Sibelius' possession and was displayed in Ainola. Sibelius' reaction does not therefore represent the rejection of the visual interpretation of his art in general.[5] More than that, he knew that the fragment of the music would not have suitably represented the complex orchestral work *En saga*, and the composer was not inclined to fetishism about melodies. A handwritten theme would have been like a musical signature, blessing an interpretation of the work reduced to an image. That was going too far for an artist sensitive to the inter-medial – whether or not he found the illustration of his ideas mistaken, possible or successful. This reticence may also have signified a strategic distance from the painter, since both artists together would have immortalised Gallen-Kallela's idea in an actual work of art, and given priority to the painter. Occasionally, as during the celebrations of the painter's fiftieth birthday, there was a lot of room for vanity in Ainola on this matter: 'The newspapers under Gallén's sign [i Galléns tecken]. Exaggeration and sentimentality.'[6] In his thank-you letter to Sibelius after his birthday, in April 1915, where Sibelius had failed to show up, to general perplexity and without apology,[7] Gallen-Kallela wrote: 'You, Sibelius, were an equal and close comrade-in-arms at that time when we embarked on our respective paths, and since then you have been for me an admired paradigm. We both have so much work to do that we have no time to spend in each other's company, but it often seems to me that our emanations meet.'[8] Sibelius focused on the phrase 'You [...] were an equal' and was hurt. He felt superior. One topical reason for his sensitivity was the publicly expressed assertion that Gallen-Kallela had provided Sibelius with important inspiration.[9]

Since 1892 Sibelius had been trailing the painter, who was only slightly older, by

[1] As early as 1894 he produced *Symbolist Landscape* and *Koli, Metsämaisema* in 1895; see Waenerberg 2002, pp. 214 ff.

[2] Lindqvist 2002, p. 126, quoting Järnefelt's diary for 9 February 1934.

[3] Tawaststjerna 1989, vol. 1, p. 276; the reference is not in Tawaststjerna 1976, pp. 254–5.

[4] For an illustration, see Becker and Melchior 2002, p. 112.

[5] Gallen-Kallela-Sirén 2001, p. 198.

[6] Diary, 25 April 1915.

[7] JS justified the decision to himself by referring to his work composing; see Diary, 26 April 1915.

[8] Erik W. Tawaststjerna 1997b, p. 117.

[9] Diary, 27 April 1915.

an increasingly smaller distance, only to overtake him around 1895 in the chronology of the completion of similar projects. In terms of quality – insofar as it is possible to judge – that happened around 1904. Gallen-Kallela, though born in the provincial town of Pori on the west coast of Finland, had lived in Helsinki since the time of his secondary schooling. From a very early age he was certain of his profession. At sixteen he broke off his studies at high school, whereas Sibelius began studying law after graduating from high school and only defined himself as a professional musician (violinist) at twenty-one and as a composer at twenty-six. Gallen-Kallela was working in Paris at nineteen, while Sibelius travelled to Berlin for the first time at twenty-three. At twenty Gallen-Kallela had already painted his first masterpieces, coached by Edelfelt and the legendary Adolf von Becker in Helsinki. In Paris, around 1885, he produced a self-portrait that shows a critical painter: 'I hope that something comes of him. Fortunately, he does not spend time with other Northerners and so he can distance himself from the influence of the internal glorification that otherwise destroys all talents.'[1] Edelfelt's reserve seems overcautious in view of the level of his technique and the modern orientation of the circle of Nordic artists around 1890. Edelfelt belonged to the generation of Realists – albeit on a level that was reached only by Edvard Grieg of the Nordic musicians. None of Sibelius' teachers – neither Wegelius nor Albert Becker in Berlin, not Robert Fuchs in Vienna and not even Karl Goldmark – could hold a candle to Gallen-Kallela's teachers as artists. Gallen-Kallela's decision to go to Paris was influenced by Edelfelt. Finnish academics, musicians and politicians still clearly looked to Germany for orientation – the literary historian and philosopher Yrjö Hirn, a friend of Sibelius', was an exception. By contrast, after the period of the dominance of the Düsseldorf school of painting – represented from 1853 onwards by Werner Holmberg, Hjalmar Musterhjelm and others – young painters were already looking for their masters in Paris, as many young composers would do after the First World War.

In 1890 Gallen-Kallela had spent his honeymoon in Karelia.[2] His role model was Edelfelt, who had visited most eastern parts of Savo in 1887 and painted in 1890 a hybrid archaic Finnish and pan-European, proto-Symbolist masterpiece, *Christ and Mary Magdalene*, on a subject from Elias Lönnrot's *Kanteletar* collection of folk poetry. Sibelius followed in summer 1892 with an assignment to document the place and its musical culture; he too brought his young wife,[3] as well as a square piano. He returned to civilisation with a few ethnological notes and a series of conventional art songs.[4] The original version of Gallen-Kallela's first *Kalevala* painting, the three-part *Aino* legend, was produced three years before Sibelius' premiere of a work based

[1] Albert Edelfelt to his mother, 18 April 1885, from Paris; quoted in Gallen-Kallela-Sirén 2001, p. 74.

[2] Gallen-Kallela-Sirén 2001, pp. 122 ff.

[3] The wedding took place on 10 June 1892.

[4] See, for example, Talas 2000, pp. 108 ff., and Erik W. Tawaststjerna 1976, pp. 121 ff., and Pentti Kivinen's memoirs (National Library Coll. 206: 20; Pentti Kivinen to JS, 19 December 1944); for a detailed discussion see chapter 3.2 of the present volume.

on the *Kalevala*: *Kullervo* in spring 1892 — at a time when the composer was also preoccupied with the *Kalevala*. The final version of Gallen-Kallela's *Aino* was completed in 1891. A year later, the same year Sibelius' *Kullervo* was premiered, it was published and received a prize. At the time, Gallen-Kallela was still clearly superior to Sibelius. His '*Kullervos*' in oil — *Kullervo's Curse* of 1899 and *Kullervo Goes to War* of 1901 — were produced after Sibelius' symphonic poem *Kullervo* and in a different spirit. Sibelius never took up the themes of Aino and Väinämöinen, which had already been staked out by Gallen-Kallela. His sketches do include 'Aino' notes, but they refer to his wife, since the names of his daughters (Ruth, etc.) also occur.[1] His reticence towards the fascinatingly erotic subject of the maiden Aino (Gallen-Kallela too concentrated on the way Väinämöinen tries to seduce the virgin, and at the time Sibelius liked to compose works with an erotic component) might be explained by the fact that Kajanus had become famous with his *Aino*. Sibelius would have had an opportunity to hear the tone poem *Aino* in 1885, during the *Kalevala* anniversary in Helsinki, but probably he did not;[2] he did, however, know about the performance and knew the work's title. Later it was important to Sibelius that Kajanus' reputation as the 'inventor' of the Finnish character should not be consolidated, which may be why he could not acknowledge the significance of *Aino*. On 5 September 1912 he got excited about notes to that effect in the newspaper, and in 1913, after he had supported with his signature Kajanus' application for a state pension, he was very concerned that the application contained the formulation that Kajanus had invented the original Finnish sound ('finska folktonen (!)'; Diary, 14 April and 6 May 1913); as a 'Finnish artist', he was almost paralysed by the idea that Kajanus, rather than he, would be recognised as the leading figure of the first period of essentially Finnish art music.

During one 'symposium', Sibelius got the idea from Gallen-Kallela, Erik Tawaststjerna conjectured,[3] to set the tragic legend of the hero Lemminkäinen to music. A watercolour sketch for Gallen-Kallela's later masterpiece in oil *Lemminkäinen's Mother* dates as far back as 1894. Another early work on this theme, also important for Sibelius, *Lemminkäinen and the Maidens on the Island*, dates from 1895.[4] By contrast, Gallen-Kallela's *Lemminkäinen's Mother* (also known as *Lemminkäinen in Tuonela*) was not completed until 1897, whereas Sibelius had composed at least the first versions of his four *Lemminkäinen Legends* between 1894 and 1896. The most famous of these legends, *The Swan of Tuonela*, has no textual relationship to the *Kalevala*, which is why the association with the highly symbolic swan in Gallen-Kallela's sketches for *Lemminkäinen's Mother* held such attraction. When a music critic in Berlin compared *The Swan of Tuonela* to Böcklin's *Isle of the Dead* in 1901, Gallen-Kallela was not yet famous enough in Berlin to replace Böcklin in the critic's imagination. Around

[1] See, for example, sketches in National Library Coll. 206: 1.A.33. See also sketches on 'Dolce far niente' ('Aino'), illustrated in Tiilikainen 2003, p. 48.

[2] Salmenhaara 1984, p. 44, and Erik W. Tawaststjerna 1976, p. 58.

[3] Erik W. Tawaststjerna 1992, p. 51.

[4] Illustrations in Gallen-Kallela-Sirén 2001, pp. 239 ff.

1895 the lines of development of the two artists crossed, and Sibelius overtook his precocious painter friend in the chronology of comparable ideas. There is only one exception thereafter: in 1898 Gallen-Kallela painted *Fratricide*, which was also the title of Sibelius' fifth folk-song arrangement in *Finnish Folksongs* of 1903. In his *Lemminkäinen Legends* Sibelius had not yet achieved the same level in his craft that the painter showed. Consequently, the final completion and publication of two of the *Legends* was delayed for some fifty years. The painter surpassed his personal high point as an artist in 1903 with the frescoes for the mausoleum of the Juselius family in Pori in western Finland, which only survive as a reconstruction and sketch: a mixture of Symbolist, Neo-Primitivist, Surrealist and Neoclassical tendencies.[1] Sibelius was also occupied with similarly heteronomous stylistic ideas, as is evident above all from his Third Symphony but also from the slightly later Fourth Symphony and the orchestral song *Luonnotar*. And above all, the peak of his artistic career was still in the future.

Although Sibelius and Gallen-Kallela were still vital 'Fennoman chiefs' (Paul) in the eyes of the public around 1910, their younger colleagues gradually began to see them as outdated, conservative in their values and regionally limited, which is paradoxical since their style had defined the national as a form of artistic expression in the first place. Thus their restriction to the national merely meant holding on to what was their own, not any form of limited regionalism. In the eyes of the younger generation, however, for Gallen-Kallela, there was no room in the contemporary context between Neo-Impressionism and Expressionism, and Sibelius' position in the perception of young composers of the time could be described in similar terms, even though he (unlike Gallen-Kallela) had not yet composed his finest and most progressive works. The last opportunity to portray the style of these two artists in the same context of the European avant-garde would seem to be Gallen-Kallela's Expressionist paintings from Africa (1909–11) and Sibelius' Expressionism as manifested in *Voces intimae*, op. 56; the Josephson Songs, op. 57 (both from 1909); the Fourth Symphony, op. 63 (1911); and the Three Sonatinas for Piano, op. 67 (1912). After that, Gallen-Kallela produced only isolated important works outside of the mainstream of conservative values, whereas Sibelius continued to publish major modern works until the mid-1920s. Although by around 1925 the *Kalevala* had long since ceased to be a progressive subject in Finnish art, Gallen-Kallela stopped producing his *Kalevala* works in 1931 only for reasons of health. In his final years, however, his Karelianism acquired Expressionist qualities. Other parallels in Sibelius' work can be found in the late works sketched in Rome and on the island of Capri, *Tapiola* and *Väinämöinen's Song* (both 1926). The latter was his final *Kalevala* setting, followed only by corrections to the *Lemminkäinen Legends*.

At the time of his revisions to the *Lemminkäinen Legends* around 1944, he noted in his diary this incomplete final thought: 'The possibilities of musical poetry …

[1] Cf. Gauguin's 'notes synthétiques' (1884–5, in Cogniat and Rewald 1962, pp. 2–3; see also Rookmaaker 1972).

were offered by the *Kalevala*.'[1] While Sibelius was composing *Tapiola*, Gallen-Kallela was working on *Kalevala* frescoes for the new National Museum of Finland in Helsinki. After they were completed in 1928, he planned to illustrate a deluxe edition: the *Suur-Kalevala* (Great Kalevala). This pioneering project was characterised by an archaic-modern symbolic language that emerged from the illustrations to the text and formed the text into an image by integrating it into the colourful visual depiction. Its bringing together of different styles and the many references and self-citations that run through the work, combined with quotations from petroglyphs and shamanistic symbolic figures, was not modern but rather post-modern, or at least ignored the usual boundaries of a medium and genre. His illustrations for the *Koru-Kalevala* (Decorative *Kalevala*) of 1922, on the other hand, were Expressionist and Modern. Whereas Gallen-Kallela found many opportunities to employ his Karelianism in the decorative arts, the help putting out melodies to the *Kalevala* around 1895 was the composer's contribution to the applied arts rather than folklorism.[2] One key figure in Sibelius' early study of the *Kalevala* was probably Arvid Genetz, who in 1895 was the chairman of the Suomalaisen Kirjallisuuden Seura (Finnish literary society). In the 1880s, he and his younger brother, the singer and composer Emil Genetz, had been Sibelius' secondary school teachers. Because Arvid had done research in Karelia with Borenius in the 1870s and was working a lot with Emil, they both may already have begun to influence Sibelius' Karelianism in Hämeenlinna.[3] Later Sibelius was familiar with the rich collections in the possession of Aksel August Borenius on which the edition was based. Borenius and he were well informed about the nature of Karelian song. It is difficult to say whether more evidence will emerge for the conjecture that as late as *c.*1920 Sibelius was even involved in a film project on the *Kalevala* (which had conditional financing).[4]

The Authentically Finnish

These young artists sought access to the elements of existence in their own homeland, where they believed they were most likely to find — helped along by their own childhood — genuine landscapes. This attitude, common at the time, was in keeping with Vladimir Stasov's simple premise: 'be what you are', or Horace's words (*Epistles* 1.10.24–5): 'Naturam expelles furca, tamen usque recurret, et mala perrumpet furtim fastidia victrix' (You may drive out Nature with a pitchfork, yet she will ever hurry back, and, ere you know it, will burst through your foolish contempt in triumph), since the artist can only master that which he truly knows and is inside him.[5] The

[1] Diary, n.d. (14 January 1944?): 'De möjligheter till musikalisk [*sic*] diktverk kring Kalevala erbjöd'.

[2] On Borenius' *Kalevala* work and a publication in 1895 with seventeen examples, selected by JS, see esp. Laitinen 1976, pp. 168 ff, with examples of the music from 1895.

[3] See ibid., p. 161.

[4] See chapter 3.3 in the present volume.

[5] See Waenerberg 2002, pp. 212 ff. Horace, *Epistles*, 1.10.24–5 (trans. H. Rushton Fairclough).

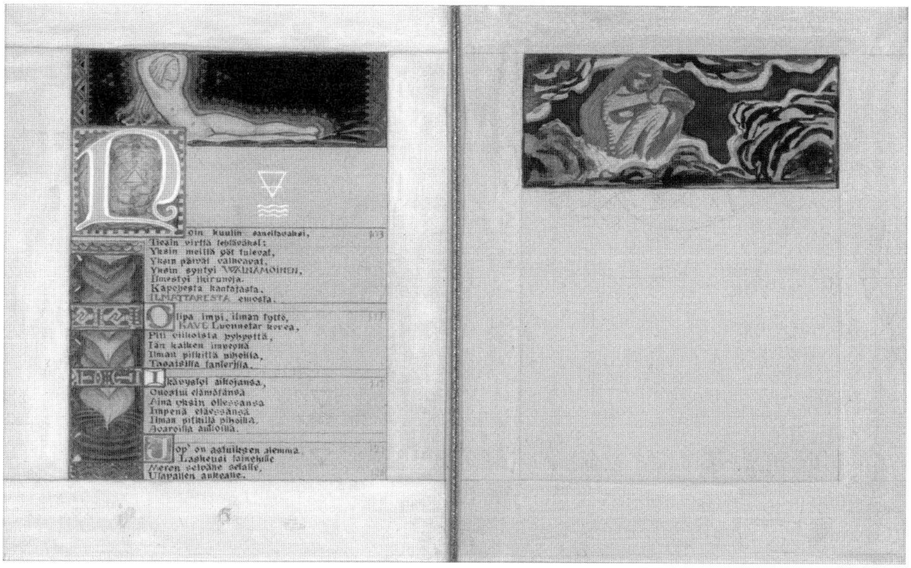

FIG. 16. Akseli Gallen-Kallela, *Great Kalevala* (1930). Detail of Gallen-Kallela's deluxe edition with a poem on the creation of the world, about Luonnotar and Ilmatar ('Noin kuulin saneltavaksi'). *Luonnotar* is one of Sibelius' finest compositions.

regional offered an opportunity to break with the universally valid — in the pejorative sense, in that it is suspected of carrying the seed of the indifferent — and to develop a significant individuality and naturalness. Most of them failed to recognise that their own surroundings were just part of the whole — along with East Africa or even the South Pacific, as Gauguin hoped in 1891 and Gallen-Kallela in 1909 (much as Debussy was inspired by Indonesia, Camille Saint-Saëns by Arabian Africa, Stravinsky by Japan and Mahler by China), and northern Karelia (Edelfelt, Gallen-Kallela, Järnefelt, Sibelius and others). They did not seek to rework trivial and romantic myths by using them in titles or creating marketable programmes but wanted to discover as a collective the core of the primal essence of humanity with the indirect aid of all previous attempts, including myths, throughout the world. With their works they were creating a new irrationalism.

The topical modern subject of the pure, the primitive and the original, which was one of the foundations of the *Kalevala* movement in the 1890s, was interpreted somewhat differently in the North than in Paris, Vienna, Munich and Berlin. The specific Finnish quality was not just the pristine Nordic sunlight or the north wind but also the way of dealing with subjects such as nature, history and mythology. It was not presented in a narrative way but in a symbolic, idea-based visual language removed from reality and the mythical world of fairy tales. Broadly European and ancient materials were interpreted in a regionally specific way and mixed with one's own reality or with Nordic myths. *The Dryad* and *The Oceanides* are two such works in Sibelius' oeuvre.

The 'myths of the beginning'[1] were immediately understood in the North, since the zero hour still seemed tangible. This is what makes such works as Sibelius' *Luonnotar* so convincing (more so than, for example, Darius Milhaud's *La création du monde*). The *Kalevala* symbolised the imagined primal magnificence that idealised a Finnish 'people' whose existence was lacking at the time. In Helsinki, a city of the modern era, people felt particularly close, geographically and historically, to the origins of the regional culture, but did anyone seriously consider the *Kalevala* anthology a historical epic? Hardly. Arcadian realms that exist only in daydreams and parlour games could be imagined not far from Helsinki, since Finland did not yet seem to have moved away from the harmony between human beings and nature, and the distance from nature that had to be overcome was not yet radical. For example, its melancholy was not so much that of a yearning for a lost paradise, as it was for the Symbolists of Central Europe.[2] Rather, it was about an awareness of the impossibility of actually founding a utopian world. Even when the subjects were not provided by the *Kalevala*, and even when nature (landscapes, plants, etc.) were only suggested in passing, one finds perspectives in Symbolist images that are now considered typically Finnish but were originally just aspects of the personal style of individual artists. Gallen-Kallela's *Ad Astra* (1907), for example, is placed in the ordinary genre of allegorical symbolism. But the facial features of the girl – for which a peasant girl modelled in the nude – are emphatically Finnish and derive from realistic aspects of the image of the region, and something of that can be said of Gallen-Kallela's *On the Road to Tuonela* (1888–94) as well. Eero Järnefelt, in turn, included a Nordic spruce tree in his *Per aspera ad astra* (1890/93), and Magnus Enckell's classicistic *Melancholy* (1895) includes birches and a fishing boat in a typical Baltic landscape.[3] Sibelius admired this painting at the Symbolist exhibition of 1895.[4] But it was thoroughly speculative of Tawaststjerna to associate the painting with Sibelius' *Malinconia* (1900), when he himself suspected the death of Sibelius' daughter Kirsti was the primary motivation for this pathos-laden piece for cello.[5] Enckell himself was of the view that his conception of Symbolism had a great deal in common with Sibelius' art. Encouraged by Sibelius' interest in the indeed masterly and Classicistic-Modernist *Melancholy*, he even planned a joint project in November 1895. Sibelius did not respond. The proposal had been conveyed by the prominent art theorist Yrjö Hirn.[6]

The genius of Gallen-Kallela, whose *Kalevala* paintings retain an unrivalled dominance in today's conception of Finnish Symbolism, made it possible that the visual arts, and not just literature – which cultivated the language of the new nation in the

[1] Jauss 1989, pp. 24 ff.

[2] Sarajas-Korte 1966, pp. 160 ff.

[3] Cf., Munch's *Melancholy* of 1892, which despite the similarity is less region-specific and representational, and more related to the psyche. Illustrated, for example, in Vaughan 2000, p. 85.

[4] Magnus Enckell to his mother, 27 October 1895; quoted in Erik W. Tawaststjerna 1976, p. 165.

[5] Ibid., p. 224.

[6] Erik W. Tawaststjerna 1992, p. 22.

battle against Runeberg's Swedish-language national poetry — helped establish a national identity in the radically visionary sense. The previous generation had already begun this: Robert W. Ekman with his *Ilmatar* (1860) and *Väinämöinen's Play* (1866). But Ekman's efforts relating to the *Kalevala* were not understood, nor did he succeed in establishing a national identity with his conventional *Kalevala* projects. He was better able to do so with his idealised yet realist rural scenes (such as *Kreeta Haapasalo Playing the Kantele in a Peasant Cottage* of 1868). During that same period, Ferdinand von Wright inspired nationalist emotions with his symbolic, idealised depictions of nature, such as *Fighting Capercaillies* (1886). The most important difference between Ekman and Gallen-Kallela or between Ekman and von Wright was the ability to deal with impulses convincingly; the relationship between Kajanus (*Kullervo's Death* of 1880 and *Aino* of 1885) and Sibelius (*Kullervo* of 1892) was much the same. What was later thought of as 'nationally motivated' resulted from the creative power of several individuals and was elevated to the 'national' only later. This perspective becomes more plausible if one considers how important foreign influence was on Gallen-Kallela's and Sibelius' development, and how easy it is to show parallels in technical detail between them and famous and less famous artists in France, Germany or even Belgium. Even Gallen-Kallela's decision to travel to East Africa in 1909 to search for ideas, colours and light could be traced back to his contacts since 1905 with groups such as Die Brücke and directly with Kandinsky and Munch.[1] It was, in any case, not an original reaction to Parisian Modernism.

Whereas Gallen-Kallela's *Symposium* is a regional interpretation of a mythological theme whose most famous treatment is probably Oscar Wilde's 'The Sphinx' (1894),[2] in *Waterfall in the Pine Forest* (1892–4) he makes synaesthesia his theme, with five gold stripes (staves) that suggest the primal sound of the waterfall but can also be seen as rays of light — a typical detail of the synaesthetic Symbolism of a Finnish forest scene. Originally, Gallen-Kallela wanted to depict a forest nymph — one should perhaps think of Sibelius' contemporaneous composition *The Wood Nymph* here — and a *runo* singer (the vocal tradition of *Kalevala*) with a traditional five-stringed *kantele*,[3] but he decided in favour of a regionalism that was less concrete. A similarly tangible example of a 'Sibelian' synthesis of Finnish and pan-European stylistic elements is Väinö Blomstedt's *Archer* (1894), in which classical Arcadia is blended with the story of Lemminkäinen. In addition to a Lemminkäinen who wants to kill the swan of Tuonela, the painter planned a white swan. Blomstedt found the revolt against the superhuman too powerful for his final composition, in which an archer is merely drawing his bow without a target.[4] This naturally gives the painting a semantic openness that can be interpreted patriotically as well. And hence a work adapted to the *Kalevala* became pan-European. All these elements, not least those from antiquity, play a role

[1] Sinisalo 2001b, p. 81.

[2] See Praz 1970, pp. 256–8.

[3] See *Kalevala*, Canto 40; Gallen-Kallela-Sirén 2001, pp. 170–71.

[4] Huusko 2001, p. 47.

in Sibelius' work as well. It is in that spirit that the Finnish cultural historian Rainer Knapas has claimed that Sibelius' work and influence incorporated simply all of the aesthetic, cultural and political trends from 1880 to 1930.[1]

Kandinsky's essay *Über das Geistige in der Kunst* (translated as *On the Spiritual in Art*) was not published until 1912, but the essential ideas had been considered by like-minded artists years before, when the book was being written: 'The year 1912 is a high point for European art. What was begun in many places and from different approaches has led to the same or similar solutions. The great lines of development of European art are beginning to converge.'[2] In Finland, Alfred W. Finch, a childhood friend of Paul Signac and Georges Seurat, rigorously implemented the art of colour. After just a few years in Finland, he produced 'genuinely Finnish' art. Ellen Thesleff, a painter who had been part of Kandinsky's most intimate circle in Munich, offered him competition. With regard to Sibelius, the relationship of plane and form and the emphasis on two-dimensionality were important technical aspects of Symbolist modernism in painting. The focus was not just on the line and colour, as in Kandinsky's *Composition v* of 1914, but also on the synthetic approach to a kind of Impressionism in pictures whose ideas are not obvious and by no means determined by mythology but nevertheless call for sensitive contemplation.

Helen Schjerfbeck's *Skuggan på muren* (The shadow on the wall; 1884) is a masterpiece of this sort: a composition of shades of grey and wan lines in which form becomes the bearer of meaning and in which the combination of details is synthetic, like many of the painter's oil paintings (*Familjesmycket* (Family jewel; 1915–6); *Flicka i sandgrop* (Girl in the sand pit; 1912), *Kostymbild I* (Dress painting; 1908) and Thesleff's paintings of Italy (e.g., *Firenze* of 1907 and *Ponte Vecchio* of 1907). Cubism, in which two-dimensionality is questioned and a new spatiality is created, was also familiar in Finland through the work of Alvar Cawén and Ilmari Aalto. In Cawén's *Asetelma* (Still life; 1916), the front cover of a book of sheet music by Sibelius is a cornerstone of the composition — instead of words such as 'Mozart' in Braque's *Violin: 'Mozart/Kubelick'* or 'Bach' in *Hommage à J. S. Bach* (both of 1912) or various sheets of music in the work of both Picasso and Braque. Sibelius himself spoke of 'cubism' in Schoenberg's work, surely inspired by the language of the arts pages of the day rather than by Schoenberg's genuinely Cubist approach to musical time. Sibelius' own Fourth Symphony has been considered 'cubist'.[3] Gallen-Kallela attacked the Cubism of Braque and Picasso for being degenerate and at best 'on the level of a circus variety show': Sibelius also criticised the 'circus' in modern music around 1910 — as well as 'Kapellmeisters with their circus showmanship' (i.e., professionally conducting composers like Felix Weingartner, but also Mahler and Strauss), in a letter to Axel Carpelan of 20 July 1909.[4] He was reacting to the protesting attitude of young Modernists,

[1] Knapas 2001, p. 38.

[2] See Osten 1962, p. 9.

[3] Erik W. Tawaststjerna 1986, p. 241, quoting Henry Krehbiel's review in the *New York Tribune*. William J. Henderson (*New York Sun*) even spoke of a 'Futurist'.

[4] JS to Johannes Öhquist, 25 October 1910, quoted in Sariola 2001, p. 197, citing a document in the

FIG. 17. Alvar Cawén, *Still Life* (1916).

for whom his Fourth Symphony – though without consequences for his later works, much like Gallen-Kallela's paintings from East Africa – was supposed to represent, according to an oft-cited letter from Sibelius to Rosa Newmarch, the ultimate solution with 'absolutely nothing of the circus about it'. Whereas Henri Matisse avoided the figurative and cultivated colour in its artful naturalness, Gallen-Kallela found his own opportunities for representation, especially in the context of nature, with objects outside the Western world.

Sibelius' brother-in-law Eero Järnefelt, self-confident and enlightened, pursued paths unlike those of most Modernists. Although in the 1880s and 1890s he created several important role models for nationalist Modernism,[1] he was unjustly overshadowed as a leading national artist by Gallen-Kallela's utter brilliance and modernity. Järnefelt's qualities are unmistakable: his portraits are flexible, while Gallen-Kallela's

archives of the Gallen-Kallela Museum; on JS, see JS to Axel Carpelan, 20 July 1909; quoted in Erik W. Tawaststjerna 1986, p. 129; Swedish original in Dahlström 2010, p. 246; JS to Rosa Newmarch, 2 May 1911, in Erik W. Tawaststjerna 1986, p. 172.

[1] A recent contribution on this context is Konttinen 2001; on Järnefelt's role in the Nuori Suomi (Young Finland) movement, see ibid., pp. 73–9; see also Lindqvist 2002.

usually took on features of the artist. His *plein-air* scenes can scarcely be misinterpreted as trivial echoes of realism. Indeed, they were part of a family tradition: his uncle was a famous painter from St Petersburg, Mikhail K. Clodt, Baron von Jürgensburg, who belonged to Ilya Repin's circle, and his father was a military cartographer; the family included several other very famous artists, such as the sculptor Peter Clodt von Jürgensburg. Järnefelt was, however, only marginally interested in modern, significant decorative arts or in the *Kalevala* and Symbolism.[1] In that respect, he is an outsider in the constellation of Böcklin, Munch and Gallen-Kallela. Presumably for that reason, Järnefelt's relationship to Sibelius has barely been studied at all, but he is nevertheless interesting, especially as music was important to him. Even as he lay dying, he thought of Schubert,[2] a composer whose significance for Sibelius, even apart from similarities in terms of the creative process, also deserves detailed analysis. Whereas the friendship between Sibelius and Gallen-Kallela had already been cooling since the mid-1890s, and was not without its tensions even earlier, Järnefelt became Sibelius' closest artist friend early on. In that same period, Sibelius began to be interested in the work of Edelfelt, the classical realist. He distanced himself from Gallen-Kallela, whom Edelfelt had criticised as 'dark' and demonic,[3] and his style was modified accordingly.

As Aino's brother, Eero had known Sibelius since 1889.[4] Their connection as family and later as neighbours was so close that professional interests seem secondary in the written documentation. They saw each other too frequently to have much need to correspond at length. In 1926 Sibelius jotted down a brief note that sums up his relationship to Järnefelt: 'Erik is a good neighbour and good artist.'[5] The sentence was written in the context of profound doubts about himself: 'But how are things with you, my splendid J. S.?' It revolved around the question whether he could finish *Tapiola*. The characterisation of Järnefelt as 'Europe's best teacher' is another sign of how different he and Sibelius were.[6]

Järnefelt's influence on *Kullervo* is documented, since on 14 March 1892, Sibelius wrote to his bride about Järnefelt's portrait of the industrialist Hugo Robert Standerskjöld (1892): 'Do you know, Aino, my angel and friend, that the scene on which I am working right now (the "läksi soitellen sotahan, ilotellen tappelohon") was already finished, but it did not have the effect it should have had, even though the idea was very naturally executed. For I saw the portrait at Erik's yesterday and realised that my scene lacked what his had: namely, wholeness. My scene was too rhapsodic, you know, my angel, just loose pieces.' In addition to 'wholeness', nature was important to

[1] On this subject, see Waenerberg 2002, pp. 217–18.

[2] Lindqvist 2002, p. 148, quoting Järnefelt's diary.

[3] Erik W. Tawaststjerna 1986, p. 36.

[4] Erik W. Tawaststjerna 1976, p. 430.

[5] Diary, 11 September 1926.

[6] See Lindqvist 2002, p. 127, which quotes a letter from Matti Warén to Järnefelt from 13 November 1933.

Järnefelt. Järnefelt himself argued provocatively that although art did not mean 'copying nature', at the same time 'you have to copy nature'. In fact, nature was supposed to achieve organic wholeness and 'economy of composition (putting together)'.[1]

Järnefelt's relationship to nature was ultimately shaped as well by the desire to achieve a fusion. As early as 1895 he explained his position in the face of the Italian spring in terms that have been interpreted as pantheism and in the intellectual tradition of Philipp Otto Runge, but which in fact make elemental harmony seem problematic: 'But faced with that one feels detached from the earth and the body; one wants to lack all will and disappear with the sun.'[2] Sibelius and Järnefelt also shared an emphasis on verity – in Järnefelt's case under the direct influence of Vissarion Belinsky and the Russian school of 'naturalness'.[3] The similarity of these ideas with those of Sibelius is astonishing, and it can perhaps be explained as the conceptual influence of the brilliant thinker Järnefelt on the intuitive and as a rule receptive composer.

Tawaststjerna associates only one composition with Järnefelt: the Allegretto moderato movement of the Sixth Symphony. This subtle work has also been compared to Mozart and Palestrina.[4] The striking thing about the movement is its simplicity. It brings 'Järnefelt's early Finnish landscapes to mind. Nature rests, cow smoke [a fire to repel mosquitoes while milking] is rising; the weather vane is sleeping.'[5] The painting Tawaststjerna associates with the Sixth Symphony is *Lehmisavu* (Cows in smoke) of 1891.[6] More appropriate, perhaps, would be a scene without cows, such as the one with a blond youth in central Finland, *Heinäkuun päivä* (A July day) of 1891.[7] The pastoral sounds in the music find their analogy there, but the relationship cannot be proven biographically or analytically. That makes Sibelius' letter to Aino from Vienna on 15 April 1891 all the more remarkable; it also contains important remarks about Järnefelt and dates the beginning of his autonomy. Sibelius reflected at length about his relationship to Pietro Mascagni's *Cavalleria rusticana*. The opera was a key work in Sibelius' awakening to nationalism and shaped his interest in regional aspects of Modernism. The letter is one of the longest coherent analyses of a work of art he wrote:

> *Cavalleria rusticana* is also very powerfully national, and many passages can only be understood by a Sicilian. As you know, the naive has an important function in their music. We Northerners tend more to the 'contemplative'. But when we manage to get free of our philosophising, we too can produce talents. I am certain that the time is not far distant when people will realise what is hidden in our old Finnish folksongs. They will see that the ancient Finns who created the *Kalevala* were on a high level musically. I am working on a new

1 Konttinen 2002, p. 171, quoting Järnefelt's diary for shortly after 1910.

2 Waenerberg 2002, pp. 203–4, quoting Järnefelt's diary for 12 April 1895.

3 Ibid., pp. 209–10.

4 See Erik W. Tawaststjerna 1997b, p. 281.

5 Erik W. Tawaststjerna 1997a, p. 152.

6 Illustrated in Konttinen 2001, p. 187, and Lindqvist 2002, p. 83 (in colour).

7 See Lindqvist 2002, p. 84 (a slightly different version in Konttinen 2001, p. 201).

symphony, which is thoroughly Finnish in spirit. The authentically Finnish has turned into flesh and blood in me. I am the best for that sort of thing. Moreover, the Finnish has become sacred to me. It was before as well. I am convinced that a Finnish man should feel and think Finnish.

As to Eero and Edelfelt, he pointed out: 'What I don't like about Edelfelt is that he is not very Finnish, at least in terms of subject matter. By what power should Erik [Eero] have the greatest success from our painters if not by founding everything on the principle of nationalism?' In 1891, Järnefelt had captured in a gouache the atmosphere that caused many artists of all nationalities abroad to be intensely occupied with their own homeland. He sketched fellow painter Pekka Halonen in an apartment in Paris playing a *kantele* on his knees, deeply engrossed by the imagined world of sounds from home.[1]

In the above-cited letter of 1891, Sibelius wrote of his own situation and the Finnish character in a way that may seem alien today. As always, however, he expressed himself 'with an eye to the recipient' and influenced by the current discussion. Possibly he was taking into account that Aino's mother might be reading it as well, since letters prior to marriage were not supposed to be too intimate – the route for secret letters to Aino passed via her brothers in a separate envelope. In another letter, Sibelius courted her parents more adroitly: 'Believe me, the time will come when Erik [Eero] will be the greatest painter of our country and Armas the greatest musician.'[2] Sibelius analysed the soul of the Järnefelts and determined that it would not 'emancipate' itself too soon. It is reasonable to assume that this was concealed criticism.

In his monumental painting from the *Kullervo* era that was so fundamental for Sibelius, *Raatajat rahanalaiset* or *Kaski* of 1893 (Under the yoke, or Burning the brushwood), which was at the same time a profound insight into the Finnish forests, which even in *Tapiola* (1926) are still the object of symbolic interpretation, Järnefelt illustrated, so the naturalist semantics tells us, landless peasants working to clear a stony forest. As a close-up, the large painting also offers insight into details of the large Koli panorama of 1899, which is of some relevance to the Fourth Symphony. All in all, the painting is as far as one can imagine from the 'symposiums' of 1894. In the middle stands a girl, who in comparison to the adults seems unreal and extra-territorial. Realist, Naturalist and Symbolist aspects supplement one another in this painting. Järnefelt was a follower of Jules Bastien-Lepage and Ilya Repin, which supports the Realist-Naturalist interpretation. He believed in the 'true', which an artist has 'experienced and understood' himself.[3] This intention shapes his portraits in particular;

[1] Illustrated in Lindqvist 2002, pp. 144–5; see also Talas 2000, pp. 84ff.: Saimi Järnefelt to Aino, 7 February 1891, in which Halonen is described playing the *kantele* and the winter drink on the table in the painting is identified as 'toti' (grog).

[2] JS to Aino, 24 February 1892, from Vienna.

[3] Ludwig Wennewirta, *Eero Järnefelt* (1950), quoted in Levanto 1987, p. 91. See also Konttinen 2001, pp. 185ff.

his portrait of Karelian folk-singer Larin Paraske was highly relevant to Sibelius.[1] Järnefelt's experiences with the singer, who lived with him, were published in 1921:

> I asked myself, very concerned, whether I would get by asking everything I wanted to see and hear from this child of nature (she was illiterate). But from the first moment I noticed that she regarded her task as completely natural. I asked her to sing a lament as if she were actually standing by a grave. She bent over the back of a chair and began to sing slowly this strange, wistful melody in which a long-since-forgotten past shines through in mysterious, foggy images. I drew and painted and listened, enraptured, to her song. Gradually her eyes grew damp and soon tears were streaming.[2]

Sibelius must have had a similar encounter in the autumn of 1891.[3] His analysis of her personality enabled Järnefelt not only to portray Paraske – which he did more than once – but to report about her and her art. It was not only information about the emotional background of a *runo* singer but also the capturing of idealistic naturalism that was inspiring for Sibelius at a time when he had not yet finished *Kullervo*.[4] *Kaski* and *Kullervo* thus represented a strong parallel between Järnefelt and Sibelius, especially since *Kaski* contains, despite its realism, a striking reference to the *Kalevala*: 'piika pikkarainen' (the little maid; cf. *Kalevala*, Canto 50). Moreover, a Symbolist worldview becomes possible: an interpretation derived from Tolstoy would concentrate on the unreal glow of her eyes and on the light surrounding her head. The girl is 'holy'. This interpretation was inspired by the Tolstoy adherent and writer Arvid Järnefelt. A Symbolist reading that goes beyond that is also possible: the work of clearing the forest is an allegory of life and death, whereas the maiden ('piika pikkarainen') is independent of the reality that surrounds her and, like a fairy angel, bears the suffering of the peasants on her shoulders. As a beautiful girl, she is also a symbol of the future, an opportunity for the weaker – Järnefelt's contribution to the question of woman in *Symposium*. Eros and Thanatos stand side by side in the painting.[5] The parallels to Sibelius lie in the mixture of Realism, Symbolism and Impressionism with a strong inclination to Classicism and the elemental. Although Järnefelt did not accept the Symbolist worldview either, he did attempt to come to terms with the typical stylistic elements and aesthetic ideas of the Symbolists as important modern innovations.

The small painting *Ahvenruoho* or *Vesileinikki* (an aquatic plant of the North, pond

[1] Née Paraskeva Nikitina (1833–1901), a *runo* singer from Sakkola in Ingermanland or Inkerinmaa in south-east Karelia, whom Adolf Neovius discovered for the world of academia in 1887.

[2] Järnefelt, 'Muistelmia Larin Paraskesta', in *Kalevalaseuran vuosikirja*, no. 1 (1921), pp. 94–9; quoted in Zeitler 1990, p. 115.

[3] JS to Aino, 29 October 1891, and 1 November 1891. It is remarkable how knowledgeably JS writes about Paraske's art before the planned meeting.

[4] On this interpretation of *Kullervo*, see chapter 3.2 in the present volume.

[5] On the expressive forms of Symbolism, such as allegory, see Hofstätter [1965] 1978, pp. 30 ff.

water-crowfoot; 1895) is a special case and is probably best categorised in the *ad astra* genre. The symbolism in Järnefelt's *Ahvenruoho* is biological. The artist discovered the symbolism in nature by contemplating and experiencing his milieu (his artistic programme was to 'experience and understand'). It remains within the framework of the realist tradition and runs the risk that its Modernist potential will not be recognised. There is a clear attempt to focus on nature in detail and discover its secrets. The plant is a metaphor for the human being. It strives to move out of the deep water towards the light and begins to flower on the surface, only to learn that it will not go further but only die. The basic elements (water, stone, light) and the two basic categories of Symbolism — life and death — are contained here. If the plants are replaced by a person, the painting can be compared to Alphonse Osbert's *Le Calme de l'eau* (1895) or *Rêverie* (1906), and Armand Point's *Baigneuse* (1900). The calm water is a flowing Arcadia, the magnificence of summer symbolised by the flowers of the warmest days.

The panorama of the autumnal landscape of Pielisjärvi and Koli (1899) is Symbolist,[1] if one agrees with Hofstätter and Carl Gustav Carus that human emotion can predominate in landscape painting, despite the lack of human forms, and that the landscape can become 'not nature but symbol' — especially since the Koli Mountains stand opposite Russian forests on the other side of Lake Pielisjärvi. The symbolic function of landscape is possible, according to Hofstätter, even without the addition of a mythical figure linking the symbolic meaning to an implied story (as in Böcklin's *Isle of the Dead*) and without a powerful scene in the style of *Kaski*, with a girl who is by nature holy (as a snapshot or a long chain of events). Landscape is not literary and mythological but universally human: 'Landscape painting creates symbols for human loneliness, for our inferiority to elemental forces, and for the mysterious omnipotence of God, which it tries to symbolise in infinite space and in the effects of cosmic forces.'[2] Järnefelt himself wrote: 'With landscape, one can depict so many human ideas and moods, seriousness, joy, despair, hate.'[3] Limitless space is the 'ur-symbol of the Faustian soul in contrast to the Apollonian symbol of the sensory presence of the individual body'.[4] Examples of limitless space include the *Pielisjärvi* panorama of the scenery of the walks in the forest he took with Sibelius when he was working on the Fourth Symphony or the background of *Kaski* — the landscape of Kullervo and his sister — and finally the deep water in *Ahvenruoho*. In the context of Symbolism, the 'Faustian' interpretation of *Pielisjärvi* is also plausible.[5] The problem of perception is also typical of music, which inherently lacks the clear meaning of the symbolic figure. It is found only to some extent in singing accompanied by orchestra, for example, in Sibelius' *Luonnotar* or in *Autrefois: Scène pastorale*. That piece exists either with programmatic vocalisation for two sopranos, clarinets with orchestra or for piano

[1] See more recently Waenerberg 2004b, and Lukkarinen 2004.

[2] Hofstätter [1965] 1978, p. 162.

[3] Järnefelt, quoted in Konttinen 2001, p. 219.

[4] Hofstätter [1965] 1978, p. 162.

[5] See also Waenerberg 2002, pp. 214 ff.

FIG. 18. Eero Järnefelt, *Evening Fog near Koli* (1928). Järnefelt produced many illustrations of the landscape near Koli and Lake Pielisjärvi. *Autumn Landscape near Pielisjärvi* (1899, 61 × 197 cm) is perhaps the best known example; it served as an illustration for festive paper for telegrams and contributed to the sense that landscape was a means of establishing national identity. In the company of Juhani Aho, Järnefelt climbed Koli Mountain for the first time in 1892. He knew the region from his childhood in Kuopio. He climbed Koli with his brother-in-law Jean Sibelius in 1909, during the formative phase of developing material for the Fourth Symphony.

(1919–21) or as a song with text, Hjalmar Procopé's 'Ej av jaktens lekar' (Not loud of hunt). The effort to dispense with obvious symbolism and exhaust the elemental symbolic power of nature was typical of the style of the period.

'Jugendstil', by contrast, existed only from 1896 onwards. The term is at best appropriate for the applied arts (based on Arts and Crafts and Art Nouveau, as a reaction to the earlier industrial aesthetic) and hence should preferably not be applied to Järnefelt and Sibelius. Jugendstil may have influenced techniques where the label would otherwise be inappropriate. Very significant for the music of this era – and that includes, for example, Strauss and Mahler, – is Jugendstil's concept of the line, since 'it is not the course of a line as such that is essential but rather the motivation that determines it'. In composition, the technical is relevant as a motivation for quasi-absolute music.[1] The influence of Jugendstil on the modern concept of the line in music can easily be exaggerated, however, causing the concept of the line in Munch, Bergson and van de Velde to be overlooked.[2]

1 See Pevsner 1991, pp. 85 ff., where he speaks of a 'new ornamental style' in painting.

2 See Asendorf 2003, pp. 86 ff.

If only I could realise my ideas in music now.[1]

2.3 First Appraisal: 'L'homme naturel' versus 'L'homme civil'

'You Magnificent Jean'

Sibelius' personality and way of creating art fitted the pattern of his time, but in their details they are unique. Processes and mental states characteristic of his era seem genuine in him but often somewhat naive as well. Certain aspects of late modern individuality can be demonstrated clearly using him as an example. Several of the characteristics of his day were fashions, provoked in no small measure by modish philosophy and art (Nietzsche, Böcklin *et al.*). In Sibelius' case, however, it would be wrong to presume fashions were the motive of his actions. We find the split identity of the time, the effort to understand nature, the critique of linguistic systems, the primacy of the imagination, the synthaesthesia and the anti-materialism that constituted the '*Zeitgeist*' both in documents of his life and in his compositions precisely where they do not seem learned. The harmony of contemporary and intimate features could even be coincidence. The correlation has consequences for the history of his reception, however. Anyone who describes Sibelius as an artist of nature of the late nineteenth century, for example, is not offering an original picture, since many artists of the era strove for *Naturzusammenhang* (identity with nature).[2] But anyone who demonstrates that qualities of this sort exist in Sibelius' letters, diaries and compositions without reference to such popular role models as Schopenhauer, Wagner and Nietzsche gets closer to the essence of his art.

In his diary, Sibelius addressed himself (often in quotation marks) in the second or third person: 'you ego', 'you Jean Sibelius' or 'you magnificent Jean'. In a letter to Carpelan he wrote analytically: 'my inner human being has changed.'[3] In addition to his intimate letters and the diary — his 'jardin secret' — this penchant is also reflected in his adoption of a foreign first name at the age of twenty: 'Jean is my music name.'[4] It would be an exaggeration to suspect that this was a psychological defect rather than a division of the ego typical of the time. Yet the clinical psychologist Abram Chipman sees Sibelius as 'one of music's most frustrating instances of "early burnout"', who was searching for a substitute for his lost father, which supposedly also explained his late interest in the forest god Tapio (cf. *Tapiola*). That Sibelius had only daughters was, in Chipman's view, tragic.[5] Yozan Dirk Mosig was on the same track, citing Edvard F. Eddinger's *Ego and Archetype* in a way that fits Sibelius: 'A kind of hole is left in

[1] JS to Aino, 2 September 1894.

[2] See Adorno 1991, p. 137.

[3] JS to Axel Carpelan, 3 June 1904, in Dahlström 2010, p. 182. See also JS to Georg Boldemann, 18 May 1915. The expressions quoted here are common in the diary after 21 June 1910.

[4] JS to Pehr Sibelius, 30 March 1886, in Goss 1997, p. 85.

[5] Chipman 2000, pp. 429–54, esp. pp. 429 and 443 ff.

FIG. 19. Hämeenlinna (Magnus von Wright's lithograph, c.1850). This picture shows the city fifteen years before Sibelius was born. In the background is the fortress, surrounded by lakes. Very early remains of permanent settlements have been found in this region.

the psyche through which emerge the powerful archetypal contents of the collective unconscious. […] If, however, the Ego can survive this danger, the hole in the psyche becomes a window providing insight into the depths of being.'[1] Such things do not, however, find expression in Sibelius' diaries, letters and anecdotes. Although Chipman diagnosed his depression as clinically 'low-level', one reason for his frustrations with the Eighth Symphony was allegedly that *Tapiola* was matchless as cathartic release: 'After playing the sounds of nymphs gamboling and the most fearsome storm in music, the fatherless boy comes to rest, with the greatest of finality and resignation, in the arms of the all-powerful spirit of eternal nature.' He also believed it was important that Sibelius, unlike Janáček, had no revitalising 'love objects' after 1894. Thus in the hands of psychologists Sibelius' model behaviour as a husband is almost turned into a reproach against the artist.

After the early death of his father in 1868 – there were devastating famines and epidemics in Finland that year[2] – Sibelius spent his childhood under the watchful eye of his grandmother. His father, Christian Gustaf Sibelius, had been a physician, but he succumbed to the consequences of his irresponsible lifestyle, including alcohol, not just extreme overwork. The son's character, as he himself admitted, resembled that of his father in many respects. On 10 February 1891 he wrote to his confidante

[1] Mosig 2003 and Edinger 1973, p. 132.
[2] See Klinge 1997, pp. 237 ff.

Aino Järnefelt from Vienna: 'I firmly believe that one always inherits one's worst characteristics from one's father. Papa drank and played cards, as you probably know. That is why we Sibeliuses, who were once so rich, are now so poor.' Since Sibelius can only have known that because someone (most likely his grandmother) had told him – probably to warn him about his father's mistakes – it is astonishing how painfully present and important his father was to him as a (negative) role model. But his daily life as a child did not consist entirely of atonement. In the home of Katarina Juliana Borg, the provost's widow and Sibelius' maternal grandmother, a lot of time was spent reading and playing music. The idyll of Hämeenlinna corresponded probably quite precisely to the clichéd notion of Protestant, bourgeois salon life in a provincial small town anywhere in the Western world. Daily life was dominated by the domestic activities of widows of two generations and by two unmarried, sensible aunts (Julia and Thekla Borg). Their financial circumstances were more or less in keeping with their class but not especially lavish.

Early childhood was followed by the second, equally important phase of conquering the world and becoming an individual in Hämeenlinna's surroundings, which the schoolboy Sibelius explored on his own or with like-minded friends. The third phase of socialisation followed – in part in parallel with the second – at a new Finnish-language model high school, with schoolmates who were often from better-off homes and from families who served the Grand Duchy or the Russian military in high positions, and hence were multinational and idealistic about education. The imperial army made an essential contribution in the heterogeneous, almost 'multicultural' life of Hämeenlinna. One element that linked these various segments was classical music, overwhelmingly of German, Italian or French provenance. Already in Hämeenlinna, Sibelius established his first friendships based entirely on musical interests, above all with August F. Ringvall and Anna Tigerstedt.

Life as a student in Helsinki, which was enriched by encounters with renowned foreign artists, slowed the formation of a sharply defined cultural and personal integrity – to a degree that was unusual for that generation, when seen from a Western European perspective – that could otherwise easily have been the precondition for a rigid regionalism, nationalism and chauvinism. It increased the distance from his childhood in both a geographical and emotional separation. Sibelius hardly ever returned to Hämeenlinna after he left for Helsinki. In Vienna, at the age of twenty-six, the skeleton of his personality, whose cultural topography was already becoming extremely far-ranging, was supplemented by the fascination he had for Catholic rites, for the culture of a southern European imperial capital and for Hispanic influences in the old Habsburg Empire. One year earlier, in 1889, he got to know Berlin at a time when the young capital of the German Reich had just become an industrial metropolis with a leading international position and a prolific, multicultural (by no means only West-European) population. As difficult as it is to imagine today, Helsinki, too, when Sibelius first went there around 1886, was still in a kind of limbo between a classically embellished fishing village, looking like a stage set amid rocky cliffs and islands with two midsized cathedrals and an island fortress; a regional centre of the social and cultural reforms of Emperor Alexander III Alexandrovich; a stage for the first phase of national idealism; and a cultural scene that could not conceal its provincialism. Seen from a distance, it was *de facto* a satellite town of St Petersburg, but, at times at least, especially in summer, it had the cosmopolitan pulse of a small Paris. A popular trade and touristic route to the Russian capital passed through Helsinki's harbour.

The intensity with which Sibelius experienced the changes of the late nineteenth century in Helsinki, Berlin and Vienna was characteristic of him. He was not in a position to question the new and 'other' in terms of his own region, language, family or ethnicity. He had to remain open to external influences instead of defending a strong sense of self. This openness did not make his path easier. Even in music, he lacked clear orientation and role models. Drifting without a rudder has its advantages, though: his imagination moved freely without conventional constraints. His musical and cultural impressions had already been mixed in Hämeenlinna. While the popular areas of Viennese Classicism (including Schubert) and Romanticism from Charles Auguste de Bériot to Henryk Wieniawski formed the primary repertoire in his family home,[1] as a student he realised that very different things already determined the grammar and vocabulary of contemporary musical life in Central and Western Europe – in particular a very different kind of Classicism, one based on Bach and Beethoven. He responded to this experience with the radicalness typical of him. Later he protected his subjectivity, having learned to get by without strong role models, from all-too-powerful impressions from Wagner, Swedenborg and other fashionable ideologues.

The lack of any restrictive corset that was typical of Sibelius was not unusual in *fin-de-siècle* modernity as such. The subsequent polarisation, the search for more solid alternatives that distinguished the later Sibelius as well and the almost limitless courage to carry them through was a reaction to the relativity, freedom and diversity of expression around 1900. Decentring, the loss of the 'aura of the autonomous self', the existence of the 'subject as multiplicity' and the gradual expansion and redefinition of the limits of the subject in general have constituted the challenge of individuation not just since Darwin and Freud but since the Renaissance in the fifteenth century.[2] The Renaissance philosopher Michel de Montaigne already understood a person's individuality as a whole composed of segments and moments.[3] Long before late nineteenth-century Secessionism, the individual had been revealed as a 'dividual'.[4] The poetic subject of the modern era in the broadest sense (the Modern Age) is fundamentally disparate, divisible not only into the perceiving and feeling self but also into facets that change their composition from hour to hour. In its heyday around

[1] See detailed discussion in chapter 3.1 of the present volume.

[2] Jauss 1989, pp. 248–9.

[3] Michel de Montaigne, 'Of the Inconsistency of Our Actions', in Montaigne 1973, p. 243; cf. Bürger 2000, p. 39.

[4] Jauss 1989, p. 24.

1900, this took on dramatic features — especially for all those who, like Sibelius, had a natural inclination to nonconformity. Western culture's horizon of self-reflection expanded to include new approaches to dealing with the question of the relationship of the subject to nature and to the essence of nature itself, as landscape or as essence of every single existence. Political, scientific, religious and technical perspectives likewise opened up and influenced specific segments of the 'dividual' in a more or less comprehensive way.

Sibelius responded to the challenges of the day musically. Only sparse first attempts to write down his ideas can be found in his letters, diaries and the quite chaotic (and naive) draft for his sample academic presentation of 1896.[1] However, it is not even clear from a look at his draft lecture that Sibelius was aware that his anti-rationalist action was in fact typical of his period in the history of ideas and not genuinely his own invention. It is certain that his childhood, his later familial environment and his artistic development all made him an artist typical of the era, when the relationship of civilisation and nature and its delicate nuances became an issue.

Given the uncertainty about the ideological and philosophical background of his art — and in light of the suspicion that close parallels between the contemporary history of ideas and of science could be purely coincidental — the question of musical 'communication of truth content' is relevant far beyond 'technical coherence'.[2] Adorno asked whether it might not be the case that 'under particular circumstances the proper, adequate depiction in art of a mental state, however inherently dubious, ranks higher than if one were to attempt to depict the supposedly higher mental state in an era that no longer permits it to be depicted'.[3] The question deserves our attention here, since Sibelius (and not just Wagner and Mahler) may indeed have inspired the author to these lines. If Sibelius' artistic honesty and genuineness have impressed us, not only should we like his compositions, but it also becomes plausible that 'identity with nature' can be restored by means of art.[4]

Sibelius was, however, not only someone who could establish contact with nature and who saw through the trap of the supposedly unspoilt nature of the mythological but was also an elegant 'homme civil', who moved about big cities like a 'fish in water'.[5] His oeuvre is also self-contradictory if viewed superficially: he was a symphonist with an architectonic intuition (consequently by no means a Finnish Grieg), but he also wrote a great deal of programme music, tremendous incidental music and subtly staged historical tableaux. The letters and notes he wrote with an eye to their recipient — for example, explicitly in the 'Strindbergian style' in the case of Adolf Paul[6] — and

1 See, for example, Oramo 1983.
2 Adorno 1984a, p. 579.
3 Ibid., p. 578.
4 Adorno 1991, p. 137.
5 JS to Eero Järnefelt, 1 December 1900, from Berlin.
6 See Jussi Snellman's draft letter, discussed in chapter 1.3 of the present volume.

his visual, visionary predisposition, embedded in the late phase of an era of monumental theories and brilliantly verbalised systems to explain the world, are the building blocks of a disparate picture that must be revealed bit by bit.

Conquering the Unspoilt

Sibelius' linguistic and cultural formation can be traced back to the time he spent in Hämeenlinna. This multifaceted context demands the use of powerful conceptual tools if it is to be properly deconstructed and the trivial transcended. Whereas philosophers such as Jean-François Lyotard, Manfred Frank and others emphasise the role of language in human development, according to Jacques Lacan the subject is constituted by the fixation on his own mirror image, long before linguistic competency is obtained. For Lacan, the 'ego' is formed gradually by a separation of other people and the imaginary 'I'.[1] His concept of the subject, dominated by 'prelinguistic' and emotional aspects, and tending already to split identity in early childhood, helps explain Sibelius' playful approach to musical *topoi* and styles and the fact that in his letters and diaries he changed not only his style but also his language, and could switch between Swedish, Finnish, German, French and Latin within a few sentences. No verbal language helped him find himself; no verbal language could be used by him in a unique style. Music alone was intended for the ineffable.

According to René Descartes, the subject finds himself not through an all-embracing engagement with the world and other people but through the cognitive, which makes completely developed language possible.[2] 'Progress' means the separation of the human from nature by virtue of the articulated thought. 'Cogito, ergo sum', and not, paraphrasing Diogenes Laertius, 'naturalia non sunt turpia' (natural things are not vile) is the guiding principle of the Cartesian modern age. Artists such as Sibelius who for many seem to represent an unusually high degree of organic connection between mind and nature appear naive and regressive in this light. The Cartesian model does not permit any friendly encounter as equals between human being and nature. But that is precisely the relationship that is evident in anecdotes about Sibelius' contemplations of nature and in some of his most authentic statements; it conditions the conflict between his essence as an artist and the still dominant Cartesian tradition of the modern age. In Descartes, nature became the 'ob-ject', from the Latin for 'thrown in the way', of 'conscious manipulation'. This went hand in hand with the conquering of nature by the human subject – Adam becomes God's gardener in Genesis 2.15 – and a sharp distinction between inwardness and the outside world.

In Sibelius' work, an anti-Cartesian ideal evolved on a foundation expressed more recently by Lacan. Sibelius realised it within the framework of his own means of expression. Sound was for Sibelius what the carefully considered word was for Henri

[1] Lacan [1953] 1966, pp. 237 ff.

[2] On this subject, see Jauss 1989; Bürger 2000; and Taylor 1989.

Bergson. Both Sibelius and Bergson questioned the existence of a solid link between these elemental building blocks and any rational system. The degree to which the ideal is achieved, the 'appropriateness of means to ends', must of course be analysed critically even in the case of Sibelius. If 'thinking' is understood a little more broadly, the formula 'cogito, ergo sum' leads not only to the hubris of the analytical word and rational reasoning as the characteristically human but also away from the gradual verbalisation of thinking into the experience of the world through the cognitive imagination, calling into question the clear boundaries of the rational. The latter path, which can certainly be associated with Sibelius as well, is not an easy solution to stabilising the artistic ego but rather merely forces creative development of the open 'experiential subject' à la Montaigne.[1] Essential conflict is inevitable.

The world-weariness that is one of the clichés about Sibelius as an artist and causes the conflict was, according to Blaise Pascal in the seventeenth century, not a problem of the age — and certainly not a quality of a specifically Nordic melancholy[2] — but the tragic foundation of all civilisations. The alternative track of the imagination and creative cognition — a parallel path of Cartesian Modernism — was supposed to bypass this crisis.[3] The instability of the creative[4] was the reason for the melancholy of great artists of the late modern era, as it certainly was for Sibelius. One solution was offered by Jean-Jacques Rousseau's polyvalence of the subject: the utopian vision of the ideal human being, who somehow manages in a corrupt world to be an unconflicted and not yet alienated 'homme naturel' — the genuine man of nature, not the modern man of society ('homme l'homme' or 'homme civil').[5] This recalls the description of Sibelius as a Dionysian artist of nature, like Silén in Adolf Paul's novel,[6] but simultaneously lends him a less disreputable image in the late Victorian context. The enlivening effect of nature of which Rousseau dreamed and Nietzsche developed in his 'book on the Greeks',[7] and subjective harmony with oneself are supposed to protect the man of nature from his environment.

For Sibelius, these problems took concrete form even in established composition courses, dominated by 'professors' and 'their methods'. But he did not find a simple solution either, since the dialogue with nature, the experience of nature in one's self and not outside, is only possible for the true 'man of nature'. Many shared this goal with him. What was for Rousseau a thought experiment in the heyday of the

[1] Bürger 2000, p. 48.

[2] 'Man's unhappiness arises from one thing alone: that he cannot remain quietly in his room.' Pascal 2005, p. 38; cf. Bürger 2000, p. 51.

[3] 'Do not be surprised if right now it does not reason well: a fly is buzzing in its ears.' Pascal 2005 p. 17; cf. Bürger 2000, p. 52.

[4] Bürger spoke of Pascal's 'anxious self' in contrast to Descartes's 'thinking self'; see Bürger 2000, p. 68.

[5] Rousseau 1995; cf. Bürger 2000, pp. 104 ff.

[6] Paul 1891.

[7] Nietzsche 1967, pp. 37 ff.

FIG. 20. Sketch with drawing by Sibelius (autograph, *c.*1890–91), documenting narcissistic self-reflection — surrounded by melodic sketches. His stay in Vienna in 1890–91 triggered a crisis of identity for Sibelius that led to *Scène de ballet* and *Kullervo*.

mid-eighteenth century shaped the attitude of many artists around 1900 who (like many today) hoped to find in 'nature', in this sense something critical of civilisation, a solution to the recent misery of urbanisation, industrialisation and incipient globalisation. This attitude was, however, rarely as solidly anchored in a personality already manifested in childhood as it was in Sibelius' case. Fair enough, hardly any other composer was so consistently perceived, for decades, as a Rousseauian 'man of nature', although this foundation of his reception was never made explicit.

The general direction of his reception as a Rousseauian artist does not call for correction, only its details. A cautious agreement requires that we ask to what extent Sibelius represented an isolated case or eccentric (perhaps one who was misunderstood). The German literary scholar Hans Robert Jauss observed that many artists of the *fin de siècle* compared themselves to the 'homme naturel' who was capable of 'immediate experience of nature' and needed no language for this. Paul Gauguin, Akseli Gallen-Kallela, Sibelius and the rural 'regional artists' (*Heimatkünstler*, 'homeland artists', as they proudly called themselves in Germany) all sought, each in his own way and under different conditions, to come into contact with unspoilt landscapes, domestic or exotic. All of them were probably aware of the conflict between the utopian ideal of the 'homme naturel' and the dissolute state as 'homme l'homme', the fragmented self of civil society and the dominance of rational language, whose universality was cast in doubt with regard to an immediacy that had been lost for ever. The experiments of Knut Hamsun and others with irrational narrative techniques, like Sibelius' use of sound and structure, were desperate rescue attempts. Jauss suspected that their origin lay in metaphors 'that combine with the voice of nature insofar as they are able to evoke the lost immediacy' and 'whose tone cannot yet be separated from music'.[1] Rousseau was already of the view that the natural and organic is present in all of us as an option, but that it is not possible to stabilise the otherness of the 'homme naturel'. This insight could not, however, prevent several artists attempting it in art.

The 'homme naturel' seems unusually real in Sibelius' case. It does not seem like a fashionable attitude but rather like the primal conflict between the individual and the surrounding civilisation. Nevertheless, it is by no means imperative to extol his particular type of artist, since it is also possible that his contemporaries who grew up in big cities – and thus learned Rousseau's principles only on paper or in landscape parks, saw wild, sublime nature only in the work of the painter Caspar David Friedrich and thus had a correspondingly abstract and literary view of nature – would in fact present a more coherent profile as artists and personalities. For however honest his desire for its ecstatic fulfilment may have been, the Rousseauian utopia remained a utopia for him as well. Sibelius did not grow up as a pure 'homme naturel' either, although his experiences of nature as a young child might have been more extensive and essential than those of a child of the city. The difference between him and, say, Richard Strauss was perhaps great in that respect but still only one of degree. He was

[1] Jauss 1989, 28 ff. On these same themes, see also Derrida, among others.

perhaps more originally and authentically an artist of nature than others around 1900 who wished to be, but he too was a prisoner of tradition and did not reach the goal. The conflict between *Naturzusammenhang* and compositional *Naturbeherrschung* (dominion over nature)[1] – not the solution to that conflict – shaped even his life and production.

Whether or not Sibelius himself thought of Rousseau and the myth of the genuine divinity of humankind, and whether or not he believed its restoration to be a sensible vision in his environment – another interesting question in relation to the true significance of Karelianism – Rousseau's desire was not alien to him. Most artists of his generation understood nature aesthetically as the 'Other [...] without senses by which to apprehend us'[2] and remained free of existentialist disturbances in their artistic creativity, so nature remained a programme for them rather than an essence. But Sibelius could not escape the conflict rationally. His childhood and youth left him no alternative; he was driven into the middle of the turbulence. The 'aesthetics of nature', which by its own admission was an anti-modern turn from the modern concept of art as anti-nature (Marquis de Sade, Charles Baudelaire, Paul Valéry), helps all the more to explain Sibelius' despair in the face of the impossibility of finding an organic solution to the idea of creating art as nature. The cause was his instinctive rejection of academic idealism and materialism and a fashionable but nonetheless genuine conviction that morality was a matter of art, not of nature. In his heart of hearts, Sibelius probably indeed believed that a synthesis of nature and civilisation was possible through art.[3]

In realising his goal, Sibelius was confronted with the usual obstacle; many an important work remained but a fragment or became more conventional by the end of the compositional process than initially planned. The conflict between his personality and limitations of this kind could easily have led to the melancholy of an 'awareness of lost naivety'[4] of the period, and to a rigorous cultivation of the archaic as a programme – if not in the sense of the negative dialectics of the Enlightenment in search of the ineffable then at least introspectively. In a genre of art (music) that understood itself as the language of the soul but for centuries had developed its techniques within the context of consumer and representative art, the modern discontent consisted in the recognition of its own (including technical) inadequacies. This conflict hit Sibelius especially hard. The accelerated pace at which the conventional means of musical expression went out of style, especially evident in mid-nineteenth-century historicism, generally contributed to this state in and around 1900. Sibelius in particular had to realise that his nature-related goals could not be achieved either with the technique whose rudiments he had been taught by conservative teachers or with what he had

[1] See Adorno 1991, p. 137.

[2] Rilke 1986, p. 80; cf. Jauss 1989, p. 18.

[3] Jauss 1989, p. 81.

[4] Ibid., p. 29.

been able to acquire laboriously on his own. The classicistic unity of ends and means was history in any case. The experience of a loss of the binding unity of a vital era of progress – which had been the goal of the first Secessionists too, after all – common to all the arts around 1900 intensified the feeling of difference from history and freedom from binding laws of any kind. That is a possible explanation both for Sibelius' masterpieces and for the struggle with the Eighth Symphony. At the same time, nearly the entire history of Western music and many non-European practices (including old Karelian popular culture), whose existence had previously been unknown to the average European, became generally accessible. Sibelius experienced this process, long before he had brought his own craft to perfection, in Helsinki, where musicians lived surrounded not by the sea and woods but by other artists and academics. Ilya Repin's nostalgic oil painting *Finland's Great Men* (1922) illustrates this perfectly: a realistic depiction of an evening entertainment of all the ranking Finnish personalities some time before 1920.[1]

With an eye to the modern concept of melancholy, Peter Bürger has observed that artists discovered 'in ennui a power that can be exploited aesthetically'.[2] For Gustave Flaubert, 'the gaze of the modern melancholic discloses a world that does not, of course, exist in historical time'.[3] Accordingly, modern art in particular was, in Bürger's view, an attempt to explore the so-called 'other' and a response to the desire for the 'other'. Art can, however, merely articulate this desire. Adorno calls that 'sublime' and 'true'.[4] Sibelius strove to achieve more than the artistic articulation of this desire. Unlike the 'modern melancholic' Gustav Mahler, he did not want to 'disclose' the world (and thus failed 'sublimely' in Adorno's sense), *de facto* making an artistic contribution to philosophy rather than resolving Cartesian objectivity. That was a properly understood Rousseauian task. Sibelius' unique quality as one of many followers of Rousseau at the time was that he cultivated neither desire nor nostalgia as a parlour game but did indeed wish to explore an overarching reality and did in fact do so (whether from hubris or not), or at least took the first steps, by trying to capture 'moods' – but then again: 'If only I could realise my ideas in music now.'[5]

We can without reservation describe as 'sublime' – precisely in Adorno's sense – the fact that Sibelius did not simulate the 'other' – programmatically or imitatively – as something existing, much less employ the work of art as means to reconcile man and nature, as an instrument of deliberate deception. In his case, rather, the Dionysically dreamed becomes effective as a utopia. The Surrealist potential in his art overcomes the simple and real and the rational, without resorting to visually

[1] See illustration 3 on page 13 in chapter 1.1.

[2] Bürger 2000, p. 137.

[3] Ibid., p. 148.

[4] These concepts are omnipresent and at the same time hidden in Adorno's writings (even in the late *Aesthetic Theory*), as demonstrated by Welsch 1989. For further details, see also chapter 5.2 in the present volume.

[5] JS to Aino 2 September 1894.

powerful objectification in the figurative sense (à la Charles Ives or Impressionism) – any citations and stylistic borrowings there may seem unintentional, not aspects of inter-textual over-painting – but rather by avoiding the primacy of the control of reason in the ecstasy of creativity. His expansion of consciousness is neither playful nor anarchic; his hallucinations and dream-like quality are the unmannered result of his individuation and socialisation as 'homme naturel' in the society of 'hommes civils' and in the era of utopian melancholy. Unlike the programmatic Surrealists of his era, he was not interested in the logic of dreams or the repressed experiences of the individual but rather in the universe and the 'wonderful logic – let us call it God – that dominates the work of art'.[1]

Surreal and Heteronomous

Sibelius' compositions are similarly insistent and involving as the anti-rationalist art of Hamsun and Munch. Nor do his works feign anything. The sincere subject of the composer is palpable as a mediator, lacking any sign of Bretonian automatism. Sibelius' true, composing self translates the worlds of his experience into a medium that does not replace the limits of the technically familiar by standardised alternatives (whose existence it denies) and does not define itself as a polished language. Depending on one's point of view, this might give the impression of being imperfect and inconsistent. Since 'an art that [...] emphasises the primacy of the imagination, that wanted to penetrate behind definable forms of appearance, because it did not have its eye on perceiving the outside world but rather wanted to experience the world first by itself, began by blurring the optical clarity of appearances'.[2] In the process, elements of the real were misused as the material of a new reality shaped by a surreal-seeming self that created from dreams.[3] Sibelius determined his own reality and drew his power from his ability to see the 'other' in dreams and to reinterpret convincingly elements of reality independently of the constraints of the material.

The mixture of contemporary and classical that characterised Sibelius not only in his schooling (Greek, Latin) but also in his artistic, aesthetic and ideological interests was also typical of the Surrealists and, simultaneously, was an essential component of Finnish Modernism. The influence on his contemporaries of French 'neo-Hellenism' – followers of the Parnassians – and of Louis Bertrand's *La Fin du classicisme et le retour à l'antique* (1897) is well known,[4] but even the Adolf Hildebrand of *Das Problem der Form in der bildenden Kunst* (1893) and the Heinrich Wölfflin of *Die klassische Kunst* (1899), as well as Goethe, Schlegel and Nietzsche, were well known in Helsinki around 1900 as connoisseurs of antiquity. Emil Zilliacus, who like Sibelius was

[1] JS to Axel Carpelan, 20 July 1909, in Dahlström 2010, p. 246.

[2] Hofstätter [1965] 1978, p. 91.

[3] See also Bürger 2000, pp. 164 ff.

[4] Riikonen 2000, pp. 260–72.

a member of the 'neo-Hellenist' *Euterpe* circle in Helsinki, published in 1905 a sound study on Symbolism and the reception of antiquity in France: *Den nyare franska poesin och antiken* (Modern French poetry and antiquity).[1] Zilliacus provided an introduction to modern Symbolist trends (Stéphane Mallarmé, Jean Moréas, *et al.*), including the efforts to create a poetry 'like music'.[2] There was increasingly a call for artistic individuality and freedom from standardised schemas. In lieu of logic and economy of expression, there were expansive forms and unusual structures (a larger orchestra, new kinds of texture, unusual lengths), to at least hint at the ungraspable. The compelling design of self-contained, modest forms was pushed out by oversized questions (e.g., Schopenhauer's 'what is life?'[3]). This emphasis on content rather than form explains projects such as *The Wood Nymph* (1895) that seem to negate the traditional laws of musical architecture and thus have been seen as real challenges for performers. As Beethoven did in his symphonies in Schopenhauer's view,[4] Sibelius too developed an instrumental symphonic style with a subtly concealed programme as the main field for pseudo-philosophical suggestion. In Finland, the main Symbolist current led to a life-affirming 'Vitalism',[5] which was also relevant to Sibelius — for example, *War Song of Tyrtaeus*, literally 'Song of the Athenians' (1899), and *Finlandia* (1900), whose potential nationalism can only be understood within the Vitalist context.

In contrast to the programmatic Surrealism of André Breton, Giorgio de Chirico and Salvador Dalí, the surreal in Sibelius is neither eccentric nor cynical nor provocative and apocalyptic. His music is a monument to cultural failure, but at the same time it symbolises a hope that Rousseau's utopia can eventually be achieved and that Arcadia still exists. This ambivalence is articulated by the mixture of Classicistic and Vitalist elements. His music was not intended to 'disclose' some external world by the most progressive artistic and intellectual means or to articulate the insatiable desire for fulfilment but rather remained, at once modest and presumptuous, a fragment of the synthesis of nature and civilisation that could only begin to be fulfilled. Mahler, not Sibelius, was the source of the pseudo-Bretonian illusion: 'One does not compose; one is composed.'[6] For Sibelius, the task of the artistic subject was that of a medium: producing equality with one's surroundings, not upholding the idea of a composing God or the fundamental superiority of the mind. More important to him than automatism was the 'Surrealistic way of relating to life and to art', since Surrealism was the most advanced form of the contemporary reinterpretation of Romantic maxims after Symbolism and Jugendstil.[7]

[1] Ibid., pp. 267 ff.

[2] Zilliacus 1905, pp. 283–4.

[3] Schopenhauer 1977, p. 176.

[4] Ibid., p. 235.

[5] See Viljanen 1950, and Rajala 1988; in general cf. Martens 1971.

[6] Danuser 1991, p. 54. Cf. 'écriture automatique' in Breton's *Manifeste du surréalisme* (1924 and 1930) and Motte-Haber 1983, pp. 458 ff.

[7] Hofstätter [1965] 1978, p. 148.

Although not automatic and without will but rather explicitly under the control of the all-powerful artist-subject, thanks to careful sketches and intense correction (even recomposition), the dreamy invention of images and the 'faith in the higher reality of certain previously neglected forms of association'[1] were nevertheless important to Sibelius. The formation of the music incorporated experiences both of the figurative and programmatic and of absolute music that were not real but otherworldly, not transcendent but surreal. His creative method deviated from the practice common before him, but without making its differentness a programme for the listener as a system or method, as was the case in Cubism (Picasso *et al.*) and dodecaphony (Schoenberg *et al.*). His art avoided the appearance of fundamental difference for the sake of an overwhelmingly suggestive effect.

His aggressive lack of method-based principles and distance from all systems is still a model for those who wish to break free of the spell of Modernism. Consequently, those critics who turn their backs on nature, in keeping with the Hegelian 'spirit', sensed the presence of 'all nature' in a power that threatens the rational – and hence rejected Sibelius. Others – those who, like Adorno, followed Rousseau but did not share his optimism – found highly pretentious the suggestion that a state of nature could be achieved – or even, in the opinion of many uncritical adherents, had already been achieved. In fact, it was one of Sibelius' maxims that form should never come at the cost of expressive power. The appearance of the traditional remained, however, for the benefit of identification, and he did not rigorously avoid the impression of the conventional. Anyone who looks at a painting by Salvador Dalí or Giorgio de Chirico from a distance will recognise a composition of figures that seems at first to deviate only slightly from the painting of earlier times, especially of the pre-modern era.[2] On moving closer, however, the figurative surface of the surreal over-painting becomes evident and counteracts the familiar. The reception of Sibelius' work is very similar. Only a willingness to engage with the immanent law of each work makes it possible to access the surreality that is required by the Bretonian postulate of artistic automatism and dreamy pictorial inventions, but it functions only rarely, and usually as a metaphor.[3]

Because music in its usual form of representation is not figurative anyway, the compositional practice of the Classical-Romantic epoch – which according to Jauss was the last true 'epoch'[4] – represented the current reality towards which Sibelius took a position similar to that of de Chirico and Dalí relative to the figurative. One unspoken goal of the Surrealistic could be described, according to Immanuel Kant, as the 'perfect art against nature'.[5] Or as in John Ruskin and Charles Baudelaire: 'No

[1] See ibid., pp. 148–9.

[2] De Chirico's model was the quattrocento. Cf. de Chirico 1971, as well as Schmied 2002 and Schmied 1989.

[3] On transitional forms between Symbolism and Surrealism, see Hofstätter [1965] 1978, pp. 148–9.

[4] Jauss 1989, p. 82.

[5] Ibid., p. 51.

longer the nostalgic return to the childhood of individual or historical life but rather the conscious, analytical restoration of an original condition and the sensory wealth of the experience of the world is the task and opportunity of modern art in the face of an alienated reality.'[1] The goal in this tradition of thought was to keep it from resulting in the illusion of reconciliation. That was exactly what Sibelius was able to do. Kant returned to art the possibility of bringing into being a different modern age by cultivating the aesthetic power of the subjective – rather than rational competencies. For Sibelius, however, the aesthetic was not that of the classicists of whom Kant was thinking but rather the anti-aesthetic of the beyond, the emphasis on the unperceivable. This premise explains the gulf between the Classical-Romantic tradition of academicism[2] and the world of ideas of the young Modernists of the Secessions in Helsinki, Munich, Berlin and Vienna – and among them Sibelius.

Whereas philosophy discovered in nature a kind of past that art required in order for its otherness to be experienced, so that it became the 'aesthetics of nature' – or, according to Odo Marquard's reading of Kant: 'It interprets art in order to understand not art but the world'[3] – Sibelius found in nature a reality in the here and now, which did not coerce him into mimesis, illustration or distanced interpretation but instead demanded immediate experience. He gave into it and composed surreally, pseudo-programmatically, in the spirit of extended romanticism that was not intended to be anti-nature à la Baudelaire, second nature or naturalistic over-drawing of nature. His action was muse-like in the Dionysian sense; he believed in ecstasy as a better way to access nature. Although he shared many goals with philosophers who were also striving for such access, he rejected the pact with the traditional and philosophically proven concept and searched for individual fulfilment. For him, the philosophical *métier* seemed opposed to his own. There are statements to that effect in the letters and diary from all phases of his life. Where philosophers in the late nineteenth century – and later Adorno – tended to melancholy, or cultivated it because they wanted to enjoy the moment of contact with the intangible, Sibelius continued the Dionysian search for fulfilment.

Considered formally, according to Hegel, 'even a useless notion that enters a man's head is higher than any product of nature, because in such a notion spirituality and freedom are always present.'[4] Sibelius too ultimately had to grant this, in order to be able to keep working at all, but he had to put it into context – namely, through his work. By his own approach – which can ultimately be understood as the formulation of a language-like material to contribute to a better existence – Sibelius came closer not only to Schopenhauer and Bergson but also, in a roundabout way, to Descartes. The premise of the unquestionably superior, which casts the shadow of Western ar-

[1] Ibid., p. 65.

[2] Cf. Wiegandt 1997.

[3] Marquard 1987, p. 136.

[4] Hegel 1974, 2:1; cf. Jauss 1989, p. 129.

rogance even on Hegel's 'spirit', does not apply to him: the creative individual and his or her art is not superior to nature but rather part of it, even if he is unable to make that integration materialise.

Because human abilities to perceive nature are in fact limited, Sibelius had to doubts the superiority of the mind and attempt to realise nature and its 'wonderful logic'[1] in his art. Hegel's concept of nature as the 'other of spirit' and the late Romantic doubt about the harmony of soul and landscape, self and nature, as well as about the '"strange religion" of the pantheist friends of nature',[2] are sublated and, as it were, resolved in Sibelius under the category of contemplation and the primacy of the imagination as a medium of assimilation. He was not interested in a 'romantic-sentimental correspondence of subject and nature or of sensory and extrasensory experience',[3] but rather in an aesthetic of the surreal anchored in the personality and in imaginative, synaesthetic perception that provides art with a way out of inverted contemplation. Although Sibelius knew the pain that probably everyone feels on recognising his or her own inadequacy, he sought a previously undiscovered way out. In his work, in contrast to some of his renowned contemporaries, he did concentrate on artistically refined, at times artfully mannered expressions of the conflict between what is suspected and what can be achieved. He conceived plans to give musical materiality to utopia. His faith in his ability to achieve what several generations had attempted seemed naive to some critics, especially to Adorno. Yet what is more worthy: attempting it or declaring clever mourning over impossibility being the goal of art?

True Surrealism, not limited to Breton's famous ideas, destroyed the unity of the self just as much as the unity of nature.[4] This latter supposed unity is not, however, a legacy that must be protected at all costs. Rather, in the diversity of nature (and of the organic) lies the point of contact for synaesthetic experience and for the 'auratic' quality of the realistic depiction of nature[5] — for the feeling of distance despite actual closeness. Surrealism achieves this only when it redefines musical reality and works with original 'conceptions of space'.[6]

If one attempts to reconstruct Sibelius' thinking — no clear statements on the subject have been passed down — the approach, largely influenced by literature, and the depth of its complex thinking turn out to be the main problem of Symbolism. The trivialisation and the unliterary yet popularised condensation of Symbolism in

[1] JS to Axel Carpelan, 20 July 1909, in Dahlström 2010, p. 246.

[2] Jauss 1989, p. 134, paraphrasing a *Festschrift* of 1855 by followers of Baudelaire.

[3] Ibid., p. 136.

[4] Ibid., p. 145.

[5] Ibid., p. 195. Jauss referred to Benjamin's concept of 'aura' (among other places, in Benjamin 1999, p. 447).

[6] Hofstätter 1972, p. 18: 'unreal conceptions of space' (John Martin *et al.*) are a stylistic means of Symbolism.

Jugendstil[1] was no solution for him, either — Jugendstil's concern was too materialistic for that. However, this inspires us to reflect on external analogies between the general theory of art and some of the developments in compositional technique of that period — in Sibelius' work as well — concerning, for example, the independence of the concept of the timbral line: 'Its handling has to derive just as much from sensation as the depiction in music of an emotional value does. It depends on the person drawing the line having a delicate sense, an expressive individual style, a profound insight into the soul of the forces to be expressed by the line.'[2] Several prominent artists (e.g. Munch) emphasised the linear traces of the material in woodcuts and objects carved from long lengths of timber; however, the prehistory of ornament as a design principle goes back to figures and symbols with a linguistic character and semantic contexts. Thus the kind of naturalness that Gallen-Kallela, say, sought in his archaic paintings by emphasising the strikingly coarse fabric — hand-woven by his wife rather than industrially produced — can only be appearance, the superficial illusion of the organic, not an artistic necessity. Such games with materials were foreign to Sibelius, while several of his contemporaries, even Mahler, attempted similar things by using everyday instruments such as cowbells.

Gauguin's harsh critique of Impressionism can be applied to mannered Jugendstil, and probably very much in Sibelius' spirit: 'the surface is immaterial, the casual arrangement of objects in nature is no more than a stimulus for the conception of a picture. The essential process is to condense from the impression received something which contains all the factors of lasting significance.'[3] Sibelius' characteristic, imaginative synaesthesia also evolved free of any external significance and thus helped the complexity of the natural to stand out. Gauguin articulated a supposed problem, to which music would be especially subject, in his sketchbook in 1889: 'Like music, it [painting] acts on the soul through the intermediary of the senses; harmonious colors correspond to the harmonies of sounds. But in painting a unity is obtained which is not possible in music, where the accords follow one another, so that the judgement experiences a continuous fatigue if it wants to reunite the end with the beginning. The ear is actually a sense inferior to the eye. The hearing can only grasp a single sound at a time, whereas the sight takes in everything and simultaneously simplifies it at will.'[4] He overlooked the human ability to be influenced completely by hearing, whereas the sense of vision in particular is rigorously trained as an analytic organ of perception and consequently functions schematically: 'the whole' can never be spontaneously surveyed visually. Just how well Gauguin understood music's potential is revealed in a letter he wrote to the American collector Daniel de Monfreid: 'In painting, one has

[1] Hofstätter [1965] 1978, p. 165: Jugendstil landscape painting is a condensation into an 'elemental or atmospheric symbol' without 'clarifying staffage'.

[2] Hofstätter 1972, p. 11.

[3] Pevsner 1991, p. 74.

[4] Quoted in Hofstätter [1965] 1978, p. 144.

to suggest and not describe, which is, by the way, also what music does.'[1] Like Paul Sérusier, Maurice Denis and Odilon Redon, Gauguin developed a new aesthetic based on an analogy between painting and music, as opposed to literature and philosophy. Art music is not always suggestive, but Sibelius in particular is an example of the tendency Gauguin describes. In his work, the suggestive is an alternative to the absolute or programmatic in the tradition of Brahms and Liszt.

Not only because of its synaesthetic, inter-medial mediation and its search for parallels, but also because of the acceleration in the change of taste and the function of public art criticism — the demand-driven compulsion to verbalise that seized artists as well — Secessionism was overflowing with new styles, trends, schools and attitudes. Frequently each of these was represented only by a few rebels. The determination of aesthetic location and the topography of styles cannot therefore deny the internal ambivalence of late Modernism as a time of distinguished individualists. Sibelius' oeuvre does not fit entirely into the set patterns of a conventional theory of styles either. The German musicologist Michael Mäckelmann characterises him convincingly as an 'aesthete of heteronomy of the purest shade',[2] and as a 'composer, who was at once an *aesthetician of content* and an *aesthetician of form*'. 'That stance is all the more remarkable since both positions were, famously, then considered irreconcilable.'

Sibelius' at least partly heteronomous solutions were connected with his genuinely visual, visionary orientation. The historical assertion that the aesthetics of form and the aesthetics of content are 'irreconcilable' can be explained by reference to the primacy of the literary, whereas in the world of visions and imaginary images or of Symbolism and Surrealism the distinction between form and content can never be plausible. Mäckelmann also drew attention to this when he commented on Sibelius' '*images of mood*' and reminds us that the subjective explodes all dichotomies. 'The *images of mood* are more *meaning* ['*Ge*-halt'] than *content* ['*In*-halt']. They do not describe an action but rather represent a musical reflection.'[3]

Both the synthetic and the post-Impressionist aspects, including the Surrealist, can also be traced back to Sibelius' personal artistic individuality, instead of typical movements of the era. Like few others, the composer perceived his environment — nature and cities — synaesthetically, making his comprehensive view the object of artistic elaboration and thus employing means of his own choice, almost without regard to the history of musical genres and the artificially objective state of development in the history of composition. Thus he lent perceivable form to 'mood'. He was neither an eclectic nor an uncontrolled pluralist; he created genuine synthesis as an 'aesthete of heteronomy of the purest shade'.

1 Ibid. Cf. also Bernard, according to Hofstätter 1972, p. 71.

2 Mäckelmann 1983, p. 129.

3 Ibid., p. 130.

The day is magnificent. Poetry in the air.
Nature is speaking.[1]

3 INFLUENCE AND RESISTANCE FROM 1880 TO 1929

3.1 The 'Post-Romantic' Foundation

Sibelius' Place in the History of Style

CARL DAHLHAUS DISCOVERED in Sibelius a master of sub-thematic processes whose analysis has to delve a level 'below' the motivic, close to the processes he already called 'sub-thematic' in his analysis of Beethoven's late piano sonatas.[2] 'Below' does not refer to the structural elements that are fundamental in a solid hierarchy of segments (in the manner of Heinrich Schenker), but rather a veiled strategy of form that is not more closely defined in regard to Sibelius. It is not about another, subliminal level of design but rather about a method of composition, about how to form the 'rhapsodic' without succumbing to dogma. In the history of composition, this is not an alternative to but rather supplements the common practice since Bach and Haydn and even earlier. This picture of Sibelius, whose succinctness analysts have yet to outdo, drew the attention of many specialists to features of the texture that are otherwise often associated with the successors to Liszt and Wagner. Dahlhaus probably provoked that association without intending to make Sibelius a direct follower of Liszt's and Wagner's New German style, but the consequence is inevitable.

Sibelius' own statements are not consistent with regard to his impressions of and influences from the representatives of the New German reforms. One reason for the occasional rejection of this trend was perhaps the vexation often triggered by related but overpowering predecessors. According to Karl Ekman's account, Sibelius spoke self-critically about his own uncertainty: 'My decided antagonism to Wagner in my youth was, I fancy, dictated to some extent by the fear of being subjected to an influence that I had seen taking possession of so many of my friends, both old and young. And yet I still place Verdi higher than Wagner. Opera is, after all, a conventional form of art and should be cultivated as such.'[3] Rarely has an artist spoken so candidly about his anxiety regarding his elders. One reason for his critical attitude towards Wagner was perhaps that in his *The Swan of Tuonela* of 1893 he only narrowly avoided crudely plagiarising the opening bars of the prelude to *Lohengrin*. Moreover, he lived

[1] Diary, 4 June 1911.

[2] Dahlhaus 1980b, pp. 309–10; Dahlhaus 1980a, pp. 81–98.

[3] Ekman 1946, p. 263.

in a country whose artists were increasingly distinguishing themselves from German role models and turning to France – which in a sense ran counter to nationalism in Finland, since Russia was an ally of France in the 1890s. In Finland, France was trendy long before the World Wars.

On 19 August 1894 his enthusiasm for Liszt reached a climax, and he wrote to Aino from Munich in poor Finnish: 'I am really a tone painter and poet. Liszt's views about music are most closely related to my own.' This moving closer to Liszt occurred during a trip to Italy and a subsequent stay in Berlin at Ferruccio Busoni's home. Busoni too admired Italy and rejected Wagner, which formed the basis of his *Junge Klassizität* (Young Classicism). Inspired by Busoni, Sibelius studied not only Liszt's *Faust Symphony* but also George Bizet's *Carmen* (a work remembered in Pauline Lucca's Viennese interpretation), Bedřich Smetana's *Bartered Bride*, Giuseppe Verdi's *Falstaff* and other compositions, not all of which pleased him,[1] but their stylistic diversity reinforced his own personality. 'I'm much more autonomous than I was when I departed [Finland]', he reported in awkward Finnish.[2] In 1905 he had another opportunity to hear the fascinating, progressive tonality of Liszt's works at Busoni's home – 'Busoni played like an angel'[3] – when Busoni was preparing his legendary Liszt concerts. He could also look at rare scores in Busoni's library. Little is known of their conversations, however, since Busoni's notes too are sparse. Remembering the years 1888 to 1890, when he was surely grateful for any stimulating entertainment during the long November evenings, Busoni wrote to Egon Petri on 13 June 1908: 'When I was in Helsinki, and younger than you are now, I had Sibelius and the Jaernefelt brothers for stimulating company; I learnt a few things from my director, Wegelius, an extremely fine and cultured man. The country too was delightfully exotic and, despite the Nordic way of life, more cheerful than Manchester.'[4] That was the beginning of a beautiful friendship.

Busoni's letter to Adolf Paul of 10 November 1921 is very revealing about the relationship between Busoni and Sibelius:

> Once again I had the privilege of paving the way for Sibelius (even though it should no longer be necessary for him!) But that's the way of the world, and I was happy that my effort succeeded. Hopefully you have shared your good impressions with him. (Would like to know what he thinks of the incident; he is so abstract and difficult to understand, and my love for him always remains one-sided.) They are all alike; I know all <u>their</u> works; none of them know <u>mine</u>. I admire the Fifth Symphony very much. The Fourth is closer to me. I don't know the Third. I performed the Second last April in Rome. Despite all my affectionate sympathy, S. behaviour towards me is always somewhat embarrassed and at the same time childishly flattering, which astonishes me.

[1] JS to Aino, 2 September 1894, and subsequent letters from Germany and Italy.

[2] JS to Aino, 2 September 1894.

[3] JS to Aino, n.d. (*c.*21–2 January 1905).

[4] Beaumont 1987, p. 91.

> I last saw him in London and [in Berlin] in February. Nevertheless, I like him very much.[1]

On 22 November 1921, Sibelius replied cordially, if not effusively, in idiomatically flawed German directly to Busoni: 'My dear friend Busoni, [...] Without you, the symphony would have remained on paper, like an apparition from the forests. I would probably come to Berlin in the spring and look forward to hearing your works and seeing you.'[2] Because the formulation 'apparition from the forests' – which also appears in German in his diary on 13 May 1910 – was not intended seriously, and because Sibelius expressed himself with restraint and diplomacy anyway, we get a sense of the bitter irony he wanted to articulate with it. Following Busoni's essay in the *Zürcher Theater-, Konzert- und Fremdenblatt* of March 1916 – Busoni conducted the Second Symphony in Zurich on 15 March 1916 – he had occasion enough to do so: 'Sibelius evolved quickly and confidently on the solid ground of Finnish folk music – ground he never left, except when he was forced into a detour by a Tchaikovskian wave.'[3]

Despite the efforts to achieve independence and an 'honest nature' that begin around 1890, Sibelius' oeuvre contains some striking facets of the fashionable New German style. Later – outraged by public distortions of his statements and perhaps also by his own all too obvious borrowings (albeit typical of the era and indeed perhaps unconscious) – he said nothing about this influence.[4] In the literature on Sibelius this is taken as reliable evidence that as an artist he rejected Wagner and Liszt. Sibelius did indeed reject the trivial Wagnerism of his colleagues, even in the months when he was interested in the compositional technique of Wagner's original works. For example, he wrote from Munich on 22 August 1894: 'I was terribly enthusiastic about *Die Meistersinger*. But, strangely, I am no longer a Wagnerian. I cannot help it. My own voices are guiding me.'[5] Nevertheless, he had previously been, at least in musical and aesthetic terms – certainly not in terms of philosophy and literature[6] – a Wagnerian. But his enthusiasm for Wagner took an obsequious form for only a few years. On the basis of the *Kalevala*, he worked on practicable ideas for operas that would continue the Wagnerian tradition. One of these was even based on a libretto he wrote himself.[7] By contrast, a subliminal New German tendency in the fundamentals of his composition can be traced far beyond this naive enthusiasm and is one of the main features of his oeuvre. His writing of programmatic, symphonic tone poems after completing his studies and, somewhat later, the idea of the 'Symphonic Fantasy' were consequences of his masterful approach to the impressions of the New German

1 Busoni to Paul: Åbo Akademi.

2 In Staatsbibliothek, Berlin, Mus.ep. J. Sibelius 6.

3 Quoted in Tanzberger 1962, pp. 17–18.

4 The quotation in Ekman 1946, p. 263, in note 3 above is an exception.

5 JS to Aino, 22 August 1894. On 17 August 1894, after a 'brilliant' performance of *Götterdämmerung*, JS had written to Aino from Munich: 'I cannot be a "Wagnerian" like the others.'

6 On this distinction, see Schwartz 1999.

7 See chapter 3.3 in the present volume.

style he had acquired in Helsinki, Berlin and Vienna. These were filled out with the Russian modernity of Alexander Borodin, Mily Balakirev and Alexander Glazunov.[1]

Here it pays to compare styles, even when the specific demonstration of influence does not stand. One such case is the Moscow composer Vasily Kalinnikov, whose First Symphony of 1895 (performed in Helsinki on 1 December 1902) reveals striking similarities to Sibelius' style of the early 1890s (*Kullervo*, etc.), who chose similar subjects for his symphonic poems (for example, *The Nymphs* of 1889) and whose reception was influenced by qualities of the Russian landscape. Like Sibelius, Kalinnikov was a follower of Tchaikovsky and Borodin, and explicitly not Rimsky-Korsakov.

Sibelius' piano music has reminiscences of Liszt. His *Impromptu*, op. 5, no. 5 (1890–3) invites comparison to *Les Jeux d'eau à la Villa d'Este* (*Troisième année de pèlerinage*).[2] In the first section (Largamente-Allegro) of the *Kyllikki* cycle (1904), Lemminkäinen, the Don Juan figure of the *Kalevala*, seduces the young Kyllikki with Lisztian gestures. In his piano music, Sibelius generally followed the line of orchestral pianism in order to achieve a multidimensional sound space. The roots of this attitude lay not in the virtuoso pianism of the composer — as they did for Liszt and his students — but in orchestral practice or in a conception of sound that was entirely free of the idiom of a specific instrument. Contrary to what Eero Järnefelt's lively sketch *Sibelius at the Piano*, 1892, suggests, he was no pianist. He played imaginatively, but the piano did not interest him as an instrument for performance, since 'it cannot sing'[3] (which was, admittedly, a violinist's pretext). He found Liszt too pianistic in his orchestral works, and too orchestral in his works for piano.[4] Above all, he considered Liszt's textures, in which masses of sound move independently of motifs, to have been a failure. As a violinist, he suspected — somewhat presumptuously — that it was a result of an overzealous use of the pedal when playing the piano and a consequent distortion to the sensitive ear. This critique indicates that his rejection was well grounded and also documents an increased, unusual interest. Already in the Piano Sonata in F major (1893), Liszt's influence is unmistakable; there are only isolated similarities with the equally complex pianism of Grieg and Beethoven. In *Tapiola* and in other orchestral works, he continued his sonic experiments on the basis of the New German reforms. No less an authority than Glenn Gould emphasised the orchestral quality of his recordings of the Sonatinas and the *Kyllikki* triptych by employing a modified multi-track recording technique he called 'acoustic orchestration' — a method Sergey Prokofiev analysed as 'inverted instrumentation' in Sergey Eisenstein's monumental film *Alexander Nevsky* ('inconceivable for symphonic music').[5]

[1] Murtomäki 1998b, pp. 153–61, quoting Ringbom, *Helsingfors orkesterföretag, 1882–1932* (Helsinki: Helsinki Philharmonic Orchestra, 1932).

[2] Ostrovsky 1998, pp. 293–6.

[3] Törne 1937, p. 29.

[4] Ibid., p. 31.

[5] See booklet to the CD Sony SM 2K 52654, 1992/1973–7, and Sergey Prokofiev, 'Music for Alexander Nevsky', in Shlifstein 2000, p. 114.

Bengt de Törne quoted Sibelius: 'I am myself a man of the orchestra. You must judge me from my orchestral works. [...] I write piano pieces in my free moments. [...] And I never go to piano recitals except when they are given by real geniuses like my friend Busoni.'[1] His finest works for piano, the Sonatinas, 1912, live from this tension: as an act of resistance to the temptation to write complex polyphony for an inappropriate medium, especially in the face of the unattainable pianistic genius of Liszt and Busoni. Sibelius was always prepared to discuss this theme ('I could talk to you about the orchestra every day for a year, without exhausting the subject'), and even as a conductor he was enthusiastic about the sound of individual instruments and the sensory effect of the orchestra.[2] The shaping of form made possible by sound was important to him as an idea – much as for a painter who can design the form from planes of colour and clear lines without losing sight of traditional laws of form: 'He emphasized the necessity of balancing the masses against each other and the importance of defining the outlines.'

He realised the truly all-embracing quality of a practical conception of texture without regard to conventional standards: 'he had never stopped to ask whether he infringed the orthodox rules of good orchestration. On the other hand, he had not abandoned the main road expressly, to create sensation, but only when it had suited his purpose. This statement expresses his entire artistic creed: innovation must come from within and not be aimed at deliberately. [...] "You know, I am not legitimately married to the orchestra; I am its lover."'[3] His explanation of details of orchestral pedal effects or the means he employed to counteract them also distinguishes this sound-orientated composer.[4] His recommendations were precise: 'I always fit in some second violins or violas in the medium register, which has no characteristic colour of its own. You practically only hear the wind, but the continuity is there.' He analysed in detail specific phenomena such as the soft orchestration of harsh dissonances or echo effects.[5] His principle was: 'You must never write anything without knowing exactly how it will sound.'[6] Rosa Newmarch quoted the same idea: 'I feel absolutely sure how my instrumentation will sound before I put it on paper.'[7] We must suppose that his entire attention was focused on shaping the sound. Consequently, the level of rhythmic-melodic and harmonic invention and shaping of form correspond to the originality of the sound: his most artful harmonies are to be found in works that are

[1] Törne 1937, p. 29.

[2] Ibid., pp. 18–19.

[3] Ibid., p. 30.

[4] Ibid., pp. 30–31. Adorno used the same pedal metaphor to describe Wagner's orchestral sound in Adorno 1991, p. 78.

[5] See Törne 1937, app. 1.

[6] Ibid., p. 37.

[7] Newmarch 1939, p. 61.

his most original in terms of sound and vice versa: 'Sound [is] largely dependent on the purely musical "Satz" [setting].'[1]

The Repertoire in Hämeenlinna and Helsinki

Although Georg Göhler wrote cuttingly in 1908 that Sibelius could only be understood once the '[Richard] Strauss mania' of superficial orchestral effects and sentimental themes in the strings had passed, Erkki Salmenhaara discussed Sibelius, in his study of György Ligeti, alongside Strauss, Mahler and Scriabin as sound-conscious 'post-Romantics', in contrast to the 'Impressionists' (Debussy, Ravel), the 'anti-Romantics' and 'Neoclassicists' (Bartók, Hindemith, 'Les Six', Prokofiev, Stravinsky and Shostakovich), and the 'anti-tonal group' (Varèse, Schoenberg, Berg and Webern).[2] Although the term 'post-Romantics' neither permits precise stylistic categorisation nor leads to a more subtle understanding, any more than the term 'national Romantic' often used by Walter Niemann, Salmenhaara confirms the absorption of a Romantic stance (Schumann, Schubert, Berlioz, Liszt and Wagner) as a basis for style. Scholarship on Sibelius has often passed these names by and postulated a direct succession from Beethoven, seeing that as the truly progressive quality, which sometimes makes Sibelius out to be the only truly progressive composer of the era around 1900. Everyone else had supposedly been on the wrong track since Beethoven. The originator of this ultra-classical approach was Cecil Gray in 1931, supported a little later by Constant Lambert, who is usually cited in abridged form by later Sibelius scholars.[3] Rather than disqualifying Gray's position as cheap polemic, we should consider how much the repertoire before Schubert and Schumann played a role for Sibelius, and in what form he avoided following the immediately preceding generations.

It presents an appealing challenge, which should not therefore be underestimated, to demonstrate when and how Sibelius first came into conscious contact with the aesthetics and compositions of Liszt's circle, having heard in his childhood almost exclusively earlier repertoire of a lighter character — almost no operas, few symphonies. Alexandra (Alie) Lindberg, a Finnish student of Liszt and Carl Tausig, would be a tempting point of reference, but in fact she played no essential role, since after 1878 she gave only a single concert in Helsinki (in 1890).[4] Impressions of the New German style apparently reached Sibelius filtered and without a direct connection; his view of art — which he himself referred to ambiguously as his 'nature' — was able to evolve freely from progressive poetics: liberation of musical structures from traditional paths and genres in favour of a new sensuousness of the language of the soul. In the period prior to his studies in Berlin and Vienna from 1889 to 1891, he did not feel op-

[1] Diary, n.d. (*c.* 9 June 1910).

[2] Salmenhaara 1969, p. 14. Göhler's essay appears in translation in *Kalevalaseuran vuosikirja*, no. 6 (1926), pp. 3–26.

[3] Lambert 1934, p. 277. See also chapter 1.2 in the present volume.

[4] See Rahkonen 2004, p. 232.

pressed by either tradition or progress. In Helsinki in 1884 he heard Liszt's legendary student Sophie Menter play paraphrases and transcriptions of Liszt – at the height of her career, a year after taking up a professorship in St Petersburg; and in 1887 Alfred Reisenauer and Eugen d'Albert performed in Helsinki.[1] Because such performances were big events, and it can be shown that Sibelius was in the area, it must be assumed that he attended these concerts, even though he did not write about them. During his year in Berlin and Vienna, he also had many opportunities to gain impressions, though they have not been documented; he definitely heard at least Strauss's *Don Juan* under Hans von Bülow in Berlin, expressed enthusiasm about many works by Wagner and Bruckner and learned to despise the German conservative August Bungert.[2] In Helsinki in 1891, two years later, he met William H. Dayas, an American student of Adolph Kullak and Liszt, who at the age of twenty-six had succeeded Busoni as piano teacher in Helsinki.[3] Sibelius even met Reisenauer in the context of Gallen-Kallela's and Kajanus' 'Symposiums', since he regularly performed in Helsinki on his way to St Petersburg and appreciated its original circle of young artists.[4]

In addition to travelling artists, there were three people in Helsinki around 1889 who seriously, enduringly advocated the contemporary even beyond their field: Wegelius, Kajanus and Busoni. In 1889, the focus of Busoni's interest was still Schumann. After a Busoni recital of *Kreisleriana*, the enthusiastic Sibelius conceived, surely not coincidentally, his own piano suite on Florestan's theme. As early as 1889, Busoni played Liszt's *Don Juan* Fantasy (as well as Beethoven's Piano Sonatas op. 35 and op. 111) in a concert in which Sibelius joined him, playing second violin, in a performance of Schumann's Piano Quintet, op. 44.[5] In his performances of Schumann, he was able to experiment with the idea of the poetic, that is, with musical structure in service of an idea from the Classical-Romantic world. Schumann was a bridge between Liszt and the method of Sibelius' composition teacher Martin Wegelius, who in practice, despite his latent Wagnerism, referred to Ludwig Bussler's conservative textbook on harmony. When teaching beginners, Wegelius set great store by Viennese Classicism (above all Mozart) and only rarely recommended studying Liszt and Wagner.[6] He had no advanced composition students. According to a legend started by Sibelius, his students were even prohibited from attending Kajanus' mixed-programme orchestral concerts.[7]

By contrast, from 1885 to 1889, in the concerts of students and teachers at Wegelius' institute, which initially (following the model of the conservatory in Leipzig) was limited to the fields of piano, singing and composition (organ and cello were

[1] Lappalainen 1994, pp. 78–9.

[2] See Ringbom 1954, p. 20.

[3] He remained in Helsinki until 1894; see Karvonen 1957, p. 276.

[4] Erik W. Tawaststjerna 1976, pp. 90 and 138.

[5] Ibid., p. 102. Cf. Goss 1997, p. 104.

[6] Erik W. Tawaststjerna 1976, p. 35.

[7] Ibid., p. 29. There were, however, exceptions, see ibid., p. 38.

FIG. 21. Eero Järnefelt, *Jean Sibelius Plays the Violin* (1890). At first glance, the portrait of Sibelius may seem unflattering, but Järnefelt depicts him as a violinist with a natural touch and bowing. The painting is a unique document of Sibelius as a violinist.

soon added), Sibelius had the opportunity to hear compositions by Beethoven, Schumann and Liszt; some Chopin, Mozart and Haydn; and Grieg, Tchaikovsky, Anton Rubinstein, Saint-Saëns, Johann Nepomuk Hummel, Georg Goltermann, Goldmark, Mendelssohn, Schubert and even selected scenes from early Wagner operas. In his Philharmonic concerts, Kajanus conducted Beethoven, Haydn, Mozart, Louis Spohr (who had been heard frequently in Helsinki since Fredrik Pacius' time, beginning in 1835), Max Bruch, Schumann, Brahms, Mendelssohn, Grieg, Tchaikovsky, Rubinstein, Berlioz (*La Damnation de Faust* alone eleven times in the 1894–5 season), Wagner (overtures and the *Siegfried Idyll*) and Liszt (Piano Concerto in E flat major, *Faust Symphony*, *Tasso* and *Les Préludes*).[1] The anecdote commonly told in the literature that students were not permitted to attend these pioneering Philharmonic concerts cannot be true — and it is not as if Sibelius had ever been such an obedient student. Nevertheless, it contains an important clue: the conflict between the two champions of Wagner demonstrates perfectly the presence of two different forms of the Wagnerian reform stance in Helsinki, which was far from small-town narrow-mindedness. Wegelius, who was primarily a teacher, represented the Apollonian track with a New German brand. Kajanus, the highly talented conductor — who, in Busoni's subjective opinion, understood nothing of Viennese Classicism[2] — saw himself as a visionary of modernity and was a worthy representative of the Dionysian element. Both of them, Apollo and Dionysus, wanted to occupy the leading position in Helsinki's musical life.

Sibelius was a natural talent who, because of inadequate professional support as a youth, was exposed to influences of an adequate standard only as an adult. To that end, he had the pleasure of attending a small but dynamic music institute, which had been established only a few years earlier. In order for the nineteen-year-old to attend courses at Wegelius' school in parallel with his regular university studies, however, Sibelius was dependent on the financial support of his family.[3] Only later did he attract the attention of wealthy patrons. He himself reported that music first 'took hold' of him as he approached the age of fifteen.[4] Before he began to play the violin seriously,[5] he dedicated himself to the piano for at least eight years — in part on his own, in part probably with instruction from his aunt Julia Borg. Because his uncle Pehr Sibelius supported him with a monthly allowance, and especially by making available two violins from his private collection, Sibelius obediently informed him in particular about his alleged reason for wanting to study law: in order to qualify 'for well-nigh every profession there is except medicine'. Only the undertone of his letter to his uncle makes it clear how important music already was to him.[6] Only towards the end of 1885 was it announced that he was already studying music. At the time, he was being taught the violin by Mitrofan Vasiliev, the son of a 'famous music professor in Berlin'. This is merely an anecdote, since all that is really known is that Vasiliev served as chamber musician to the court in St Petersburg.[7]

In March 1886 Sibelius applied for a music scholarship from Helsinki University and was able to submit favourable but by no means effusive recommendations from

1 Kilpeläinen 2001, pp. 228–9; see also Lappalainen 1994, pp. 76 and 80.

2 Ferruccio Busoni to Henri and Kathi Petri, 17 October 1888, from Helsinki, in Beaumont 1987, p. 40.

3 JS to Pehr Sibelus, 4 August 1885, in Goss 1997, p. 73.

4 Ekman 1946, p. 27.

5 Goss 1997, pp. 134–5 and 20 ff. (summary in the introduction).

6 JS to Pehr Sibelius, 17 September 1885, ibid., p. 77.

7 Ibid., pp. 20 and 80.

Wegelius and the music director of the university, Richard Faltin. He carefully transcribed them for his uncle Pehr. On this occasion, on 31 March 1886, he announced his artistic name: 'Jean is my music name.'[1] The public debut of 'Jean Sibelius', the cosmopolitan with a French name but Finnish-Swedish heritage, was in May.[2] In November 1886 he reported the still not exactly effusive diagnosis of his harmony, piano and composition teacher that he 'undoubtedly [had] a musical future' ahead of him.[3] His letters to Pehr Sibelius also provide information about his first compositions, such as a more substantial chamber music work with horn in the central movement,[4] about his studies of music theory and about experiments with chords that even he considered 'radical'. On 24 October 1888, he wrote about a 'sixteenth chord' composed of triads in C major and D flat major. It is confusing that in these reports he often fails to distinguish between important and everyday artistic events. Moreover, their naive tone is striking, given his age. For example, his performance of Schumann with Busoni is mentioned only in passing[5] — the occasion of the first encounter onstage between these representatives of an alternative modernity, when Sibelius could truly play music with an artist of his own future stature.

The collection of music he left behind testifies to an unsystematic occupation with Classical and Romantic chamber music. It is documented that not only religion but also music played a relatively central social role in his childhood in Hämeenlinna. The fact that he never had the support to pursue a professional career — in contrast to competitors the same age such as Busoni, Mahler, Hugo Wolf and Strauss — but nevertheless had sufficient creative impulses of his own meant that he discovered early on unusual ways of making music, some quite far from the traditional curriculum. Classical and Romantic music were supplemented or even replaced by his own inventions, not by Berlioz, Wagner and Liszt, and only secondarily by Tchaikovsky and Grieg. He was second violin in a string quartet with fellow students in Hämeenlinna from 1882 onwards,[6] and he also played the violin in a quartet at the Wegelius Institute from 1887. The level of the latter ensemble must have been respectable, since all its other members were teachers.[7] It is notable that experienced musicians such as Hermann Czillag, whom Leevi Madetoja, quoting Sibelius, in 1915 called an 'extraordinarily precise and strict man',[8] and Karl Fredrik Wasenius accepted a student in their quartet at all.

Sibelius himself mentioned the Haydn sonatas and quartets, along with various pieces by Schubert and Mendelssohn, as important parts of his repertoire in Hämeen-

[1] JS to Pehr Sibelius, 31 March 1886, ibid., p. 167.
[2] Ibid., p. 77.
[3] Ibid., p. 86.
[4] JS to Pehr Sibelius, 31 May 1887, ibid., p. 88.
[5] JS to Pehr Sibelius, 20 March 1889, ibid., p. 104.
[6] Ibid., p. 142.
[7] Kilpeläinen 2001, p. 224.
[8] Quoted in Salmenhaara 1987, p. 78.

linna. Viennese Classicism became for him, influenced by the preferences of the Tigerstedt family (Sibelius' father and the father of fellow student Anna Tigerstedt were colleagues), a lifelong role model.[1] Even much later he dreamed of a private visit from Haydn to Ainola.[2] At sixteen, he expressed himself quite poetically about Haydn's compositions and the violin: 'When I play on it [my violin], I am filled with a strange feeling; it is as though the insides of the music opened up to me, and Haydn's sonatas with their deep, serious sounds almost make it holy.'[3] This letter is one of the pearls of this period, and it provides a hint of an artistic attitude that is more Apollonian than Dionysian. The Beethoven trios came only later.[4]

The high value he placed on Schubert is clear from his music collection and from other important documents. Sibelius was enthusiastic about Schubert's chamber music – especially the 'Trout' Quintet and the String Quartet in D minor, 'Death and the Maiden' – and he rightly admired the Lieder as the perfect way to exploit the possibilities of the human voice. In Helsinki, too, before tackling Schumann's Piano Quintet, op. 44, he performed a lot of Haydn, Mozart's Quintet in G minor, Beethoven's String Quartets, op. 18, Schumann's string quartets, and isolated compositions by Robert Volkmann, Liszt, Rubinstein, Alexander Fesca, Carl Reissiger, Tchaikovsky, Bellini and Moritz Kässmayer.[5] Nevertheless, it is difficult to assess his level as a violinist. He first performed as a soloist in April 1883 – while still in Hämeenlinna and supposedly after less than three years studying the violin with a local military musician, Gustaf Levander – in a performance of Miska Hauser's *Liebeslied* (Love song).[6] In the autumn of 1883 he considered playing Bériot's *Air varié* no. 7, and in the summer of 1885, he is said to have rehearsed another ambitious piece by Bériot, the Concerto for Violin and Orchestra no. 7.[7] That was followed by Giovanni Battista Viotti's Violin Concerto in G major, Pierre Rode's Concertos in A minor and E minor (final movement) and finally by the Adagio from Conradin Kreutzer's Concerto in E minor.[8]

The archive of his collection of sheet music includes material from his youth as well as purchases from Vienna and a few later acquisitions, most with no indication of the year they were purchased or any dealer stamp. The pieces listed under nos. 6–8 are probably mostly from his years of study in Berlin and Vienna or possibly even from later trips there:[9]

1 Shorter salon pieces for and with violin (Hummel's *Im Frühling*, op. 37; Spohr's *Salonstück*, op. 145, no. 4: Tchaikovsky's *Serenade*, op. 26; Schumann's

[1] Jalas 1981, p. 61.
[2] Diary, 11 July 1912.
[3] JS to Pehr Sibelius, 1 August 1882, in Goss 1997, p. 54.
[4] Ibid., p. 64, cf., for example, JS to Pehr Sibelius, 24 February 1884.
[5] Kilpeläinen 2001, p. 225.
[6] Goss 1997, p. 59.
[7] Ibid., pp. 63 and 72.
[8] Kilpeläinen 2001, pp. 225–6.
[9] National Library Coll. 206: 94–9.

Schlummerlied from *Albumblätter*, op. 124, no. 16 with markings; Schubert, op. 137, no. 3; François-Hubert Prume's *La melancolie pastorale*, op. 1; Henryk Wieniawski's *Souvenir de Moscou*, op. 6 and *Thème original varié*, op. 15; Henri Vieuxtemps's *Voix intimes*, op. 45; Schubert's *Preghiera* 'Andante cantabile', etc.).

2 Sonatas, trios and quartets: Carl Maria von Weber's Sonatas nos. 1–6 (with markings); Mozart sonatas and trios (with Sibelius' signature); various Beethoven trios; Schubert Trio, op. 100; Schumann Quartet, op. 41, no. 1.

3 Arrangements: the overture from Beethoven's *Fidelio* for string quartet; Gustav Ernst's *Il pirata de Bellini*, op. 19; Andante of Haydn's Symphony no. 94 in G major ('Surprise' Symphony) for string trio, etc.

4 Violin concertos: Vieuxtemps's op. 37; Spohr's op. 2 (signed by Sibelius in Helsinki in 1886 with a few performance markings), op. 47 (with many agogic and performance markings) and op. 55 (with the stamp of Beuermann's music store in Helsinki); Bériot's no. 7 with markings; Viotti's no. 23 (with one ornament added by hand: the so-called Sibelius triplet, which is typical of his Violin Concerto); Vieuxtemps's op. 10; Viotti's *Duo Concertant*, bk. 4, no. 1 (a copy borrowed from the library of the music institute in Helsinki but apparently never returned), etc.

5 *Collection de tous les Duos Concertants par Viotti, Violino Primo* — with a note in his teacher's hand: '*Skalor, terzer, sexter och oktaver / Etyder 12 af Rode, 7 af Sont samt Spohrs arpeggien / Gesangsscene* [op. 47] *af Spohr / Serenade melancolique af Tchaikofsky / Concert i.e. af Mendelssohn / Sonate D dur af L. van Beethoven.*'

6 Scores of larger orchestral works and other works from the standard repertoire: J. S. Bach's motets (signed and dated 1893, stamp of Bote & Bock, Berlin) and chorales and sacred arias (ed. Ludwig Erk; signed); Handel's *Messiah*; Mozart's *Magic Flute* and Requiem; Weber's *Freischütz*; Wagner's *Meistersinger* overture; Strauss's *Also sprach Zarathustra*, op. 30 (signed and dated 1901, stamp of A. Stahl, Berlin: Sibelius corrected the number of trombones in the list of instruments: three rather than two); Goldmark's overture to *Im Frühling*, op. 36, for orchestra (two copies of large score) and *Merlin* prelude (also as score);[1] Scriabin's *Prometheus*; Schoenberg's *Gurre-Lieder*, Chamber Symphony, op. 9, Three Pieces for Piano, op. 11, Five Pieces for Orchestra, op. 16 and Six Little Pieces for Piano, op. 19.

7 Choral exercises from the Münchener Musikschule (signed), perhaps purchased in Munich in 1894.

8 Gevaert's *Neue Instrumenten-Lehre* of 1885 (trans. Riemann) (signed, stamped 'Emil Berté, Wien').

[1] JS heard both works in Vienna, see Revers 1996, p. 16.

With regard to his own compositions, the remarkable thing about this collection is the central position occupied by Spohr's violin concertos. The compositions by Vieuxtemps, Viotti and Wieniawski contain isolated seeds for the rhythms and gestures characteristic of Sibelius. This comparison with the semi-popular music of the nineteenth century has already been made by Erik Tawaststjerna with reference to an early suite,[1] but Sibelius' later scherzos and individual themes in the symphonies and piano and chamber music works evoke the same associations. As a student in Helsinki, Sibelius had already read on his own initiative Johann Christian Lobe's old textbook *Lehrbuch der musikalischen Composition* and perhaps also Adolf Bernhard Marx's *Lehre von der musikalischen Komposition*, in part in order to put his knowledge of German to the test. He wrote to his uncle on 24 February 1884:[2] 'It [Lobe's book] is in German and hence doubly useful.' He purchased François Auguste Gevaert's textbook on instrumentation later in Vienna.[3] As a young violinist, he used Carl Henning's *Praktische Violin-Schule nach pädagogischen Grundsätzen*, 1843.

The concert repertoire that the young Sibelius knew before travelling to Berlin and Vienna can be approximately evaluated using Kari Kilpeläinen's summary.[4] Even before 1885, he had one opportunity to hear a fairly large Austrian orchestra, various virtuosos from Finland and abroad, potpourris played by military and town bands, choral singing, domestic concerts and isolated scenes from Tchaikovsky operas. The comparatively active musical life, given the size of the city, was probably in part connected to the building of a railway line from 1857 onwards. After Hämeenlinna, the line continued via Riihimäki and Lahti to St Petersburg in 1870, having been dramatically delayed by famine and epidemics. Although Hämeenlinna had only about three thousand inhabitants at the time, it was a centre of education influenced by teachers and officers.[5] The institutional level of the musical culture of the city was still modest – especially by the standards that Sibelius would soon be establishing himself – but he and his friends balanced it out with improvised events. The artistic success of the student ensemble organised by August Ringvall and Sibelius was probably at least as important to his development, along with free improvisation in nature, as was the chamber music played in his home. In 1876 he visited Helsinki for the first time and heard a large orchestra. Although later too he had opportunities in Helsinki to experience some of the finest virtuosos of his day, impressions from the world of opera were particularly sparse, even though Sibelius himself sometimes performed in the orchestra in modest opera performances – for example, in the school orchestra in Hämeenlinna in 1882, when apparently Vincenzo Bellini's *Norma* was performed (or at least

[1] Erik W. Tawaststjerna 1976, pp. 49 ff.

[2] Goss 1997, pp. 20, 27 and 64.

[3] See also Salmenhaara 1984, p. 67.

[4] Kilpeläinen 2001, pp. 226 ff.

[5] See Klinge 1997, p. 192.

highlights from it).[1] These opportunities, some of them at a rather early age, to play in the orchestra himself may have helped Sibelius evolve into an orchestral composer of the first rank, who in his *Scène de ballet* of 1891 produced orchestral writing that was experimental down to its tiniest detail but also persuasive in terms of technique. Similarly significant were his first reflections on tremolo[2] and other elementary aspects of music with an eye to his innate interest in shaping sound. In 1888 Sibelius was no longer a child prodigy, but the sources demonstrate how originally he approached fundamental problems of composition even before studying in Berlin and Vienna.

When he arrived in Berlin in 1889, he had never seen a Mozart or Wagner opera staged. While he was studying in Helsinki (1885–9), there were performances of Adolphe Adam's *Si j'étais roi*, Bizet's *Carmen*, Ignaz Brüll's *Das goldene Kreuz* (The golden cross), Alexander Dargomyshski's *Rusalka*, Friedrich von Flotow's *Stradella*, Mikhail Glinka's *A Life for the Tsar*, Charles Gounod's *Faust*, Giacomo Meyerbeer's *Les Huguenots* (excerpts), Stanislav Moniuszko's *Halka*, Offenbach's *Les Brigands* and *La Belle Hélène*, Pacius' *Loreley*, Johann Strauss II's *Der Zigeunerbaron*, Franz von Suppé's *Donna Juanita*, Verdi's *La traviata*, *Il trovatore* and *Rigoletto* and Weber's *Der Freischütz* as well as scenes from Mozart's *Le nozze di Figaro* and Rossini's *Il barbiere di Siviglia*. The first Finnish opera (in Swedish), Pacius' *The Hunt of King Charles* (1852, 1875, 1880), was first performed again in 1909, after a long interruption, so that Sibelius was never able to hear it as a student. But on his very first evening in Berlin, he attended *Don Giovanni* (with the legendary Francesco d'Andrade in the title role) at the Krolloper and found the performance 'very fine'.[3] During his first weeks in Berlin he spent more time being astonished and surprised than composing and studying. The opportunity to see Mozart's *Don Giovanni* repeated itself a year later at his first visit to the Hofoper in Vienna.[4] Clearly, it could scarcely be said he was uninterested in the genre, rather that he thirsted for more.

Furthermore, intimate knowledge of the more recent history of composition (contemporary world premieres of note) was virtually closed off to him prior to autumn 1889. Not even the Classical and Romantic canon was completely familiar to him, at least not from the concert hall. Until 1886, his focus was on semi-serious genres, which is indeed reflected in his early compositions both stylistically and in specific melodic and rhythmic figures. It may therefore seem plausible to regard Sibelius – especially in comparison to Strauss and Mahler – as not a 'native speaker' of Central European Modernism.[5] This characterisation by James Hepokoski applied also to his musical education. It was, however, 'Austro-Germanic' – as Hepokoski wrote

[1] Goss 1997, pp. 33–4, makes that assumption, but it was only overtures, scenes and so on, not entire operas.

[2] JS to Pehr Sibelius, 24 October 1888, ibid., pp. 30–31 and 98.

[3] JS to his brother Christian Sibelius, 18 September 1889, and JS to Martin Wegelius, 29 September 1889; quoted in Erik W. Tawaststjerna 1991, p. 123, and Erik W. Tawaststjerna 1976, p. 55.

[4] Erik W. Tawaststjerna 1976, pp. 73–4.

[5] Hepokoski 1993, p. 3.

of Strauss and Mahler – already in Hämeenlinna, and not characteristically Slavic (Russian) or even 'Nordic'. The difference between Sibelius and his 'Austro-Germanic' competitors was not so much the nature as the intensity of his schooling. That is made clear by a comparison of the development of Strauss, Mahler and Sibelius until the age of eighteen. Around the age of eighteen, Sibelius first performed a salon piece in public and had written a few smaller pieces that are difficult to date. Strauss, by contrast, had had a respectable Symphony in D minor premiered under none other than Hermann Levi in Munich and had already published a string quartet and five pieces for piano. At the age of five, Strauss was getting piano lessons from one of the finest teachers of the period in Munich, August Tombo. Nothing comparable ever happened to Sibelius. Mahler, by contrast, gave his first important piano recital at the age of ten and played Sigismund Thalberg's *Grande Fantaisie et Variations sur des motifs de l'opéra 'Norma' de Bellini* at the age of thirteen. A little later, he wrote an opera and studied harmony and counterpoint with Fuchs and piano with Julius Epstein. By the time he was eighteen, he had won several first prizes and had composed a piano quintet, among other works. At that stage, the head start the two Central Europeans had was enormous, and it is well known that Sibelius was later extremely frustrated by such 'hothouse plants', even less prominent ones. The difference should not, however, be interpreted along a cultural axis between 'inside' and 'outside' (in relation to the European mainstream) but rather by weighting differently the elements from the same tradition of music of the second half of the nineteenth century and above all by the respective family circumstances, which still today explain similar differences in the development of great talents.

One example of the Central European foundation of the original 'native speaker' Sibelius is the waltz.[1] It remained alive even after his studies as a monument to the small salons of his youth and as genuine proof of his clear membership in Central European culture, despite his belated professionalisation, and did not simply become a way of earning money. His provisional 'Opus 1' (1887) was a 'Walse fantastique' [*sic*]. It was preceded by a 'Con moto, sempre una corda' ('Minne af J.S. 1885' in 3/4 time), and later in 1888 he wrote three short waltzes for piano. In Helsinki, these were followed by a quick 'Tempo di valse' (1888) for piano and cello and – somewhat more finished, for piano alone – a waltz in A flat 'À Betsy Lerche' (1889), dedicated to his Finnish girlfriend prior to his engagement to Aino Järnefelt. He alluded to the style of the Viennese salon when he composed *Scène de ballet* in stylised waltz rhythm in 1891.[2] Later the composer wrote several waltzes when he had to produce something lucrative quickly. Yet even decades after *Scène de ballet* and *Valse triste* (1903), the waltz kept its very special position in his serious works as well. One notable special case – not least because of Aino's antipathy – was the uncomplicated salon piece *Valse chevaleresque* (1921–2). For the composer's wife, this composition symbolised

[1] Cf. Baranova 2003.

[2] For more detail, see chapter 2.1 in the present volume.

that aspect of her spouse who not only composed and conferred in chic hotels but also celebrated and was celebrated there.[1] Those qualities did not suit the symphonist Sibelius inspired by Nordic nature whom Aino loved and whose myth she cultivated.

A penchant for semi-public salon culture was, however, truly one of his characteristics. That not only came from his first experiences as a violinist (Bériot, Wieniawski and Vieuxtemps) but also expanded his stylistic horizons far beyond the trail reaching from Viennese Classicism via Beethoven's Ninth to the New German style by adding important impulses. The characteristic citation at the end of the Seventh Symphony (1924) of a sequence of chords from the *Valse triste* marks unmistakably the intended connection between his symphonic writing and semi-popular practice – and is also the only instance of conscious inter-textuality – whereas the similarity between *Scène de ballet* and the waltz 'A Spring in the Park' from the *Pelléas et Mélisande* Suite (1905), for example, may be coincidence. In the very last work he completed and published, Three Pieces, op. 116 (1929), composed out of inner inspiration when he no longer had financial worries, there are two characteristic dances for violin and piano, an interesting experiment with the *topos* in 3/4 or 6/4 time. Thus the arc of the waltz spans more than forty years of composition history from his 'Opus 1', 'Walse fantastique' (1887), to his last completed works, *Scène de danse* and *Danse caractéristique* (1929).

Berlin and Vienna, 1889–1891: Becker, Fuchs and Goldmark

In 1889, Sibelius wrote that his teacher Albert Becker, an experienced pedagogue from the inner circle of Franz Xaver Scharwenka's conservatory, was following Bussler's method, with polyphonic exercises and much annoying homework.[2] Becker was a specialist in musical historicism, and in his compositions for the Berlin cathedral (where they can still be heard) he repeatedly referred to sixteenth-century music. Sibelius, by contrast, was a rebellious advocate of the freedom of inspiration. Only twenty years later did he recognise the need for studies of counterpoint and even considered getting further training in composition.[3] After only a few days in Berlin, he remarked: 'Certainly here in Germany they know how to put you down. The only thing for it is to put them down in return.'[4] Although Becker's name was not mentioned, he was intended. In Adolf Paul's portrait of the Berlin period, *En bok om en människa*, Sibelius alias Silén says: 'Everything the teachers tell you is humbug! At least in my case, they taught me nothing but their methods! […] If you show me a teacher whose method is not to have one, then I'll go to him! Otherwise I'll make more progress without any teaching.'[5] Becker wrote in an evaluation that Sibelius was

[1] Erik W. Tawaststjerna 1997b, p. 215.

[2] JS to Pehr Sibelius, 3 October 1889, in Goss 1997, p. 109.

[3] Erik W. Tawaststjerna 1986, p. 141.

[4] JS to Pehr Sibelius, 3 October 1889, in Goss 1997, p. 109.

[5] Paul 1891, p. 206.

a dutiful student and 'hardworking', but more interesting than such formulations, which every evaluation must have, is Becker's cautious assessment of the 'Nordic, rougher character', which had posed a problem with exercises in the Netherlandish-Italian-German (or 'Franco-Flemish') style of the Renaissance.[1] Such formulations suggest that Sibelius was rather headstrong in carrying out his exercises, not entirely conforming to his teacher's expectations.

In his letters to Wegelius, too, Sibelius was critical of Becker: 'in particular, he could not express enough surprise that I use [in his quartet] the same note in its major and minor triad in alternation'.[2] This simple trick was later part of his personal style. Sibelius also reported that Becker charged 10 Reichsmarks for an hour's lesson – a rate similar to that of Fritz Struss, his violin teacher. This information suggests that Sibelius did not, as Madetoja reported in 1915, study with Becker at Scharwenka's conservatory, which had been founded in 1881, but rather privately.[3] Nor can Madetoja's claim be proven that Becker later used the results of Sibelius' exercises in his textbooks.

Sibelius remarked that a non-harmonic false relation ('Querstand') that Becker – who assessed the compositions without a piano, supposedly because he could not even play one, which is a presumptuous statement to make about a German church musician of Becker's standing – had found was intended as a deliberate 'sound effect': 'He said that it was a false relation, but he should hear how the phrase is played by us [that is, by his string quartet] an octave lower. Naturally I was thinking of the sound effect there.' That remark put a great strain on the trust between the young radical and the old academic, and the difference between two artistic concepts was evident. While still in Vienna, Sibelius reflected on his 'deplorable professors', who had managed to praise him for a weak work: 'They are not worth a single pfennig as artists.'[4] When he wrote to Aino on 15 February 1891, that 'now I can do more than Martin [Wegelius] or Kajanus', he was referring to technique, since he had known that for a long time where 'art' was concerned.

Ekman and Tawaststjerna claimed to quote a letter Busoni wrote in the autumn of 1890 characterising his friend Sibelius immediately before his second year abroad. Ekman quoted in German and offered a parenthetical translation: '"Seiner nordischen Herkunft gemäss", Busoni wrote, "ist er später entwickelt wie wir …" (True to his Northern origin, he has developed later than we …).'[5] Tawaststjerna quotes the phrase in German, but differently in one detail: 'als wir' rather than 'wie wir' – the latter an idiomatic mistake typical of Sibelius. The original letter, which Ekman and Tawaststjerna claimed was addressed to Brahms, was supposedly lost, so that Ekman's

[1] Quoted in Gleissner 2002, pp. 43–4.

[2] National Archive Box 121 (referred to hereafter by date alone): JS to Martin Wegelius, 29 September 1889.

[3] Quoted in Salmenhaara 1987, p. 79.

[4] JS to Aino, 3 February 1891.

[5] Ekman 1946, p. 93; quoted in Erik W. Tawaststjerna 1976, p. 72.

notes of his conversations would be the only surviving source. In the National Archive in Helsinki, however, there is a letter from Busoni to Heinrich Freiherr von Herzogenberg, dated September 1890, with a strikingly similar phrase: 'The person in question, Mr Jean Sibelius, is a very talented composer who, in my opinion, may best be able to achieve his final development with you. In keeping with his Northern homeland [*Seiner nördlichen Heimat nach*], he has come to maturity later than usual, but in return he has remained unusually pure and unspoiled for his age.'[1] It is difficult to believe that this letter from Busoni to a famous composer could have been overlooked for so long. In his letter, Busoni refers as a personal reference to a meeting in Leipzig in 1885, when he, himself still a 'beginner', met Herzogenberg.[2] In light of this document, it is unlikely that another letter of recommendation to Brahms exists, especially since Busoni knew the scene too well to suppose that Brahms would accept a new student, and he also knew that Herzogenberg might well do so. Ekman, who was quoting Sibelius, quotes the central passage in German with minor differences and a grammatical error that was typical of Sibelius. It should therefore be assumed that Sibelius was quoting Busoni's letter from memory, and for some reason had forgotten its recipient. It is, of course, also conceivable that he merely mentioned that Herzogenberg was a friend of Brahms, and Ekman understood only 'Brahms'. It is also conceivable that Sibelius deliberately substituted Brahms for the lesser-known Herzogenberg.

Ekman falsely describes the tone of the letter as 'jesting', which indeed proves he never saw it. Busoni wrote elegantly. He did not use, unlike Ekman and Tawaststjerna in the original editions (not in all translations), either the word 'nordisch' (Nordic), which is most unfortunate in the wrong hands, or 'Herkunft' (ethnic origin),[3] but rather the more neutral 'nördlich' (Northern) and 'Heimat' (homeland). Moreover, he avoided the modernist category of *Entwicklung* (development) and wrote, sympathetically, 'Reife' (maturity). The words 'nordisch' and 'Herkunft' have to be traced back to Sibelius and the style of the 1930s. Because Herzogenberg and above all his wife, Elisabeth, were among Brahms's closest friends, Busoni may have been thinking indirectly of an acquaintance with Brahms as well. In this letter, however, it is clear that he intended for Sibelius to study with Herzogenberg. Herzogenberg had been active in Berlin since 1885 and only in the autumn of 1889 did he continue, after an interruption of a few years, his master class for 'advanced composition' in the famous Berlin school of Joseph Joachim and Philipp Spitta. So Busoni and Sibelius, who spent a year studying in Berlin in 1889–90, could assume that Herzogenberg would be looking for new students in autumn 1890 in order to continue to develop his course of study at what was then one of the most progressive conservatories in the world. Dur-

[1] Cf. Mäkelä 2003a.

[2] See Heinrich Freiherr von Herzogenberg to Philipp Spitta, 14 March 1885: 'We now have a very splendid nineteen-year-old here: Busoni. Pianist and composer, matured prodigy, but used to be very serious and brimming with talent.' Quoted in Wiechert 1997, p. 53.

[3] Busoni was also familiar with the word 'Nordic'; see Ferruccio Busoni to Egon Petri, 13 June 1908, in Beaumont 1987, p. 91.

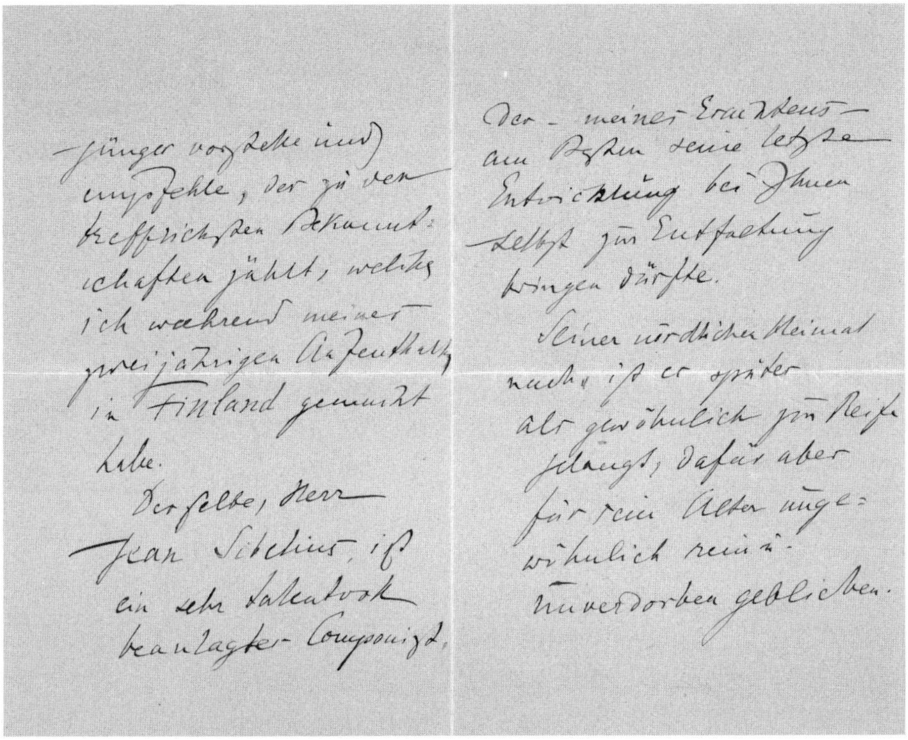

Jünger vorstelle und
empfehle, der zu den
trefflichsten Bekannt-
schaften zählt, welche
ich während meines
zweijährigen Aufenthalts
in Finland gemacht
habe.
Derselbe, Herr
Jean Sibelius, ist
ein sehr talentvoll
beanlagter Componist,

der – meiner Erachtens –
am besten seine letzte
Entwicklung bei Ihnen
selbst zur Entfaltung
bringen dürfte.
Seiner nördlichen Heimat
nach, ist er später
als gewöhnlich zur Reife
gelangt, dafür aber
für sein Alter unge-
wöhnlich rein u.
unverdorben geblieben.

FIG. 22. Ferruccio Busoni's letter of recommendation for Sibelius to Heinrich von Herzogenberg (September 1890).

ing Herzogenberg's illness, Woldemar Bargiel had substituted for him — expressly not Becker, who, in the opinion of Joachim, would have been 'too insignificant' for Herzogenberg's tasks at the school.[1] Moreover, it may have worked against Becker that he was already teaching for Scharwenka. On 11 January 1890, when Sibelius was still in Berlin, Herzogenberg was appointed an ordinary member of the Königliche Akademie der Künste (Royal Academy of the Arts). In that winter especially, he was inundated with honours,[2] so Sibelius must have known his name. Nor would the

[1] Joseph Joachim to Philipp Spitta, 3 August 1884; quoted in Wiechert 1997, p. 62.
[2] Ibid., pp. 77 ff.

competition between Becker and Herzogenberg or Bargiel (and beyond that between the leading Berlin conservatories of the late nineteenth century) have negatively affected his impression, since Sibelius did not admire Becker either. Because he had spent several days in Berlin before arriving in Vienna, it is conceivable that he tried to reach Herzogenberg. His letters to Aino seem to prove, however, that Vienna was his destination on that trip and Berlin was merely a stopover.

In September 1890, in any case, it was not clear where and with whom Sibelius would continue his studies. Sibelius may have decided relatively spontaneously (even as he was still in Berlin, perhaps advised by Berlin musicians) to study in Vienna, since as late as 29 October 1890, he did not know with whom he could study there, though he was already there: Bruckner and the conductor Hans Richter were recommended to him after his arrival, which shows how chaotic this undertaking was. Sibelius himself noted: 'Richter does not accept any students and Bruckner is sick.'[1] One obvious explanation for his indecision could, of course, be a failed plan by Sibelius or his Finnish teachers to spend another year in Berlin, but this time with a suitable teacher (like Herzogenberg). The great Wagnerian conductor Hans Richter supposedly recommended Robert Fuchs, which was a bold suggestion in light of the documentation of the Brahms–Bruckner(–Wagner) controversy – or alternatively strong evidence that this conflict existed primarily in the press. In the end, Sibelius began to take private lessons from Fuchs. He also visited Karl Goldmark, famous for the opera *The Queen of Sheba* (1875), several times. Sibelius' letters from Vienna (e.g., a letter to Aino, 13 February 1891) indicate that Goldmark wanted to see 'something' four times a year, and then only if Sibelius had something to show. It is not known how often he went to Goldmark. Nevertheless, Goldmark later proudly introduced himself as 'Sibelius' teacher'.[2] Both statements should be treated with caution: Sibelius consistently emphasised his independence, and Goldmark had no other distinguished students to show.

Sibelius never allowed himself to be influenced by the style of a traditionalist teacher like Fuchs, even though he valued him as a conversation partner. The openness and curiosity of Sibelius are demonstrated by the enthusiasm he showed for Bruckner, whose Third Symphony he heard on 21 December 1890, when its new version was premiered, and by the fact that he sought inspiration from Goldmark of all people, who had been known for his emphasis on Wagner. Sibelius was astonishingly negative in his attitude towards Brahms, whose 'new' Quintet in F major, op. 88, of 1882 he characterised as 'beneath all criticism' in a letter to Aino on 27 January 1891 – with a similar comment, by the way, about Busoni's Sonata for Violin and Piano. His judgements in general were unrestrained and at the same time refreshingly unconventional during this period: he considered Anton Rubinstein even weaker than

[1] JS to Maria and Evelina Sibelius, 29 October 1890, in Goss 1997, p. 112.

[2] Erik W. Tawaststjerna 1991, p. 173, quoting Wilhelm Altmann, 'Jean Sibelius', *Nord und Süd* (December 1908).

Tekla Bądarzewska's piano piece *La Prière d'une vierge* (1856), and Rubinstein was, after all, Goldmark's mentor. Perhaps this was a sign of Sibelius' generally negative (nationalist) position on artists of Russian origin.

Fuchs took over Beckmesser's task of detecting banalities of compositional technique, rather than interpreting them as signs of outstanding talent. But even Fuchs had ambitions. During the time Sibelius spent in Vienna, Fuchs himself was working on opera projects. One of the most important of them was *Die Teufelsglocke* (The devil's bell; 1893), with a great deal of wind and storm. Hanslick commented critically on Fuchs's operas, although with some sympathy. Fuchs lacked, in Hanslick's view, the dramatic, the 'gripping force of rhythms, convincing immediacy of melodies, vigorous forward movement and rapid conclusion'.[1] Peter Revers believes with good reason that Sibelius was greatly influenced not by Fuchs but rather by Goldmark's aesthetic, his general advice on an advanced level ('Rework your ideas more thoroughly, so they have more inner character' and the like) and his deftly formulated criticism of the Overture in E major — the last of the not yet very interesting orchestral works — as 'artificial'.[2] Madetoja reported, however, that Goldmark's criticism was by no means always so deftly formulated.[3] When Sibelius responded: 'But I wanted to emphasise …', Goldmark supposedly interrupted him (in Viennese dialect): 'You aren't allowed to want here.' In Vienna, in any case, Sibelius was made into a 'routined orchestrator'.[4] He purchased Goldmark's scores but did not mark what he found interesting. We do not even know whether he actually read them or which of the many performances of Goldmark's or Fuchs's works in Vienna he attended.[5] By his own account, not even Goldmark was 'of much importance' for his 'inner development',[6] so that it would be risky to assume he was a faithful student.

Just as Wegelius had, Goldmark recommended Mozart, Haydn and Beethoven as role models.[7] He was no avant-garde ambassador of the New German movement but rather an older colleague who inspired him to self-confident independence. He supposedly said of Wagner: 'It is a great danger for the youth of our day that they begin with Berlioz and Wagner.'[8] He advised Sibelius to remain 'modest' (*bescheiden*) for several years and dedicate himself to the classics, which had been Goldmark's own method as a self-taught composer many years ago.[9] Sibelius, who was, after all,

[1] Hanslick 1889, pp. 95 ff.; quoted in Grote 1994, p. 36.

[2] Revers 1996, p. 16; he emphasises Goldmark's influence as a master of orchestration (p. 23).

[3] Leevi Madetoja, 'Jean Sibeliuksen taiteilijanuran yleiset piirteet', *Helsingin Sanomat*, December 8, 1915; quoted in Salmenhaara 1987, p. 80.

[4] Ringbom 1954, 24.

[5] A list that suggested he attended is found in Krones 2003a, pp. 26–7.

[6] Ringbom 1954, p. 24.

[7] Revers 1996, p. 16; see also Erik W. Tawaststjerna 1976, p. 88.

[8] JS to Martin Wegelius, 12 February 1891. On Goldmark's view of Wagner, which was by no means negative, see also Botstein 2003, pp. 56–7.

[9] Pfannkuch 1956, col. 482.

a grown man and not a young student (in that sense Goldmark's advice came too late and ignored Sibelius' belatedness), nevertheless immediately plunged into the New German wave. Goldmark's dealings with him may reflect a certain restraint. In particular the word 'modest', which Sibelius quoted in German, implies that Goldmark suspected he was too impulsively self-assured.

Fuchs, by contrast, was a widely admired, experienced teacher of harmony and counterpoint. He taught advanced composition only after 1895, at least at the conservatory, after his brother and predecessor, Johann Nepomuk Fuchs, took over as rector.[1] Although Sibelius was unable to study with Fuchs in the established framework of an academic curriculum, he was dealing once again – as with Wegelius and Becker – with a technically extremely precise composer who also knew how to foster different types of students. The list of Fuchs students (including his harmony and counterpoint class) reads like an encyclopaedia of Viennese modernity. Sibelius was a member of the student orchestra under Fuchs's direction and showed him his own compositions.[2] For Sibelius' Finnish sponsors, Fuchs provided a glowing recommendation. With him, Sibelius was not far from Brahms's circle of influence, whose advocacy had helped Fuchs obtain his very first lectureship in harmony in 1886.[3] However, Fuchs could not or did not wish to – which is more likely – introduce Sibelius to his mentor; there was only a brief encounter in a Viennese café (perhaps Zum Rothen Igel at the Tuchlauben). Two characters could hardly be more different, even overlooking the difference in age. Only later did Brahms show an interest in a Sibelius song, 'Se'n har jag ej frågat mera' (Then I ceased to ask those questions) from op. 17, and said to the soprano performing it: 'He will be something someday.'[4] For Brahms, that was presumably a compliment.

In contrast to the impressions Sibelius gained in the circle of his artist friends in Helsinki, Berlin and Vienna, through the *Kalevala* and from nature, all of his composition teachers were traditionalists who tended to pedantry. This made successful practitioners such Alois Rosenberg, Pauline Lucca, Aino Ackté, Busoni and Kajanus all the more important. Their influence explains the self-confidence with which Sibelius kept his distance from the established aesthetic bastions of his day. Whereas he accused his three official composition teachers (and probably Goldmark as well) of not understanding him, he singled out Kajanus for precisely showing the

[1] Grote 1994, p. 164.

[2] Erik W. Tawaststjerna 1976, pp. 74 ff. For Fuch's letter of recommendation (28 February 1891), see Erik W. Tawaststjerna 1991, p. 171. Layton's abridged translation of Tawaststjerna mentions only that the letter is a 'glowing testimonial' (1976, vol. 1, p. 87). In fact, it reads as follows (and, for a Viennese tutor, its tone is rather moderate): 'With pleasure I confirm that Mr Jean Sibelius, who is at present studying music with me, possesses quite an outstanding talent for composition that we can expect to produce the finest fruits in the future.'

[3] Grote 1994, p. 37.

[4] On the report (1942) by Ida Ekman, who was permitted to sing the Lied twice for Brahms, see Erik W. Tawaststjerna 1976, p. 180.

required insights into his art, as Jussi Jalas has noted.[1] It would be an exaggeration to say that Sibelius' development as a composer would have been inconceivable without Kajanus, but Finland's leading musician of the 1880s was not unimportant, not only as a powerful defender of the ideas of the New German reform in a context that was typically Finnish rather than classicistic but also as a charismatic fellow artist.

Some early reporters exaggerated Kajanus' importance. Therefore, to his annoyance, Sibelius found it necessary to speak of Kajanus and his influence often, as is documented, for example, in a manuscript written by Jussi Snellman, at Sibelius' request, and dated 24 December 1943; it was a draft letter to the editor in response to a problematic report in the newspaper *Kaleva*.[2] It corrects the information that Bargiel[3] and Busoni had been his 'teachers'. It also comments on the style of Sibelius' letters (always in the style of the recipient, etc.[4]), on his relationship to Larin Paraske as regards *Kullervo* and emphatically on the question of unpublished works: 'Any possible surviving manuscripts of mine may not be published. Publishers often use those that composers themselves have not cleared.' His relationship to Kajanus is summed up in accordance with Jalas's notes: 'All three of my teachers – Martin Wegelius, Albert Becker/Berlin/ and Robert Fuchs/Vienna/ – had little understanding for my artistic efforts. Robert Kajanus, by contrast, recognised immediately that an artist like me has to find his own way.' Defending him, Mikko Slöör wrote to Sibelius as early as 16 May 1898: 'You know that in Kajus [Kajanus] you have a true friend to a much higher degree than you perhaps believe. Don't let gossips separate you; it is my conviction that he can report in good conscience about all his activities concerning the application for a position.'[5] The reference is to the obscure events surrounding Sibelius' application for the position of music director at the university in 1896. The climax of the conflict came in 1952, when a new Kajanus biography offered the view that Sibelius was dependent on Kajanus' advice up to the time of the Fifth Symphony.[6]

For various reasons involving the structure of their respective personalities, Sibelius' relationship to Kajanus was always complicated, even though Kajanus performed Sibelius' work at every opportunity, asked for advice on such occasions and even made his orchestra available as a kind of sonic laboratory.[7] For a time, Sibelius tried to convey the impression he had not even known Kajanus until 1890 and did not learn anything from him afterwards, but this was a strategy of public defence as he had the impression of standing in Kajanus' shadow. On April 9, 1891, Sibelius wrote diplomatically – *nota bene*: shortly before the world premiere of *Scène de ballet* under Kajanus

[1] Jalas 1981, p. 57.

[2] In National Archive Box 41.

[3] See Niemann 1917, p. 9.

[4] See chapter 1.3 in the present volume.

[5] National Library Coll. 206: 36.

[6] Suomalainen 1952, p. 89.

[7] Erik W. Tawaststjerna 1976, p. 137.

on 28 April — that he envied him for his most recent composition.[1] In the early 1890s, the problems were probably minimal. For example, in 1892 Sibelius began to teach at the orchestra school Kajanus directed, which competed with Wegelius' institute. Like every written document on influence or antagonism in Sibelius' case (both reports and Sibelius' responses), those concerning Kajanus should be read carefully. The clues do not point to Salieri syndrome, but the anxiety of influence is evident.

[1] Vainio 2002, p. 213.

> [...] but I have no folkloristic intentions in the music so you must approach it [*Kyllikki*] quite abstractly like a sonata and just closely follow the musical signs.[1]

3.2 From *Kalevala* to *Kullervo*

Beyond Grieg

When Sibelius was studying the *Kalevala* in the autumn of 1890,[2] he was building on the few advantages he had over his fellow students in Vienna. Because he had to learn Finnish at the same time, however, his goal in studying the *Kalevala* was not to find his own roots. Although it had been required reading at his high school in Hämeenlinna, and Kajanus' performance of his symphonic mystery play *Aino* in Berlin in 1890 – the first time a conductor from Finland conducted his own work with the Berlin Philharmonic – had surely been unforgettable, it was in Vienna that Sibelius first discovered the artistic possibilities of that collection of folk poetry. The influence of his fiancée, Aino Järnefelt, who was steeped in nationalist idealism, was considerable. Personal reasons – on the one hand, his desire to please the Järnefelts and, on the other, establishing himself in Vienna – made Sibelius the ideal agent for the *Kalevala* cult, which was in any case raging around 1890. In an effort to curry favour, the composer asserted in a letter from Vienna: 'Right now all my moods are stolen from the *Kalevala*.'[3] At almost the same time, however, he enthused about the Third Symphony by Bruckner, whom he considered 'the greatest of all living composers' (though he called Bruckner 'ridiculous' from the point of view of form), and about Pietro Mascagni's opera *Cavalleria rusticana*.[4] Another source of musical pleasure at the time was Beethoven's Ninth Symphony, which he heard under Hans Richter.[5] Mozart's *Don Giovanni* completed the 'cocktail' of influences that led to the symphonic cantata *Kullervo* in the spring of 1892.

The suspicion that Grieg influenced Sibelius – especially with regard to his interest in regional, Nordic and rustic subjects – is based largely on the trivial fact that until a few decades ago Grieg and Sibelius were the only internationally known composers from the North. Niemann, who established the premises of the reception of the North in the German music press, reduced the two composers to an aesthetic common denominator and considered them 'Heimatkünstler' – or 'artists of the

[1] National Archive Box 35. JS to Helen Levin (in Chicago), 8 May 1936, concerning *Kyllikki* (based on the *Kalevala*).

[2] There were three versions of Lönnrot's anthology: 1835, 1849 and 1862. The most extensive of these was the 1849 version, which set new standards, and it was the one JS most likely used.

[3] JS to Aino, 18 April 1891.

[4] See Erik W. Tawaststjerna 1976, p. 77. Cf. JS to Aino, 21 December 1890.

[5] JS to Martin Wegelius, 13 April 1891.

homeland', which he intended in a positive sense — 'from abroad'.[1] By doing so, he neglected Sibelius' complex regional identity in particular. Sibelius was referring to this misunderstanding of an essential equivalence, which apparently often occurred long before Niemann, when he wrote from Vienna in 1891: 'People are always saying to me: "Your compatriot Grieg." That's how little they know about us Northerners.'[2] Ida Ekman's postcard from Berlin, dated 7 April 1903, is revealing about Grieg's relationship to Sibelius: 'Maestro Grieg is magnificent! [...] Grieg would be delighted if you were to send him your "Christian Suite". He is delighted by your songs and says, unfortunately, he knows far too few of them. [...] Grieg loves Finland.'[3] But even in 1903 one could hardly say that Grieg had appreciated Sibelius' work beyond a love for Finland. Whereas Constant Lambert explicitly warned against taking Sibelius, in the wake of a 'Nordic nationalism', for a 'local *petit-maître*, a Finnish Grieg',[4] other authors such as Tawaststjerna have seen the influence of Grieg in the dominant ninth chords of his early work, especially given that as a youth Sibelius had heard Grieg's violin sonatas.[5] Considering Grieg's popularity around 1880, this is hardly surprising; Henryk Wieniawski and Louis Spohr were similarly important to Sibelius, albeit less 'Nordic'.

Grieg and Sibelius, who never met, have independently given reason to suppose that traces of the 'genuine' folk music of the North can be found in their work. Although Grieg also integrated regional elements and melodies into a contemporary, universal art-song texture — for example, in 'Aften på höyfjellet' (Evening on the mountain) of 1882 — rather than imitating or quoting them, he is never accused of being a 'folk-song nationalist'.[6] Perhaps Grieg's relationship to Norwegian folksong was not as complicated as the function of folk culture in Sibelius or Bartók, for example. The range of the aesthetic framework is not entirely unimportant for the differences in the effect of the folkloristic elements in Grieg and Sibelius, respectively. Whereas Grieg defended his penchant for the miniature (Lied, lyrical piano piece) until the end of his life, and encouraged younger Norwegians such as Johan Svendsen to establish the national symphonic style instead, small forms were secondary for Sibelius (and often occasional works). The folk quality of Grieg's work has the effect of having emerged directly from the bourgeois salons of the Romantic era, using their genres to express himself.

Despite Grieg's self-proclaimed 'total absorption in nature', there are statements by him that reveal that his understanding of nature, even in the 1890s, did not have the profundity or the sublime ambition of the Symbolists that was characteristic of Sibelius. Grieg represented another generation. In Norway, Knut Hamsun and

[1] Cf. the table of contents in Niemann 1913a.

[2] JS to Aino, 11 January 1891.

[3] National Archive Box 18.

[4] Lambert 1934, p. 305. He was (for good reason) attacking the British critic Walter J. Turner, who in 1933 had described *Tapiola*, of all works, as 'neo-Grieg'.

[5] Erik W. Tawaststjerna 1976, pp. 33–4, etc.

[6] Alfred H. Meyer 1936, p. 68. For more on this topic, see Grimley 2006.

Edvard Munch stood for the same direction of Modernism as Sibelius. In any case, Sibelius never made statements establishing a direction for or restricting the function of art as Grieg did, who on 21 February 1875 saw his artistic ideal as 'painting in sound Norwegian nature, Norwegian folk life, Norwegian history and Norwegian folk poetry'; or in 1869: 'because it is my life dream to form in sound the nature of the North.'[1] These are the ideas of a realist anchored in the regional,[2] not those of the Surrealist or Symbolist. Although Grieg spoke of 'bathing in authenticity' and of nature as 'Shakespeare, Beethoven and whatever else you will in a pure concentrate' and lived in constant conflict between the desire for the peace of the countryside and the excitement of large cities, he did not become absorbed in his fantasies in nature in the spirit of Symbolism.[3] For him, nature was an 'other', albeit the loving mother's bosom:

> I really know only one cure, but thank God I know that, and it is mentioned in your letter, because it is your medicine as well. 'A little mouse hole in which to hide or a little hut in the mountains.' I would like to formulate it a little more broadly and say: life in the (western) Norwegian mountainous nature as a whole. [...] How wonderful it is that nature is superior to man in such relationships. For a man, however much one may like him, can only disappoint [one]. But nature never can. Whatever happens, one does not seek refuge in its bosom in vain.[4]

The idyll Grieg describes here is not identical with Sibelius' elemental experience of nature. It is also characteristic that Grieg locates his idyll so precisely – which is untypical of Sibelius.

Considering the works of Bartók and Janáček, 'in spite of [...] folkloristic inclinations', as 'nonetheless among the most progressive in European musical art' and not part of the 'nationalistic reaction', as Adorno did,[5] applies to Sibelius as well, especially since Bartók and Janáček did not compose only 'extra-territorial' music, but not so much to Grieg, whose art, despite remarkable modernity in its details, still represented the Romantic-Realistic era. In Sibelius, this 'extra-territorial' quality involved taking gestures that emerged in the context of traditional folk music and integrating them into contemporary compositional practice. In the process, he employed elements from folk music that aggressively negate their regional function. Moreover, there is his aesthetic stance, already influenced by Impressionism and Symbolism, and the metrically and semantically regulated art of *runo* song in the *Kalevala*. In his most important works he demonstrates that, although he is dealing with archaic materials in a masterly way, he questions the conventions in practice. He permits motifs,

[1] Edvard Grieg to Bjørnstjerne Bjørnson, 21 February 1875, and Edvard Grieg to Gottfred Matthison-Hansen in 1869, quoted in Schwab 2001a, pp. 397–8 (which in turn cites Hauch 1922).

[2] Cf. Dahlhaus 1985, pp. 106–13 ('The Natural World and the "Folklike Tone"').

[3] Quoted in Benestad 2002, p. 183.

[4] Edvard Grieg to Franz Beyer, 29 December 1894; quoted in Vollsnes 2002, pp. 75–6.

[5] Adorno 1985, pp. 35–6 n. 5. For a detailed discussion, see chapter 5.2 in the present volume.

rhythms, metres and phrasing — gestures small and large — that are rooted in the design principles of Finnish folk culture. It is, however, not possible to identify specific folkloristic models for his melodic invention.[1] Whereas Wagner, say, created the regionalism of his art on a historical and mythological basis, and composers such as Grieg, Smetana and Vincent d'Indy made use not only of a quite complex integration of folksong but also of flourishes borrowed directly from it, the relationship between Sibelius and Finnish folk culture is structural and sub-thematic. Even where many suspect folklorism — in *Kullervo* and the early symphonies — it is actually a critical position vis-à-vis late Romantic musical language and academism.

In Sibelius' works, such motifs are heard unmediated and in an unusually modern context. Even in *Tapiola*, where they are part of an avant-garde concept of the work, the simple third motif in bar 569 concludes a section begun already in bar 513 that is without a doubt one of the most radical in the orchestral literature of the period. In bar 552, rising motifs suggest that the chromatic field of the strings will soon come to an end, but their rhythmic profile is unprepossessing in comparison to bar 569. The motif in bar 569 is derived from the motivic basic cell of the work in bars 1–3, but the rhythm gives it a unique quality whose folkloristic form contrasts with the sound fields. One reason for this impression may be that listeners in the twentieth and twenty-first centuries, thanks to a growing culture of folk music in the media, hear far more often (and not always willingly) the folk music of their regions and beyond in 'world music' than was possible around 1900 and earlier. Over the course of the twentieth century, many folk music cultures have become so omnipresent in media that trivialisation is inevitable. By contrast, when Chopin in his mazurkas works with a specific culture of dance music that remains almost unknown today — and that even in his lifetime was viewed from a respectful distance by the academically educated and only occasionally practised, precisely as a form of exoticism — his work does not suffer from this problem. The enjoyment of his art is not affected by folkloristic associations. Chopin was the first to employ folklore as a vehicle of defamiliarisation, making him a true precursor of Grieg, Sibelius, Janáček and Bartók.

His occasional direct contact with folk music — beginning in 1889 with a student masquerade as a *kantele* player[2] — helped Sibelius truly to absorb folk music, not just objectify it in a programme or quote from it. In some songs, especially in 'Drömmen' (The dream, op. 13, no. 5), a Lied he composed in Vienna in 1891, it is clear he was striving for a Finnish sound. He wrote to Aino on 8 January 1891 about this 'melancholically monotone' song and how he 'believes in Finnish music'. Only for his six piano arrangements of 1903 did he actually start with folksongs. With regard to the piano cycle *Kyllikki* (1904), whose overall title and names of the movements refer to the *Kalevala* legend of a girl from Lemminkäinen's circle, he wrote even more clearly to the pianist Helen Levin on 8 May 1936: 'but I have no folkloristic intentions in the

[1] Cf. the models of assimilation, imitation and incorporation in Bartók [1920] 1976b.

[2] JS to Pehr Sibelius, 3 February 1889, in Goss 1997, p. 102.

music so you must approach it quite abstractly like a sonata and only closely follow the musical signs'.[1] This was not about denying the all-too-obvious but about providing important information about the compositional process, in which the exotic title had little meaning as a programme; Sibelius did not want the programme to preclude formal order and believed the challenge for the performer was to work out the structure.

While working on *Kullervo*, his opportunities to hear genuine *Kalevala* sounds were limited in any case. Sibelius had a supplement to Elias Lönnrot's *Kanteletar* that included music and an edition of *runo* melodies by Kajanus published in 1888, and in 1891 he got to know Ilmari Krohn's 'Paimenessa' (Shepherd's song), which featured passages in 5/4 time.[2] More important still was his encounter with the *runo* singer Larin Paraske, who since 1887 had been celebrated in the national press as a representative of an old tradition. The very knowledge of her existence – like a figure from mythical worlds, the 'other' personified – inspired contemporary artists for whom archaic Finland was otherwise something imaginary. Not until summer 1892, on the trail of Albert Edelfelt and Akseli Gallen-Kallela, did Sibelius visit Karelia. His studies there, for which he received stipends of 600 Finnish marks – one third paid on completion – were not especially detailed. By his own account, he did not find 'any Finnish sound', but he heard several singers, reported on the significance of their mannered, hysterical laughter as the climax to ritual weeping, notated dance songs (some of them cheerful) and observed that Karelian folk music was by no means always melancholic. Thus he discovered that there was an important difference between the folksongs known in Helsinki – selected for publication using one-sided aesthetic criteria by artists such as Kajanus – and the living tradition.

One of the high points of his journey, via Toijala, Imatra and Joensuu, was a stop with Aino near Lieksa, with a view of Mount Koli, which Sibelius would later climb in 1909 with his brother-in-law Eero Järnefelt. Around 20 July 1892, the young couple parted ways, for some ten days, in Joensuu, a port city on an inland sea. This period is relevant as a research trip. The route was determined by the traffic routes at that time, travelling whenever possible by ship, on a few legs by train – for example, from Helsinki to Imatra (an old stretch of track via Riihimäki, Lahti and Kouvola on the way to St Petersburg via Vyborg) – and from Helsinki to Hämeenlinna. Old country roads were used only for local traffic. Sibelius continued the journey on horse trails, while Aino took the ship from Savonlinna to Kuopio to see her aunt, as documented in her letter to Sibelius of 20 July 1892. In his final report, however, he was vague about dates in general but wrote that he 'departed Karelia in mid-August',[3] which means that he generously extended his study trip on paper to include the time with Aino's relatives in the provincial city of Kuopio and above all on the Monola estate in

[1] National Archive Box 35.

[2] See Goss 2004, p. 27 (with musical example).

[3] Archives of the University of Helsinki. See also Erik W. Tawaststjerna 1991, p. 232.

Lieksa.[1] He was exaggerating the length of the professional part of the trip, but (and more importantly) he was successful: in Mysysvaara, near Korpiselkä (today mostly in Russia, thirty miles north of Lake Ladoga), Sibelius met Petri (Pedri) Shemeikka, one of the most famous *runo* singers of the era.[2]

Three years passed after completing the journey before the *Kalevala* supplement with music that Axel August Borenius (later Lähteenkorva) had wanted to edit, with Sibelius' assistance, was finally published.[3] Salmenhaara considered it possible that Borenius might have shown the young composer his extensive collection of some eight hundred melodies much earlier.[4] More interesting than a precise date would be information about how thoroughly he studied Borenius' archive of folksongs. In the first edition of *Kalevala: II. Selityksiä* (Commentaries), it misleadingly states that Borenius helped Sibelius edit it. In the second edition (1901), that indication was not only corrected but Sibelius' name was removed — according to his express wish.[5] The original listing of Sibelius' name first was probably connected to the national resonance of his name. At the same time, it was hinted that the sparse selection of examples from Borenius' collection must have been made by Sibelius and probably was not approved by the folklorist at all.[6] In 1901, in turn, Sibelius suddenly no longer wished to be associated with this activity (or with folk music in general). His activity as a collector and editor was, in sum, less important than his general enthusiasm for Borenius' archive and recognition of his work.[7]

Between Cavalleria rusticana and Le Sacre du printemps

Kajanus observed — whether ironically, enviously or respectfully — after the premiere of Sibelius' Second String Quartet on 29 May 1889, that 'one' need not compose in Finland any longer since the 24-year-old could clearly do it much better.[8] He also revealed to the public the young artist's creative competencies by presenting *Scène de ballet* in Helsinki on 28 April 1891. Nevertheless, Sibelius' career as the successor to the older national composer Kajanus effectively began a year later, on 28 April 1892, with the premiere of the 'symphonic poem' *Kullervo* for soprano, baritone and chorus. The year of its premiere was a political bull's-eye. In the context of the heated

[1] Emma Järnefelt to Aino in Kuopio, 5 August 1892, in Talas 2000, 108 ff. Cf. the correspondence between Aino and her relatives, quoted in Talas 2000, pp. 108 ff. (with comments by the editor), as well as between Aino and JS.

[2] Väisänen 1921, p. 77.

[3] Erik W. Tawaststjerna 1991, pp. 269 ff., and Erik W. Tawaststjerna 1976, p. 164. See also Laitinen 1976.

[4] Salmenhaara 1996b, pp. 73–4.

[5] See the correspondence between the Suomalaisen Kirjallisuuden Seura and JS in 1895 and 1901; National Library Coll. 206: 26 and 50.

[6] Laitinen 1976, pp. 166–7.

[7] Ibid., p. 159; musical samples on pp. 168–70. Cf. also the sketch of a folksong by JS illustrated on p. 175.

[8] Salmenhaara 1996b, p. 86.

debates over the constitution for the Grand Duchy of Finland,[1] Alexander Järnefelt wrote with inner conviction to his future brother-in-law that 'with *Kullervo* you have entered the service of the Finnish cause'.[2] The years of oppression had not yet begun; a show of cultural and political strength still seemed possible.

The idea *per se* of selecting the subject of Kullervo from the diverse material of the *Kalevala*, which by no means forms a homogeneous narrative line, was not original and may in fact have had a populist motive. Compared to the legend of the *sampo*'s robbery (*Kalevala*, 1849, Cantos 39–44; cf. Gallen-Kallela's painting of 1905–6), it was not just politically coded but quite harmless. Aleksis Kivi had received the grand prize of the Suomalaisen Kirjallisuuden Seura (Finnish literary society) in 1860 for his one-act play *Kullervo*, and Filip von Schantz composed an overture for Kivi's play. Kajanus' *Funeral March of Kullervo* (1880) was another precursor on this theme.[3] Although Sibelius' work also reflects a naturalistic and social critical updating of the material that was common around 1860, Kivi, because he was working in spoken theatre, was in a better position to treat current themes in a forceful way. Moreover Sibelius' interpretation of the *Kalevala* was 'modern', but at the same time it was 'pure music':[4] Kullervo's war against the enemy is purely symphonic, and the enemy is not the Ilmarinen of the 'East' but rather a certain Untamo (Kullervo's uncle).[5] Nevertheless, Sibelius' *Kullervo* is closer to Kivi's take on the theme than its archaic-mythological, trivially neoclassical reception in the twentieth century might lead one to believe.

The composer and organist Oskar Merikanto played a role in the success of *Kullervo*, which became of eminent significance for Finnish art and for the nationalist project of cultural development in general, positioning it in the regional culture. His interpretation, which drew attention to the work's political power, was distributed to the audience before the premiere. This prevented the performance from causing outrage because of its musical difficulties (unusual chords and rhythms, far from the popular style of patriotic cantatas and the nationalist, idealist classicism of the previous generations). It was feared that some of the Swedish-speaking elite would scheme against the work if only because it had a Finnish text. In addition to the language, which was a novelty in a work of this size, there are modal scales (popular and historicist) and asymmetrical 5/4 time. This metre had been used previously by Axel G. Ingelius in his rustic *Scherzo finnico* of 1847, but it is also found in Russian folk music. It can therefore function as a Russian element, made socially acceptable in Tchaikovsky's Sixth Symphony. In the Western European or Swedish context, the metre sounds 'Eastern', but in Finland that could just as easily mean 'Finnish'.

In his essay Merikanto explicitly warned of 'strange harmonies and unusual

1 See Klinge 1997, p. 322.

2 Salmenhaara 1996b, p. 90.

3 On the context, see Klinge 1997, pp. 201 ff. See also Salmenhaara 1996b, pp. 46 ff.

4 Erik W. Tawaststjerna 1976, p. 76.

5 The various versions of the story are discussed later in this chapter.

melodies'. He wrote that these were national features — not naturalism, much less 'modern'. Correspondingly, the first main theme in E minor has been compared not only to Bruckner's Third Symphony and to Dvořák but also to the Finnish folksong 'Niin minä neitonen sinulle laulan' (Thus I sing for you, maiden).[1] The composer did not support any such an interpretation. One of the features of the theme is a syncopated rhythm (short–long) on the fourth count of the first bar, which is actually a feature of the Celtic vocabulary.[2] This example shows how arbitrary the search for reminiscences is, since the theme in question is neither a quotation from a folksong nor a variation on Bruckner or Dvořák, despite its heavily dotted rhythm. The question remains: what significance do such similarities have?

The compositional originality of *Kullervo* is astonishing in comparison to the works that preceded and immediately followed it. *Kullervo* was a unique, ripe fruit of his nine months in Vienna — the result of his artistic and human development. In Vienna on 18 April 1891, Sibelius sketched the archaic 'basic idea of the first theme' as the theme for a 'symphony'.[3] Even without an intense study of folklore, he was able to simulate the motifs, scales and rhythms of Finnish folk culture — much as he did in passages in the Overture in E major, which premiered on 28 April 1891. As creative as a *runo* singer, a Finnish Homer, he reworked the archaic stories he had studied so intently in Vienna. Sibelius achieved effects that presage Stravinsky's *Le Sacre du printemps* (1913) — for example, the horn version of the *runo* theme in the second movement. Salmenhaara even compared the rhythm of the fourth movement to *Petrushka*.[4] In Helsinki in 1892, Sibelius could not take the same risk that Stravinsky could twenty years later in France. If the history of performances of *Kullervo* had not been so limited geographically — although it is not documented which musicians from St Petersburg attended the performances in 1892 and 1893 and may thus have served as mediators — then one might have thought that not only Stravinsky but also Zoltan Kodály and Béla Bartók must have known the work in light of their own developments several years later. *Kullervo* is like a surreal link between *Cavalleria rusticana* and *Le Sacre du printemps* (with certain motifs that also recall Stravinsky's *L'Oiseau du feu*). On 14 April 1891, just before sketching the first version of the main theme of *Kullervo*, Sibelius had seen Mascagni's opera.[5]

In the circle of Alexander Borodin in particular — one thinks of Vasily Kalinnikov, for example — there are of course other works that could help to explain the links between *Kullervo* and Stravinsky. Nils-Eric Ringbom believed that Sibelius had almost no opportunities, at least during his early years in Helsinki, to hear Russian orchestral music — other than Tchaikovsky — because he was in Vienna when Borodin's 'musi-

1 See Salmenhaara 1984, pp. 89–90.

2 On rhythms of this sort, see Monelle 1997, pp. 87 ff., and Latham 2002, p. 1131.

3 JS to Aino, 18 April 1891, with musical example. On the biographical context of this time, see chapter 2.1 in the present volume.

4 See also Salmenhaara 1996b, pp. 78–9.

5 JS to Aino, 15 April 1891.

cal tableau' *In the Steppes of Central Asia* (1880) was performed on 5 March 1891, for example.[1] When Borodin's First Symphony was played on 15 October 1896, however, he was in Helsinki. He visited Russia only briefly (and rarely indeed considering how close it was), for example on his train journey south or four times as a conductor (in December 1906, November 1907, November 1908 and February 1911). Kalinnikov's First Symphony, with its astonishingly Sibelian first movement, was first performed in Helsinki in December 1902. Kajanus, at least, was well informed and in a position to introduce Sibelius to Russian scores and sounds on the piano as well, though this is not documented. Nor is anything specific known of Sibelius' encounters with Russian music in Berlin and Vienna, apart from Tchaikovsky and Anton Rubinstein.

The first movement of *Kullervo* ('Introduction' in E minor) is dominated by a gesture that has been compared to Bruckner, because of its main theme and some of the transitions. The influence of Brahms on the energetic gravity of the bass leading voice is also obvious. The movement, written between April and December 1891, heeds with surprising diligence the rules of sonata form for a main movement with a coda, and it is one of Sibelius' most vital creations. The flexible harmonisation of the theme helps make it so. The second movement ('Kullervo's Youth') also lives from ideas that put the parallels to Russian orchestral music of the period into perspective. The mixture of triads in B major and B minor is noteworthy, enriched by the note *g* as an accented suspension within the carefully balanced instrumentation of the folkloristic, initially delicate formation of the first idea. Throughout the progression of the melody, which together with the harmony points towards the future by means of percussive repetition, Sibelius produces variations of specific details. The second thematic idea is a mixture of three textural segments: folksong, flexible bass accompaniment and descending scales in the strings. Among the most powerful effects in the further course of the work are chromatic, modal bass runs that accompany the first theme and in that sense represent a synthesis of the high scales of the strings in the second theme and the motifs of the first. The fascinating processes of this movement include the presentation of the melodic ideas, which form a rondo sequence in kaleidoscopic simultaneity. The rhythmic effects near the end of the development and before the repetition of the beginning are unmistakable, anticipating the gestural power of Stravinsky scores, and are derived from the first motif (repetition of one pitch).

The beginning of the third movement ('Kullervo and His Sister') is one of the composer's most original designs. The ambiguity of the metre, in the tradition of Beethoven's scherzos, is charmingly implemented. The wild dance motifs are based on a consistent 5/4 time (Allegro vivace) with no upbeat, but it is barely recognisable owing to the asymmetrical accents prior to the entry of the choir. The movement is the centre of the cycle. In the archaic rigour of the hymn, the monophonic, Doric singing of a male choir with many octave doublings introduces the tale of Kullervo's

[1] Ringbom, *Helsingfors orkesterföretag, 1882–1932* (Helsinki, 1932), quoted in Murtomäki 1998b, pp. 160–61.

fall. The effect of this simple measure is overpowering. The phrasing has less to do with the melody of *runo* singing than with medieval psalmody of the not infrequent type of the archaic-sounding monophonic choral song. The modal scales that Sibelius uses here, and in many other compositions, can also be associated with Gregorian chant and stylistically with late nineteenth-century historicism — not just with folk music. (Sibelius became familiar with and learned to appreciate the Catholic liturgy in Vienna.) After a few strophes, the text leads to the first important events: the first of Kullervo's three encounters with a woman, namely, his sister who has been missing since childhood. In the literature, it is taken for granted that it is always the same sister. Sibelius simply calls the solo role 'Sisar' ('sister', which in Finnish can also simply mean 'girl'). The text might also mean that Kullervo tries to seduce all the women he sees en route and is successful with, of all people, his own sister.

One of the achievements of the construction is the extensive dramatic intensification that works towards the successful seduction, which is naturalistically imitated in the orchestral interlude. The dramatic highlight, however, is the simultaneous entry of the soprano (sister) and the choir, when the sister articulates her resistance: 'Päästä pois minua tästä, / laske lasta vallallensa / kunnotointa kuulemasta, / pahalaista palvomasta, / tahi potkin pohjan puhki, / levittelen liistehesi, / korjasi palastehiksi, / rämäksi re'en retukan!' (Let me out of here, let me go [...] or I will pound through the bottom [...] destroy your sled.) Apart from this passage, the setting of the text leaves plenty of time for the narrative. During the dialogue, the choir declaims lines that precede the dialogue in the *Kalevala*, describing Kullervo's silent actions as a ruthless seducer: 'Reualti rekosehensa / asetteli taljoillensa, / alle viltin vieretteli.' (Lingered in his sled, sat down on his pelts, rolled under the deck.) The simultaneous presentation of the verses contributes to the presentation of a struggle.

The first pause in the action, which in the sections with singing initially concentrates for the length of one movement on the encounter between Kullervo and his sister, is a striking choral strophe that comments on Kullervo's love-crazed success. The text indicates that the young woman ('sisar') abandons her resistance on seeing the gold. Glenda Dawn Goss has proposed another version of the text, which seems plausible in light of the struggle that Sibelius stages dramatically: She demonstrates that Sibelius' text — unlike the commercial study score (a facsimile of an autograph copy), in which a later correction of the text is evident — changes the line 'money changes the bride's attitude' from the *Kalevala* to 'desire changes the bride's attitude'. In the end, the difference is not great, since the desire may refer to the gold rather than the body of Kullervo. The reason for deviating from the *Kalevala* may have been motivated more by the melody of the language: 'halu' sounds softer in Finnish than 'raha'. Moreover, it is conceivable that Sibelius preferred the ambiguity of the word 'halu' ('desire', 'lust', 'greed') because it articulates various motives at the same time and does not make the woman seem like a cheap prostitute. The ambiguity of the term makes it easier, in any case, to interpret the scene after they make love, in which the 'sister' asks about the origins of her seducer, as if she were in love with him al-

FIG. 23. *Kullervo*, third movement, bars 238–9 (score in the *Jean Sibelius Complete Works*).

ready. An orchestral interlude in 5/4 time and in a tragic, melancholy tone throughout shows how Sibelius had mastered, decades before Dmitry Shostakovich's opera *Lady Macbeth* but after Wagner's *Tristan und Isolde*, the difficult art of orchestrating the act of love without descending to the trivial. At the melodic (and sexual) climax, he shifts from the distinctive 5/4 time to a spherical, floating 3/2 time. Sibelius feared that the passage was too 'illustrative' for the taste of the 'women in the choir', as he wrote to Aino on 4 March 1892. In the end, he decided not to have women's voices in the choir. Originally, Aino was supposed to help select the texts. The love scene had been planned out in full (*c.* a hundred measures, broad melody, rhythmic accompanying figures in the trombones, extreme intensification, etc.), Sibelius reported to her on 17 December 1891. In the end, however, the passage had only about fifty measures in 5/4 time. On 9 December 1891, he was already working on the first movement — 'with all the ideas of the whole work'.

The dialogue of the siblings after the act of love constitutes its own section. In involved monologues, they determine they are related. The naturalist character of the dialogue is not brought out, however, owing to the strict metre of the verse. The sister is immediately active after the act: she asks about the origin of her seducer and recognises what precisely has happened. Her salvation, suicide, she decides on herself; a Finnish Siegfried would not be born in this moralist fairy tale. The following passage is already a model for Sibelius' later vocal style: 'Elä huua, hullu tyttö, / Elä, mieletön, melua! / Ei se kuulu kumminkana, / Ei kuulu kotihin huuto.' (Do not scream, mad girl [...] no one at home hears you.) Here the sister quotes, within the framework of her own legend, the reply of the forests ('salot vastahan saneli, kankahat kajahtelivat': the wilderness replied, the meadow echoed) to her desperate cries as an abandoned child. In the *Kalevala*, these sentences are given particular weight. After all, nature — 'vaarat' (mountains) and 'kankahat' (meadow) — had given similar answers to Kullervo's mother and sister (Canto 34, lines 241 ff.). Sibelius underscores these lines with free metre. In both the song 'Kaiutar', op. 72, no. 4, and the tone poem *Luonnotar*, this becomes an unmistakable part of his vocal style. The sister's monologue of suffering ends with a climax. Final chords in C sharp minor mark her death with sounds of sorrow and repentance. The movement ends only after Kullervo's isolated lament (Largamente, F minor, 4/4 time). Sibelius confronted his audience with his sense of guilt with a curse in simple, folksong form (ABA′) that is accompanied ascetically by brief beats from the orchestra but lasts just two minutes. The tripartite final chord alone lasts sixteen measures, about fifteen seconds.

The fourth movement ('Kullervo Goes to War') serves as a release of tension; the gesture of the movement recalls John Williams's galactic sound scapes. The concluding nine orchestral beats in C major — a gesture typical of Sibelius, most effectively in the finale of the Fifth Symphony, though only in the later, not in the original version and with changing chords — take up more than fifteen seconds by themselves. Listeners unfamiliar with the *Kalevala* may be perplexed on looking at the programme and listening to cheerful music with few minor-key chords. But Canto 36 (lines 155 ff.) reads: 'läksi soitellen sotahan, / iloitellen tappelohon. // Soitti suolla, soitti maalla, / kajahutti kankahalla, / rojahutti ruohokossa, / kulahutteli kulossa.' (Went to war making music, went cheerfully to battle, played in the swamp, in the country, resounded in the meadow.) These words not only point to a generally cheerful ('iloitellen') battle atmosphere but also a specifically musical one ('soitellen'). Not even the news of the death of his father and siblings dampens Kullervo's mood. Only the death of his mother (Canto 35, lines 205 ff.) causes him to lament loudly. This in turn draws attention to an important detail in relation to his mourning the death of his sister, since then he cries because he spoiled the child of his mother ('turmelin emoni tuoman!' or 'I spoiled the fruit of my mother') – and not because of the girl as such. The youth is fixated on his mother and sees any other woman either as a random quarry or as the daughter of his beloved mother. Only after this emotional turn does he decide to take revenge on Untamo.

The final third of the movement accentuates sombre tones. If we assume there is a programme based on the text in the *Kalevala*, it represents Kullervo being confronted with the death of his mother, which motivates his own death in the last movement: ritual suicide in the place where he seduced his sister – but not as she did, by drowning in the river, which would be a symbol of their equal value, but gender-specifically, using his own knife (in the Nordic tradition as well as other rural traditions an intimate instrument of a strong male). This is apparently the consequence of his mistake, but in the end he thinks of his mother, not of the young 'spoiled' one. Death by knife brings him close to his dead mother. There is a central scene in the *Kalevala* in which Kullervo returns home after destroying Untamo's house and discovers the death of his mother and his entire family. There his mother speaks to him from the earth, like Erda of the *Nibelungenlied* once did, or at least Kullervo hears her speak. The mother's words would have called for a psycho-social interpretation of the theme. Sibelius concentrates instead on the consequences of confronting the death of his mother, and his music does not accompany the audience through the episode in the *Kalevala* in which the son's relationship to his mother is materialised onstage. The final episode ('Kullervo's Death', the fifth movement) resounds in effectively reduced choral and orchestral writing with broad arcs of increasing tension and extended pedal points. This movement's final chord alone lasts a good fifteen seconds. The cyclical coherence of the work as a whole is confirmed in the final movement by the Brucknerian brass sound of the orchestra. After all, it is quoting the first theme of the first movement as a coda. Originally the composer had considered further orchestral painting of the narration in the *Kalevala* but rejected such ideas as 'banal and theatrical' in favour of the sober monophony of the chorus.[1]

Countless musical ideas and their striking repetition produce a dramatic fresco lasting seventy minutes. From the perspective of the usual temporal scale – to say nothing of extreme examples lasting several hours, such as August Bungert's monumental *Homerische Welt* (1898/1903) or Felix Draeseke's tetralogy of complete oratorios, *Christus* (with Prologue or 'Vorspiel', 1895) – Sibelius' poem seems brief. Sibelius sought a path far from modish pomp and skipped long passages of the tale to achieve an exemplary succinctness. All of the movements have a unique character,

[1] JS to Aino, 16 February 1892.

despite more or less obvious similarities in the motifs, to which Sibelius gave much thought from the outset, and regardless of the cyclical quotations in the end of the final movement. In a letter to Aino of 9 December 1891, he already knew that the first movement in the style of an introduction contained 'the ideas of the whole work'. The predominance of instrumental writing in three movements, which could certainly be performed *concertante* as a symphonic cycle – (1) Allegro moderato in E minor; (2) Grave in B minor and B major; (4) Alla marcia in C major – and the formal autonomy of the movements with vocal elements (3 and 5) emphasise that the overall structure is multidimensional. Such considerations are legitimate within the process of its creation, since Sibelius was working on conventionally 'symphonic' projects in Vienna when *Kullervo* began to take form. Initially, the basic form of his experiments was the overture ('Introduction'); the rest was supposed to become 'a kind of suite or really a symphony'.[1] He composed two autonomous overtures in Vienna. These ideas are also reflected in *Kullervo*, a work that as a cantata symphony is also somewhere between a suite and a symphony in the history of musical genres.

Incidentally, his letters to Aino demonstrate that the martial fourth movement was originally supposed to follow the seduction scene – rather than functioning as a final movement in a three-movement symphony.[2] In late January 1892, it was already clear that the problem of seduction would be treated in the third movement of the 'symphony' (as the project was still called just four months before the premiere), and at that time still with the dramatic support of recitation. This is an early example of how much more radical and correspondingly more interesting Sibelius' original versions can be than the final ones, which are characterised by polish and abstraction. The movement caused Sibelius great difficulties, until early March 1892 when he discovered the phrase 'läksi ilotellen sotahan' ('went jubilantly to war', quoting his source imprecisely by conflating two lines) and hence the idea of jubilant war, which he wanted 'to treat quite literally'.

Even after completing *Kullervo*, Sibelius sometimes referred to it as his first symphony. Jussi Jalas derived from that the idea that his oeuvre was cyclical (based on the Golden Section).[3] In this view, the four *Lemminkäinen Legends* also form a genuine 'symphony' – after all, the first legend, like the first movement of *Kullervo*, adopts a conventional sonata-allegro form. Sibelius himself knew that a symphony needed more than a classical framework (such as the sonata form of early Beethoven). That is why he tolerated more as a joke certain associations that certainly suggest themselves in the face of the resulting sequence of nine symphonies. However, he drafted a letter with a striking correction: 'whether there will really be a ~~VIIIth~~ IXth Symphony',[4] and writing to Newmarch – in English, a language in which he was not comfortable

[1] JS to Aino, 10 February 1891.

[2] JS to Aino, 31 January to 6 April 1892.

[3] Jalas n.d., p. iii, and Jalas 1981, p. 65.

[4] National Archive Box 35, draft letter.

– he described *Kullervo* simply as 'an independent symphony'.[1] But the conceptual distance between *Kullervo* and his genuine symphonies is greater than the difference between the symphonic prototypes (serenades for orchestra, etc.) and the later symphonies of Bruckner or Brahms, for example.

The Relevance of the Legend

Faced with the great detail typical of the *Kalevala* and the many playful, distanced, ironic explanations in Lönnrot's narrative, Sibelius concentrated his selection of texts on a few instructive events. To sum up, the young man begins a journey (Canto 35, lines 69 ff.), meets a girl and seduces her. The young lovers realise they are related by blood (Canto 35, lines 199 ff.) and they seek spectacular suicide in keeping with late Romanticism's fondness for death – not to fulfil their love but as a naturalistic depiction of self-punishment as they felt desire for one another without true love. The orchestra is supposed to illustrate Kullervo's youth and bloody war of revenge (Cantos 32–3 and 36), but it does so only with programmatic abstraction and interchangeable, conventional means. Just as abstract is the illustration of the sister's suicide after her brief lament (Grave, beginning in G sharp minor), which breaks off at its climax: the orchestra responds to her suicide with a radiant C sharp minor chord in a high register in the woodwinds, framed by general pauses (Canto 35, lines 257 ff.): 'Sai toki sanoneheksi, / kerran kertoelleheksi: / heti repsahti re'estä, / siitä juoksihe jokehen, / kosken kuohu'un kovahan, / palavahan pyörtehesen. // Siihen surmansa sukesi, / kuolemansa kohtaeli; / löyti turvan Tuonelassa, / armon aaltojen seassa.' ([...] suddenly she plunged from the sled, ran into the river [...].) Harmonically too, Sibelius went his own way. For example, in the lament he dispensed with the obligatory modulation from C sharp to F minor, replacing it with four long measures of silence. Whereas he savours the musical illustration of the act of love, which in the *Kalevala* is merely suggested, he marks the sister's suicide by refusing to illustrate the event in music. In comparison to the *Nibelungenlied*, the moral severity of Kalervo's children is surprising; their uncle Untamo had robbed them and sold his own nephews as slaves to the smith Ilmarinen in the East (Canto 31). Granted, the tale of the Nibelungen is more explicitly connected to the world of gods and demigods, which permits exceptions to accepted moral norms (compare the unequal pair of Brünhilde and Siegfried; Siegmund and Sieglinde in particular are merely human, as well as naive and unenlightened). The comparison with the *Nibelungenlied* draws attention to the extreme moral position of Kullervo and his sister, which in the *Kalevala* itself seems isolated, since after the shameful act Kullervo travels to his parents in order to confess, rather than immediately taking his vengeance, which seems legitimate in the context of the narrative.

The behaviour of the siblings is neither exemplary nor typical for the genre but is

[1] Newmarch 1939, p. 11.

FIG. 24. Louis Sparre, *Kullervo and His Sister in the Sled* (1891).

rather sociopathic. The story of Kalervo's family is — quite unlike Siegmund's — a tale of a modern nuclear family, whose cohesion and honour in difficult times, under the threat of foreign rule, are more important than overarching, archaic motifs. Unlike most of the other legends in the *Kalevala*, this subject matter is naturalistic. In his *Kullervo* opera, this led the Finnish composer Aulis Sallinen — and to some extent Aleksis Kivi in his drama — to the view that there are little Kullervos everywhere: children in a hostile environment who evolve into debauchees. For the German premiere in Lübeck in 2001, the German theatre director Elmar Fulda took the view that Kullervo was *de facto* a debauchee — a perspective Sallinen had regarded with interest but one that deviates radically from previous performance practice, which was more nationalist and mythologising than politically naturalistic. Kullervo is thus no hero who had escaped from one of Gallen-Kallela's paintings (i.e., *Kullervo's Curse*; 1899) but more the wiry youth of Väinö Blomstedt's *Kullervo* (1897; see Fig. 2), who is sketched before he kills the innocent cows. The Finnish baritone Jorma Hynninen's performances in the role of Kullervo, thanks to his masculine charisma, have also contributed to the heroising interpretation of the works of Sibelius and Sallinen.

The *Kalevala* also underscores the pedagogical aspect. In the final lines of the legend, Väinämöinen speaks with his sonorous chest voice: 'Elkötte, etinen kansa, / lasta kaltoin kasvatelko, / luona tuhman tuuittajan, vierahan väsyttelijän! // Lapsi kaltoin kasvattama, / poika tuhmin tuuittama, / ei tule älyämähän, / miehen mieltä ottamahan, / vaikka vanhaksi eläisi, / varreltansa vahvistuisi.' (Ancient people, you should not raise children badly, leaving them with an evil caretaker [...]. A badly raised boy [...] will not understand how to become a man even if he should grow older [...].) Thus Väinämöinen (as Lönnrot's alter ego) warned his people of the consequences of neglecting the youngest members of society and established the basis for the Finnish primary education system. Not utopian archaisms but the ideas of Jean-Jacques Rousseau and Johann Heinrich Pestalozzi provide the context for his statement in the *Kalevala* of 1849.

The original version of the *Kalevala* from 1835 (Canto 19, lines 1–530) tells the saga without his sister and mother. There too Kullervo wages war against his oppressors (not Untamo but rather Ilmarinen's wife), but he responds indifferently to the news that his family has died. In this version, too, the war consists of Kullervo's music, explained as powerful magic. Ilmarinen's wife is destroyed by a magical evocation: 'Oi Ukko yli jumala! / Tapa Ilmarin emäntä / Rakehilla rautasilla, / Niekloilla teräsnenillä, / Kapehilla kartanoilla, / Oman pirttinsä pihalla.' (O old supreme god, kill Ilmarinen's wife, with hail of iron [...] in front of her own home.) Kullervo himself is not a debauchee but rather evokes the powers of nature by music against the enemy in the East, behind the mental Iron Curtain. Consequently, the 1835 version would be better suited to the mythological interpretation still common today – including Hynninen's gripping achievement as Sallinen's first Kullervo and also a regular interpreter of the role in Sibelius' work – than the naturalistic version of 1849, which concentrates on Kullervo's family and downplays the cultural and political dimension of the ancient conflict between East and West. In the later version, whose narrative is also smoothed out, Kullervo asks the supreme god for a sword (Canto 36, lines 237 ff.) with which to kill his uncle Untamo; in this version, he destroys Ilmarinen's wife in Canto 33 (lines 277 ff.) with the help of Ukko, the great god of the Finns. In the 1835 version, there are two lines (Canto 19, lines 495–6) that make clear the devastating effect of Kullervo's trumpet: 'Suo järähti, maa tärähti, / Kangas vastahan kalahti.' (The swamp trembled, the earth shook, etc.). The reverberation of the universe is described almost identically in Canto 34 of the 1849 version (lines 15 ff.: 'suo sorahti, maa järisi, / kangas vastahan kajahti, / Kullervoisen soitantoa, / ilkeän ilonpitoa' [The swamp trembled; the earth shook; the meadow echoed back, after Kullervo had played, the cheerfulness of the mean warrior]); the last line emphasises Kullervo's psychologically sick essence, playing music and rejoicing in the wake of his battle). Sibelius sets that galactic echo to music in the orchestral part of 'Kullervo Goes to War' – in the second section, among other places – without having found any occasion for doing so in Canto 36 of the new *Kalevala* of 1849, which is about the psychological tension and the news of the deaths of family members. The latter are strangely underemphasised in the musical setting. They are indeed present, if hidden, in the fourth movement, but weakly articulated, as in the old (1835) edition of the *Kalevala*. It is beyond doubt, however, that Sibelius used the newer edition. Sibelius' *Kullervo* is emancipated from Gallen-Kallela's mythological reading of the *Kalevala* and from the insight that the Kullervo saga in particular is linked to the naturalistic, psychologically and socially critical modernism of Ibsen and his age. This tradition does not ask about the universal meaning and archaic significance of suicide; it is necessary to do what Sallinen and Kivi also did, namely, recognize psychoanalytically, and without forgetting Nietzsche, the doctrine of the antihero's pitiable childhood in the beginning and regard the events as a demonstration of the consequences.

Sibelius was rather reserved when it came to the dissemination of his setting of the *Kalevala*. There are several possible reasons for this, such as its apparently folkloristic aspects. In the years immediately following its completion, his aesthetic ideas transformed, and possibly he lacked the self-confidence to appreciate the timeless qualities of his early masterpiece. The classic and universally valid qualities of the folkloristic were defined as follows by Merikanto in his essay on the day of the premiere: 'He caresses our ears with Finnish tones, which we recognize as our own, even though we had never heard them before.'[1] The 'Finnish' quality consisted of metre, rhythm (frequent repetitions of notes at the end of the phrase) and, with regard to the history of composition of past centuries, unusual modal scales. Sibelius always acknowledged the importance of the premiere of *Kullervo* as the beginning of his career,[2] but the publication of the score, which had already been announced, never materialised during his lifetime. Although *Kullervo* was not one of the early works, versions or fragments whose performance Sibelius expressly prohibited, the work was not performed again in full until 1958, following a break of more than sixty years. Even in the 1890s, a performance was planned in Vienna, where Sibelius had written the sketches for the main theme. There existed substantial materials to aid the preparation of the work, such as a reduction for piano four-hands and a German translation of the text. But it was never premiered. The erosion of the symphonic unity of the work – or at least cycle – began in the twentieth century: the final piece of the third movement, 'Kullervo's Lament', was performed together with *Finlandia* and *The Swan of Tuonela* (with a mythologising and historicising programme note) under Kajanus in February 1905.

On 1 March 1935 the third movement, 'Kullervo and His Sister', was performed as part of the anniversary of the publication of the 1835 version of *Kalevala*. On 8 December 1950, on the occasion of the composer's eighty-fifth birthday, the instrumental fourth movement was performed in Turku. Both performing isolated bits and pieces of the work and the celebratory occasion made it more difficult to appreciate the grand socio-critical aspects of the work. Five years after the third movement was

[1] Goss 2005, p. xii, quoting *Päivälehti*, 28 April 1892.

[2] See, for example, Hauch's questionnaire, discussed in detail in chapter 5.3 of the present work.

performed in 1935, Sibelius drafted a letter in which he expressed his gratitude for an unknown recipient's interest in *Kullervo* and clarified the problem from his perspective:

> This youthful work is still close to my heart. Probably for that very reason, I would not want to see it performed abroad in an era that is, in my view, very far from the spirit of *Kullervo*. [...] I am not certain whether the public would see the work in the proper historical context [...]. I did not even want to permit *Kullervo* to be performed in my own country, apart from exceptions such as my birthday five years ago. Here the circumstances are very different from the world at large, and so I felt obliged to respect the wishes of the government.[1]

The text was written in Finnish by someone else, but Sibelius added to it and signed it. All this makes it authentic. If his remark about an 'era that is, in my view, very far from the spirit' of *Kullervo* refers to the cultural and political climate around 1940, which would certainly have been conducive to a large-scale realisation of the work that would contribute to nationalist pathos during the World War (which many Sibelians today would expect him to have supported), he must have recognised that any performance could only be in a mythologising and one-sidedly classicising spirit – lacking socio-critical naturalism, unhappy children and mad warriors. Apparently he was apprehensive of a classicising approach to a work that was, as he alone still realised, deeply rooted in the social naturalism à la Gerhart Hauptmann of the late nineteenth century, especially since the first reviewers (such as Merikanto) had given the work a very different meaning in relation to the regional and cultural politics of the time.

[1] National Archive Box 36.

> I see clearly, for example, that the opera I shall write ought not to have any words. Only architectural backdrops and singers who sing A; above all, no words. That would be an opera of the mind. The whole thing should be beautiful, singing and colours, music and accompanying gestures. No intrigues?! Yes, that's right, gentlemen.[1]

3.3 Theatrical Works

The Utopia of an Abstract Opera after 1893

In prophesying a 'religious age',[2] Sibelius referred to Scriabin and contemporary opera as the basic requirements for the 'religious' music of the future.[3] Sibelius had rejected 'absolute' music since 1893, ten years after Wagner's death: 'It arouses feelings and induces certain states of mind but it always leaves some part of one unsatisfied: one always asks questions, why just this?'[4] The what was not enough for Sibelius; in the Symbolist spirit, he was also interested in the why. He said music is 'like a woman, it is only through man that she can give birth and that man is poetry. Music attains its fullest power only when it is motivated by poetic impulse. In other words when words and music blend.'[5] The significance of these ideas at the time he wrote this note is not diminished by the fact that Sibelius was in effect (without saying as much) paraphrasing Wagner's *Oper und Drama* (1852; translated as *Opera and Drama* in 1913).

Once *Kullervo* was completed in 1892, Sibelius planned a *Gesamtkunstwerk*, or 'total work of art', titled 'Veneen luominen' (The creation of the boat, with a text by Juhana H. Erkko based on the *Kalevala*): a Symbolist story with nationalist significance: the mythological and nationalist value of the boat in the *Kalevala* is comparable to Nauplius' chest. On 28 July 1894 Sibelius wrote to Aino from Munich pensively (in poor Finnish): 'The opera, for instance. The material in it is great indeed. The greatest.' Possibly — especially given that he intended to give the composition a decidedly national and popular stamp ('folkprägel') — Sibelius was reacting to an announcement of a prize to be awarded by the Suomalaisen Kirjallisuuden Seura (Finnish literary society): in 1891 the society had published a plan to award a prize of 2,000 Finnish marks in 1896 for the best Finnish-language opera on a mythological or historical text. Sibelius' only completed 'opera' *The Maid in the Tower* (1896; a one-act ballade on a text by Rafael Hertzberg), was delivered on time in 1896, but in Swedish. Not

[1] Diary, 18 May 1912. Salmenhaara 1984, p. 292, compares these ideas to Boris Blacher's composition *Abstrakte Oper Nr. 1* (1953).

[2] JS to Axel Carpelan, 28 August 1914, in Dahlström 2010, p. 369.

[3] JS to Rosa Newmarch, 18 April 1913; quoted in Erik W. Tawaststjerna 1997b, p. 3.

[4] JS to J. H. Erkko, 8 July 1893; quoted in Erik W. Tawaststjerna 1976, p. 141.

[5] Ibid.

until 1899, when the deadline had been extended and Sibelius himself was a member of the jury, could the prize be awarded: to Oskar Merikanto for his lyric three-act opera *Pohjan neiti* (The maiden of the north, text by Lorenz Nicolai Achté and Antti Rytkönen, based on the *Kalevala*). Because the second prize was not awarded, the money was used to finance Leevi Madetoja's opera *Juha* in 1935.[1] Another plan may also have been an attempt to write a kind of national opera: an opera with a libretto he would write himself, in the spirit of verismo (Mascagni, Leoncavallo) and with a historical framework: in the seventeenth century, a student engaged to a Finnish peasant girl falls in love with foreign dancer, whereupon the peasant girl dies. In a letter to Aino on 28 July 1894, Sibelius characterised this sketch as modest material, 'realistic' and 'common' in comparison with anything related to Wagner or the *Kalevala*.

The musical motifs about which Sibelius wrote in his letters end up either in the *Lemminkäinen Legends* or in *The Wood Nymph*. The operatic ideas may easily be traced further even in the orchestral song *Luonnotar* (1913). The *Kalevala* was supposed to replace the *Nibelungenlied* as a vehicle of archaic culture, and Väinämöinen was allowed to try on Wotan's garment in a mythological opera with a nationalist tone. Tawaststjerna had his doubts whether the composer had internalised the complex idea of the Wagnerian *Gesamtkunstwerk*, or merely found isolated visions and concepts (possible explained to him by his literary friends) appealing.[2] Probably it was indeed just a gust of Wagnerian wind in which Sibelius was briefly caught up.

While working on the *Kalevala* opera 'Veneen luominen', which continued *Kullervo* within a nationalist and mythological framework rather than a naturalistic and socio-critical one and occupied the composer from 1893 to 1895, preceding the work on the *Lemminkäinen Legends*, Sibelius visited Bayreuth.[3] He was immediately enthusiastic about *Parsifal*. In light of such statements as 'Nothing in the world made such an impression on me; it moved the innermost depths of my soul' or 'I cannot even say how much *Parcival* [*sic*] enchanted me',[4] it is remarkable that his own attempts to carry on this tradition remained unfinished. Apart from the genre, numerous passages from the third act – especially the beginning of the prelude and 'Karfreitagszauber' (Good Friday spell) and the orchestral texture of 'Ihn selbst am Kreuze kann sie nicht erschauen' ([All creation] cannot see him on the cross) had far-reaching consequences for his style. By contrast, in July 1894 he found *Lohengrin*, of which he had a piano score and whose beginning he seems to quote in A minor in *The Swan of Tuonela*, old-fashioned and too theatrical; he did not even comment on *Tannhäuser*. To judge from notes for letters, during these two performances in Bayreuth he was thinking only of his own opera plans, although he had not been inspired by the performances. By contrast, he reported openly about a performance of *Tristan und Isolde*

1 See Suomalainen 1950, pp. 93–4, and Sola 1952, p. 99.

2 Erik W. Tawaststjerna 1976, p. 142.

3 Ibid., pp. 152 ff.

4 JS to Aino, 19 July 1894 and 1 August 1894, etc.

in Munich: 'Not even *Parcival* made such an impression on me; everything else is "feeble".'[1] On 12 August 1894, he heard *Die Walküre* in Munich but was not enthusiastic. On 16 August he found *Götterdämmerung* largely 'brilliant'.[2] The chromaticism of these works is audible in Sibelius' harmony of the 1890s and even beyond.

He had had his first experiences with Wagner operas in their entirety in Berlin in 1889 (*Tannhäuser* and *Die Meistersinger*). For a time, he was 'crazy about Wagner'.[3] He remarked to Martin Wegelius, however, that (and this is almost common sense) the overture to Wagner's early opera *Die Feen* (The Fairies) was 'all but plagiarised from Weber', and of *Tannhäuser* and *Die Meistersinger*, which he saw in September, he wrote: 'In my innermost soul was such a strange mixture of admiration, disapproval and rejoicing.'[4]

Wagner's art inspired him to write his own opera, for which he initially planned a mythological theme and then later (after seeing *Die Meistersinger* in Munich) a historical one, but Wagner's model also made him feel how difficult it was to invent expressive, 'genuine' musical motifs. One theme from his opera sketches – a folk-like theme intended to characterise a female figure in the mythological underworld – was already employed in *The Swan of Tuonela*. Here, as for Sibelius in general, striking passages characterise the solo part for the cor anglais. In Vienna in 1891, an oboist had initiated him into the mysteries of his instrument.[5] That knowledge proved crucial to the solo for cor anglais as well as for *Scène de ballet* of 1891 and numerous other works. His woodwind-heavy Wagnerian sound had begun to form in Vienna, not after hearing the acoustic of the Festspielhaus in Bayreuth, which is particularly favourable to woodwinds (softening the brass).

It was not just his own motifs but also Wagner's that he criticised as not 'immediate' enough and excessively calculated. This attitude reveals his passion. Nothing was indifferent; everything was questioned. The problems with leitmotifs demonstrate how thoroughly he analysed Wagner's compositional method and also uncovered weaknesses.[6] Anyone who claims that Sibelius was the only composer of the time whom Wagner did not influence and who did not react against him is mistaken.[7] Because Sibelius, who was just thirty and had little experience with orchestras, wanted to start where Wagner had left off at the end of his life, he was forced to recognise his

[1] JS to Aino, 10 August 1894.

[2] JS to Aino, 12 August 1894 and 17 August 1894.

[3] Erik W. Tawaststjerna 1991, pp. 128–9; see also, for example, Salmenhaara 1984, p. 57, who doubts that JS saw the Berlin *Ring* in 1889 because he did not write about it. Other operas and concerts that he very likely did experience were not mentioned either, so that the lack of evidence in his correspondence and notes does not prove much.

[4] JS to Martin Wegelius, 29 September 1889 (on *Tannhäuser* and *Meistersinger*) and 6 November 1889 (*Die Feen*).

[5] JS to Martin Wegelius, 11 January 1891.

[6] On this subject, see Schwartz 1999, pp. 121ff.

[7] See, for example, Cecil Gray 1931, pp. 202–3.

own technical inadequacy.[1] Later he told chroniclers only about insignificant performances of *Lohengrin* and *Tannhäuser* but did not say a word about *Parsifal* or *Tristan*. As a comparison of *Lohengrin* and *The Swan of Tuonela* shows, and many other works lead one to suspect, it is necessary to distinguish between performances that may well have been unsatisfactory and the scores themselves. It is not possible to reconstruct when Sibelius studied *Lohengrin* and *Tannhäuser*, nor did he keep track of performances he attended. So it is legitimate to speculate about the influence of specific performances he might have been able to attend and works that he must have known.

The one-act opera *The Maid in the Tower*, written a few years later, was one Mark Twain supposedly enjoyed. 'Did we ever tell you that Mark Twain himself was a great admirer of your glorious music, especially the opera Tornissa', wrote Cyril Clemens of the Mark Twain Society in Missouri to Sibelius on 17 July 1941 (referring to its Finnish title: *Neito tornissa*).[2] Sibelius became honorary chairman of the society in 1947. From the history of the work's reception, however, it is difficult to account for Twain's fondness for the work: the first recording came out 1984, and there is no printed music for the piece. In it, the expressive world of Charles Gounod replaced Wagner's *Gesamtkunstwerk*. The fate of the genre was thus not linked to Wagner, and the failure of Sibelius' various plans — 'Veneen luominen' (The creation of the boat), a number of reflections on Boldemann's libretto, Adolf Paul's *Blauer Dunst* (Blue haze)[3] and progressive texts by Jalmari Finne[4] and Juhani Aho,[5] not to forget Walter von Konow's 'Ljunga Wirginia' of 1885[6] — merely demonstrates how inappropriate the traditional opera was for him. His strong interest in music drama is clear, however, from the diversity of these plans and his self-criticism.

Jalmari Finne's plan for 'Marjatta' is noteworthy, since he had presumably understood best what Sibelius wanted: 'a form between the lyric and the epic',[7] not an ordinary opera. Finne wrote on 1 January 1908 that his plan could not be carried out:

> Marjatta cannot become an ordinary oratorio; the theme [Jesus and Mary] is too fantastic; it cannot be treated within the framework of an oratorio. As an opera, it would destroy everything fantastic. I see the theme as something in-between, as a new form that combines the mystical quality of the oratorio and the dramatic quality of an opera and drives the listener's imagination to unimaginable heights. [...] You once ordered me to finish the text, and after

[1] See Erik W. Tawaststjerna 1976, p. 157.

[2] National Library Coll. 206: 8

[3] On 22 March 1913, Paul showed JS the contract (Åbo Akademi).

[4] National Library Coll. 206: 11.

[5] The reference is to Aho's *Juha*, later set by Aarre Merikanto (*c.* 1922) and Madetoja (1935).

[6] JS to Pehr Sibelius, 4 August 1885, in Goss 1997, p. 74. 'Ljunga' means 'flaming and armoured'.

[7] National Library Coll. 206: 11; Jalmari Finne to JS, 27 August 1905.

> that you would create it alone. [...] Let your wife read my letter; I am certain that she understands.[1]

Finne enclosed sketches – some of which were in German, so apparently he was speculating about presenting it internationally – after all, Sibelius had supposedly 'ordered' the text. That remark suggests that Finne's idea had interested him. The genre would not let him go; along with his Eighth Symphony, it was one of those central utopias that mark the essence of the artist just as fundamentally as, say, Schoenberg's futile struggle with the ineffable, which explains his great fragmentary works like *Moses und Aron* and *Die Jakobsleiter*. Again and again – for example, in 1910 by a performance of Jules Massenet's opera *Thaïs*[2] – Sibelius was inspired to new attempts. Massenet's opera made big waves in Finland, in comparison to its rather marginal role in the international canon, especially since the Finnish diva Aino Ackté (famous as Strauss's *Salome* in Paris and London) took the lead role in the Finnish premiere in 1910, and Anatole France's novel was translated into Finnish by Madetoja's wife, L. Onerva alias Hilja Onerva Lehtinen, in the same year.[3] A Finnish version of *Thaïs* was even performed in 1934.

Sibelius had gained early dramaturgical experience as a successful composer of incidental and tableau music as well as a cantata-symphony (*Kullervo*). However, his reaction to an inquiry from a libretto author named G. Arbour Stephens, at a time when Sibelius was no longer publishing any new orchestral works, is open to speculation: 'I am very much occupied with my own music and have no intention for writing an opera.'[4] This sentence could mean that his 'own music' precluded on principle opera as a genre. Stephens had proposed a Celtic theme. The reply to Stephens in 'Swansea, USA' is in the Sibelius collection because the letter was returned, stamped 'retour'. It seems possible that G. Arbour Stephens was George Arbour Stephens in Swansea, Wales, which would explain why the letter could not be delivered.

Newmarch reported in detail on a discussion of the genre and of the *Kalevala* as source material: 'But his manner when referring to this opera gave me the impression that he has left this early work far behind him and attaches no great importance to its future. If The Kalevala is eventually to find its Richard Wagner, there does not seem to be any immediate prospect of his being revealed in Jean Sibelius.'[5] Cantos from the *Kalevala* had, of course, already found their dramatisation in *Kullervo* and *Luonnotar*. As far as other possible sources are concerned, Sibelius' comments on Juhani Aho's *Juha* are informative, especially since two younger composers (Aarre Merikanto and Madetoja) have demonstrated how appropriate this novel could be to the modern context. A letter of 18 October 1914, to the soprano who had turned *Juha* into a li-

[1] Jalmari Finne to JS, 27 August 1905 to 1 January 1908 (National Library Coll. 206: 11).

[2] Diary, 21 April 1910.

[3] See, among others, Sivuoja-Gunaratnam 2003, p. 181.

[4] National Library Coll. 206: 37; JS to G. Arbour Stephens, 7 January 1937.

[5] Newmarch 1906, p. 24.

Fig. 25. Albert Edelfelt, *Aino Ackté* (1901, detail)

bretto titled 'Marja' (with a not exactly selfless emphasis on the female lead), makes it clear how seriously Sibelius took his potential material:

> An opera composer of the 'old school' could, in my opinion, write one unique virtuoso role: Marja. But others? Juha, for example, would have to be a silent role. In the operatic style of which I am dreaming, the music has to be written first, that is, absolute music – singing – has to be the main thing. The text is added to the music but it has to be completely subordinated to it. And Juha is a masterpiece in the form Aho gave it.[1]

Ackté's anger at Sibelius and the failure of her plan was manifested the following day, 19 October 1914, in a letter to the distinguished writer Aho in which she said that Sibelius did not have 'the slightest idea what dramatic theatrical art is. Sibelius cannot compose opera music.'[2]

[1] National Library Coll. 4: 13 (Ackté–Jalander).

[2] Suomalaisen Kirjallisuuden Seura, Juhani Aho Collection, quoted in Sivuoja-Gunaratnam 2003, pp. 186–7.

Annoyed by problems with the 'Raven' (Edgar Allan Poe) project in 1910, when Sibelius rejected the marketing of his composition as a 'commodity' presented by Ackté,[1] Ackté had already offered the *Juha* project to Armas Järnefelt in August 1912,[2] then to Erkki Melartin and a year later even to the young Ilmari Hannikainen. If Sibelius, who at the time was cooperating with Ackté on the orchestral song *Luonnotar*, had been informed of this long chain of requests, he would surely have turned the proposal down immediately. Ackté had, however, chosen an imposing messenger: Aho himself. But Sibelius was already 'dreaming' of an 'operatic style' that, if possible at all, would have been far more original in its conception than Merikanto's and Madetoja's later projects. His description of Juha's role as the protagonist can even be compared to Schoenberg's speaking roles (Moses, etc.) that are only conceivable without singing. *Sprechgesang* and recitative were alternatives that would probably have seemed too radical to Sibelius, although he had mastered them through his work on the genre of the melodrama. Notwithstanding François Auber's *La Muette de Portici* of 1826, a silent lead would have been even more daring from a theatrical perspective than a speaking role. It is not surprising that he did not wish to be an opera composer of the 'old school', although it is uncertain whether he was thinking of Wagner or Mascagni, Goldmark or Puccini, Gounod or Tchaikovsky. In any case, he imagined an emphatically 'new' practice, a kind of contemporary *seconda pratica*, an opera 'even without words', to borrow an expression he used to describe his Lieder.[3]

Salmenhaara observed that Sibelius' sensitivity to musical dramaturgy is expressed in his incidental music.[4] The conductor Osmo Vänskä too has emphasised that 'He was very good at incidental music, and had a genuine understanding for drama. And he was extremely good at writing short pieces of music, especially in *The Tempest*. He knew exactly what to do.'[5] Ackté's verdict, 'Sibelius cannot compose opera music', need not be taken seriously. Nevertheless, even Salmenhaara believed that the opera did not fit with Sibelius' 'symphonic conception' (much as this was true of Gustav Mahler). Was this the main reason for renouncing traditional opera, or was it the professional and artistic difficulties he had dealing with texts? Or was it plainly and simply the lack of solid performance practice for opera in Helsinki or the impossibility of composing as experimentally as he would have wanted? The answer is, as so often, a mixture of all the possibilities. In Hämeenlinna he had performed in children's theatre and worked on plays;[6] and his songs and incidental music such as *Kullervo* and *Luonnotar* prove that he was capable of unusual dramatic ideas. His struggle is tangible in letters to Georg Boldemann, supplemented by parallel diary

1 See Vainio and Salolainen 2002, pp. 315 ff.

2 Salmenhaara 1996c, pp. 251 ff.

3 For more detail on this, see chapter 4.3 in the present volume.

4 Salmenhaara 1984, pp. 129–30.

5 Grimley 2004b, p. 240.

6 Erik W. Tawaststjerna 1976, p. 17.

entries.[1] On 2 September 1909, he wrote to this German-Danish businessman and amateur writer that he was firmly convinced of Boldemann's qualities as a librettist. As a composer, however, he recommended in the end an Italian: Mario Enrico Bossi: 'I know him well. Although he did not earn his reputation as an opera composer, like the other stars.'[2] From Moscow, Sibelius wrote to Aino on 15 November 1907: 'Bossi is here, and I have often spent time with him.' In 1913, Sibelius arranged a scholarship for Toivo Kuula to study with Bossi in Bologna. On 12 May 1910, he wrote: 'In my life I have always suffered from "lifsångstet" [life angst] and "allein-Gefühl" [feeling alone]. You are a shining light. [...] As far as opera is concerned, your text is excellent. [...] You know that I have always been averse to writing operas. But it seems to me as if I will think differently someday. I will write more about that. [...] Life is short, deep, full and infinitely fantastic.' On 9 May 1911 everything seemed set as he wrote to Boldemann:

> I received a letter from Berlin from your friend Bart, the opera singer. I will compose the opera! (You know the text you gave me.) [...] Perhaps you will come with me to Rome? We have to prepare the thing thoroughly. Then composing won't take a long time. [...] A fair copy of my new symphony (IV) is being made now. A splendid work, I believe. [...] Please tell no one about my opera plans![3]

The diary suggests the reason the opera project in question could not be completed: 'Tending in the direction of "symphonic poem" today. Find operatic style banal. If I had lived my life in the wings, it would presumably be different.'[4] On 16 November 1911 he wrote in another letter to Boldemann: 'Operatic form is and will remain conventional. I believe the subject has no place here.' On 29 November he was working on details again: 'please, as much as possible avoid "names" and other "unpoetic" words. I get vertigo every time I hear bohemians set to music words like "I have to write a newspaper article" or "there is the encyclopaedia". Where the plot goes "faster", then please make the dialogue absolutely as brief as possible. I find the beginning too long.' On 15 July 1911, too, in a letter to Boldemann things sound more promising: 'I am very excited about the opera libretto! Can you send it here? Otherwise I am coming to Europe again at the end of September. [...] But if it is necessary, I will come to Berlin sooner for the opera, for example.' On 23 August 1911, doubts predominated: 'This text is excellent. It may be that I am not composing the opera well. [...] At the moment, I have a lot of "bread-and-butter work", readying old things for publication. But soon I will begin work.'

[1] All letters in the collection of the Åbo Akademi. On this project, see also Erik W. Tawaststjerna 1986, pp. 205 ff. Boldemann's letters to JS are in the National Library (Coll. 206: 4).

[2] Erik W. Tawaststjerna 1994, p. 172.

[3] All letters in the collection of the Åbo Akademi.

[4] Diary, 4 June 1911.

On 16 October 1911 his correspondence with Boldemann is about business again: 'What's up with the licence? If there are expenses for it, I should pay a share in proportion to the profits I can claim. I believe this letter is the first business letter between us.' On 14 January 1912, the project had suddenly lost its attraction, especially since the text suddenly seemed too realistic. He wrote to Boldemann:

> I am having many doubts about the opera. If I do something truly good, it will be recognised only after a long time. My saga was printed twenty years ago [*sic*; in fact, *En saga* was printed in 1903], and only now is it found everywhere. That's just an example. And above all music history speaks a clear language. Then I fear that the milieu — French officers, etc. — does not suit my music. Then the whole opera is too realistic for me. And finally: despite everything I find it very difficult to separate myself from this wonderful text. [...] I wrote that the day before yesterday. Last night I had firmly decided to compose your text as it is. Today the French traditions are the sticking points again. Please write me to say when I must decide at the latest.

On 3 February 1912, he could not identify specific progress either: 'I will indeed start working on the opera. [...] Leave the text as it is for now.' Other ideas about the text followed on 20 April 1912: the action should take place not in France but southern Sweden, and so on.[1] That makes it clear how vague the project still was. He fortified himself by reading texts on opera theory in specialist journals. 'A very rewarding essay about opera in *Signale*', he wrote in his diary on 13 March 1912. He was clearly referring to Emil Petschnig's two-part article 'Die Oper der Zukunft' (The opera of the future) of 28 February and 6 March 1912. The author wrote that the opera of the future must 'mean a turn away from the present style of dramatic composition, a turn away and around, which does not by any means necessitate a step backwards'.[2]

The few musical ideas for the opera were competing with reflections on the symphony, which in the months that followed took on fascinating features.[3] 'In opera, absolute musical talent counts for less. "The exciting"!!' he wrote on 24 April 1912, whereas by 12 May 'the opera has gained the upper hand' over the alternative symphony and the 'symphonic fantasy'. On 18 May he observed that an opera 'of the mind' cannot have a text or any intrigues. The unhappy ending was reached on 7 October 1912, three years after the first sketches:

> Just back from England — my Symphony no. 4 was a success at the Birmingham Festival. Under no circumstances can you spend anything for any concerts in Copenhagen. Money can never come between us. I value your friendship too highly! And thousand mark notes always have something bad about them. [...]

[1] Diary, n.d..

[2] Emil Petschnig, 'Die Oper der Zukunft', *Signale für die Musikalische Welt* 70, no. 9 (February 28, 1912),p. 279.

[3] Documented in detail in chapter 3.4 in the present volume.

I have to send your opera libretto back, because I find it unjust of me to delay the setting of your magnificent works. I cannot bring myself to do it. I am very, very unhappy.

The Incidental and Tableau Music: From Karelia to The Tempest

The possibilities within the framework of the genre are diverse enough for Sibelius to have been able to find his niche with the help of a specialist in theatre – especially after 1927 when he was increasingly free of dependence on financial success. Despite (or precisely because of) her experience in the large opera houses of the world, Aino Ackté was not able to fill the role of the helpful specialist. The causes of his failure were his music theatre and vocal scores of other kinds and his experimental vision.

The ritual music for Freemasons after 1930 also testifies to dramaturgical talent. Even more important, however, was the progressive genre of incidental music, which was popular throughout Europe around 1900, which Sibelius actively influenced, as well as the fact that opera – like the symphony, the solo concerto and piano music – found itself in a crisis and had already found gifted reformers in Strauss and Janáček. Sibelius had gained knowledge of the field through theatre projects for which he was almost always responsible as conductor, but there was no appropriate text for an opera to be found,[1] and the genre was more influenced by conventions and commerce than non-musical theatre was. One of his convincing masterpieces from the world of incidental music is *Valse triste* for Järnefelt's *Kuolema* (1903), op. 44, no. 1, which has unfortunately lost some of its original significance by being separated from the stage.

Valse triste in particular – which is, according to Salmenhaara, an example of 'sublime salon style', as opposed to (somewhat less aptly) 'pathos-laden salon style'[2] in the tone poem *Finlandia* – became a 'concept' early on, to which references could be made in poems, novels and films without further particulars.[3] In the original, it accompanies a morbid dream: a dying woman lives through a scene at a ball from her youth. Someone knocks at the door, and Death enters – a free adaptation of Maurice Maeterlinck's *L'Intruse* (1891).[4] Another important episode in *Kuolema* is *Scene with Cranes*, which in the concert version of 1906 (op. 44, no. 2) consists of two pieces of incidental music: 'Eilaa, eilaa' and an untitled passage accompanying the

[1] On the fundamental closeness of opera and incidental music as genres around 1900, see Schwartz 2000, pp. 151ff., and Schwartz 2002.

[2] Salmenhaara 1996b, p. 182. Cf. Erik W. Tawaststjerna 1997b, p. 252, quoting JS to the newspaper *Politiken*, 9 October 1924, concerning *Valse triste* and *Valse chevaleresque*: 'salon music of genius' versus 'pure salon music'. Neither *Valse triste* nor *Finlandia* is truly related to salon culture.

[3] Worthy of study, in part as an attempt at explanation, is Gottfried Benn's poem *Valse triste* (1936; in Benn 1965, pp. 104–5; see also chapter 6 in the present volume): 'Danced before the Finnish skerries – *Valse triste*, bosom of dreams'. *Valse triste* serves as a symbol for the 'other trail' and the 'bosom of dreams'.

[4] On this, see Kurki 1997, p. 45.

cranes. This score has motifs that relate to the Fifth Symphony,[1] whereas *Valse triste* features the characteristic sequence of chords that concludes the Seventh Symphony.[2] Canzonetta, op. 62a ('Rondino of the Lovers', originally music for *Kuolema*), which Stravinsky arranged for four horns, two clarinets, harp and double bass in 1963, is also incidental music.

The public presence of his incidental music suffers from the shortcomings of theatre history, which shows no interest in reconstructed historical performances – particularly in the case of minor texts for the theatre. The ambitious release on CD of the complete incidental music of Sibelius has, by contrast, been ongoing for several years.[3] The works contain brief, quite charming music for fleeting appearances and events on the stage, such as 'Ariel flies in' (in several variations) in *The Tempest*. Most of the incidental music is available in suites of selections or collections of arrangements of individual pieces:

> *King Christian II* Suite (1898, Paul), but lacking the famous 'Sången om korsspindeln' (Fool's song of the spider);
> *Pelléas et Mélisande* Suite (1905, Maeterlinck, trans. Gripenberg), a single song: 'De trenne blinda systrar' (The three blind sisters);
> *Belshazzar's Feast* Suite (1906–7, Hjalmar Procopé[4]);
> *Swanwhite* Suite (1908, Strindberg);
> *Canzonetta* and *Valse romantique* from *Kuolema* (1906/11, Arvid Järnefelt);
> single passages from *Scaramouche* ('tragic pantomime' by Poul Knudsen and M. T. Bloch:[5] *Danse élégiaque* and *Scène d'amour* 1914[6] as well as Eyvind Alnaes's piano paraphrase *Choix de mélodies tirées de la Pantomime tragique* 1923);
> single pieces from *Everyman* (1925/6, Hofmannsthal, trans. Huugo Jalkanen): *Episodio*, *Scena* and *Canzone*;
> *The Tempest* Suites (1927, Shakespeare).

[1] Ibid., p. 76.

[2] On this, see Cecil Gray 1935, pp. 76–7.

[3] It began with *The Tempest* (Shakespeare): BIS-CD-581, 1992; Järnefelt's *Kuolema*: BIS-CD-915; Strindberg's *Svanevit*: BIS-CD-815 – each include all the songs and melodrama movements.

[4] Kurki 1997, p. 128.

[5] JS was sceptical in the initial phase of the project because he considered the text to be an imitation of Arthur Schnitzler's *Der Schleier der Pierrette* (National Archive Box 45; correspondence with Hansen Publishing Company, 1913). Hence he was not prepared to work with Knudsen later when Knudsen wrote *Ocon fuoco* for him (National Archive Box 45; JS to Hansen, 9 June 1923). Madetoja wrote music for a ballet based on this text. In 1927, Diaghilev planned a performance of *Scaramouche* in Paris (Erik W. Tawaststjerna 1997b, p. 221), but it was performed by the Danish Ballet (Tyrväinen 2003, pp. 54–5).

[6] There is an important document on the *Scaramouche* Suite in National Archive Box 52 (Hansen Publishing [no name mentioned] to JS, 6 December 1946, in German). The arranger of the suite – the minuet and waltz from the original score were missing – was reflecting on how to put the movements together: the disadvantage was the metre being the same and all the movements ending in a diminuendo; the advantage was the symphonic form of the whole.

Only a few examples of his incidental music, such as *Ödlan* (Lizard; text by Mikael Lybeck) from 1909 and *Die Sprache der Vögel* (The language of birds; text by Paul) of 1911 exist neither as a suite nor in an arrangement for piano. *Pan and Echo* (Dance Intermezzo, op. 53a, 1906) was arranged in 1921 as incidental music for Hofmannsthal's *Elektra*.

Strindberg's fairy tale *Swanwhite* inspired bold sounds. Even as a youth, Sibelius had discovered the author as a fascinating Modernist.[1] His friend Adolf Paul knew the Swedish poet personally, but the specific occasion for the incidental music came via Harriet Bosse, who had a theatre engagement in Helsinki between 1904 and 1906 and met the composer when she played Mélisande in 1906. She asked Strindberg, her ex-husband, if Sibelius could compose music for *Swanwhite*, which had been an engagement gift to her. Once Strindberg had granted his consent on 18 March 1906,[2] Sibelius began working on it, completing the score in April 1908. Since Strindberg had planned to compose his own music for it,[3] this consent was by no means taken for granted but represented a special honour. Sibelius esteemed Strindberg highly, and so he was hurt by the poet's distant-sounding reply to the composer's unbridled enthusiasm. Strindberg later tried to help arrange additional performances of Sibelius' incidental music, but it was repeatedly rejected for financial reasons.[4]

In this case, the orchestral suite represents an exceptionally complete, albeit coded summary. Moreover, Sibelius used material from *Swanwhite* in his Fifth Symphony (the Andantino is from no. 11), in *Pelléas et Mélisande* and in *The Bard*,[5] so that apart from a few measures this music is performed. The seven movements of the orchestral suite correspond to the following numbers from the music for *Swanwhite*:

- Movement I ('The Peacock'): no. 2 (an expectant Comodo movement in 2/2 and 6/8 time: 'Tyst dufvan, min prins kommer' (Quiet dove, my prince comes)), no. 3 ('En svan flyger förbi' (A swan flies past)), and no. 5 (the mother of the prince as swan);
- Movement II ('The Harp'): no. 4 (setting of the sad atmosphere of a scene in which Swanwhite's mother washes his feet) and no. 11 (a 'symphonic fragment' with the king, Swanwhite and the prince);
- Movement III ('The Maiden with the Roses'): no. 9 (a delicate waltz as wedding scene);
- Movement IV ('Listen, The Robin Is Singing'): no. 6 (a dream idyll and complex vision) and no. 7 (an atmospheric scene of yearning);
- Movement V ('The Prince Alone'): no. 8 (Funerailles);
- Movement VI ('Swanwhite and the Prince'): no. 10 (Wedding night);

[1] Erik W. Tawaststjerna 1976, p. 20, etc.

[2] August Strindberg to Harriet Bosse, 18 March 1906; quoted in Erik W. Tawaststjerna 1986, p. 88.

[3] JS, according to Ekman, quoted ibid., p. 89.

[4] See Kurki 1997, pp. 149, 173–4 and 180.

[5] Ibid., pp. 167–8 and 170.

Movement VII ('Song of Praise'): no. 13 (Pantomime) and no. 14 (Finale: 'I believe, I want, I pray' with organ and orchestra; the prince is called back to life by Swanwhite).

No. 1, which lasts eleven seconds, consists solely of a fifth in the horns: 'En hornsignal i fjärran'[1] (A horn signal in the distance), while no. 12 is a dialogue of horns.

Another original masterpiece is the incidental music to *The Tempest* (1925–6)[2] – a timelessly contemporary work for the stage, which has a lot of music of its own (not just the 'soft music' of Iris, Ceres and Juno but also a 'scurvy tune'), and it inspired Ludwig Tieck to imaginative experiments.[3] In comparison to the first movements – Overture (no. 1), 'Miranda is lulled into slumber' (no. 2) and 'Chorus of the Winds' (no. 4) – the others are more in the composer's usual style, but no. 18, 'Ariel as Harpy (Melodrama)', is noteworthy. In 1927, Sibelius' daughter Ruth Snellman was the first to perform Ariel in Helsinki. Every single movement has the seed of a bizarre orchestral style that is not even continued in *Tapiola*. An atonal overture, which as an orchestral piece lacks any visual effects, introduces the incidental music. With a little imagination, these effects can be derived from Debussy's *Nocturnes*, which Sibelius had known at least since visiting London in 1909 (especially no. 3, *Sirènes*, with its striking vocalises in the choir).[4] The overture concludes with characteristic experiments with chords based on the notes E, B flat, A sharp, D′, and G flat′ that shift and are supposed to form a kind of *Klangfarbenmelodie* (timbral melody) like the orchestral piece 'Farben' (Colours), Schoenberg's op. 16, no. 3, a score that Sibelius owned.[5] The duet of harmonium and harp ('Miranda is lulled into slumber') reflects a similar intention and is at the same time fascinating for its harmonies, even though they are based on a simple E flat minor triad. 'Ariel flies in' is a brief proof of Sibelius' brilliance as an orchestrator, and similarly in no. 5 or no. 29: 'Ariel hastens away' and no. 21 or no. 28 and no. 30 (once again titled 'Ariel flies in'), which leads into a magical world evoked by vocalises in the choir, harp and harmonium ('Chorus of the Winds'). Without the obvious influence of Russian and French orchestral music, this movement would have seemed original even in 1925. In 'Ariel's First Song', the Sibelius of the 'middle' years of 1900 to 1910 is unmistakable. The interjections of the male voices are dramatic and operatic, introducing a style totally different from the late symphonies or *Tapiola*. This stylistic change could not be explained without reference to Schoenberg's op. 16 and *Gurre-Lieder*. In some passages, Sibelius imported charac-

[1] His handwritten notes for the incidental music are printed in part ibid., appendix 4.

[2] The Danish title, *Stormen*, would also be appropriate since JS composed the work for a performance of Edvard Lembecke's translation at Det Kongelige Teater. The premiere took place in Copenhagen on 16 March 1926.

[3] See Cloot 1999, pp. 46–7.

[4] Erik W. Tawaststjerna 1986, p. 107.

[5] See, for example, Doflein 1969; cf. Sibelius' scores by other composers (including Schoenberg's op. 16, without autograph markings), National Library Coll. 206: 94.

teristic tropes from English music – by Edward Elgar, among others (no. 16 contains elements of *Falstaff*) – into his texture, which almost has the effect of adding local colour to music for Shakespeare.

His incidental music has been accused of 'squandering musical ideas'.[1] Indeed, Sibelius did not work out his ideas as symphonic suites, as Tchaikovsky, Stravinsky and Prokofiev did. Eija Kurki responded to the reproach by pointing out that motifs from the incidental music turn up in the symphonies. The fundamental critique of 'squandering' cannot be refuted in this way, however. When they were composed, both the tableaux and the incidental music were social events.[2] Consequently, Sibelius conducted all the premieres himself. We can only guess, moreover, what value these genres would now have if the art of the cinema – and by no means just the sound film – had not overshadowed the diverse developments in musical theatre and incidental music that occurred around 1900. Taken together, the fragments of work on musical theatre seem like blueprints for a new, extravagant genre that, on the trail of the Symbolist opera and the great ballets of the turn of the century, reveals a direction completely different from that of the great operas.

From the Tableau to the Film

Alongside the incidental music, individual pieces of which number among Sibelius' most interesting fragments, his tableau music for scenes from Finnish history looms as a dramatic genre that can scarcely be understood today in isolation from their contemporary standing and their context as stage drama. Despite its roots in Romanticism and its celebrated parallels to the political enthusiasm of such works as Beethoven's *Wellington's Victory* and the patriotic cantatas of the period around 1814 and again around 1870–1,[3] Sibelius' tableau music around 1900 can best be compared to music for silent films. Like music for the theatre and film, tableau music loses its intended effect outside its original context. Sibelius composed several masterpieces of tableau music such as the tone poem *Finlandia*, op. 26 (1900, initially known as 'La Patrie', 'Vaterland' and even 'Suomi'), the *Karelia* Suite, op. 11, and the *Karelia Overture*, op. 10 (1906). The Suites for Orchestra, op. 25 and op. 66, are known as *Scènes historiques* Nos. 1 and 2, even though the latter are not based on a tableau. Opus 25, in its present form, consists of three movements: 'All'Overtura', 'Scène' and 'Festivo' (originally titled 'Quasi Bolero'). In 1899, there had been a four-part version, whose last movement, 'Finale', has, under the name *Finlandia*, conquered the world in a more lasting way than anything else from Finland (including Nokia). The premiere of the original cycle followed on 4 November 1899, as part of an event to benefit the

[1] See Salmenhaara 1984, pp. 223–4, and Kurki 1997, p. 135.

[2] Salmenhaara 1996b, p. 174. With regard to the political significance of the events, Salmenhaara points especially to *Breaking of Ice on the Oulu River* and to passages in 'Sången om korsspindeln'.

[3] See Steiner 2001.

journalists who had been made into martyrs of cultural independence by pan-Slavic 'Russification'. The music included a prelude and six tableaux:

> 'Väinämöinen delights in nature and the people of Kaleva and Pohjola with their song' (later op. 25, no. 1);
> 'The Finns Become Christians' (thirteenth century);
> 'From the Court of Duke Johan' (Turku in the sixteenth century; op. 25, no. 3);
> 'The Finns in the Thirty Years War' (early seventeenth century; op. 25, no. 2);
> 'Great Wrath', eighteenth century.
> 'Finland Awakens' (nineteenth century; op. 26, no. 7 as hymn, text by V. A. Koskenniemi; see also *Musique réligieuse*, op. 113, no. 12, 1938, text by Wäinö Sola).

For 'Finland Awakens', a locomotive stood on the stage, which has inspired some to associative explanations of individual motifs in *Finlandia*: with a little imagination, one can indeed compare isolated effects to the acceleration and signals of a steam locomotive.[1] This interpretation is also in keeping with the information that while composing it Sibelius thought of the landscape around Hämeenlinna, through which Finland's first railway tracks passed.[2]

Similarly, four movements of his first tableau piece, composed in 1893 to support the Vyborg student body and idealistic popular education in the eastern province of Finland – 'Overture', 'Intermezzo', 'Ballad' and above all 'Alla marcia' – are still commonly heard in the form of the *Karelia* Suite. That selection was premiered in 1894. The suite of 1893 contained three movements: 'Runo Singing', Allegro and Finale. The original tableaux were:

> 'Oi ukko ylijumala' or 'A Home in Karelia, 1293' – six hundred years before the premiere in 1893;
> 'Laying the Foundation Stone of Vyborg Castle';
> 'Marimont, Duke of Lithuania, Raises Taxes in Käkisalmi Province' (cf. op. 11, no. 1);
> 'Tempo di menuetto non troppo lento. Dansen i rosenlund' or 'Karl Knutsson in Vyborg Castle' (op. 11, no. 2);
> 'March on an Old Motif' or 'Pontus de la Gardie before the Gates of Käkisalmi, 1580' (op. 11, no. 3, i.e., 'Alla marcia');
> 'A Scene from the Siege of Vyborg, 1710';
> 'The Unification of Old Finland [Karelia] with the Rest of Finland, 1811'.

It was followed by Fredrik Pacius' *Maamme* or *Vårt land* (Our country), which since

[1] See Hepokoski 2007; the image is originally by the Finnish avant-garde composer and writer Jouni Kaipainen.

[2] Koskimies 1990, p. 16.

1848 had been the hymn of the 'nation'. The significance of the 'old motif' in the March, op. 11, no. 3 ('Alla marcia') is a mystery.[1]

The dramaturgical principle was, on the whole, similar to that of the press tableaux of 1899, but better suited as patriotic battle music for the Finnish independence movement. Certain passages from these two complexes have become better known than the symphonies, and many listeners learn about the composer from concert performances (especially of 'Alla marcia' from the *Karelia* Suite or even *Finlandia*). Sibelius' own commentary on *Finlandia* is worth noting: 'Why do people like this tone poem? Probably because of its "plein-air" style. It is indeed constructed entirely of themes that come from above. Pure inspiration!'[2] The composer, who seemed surprised by the music's popularity, ruled out symphonic complexity and emphasised instead the inspiration that accounted for the quality of this composition but did not make it resilient. The result of pure inspiration was, in his view, ephemeral. *Valse triste*, by contrast, was the fruit of spontaneous inspiration: 'I composed "Valse Triste" originally for string orchestra. The composition with all retouching was finished in a week.'[3] Many masterpieces are composed that way.

Sibelius' royalty statements from GEMA in Germany provide an insight into how often specific works are performed. This provides us with an opportunity to use this rather controversial source to determine precisely the relative popularity of specific pieces and to demonstrate the extreme popularity of compositions from his incidental and tableau music in particular. The available GEMA figures from 1917 to 1925 reveal in the case of the most popular works that *Finlandia*, which was originally a tableau movement, was as a tone poem only rarely surpassed by works originally composed as concert pieces and that many of the other most popular works also derive from a theatrical context:

1917–18: Art music: *Finlandia*, 576 points; *The Swan of Tuonela*, 576; *King Christian II* Suite, 432; *Dance Intermezzo*, op. 45, no. 2, 864; *Valse triste*, 6,816. Popular music: *Finlandia*, 576; *Spring Song*, 2,496, 'Fool's Song of the Spider', 180; *Romance* for Strings, 2,496; *King Christian II* Suite, 144; *Valse triste*, 4,464.

1918–19: *Valse triste* as art music (Art), 144 points; as popular music (Popular), 3,978; *Finlandia* (Art), 2,016; (Popular), 840; Violin Concerto (Art), 648; Third Symphony (Art), 1,728; *The Swan of Tuonela* (Popular), 162.

1919–20: *Valse triste* (Art), 1,728 points; (Popular), 5,382; *Finlandia* (Art), 2,016; (Popular), 960; First Symphony (Art), 432; Second Symphony (Art), 2,592; *Voces intimae* (Art), 162; Violin Concerto (Art), 648; *The Swan of Tuonela*, 216.

[1] There is already a complete recording of the surviving incidental music. Certain movements were set to music anew by Kalevi Aho for the recording under Vänskä (BIS-CD-915).

[2] Diary, [22–]23 December 1911 (subsequent undated entry).

[3] Ekman 1946, p. 172. Cf. Kurki 1997, p. 46.

1920–1: *Finlandia* (Popular), 1,176 points; (Art), 1,008; *Valse triste* (Popular), 8,451; (Art), 912; Violin Concerto (Art), 288; First Symphony (Art), 864; Second Symphony (Art), 1,296; *The Swan of Tuonela* (Art), 288.[1]

In the fiscal year 1924/5, *Finlandia* received what may have been a record-breaking 12,000 points in the popular music category and another 1,244 points as art music, as well as 48 points for radio, which were especially valuable. *Valse triste* received 3,700 points in the popular music category and 252 in the art category as well as 54 radio points; the Violin Concerto 1,120 art music points; the First Symphony, 27 radio points; the Second Symphony 864 art music points; the Fifth Symphony, 432 art music points; and the string quartet *Voces intimae*, 144 art music points.

So for decades a majority of music listeners were aware only of *Finlandia*, which Sibelius himself regretted on the occasion of a Europakonzert in 1943: 'Heard Europakonzert from Germany tonight. All the composers were represented by their best works — in my case, by *Finlandia*. From now on — that's certain! — I will be taken for a *fait accompli*.'[2] The scene is typical, since Sibelius spent a lot of time listening to the radio. A few days earlier, on 20 September, he heard a Swedish broadcast of Ralph Vaughan Williams's Fifth Symphony, which is dedicated to him, and noted: 'Culture and rich humanity! I am profoundly grateful. Williams gives me more than anyone can imagine.' He responded quite similarly as in 1943 to the Internationales Musikfest of 1935 in Hamburg, in which he was represented by the *Karelia* Suite.[3]

Just how universally appropriate and effective his music can be outside the context of a concert is demonstrated not only by *Pelléas et Mélisande* in Al Jolson's *The Jazz Singer* (1927) and *Valse triste* in Charlie Chaplin's *The Gold Rush* (1925),[4] but also by a German project from 1955, a documentary film on Friedrich Schiller with the tone poem *Night Ride and Sunrise* as background music. The correspondence between the AWA production company in Berlin and Sibelius documents the plan: a mail coach travels quickly along a country road (20 sec.), a long shot of Mannheim Castle (10 sec.), two people walking along a mountain road (49 sec.), pan from a bridge into the water (12.5 sec.), falling leaves (6 sec.), meadow stream (19 sec.).[5] Because his German publisher was not enthusiastic about the project, the producers contacted Sibelius directly — unsuccessfully. This tone poem is based on particularly complex

[1] National Library Coll. 206: 45.

[2] Diary, 5 October 1943.

[3] Diary, 17 June 1935.

[4] Cf. Erik W. Tawaststjerna 1997a, p. 287. The only source on *The Gold Rush* is Adolf Paul's letter to JS on 29 December 1929 from Berlin. Neither Paul nor Tawaststjerna seems to have considered that film music of that era could vary from performance to performance, even if Chaplin had released music lists. *Valse triste* was probably only used occasionally in the melancholy scene with Georgia in the saloon. It was not used in the 1942 version of the film, nor is it on the DVD of the 1925 version with the pianist Neil Brand, based on the original music list for the USA. German lists (if they ever existed) are lost.

[5] See National Library Coll. 206: 43; AWA to JS, 5 December 1955.

autobiographical experiences: an overnight coach ride from Helsinki to Kerava one summer prior to 1904 or a trip from 'Suolahti' or Soanlahti[1] to Wärtsilä (in Karelia, south of Korpiselkä) in the summer of 1892, 'through deep forests to Aino'. In 1912, Sibelius had yet another night ride in summer, between Kuhmoinen and Orivesi, and his own impressions of Rome in 1901 are said to have played a role as well.[2] This example demonstrates the complexity of inspiration and choosing a title — there are similar stories for *Pohjola's Daughter* and the symphonies. Tawaststjerna expresses the opinion that the light of the sunrise is not 'Central European' but Nordic,[3] but that is a subjective reservation and could scarcely be proven.

In numerous other films, Sibelius' music is used for dramatic decoration. The GEMA statements in his archive include the following film titles just for the fiscal year 1931/2:[4] *Galgenvorspiel* (with 784 points), *Tannenberg* (17,244), *Der weisse Teufel* (2,247) and *Illusion* (956).[5] His correspondence with Breitkopf & Härtel also mentions: *Eine Nacht* (1931, with 'War Song of Tyrtaeus' (Song of the Athenians)), *Monga ma loba – Der Götterberg* (Berlin, 1955, music from *Finlandia*), *Wings for the Navy* (Canada, 1955; music from *Finlandia*), *Land des Lichts* (Upper Bavaria, 1957, various compositions). In 1939 the correspondence with Breitkopf includes an appendix (n.d.) with the following titles: *Arbeit bricht Not, Arbeit schafft Brot!* (Germany; parts of *Valse triste*), *Suomi kutsuu* (Finland calls, Finland; *Karelia* Overture, *Lemminkäinen's Return* and *King Christian II* Suite), *The Medium*, *The Rasp* (United Kingdom; *Finlandia*), *The Great Gambini* (USA; parts of *Valse triste*), *Jääkärin morsian* (The bride of the soldier, Finland; *March of the Finnish Jaeger Battalion*), and *Helmikuun manifesti* (The manifest of February, Finland; *March of the Finnish Jaeger Battalion*). In 1959, for example, *Ultima Thule* was produced by Documentari geografici in Milan, with music from the First and Second Symphonies. *Tapiola* and *En saga* were selected for a French film on Lapland, whereas *The Swan of Tuonela* was used in a Swiss film about mountain guides.[6] The publisher Robert Lienau's statements from 1907 to 1957 show how often the just the music for *Pelléas et Mélisande* and *Belshazzar's Feast* were used in films.[7] Film had truly become a major source of income for Sibelius.

The distinguished German producer and director Jürgen Neven-du Mont suspected that the programme of *Valse triste* concerned the death of Sibelius' first wife from tuberculosis, which he told the composer because he was firmly convinced he could do the music a favour interpretively by producing a film.[8] Sibelius' reaction has not survived, but after all (as far as we know) he had had only one wife, and she

[1] Jalas's note from July 1942, quoted in Sirén 1999, pp. 39–40.
[2] See Erik W. Tawaststjerna 1986, p. 101.
[3] Ibid., p. 104.
[4] National Library Coll. 206: 45.
[5] National Archive Box 43.
[6] National Archive Box 44.
[7] National Library Coll. 206: 48.
[8] National Library Coll. 206: 27; Jürgen Neven-du Mont to JS, 25 November 1948.

was still alive. In the fiscal year 1925/6, *Valse triste* received 12,200 GEMA points – and *Finlandia* 12,000 – for the silent film industry alone. These figures explain, on the one hand, the financial salvation of the composer and his family and also, on the other hand, the attacks of modernist critics, for he had truly become the greatest 'star' (Adorno) among the living composers of art music.

And I dreamed of orchestral fantasies [as]
'something that has not yet existed'.[1]

3.4 The Post-Wagnerian Dilemma of Orchestral Music after 1894

The Problem of Naming

Sibelius reflected on whether the title 'symphony' was relevant to his time, something that the catalogue of his works, with its distinctions between 'symphony', 'symphonic poem' and 'tone poem', makes clear. The context of his ideas, as manifested especially in his diary, was inspiration derived from Berlioz and Liszt and from the ongoing crisis of the symphony. The latter was reflected in the gap between Brahms's Fourth Symphony (1885) and Mahler's 'Symphonic Poem in Two Parts' (First Symphony), *Titan* (1889), preceded by, among other works, Schumann's 'Spring' Symphony, op. 38 (1841). Sibelius was not doing what Schumann, Glazunov, Mahler and others had conceived and in part also achieved. He developed his own solution to a problem that was far from occupying him alone; nor can it be said that the problem had already been solved even by the highly progressive symphonic universe of Mahler.

In 1914 he commented on the word 'symphony' (Diary, 21 November 1914): 'The concept must be expanded. I've at least helped with that!' On 18 October he had noted that this eighteenth-century title had done his works more harm than good. On 5 February 1918 he noted this remarkable idea: 'Strange that the name of my symphonies should be their greatest enemy. These old gentlemen with their "concepts" would of course prefer to call them "fantasies" or something else – what do I know? [...] The name "symphony" can be expanded in its meaning. It has always been that way. An example of infinity.' The occasion was Carl Krebs's review in the Berlin newspaper *Der Tag* on 19 November 1921: 'The piece [the Fifth Symphony] is more a fantasy than a symphony.'[2] Berlioz's use of the concept of 'fantasy' to designate the genre of a large orchestral work is used by Sibelius as an alternative even earlier – for example, in a letter to Aino of 23–24 January 1905 – to contrast with symphony: 'I no longer write "symphony" but rather "symphonic fantasy for orchestra". I can move freely there, since there is no tradition.' In Berlin around 1890 he encountered Berlioz's *Symphonie fantastique* and Liszt's *Faust Symphony*. He assessed Berlioz in a note written in Berlin on 2 March 1898: 'O santa inspirazione! O santa dea!'[3] The First Symphony benefited from that influence.[4]

[1] Diary, 14 September 1912.

[2] Erik W. Tawaststjerna 1997b, p. 211.

[3] Erik W. Tawaststjerna 1976, p. 201.

[4] Tawaststjerna writes that an early version of the Fifth Symphony was called 'A Dramatic Fantasy for Orchestra' (Tawaststjerna 1994, p. 312). He quotes a letter of JS to Axel Carpelan, '28 May 1913'. This letter is also in Dahlström 2010, p. 177, but with the remark: 'incorrect date by unknown hand', and: 'most likely January 1904'. If the new dating is correct, the work in question is not the Fifth.

Such reflections on the choice of titles led to fundamental questions about genre and its significance. In that spirit, Sibelius wrote in his diary on 13 September 1943, while working out the unfinished but apparently not yet abandoned Eighth Symphony: 'What I want from and want to do with the symphonic is something very few people in the world understand. Most of them do not even suspect what it is about.' His critical ideas were connected with the anticipated failure of his great symphonic project, the Eighth. Even he could not immediately implement the particular, the ineffable, even though his effort was honest and the goal almost tangible. His struggle with the genre designation became extraordinarily fraught in 1912, in the context of the first phase of composing the Fifth Symphony. After the sinking of the *Titanic* put him in a contemplative mood on 17 April, he decided on his project for the coming weeks and wrote on 18/19 April: 'The "new" one: a symphony (?) and symphonic fantasies (?).' On 19 April 1912 he reflected more generally on a 'new symphonic task', which, after several detours, would lead to the Fifth Symphony. This challenge was related to open questions on the revision of the Fourth Symphony and – though this is often overlooked – Georg Boldemann's opera project.[1] On 22 April 1912 his time was initially divided between opera and string quartet ('from one extreme to the other'), but the afternoon was spent entirely 'under the sign of the opera. Sketching and planning. On the right course!' The very next day he abandoned the opera and planned a 'symphonic fantasy' ('my prayer') 'with or without a programme'. For a time from that point onwards, it was only generally about 'the new'.

On 5 May 1912 he sketched the title (in German from the very beginning): '"First Fantasy for Large Orchestra, op. 67"!! "Second" and so on!! That might be the solution! Opera?! Symphony? Yes, yes! You have to approach the thing calmly.' On 23 May he wrote: 'Worked intensely on the "new one" – the difficult-to-define "new one"', after writing as recently as 20 May: 'Worked: Symphony no. 5?! A splendid day', and the day before that: 'Worked: symphony or opera?!' On May 13 he had been reworking the material 'under the sign of the opera' and four days later 'under the sign of a symphony again! This unfortunate friction is driving me crazy!' On 18 May he remarked, frustrated: 'Friction between symph. and opera. How will it end?' The project hovered between the two large genres and did not want to take on definitive form. On 14 September 1912 he wrote: 'And I dreamed of orchestral fantasies [as] "something that has not yet existed".' In November, Aino Ackté's libretto 'Juha; or, Marja' was mentioned only in passing, as an isolated project at an early stage. In March 1913 the title 'orchestral fantasy' caught on for a time, but in the same context he also discussed the ephemeral, very first ideas for the 'tone poem' *The Bard*, op. 64. Several weeks later (Diary, 4 May 1913), the plans for 'the new one' and op. 64 went their separate ways again. On 27 April the distinction had been lost: 'I [am a] "tabula rasa": opera, symphony or symphonic fantasy.'

In lieu of the common genre description 'symphonic poem', Sibelius often used

[1] See chapter 3.3 in the present volume.

the term 'tone poem'. Another original, modest name was 'improvisation' for choral works such as *Sandels* (to a text about the Swedish officer Johan August Sandels by Johan Ludvig Runeberg, 1898), *Snöfrid* (Snowfreed, text by Viktor Rydberg, 1900, with recitation), *Breaking of Ice on the Oulu River* (text by Zachris Topelius, 1899, in this case as a subtitle) or for the first version of *Spring Song* (1894) as a main title. Clearly, 'tone poem' and 'symphonic poem' are no arbitrary terms for Sibelius, although they are used that way in the literature.[1] Pierre Vidal speaks of the 'model of the Sibelian symphonic poem' being established in *En saga*.[2] He believes that brevity is the most important criterion for the new model – with one exception: *Tapiola*. But *En saga* is longer than *Tapiola*, and the score for *The Wood Nymph* is similar in length, as is Richard Strauss's *Don Juan* (*c.* eighteen minutes). Liszt's *Die Hunnenschlacht* lasts about fourteen minutes; *Les Préludes*, about sixteen minutes; *Mazeppa* and *Hamlet* are similar in length. Sibelius was by no means deviating from the tradition in terms of brevity (even *Spring Song* and *The Bard* last more than eight minutes). The highly formal scope and, apart from *Tapiola*, minimal density of the structures are nevertheless probably the main reasons Sibelius himself avoided the word 'symphonic' (or rather reserved the term 'symphonic fantasy' as an alternative to 'symphony') and spoke instead of 'tone poem'. Another reason may be that the newer title made clear his conscious decision and represented his reflections on the history of the genre in general, which in the case of the symphonies ceased just prior to publication.

After various other projects, Sibelius began to reflect again on the 'new one, symphony?' in 1914.[3] He always used the adjective 'new' emphatically, not as a synonym for 'next'. On 17 September, the title 'Symphony no. 5' occurs. On 19 September he wrote: 'Worked on Symph. no. 5 yesterday. What will become of this child?!' And on 2 October: 'This morning a terrible depression, but: bathed in my new symphony and my innermost soul lit up.' Whereas on 18 October he had doubts about the acceptance and suitability of the term even for his previous symphonies, on 26 October he was once again emphatically using the title 'Symphony no. 5 (!)' and began 'serious' work on its composition. There are entries in the diary on specific themes and movements. On 16, 17 and 21 December 1914, the titles 'Fantasia 1', 'Symphonic Fantasy' and 'Orchestral Fantasy' ('how close my heart is to this form!') were all given as possible names for the current symphony and even for the Sixth Symphony, which was conceived in parallel with the Fifth and in part without separating the musical material;[4] he is supposed to have said of the Sixth that it was really 'a poem'.[5] In 1915 he had a 'powerful impression' of the 'Symph. no. 5. The new one!'[6] In November, with four

1 See, for example, Tanzberger 1943; Werbeck 1996.

2 Vidal 1995, p. 204.

3 Diary, 2 August 1914.

4 Erik W. Tawaststjerna 1997b, pp. 8–9 and 26.

5 Howell 1989, p. v.

6 Diary, 18 April 1915.

movements of the first version finished, he was still writing only about a 'symphony',[1] and a little later the Sixth is also identified as 'Symph. no. 6'.[2] In the meanwhile – during the revision, which came to a merely temporary conclusion on 24 November 1916 – the Fifth was called only that. By contrast, there were other 'Fantasies': 'Plan a new orchestral work with or without singing (?): Fantasies? Or?'[3] The work on the Fifth or Sixth Symphony was taken up again in January 1917, also under the designation 'symphony'.[4] Another project was now 'the new one'.[5] Even as he was finishing the final version of 1919, he was unsure what the still undefined work would be called in the end: 'Should I call it "Symphony in One Movement" or a symphonic fantasy, "Fantasia sinfonica I"?'[6] These thoughts are followed by the suggestive, undated addition: 'Bosh!' Interestingly, he knew on 22 April 1919 that the symphony was now finished. His hands were shaking so much that he could barely write: 'Nerves!' On 28 April he cut out the second and third movements and thought about the title, but on 6 May he took back the changes: 'The symphony will be in three movements as originally planned.' Only now did the copyist receive the score.

He was still marking the Sixth, which was 'the new one', with a question mark – ('Symp. no. 6?!') – as late as 11 November 1920; it was not premiered until 1923. On 12 September 1926 the Eighth was his youngest 'child', 'the new one', the Seventh having been premiered in 1924; referred to as the '8th Symphony' on 18 December 1931, it made him feel strangely 'youthful', and on 13 September 1943, he still had it 'in [his] thoughts'. Despite the 'youthful' energy his plans for the Eighth Symphony contained, the project could not be completed.

The Seventh Symphony, whose title was first established on 18 December 1917 (in parallel with the Sixth[7]) and was mentioned in the diary on 2 March 1924, the day after Sibelius finished the manuscript during the night, under the once again freer title 'Fantasia sinfonica I'.[8] This symphony was also discussed with Gunnar Hauch as 'Sinfonia continua' and only called 'Symph. 7' in the diary on 5 September 1924, but from then on for good. Its one-movement structure – modelled, probably unconsciously but nonetheless consistently, on Schumann's Fourth Symphony – was its distinguishing feature, whereas it had been only a passing idea for the Fifth. Again and again, he worked on a new work without knowing whether it should be a symphony or indeed something quite different: 'Forging the new one. Symphony?'[9]

[1] Diary, 1–17 November 1915.

[2] Diary, 27 January 1916.

[3] Diary, 11 February 1916.

[4] Diary, 12 January 1917.

[5] Diary, 4 July 1917.

[6] Diary, 28 April 1919.

[7] Diary, 18 December 1917. JS had the Sixth and Seventh 'in my head' and continued to work on the Fifth Symphony.

[8] Erik W. Tawaststjerna 1997b, p. 243.

[9] Diary, 2 August 1914.

For Sibelius, symphonic writing represented the highest level for the artistic development of the material. The purely musical raw material mostly exists first; only later did he think explicitly about the title. This uncertainty applied to other genres as well, such as works for piano (Diary, 30 May 1912): 'Working on piano things — Sonatinas?' They were finished on 3 July and were indeed called Three Sonatinas, op. 67. On 30 April 1912 (Diary), he saw through the process: 'Organise my material from musical ideas. Interesting to see with what result!' Where the Sixth and Seventh Symphonies were concerned, the work overlapped with the *Kalevala* project 'Kuutar' about the Lady of the Moon (1919–20). In a large sketchbook there is a rich selection of themes with programmatic references to the *Kalevala*.[1]

On 25 November 1920 he wrote about the Sixth in his diary using a question mark and in close connection to another project: 'Doubts about symphony or "Runes historiques".'[2] The titles 'Runes historiques' and 'Runes symphoniques'[3] were his most original attempts — and at the same time, with regard to the eventual future reception, most fatal as an invitation to regionalist misunderstandings) — to develop terms for a new genre from 'symphony', 'symphonic poem' and 'symphonic fantasy'. In a draft letter Sibelius asked a friend to help choose an appropriate title. He made it clear that it was not about 'runes' in the sense of characters and feared that these titles — in any language — could have a 'negative connotation of ethnography'. If the date of 1928 is correct, the sketches must have been for the Eighth Symphony. Despite everything, the Seventh was finished as a 'symphony' after various transitional stages; likewise, the Eighth was begun, and nearly completed, as a symphony — not, say, as a new 'Fantasia sinfonica'. Consequently, it is evident that even this new genre was not the goal but rather the symphony. Sibelius' position corresponds to the Austrian music theorist Friedrich von Hausegger's dialectic of 1885: 'Great artists have extended forms without the basic character of the musical form suffering by it. The perfect, true artist does not feel superficially bound to the form; he defines it according to his needs.'[4]

In his late work, Sibelius was to overcome the distinction between 'symphony' and 'symphonic poem' or 'tone poem', which, apart from *Kullervo* and *Lemminkäinen*, had been his elegant name for this type of work. He was even about to develop the 'symphonic fantasy' from this synthesis.[5] His awareness of tradition kept him from doing so: he lacked either the courage or a good reason to introduce a new term to the public. The understatement 'tone poem' — apparently without symphonic ambitions — suited his character. Privately, he had made the leap since his work on the

[1] National Library Coll. 206: 1.A.33.

[2] Diary, 25 November 1920.

[3] National Archive Box 36: draft letter to unknown recipient, n.d. (subsequently dated 1928 in another hand), on the terms 'Runes symphoniques', 'ton-runa', 'symphonic *runo*' and 'runa sinfonica'.

[4] Hausegger 1885, p. 165.

[5] Murtomäki 1996, pp.147ff. He elaborated Tawaststjerna's formulation (Erik W. Tawaststjerna 1997a, p. 187): 'In the Seventh Symphony, Sibelius finally realised his idea of composing a one-movement symphony.'

Third Symphony, but a specific term does not occur until *Pohjola's Daughter* (1905–6), which was ultimately called a 'Symphonic Fantasy for Large Orchestra'. One title proposed by Sibelius for it was rather pompous: 'L'Aventure d'un héros', perhaps after Strauss's *Ein Heldenleben*, although most *Kalevala* connoisseurs suspect that the hero is old Väinämöinen (Cantos 1–10). Originally, Sibelius preferred 'Väinämöinen'.[1] The final title, after a major female character (the daughter of the sinister Lady of Pohjola), was Robert Lienau's proposal. Lienau also took the 'Symphonic Poem' as subtitle for granted. He wrote Sibelius a postcard on 22 July 1906: '"Wainamoinen" [*sic*] is [...] too striking a word for us Germans. Can we not say, perhaps: "Pohjola's Daughter" or very generally: "Finnish Fairy Tale" or the like?'

The debate was continued on 30 August 1906. Lienau wrote Sibelius: 'The title you proposed, "L'Aventure d'un héros", does not really please me at all. For the word "héros" implies as a consequence of its German meaning above all the powerful, the violent as such, and in that sense your symphonic poem is not really heroic. But why not "Pohjola's Daughter"?' This example shows how much publishers welcomed Finnish and Nordic references. Although this title from the *Kalevala*, *Pohjolan tytär*, could be translated literally as 'Daughter of the North' – much as *The Swan of Tuonela* is literally 'The Swan of Hades' or 'of the Afterworld' – Lienau preferred the Finnish word. And indeed: Pohjola is not only a synonym of 'North' but also a name – today the surname of a dynasty of musicians and in those days a mythological name in the *Kalevala*. For Lienau and contemporary audiences, the exotic (Finnish) was attractive, at least in small portions. One reason for Sibelius' reluctance to use 'fantasy' as the name of a genre may have been Berlioz's *Symphonie fantastique: Épisode de la vie d'un artiste* – another musical setting of the composer's own 'state of mind'.[2] The thoroughly feminine title *Pohjola's Daughter* should not mislead here, since the myth is primarily about the masculine main character, Väinämöinen. Living with Sibelius means living with problematic titles.

Lemminkäinen, The Bard, The Oceanides and Other 'Tone Poems'

Ever since Monteverdi, the development of an expressive orchestral language was primarily the domain of opera orchestras. In the nineteenth century, especially, opera scores substantially expanded their vocabulary of sounds and gestures. So it is not surprising that Sibelius' generation, even when constructing symphonies in the tradition of Beethoven and Brahms (or at least titling their works accordingly), were suspected of being inspired dramatically and programmatically. In terms of harmony and orchestration, the orchestral language of the *fin de siècle* was, even among its less advanced representatives, so rich in expressive gesture that to this day many involuntarily perceive a narrative sequence of states of mind and regard this music as

[1] National Archive Box 46; correspondence with Lienau.

[2] Ibid.

a 'psychologically accurate course of ideas'.[1] In the hands of Wagner, opera became increasingly 'symphonic', and 'absolute' symphonic writing was designed – not only in Tchaikovsky, Sibelius and Mahler but also in Schumann, Brahms and Bruckner – to be dramatic in its syntax.

Like Liszt – who, in contrast to those who were 'specifically symphonists', saw himself as a 'poetic symphonist' and 'tone poet'[2] – Sibelius labelled himself a 'poet' (in the Lisztian sense) and thus distinguished between the tradition and his own efforts to create the fantasy, 'tone poem', 'symphonic poem' and 'rune symphonique'. It was about more than just the form, namely, about the 'poetically' moving and the 'why' of sounds. His distancing himself from Wagner and moving closer to Liszt are already evident from the *Lemminkäinen Legends* (1893/5) in the way that the protagonists are not assigned leitmotifs. The programme unfolds within the framework of a motivic kaleidoscope, and the melody tends to the 'sub-thematic' and 'structural'.[3] Around 1895 Sibelius made a transition from traditional motivic to 'structural' logic. The emancipation of poetic, lyrically expressive and ultimately programmatic dissonance determined both the melodic lines (in the style of a recitative) and his orchestral textures. It permitted the flexible leading of lines and harmony necessary to depict complex moods and objects. Liszt's *topoi* consist, on the one hand, of melodic details that are difficult to grasp and, on the other, of crescendo waves of tremolos and other grand effects. *Tapiola* (1926) reveals experiments with sound fields that after 1960 would lead to the emancipation of timbre as a formal parameter.

Sibelius' poetically motivated pathos is also something he shares with Liszt. In terms of orchestration, the *Lemminkäinen* cycle, moreover, has passages that would have had a revolutionary effect before Wagner's *Parsifal*. Sibelius achieved 'an extremely sensitive way with colour, surprising in its timbral effects, that is downright genius', as the *Berliner Tageblatt* wrote of *The Swan of Tuonela* in its report on the June festival of the Allgemeiner Deutscher Musikverein in Heidelberg in 1901.[4] It was not the sound but the melodic invention that impressed Richard Strauss, who was also present, noting in his diary that Sibelius was the only Nordic composer with depth;[5] in Strauss's view, he was not only capable of masterly orchestration but also of composing music with a freshness that revealed an almost inexhaustible talent for melodic invention. If Strauss was recorded expressing that view immediately after hearing the performance of *The Swan of Tuonela*, without knowing anything else, then his characterisation is understandable. Only after his success in Heidelberg did Sibelius write his Second Symphony, whose extensive structures are derived, as in Beethoven and Liszt, from the tiniest motifs but then worked out in playfully minute ways. In his First Symphony (1899–1900), which would probably have been better

1 See Newcomb 1984; Newcomb 1987; and Newcomb 1981.
2 Dömling 1998, p. 107.
3 See Dahlhaus 1989, p. 367, and, on the 'sub-thematic', Dahlhaus 1980a.
4 Erik W. Tawaststjerna 1992, p. 160, quoting Adolf Paul's report.
5 Erik W. Tawaststjerna 1976, p. 241.

FIG. 26. Akseli Gallen-Kallela, *The Maidens of the Island* (1895). This depiction corresponds to the first of the *Lemminkäinen Legends* and shows the girls mourning the young hero. The symbolism of the red swan is risqué, but the erotic scene on the left edge is barely recognisable. The one painting narrates several episodes of the legend.

suited to the artistic ambitions of the Allgemeiner Deutscher Musikverein, apart from its considerable length, one finds, despite its simplistic elaboration, a striking, catchy motif common in Edvard Grieg's music — G, F sharp, D — as well as isolated other elements of Lisztian gestures, such as imposing chromatic runs, fields of sound, recitative-like themes and fermatas. The melodies of the First Symphony are lyrical and vocal ('cantabile') in their gestures. The orchestral texture evokes changing moods, emphasises contrasts, permits musical flow and articulates dividing lines between sections.

Sibelius' studies of Liszt were concentrated in the period between the *Lemmin-*

käinen Legends and the Second Symphony. His study of Wagner, which had occurred somewhat earlier, provided the foundation for his reception of Liszt. Echoes of *Lohengrin*, *Tristan und Isolde* and *Parsifal* are indeed characteristic of this phase. Whereas Wagner's chromaticism functions differently within the framework of the tonal system than the modal does in Sibelius, the orchestration in the *Lemminkäinen Legends* recalls Wagner in places. The first legend, *Lemminkäinen and the Maidens of the Island*, is influenced by Liszt, Wagner and Tchaikovsky. Comparisons with Debussy's *L'isle joyeuse* are by no means far off the mark, and *The Swan of Tuonela* can also be compared to *Prélude à L'Après-midi d'un faune*, which was written at nearly the same time. *The Swan of Tuonela* takes up the ancient theme of the swan, and *Lohengrin*, of all things, is echoed (albeit in A major): for example, in the beginning where the static A minor chord is transposed up octave by octave. The still somewhat naively programmatic, possibly autobiographical orchestral ballad *The Wood Nymph* (1893–5?), after a poem by Viktor Rydberg, is based on Liszt's ideas in concept but follows the poem closely in its setting. (There is also a version as melodrama that was premiered in March 1895, roughly a month before the orchestral ballad.) *Lemminkäinen* is influenced by the overall poetic idea of various cantos from the *Kalevala*. At the premiere in 1896 the *Legends* were still called 'Symphonic Poems (Subject from the Legend of Lemminkäinen)':

first movement: *Lemminkäinen and the Maidens of the Island*, *Kalevala*, Canto 29, lines 1, 77–8, 223–6, 345, 347–50, 357–60;
second movement: *Lemminkäinen in Tuonela*, Canto15, lines 115–16, 179–82, 186–90, 239–42, 273, 275–6, 603–6, 611–15 [later no. 3];
third movement: *The Swan of Tuonela* [later no. 2];
fourth movement: *Lemminkäinen's Return*, Canto 30, lines 481–4, and Canto 29, lines 454–8.

In 1901 Sibelius had his first great success with international critics with this work, and its third movement has remained one of his most popular pieces in concert ever since, as well as the main reason for the suspicion that the cor anglais was his favourite instrument. It would occupy him again towards the end of his life: during the so-called silence of Ainola after 1929, he was working intensely on an edition of the two legends that had not been published: *Lemminkäinen and the Maidens of the Island* and *Lemminkäinen in Tuonela*.[1] The manuscript was completed, after substantial changes, in May 1939. After that only details were changed, and these were among his last published musical ideas; the score was published in 1954.

Although the tone poem *En saga* (1892/1902), which had been composed in 1892 but is known only in a later version, is occasionally associated in the specialist

[1] National Archive Boxes 43 and 44; correspondence with the publishing house from 1935 onwards: see, for example the letter from one of JS' children, 18 January 1954, which stated that JS would permit publication only after his death and with the date of composition indicated: '1893/95'.

literature with sagas and epics, it is a 'self-portrait',[1] freely based on the subtitle of Berlioz's *Symphonie fantastique*. The composer prepared an explanation for Gunnar Hauch in 1913: '*Saga*'s music depicts moods and — why not? — various phases in a saga for which every listener can compose the "subject matter".'[2] Niemann — who responded to *En saga* by saying: 'The saga itself becomes the music here'[3] — instinctively got the point. The musical form is adapted to the 'expression of a state of mind', as the composer himself put it in the 1940s: this work was 'among the most profound, psychologically; I could almost say my entire youth is contained within it'; 'I had undergone a number of painful experiences at the time and in no other work have I revealed myself so completely.'[4] This pointed confession, which recalls the background to *Scène de ballet* of 1891,[5] is elegantly summarised by Ringbom: the point is 'to take it simply as a legend *without* any literary or programmatic basis, as one that Sibelius *himself* invented and that he, even had he wished, could not perhaps narrate with words — to take it purely as a fantastic legend.'[6] Apart from *En saga* and the popular *Spring Song* (1902; originally 'Improvisation for Orchestra', 1894–5), which Mahler heard in Helsinki in 1907 along with *Valse triste*, Sibelius published all of the orchestral pieces that are not explicitly related to the *Kalevala* — such as *The Dryad*, with the English subtitle 'tone picture for orchestra' (in German, less unconventionally: 'Tonstück'; 1910), *The Bard* (1913) and *The Oceanides* (1914) — without offering the listener a programme. The three-movement suite for string orchestra *Rakastava* (The lover; 1911–12) must also be mentioned in this context. It originally became known in 1893–4 as a work for male chorus with tenor solo, then in 1894 for male chorus with strings and in 1898 in a version for mixed choir with two soloists. The text of the choral work is from the *Kanteletar* and in that sense the programme forms a suite. The titles of the movements are: (1) 'The Lover'; (2) 'The Lovers' Path'; and (3) 'Good evening, my beloved! — Farewell!'.

Of *The Oceanides*, Newmarch remarked: 'It records individual impressions of an awakening sea, stirring under the cold caresses of the dawn-wind; echoing of light on the deep; presently Oceanus stretches his night-benumbed limbs, tingling with full remembrance of his potency, and the music swells to a grand tidal climax. This is no authentic programme; the work needs none.'[7] *The Bard* may have been inspired primarily by Runeberg's poem of that name. Certainly the title does not intend

1 Salmenhaara 1996b, p. 93.

2 National Library Coll. 206: 61: draft letter from JS to Gunnar Hauch, 20 April 1913.

3 Niemann 1917, p. 27.

4 Salmenhaara 1984, pp. 98–9, and Erik W. Tawaststjerna 1976, p. 130.

5 JS mentioned the as yet unfinished first version of *En saga* yet again as 'Ballet Scene no. 2' (copy of a letter to Adolf Paul, 13 November 1892, in University Library Coll. 206: 62, all originals in Stockholm).

6 Ringbom 1954, p. 40.

7 Newmarch 1939, pp. 52–3. In Aino's diary (14 May 1914), the project is referred to with a German title: 'Rondeau der Wellen' (Rondo of the waves). As of 2002, this composition too exists in two versions, since the premiere of the score JS left behind in America (the 'Yale Version' of 1914).

a Karelian singer. Even Tawaststjerna considers the association between *The Bard* and Runeberg's elegiac poem unimpeachable, especially since he can prove that during its composition Sibelius was indeed working with Runeberg's collection of poems, which includes this one.[1] It is also difficult to imagine that Sibelius would have forgotten, within a couple of weeks, the title of a Runeberg work he knew, and then unconsciously given his own work the same title.

Runeberg's portrait of an artist who lives in harmony with nature and the universe could indeed be the programme for the brilliantly compact 'tone poem' *The Bard*, but the poem is not commonly included in programme notes. Tawaststjerna explains the composer's secrecy by suggesting that he identifies with Runeberg's bard. This is plausible. The end of the poem depicts a death scene using the metaphor of the seasons to which Sibelius was receptive: winter brings death; the bard goes home for one last time, having roamed the world and enchanted everyone with his singing. He strums a deep chord on his lyre (in the tone poem it is a harp) and passes away. In the Elysian Fields, he relinquishes his own soul. The tone poem's form of expression is very similar to the final lines of the poem. Thus *The Bard* lacks the Impressionist character it is occasionally said to have and becomes a pensive example of romanticising Symbolism. Sibelius has succeeded with a tone poem in miniature that without any great mythological effort captures the essential quality of Strauss's *Tod und Verklärung* (Death and transfiguration) in an up-to-date, intimate and lyrical form.

Originally, *The Bard* was supposed to be the first part of a triptych: 'Concerning The Bard, I have the following in mind: namely, a Scenes hist. III: 1. The Bard; 2. The Knight and the Elf; 3. Rondo (conceived as round dance). But I would like to sell these tone poems separately.'[2] He wanted to sell the first part — an extraordinarily artful, compact composition — to the highest bidder. Including it in a cycle was intended to increase its market value and to respond to publishers' concerns about its impractical brevity (forcing the piece into unsuitable combinations in concerts and on recordings, for example, between *Spring Song* and *Valse lyrique*, op. 96a). On 3 May 1913, he confirmed that *The Bard* was part of a planned suite and on 12 June 1913 was still referring to 'The Bard: Triptych for Orchestra, op. 64'.

Sibelius recognised early on the imminent danger of 'trivialization' within the New German style,[3] which did indeed later become the basis for emotionally superficial film music. He wanted to develop his initially Symbolist and late Impressionist then later Surrealist poetry of the soul and of nature. It was not just folkloristic elements in the music but also programmatic ones that caused principled reservations or even the complete rejection of a subject — not least because of the banality of many of the proposals for symphonic poems. A late example of this is documented in a draft letter to his 'honoured brother', the distinguished opera singer and active Freemason

[1] Erik W. Tawaststjerna 1997b, p. 247.

[2] National Archive: copies in the Tawaststjerna Collection; JS to Breitkopf & Härtel, 23 April 1913.

[3] See also Dahlhaus 1989, p. 255.

Wäinö Sola, who wrote to him on 27 July 1928: 'The "Imatra Symphony" will become your most tremendous symphony.'[1] To assess this idea, it is important to know that the Imatra Falls, close to today's Russian border, mark the route along which water from the lake areas of eastern Finland makes its way directly to the Baltic Sea; in 1929 their power was made available to industry. Sibelius rejected the plan: 'I have thought carefully about your proposal. My composition should be decorative, so to speak. I have written many ~~such~~ works of that sort, most recently the overture to *The Tempest*, so that now I am bored and [it is] completely impossible. As a symbol, ~~such an~~ this art has a certain interest, but — .' The 'tremendous' work was supposed to be performed in 1929 on the occasion of the official opening of the hydroelectric power plant.[2] Another draft of this letter is almost identical: 'I have thought carefully about your proposal. The "Imatra Symphony" should be decorative, so to speak.'[3] 'Decorative' is an instructive term for the 'programmatic', but in the present case it is limited precisely to the kind of programme that Dahlhaus intended when he spoke of the risk of trivialisation. The masterpieces of the genre, such as *The Bard*, *Luonnotar* and *Tapiola*, are neither decorative nor trivial but rather alternatives to absolute symphonic writing — indeed orchestral 'fantasies'.

The Imatra project was never realised, but, according to Sola, it was not just a passing idea either.[4] Sola himself worked on a detailed schema for the programme, and Sibelius was prepared to attend planning discussions near Imatra. It is difficult to say, however, to what extent this was done more for reasons of politeness and whether the trip was motivated by Sibelius' curiosity to see from up close both the water, which was then still flowing freely, and the effort to focus nature's energy to benefit civilisation in the young national republic. It is possible to imagine that Sibelius was deeply distressed by this project, which was important for Finnish industry. It would be bold to see a connection between the destruction of what was perhaps nature's most sublime monument in north-eastern Europe — especially with the active participation of his fellow Freemasons — and Sibelius' lack of productivity, which began at the same time. Certainly the dam was one of many projects that Sibelius saw as a sign of an increasing rift between his own mentality and the modernist tendencies of the present. In a way, Imatra has become a symbol of that.

The Lyrical Programme Music before Tapiola: 'Where the Word Ends'

Sibelius' best compositions are the results of a fundamental, perhaps intuitive reform of the New German style. With all due allowances for the complexity of their themes, and despite countless attempts (not least by Sibelius himself) to prove the opposite,

[1] National Archive Box 36. The unnamed addressee was Wäinö Sola; cf. Wäinö Sola to JS in National Archive Box 30.

[2] On this work, see Salmenhaara 1998, pp. 15–26, quoting the text of the letter (dated 4 August 1928) from Sola 1952, p. 219. See Sola's collection in the National Archive and the letters from JS in it.

[3] National Library Coll. 206: 63.

[4] Salmenhaara 1998, p. 17.

the currently known facts provide a portrait of an artist 'who did not draw his musical ideas out of nowhere but instead needed for their development something tangibly programmatic or an atmosphere into which he could place himself'.[1] With this summary, the Finnish composer Kalevi Aho supports the old suspicion of a secret programmatic content even in the symphonies, which have allegedly 'almost' lost the traces of their extra-musical inspiration over the course of their composition. Aho assumes that the absolute, structural qualities come into being only at the end of a creative process whose beginning is characterised by the programme and by extra-musical inspiration. He offers the Fourth Symphony as a famous example of this. Its original occasion was connected with experiences in the region of low mountains near Koli in 1900 – hence its working title: 'La Montagne' (as in Liszt's *Ce qu'on entend sur la montagne* after Victor Hugo). At the end of the composition process, however, the work represents an architectonic construct in which Aho perceives a 'music of inner voices', though the listener can also associate them with Koli (voices of the landscape or the moods of a hiker). Aho summarises the process of composition as a goal-directed path towards absolute music and increasing abstraction – that is to say, a process that is recognisable in every single work as a reduction. Studies of the sketches confirm this thesis.[2] Although the original occasion for forming the core material, even in the symphonies, may have been an experience of nature, a high degree of abstraction is achieved in this genre. Often the original occasion can no longer be reconstructed by looking at the finished work of art.[3] The lengthy process of elaboration of the ideas that follows the first flush of inspiration does not allow us to recognise the project in the sketches but instead forms a fund of material for a number of works.

Carl Dahlhaus's suspicion that the 'symphonic poem succumbed to a resistless process of trivialization following, if not in the hands of, Strauss and Sibelius'[4] does not pertain to Sibelius in his technique or in his ideas – particularly not in the works after the Fourth Symphony of 1911 (*Luonnotar* and *The Bard*), whereas *The Wood Nymph*, *Spring Song*, *Lemminkäinen* and other early orchestral works (*En saga*, *The Dryad*) are marginal cases. Others include *Finlandia*; *Pohjola's Daughter*, which as a 'symphonic fantasy' aggressively approaches Strauss's idiom;[5] and *Night Ride and Sunrise*. Of this last work, Rosa Newmarch wrote (very relevantly with regard to the risk of trivialisation):[6]

> I remember that he once asked me if I thought the title was judiciously chosen, or whether it might lead people to expect in it a reflection from the older

[1] Aho 1998, p. 58.

[2] See, for example, Virtanen 1999, p. 247.

[3] Aho 1998, p. 58.

[4] Dahlhaus 1989, p. 255.

[5] Just how complex the category of the trivial is in this context is demonstrated by Virtanen 1998. See also Fanselau 1992.

[6] Newmarch 1939, p. 47.

romanticism of Raff's day, whereas the music is concerned rather with the inner experiences of an average man riding solitary through the forest gloom; sometimes glad to be alone with Nature; occasionally awe-stricken by the stillness or the strange sounds which break it; not filled with undue foreboding, but thankful and rejoicing in the daybreak.

Although the basic principle of his creativity was a parallelism of different approaches, dispensing with song and other texts marks a consistent development in Sibelius' approach to programmatic music: following the 'symphonic poem' *Kullervo*, a symphonic cantata with solo and choral voices (a recitation was planned as well), and the 'ballad' *The Wood Nymph*, which was also conceived as a melodrama, he concentrated on instrumental forms of expression based on lyrical inspiration. *Kullervo* makes the boundaries between forms of verbal expression problematic by dispensing with the spoken word in three of the programmatic movements. The text of *Kullervo*, which is at heart social criticism, is, so to speak, performed by instruments. For *Pohjola's Daughter*, Sibelius conceived his own programmatic text on the basis of Canto 8 of the *Kalevala* (only the final strophe of the programmatic poem printed in the score is not by Sibelius), whereas the tone poem *The Bard* exists without a text and in that sense without a programme. There is, however, a great deal to suggest that this work concerns a salvation of the soul similar to the one at the end of Runeberg's poem. The study score for *Tapiola* contains a brief poem intended to be read as a programme, but apparently it was first written by the editorial department of the publishing house in Leipzig, on the basis of an idea from the composer: 'Da dehnen sich des Nordlands düstre Wälder / Uralt-geheimnisvoll in wilden Träumen; / In ihnen wohnt der Wälder grosser Gott, / Waldgeister weben heimlich in dem Dunkel.' The English translation published with it reads: 'Wide-spread they stand, the Northland's dusky forests, Ancient, mysterious, brooding savage dreams; Within them dwells the Forest's mighty God, And wood-sprites in the gloom weave magic secrets.'[1]

The title and subject matter of *Tapiola* were, by contrast, established quite early, at the beginning of April 1926, a couple of months before work started. Moreover, Sibelius himself felt the need to explain the title. In early June 1926 he was corresponding with the New York-based conductor Walter Damrosch about the title. Damrosch came up with the formulation: '"Tapiola", a wild Nordic barren landscape, where the forest god and his wood nymphs dwell.'[2] No poem had a 'programmatic' function for the work; rather, it was about familiar themes that could be communicated by a title.

Unlike in *Kullervo* and the *Lemminkäinen Legends*, the latter of which Tawaststjerna suspected was a 'Sinfonia quasi una fantasia' or even a traditional symphony,[3] the poem for the programme of *Tapiola* was not from a published collection of

[1] See Erik W. Tawaststjerna 1997a, p. 240.

[2] Erik W. Tawaststjerna 1997b, p. 269, and Erik W. Tawaststjerna 1997a, p. 240.

[3] Erik W. Tawaststjerna 1976, p. 177. He believed that JS' choice of the title *Legends* was influenced by contemporary aversions to the genre of the symphony.

pseudo-mythological folk poetry. According to a statement credibly attributed to Sibelius, he got his inspiration 'entirely in nature or in something that cannot be expressed in words'.[1] In the spirit of desubjectivisation and the anti-lyrical, in its core Debussian Symbolist attitude, he drew here the obvious consequences from the crisis of the New German tradition. He was not composing epic tone poems in any case, so he quickly progressed from the slightly epic but at the same time – following Aleksis Kivi's lead – dramatic *Kullervo* by way of the romantic and lyric (*En saga*) to Symbolist tone poetry (*Lemminkäinen*, *The Bard*, etc.) to *Tapiola*. This evolution reflects the general history of culture and style between 1891 and 1926.

The First Symphony only had programmatic features in the conceptual phase – he had planned a three-part programme with literary allusions to Heinrich Heine, Adolf Törneros and Juhani Aho[2] – and unlike Mahler's first symphony (*Titan*, 1889), for example, it was never called 'Symphonic Poem'. By contrast, the history of the writing of the Third Symphony raises the question of leftover programmatic references to the *Kalevala* (the stories of Luonnotar and Marjatta).[3] The Second Symphony, in turn, justifies the question about the difference between symphony and tone poem, despite the unambiguous title, since while sketching the second movement, in 1901, the composer considered a scene with Don Juan and on another occasion, in 1902, associated the figure of Christ with one theme – in both cases mixed with autobiographical details. He even considered the idea of a sequence of four tone poems for orchestra on the subject of 'Feast'.[4]

The common image of Beethoven, handed down by his student Ferdinand Ries and others,[5] conjuring up a 'specific object' as he composed – which was interpreted by early-nineteenth-century authors such as Anton Schindler and Franz Anton Hoffmeister as a latently 'poetic idea'[6] – was connected with such visions in Sibelius' thinking. He knew the anecdotes about Beethoven and decisively rejected the often misunderstood idea in his own work.[7] For him, there was no inspiration by the 'object' but rather a 'language of the soul' and sequences of lyrical and subjective moods that could be connected in a noncommittal way to interchangeable objects. Whereas

[1] Levas 1960a, p. 129; see also Salmenhaara 1970, p. 23.

[2] See National Library Coll. 1472, pp. 38 ff., and Coll. 1540, 2. The question arises to what extent the gesture of the score is still connected to the original visions – for example, the main theme of the second movement with the idea 'Det blåser kalt, kalt väder från sjön' (A cold wind is blowing, cold weather from the sea) as the motto of the first movement or with that of 'Vintersaga' ('Carmina Jormae' after Aho's *Pan*) as title of the third movement.

[3] Cf. Virtanen 2005, pp. 125 ff.

[4] Erik W. Tawaststjerna 1976, pp. 237 ff. On the possibilities for interpreting the symphonies of JS speculatively based on knowledge of the region, see Krohn 1945–6, vol. 1, pp. 99 ff.

[5] Floros 1978, p. 8, and Schmitz 1927.

[6] Schindler [1840] 1977, p. 472.

[7] Murtomäki 1996, p. 147.

Salmenhaara sees the influence of Brahms in the Second Symphony,[1] David Haas suspects that this work marks the beginning of 'symphonic lyricism' in the spirit of Liszt. Richard Pohl believes it began with Tchaikovsky, though Salmenhaara vehemently rejects that relationship.[2]

Traces of Tchaikovsky are evident in the First Symphony. The formal strategy alone clearly recalls Tchaikovsky's Fifth (also in E minor), with a solo beginning, a solo clarinet in both cases, and a reminiscence of this section at the beginning of the final movement. At the same time, however, the differences are clear as well: what sounds like simple division into periods and harmonic accents in Tchaikovsky in 1888 evolves in Sibelius in 1899 into one of the freest strategies for a beginning in the late nineteenth century. The movement is introduced in the spirit of free improvisation with a B minor that has been distorted modally — the symphony is actually in E minor. The question of isolated influences is not essential, however, especially as the similarities could just as well be coincidence — and by no means components of an inter-textual construct. Both tone poems and symphonies are about the subjective expressions of a lyrical subject. Despite its different context, Sibelius' music is fundamentally a lyrical 'language of the soul'. The musical form suits the 'expression of a state of mind', as Sibelius himself supposedly said about *En saga*.[3] Although his remarks on that subject are rarer than those of Tchaikovsky, for example, David Haas's approach of analysing the 'lyricism' of Liszt, Tchaikovsky and Sibelius as an aesthetic and compositional stance similar in many respects for each of them is a plausible one. The only thing that argues against it is an equally plausible interpretation that Sibelius' orchestral work is not so much 'symphonic lyricism' as it is a gradual solution to crucial problems of the genre, which in turn supports Salmenhaara's critical position.

Sibelius' position in modernity is defined precisely by the dominant heteronomy and the simultaneity of disparate forms. The aesthetic ambiguity and independence from common lines of development that went hand in hand with that were characteristic of him. This is apparent not only terminologically (symphony, symphonic poem, tone poem, symphonic fantasy, 'Runes symphoniques', etc.), but also in the ambiguous categorisation of specific masterpieces such as *Kullervo* — 'symphonic poem' or 'symphony'? Sibelius indeed also referred to the work as his 'first symphony',[4] which made the incomplete Eighth Symphony his Ninth (or Tenth if the *Lemminkäinen Legends* are included). Today, for lack of a better solution, *Kullervo* is occasionally — in the strict, standardised pigeonholes of guides to the repertoire — even treated in the context of the oratorio[5] or described as a symphonic cantata.[6] The four *Lemmin-*

[1] Salmenhaara 1996b, p. 145. But Brahms is also the ultimate source of the metrical dynamics of the First Symphony. The role of Dvořák's Sixth Symphony also deserves attention.

[2] See Haas 1996, pp. 77 ff.

[3] Erik W. Tawaststjerna 1976, p. 130, and Salmenhaara 1984, pp. 98–9.

[4] Jalas n.d., p. iii.

[5] Mäkelä 2000d.

[6] Mäckelmann 1983, p. 129.

käinen Legends can indeed be performed as a symphony, with *The Swan of Tuonela* as the slow movement — if one relaxes the standards for the architecture of a symphony that actually apply in Sibelius' case — since the expressive character of the four movements largely conforms to symphonic practice.

If one respects the titles chosen by Sibelius for his works as the conscious decisions of a critical artist, rather than dismissing them as remnants of an outdated tradition, the tight framework of tone poems around the seven symphonies demands explanation. In doing so, we must take into account Salmenhaara's critique of Harold E. Johnson, who viewed *Tapiola* in the context of the poetic and programmatic early work, whereas Salmenhaara does not take note of the young composer's statements, especially since Sibelius later said nothing about his positive impressions of Liszt and Wagner.[1] Salmenhaara, who says nothing more about Liszt's oft-misunderstood idea of *poesis*, accuses Johnson of not recognising Sibelius' professional development over a thirty-year period. The tone poems, and with them the idea of a lyrical and subjective, poetically motivated single tone, not only represent the point of departure if only in the chronological sense but also the conclusion of the sequence of major works from 1891 to 1926. The following list clarifies the ambiguity of certain categorisations through the use of parentheses and a programmatic reference in the title to the *Kalevala* with a superior K, whereas a superior A indicates a well-founded or confirmed suspicion of autobiographical material and the N indicates a nationalist or patriotic background; very vague references are indicated by enclosing the superior letter in parentheses:

symphonies, 1899–1924: nos. [(N)] 1, [(A)] 2, [(K)] 3, [(A)] 4, 5, 6 and 7;

tone poems and the like (symphonic poem, symphonic fantasy, orchestral ballad, tone piece) 1892–1926: ([K(A)] *Kullervo*,) [A] *En saga*, [A] *The Wood Nymph*, *Spring Song*, [K] *Tiera* (for horn septet and percussion),[2] [K(A)] *Lemminkäinen Legends*, [N] *Finlandia*, *The Dryad*, [K(A)] *Pohjola's Daughter*, [A] *Night Ride and Sunrise*, [A] *The Bard* ([K] *Luonnotar*), *The Oceanides*, [K] *Tapiola*;

orchestral songs, 1894–7, 1913: *Arioso*, [N] *The Rapid-Rider's Brides*, [K] *Luonnotar*;

choral and orchestral songs, cantatas and cantata-symphonies, 1892–1926: [K(A)] *Kullervo*, [N] Cantatas for the University Graduation Ceremonies of 1894 and 1897, [N] Cantata for the Coronation of Nicholas II, *Impromptu (Livslust)*, [N] *Sandels*, *Snöfrid*, [N] *Breaking Ice on the Oulu River*, [K] *The Origin of Fire*, [N] *The Captive Queen*, [N] *My Own Land*, *Song of the Earth*, *Hymn of the Earth*, *Autrefois* (from Three Pieces for Piano or Orchestra), [K] *Väinämöinen's Song*;

incidental music and orchestral suites, 1893–1925: *Ödlan*, [N] *Karelia*, *Rakastava*, [N] *Scènes historiques I*, *King Christian II*, *Kuolema* (with *Valse triste*), *Pelléas*

[1] Salmenhaara 1970, pp. 23 ff.

[2] Tiera is Lemminkäinen's fellow warrior (*Kalevala*, Canto 30, lines 48 ff.). This chamber music 'tone poem' was later published in 1934.

et Mélisande, *Belshazzar's Feast*, *Swanwhite*, ᴺ *Scènes historiques* ɪɪ, *Scaramouche*, *Everyman*, *The Tempest*;

solo concertos, etc., 1903–29: Violin Concerto and other works, primarily for violin and orchestra;

other orchestral works, 1891–1922: Overture in E Major, ᴬ *Scène de ballet*, *Cassazione*, *Romance* in C major, *Dance Intermezzo*, op. 45, *Pan and Echo*, ᴺ⁽ᴬ⁾ *In memoriam (Marche funèbre)*, *Valse lyrique* and ⁽ᴬ⁾ *Valse chevaleresque* (from Three Pieces for Piano or Orchestra), *Suite mignonne*, *Suite champêtre*, *Suite caractéristique*.

The list shows how complexly Sibelius, in contrast to Mahler and Strauss, dealt with the palette of genres common around 1900, though he too was starting from the crisis of orchestral music after Berlioz, Liszt and Wagner.

It is a mystery how Cecil Gray, the first author who could have been familiar with nearly all of Sibelius' work published in his lifetime, could assert that Sibelius began where Beethoven left off – without any influence from Berlioz, Chopin, Weber, Liszt ('no repercussion') or Wagner.[1] The New German style, filtered through composers such as Borodin and perhaps Glazunov and even Tchaikovsky, was in fact the omnipresent stylistic foundation to which Sibelius referred even when he followed original paths or when the specific influence is not detectable. Because of daily train and ship travel between St Petersburg and Helsinki, it is difficult to trace which musician attended which performance. Until the late work *Tapiola*, the traces of this orientation were evident. Yet Gray rigorously dismisses them, because he was a euphoric adherent of the absolute symphonic spirit. Similarly ideological is Sibelius' own 'standpoint', as cited by Ernst Tanzberger, from which he perceived a clear separation between symphonies and symphonic poems or tone poems:

> Since Beethoven's time, all so-called symphonies, with the exception of those of Brahms, have been symphonic poems. In many cases, the composers have offered, or at least suggested, a programme [...]. That is not my ideal for a symphony. My symphonies are music – conceived and worked out as music's expression, without any literary basis. I am not a literary musician; for me, music begins where the word ends. [...] Of course it happens that an intimate mental image involuntarily clings to a musical movement I have written, but my symphonies have always been purely musical in their emergence and inspiration. When I write symphonic poems, the relationship is different, of course, but neither do I require that they be regarded as symphonies. [...] I do not wish to speak about my works ... My works should speak for themselves.[2]

Although Sibelius occasionally assumed there would be structural overlapping be-

[1] Cecil Gray 1931, pp. 202–3.

[2] Tanzberger 1962, p. 9; see also Legge's interview in *Hufvudstadtsbladet* (1934), in Legge 1935, esp. p. 219.

tween genres, and by no means treated programmes and purely formal conceptions as mutually exclusive antitheses in his own work, the provenance of this passage, which Tanzberger took from Ringbom and Legge and can be dated to 1934, can be considered relatively authentic, especially since there are consistent references to a 'literary basis' in unquestionably genuine sources. He was not ruling out here that a symphony could have a programme – indeed it is clearly implied in the turn of phrase 'an intimate mental image involuntarily clings to'. He is referring not to the listener's expected associations but rather to inspirations as such images. Completely independent of that, the origin and above all the so-called inspiration remain 'purely musical'.

Whether or not the sounds were inspired by poetry (as in the 1890s) or were supposed to be 'always purely musical', as in 1934, what remained constant was the rejection of the idea that music has to have literary roots. It would be possible – and this would imply that his 'standpoint' had been carefully considered – to sum it up by saying the inspiration was musical for him but that something other than the word – namely, 'intimate mental images' – was to be inspired. The inspiring thing for Sibelius is not 'poetry', as it was for Liszt and Wagner, but rather 'music', and the thing to be inspired was the intimate 'image'. Unfortunately, Sibelius said nothing about the supposed 'completely different' relationship in the symphonic poems. Presumably he meant that the 'image' or even more concrete images and ideas could 'inspire' the origin. Around 1900, however, it would be more reasonable to assume a mixture of symphony and symphony-poem, of symphonic and poetic intentions, which, on the one hand, was anchored in the optimised formal design and, on the other hand, was intended to sum up – programmatically, in the tradition of Liszt – the dignity of the new era and its ideals.

From the outset, Sibelius' 'tone poetry' was also innovative. His experiments in dealing with a programme were decisive, and the poetry and programmatic was not limited to the title. In contrast to Liszt, whose subjects often seem a bit academic (rarely nationalist and in a limited sense Hungarian[1]), Sibelius' themes from the *Kalevala* certainly contributed to the formation of Finnish culture, to forging the mythological *sampo* as a work of art on the basis of a cultural heritage that had not yet been established but was nonetheless extremely fashionable at the time. Whereas Liszt's symphonic poems can be read as manifestations of a desire for education for those who were willing to be educated academically (including, of course, Liszt himself), such ambitions were foreign to Sibelius. Even titles such as *Pan and Echo*, *The Dryad* and *The Oceanides*, which followed the trend around 1900 for subjects from

[1] See Jäker 1998. Whereas Alfred H. Meyer (1936, p. 68) drew a line between the folksong nationalism of Grieg and Smetana and JS' 'mythical and historical', 'topographic and climatic' nationalism, according to Altenburg (1998, col. 166), Sibelius' 'symphonic poems', because of their relationship to the *Kalevala*, are close to Smetana's *Má vlast* (1872/9). It is not known whether JS knew any of Smetana's works, much less the opera *The Bartered Bride*.

classical antiquity,[1] also refer to Finnish nature and are given only as vague hints, not with academic references. For Sibelius, the formation of identity was only indirectly related to a national context. Autobiographical impulses were often the deciding factor. Although the aspect of sophistication was secondary — Sibelius knew the classics as well — their responses to contemporary questions were not sufficient for him. He did not search within the cultural context to which he belonged (in Runeberg, Ibsen, Tolstoy and Nietzsche) but rather in the archaic folk culture of the *Kalevala* or in nature. Vidal has written of an avoidance of metaphysical, philosophical and idealistic themes; in that respect, Sibelius' programmes could be compared to those of Mily Balakirev's *Thamar* (1882), Nikolai Rimsky-Korsakov's *Sadko* (1867/92), Tchaikovsky's *Romeo and Juliet* (1870) and certainly also to Vasily Kalinnikov's *The Nymphs* (1898), but not to Strauss's *Ein Heldenleben, Tod und Verklärung, Alpensymphonie* or *Also sprach Zarathustra*. But this distinction is also exaggerated, since the tales from the *Kalevala* certainly have a metaphysical and philosophical depth. In lieu of Horace, Dante, Schiller, Goethe, Hugo, Nietzsche, Byron and Tasso, Elias Lönnrot's *Kalevala* provided Sibelius with the title characters of *Kullervo* and *Lemminkäinen* as well as of *Luonnotar* and *Pohjola's Daughter* up to *Tapiola*, but he did not neglect antique subjects (Oceanids, dryads).[2] Pursuing projects in this conflict between civilisation and nature was honourable and sublime but not easy. 'Nature speaks', as he noted in his diary on 4 June 1911, and he spoke of 'poetry in nature' on 18 February 1925, but even he — the bard who understood nature well and had an extraordinarily heartfelt relationship to it in comparison to other great composers of his generation — did not find it easy to translate it into music.

His poetic approach to the programme in question could be compared to Liszt's. The decisive thing is not the descriptive, linear narrative but rather the guiding idea — the theme of the language of the soul of a story that is not verbalised, which is sketched in a few lines or forms the abstract motto. Sibelius strove to make it possible to give form to the ideal, poetic meaning — if necessary dispensing with classical beauty. Often he confronted the audience with an ideality that he by no means motivated with the title but instead expressed in a seemingly absolute symphony. The poetic meaning of the lyrical language of the soul leads to the original form; the significant chromaticism, which is justified gesturally, to the poetic, lyrical, Symbolist or Surrealist dissonances — in any case, to indispensable details beyond the Classical and Romantic codex still palpable in the work of some of his contemporaries. The high value he placed on small, flexible motifs and 'sub-thematic' structures (Dahlhaus) is no less a consequence of poetry than of the unprepared deployment of dissonance, modality and other expressive techniques,[3] in the symphonic architecture as well as in the tone poems. The similarities with the New German tradition are also

[1] See Schneider-Seidel 2002.

[2] Vidal 1995, p. 203.

[3] Oramo 1995, pp. 150 ff.

obvious in terms of form. Traces of Classical and early Romantic principles can also be confirmed (as in Liszt and Tchaikovsky) – after all, in Symbolism and Surrealism, too, and later even in Cubism,[1] the neoclassical line is present, deviating from the realistic and naturalistic manner – but the poetic does not cover the theory of forms. Salmenhaara demonstrates this with reference to *Tapiola*, introducing the term 'principle of organic variation'.[2] This concept represents a legitimate critical reaction to Tanzberger, who saw *Tapiola* as a main movement in sonata form.[3] The principle introduced by Salmenhaara contains elements of Schoenberg's and Brahms's total, developing variation and even of formal principles that Karlheinz Stockhausen postulates in another stylistic context.[4] The motivic cells are important, not the melodic work with characteristic themes. 'Organic' means that every work represents a naturally evolved whole and yet is open in its relation to the history of style. These insights demonstrate how skilfully Sibelius implemented Lisztian innovations. His own contribution to the history of music lay in the heterogeneous totality of his orchestral music and in a specific orientation and updating of the New German track: over the course of the process of their composition, his symphonies gradually evolve into tone poems with a poetic foundation and fantasies without a programme. Or at least the reference to a programme becomes more complex, more abstract and more surreal. Yet both genres exist side by side, unlike in the work of Richard Strauss, and no decision is made about whether the absolute or the programmatic has priority.

1 As to this connection of these principles (or styles), cf., for example, Severini 1921.

2 Salmenhaara 1970, pp. 56 ff.

3 For example, Tanzberger 1943, p. 59.

4 Wörner 1973, p. 84 and passim. Wörner's account of Stockhausen and even serialism generally reveals surprising parallels between Sibelius and the post-war avant-garde.

The youth are stirring. My natural enemies!
But I like them anyway! I can't help it![1]

3.5 The Music of Youth

Helsinki, Berlin and Paris after 1900

Anyone who was over forty in 1910, as Sibelius was, could easily have missed Guillaume Apollinaire's call to form the avant-garde. After the First World War and the subsequent unrest, it was too late for his generation to find a connection to the authentic feelings of the young. But Sibelius strove to do so. He engaged directly with the work of Schoenberg, Stravinsky and other, younger artists. He travelled to Paris several times, but most often he visited Berlin when he wished to satisfy his curiosity or missed the atmosphere of a modern metropolis. As late as 1931, at the age of sixty-five and at the beginning of the legendary 'silence of Ainola', he was able to work in Berlin 'better than I have done for a long, long time'.[2]

Even on his journey to Italy in the winter of 1900–1, which would prove so important to finding his identity and during which he would visit the Eternal City while his family remained in a holiday home in Rapallo, he remained in Berlin much longer than planned. During this stay, Aino wrote numerous letters to her relatives.[3] He added, in a mixture of English and Swedish, to some lines she had written to her brother Eero Järnefelt on 1 December 1900: 'Morning, Erik! I'm like a fish in water.'[4] Only rarely did he write so enthusiastically about blending into his environment. In contrast to Aino, he had no time for museums, only for 'especially interesting concerts'.[5] He pursued his business purposefully. His most successful project was a concert in the home of Otto Lessmann, the editor of the *Allgemeine Musikzeitung*, in January 1901.[6] It led to contact with the Allgemeiner Deutscher Musikverein, the most important German music association of the day. The Runeberg song 'Flickan kom ifrån sin älsklings möte' (The girl returned from meeting her lover), op. 37, no. 5, was composed in Berlin, probably first performed by Ida and Karl Ekman at Lessmann's home and then published soon thereafter in the association's journal.[7]

In late January 1901, the family continued the journey from Berlin via Basle to Italy. The return journey in March and April 1901 was by way of Vienna and Prague to Dresden.[8] In Prague he met the composers Josef Suk and Antonín Dvořák, the lat-

1 Diary, 19 December 1914.

2 Erik W. Tawaststjerna 1997b, p. 307.

3 Talas 2000, pp. 186 ff.

4 Ibid., p. 192.

5 Aino to Anni Swan, 13 December 1900; quoted ibid., p. 200.

6 Erik W. Tawaststjerna 1976, pp. 235–6, and Ekman 1946, p. 161.

7 *Allgemeine Musikzeitung* 28, nos. 22–3 (31 May and 7 June 1901), pp. 382–7; on the event itself, see Erik W. Tawaststjerna 1976, p. 240.

8 Aino to Elisabeth Järnefelt, 30 April 1901, in Talas 2000, p. 233.

ter of whom allegedly said: 'You know, I have composed too much.' That sentence no doubt made Sibelius think, especially as he wanted to reflect critically on his artistic objectives after his time in Italy. Although Sibelius had to conduct in Heidelberg on 4 June 1901, which he learned at the end of April,[1] he travelled with his family back to Helsinki in early May as planned. He was informed by telegram in early March about the programme committee's tentative plan to perform his music in Heidelberg and requested to propose works. Sibelius chose two *Lemminkäinen Legends*, *The Swan of Tuonela* and *Lemminkäinen's Return*. The music committee made its decision on that basis and asked him to conduct the works himself.[2] On 28 May he was back in Berlin and on 31 May in Heidelberg, where the rehearsals were supposed to begin.

He made five lengthy visits in Berlin in the years from 1909 to 1914 alone – the years that, according to Hepokoski, finally led to his modern, 'condensed "classicism"'. The Third Symphony had been written in 1907, and in comparison to the first two, it was already completely new and perplexingly classicistic. It followed by just a few years Heinrich Wölfflin's *Die klassische Kunst* (translated as *Classic Art*) and other prominent publications that provided a foundation for the new classicism. Sibelius' classicism was marked by the fear that as an older artist he was increasingly 'overshadowed' by younger ones.[3] Insight into a typical mood – albeit adapted in its presentation to the anti-German sentiments of its recipient – is found in a letter to Rosa Newmarch on 1 January 1911, after a stay in a centre of Modernism: 'I had just come back from Berlin where I had been staying for two months. As usual I acquired an unconquerable distaste for the "modern tendency". And out of this grew a sense of solitude. [...] To my astonishment I see that my works are being performed a good deal on the continent, although they have no "Modernity" in them.'[4] For him, 1911 was from the outset the year of protest. On 2 May he wrote to Newmarch about his nearly completed Fourth Symphony: 'It stands out as a protest against the compositions of today.' This 'protest' symphony is considered by many critics to be adapted to mainstream Modernism – despite its quotations from *Parsifal*, the key of A minor and numerous triads.

A diary entry written in Berlin on 21 May 1909, when a shift in style was about to occur after completing the string quartet *Voces intimae*, is often cited in the context of troubles he was having with his throat and a suspicion of cancer: 'I have to go home. I can no longer work here. A change in style?!'[5] Hepokoski interprets this letter (and other similar statements from this period) in a subtle way and rightly points out that Sibelius was, despite his illness, by no means despondent around 1909–10 but as

[1] National Archive Box 16; Fritz Steinberg to JS, 24 April 1901.

[2] National Library Coll. 206: 53; Otto Lessmann to JS, 8 March 1901.

[3] Hepokoski's characterisation of the Fifth Symphony as 'eclipsed' goes well with this metaphor of shadowing; Hepokoski 1993, p. 11.

[4] Newmarch 1939, p. 24. Original (in German) in National Archive Box 121.

[5] Diary, 21 May 1909.

FIG. 27. Helsinki, 1916 (photographer unknown). This photograph shows the southern end of what is now Mannerheimintie (at the time West and East Henrikinkatu in Finnish) with the Swedish Theater (right) and the Stockmann department store (centre). In the background there is the National Museum and a construction site at the train station (right). The building from which the photograph was taken was next to the site of Martin Wegelius' music institute (Boulevard 2) where Sibelius studied.

a rule 'sure' of his 'artistic path'.[1] He even interpreted negative criticism as a sign he was on the right path. His positive mood is clear in an undated letter from Berlin to the Finnish-American architect Eliel Saarinen in April or May 1909: 'I have to return home heavy in heart since my work here [Eight Songs (Josephson), op. 57] has been a joy. What a breath of fresh air Europe brings!'[2] Such energetic tones in his private notes make it clear that his illness was by no means a psychosomatic expression of stylistic uncertainty but rather the cause of fundamental reflections concerning the sublime style he was imagining.

Aino Sibelius found Berlin and the Berliners 'repulsive and disagreeable' on her first stay in 1898.[3] Her report to her Tolstoyan mother on 25 August 1907 was equally characteristic.[4] She reflected critically on everyday life in the city, though she could not conceal her fascination for the traffic at Potsdamer Platz. Her letters say little about Jean. On 21 August 1907 she reported to her sister-in-law Saimi only briefly

[1] JS to Axel Carpelan, 20 July 1909; quoted in Erik W. Tawaststjerna 1986, p. 130; Swedish original in Dahlström 2010, p. 246.

[2] Quoted in Erik W. Tawaststjerna 1986, p. 114 (undated).

[3] Aino to Saimi and Erik (Eero) Järnefelt, 9 March 1898, in Talas 2000, p. 153.

[4] Ibid., pp. 280 ff.

in English, as a kind of exercise, about visits to the theatre after they had seen Frank Wedekind's scandalous *Frühlings Erwachen* (translated as *Spring Awakens*) at the Deutsches Theater, just a year after its premiere.[1] On 9 March 1898 she had written: 'And yesterday we were at the so-called popular concert again, in which symphonies were performed, among other things, and, imagine, to my joy the very Schubert symphony I used to play with Eero on piano four-hands. Janne [Jean] was also interested, for that very morning he had studied the symphony in the library.'[2] Staying in a small pension, she cared for their children and read Eugène Fromentin and Hippolyte Taine's still current *Philosophie de l'art* in French with 'the greatest emphasis: truly so thoroughly that I look up every word I don't know. It interests me a lot. Precisely because it is so clear that you really have to smile when reading it.' Taine was one of the authors whose theories emphasised race and milieu as topical categories in the social sciences.

Sibelius had got to know Paris in the summer of 1900 together with the members of Robert Kajanus' Philharmonic Orchestra. Carpelan, who was always enterprising, felt obliged to give advice, and he wrote to Kajanus that the first names of Ernst Mielck and Jean Sibelius should not be given in full in publications, lest they be taken for 'foreigners', and that the many German musicians in Kajanus' orchestra should not speak German to one another in Paris, as otherwise the orchestra would not be regarded as genuinely Finnish.[3] Other Finnish artists had already been represented in the Russian Pavilion at the World's Fair in 1851 and several times later as well. Finland regularly used the World's Fair to demonstrate its cultural independence as emphatically as possible. In Paris in 1900 Sibelius, too, was heard in Kajanus' Concert Finnois – following successful performances in Copenhagen, Lübeck, Hamburg, Berlin, Amsterdam, The Hague, Rotterdam and Brussels. Later he was in Paris from December 1905 (coming from England) to January 1906, again in 1909 (on the way from London to Berlin), in November 1911 (coming from Berlin) and in 1927 with Aino, who in 1926 had travelled to the Seine on her own. There, too, he was able to compose and hear more recent music. To a journalist in 1909 he spoke emphatically about the future of French and English music – in explicit contrast to the prestigious but outdated German tradition.[4] Veijo Murtomäki suspected that this statement (which is not, however, authentic) was the beginning of his 'pro Gallia contra Germania' attitude (as if one could not respect both).[5] In fact, Sibelius only began to appreciate the French tradition adequately after 1909; similarly, somewhat later, the culture of North America: 'this great country in which, I believe, the most powerful spiritual forces prevail without bonds. It will take a long time for the Niagara to find the ocean, but one day it

1 Ibid., pp. 278–9.

2 Aino to Saimi and Eero Järnefelt, 9 March 1898, ibid., pp. 151–2.

3 See, in detail, Tyrväinen 1998 and Vainio 2002, pp. 351 ff.; Kerstin Smeds, in Klinge 1997, pp. 364–5, and Smeds 1996.

4 Sirén 2000, p. 272.

5 He documents this sweeping view with diary entries from 1911; see Murtomäki 2001a, pp. 251 ff.

will happen.'[1] In fact, Sibelius never turned his back on Berlin – and his last journey in 1931 took him there, not to Paris or Rome – but his perspective had expanded.

There are, however, indications of passing problems with Berlin and Berliners. He wrote to Axel Carpelan on 30 October 1911: 'I have been here two days. Must get out of it. Everything is lacking in charm.'[2] The city radiated an industrial dynamic and urban expansion that was surely not pleasant, and the pompous excesses of conservative and nationalist Wilhelmianism were indeed 'lacking in charm'. Aino and their daughters, by contrast, were impressed by, of all things, the pomp of the Siegesallee through the Tiergarten (which in those days featured statues of Prussian royals, starting with Albrecht I, aka 'The Bear'),[3] but not at all by the 'crooked noses' of some Berliners. This anti-Semitic-seeming aversion is not known to have been expressed by Sibelius himself on any occasion. The realisation that there was a new generation of talented composers who pursued different ideals and were successful was, on the other hand, a likely reason for his discontent. In January 1911 he had reported on his aversion to the latest trends,[4] and in October he was even introduced to the young Edgard Varèse at Busoni's home.[5] On 26 October 1911 he wrote in his diary: 'All of Berlin is unbearable. I don't have enough words to express my horror.' In a letter to Aino on 1 November 1911, he sounds similarly desperate: 'Had to leave. All due respect to Germany, but ...' In the capital of critical modernism, where Busoni was active as the beloved, non-conformist maestro of young geniuses, Sibelius was feeling his age. His own interest in advising new talents (one way of staying younger) was all but non-existent.

From Paris, where he had hardly any acquaintances in musical or other circles, Sibelius wrote, with relief, on 1 November 1911: 'This wonderful Paris, this seductive Paris, with all its inadequacies, because of its old culture.' Only in Paris could he dedicate himself to the aesthetic of the everyday – note, though, its 'old culture' – especially since he had not even mastered the language; there he had no interests to represent, and no intrigues to fear. In addition to contact with Finnish painters and sculptors, he heard a lot of new music in Paris as well. To Madetoja, who had been in Paris in 1910, he wrote: 'I have heard a dozen new French symphonies. Paul Dukas's C major [Symphony] is, in my opinion, brilliant; Louis Thirion is good as well. But he has no sense of style – exactly what you possess so much of.'[6] He heard movements from César Franck's tone poem *Psyché* (with thematic and technical parallels to his own projects, especially *The Dryad* and *The Oceanides*), as well as scenes from *Ruth*

[1] National Archive: Wäinö Sola Collection; JS to Wäinö Sola, 27 November 1928.

[2] JS to Axel Carpelan, 30 October 1911; quoted in Erik W. Tawaststjerna 1986, p. 208; Swedish original in Dahlström 2010, p. 320.

[3] Aino to Elli Järnefelt, 12 December 1900, in Talas 2000, p. 198.

[4] National Archive Box 121; JS to Rosa Newmarch, 1 January 1911.

[5] Erik W. Tawaststjerna 1986, p. 147; see also Ouellette 1968, p. 9: Varèse had known his music (for example, *The Swan of Tuonela*) from his time in Turin.

[6] National Archive Box 35. For more detail on Thirion, see Diary, 19 November 1911.

and *Rebecca*. To these last, at least, he reacted indifferently: 'Both works are full of naive religiosity. Almost too much naivety. The rhythm is tiring over time.'[1] His idea of 'religious music' was more complex.[2] Thanks to Dukas, his faith in what he called 'new music' was restored: 'It is so nice that I can enjoy, truly enjoy new music, because it is no longer struggling but rather producing personalities.'[3] In Berlin in 1914, he was forced to learn that he had not assessed the state of developments and the direction of modernism entirely correctly. On 12 November 1911, he reported to Aino about a performance of Stravinsky's *Scherzo fantastique*. In 1927 he heard Florent Schmitt, Albert Roussel, Darius Milhaud and Arthur Honegger and was impressed by the new French 'technical resources and sureness of touch' as well as their 'admirable honesty'.[4]

He had travelled to Paris to enjoy life there and to be able to 'learn something new again and again'. He listened to both excitingly new programmes as in Berlin in 1914 and older music such as Mozart's Symphony in E flat major, K 543. 'We felt as if we were *purifiés* of the noise of car horns', reads a letter from Aino to their daughter Katarina.[5] Was that his view as well? Aino later admitted: 'Papa will not say what he really must think, out of pure politeness.'[6] But did she 'really' know it? For her, Mozart was one of the most important artistic experiences of the trip. A year previously, her brother Eero Järnefelt heard Mozart's 'Jupiter' Symphony in C major, K 551, with Sibelius in Paris. Järnefelt was not at all enthusiastic about the tremendous success of Glazunov (who was exactly the same age as Sibelius) and Rimsky-Korsakov. In general, Eero was impressed by the performing orchestras, regardless of the composer. In a letter to Aino from Paris on 26 January 1926, he regretted that Sibelius was virtually unknown there, whereas 'the Russians [i.e., Glazunov and Rimsky-Korsakov] can settle anywhere', which did not exactly encourage his enthusiasm for their music. Because of jealousy regarding the enduring success of the 'Russians', he underestimated the standing of Sibelius' music with the public. When Sibelius was popular among all parties of the war in 1943, Aino wrote to her brother Arvid Järnefelt with concern: 'But Janne is so ignored today, because the symphonies and his profound art are not supported by the radio.'[7] This statement was scarcely justified in the early 1940s.

Experiences during his journeys occasionally led to uncertainty and certainly to various stylistic influences (conscious or not) as well. Despite having a number of

[1] Diary, 3 December 1911.

[2] See, for example, JS to Axel Carpelan, 28 August 1914; quoted in Erik W. Tawaststjerna 1997b, p. 3; Swedish original in Dahlström 2010, p. 369.

[3] JS to Aino, 5 December 1911. See also Diary, 5 November to 3 December 1911.

[4] Interview in Paris with Anna Levertin in *Suomen Kuvalehti*, 26 March 1927; quoted in Erik W. Tawaststjerna 1997b, p. 280 (translation modified); Finnish original in Tawaststjerna 1998, vol. 5, p. 259.

[5] Aino to Katarina Ilves, 22 February 1927; quoted in Erik W. Tawaststjerna 1997b, p. 281.

[6] Aino to Katarina Ilves, 26 March 1927; quoted in Erik W. Tawaststjerna 1997b, p. 281.

[7] Eero Järnefelt to Aino Sibelius, 26 January 1926, in Talas 2000, p. 303; Aino to Arvid Järnefelt, 4 October 1943, ibid., p. 320.

significant works behind him, after 1910 he suddenly planned to study counterpoint. In parallel with that, he was thinking about 'epic' versus 'narrative' orchestration. He recognised the dependence of sound on the type of configuration of pitches, and wrote in an undated entry in his diary (perhaps 9 June 1919), without ulterior didactic motives, a few vague principles of his 'epic' orchestration. His enthusiasm for the 'linear' and for modern counterpoint explains his fascination at this time for Max Reger, as expressed in his diary on 15 October 1910: 'National, German, ornate, also boring, but good precisely because of the German type.' Carpelan expressed himself in a less muted way in *Helsingin Sanomat* on 26 April 1911 (allegedly quoting Sibelius): 'above all in Germany, its [the symphony's] birthplace, where orchestral music is becoming a mere technical operation, a kind of musical civil-engineering, which tries to disguise its inner emptiness behind an enormous mechanical apparatus.'[1] Hepokoski believes that this formulation is authentic Sibelius,[2] but Carpelan probably took various phrases from Sibelius and simplified and revised them. The artistic result – the Fourth Symphony – was supposed to be independent, 'a protest against present-day music. It has nothing, absolutely nothing of the circus about it.'[3] By that Sibelius meant the superficiality of orchestral works of his time – very much including Rimsky-Korsakov and Stravinsky,[4] perhaps Strauss and Mahler as well, or (more fittingly) composers such as Felix Weingartner and Siegmund von Hausegger. On 20 July 1909, in an oft-cited letter to Carpelan, Sibelius criticised 'Kapellmeisters with their circus pretentions', obviously meaning certain composing conductors.[5] According to Hepokoski, he meant 'the diffuse expansionism of Mahler and the technological sensationalism of Strauss and the younger Straussians.'[6] Mahler's Fifth Symphony (1904–5) may indeed have perplexed Sibelius and triggered the 'circus' reproach. Sibelius' alternative was 'this wonderful logic – let us call it God – that dominates the work of art.'[7]

1914 and the Consequences

In 1914 Sibelius went to Berlin for several months, taking with him the plan for the symphonic poem 'Rondo of the Waves' (an early version of the 'tone poem' *The*

[1] Erik W. Tawaststjerna 1986, p. 172, quoting *Helsingin Sanomat*.

[2] Hepokoski 1993, p. 15.

[3] JS to Rosa Newmarch, 2 May 1911; quoted in Erik W. Tawaststjerna 1986, p. 172.

[4] See JS to Aino, 12 November 1911.

[5] JS to Axel Carpelan, 20 July 1909; quoted in Erik W. Tawaststjerna 1986, p. 129 (translation modified); Swedish original in Dahlström 2010, p. 246: 'cirkuspretensioner'.

[6] Hepokoski 1993, p. 15. Gallen-Kallela used the word 'circus' as well: see Akseli Gallen-Kallela to Johannes Öhquist, 25 October 1910, in the archive of the Gallen-Kallela Museum; quoted in Sariola 2001, p. 197.

[7] JS to Axel Carpelan, 20 July 1909; quoted in Erik W. Tawaststjerna 1986, p. 129; Swedish original in Dahlström 2010, p. 246.

Oceanides), a work he completed only after visiting Niagara Falls. This trip to Berlin also enabled him to visit the Philharmonie there, where his Violin Concerto was performed by Alfred Wittenberg on 2 February[1] – by no means to the composer's satisfaction. Most of the concerts he attended disappointed him: his notes are laconic, but his conviction that the organic 'nature' in his own music was more valuable than the usual 'hothouse *Erzeugnisse* [products]' is clear.[2] Towards the end of his productive years, he wrote to Newmarch: 'There is so much in the music of the present day that I cannot accept. For example, that one should be able to make for oneself an ideal by reflexion (a reflected ideal).'[3]

In Berlin, Sibelius heard Arthur Nikisch in the sixth concert of the season of the Berlin Philharmonic on 11 January 1914 conducting Heinrich Zöllner's Symphony in D minor, op. 130, 'Im Hochgebirge' (In the high mountains). He vehemently criticised Zöllner's musical relationship to nature – and not just Zöllner's but also that of 'all Germans, Englishmen and Frenchmen'. In other concerts, Sibelius encountered other more or less clearly identifiable works: August Scharrer, *Sinfonische Ouvertüre* ('He is still just beginning'; Diary, 13 January); Julius Weismann, Sonata for Violin and Piano (15 January) and Piano Concerto ('plagiarised from me'; Diary, 18 January); Ziell's Symphony in B major ('beneath all criticism'; Diary, 15 January); Erwin Lendvai, *Masque* for piano (18 January); Paul Juon, Violin Concerto ('influenced by me'; Diary, 19 January); Donald Francis Tovey, Allegro and Andante for Two Cellos ('subtle but nothing new'; Diary, 20 January); Alfredo d'Ambrosio, Violin Concerto (for whatever reason, Sibelius placed two exclamation marks after it; Diary, 21 January); Rudolph Tobias, *Kalevipoeg* (Diary, 22 January); Busoni, two of his *Elegies* for Piano (Diary, 23 January); Conrad Ansorge, Sonata for Piano (probably op. 21, no. 2; Diary, 23 January); Ernst von Dohnányi, Four Rhapsodies for Piano, 1902–3 (Diary, 23 January); Paul Scheinpflug, 'Lustspielouvertüre' ('not bad', Diary, 24 January); Gustav Hollaender, Third Violin Concerto, op. 66 (Diary, 24 January); orchestral works by Frederick Delius ('a poet but alien to the orchestra in a higher meaning'; Diary, 24 January); Friedrich Gernsheim, Violin Concerto no. 2 (Diary, 25 January); Émile-Robert Blanchet, *Au jardin du vieux Sérail* (*Adrianople*), op. 18, no. 3, and *Sérénade* (Diary, 27 January); Rudolph Ganz, *Im Mai*, *Serenade* and *Bauerntanz* (Diary, 27 January).

In just a few days in Berlin, he absorbed this incredible variety of music offered 'in the spirit of the new', as he noted in his diary on 27 January – in part in concerts but in part in private homes in the salons of that era. In the case of the performances on

1 *Berliner Börsen-Courier*, 4 February 1914.

2 JS to Axel Carpelan, 26 January 1914; quoted in Hepokoski 1993, p. 17; Swedish original in Dahlström 2010, pp. 347–8.

3 JS to Rosa Newmarch, 5 February 1927; quoted in Newmarch 1939, pp. 45–6.

19 January, it was clearly a private occasion. He was staying with the Vecsey family: 'Vecsey played in the spirit of the new age.' In many works, Sibelius sensed 'something big on the way', but at the same time he noted how few of his colleagues could make anything of it (Diary, 27 January). He was aware that he himself was by no means predestined for the avant-garde, but he believed that with extreme effort he could articulate what he imagined. One of the high points of those days was Bruckner's Fifth Symphony in B flat major (1875), which even moved him to tears, as he confided to his diary on 25 January: 'What great spirit and religiousness!' A few days later, in February, there were other extraordinarily valuable concerts with Mahler (including *Das klagende Lied*: 'a wonderful composition', Diary; 1 February); Carl Nielsen's overture to the opera *Saul og David* (1898–1901); Peder Gram's *Poème lyrique*, op. 9; Wilhelm Stenhammar's Second Piano Concerto in D minor, op. 23 (1904–7); Brahms (quartets, 'poetic'; Diary, 1 February), and Schoenberg's Chamber Symphony no. 1 for Fifteen Solo Instruments, op. 9 (4 February). On 8 February he heard the *Sinfonietta* for Large Orchestra, op. 7 (1913) in the performance with which Erich Wolfgang Korngold conquered Germany. Sibelius sarcastically referred to him as 'a young eagle'.[1] Another 'hothouse product' from his days as a student had remained in his memories: August Bungert. 'His music was played a great deal and people seemed to look on him as a new Wagner!'[2] The image of Bungert as a 'successor to Wagner' was connected with his tetralogy *Homerische Welt* (1898), whereas previously he had been considered a composer of Lieder and chamber music in the circle of Brahms and Robert Volkmann.[3]

Some of Sibelius' comments can be interpreted as compensation for his fragile self-confidence. The artists whose music he heard were often those who, like himself, strove for a different modernism outside the main current. This is one variation on the argument of nature versus art — or naturalness versus construct — typical of Western philosophy, in which Sibelius wanted to distinguish himself and his 'nature' from the 'hothouse' products. It is a trail that can be traced back in Sibelius' case to his famous, partially improvised sample lecture of 1896, since on the basis of his 'birth and unimpeded habit' he believed he was in the position to write new, living music on the basis of church modes.[4] He also based his critique of the followers of Wagner and Liszt on nature and on the authentically folk quality of his inspiration.

For the years from 1912 until Sibelius stopped composing, it was characteristic of him, in Hepokoski's view, that he lent new splendour to the tradition of organic

[1] JS must have attended the final rehearsal under Nikisch on 8 February 1914. In the literature, one occasionally finds the date 14 February as well, rather than 9 February, as confirmed by the *Berliner Volkszeitung*, 11 February 1914.

[2] Ringbom 1954, p. 20.

[3] Kahl 1989, cols. 465–6, and Klein 2001.

[4] Diary, 26 January 1914. For a discussion of this expression, see Mäkelä 2008.

form derived from the essence of sound and thereby developed a kind of 'aesthetic pantheism' that can scarcely be analysed.[1] There is a lot of evidence that this attitude influenced his artistic approach to childhood, but its manifestations in self-contained works of art were more convincing. In a note in August 1912, he compared current trends – he had just looked at Schoenberg's work – to a manmade river: with an artificial floor and a rationally planned path (like a canal) but without natural water. A 'natural' symphony, he wrote, had to emerge slowly like a river from small streams, with the motifs forming organically and 'seeking their path'; 'You, great ego, noticed that early on.'[2] The similarity of this metaphor to Varèse's vision is fascinating: 'There will no longer be the old conception of melody or interplay of melodies. The entire work will be a melodic totality. The entire work will flow as a river flows.'[3] Natural laws are at work here, not constructs.

Debussy's works for piano, especially *La Fille aux cheveux de lin*, from the first volume of *Préludes* (1909–10), and the only slightly older *L'Isle joyeuse* (1904), were, from Sibelius' perspective, the most pleasing performances of more recent compositions he heard in Berlin in 1914. Sibelius had already encountered Debussy's harmony in Berlin in 1905 and in London in 1909. From London, where he heard several songs and the *Nocturnes* (1897–99) conducted by Debussy, he reported back home: 'I have something altogether new to say in my music. [...] It is absolutely vital for me to be abroad now. My artistic development necessitates it.'[4] The euphoria is surprising, since he had already heard these works in 1905; the point here was to justify staying. Sibelius dated his meeting with Vincent d'Indy precisely in his diary: 25 March 1909. He noted in conclusion: 'I have seen a lot and profited from it – what was unclear before, is no longer. Personal acquaintance with Debussy and d'Indy, Bantock, Barth, Dale and so on, as well as many compositions [...] such as Debussy's new songs and his orchestra suite *Nocturnes*, etc., all that reinforced my views and confirmed the path I have taken, am taking, and must take.' One should not conclude from that that he identified with these colleagues, only that he recognised something in conversations with them. His admiration for Debussy was by no means unqualified, either, saying his French colleague believed 'in all sorts of meaninglessness'.[5] In 1910 he called Debussy's string quartet 'ingenious but minor'.[6] Such positions testify to an approach influenced by nineteenth-century categories,[7] as well as his habit of belittling competitors, especially when he had recognised in their efforts parallels to his own.

Mahler, Strauss (*Sinfonia domestica* and *Ein Heldenleben*), Hans Pfitzner, Albéric

[1] Hepokoski 2001b, pp. 333–4.

[2] Diary, 1 August 1912.

[3] Varèse 1971, p. 25.

[4] JS to Aino, 3 March 1909, and JS to Axel Carpelan, 27 March 1909; quoted in Erik W. Tawaststjerna 1986, p. 108; Swedish original in Dahlström 2010, p. 234.

[5] JS to Aino, 1 March 1909.

[6] Diary, 21 October 1910.

[7] See Nicklaus 1989.

Magnard, Christian Sinding, Debussy and Busoni, among others, were the focus of his experience as a musician during his 1905 stay in Berlin. The primary occasion for the trip was rehearsals for a performance of the Second Symphony under Felix Weingartner. The event took place on 12 January 1905, and made Sibelius, who had not been unknown since his earlier success in 1900 and 1901, a subject for the media, although by no means all of the critics appreciated his art. Carl Krebs, for example, used the opportunity to attack the concert series in general:

> It is truly strange to behold the instinct with which Mr Busoni has brought together insignificant or eccentric compositions from all over the world in order to delight the public in Berlin; from all over the world, even though enough of such excrescences are produced in Germany, not of a natural kind but in test tubes and distilling flasks. Do these homunculi – and would that they were still homunculi! – truly have a right to live, as Mr Busoni assumes? In my view, no.[1]

His meeting with Pfitzner and Magnard, whose works were performed in the same concert, was tense. Sibelius interpreted, probably correctly, Pfitzner's hostility as a sign that he found Sibelius' reputation threatening.[2] Sibelius remarked of Berlin: 'One thing I recognise very clearly, and that is that I must come here annually, at the height of the season. Two, three months a year. Otherwise I will stagnate …'

Sibelius visited Berlin more than thirty times between 1894 and 1931.[3] On 11 February 1914 he saw *Elektra*. He found Strauss, who had interested him since 1889 (when he heard *Don Juan* in Berlin), 'brilliant'.[4] Strauss's *Sinfonia domestica* and *Ein Heldenleben*, which he heard in 1905, did not get such a reaction. Here too it is clear that he was always fascinated by compositions that were not related to his own projects – which in February 1914 would have been the more Impressionist tone poem *The Oceanides*. He was not in search of ideas he could quote. Just how tolerant his curiosity could be is demonstrated by his simultaneous interest in Max Reger, Sergey Rachmaninoff and Alexander Scriabin.[5] By contrast, he always had problems with Stravinsky. He was appalled when the Suomen Kulttuurirahasto (Finnish Cultural Foundation) awarded Stravinsky the Sibelius Gold Medal, of all things, in 1956[6] to someone who had said of Sibelius that he 'can't do much'. Sibelius replied sarcastically on 20 November 1949: 'That, I believe, is the greatest compliment I have received in my entire life! Mr I. S. is always imitating someone. I like his *Oedipus* best, in which he imitates Gluck. Musical talent is not something you learn in school with the rod. In that sense, Mr S. is certainly almost at the top of his class. And I am almost at the bot-

[1] Krebs 1905.

[2] JS to Aino, 11 January 1905.

[3] For the chronology and travels in particular, see www.sibelius.fi by Markku Hartikainen.

[4] Diary, 11 February 1914.

[5] Diary, 29 June 1910; Diary, 15 October 1910; and JS to Aino, 16 October 1910.

[6] Jalas 1981, p. 63. Stravinsky is said to have later sold the medal for charity.

tom. Poor me. But my symphonies should be compared to his stillborn affectations.'[1] Sibelius proudly held up his organic nature to Stravinsky's deliberately artificial art. On 25 February 1928, before the premiere of *Oedipus Rex* in Berlin under Otto Klemperer, Sibelius commented insincerely: 'I cannot afford to waste three times 400 [Reichsmarks] for a ticket to the premiere.'[2] Even in financially more difficult times, however, he was known for disproportionate spending (albeit of another sort).

In a different context, years earlier, he wrote with the same bias: 'Now I have listened to French composers all day long. And also to a young Russian (Igor Stravinsky), who has written a Scherzo [fantastique] based on Maeterlinck's *La Vie des abeilles*. You cannot imagine how I was laughing inside. Not in a nasty way. But all sorts of things were in there.'[3] Sibelius — who can himself be said to be an 'aesthete of heteronomy',[4] like Mahler and even Stravinsky, each in his own way — appears to have recognised Stravinsky's stylistic heterogeneity already in 1909. In another context, in conversation with the producer and writer Walter Legge around 1935, he supposedly made fun of Stravinsky's various 'styles': 'Three styles were enough for Beethoven, but I have forgotten whether the last work by Stravinsky I heard was his tenth or eleventh.'[5] Still, he knew them all. Regardless of the value one attaches to the heteronomous or heterogeneous and a specific form of classicism, Sibelius was no neoclassicist in the usual meaning of the word. Like Stravinsky, he was the type of composer for whom the process of creating a work, rather than its completion, can represent the high point. Stravinsky said: 'I love composing music more than music itself',[6] and Sibelius wrote in his diary on 25 July 1910: 'The finest moments are probably when a comp. is being planned and I carry it around in my heart. The work is a "life-and-death struggle". Is that because of self-criticism or lack of talent?' Stravinsky's position can be associated with neatly ordered sketchbooks and a clear desk,[7] whereas with Sibelius, despite interesting sketches, one thinks rather of lonely strolls.

In the second half of 1914, following the concerts in Berlin and a successful tour of North America, and several days after the First World War broke out, he wrote in despair: 'But I — or rather, it seems to me that my artistic work is, by and large, of such infinitely small meaning to the art of this world.'[8] The statement was not intended to refer to world politics, since several months later he continued the idea: 'I will probably never become the great composer Aino and I have dreamed about. [...] A profound, irresistible feeling of loneliness and disappointment over everything I have

1 National Archive Box 41.

2 JS to Aino, 29 February 1927, and '1 March 1927'.

3 JS to Aino, 12 November 1911.

4 Mäckelmann 1983, p. 129. See chapter 2.3 in the present volume.

5 Hill 1947, p. 12, quoting Legge 1935.

6 Danuser 1991, p. 54; the story was told by Paul Sacher.

7 See Mäkelä 2004a.

8 Diary, 14 August 1914.

achieved is setting in.'[1] Frustration in the face of the world on fire — on 18 August he wrote presciently: 'Probably the end of our civilisation!' — dominated his thoughts. In Schoenberg and Debussy, he sensed a persuasive aesthetic he believed he understood.

Immediately after the concerts in Berlin 1914, he seemed unfailingly self-confident. The many impressions preoccupied him subliminally, however, and a productive uncertainty in connection with thoughts about his own position set in. His mental state during this period following the 'journeyman's piece' *Voces intimae*, the Josephson Songs and the Fourth Symphony, when his goal was to move forwards despite all existential and cultural doubts, can be illustrated along two axes: first, his reflections on his own standing in the history of music with regard to his powerful awareness of his originality and 'nature'; secondly, his desire for large cities and isolation versus homesickness and his inability to leave his familiar surroundings for long. Such contradictions can be crippling. But they can also, as in Sibelius' case, be the context for creating expressive works and providing the uncertainty necessary for great art. His subsequent development shows that 'one' indeed does not 'suffer in vain'.[2]

Arnold Schoenberg

Schoenberg and Sibelius are often misused to represent opposite poles within early twentieth-century modernity. Both of them had important things in common, however: ambiguous friendships with Strauss, a distinct aversion to Stravinsky (one of the many things Sibelius shared even with Adorno), a collegial relationship with Busoni (who admired Stravinsky as well) and a tendency to materialise the ineffable, as manifested in fragmentary large-scale works. Today, every comparison between them seems absurd. That presumably explains Michael Mäckelmann's exclamation point, finding it ironic that Sibelius died six years '*after* Schoenberg (!)'.[3] But there is a great deal of evidence that it was a fatal error in the history of their reception to paint them as fundamentally different. Only in the generation of their students, performers, and critics did an unbridgeable rift open up.[4] Sibelius' collection of sheet music included Schoenberg's *Gurre-Lieder*; Chamber Symphony, op. 9; Three Pieces for Piano, op. 11; Orchestral Pieces, op. 16; and Three Brief Pieces for Piano, op. 19 — unfortunately with no notes to indicate when or where he acquired these expensive scores or what he found remarkable about them.[5] There is one clue to dating where the *Gurre-Lieder* are concerned: on 10 August 1916, Madetoja published an interview in which Sibelius indicated he had just studied that work,[6] finding its orchestration revolutionary and

[1] Diary, 11 February 1915. The word 'Alleingefühl' or 'allein Gefühl' (as in JS to Axel Carpelan, 8 March 1904, in Dahlström 2010, p. 181) was often used in German by JS, but here it is Swedish.

[2] JS to Axel Carpelan, 2 April 1901, in Dahlström 2010, p. 77.

[3] Mäckelmann 1983, p. 122.

[4] For more detail, see chapter 5.2 in the present volume.

[5] National Library Coll. 206: 96 and 98.

[6] National Library Coll. 206: 98.

the whole 'of childlike originality'. Hepokoski emphasises — to put the enthusiasm for Schoenberg in context, though there is really no need to do so — that this praise should be interpreted cautiously, since the design of sound interested him in general and inspired particularly careful appreciation.[1] Sound was perhaps the primary reason why the *Gurre-Lieder* seemed important enough to him to study in detail and to mention with such unusual specificity in Madetoja's interview. Probably he purchased the score in Berlin in 1914 and started reading it on his trip to New York.

As early as 1912 he had shown an interest in Schoenberg's *Harmonielehre*.[2] He considered Schoenberg 'one-sided', but conceded that he did not really know him yet. He may have first encountered Schoenberg's compositions in 1910, at the earliest in 1904, in Berlin. Santeri Levas quoted Sibelius: 'I was one of the first to purchase Schoenberg's works. I did so on Busoni's advice, in order to learn something. But I didn't learn anything.'[3] Hepokoski is convinced that Busoni first drew his attention to Schoenberg in 1910.[4] Levas's imprecise information argues for that. Be that as it may, it is likely that Busoni was the mediator (and could well already have been in 1904). It is understandable that Sibelius was not able to 'learn anything' from Schoenberg. Yet that does not preclude subliminal influence or productive stimulus. His critical remarks on Schoenberg are quoted exclusively by authors and journalists; there is nothing of the sort in his letters or even his diary. For example, *Stockholms Dagblad* published on 5 May 1927 a remark by Sibelius that Schoenberg should be performed more often so that the public would have grounds for a negative opinion of him.[5] If this is indeed authentic, Sibelius' opinion had changed diametrically. On 28 January 1914 he remarked positively in his diary: 'A song of Schoenberg made a deep impression on me.' On 4 February 1914 his notes on the Chamber Symphony, op. 9 were more detailed: 'This is a legitimate and valid way of looking at things I suppose. But it is certainly painful to listen to. A result achieved by excessive cerebration. People whistled and shouted. Not for weak minds or so-called talented composers. They would certainly misuse it. There is something important there all the same, even if it is not yet fully realized.'[6] Compared to Mahler's statement about Schoenberg in 1907 — 'I do not understand his music, but he is young; perhaps he is right; I am old, perhaps I no longer have the ear for his music'[7] — Sibelius' position was quite moderate.

Tawaststjerna's view that the 'extended chamber music quality' of Sibelius' Fourth Symphony corresponds to Schoenberg's op. 9 seems bold.[8] Schoenberg's chamber

[1] Hepokoski 1993, p. 96.

[2] Diary, 8 May 1912.

[3] Levas 1992, p. 366.

[4] Hepokoski 1993, p. 14.

[5] Erik W. Tawaststjerna 1997a, p. 254.

[6] Erik W. Tawaststjerna 1986, p. 262.

[7] Quoted in Danuser 1991, p. 39.

[8] Erik W. Tawaststjerna 1989, vol. 3, p. 240. In Erik W. Tawaststjerna 1986, pp. 176 ff., the comparison to Mahler is clearly forced.

music quality has less to do with the instrumentation than with the structure of its polyphonic writing. Sibelius' attitude in the Fourth Symphony is not that of 'chamber music' either; rather, its style is more the legacy of the late nineteenth century (Mahler *et al.*). Thanks to the emancipation of the dissonance, however, Sibelius is much closer to the new music of the time. The tone poem *The Oceanides*, written between the Fourth and the Fifth Symphony (*The Bard* and *Luonnotar*, both from 1913, should be mentioned as well), was supposedly a 'counter-reaction' to Schoenberg's Expressionism — an attempt to distinguish himself from a direction that had been manifested in the Fourth Symphony three years earlier.[1] First, the chamber-music 'Expressionism' of the Fourth Symphony is by no means unambiguous (Wagner's *Parsifal* is even quoted in the first movement at measure 40 and 19 measures before the end). Second, 'counter-reaction' suggests a process focused on an object. There are, however, only vague, polemical statements such as that to Newmarch about a 'protest against the compositions of today' or the passage from his diary in 1910, which could have been written about Debussy: 'Do not let all these "innovations", third-less triads, etc., keep you from your work. Not everyone can be a "pioneering genius". As a personality and as an "apparition from the woods" you will have your small, modest place. Here at home, you are presumably "defeated" in the court of common opinion. Be done with it! Nous verrons!'[2] The sentence is not intended seriously: Sibelius was not thinking of a 'small, modest place' but rather of none at all ('in Hades') in his dark hours and of a central place ('on the Himalayas') on good days. He saw himself as anything but an '*apparition from the woods*'.

Certainly in *The Oceanides* and the Fifth Symphony he was experimenting with a contrary, different style from that of the Fourth Symphony and *Voces intimae*. These four works represent two currents of equal importance — an expressive and melancholic one and a euphoric and classicistic one — and illustrate the synchronistic openness of the composer in an era of general polarisation. Just as much as *The Oceanides*, the Fifth Symphony could be seen as an attempt to 'distance' himself from the 'German', polyphonic idiom (Reger *et al.*), but in both cases it would be better to use a term that captures his distinct desire for originality and his striving to be different (in the sense of an attempt to distance himself that was more subconscious). Hepokoski notes that Sibelius admired Schoenberg's motivic integrity, rigorous logic and musical compression, although he himself took another path.[3] Possibly, though, he was interested in Schoenberg even beyond the *Gurre-Lieder* primarily for the sound and chords and various other configurations. In a letter to Aino on 5 February 1914, Sibelius described Schoenberg's work as musical 'cubism',[4] which is fascinating,

[1] Erik W. Tawaststjerna 1996, p. 14; Erik W. Tawaststjerna 1997b, p. 89.

[2] Diary, 13 May 1910: 'eine Erscheinung aus den Wäldern' is in German and is found in an earlier letter, JS to Busoni, 20 November 1921 (postmark); cf. Erik W. Tawaststjerna 1986, p. 172, and Erik W. Tawaststjerna 1997b, p. 213.

[3] Hepokoski 1993, p. 18.

[4] Erik W. Tawaststjerna 1986, pp. 241 and 262. We should keep in mind that Sibelius himself had

since Cubism is indeed about questioning the two-dimensionality of painted space. In terms of the two-dimensionality of shaping time, that was a significant aspect of Schoenberg's later relationship to tonality and already central in op. 9. But did Sibelius realise that? It is difficult to bc sure, as both Cubism and Dadaism were familiar to him first of all as fashionable terms.

In this context, one draft letter by Sibelius deserves consideration, even if its context and hence significance are obscure. Sibelius was writing to a 'maestro': 'To maestro I send my best regards and remain in ~~gratitude, Jean Sibelius~~. Maestro, I admire the great, liberating sign that you, maestro, have ~~underst~~ felt my life so ~~we~~ deeply. ~~and~~ // The Dadaist composition gave me great pleasure. Likewise, though in a different way, the old painting.' Perhaps he had Paul Juon (rather than Schoenberg) in mind, about whom Sibelius wrote enthusiastically: 'Mr Juon's sonata is simply a masterpiece. It was pure joy for me to look through the work.'[1] Juon was arranging Sibelius' music for the Berlin publisher Robert Lienau. Moreover, Sibelius sent young Finnish colleagues to him for lessons.[2] Connections to Dadaism in the circle of Juon and Busoni (Stefan Wolpe, among others) may explain Sibelius' misuse of the term.

One of the most important events on his travels was the evening of 9 February 1914, with Schoenberg's String Quartet, op. 10. This work gave him 'much to think about' (diary), which is a rare observation, and he admitted that Schoenberg interested him 'enormously'. Just under six months later, he said to the *Musical Courier* in New York that he 'greatly admired' Schoenberg.[3] In 1914, that was neither a matter of course nor necessary. Schoenberg would be the only contemporary composer about whom Sibelius ever said something that enthusiastic in public. If the remark is authentic, which is probable in this case, it may not reflect his enduring attitude but rather the effect of the Berlin performances, perhaps reinforced by studying scores (such as the *Gurre-Lieder*) on the ship to New York. After encountering Schoenberg's chamber music, he never composed anything again for string quartet or similar ensembles, although he had finished *Voces intimae* only a few years earlier and had convincingly mastered the idiom. As recently as April 1912, he had been working on a new quartet but never finished it.[4] Even apart from the key, *Voces intimae* bears striking similarities to Schoenberg's string sextet *Verklärte Nacht* (Transfigured night). It is uncertain whether Sibelius was familiar with that composition in 1909. Busoni had been in regular correspondence with Schoenberg since 1903,[5] and it concerned, of all things, the symphonic poem *Pelléas und Mélisande*, op. 5, whose score was in Busoni's

been called a 'cubist' for his Fourth Symphony by Henry Krehbiel in the *New York Tribune* in March 1913 and even a 'futurist' by the conservative opera critic William J. Henderson in the *New York Sun*. Cf. chapter 2.2 in the present volume.

1 National Archive Box 34; draft letter to Robert Lienau, n.d.

2 National Library Coll. 206: 18; Paul Juon to JS, 10 November 1909.

3 *Musical Courier*, 10 June 1914; quoted in Erik W. Tawaststjerna 1986, p. 262.

4 Diary, 22 April 1912.

5 Beaumont 1987, pp. 381 ff.

possession in October 1903.[1] Sibelius' incidental music on the same subject, *Pelléas et Mélisande*, was written in 1904 and premiered in Helsinki on 17 March 1905. He had composed it in Berlin.[2] Under these circumstances, it is likely that Busoni spoke to him about Schoenberg and Maeterlinck, especially as Sibelius was interested in orchestration. There are, however, no significant similarities between these two *Pelléas* compositions – apart from the sort of coincidental echoes that any analyst can find in two arbitrary scores from the same period. Maeterlinck was fashionable everywhere around 1904, and Sibelius' participation in the big *Pelléas* project of his generation is merely proof of his awareness of trends, not of his reception of Schoenberg. Richard Dehmel – present in Schoenberg's oeuvre in *Zwei Menschen* (cf. *Verklärte Nacht*) – began to interest Sibelius by 1906 at the latest, perhaps also because of the Richard Strauss songs opp. 31, 37, 39, 41 and 49. Sibelius set 'Aus banger Brust' and 'Die stille Stadt' (op. 50, nos. 4 and 5).

The fact that he recognised the necessity for lessons in counterpoint demonstrates his disregard for polyphony in his previous period of development and the effect of some important sources of inspiration (Schoenberg, Reger, perhaps even Busoni) rather than his lack of competence or even talent. He had already demonstrated the latter in his orchestral works from 1889–92, such as the artful Fugato in *Scène de ballet*. His concern was of a general nature. On 18 June 1910 he wrote: 'All true talents found their way "ad astra" through self-study.' And his diary for 6 November 1910 reads: 'With colossal effort, forced myself to practise counterpoint for half an hour.' On 16 June 1913, he noted: 'Meditated on linear counterpoint!!' And on 9 March 1913: 'My "style" is too homophonic.'

Tawaststjerna wondered why Sibelius would respond critically to the Chamber Symphony, op. 9, when he admired the String Quartet, op. 10, and a song made 'a deep impression'. Although his brief notes do not reveal any clear difference in argument and could be dismissed as whims, Tawaststjerna's answer is noteworthy: because of the connection to the emphatically linear writing style in op. 9 with its extreme polyphony, of which Schoenberg himself was aware, since he wrote that its main difficulty, in his view, was the 'great amount of polyphony'.[3] The quartet, by contrast, was chordal.[4] It may have been even more important, however, that the Chamber Symphony breaks with tradition more rigorously than the other works because it changes paradigms within the given symphonic context. The density of motivic and harmonic events is extreme. The motifs can seem disconnected, because Schoenberg gives the unprepared listener so little time to perceive their unfolding. Moreover, op. 9 moves between creating miniatures and large forms outside of the history of the genre, whereas Sibelius – despite his nature and his naturalness – was more con-

[1] JS later confirmed that Busoni had brought Schoenberg to his attention. See Levas 1992, p. 366. Unfortunately, this statement is not dated.

[2] Erik W. Tawaststjerna 1986, pp. 27ff.

[3] Arnold Schoenberg to Pierre Ferroud, 31 August 1922, in Stein 1987, pp. 76–7.

[4] Erik W. Tawaststjerna 1986, p. 262.

servative towards the history of the genre. Only his secret reflections on titles ('symphonic fantasy', 'Runes symphoniques', etc.) were truly original. The unusual form of the Chamber Symphony attracted him: 'There is something important there.' The assertion that Schoenberg did not achieve this 'something important' is not pretentious either: op. 9 was, after all, the first experiment of its kind — a shrunken monument and a 'hall of mirrors' visible 'from all sides'[1] — or even 'musical cubism'. Quartets and songs were already a common field for experimentation prior to 1900, whereas op. 9 is orchestral music with one instrument per part. It remains particularly successful in arrangements for orchestra and small ensemble — it was arranged by the composer for large orchestra twice (and by Anton Webern for flute, clarinet, violoncello and piano, 1923) — and most difficult in its original form. But the view that the sound of op. 9 could be balanced only through recording techniques and is otherwise 'a failure' seems exaggerated.[2]

Perhaps Sibelius was only criticising the exclusivity of Schoenberg's method:

> There are not twenty musicians in the world who could follow the structure and inner logic of any recent Schönberg work or even get a rough idea of the composer's meaning at one hearing in a concert hall. I flatter myself that I have a sensitive ear, far more sensitive than that of the average concert-goer. And yet when I hear for the first time the more complicated Schönberg works I am completely lost. I have to study the score closely to see what he is driving at. How can the casual concert-goers or the affectationists make head or tail of such music? Alban Berg is Schönberg's best work.[3]

Unlike many of his supporters, he admitted that he recognised 'what he is driving at'. The reference to Berg is not malicious but rather underscores Schoenberg's importance as a teacher. After all, Sibelius knew he was not in a position to educate composers. The fact that he spoke to Legge in the 1930s of 'recent' works shows clearly that he had not been left behind with opp. 9 and 10 in his knowledge of Schoenberg.

'My Generation is Leaving the Stage'

The First World War threatened Sibelius' career just after he had conquered the Western world from Berlin to New York. In Finnish isolation, he probably felt the war, despite the apparent military calm, more bitterly than some Berliners or even émigrés in Paris or in French-speaking Switzerland. He had no contact with friends and colleagues in Germany (including the publishing houses). Many German musicians had had to leave Finland, since the formerly Germanophile region was part of the Russian Empire, which was involved in the war. 'It seems as if the war will last a long time

[1] Schoenberg 1965, p. 11.

[2] Hirsbrunner 1982, pp. 99–100.

[3] Hill 1947, p. 13, quoting Legge 1935.

still. How will I get by?' reads his diary for 25 December 1914 — a good question, even though it primarily concerned financial issues. Performances as a conductor abroad — before the war even in the United States and already several times in the United Kingdom and on the continent — were an important source of income in the exciting years before the war as well as a way of satisfying his need to experience new sounds. Now he was cut off, at a critical moment of exchange. What once seemed a matter of course became the object of desire. It seems almost contrary when he himself rejected Wilhelm Stenhammar's efforts to organise a concert in Gothenburg (Diary, 1 December 1915): 'I will retire for a while.' In January 1915, he wrote the pathos-laden but by no means unfounded words: 'My generation is disappearing. And we can all be replaced. They say!'[1] He was reacting to the death of the Finnish actress Ida Aalberg, but for some time he had already been thinking more and more about the touchy question of the generations. In 1912 he believed that he had to consider the 'composers of the younger generation' his 'natural enemies', though he found it difficult: 'But — the instinct for self-defence!'[2] Or on 19 December 1914: 'The youth are stirring. My natural enemies! But I like them anyway! I can't help it!' In a moment of technical uncertainty back in 1910, he swore he would not allow himself to be 'impressed' by the younger generation[3] and that he would assert his 'position among contemporaries'[4] and not allow himself to be pushed into the shadow of younger artists.

Just how difficult that was is demonstrated by a note from 1922: 'The "modern" is forcing its way out and I am unhappy (*inter alia*) "for that reason".'[5] Although in brackets, the '*inter alia*' should be considered. In 1922 he was referring to the local situation (Ilmari Hannikainen, Selim Palmgren and Toivo Kuula, among others) — and *not* Schoenberg. Even earlier, on 28 April 1915, he was bitter because the public supposedly appreciated Palmgren and Kuula more than him. On 9 March 1916, he wrote: 'I see how the youth are raising their heads — Madetoja higher than the others (?) — and have to admire them.' On 20 December 1918 he even admitted that Madetoja's Second Symphony gave him 'a lot to think about'. He was only thinking of Finland again when he noted on 7 October 1921: 'The youth — composers — are gaining momentum. New ideals and new approaches.' Of all people, it was the 43-year-old Palmgren, who accepted the professorship at the Eastman School of Music instead of Sibelius and after Christian Sinding, whom Sibelius identified as the leader of the 'youth': 'The youth, with Selim P. at the fore, are taking my life from me, financially.'[6] His image of the enemy was more general on 20 February 1913: 'They think — at least

[1] Diary, 19–20 January 1915. See a similar remark on 6 March 1916, after the death of Abraham Ojanperä, the first Kullervo: 'Those born in my year are disappearing.'

[2] Diary, 7 November 1912.

[3] Diary, 18 June 1910.

[4] Diary, 8 October 1910, writing in German: 'Stellung unter d. Zeitgenossen'.

[5] Diary, 27 April 1922.

[6] Diary, 14 May 1924.

the leading orchestral musicians in the world — that I am a dead man.'[1] The Vienna Philharmonic had rejected the Fourth Symphony, and there were similar rumours coming from Berlin, although it was successfully premiered there in 1915, despite the war. Regardless of the frequent mood swings that document his interest in the opinions of others, he continued to search for his own aesthetic identity: 'it seems as if now the genuine "Jean Sibelius" will begin', he wrote while working on his new symphony.[2] He always put his name in quotation marks, as if he himself were a product and the artist in him an object, the 'other' in himself. 'Jean Sibelius' was the name of his oeuvre since 1886. He was proud of that and believed in it.

Even as a student in Vienna, Sibelius was interested in 'success'.[3] Consequently, it was with satisfaction that he wrote to Martin Wegelius on 11 January 1891: 'I have it in me to achieve something great one day.' Later, when he could look back on his 'life's work', he was annoyed when his work was not sufficiently regarded — or he had the feeling of being only a 'famous name'.[4] In 1915, too, the Finnish press was actively involved in cultural life — rather than reporting on it from a distance — and the value of 'Sibelius' depended primarily on how the newspapers were reporting foreign reviews. And so he was annoyed in 1915 — especially since he could not flee to the 'quiet', 'beauty' and anonymity of the great cultural centres of Paris, Rome, Berlin and London — about the thoroughness of the local report of a minor review. In the art magazine *La Nouvelle Revue* of 1914, the almost forgotten French composer and writer Maurice Touchard had insulted him in supposedly Walter Niemann-like terms, but (in contrast to the northern German regionalist Niemann) clearly with pejorative intent, as a 'simple and unpolished representative of the people, dressed up in the garment of the folksong'.[5] His music seemed to Touchard to be written for an uneducated public. An anecdote that was met with smiles in Paris and certainly not even read by many subscribers was puffed up in the Finnish press to be France taking a position against Sibelius and Finland. (Occasionally, too, completely insignificant reviews were turned into great successes.) The annoying thing was not the review in Paris but that it was passed on in Helsinki: 'I see clearly how people want to devalue my life's work even here in my homeland. [...] O world, how devilish you are!'[6] Nevertheless, he knew how well established he was. In 1924 he wrote to Aino that he had been told he was the only composer whose North American tour would be a financial success:

[1] Diary, 20 February 1913.

[2] Diary, 18 October 1914.

[3] JS to Aino, 18 December 1890. 'Erfolg' (success) is always in German.

[4] Diary, 4 December 1910.

[5] Touchard 1914. As to Niemann, cf. chapter 5. During the last years of existence of the magazine, Touchard contributed on a small scale to the liberal *La Nouvelle Revue* founded by the *salonnière féministe* Juliette Adam. His article on JS seems to be the one that attracted the most attention. More than a year later it was translated by Evert Katila into Finnish: cf. E.K., 'Suomalainen säveltaide: Ranskalaisen silmällä katsottuna', *Uusi Suomi*, 14 August 1915.

[6] Diary, 15 August 1915.

'Millions are at stake.'[1] It was not his doubt about such successes but self-criticism, which he had already realised while composing the Fifth Symphony was the antipode of his imagination ('Should it kill this magnificent inspiration, my self-criticism?!'[2]), that constantly increased. That presumably explains why the Eighth Symphony, parts of which had already been prepared as a fair copy for the publishing house in 1922,[3] has not survived.

The years 1923 and 1924 marked the beginning of a phase during which Sibelius did not even open up to his diary. Edvard Robert Gummerus, the son of the Finnish ambassador to Rome, Herman Gummerus, described him in Rome in 1923 as living 'in another world and was indifferent to the things going on around him, was alone with his creative muse'.[4] This statement is one of the most revealing from this period when he was working out his Sixth and Seventh Symphonies, and it is high on the list of the more successful summaries of his essence. He gradually lost hope in lasting 'success' for 'Jean Sibelius', but not his faith in his ideals. As late as autumn 1943, the 77-year-old wrote: 'Life is soon over. Other composers come and overtake me in the eyes of the world. It is our fate to die forgotten.'[5] The important core of that idea is in the phrase 'Other composers come [...]', which is necessarily part of the course of history. He hoped he would be an exception, perhaps on the model of Schoenberg, who continued to be recognised until the final year of his life and beyond. He did not always view his fate as a typical one, but in January 1924 he wrote: 'How infinitely tragic is the fate of an aging composer! Things do not happen with the same speed as before, and self-criticism grows to the point of impossibility.'[6] Before that stands: 'Hope that something can be completed. An absolute <u>must</u>. But – my life has gone off the rails. Alcohol deadens the nerves & senses!' There is no need to search for further explanations for the problem of the Eighth Symphony: self-criticism, fatigue from old age and alcohol formed Sibelius' Bermuda Triangle. Which of the three corners was most dangerous? Self-criticism, which had, after all, played an inhibiting role much earlier, was the crucial factor.

Sibelius was asked whether 'Modernism' and the music of the younger generation had influenced his works in any way. His answer was: 'No. I am, however, very interested in modern art.'[7] On this occasion, he explicitly mentioned Väinö Raitio, who is by no means the most prominent of his Finnish contemporaries but nonetheless a skilful orchestrator. New music did not have any tangible 'influence' on Sibelius before or after the First World War. Neither did he borrow technical models from

[1] See Erik W. Tawaststjerna 1986, pp. 252–3.

[2] Diary, 13 November 1914.

[3] Erik W. Tawaststjerna 1997b, pp. 316 ff.

[4] Ibid., p. 234; Erik W. Tawaststjerna 1997a, p. 130. Tawaststjerna quoted Edvard R. Gummerus, 'Roman memoires', *Palatset med kolonnerna* (Stockholm: LT, 1974), p. 188.

[5] Diary, 5 October 1943.

[6] Diary, 6 January 1924.

[7] *Svenska Dagbladet*, 23 March 1924; quoted in Erik W. Tawaststjerna 1997a, p. 165.

FIG. 28. Punavuorenkatu 7 (photo: W. W. Wilkman, *c.*1930). This photograph shows a rear courtyard typical of Helsinki; it was located near several bordellos that were the source of much outrage from 1882 to 1892, but also not far from the upper-middle-class Boulevard and several apartments belonging to the young, quite poor Sibelius family. As late as the 1970s, these central neighbourhoods were influenced by the *demi-monde* and even today it is a 'nice mix', surrounded by fancier neighbourhoods. Only a few of the wooden houses that gave the city its look in the 1930s, along with neoclassical government buildings, are still standing.

Schoenberg, Hindemith, Varèse or others or allow himself to lose his thread for any time by pursuing current trends – except perhaps after 1929, when he was publishing almost nothing. Both the wave of chamber music in the 1920s and the interest in early music, much less functional music, left him cold. He became neither a Neoclassicist nor an Expressionist but rather sought his own way. The new did sometimes stimulate and also perplex him, both in the form of Debussy and Schoenberg and the late Scriabin. Only a high degree of perplexity can explain his interest in the latest achievements in the history of composition – a quality typical of him since his youth – which was explicitly not goal-orientated and focused on a specific new project.

As a rule, this curiosity had no concrete connection to his own projects. In that sense, he remained true to his resolution of 1910 not to allow himself to be 'distracted' by the numerous 'innovations'. Being 'distracted' would presumably have meant applying them in a specific way, which he did not do. Despite the Symbolist and nationalist-romantic tinge of his early years, and despite his age, he was a presence as a listener in the early days of the avant-garde. He listened to premieres of new masterpieces and studied their scores as well. As late as 1926 he wrote to Aino from Berlin,

'I am studying modern German and French music in music shops.'[1] He was working on *Tapiola* at the same time. Even in this late work, however, one could not really point to a specific example of the influence of a younger colleague; not even chance quotations have been identified. Schoenberg and others did inspire his high artistic ambitions and his pleasure in especially bold innovation. His method of studying modern scores 'in music shops' makes it clear that Sibelius was familiar with more New Music than what he remarked on in his writings or had in his collection of music (primarily Schoenberg scores). This makes it considerably more difficult to analyse possible strands of influence.

This idea is revealing: 'We should leave, but we are tied to this place [Finland] by bonds that cannot be undone. We can no longer rebuild our life.'[2] The important thing is that the sixty-year-old wished to 'rebuild' his life somewhere else (but with his old partner, Aino). The 'bonds that cannot be undone' were probably not primarily his children but rather his function as a national composer. If one wished (and really one should) one could even sense in Sibelius' desire to flee antipatriotic feelings. It was similar with the musical avant-garde: he was more solidly anchored to the Western tradition 'by bonds that cannot be undone' than he would have believed.

1 JS to Aino, 29 April 1926.

2 Diary, 25 January 1925.

What I want from and want to do with the symphonic is something very few people in the world understand. Most of them do not even suspect what it is about. German radio plays old things they have dug out of the dust. To improve today's taste. But, as a rule, the only value they have is as antiques.[1]

Keep to the plastically symphonic, clear but subtle in timbre in your art! Do not allow yourself to be diverted from this.[2]

4 THE LARGE-SCALE GENRES

4.1 Symphonies between Utopia and Progress

'For me, they are declarations of faith'

'A symphony is not a "composition" in the ordinary sense. Rather, it is a declaration of faith.'[3] Sibelius wrote these sentences (freely adapted from Goethe's *Poetry and Truth* and Friedrich von Hausegger) which claim for the symphony as a genre the status of a worldview, while he was working on his Fourth Symphony in 1910. In 1885, Hausegger, the father of the composer and conductor Siegmund von Hausegger, wrote: 'It [the divine genius, as understood by the ancients] can be traced back to the power at work in all of us, conditioning our expression of life, which, urging expression even more so in the genuine artist, leads to the purest and strongest realization.' In his discussion of Brahms's Fourth Symphony, also from 1885, Hausegger spoke of 'declarations' in symphonic writing, albeit in another way (as 'declaration' of a particular direction in the history of music). Goethe in *Poetry and Truth*, by contrast, viewed not only his largest treatises and main works but all his works as 'fragments of a great confession'.[4]

In November 1914 Sibelius wrote: 'A better name for the symphonies would be: "prayer". Preghiera. Although misleading.'[5] Five years later, on the threshold of a stylistic metamorphosis, he repeated the old idea of 1910: 'A propos symphonies. For me, they are declarations of faith at different ages. That is why all of mine are so different. Nos mutamur, in temporibus. Or more precisely: tempora mutantur et

[1] Diary, 13 September 1943.

[2] Diary, 25 April 1910.

[3] Diary, 5 November 1910.

[4] Hausegger 1885, p. 169, and Hausegger 1903, p. 238. On Goethe, see Bürger 2000, p. 204. Cf. Goethe 1901, vol. 1, p. 240.

[5] Diary, entry, n.d. (*c.* 21 November 1914).

nos illis mutamur.'[1] Following up on this saying, popularised by Andreas Gartner's *Dicteria proverbalia* of 1598, and underscoring the historical, mutable character of both declarations and faith, he continued his reflections with a characteristic theme from nature: 'Swans & cranes & wild geese. Their sounds and essences' were associated with symphonies for him. It was April and the wild birds were moving in. A few weeks later, on 20 May 1918, he wrote to Axel Carpelan that his symphonies were 'more declarations of faith than other works',[2] and Santeri Levas, his secretary, published a statement by him saying 'every one of my symphonies has its own style. I have to work a long time to create it.'[3] The pompous term 'declarations of faith' does not occur in the latter testimony, reflecting the years after 1938 when Levas was working for Sibelius, but his general attitude towards the genre had remained unchanged.

The symphonies are the results of the most meticulous work, worthy of comparison on an equal footing with the oeuvres of Bruckner, Mahler and Strauss. And because of his tendency to perfect the symphonies over the course of publication as the final result of the creative act, it is unproblematic to separate them from the rest of his oeuvre (with very few exceptions). His concept of the work of art is clearly defined in the symphonies, and it confirms his lifelong struggle with the problematic category of the finished artefact, the *opus perfectum et absolutum*. He went on revising his symphonic works until a time he had chosen himself and without regard to deadlines. The printing plates may already have been engraved, but he would request corrections, which the publishing house often agreed to, especially when Sibelius offered to pay the costs. Further autograph corrections were made after printing, as documented in the *Jean Sibelius Complete Edition*.

It does sometimes happen that the final version — the result of abstraction and concretisation — is not considered the best. For example, some will be enthusiastic about the charms of the formal imperfection of the first complete version of the Fifth Symphony. On 14 August 1914 Sibelius wrote in his diary: 'People ordinarily console themselves by saying that "it suffices to have wanted the great"! But for me the result is indeed the main thing.' The quotation — 'it suffices …' is in German. And it appears again (less enthusiastically, with a bit of frustration and/or understatement) in a letter of congratulations to Carpelan on 15 January 1918: '"Es genügt das Grosse gewollt zu haben." That applies well enough to what each of us has done.'[4] Sibelius is quoting Sextus Aurelius Propertius' *Elegiarum liber* (2.10.6): 'In magnis et voluisse sat est.' The perfection of the result consisted in perfecting what he had called the 'wonderful

[1] Diary, 24 April 1915. Also 26 April 1915: 'sinfoniska trosbekännelse' (symphonic declarations of faith).

[2] JS to Axel Carpelan, 20 May 1918, in Dahlström 2010, pp. 422–4.

[3] Levas 1992, p. 384.

[4] JS to Axel Carpelan, 15 January 1918; quoted in Erik W. Tawaststjerna 1997b, p. 116; Swedish original in Dahlström 2010, p. 417.

IV

Finale (Quasi una Fantasia)

FIG. 29. Beginning of the fourth movement of the First Symphony, Finale (Quasi una Fantasia). The first of the seven symphonies is already distinguished by its architecture (here in particular the motivic work that closely connects the Largamente ed appassionato theme to the beginning of the first movement, Andante, ma non troppo), its striving for the new (carefully worked-out expressive characters, Fantasia *topos*, etc.), regional and supra-regional conventions, gestural simplicity and sublime clarity, without anything pompous.

logic (let us call it God)'.[1] This ambitious principle goes far beyond the limits of a single work, and it is fair to ask whether the creative process is not the ultimate 'achievement' of an artist.

No routine solutions or compromises came into question for major works, no matter how much time and work it took to reach his goal. The composition of occasional works looked quite different; there 'lavishness' of material was possible.[2] There, however, it is necessary to distinguish between commercial occasional works and those for performance at a celebration and not intended for publication — as was the case, for example, with the cantatas of 1894. Notes in his diary demonstrate that the minor works were mostly written for financial reasons and underscore the contrast to the major works: 'My affairs force me to write piano pieces', he wrote on 3 June 1909, before completing the Ten Pieces op. 58, although by 12 July they already 'interested' him and he was proud of their technique on 28 August. 'When someone is forced, as you are, Ego, to earn his bread with his "pen", everything can't be nine-year-old wine', he wrote on 28 July 1910; 'Plan piano compositions. Because of large expenses' on 27 May 1912; 'Should I sacrifice myself for the breadwinning "minor" works, or reach deeper and remain an idealist? [...] But — perhaps I could go both ways' on 7 July 1912 and 'I was supposed to compose great things, but it's not working. And these miniatures cost me more time than they should' on 14 May 1924.

Only rarely did Sibelius distance himself from the specific concept of the work of art manifested in the idea of major and occasional compositions: 'The finest moments are probably when a comp. is being planned and I carry it around in my heart.'[3] That note refers to a method of working he characterised elsewhere, with an ironic reference to painting, as '*plein air* art',[4] and many times he expressed his dislike for the 'German method' of working in a concentrated way at a neat desk. For him, walks in '*plein air*' were an important form of 'work'. But the goal was always specific compositions and Beethoven (a German, after all) was the great role model as he told a journalist writing for the distinguished *Muzykalnaja Gazeta*.[5] He was aware of the disadvantages of this '*plein air*' method, and complained accordingly: 'Oh, if only I could work!!'[6] He was often not in a position to convince himself to work in a rigorous way. An outburst a few months before *Kullervo* was completed is characteristic: 'For my symphony I have moods but no musical expression for them.'[7] At the same time, his unconventional method — based on comprehensive visions, walks and

[1] JS to Axel Carpelan, 20 July 1909; quoted in Erik W. Tawaststjerna 1986, pp. 129–30; original Swedish in Dahlström 2010, p. 246.

[2] Salmenhaara 1984, p. 80.

[3] Diary, 25 July 1910. Cf. chapter 3.5 in the present volume.

[4] Diary, 18 July 1911.

[5] Erik W. Tawaststjerna 1996, p. 10, citing an interview with Ivan Lipajev in *Muzykalnaja Gazeta*, nos. 30–31 (28 July – 4 August 1913) and nos. 32–3 (11–18 August 1913).

[6] Diary, 19 September 1914.

[7] JS to Aino, 16 April 1891.

loose motifs intended to determine the form organically – guaranteed originality. He avoids schemas and routines that would have made creative activity easier. He acknowledged his inability to control the process of composition when he identified himself as a 'vessel' of God and praised the 'wonderful logic (let us call it God)'.[1] When he wrote to Robert Lienau on 22 April 1919 that he had 'struggled with God', his wrestling was focused on this 'logic', and he sensed that some would view his avoiding schemas as unprofessional and his compositions thus as arbitrary:

> People seem not to notice ([Felix] Weingartner, Hans Richter and several others excepted) the architectonically solid form my compositions have. Probably they believe that I just wrote them down that way or carried the ideas around with me for years and then gave them a form that then stands – forgive me the word – for ever. You cannot even imagine how lacking in style and comic the additions are in these compositions where every note – I can say this in good conscience – is weighed on the gold scale. I get quite beside myself when I think of [Sigfrid] Karg-Elert – and now these new arrangements. Breitkopf has also published several (arrangements) that make me sick. I feel as if someone had desecrated my most sacred thing.[2]

Karg-Elert had arranged at least parts of *Pelléas et Mélisande* for harmonium and piano in 1907 for Lienau. On 10 July 1911 Sibelius wrote to Lienau: 'You mentioned "Sibeliana". I only need to see the word and I get almost ill and unable to work for several days.'[3]

Without mentioning the 'Sibeliana' – the many arrangements of *Valse triste*, and so on, but very much based on the orchestral works already written (including the Fourth Symphony) – Walter Niemann posed a question in his book on Sibelius that later Sibelius scholars, and the composer himself, would unanimously answer with an emphatic yes, but that several critics and Niemann himself answered with a no: did Sibelius compose 'symphonically' in the strict (Brahmsian) sense?[4] Arguments for a yes include the prominent position and the standing of the symphonies in his oeuvre as a whole and his statements about the symphonies as 'declarations of faith'. Admittedly, the name of the genre does not presume symphonic work à la Brahms, no more so than the genres of opera or solo concerto preclude it. Arguments for a no include the way he defines the significance of imagination, inspiration and thematic ideas rather than their elaboration (despite his dense work with motifs), and ultimately too his formal strategies, which from the perspective of the authentic documents do not concern his work as a whole but were conceived for particular cases.

[1] JS to Axel Carpelan, 20 July 1909; quoted in Erik W. Tawaststjerna 1986, p. 129; original Swedish in Dahlström 2010, p. 246.

[2] National Archive Box 46; JS to Robert Lienau, draft letter, 26 May 1910. The letter concerns Johannes Doebber's arrangements.

[3] National Archive Box 46; JS to Robert Lienau, 10 July 1911.

[4] Niemann 1917, pp. 47–8. See also Niemann 1913a, p. 261.

Niemann has repeatedly been accused of critiquing Sibelius without understanding him or even with ill will, making him out to have fouled his own nest and 'armed the enemy'. This critique of Niemann is such a fixed feature of the Sibelius literature and is so sweeping — often combined with generally anti-German sentiments — that Niemann has long since become a *de facto* martyr.[1] For Niemann, the art of symphonic form was a product of a degenerate civilisation in which the poetic programme in the New German manner revealed, in his view, the seeds of a future 'Heimatkunst' (art rooted in the homeland). It may be, however, that Niemann was wrong on this crucial point and underestimated the cosmopolitan in Sibelius. The militarist conclusion that Niemann put 'weapons in the hands of Sibelius' enemies' comes from Erik Tawaststjerna, characteristically defending Sibelius as if he stood for Finland.[2]

Today the question of the essence of the symphony can be analysed objectively. For Sibelius' topicality in the twenty-first century is only enhanced by any attempt to present him as not necessarily a symphonist à la Beethoven but rather as an alternative modernist who composed discursively and gave new meaning to the term 'symphony', rather than just warming up the old meaning. Another alternative would be to compare his formal language with the epic quality of the *Kalevala* tradition and its syntax. Literary scholars have already done excellent work with the structural idea of 'epic expansion': a 'chain formation'. The Finnish *Kalevala* expert Lauri Honko uses the term 'sikermä'[3] (chain, group, circle) for this. The analysis of 'rotations' in Sibelius as initiated by James Hepokoski is related to it in terminology, at least.[4] It is rewarding to connect Hepokoski's 'rotation' and the 'sikermä' technique with Søren Kierkegaard's philosophical categories of 'repetition' and 'memory' from 1843.[5] It helps get rid of classicist language for analysing music. In the morphology of the Finnish language, the word 'sikermä' is used for a loose, primitive stringing together so that the term would probably become an unfortunate provocation in the analysis of Sibelius — even though entire Bruckner symphonies have been analysed as exposition of bar form.[6] 'Sikermä' recalls Ralph Vaughan Williams's O.D.T.A.A. principle ('One Damn Thing After Another') — 'but what marvellous D.T.s they are, so what does it matter?' Vaughan Williams, who dedicated his Fifth Symphony to Sibelius, and can be considered an adherent, knew very well that syntax, too, and not just the 'marvellous D.T.s' as such, were significant in Sibelius, since 'the beauty of a theme depends almost entirely on its position in the scheme'.[7]

When Sibelius wrote in his diary on 8 May 1912 that he wanted 'to allow the musical ideas and their development in my mind to determine the form' or in an

[1] For more detail, see chapter 5.1 in the present volume.

[2] Erik W. Tawaststjerna 1996, p. 297.

[3] On the *Kalevala*, see, for example, Honko 1999, pp. ix–x.

[4] Hepokoski 1993, pp. 62 ff.

[5] See Hoerschelmann 2003, p. 11, quoting Hock 2000, p. 37.

[6] On Alfred Lorenz's theories, see Stephan [1970] 1985.

[7] Vaughan Williams [1963] 1986, pp. 262–3.

undated entry sometime around 9 March 1913 that it was 'My attempt to make the motifs, that is, the ideas, determine the form', he was justifying the expanding syntax of the *Kalevala* – presuming that he meant the 'theme' in the colloquial sense, not the motivic, harmonic and structural core formations that also 'determine' the form in the tradition of Beethoven.[1] One argument for using terminology adapted to the *Kalevala* ('sikermä') is that specific symphonies – for example, works as utterly different as the Fifth and Sixth Symphonies – grew out of a single set of sketches,[2] or, to borrow Sibelius' favourite expression, were 'forged' from them. The impression of arbitrariness in the formation from this material[3] – especially in provisional versions – would, moreover, be occasion enough to reflect on the 'mental text' in the context of the concept of the symphonic work, since it seems that, despite Hepokoski's 'rotation' model and Finnish folklore studies, there is a lack of theory in this area. Sibelius provided important stimulus to this with his fascinating concepts of 'runes historiques' and 'runes symphoniques'. On 25 November 1920 he wrote in his diary about the Sixth Symphony and, in that context, about the title 'Runes historiques' ('Doubts about symphony or 'Runes historiques'.') and noted on a sheet of paper 'Runes symphoniques'.[4]

Another revealing report, this one passed on only indirectly, concerns a private conversation with Mahler in 1907.[5] Sibelius is said to have stressed his admiration of 'the style, the strict form and the profound logic that creates an inner connection between all the motifs'. The focus is not on the 'theme' but on the motifs. He may have learned to emphasise the motivic in this fashion from the eighteenth-century music theorist Johann Christian Lobe, whom he studied on his own initiative as a youth. This classic author wrote in detail on 'formations of motifs and parts of motifs' (starting from 'ur-motifs') and even briefly discusses the idea of entire cyclically or comprehensively connected works[6] based on a single motif[7] – a feature that should be assessed in Sibelius' oeuvre but is typical of Beethoven. Mahler is said to have contradicted him in the romantic spirit of Jean Paul: 'No! The symphony must be like the world. It must embrace everything.' Sibelius thus advocated precisely what his critics have been unwilling to acknowledge in his work. If we can believe this report, it conveys the impression of two composers talking past each other, since one statement is

[1] Cf. ibid. also on form in Beethoven in comparison with Sibelius.

[2] Cf. Virtanen 2003. The author expands the spectrum of works based on a supply of motifs that were used for several projects. See also Tiilikainen 2003.

[3] See Honko 1999, pp. ix–x.

[4] National Archive Box 36.

[5] Ekman 1946, pp. 190 ff.

[6] On the history of the terminology, see Riethmüller 1988, 189 ff: A. B. Marx, whom JS probably also knew from early on, spoke of 'connected forms', whereas the term commonly used today, 'cyclical forms', was first established by Hermann Mendel (1873).

[7] Lobe 1844, 15 ff.; see also Riethmüller 1988, p. 188.

technical (and only indirectly related to a classicist worldview) and the other openly philosophical.

Another source for the conversation between Mahler and Sibelius is Jussi Jalas's notes from the 1940s and 1950s. Jalas, a conductor and Sibelius' son-in-law, noted in a conversation with Sibelius – and one should not entirely lose sight here of the notorious Beethoven–Schindler constellation and its concomitant problems as to documentation of the master's voice – that Sibelius had described to Mahler the public's disappointment with his own Third Symphony in comparison with the Second, to which Mahler is supposed to have said that he too was aware that every new symphony drove off the audience that the previous one had produced.[1]

With regard to the question whether Sibelius considered his symphonies to be a cycle or series or rather individual works, selective crystallisations of his efforts to achieve his divine 'logic', it is striking how rarely he wrote about several symphonies at once. A lengthy letter to Carpelan on 20 May 1918 is an exception:

> The Fifth Symphony in its new form – almost completely rewritten, I am working on it today. The first movement completely new, the second resembles the old one, the third is a reminiscence of the end of the first movement in the old version. The fourth movement: the old motifs but developed in a more sober, most solid form. The whole thing, if I may call it that, is a vital build up towards the end. Triumphal.
>
> The Sixth Symphony is wild and passionate in character. Gloomy with pastoral contrasts. Probably in four movements with a finale, which will build to a gloomy, wild romp of the orchestra in which the main theme disappears.
>
> The Seventh Symphony. *Joie de vivre* and vitality, with appassionato passages. In three movements – the last a 'Hellenic Rondo'.
>
> But all this only provisionally. It looks as though these three symphonies came simultaneously. [...]
>
> The planes will perhaps be changed as the musical ideas develop. As usual, I am a slave to my themes and adapt myself to their needs.[2]

In keeping with the pastoral quality of the Sixth Symphony, Sibelius considered, according to Jalas, an orchestra of no more than fifty musicians appropriate,[3] though the effect is not of chamber music but rather of impulsive vitality.

The artist's apparent wish to present specific plans (in the form of suggestions, à la Beethoven) to the enthusiastic sympathizer Carpelan poses a problem for interpretation of this letter. However, the sketches for the final symphonies do indicate a close connection in their composition.[4] Not even the Seventh was conceived as an isolated

[1] See Jalas's note on 8 January 1943; quoted in Sirén 1999, p. 37.

[2] Dahlström 2010, p. 423.

[3] Jalas's note, n.d.; quoted in Sirén 1999, pp. 34–5.

[4] See, for example, Kilpeläinen 1992.

'unity' — as the conclusion of the teleological, intertextually symphonic project — but it was born out of the same material as the Sixth, and even in the case of the Fifth, Sibelius called into the question 'the whole'. In each case, he started out with a cyclical structure in multiple movements. Only in the Seventh, which was derived from the Sixth during the creative process, and in the 'tone poems' and the utopia of a 'symphonic fantasy' — but not in the 'symphonic poem' *Kullervo* — did he deviate from this classicist formal principle in his 'major work'.

Teleology or Chronology

In the years between 1989 and 1995 three prominent scholars addressed the problem of symphonic form in Sibelius, which both critics and some otherwise sympathetic interpreters (Walter Niemann in particular) had previously called into question. In his outstanding and far too little appreciated study on the late symphonies and personal style of Sibelius, Lorenz Luyken wanted to capture the individuality of the compositions in their uniqueness and show why the best experts do not agree about the quality of the works, a scenario which would really be indicative of reaching the status of a classic. Luyken suspects that the main problem is the 'fragility of the thematic surface and the thematic forms',[1] which Adorno (in Luyken's words) rashly took to be a 'sign of serious artistic incompetence'. Luyken demonstrates that an 'erosion of the thematic surface' is evident in the last three symphonies and the tone poem *Tapiola*. The connection between the thematic configurations ('Gestalten') is either loose or non-existent. In place of the common parameters there are 'field structures of varying complexity': 'The breakdown of tonality went hand in hand with the disintegration of the thematic. Structures of functional harmony are found essentially only in connection with traditional thematic forms. [...] In its most intrepid passages, Sibelius' music is rigorously a-tonal and a-thematic.'[2] His 'spatial dramaturgy' differs in every single work and is always the focus of his symphonic experimentation. The Fifth Symphony is characterised by 'metamorphic compositional technique', which confronts the 'thematic forms in various stages of "disintegration" with field structures'. In the final movement, the 'anonymous field-structure-like quality' threatens the thematic forms as 'aesthetic subjects', which Luyken aptly characterises as a 'tragic' strategy. The athematic quality of the Sixth, by contrast, is increasingly permeated by a concentration on scale structures (modality) — in this case 'tragic–elegiac' or an 'experiment that has proceeded negatively'. Finally, Luyken sees in the Seventh the 'vision of a movement structure' in which 'the antithesis between thematic and field-like appears to be eliminated'. (That occurs despite the stylistic regression through reminiscences of past styles of his own work, which Sibelius causes to 'appear as composing subject directly in the music'.)

1 Luyken 1995, p. 248.
2 Ibid., p. 249.

FIG. 30. Second Symphony, first version (autograph, first page, with burn marks). The original version of the Second Symphony began with a natural division of the 6/4 time (Allegretto moderato), whereas the final version implies asymmetrical phrasing at the beginning (Allegretto). The composer destroyed the first version himself.

The late 'symphonic poem' *Tapiola* (a sort of Seventh and a Half Symphony) features another form of confrontation of the musically individual with the field structure that can be called (in the meaning given to the word in German critical theory) 'pessimistic', with all the 'implications in terms of structure and content' of its programme. This is Luyken's carefully formulated explanation for the 'silence of Ainola' after 1929.[1] Precisely in those passages where echoes of Beethoven's symphonies occur, he caused the 'invalidity of the ideal of the individual and of humanity associated with Beethoven's music in the age of modern mass society to be especially evident'.[2] Luyken's theory of symphonic individuality is a response to Adorno that uses Adorno's own categories, since genuine art was supposed to be precisely about revealing the invalidity of the outdated 'sublime' (the Wilhelminian style) and the pompously 'beautiful'.[3] In Luyken's successful effort to understand the symphonic style on the basis of Sibelius' late work and to explain it in terms of Adorno's critique, he focuses on the differentness of the symphonies that Sibelius himself postulated and thus takes into account the related heterogeneity of the symphonic – a quality that is found not just until the end of April 1915[4] but in Sibelius' entire oeuvre, since Sibelius' remark that every symphony has its own style, and thus he worked a long time on them, was made later.[5]

In contrast to Luyken, Veijo Murtomäki, as a Schenkerian with an emphatically Finnish point of view (not entirely free of paradigms of a national nature), presumes a teleological model in which the Seventh represents the ultimate goal of the 'unity' for which the composer strove from the beginning. The first two symphonies continue the old tradition; the Third is a 'turning point' and the Fourth, Fifth and Sixth Symphonies are important milestones on the way to the final 'goal'.[6] Murtomäki does not take into account the fact that the Eighth was supposed to have several movements.[7] For him, Sibelius' symphonic work is not a fundamental heterogeneity but rather a solidly outlined project that continues Beethoven's work and corresponds to the idea of totality of form and the idea of the perfect unity.[8] At the beginning of his creative life Sibelius stated: 'My plan is to create a new form, a kind of suite or symphony, really'[9] – which is not exactly a goal-orientated formulation. Later there are no statements about his orchestral oeuvre as a teleological whole. In other contexts, by contrast, Sibelius enjoyed reflecting on the great courses of the history of art and culture, as in a letter to Aino from Vienna on 8 January 1891:

> The Germans are following old paths too much. For example, they understand nothing about the latest trend in literature and art. They attack the French as well as the Russians. One can't even talk about Scandinavians [with them]. They consider barbaric everyone who isn't embroiled in a conservative lie. But

[1] Ibid., pp. 249 ff.
[2] Ibid., p. 266.
[3] On this, see chapter 5.2 in the present volume.
[4] Luyken refers to a diary entry on 24 April 1915.
[5] Levas 1992, p. 384.
[6] Murtomäki 1993, pp. 32 ff.
[7] Salmenhaara 1984, pp. 386 and 413.
[8] Murtomäki 1993, p. 11, and passim.
[9] JS to Aino, 10 February 1891.

> it must be said that the Germans have gambled away their role [in the history of music and art]. They have no Zola, Ibsen, Tchaikovsky, etc. They see everything through their own spectacles – usually poor ones.

Based on the idea of the *telos* at the end of a modernist progression, which is scarcely evident in Sibelius' astute critique of the modernist era, Murtomäki stresses in all the symphonies, in the interest of his theory of a 'unity' of all, the aspects that seem to lead gradually from the First to the Seventh. For example, he expresses surprise that other authors, such as the composer Mikko Heiniö, have suspected a 'step backwards' in the Fifth 'even with regard to orchestration'.[1] In this striving for unity and progress, Murtomäki sees a reflection of nature à la Goethe: following Michael McMullin, Burnett James, and David Cherviansky, Murtomäki concludes that 'the processes of Sibelius' music are dictated by nature'.[2] In this reception nature becomes a moral category. Correspondingly, the 'ethical line'[3] that Sibelius himself recognised while working on the Fifth is said to be 'an enduring challenge for the music of our time'.

Even in Beethoven – whom Sibelius 'loved', as he confessed in his diary on 27 December 1918 – he emphasised this quality: 'One can like worse gods. The ethics in his music, not the technique, which is often antiquated and not brilliant enough.' When Ferruccio Busoni played Beethoven's 'Hammerklavier' Sonata, op. 106, in 1912, Sibelius experienced the 'greatness and power of humanity' in a unique manifestation: '"Power is the morality of people", Beethoven said. What miserable little worms ordinary people are! Phooey!' (Diary, 28 October 1912). A later remark is critical (27 April 1922): 'My orchestration is better than Beethoven's, and I have better themes than he does. But: he was born in wine country, and I was born in a country where sour milk reigns.' This sentence could be discussed as a sign of a Beethoven complex, especially given that Sibelius knew both the Rhineland and Vienna. On 13 September 1943 – twenty years later – he again wrote metaphorically about sour milk in his diary: 'A talent – not to say genius – like mine does not emerge from sour milk, etc. You need different ingredients from that.'

Even in the early phase of work on the Fifth, the composer wrote: 'God opens his door for a moment, and his orchestra is playing Sym. 5.'[4] The ethical and cosmic qualities the Fifth were part of its programme from the outset. Their ambiguity is made clear by the symphony's second motto, which was already established in his diary on 10 October 1914: 'When the shadows lengthen.' As late as 1923, he used the

[1] Heiniö 1977, p. 11; quoted in Murtomäki 1990, p. 107; this view is omitted in the English version: Murtomäki 1993.

[2] Murtomäki 1990, p. 223 (omitted in the English version). This idea is derived from James 1983, pp. 144–5; McMullin 1985, pp. 199 ff; and Cherviansky [1947] 1952, pp. 141 ff.

[3] JS to Axel Carpelan, 20 May 1918, in Dahlström 2010, p. 423.

[4] JS to Axel Carpelan, n.d. [22 September 1914?]; quoted in Erik W. Tawaststjerna 1997b, p. 6; original Swedish in Dahlström 2010, p. 369.

'shadow' motto in an interview when visiting Gothenburg, Sweden.[1] An associative or even Symbolist bridge between shadow, God and cosmos suggests itself here. This gives at least a vague notion of the poetic core of the symphony.

Here it becomes clear how difficult it is to write about Sibelius' music in an ideology-free space. The ideology of the theorems and classicistic, modernist-totalitarian glorification of unity are already unmistakable in Ilmari Krohn's well-meaning attempt in 1945–6 – not yet liberated from the *Zeitgeist* of the previous years – to find a Nordic programme in all the symphonies. Much like Murtomäki, Krohn believed he had found a cyclical meaning (the seasons) relevant from work to work, which after the 'northern spring' of the Fifth led to a 'northern summer' in the Sixth and culminated in a 'harvest time' in the Seventh.[2] Sibelius reacted calmly, saying: 'I am amused by the images Ilmari Krohn believes he sees in my symphonies. They are, of course, his images, no one else's.'[3] In his notebook he continued: 'My letters to Ilmari Krohn cannot be published!' We do not know why, but it is likely that he remembered having been all too friendly when writing about Krohn's odd concepts. The tendency to formally and semantically grounded interpretations of the genre in a composer's work follows Paul Bekker's euphoric (pro-revolutionary) Beethoven hermeneutics[4] and the efforts common in the older literature to support the greatness of the individual work by pointing to the construction of an oeuvre. The first requirement for the formal plausibility of such projects is an oeuvre that is more or less unambiguous in relation to the history of the genre, and that is not the case with Sibelius. Timothy Howell, the third distinguished Sibelius specialist of the 1980s and 1990s, rightly sees the symphonies as explicitly not a 'chronological sequence of progressive stylistic development' but rather as 'a series of various symphonic experiments (notably in form of tonality)'.[5] According to Howell, certain symphonies experiment with tonality (such as the Fourth and Sixth) and others with form (Fifth and Seventh). Howell identifies a technical problem in each symphony – even those that were written in part at the same time, such as the Sixth and Seventh.

In *Ton och tolkning*, his earliest essay on Sibelius (published in the year of the composer's death, 1957), Tawaststjerna very closely followed Cecil Gray, who was the first to take as his starting point, in the manner of older biographies of Beethoven, a sequence of three creative periods – romantic and national, eclectic and cosmopolitanism and classic and universal – and thus a teleological concept.[6] Tawaststjerna

[1] Erik W. Tawaststjerna 1997b, p. 85; quoting an interview with Julius Rabe in *Göteborgs Handels- och Sjöfartstidning*, 11 April 1923.

[2] Krohn 1945–6.

[3] See JS' notebook; National Archive Box 41.

[4] Bekker 1932.

[5] Howell 1989, pp. 1–2.

[6] Cecil Gray 1931, pp. 179–80. Also summarised in Johnson 1959, p. 231. Johnson describes as a more common breakdown of periods the sequence 'Kalevala-Romantic' (1892–1903), 'European-Classical' (1903–19), and 'Universal' (1919–26).

went even further than Gray by defining three creative periods in the works for piano in particular (not in passing, but as the structuring principle of the book).[1] Thus he postulated a second (mediocre) genre that supposedly makes it possible to survey the chronology of the composer's entire stylistic development, which is a bold notion. In contrast to Beethoven, however, only in Sibelius' symphonies (if at all) is it possible to imagine a completely structured super-genre or to see the genre as an all-embracing teleological project. According to Tawaststjerna, the first creative period (from the *Kalevala* romanticism of the early work to the Second Symphony as a transition), which contains a large number of the popular orchestral works and which is preceded only by student compositions, draws on the context of the time and place in which the works were composed. The second period is characterised by a pronounced individualism and at the same time a turn to European classicism. Between 1903 and 1919, the subject matter is liberated from its regional ties: Maeterlinck, Strindberg, Shakespeare and classical antiquity — *Pelléas et Mélisande* (1905), *Pan and Echo* (1906), two songs for *Twelfth Night* (1909), *The Dryad* (1910), *The Oceanides* (1914), as well as *Belshazzar's Feast* (1906–7), *Swanwhite* (1908) and *The Bard* (1913–14) — replace the *Kalevala*. *Luonnotar* (1913) is the only exception among the major works. The third period begins in the wake of the final version of the Fifth Symphony as a monument to the transition and leads to universally human dimensions — regardless of the themes, which also touch upon the specifically European (*The Tempest*) or Finnish (the *Kalevala* in *Tapiola*) but overcome them in the realisation. In the shadow of Albert Schweitzer's categories (Wagner the 'subjective', Bach the 'objective'),[2] in his early *Ton och tolkning* Tawaststjerna postulates Sibelius as a representative of the subjective type of artist and consequently sees the development of his subjectivity in the sequence of three creative periods. The change in style can also take place within a single project, as happens precisely in the Fifth Symphony. On 26 January 1916, while working on revising it, Sibelius wrote in his diary: 'I would like to give the symphony another — more human — form. More rooted, more alive. The problem is that while working on it I have become someone else.' The Fourth Symphony, whose expressiveness provided occasion for the myth of 'confession of the soul'[3] and the Lisztian supposition of a 'Mountain' Symphony (or 'Thoughts of a Wayfarer'),[4] was indeed one of the

[1] Erik W. Tawaststjerna 1957, p. 11, and passim. In a recent discussion with this author (October 2010), the son of Tawaststjerna, the distinguished professor of piano Erik T. Tawaststjerna, emphasised that the book on Sibelius' piano music was the his father's first publication on the composer (written in a great hurry) and not representative of his later views, which were based on a better overview. Indeed, in Tawaststjerna's case the teleology looks more like a rhetorical figure, whereas Krohn and Murtomäki, for ideological reasons, obviously meant it.

[2] Schweitzer 1966, pp. 1–4.

[3] Salmenhaara 1984, p. 288.

[4] Diary, 27 September – 3 October 1909: 'Plans. "La montagne."' Or in Axel Carpelan to JS, 27 December 1909; quoted in Erik W. Tawaststjerna 1986, p. 132; original Swedish in Dahlström 2010, pp. 261–3. JS had played him passages from a 'Mountain' project and from 'Thoughts of a Wayfarer' and in that context clearly spoke of the Fourth Symphony.

fruits of an intense occupation with the principles of art that ultimately led to a desire to 'distance myself from myself' and listen to works by others.[1] But in it he appears to have accepted his proximity to progressive modernism and moved towards it in an almost jerky way stylistically. Tawaststjerna spoke of 'new expressive possibilities' around 1908 in connection with a crisis in his health.[2]

The Third Symphony also stands out on account of its accordance with classicistic trends and its 'crystallisation of ideas from chaos' by means of form, sound, rhythm and orchestration.[3] Linearity and a chamber-music quality are recognisable early on, but they can be seen in the context of less famous works (from today's point of view) such as Alexander Glazunov's Eighth Symphony (1907). In the Fifth, Sixth and Seventh Symphonies, in turn, Sibelius parted ways with fashions and the conventional history of modernism – but as the result of a profound engagement with it, not out of ignorance. The modernist category of teleological progression fails because it presumes an order that cannot hold for a synthetic, heterogeneous oeuvre and heteronomous style. Sibelius' creative work does not conform to Bekker's category of the 'modern' as a component in a consequent 'flow and change of things'.[4] Tawaststjerna also recognised that Sibelius' stylistic development did not happen consistently from work to work.[5] So the question arises why anyone should speak – in the context of teleology – of a stylistic 'development' at all; later Tawaststjerna himself did not. To emphasise the lack of stringency in the symphonies rather than any teleological process is no argument against their aesthetic value but rather represents an example of the limited validity of modernist categories.

When Harold E. Johnson asserted that Sibelius did not know the path he was on and that he was too receptive to contradictory influences,[6] he provided the necessary impulse for the important distinction between uncertainty and suggestibility. An enlightened, critical uncertainty or openness means that someone rejects the illusion of the straight path, which can indeed be said of Sibelius, but he was not suggestible even where his works lead one to suspect the influence of others. The occasional similarities with others were accidental and very probably unconscious. Anyone who wants to illustrate heterogeneity and heteronomy based on the fleeting passages where Sibelius seems to have imitated someone has understood no more than those underlining the progressive homogeneity and autonomy of his project. The sequences of brass chords à la Wagner, Chopin's piano figurations and the like, were for him not the quotable, copyrighted property of others but rather public domain. This view is plausible and legitimate.

[1] Salmenhaara 1984, p. 289, quoting JS as reported by Ekman.

[2] Erik W. Tawaststjerna 1986, p. 83.

[3] Virtanen 2005, p. 78.

[4] Bekker 1921, p. 330.

[5] Erik W. Tawaststjerna 1994, p. 67.

[6] Cf. Salmenhaara 1984, p. 258.

'The Fourth is closer to me'

No matter whether the symphonies are 'declarations of faith', 'abstraction', expressions of the 'sublime' or (as a cycle) a totalitarian project of 'perfect unity' and of progressive modernity, their significance for the history of music is beyond question. Whereas with few exceptions Wagner wrote only operas after his early work, Hugo Wolf only Lieder and Mahler and Bruckner primarily works for (or at least with) orchestra, Sibelius was a composer of nearly all genres and ensembles, albeit with clear preferences. He wrote interesting works in most genres other than opera, and a dozen individual works have come to occupy a central place along the symphonies thanks to favourable circumstances – his Violin Concerto, thanks not least to the Jean Sibelius Violin Competition in Helsinki since 1965, and a few works for piano thanks to the worldwide popularity of Glenn Gould's innovative recordings. Nevertheless, his symphonies have always been recognised as his main genre.

That fact is neither altered by the interests of specialists in, say, the orchestral song *Luonnotar*, which is on a par with Schoenberg's *Erwartung*,[1] nor by the search for pearls in his early work, just as much as the first interpreters (Niemann, Göhler, *et al.*), who (like the public) preferred the tone poems. The ultra-modernist ideas of symphonic *telos* and of abstraction as a universally valid aesthetic principle cause us to lose sight of his oeuvre's variety and the value of its enigma and diversity. At least from a multicultural and post-modern perspective, Sibelius' heterogeneous, unconventionally forward-looking work was forced into the sterile pigeonhole of a dogmatic monoculture by the apologists of a direct Beethoven tradition. Too much classicism can do a lot of harm. Sibelius' oeuvre is probably no more easily understood solely on the basis of his 'declarations of faith' than the Catholic liturgy on the basis of its creed. Without the charming character pieces, waltzes, cantatas and the imaginative turns and transformations in compositions that are as a whole somewhat trivial and lacking context, important aspects of the artist that require explanation would not be appreciated.

Just as problematic as focusing analysis on the symphonies is the glorification of another masterpiece. In countless letters and postcards Sibelius received from sympathisers in the United States, *Finlandia* and *Valse triste* were celebrated as his true and only masterpieces. For a connoisseur who admires the symphonies, this may be frustrating – true even when discussing Sibelius with faithful music lovers even today. Sibelius felt much the same way. As far as the symphonies are concerned, for many professionals the Third (1907) is the first modern one – with the exception of the second movement of the Second (1901–2). Among modernist specialists, the Fourth (1911) was long considered the first of any importance and also the ultimate high point in his oeuvre. Apparently Sibelius too esteemed this work most of all, and

[1] Salmenhaara 1996c, p. 71. According to Salmenhaara, JS was not familiar with *Erwartung* (1909), but of course that is difficult to prove.

Wolfgang Rihm called it is his 'favourite piece' and 'one of the great symphonies in general'.[1] Sibelius called it a 'psychological symphony' and divided people into its lovers and enemies.[2] Jalas's notes also testify to this preference: as late as July 1942 Sibelius supposedly said that he had not found a single note in the Fourth that he would change;[3] there was no information about the notes in other symphonies he might change. In fact, however, he had considered making changes to the Fourth Symphony, as documented in his diary on 10 April 1912. It concerned, for example, the intermediate theme in the final movement ('could have had notes twice as long'). On 21 September 1913, he decided against revising. But Jalas's notes too are snapshots of a moment rather than a first-class source.

It took years before the greatness of the Fourth was recognised. For example, in 1912 the Vienna Philharmonic was not prepared to play it under Felix Weingartner – even though the concert had already been announced; Vienna did not open up to its occasional 'dissonances' (Rihm) until the 1970s.[4] In New York in 1913, Walter Damrosch of the Philharmonic Society still considered it appropriate to warn the audience with an announcement before the piece.[5] Sibelius was aware of the problems of its reception. He recommended the Fifth and the Second to the conductor Karl Krueger, who had written on 19 March 1930 to ask which symphony he could conduct after a performance of the First.[6] In Vienna, too, Krueger conducted primarily the Second and the Fifth. For various reasons, Sibelius continued to have reservations about a recording of the Fourth. On 22 May 1943, he wrote to the Finnish conductor Georg Schneevoigt: 'I fervently hope that you could record the Lemminkäinen and King Christian and of my symphonies the First and Second and above all the Seventh but not the Fourth and Sixth.'[7] The apparent reason was that they were not suited for the medium. He had emphasised this on 23 November 1937, in a draft letter to Walter Legge, the producer responsible for the recordings: 'Because these symphonies are terribly unsuited to the gramophone, it is necessary – even though Sir Thomas [Beecham] naturally played it well – to perform much with different dynamics from those marked in the score. Sometimes one doesn't hear the many voices at all. [...] The tempi were good, but I would just like to propose that in the final movement, from letter S onwards, it be played more quietly.'[8] He was all the more impressed by

[1] Brinkmann and Rihm 2001, p. 90.

[2] Erik W. Tawaststjerna 1986, p. 175, quoting an interview in *Dagens Tidning*, 28 March 1912.

[3] Sirén 1999, p. 38.

[4] Erik W. Tawaststjerna 1986, pp. 239–40.

[5] Ibid., p. 241.

[6] Draft letter: National Library Coll. 206: 21. On Krueger as a conductor of JS, see Krueger 1946, p. 42 (with illustration of JS and Krueger). Krueger was later active in Detroit.

[7] National Archive Box 35; draft.

[8] National Library Coll. 206: 46.

Karajan's later recording with the Berlin Philharmonic: 'Karajan is a great master. His interpretation is superb, technically and musically.'[1]

Perhaps in reaction to the hegemony of the Fourth Symphony in the earlier literature, or perhaps even as the result of a paradigm shift, in recent years its primacy has been put into perspective by arguments for the Fifth. Breitkopf & Härtel was unable to pay in advance for it during the post-war economic crisis, and so the publishing house lost Sibelius for several years to its Danish competitor Wilhelm Hansen, who in July 1920 transferred to Sibelius 3,000 Danish crowns, a stable currency scarcely affected by the post-war turmoil. For negotiations for *Tapiola*, the owner of Breitkopf & Härtel, Hellmuth von Hase, later travelled himself from Leipzig to Sibelius in Berlin.[2] It is not easy to choose a favourite from among Sibelius' symphonies. Even among the works available in 1921, Busoni was indecisive when he wrote to his former student Adolf Paul:

> Once again I had the privilege to pave the way for Sibelius (even though it should no longer be necessary for him!) But that's the way of the world, and I was happy that my effort succeeded. Hopefully you have shared your good impressions with him. (Would like to know what he thinks of the incident; he is so abstract and difficult to understand, and my love for him always remains one-sided.) They are all alike; I know all <u>their</u> works; none of them know <u>mine</u>. I admire the Fifth Symphony very much. The Fourth is closer to me. I don't know the Third. I performed the Second last April in Rome.[3]

Busoni vacillated between the Fourth and the Fifth. More recently, the Fifth Symphony gained a prominent advocate in James Hepokoski,[4] but there are also connoisseurs who argue for the Sixth Symphony (1923) and its timeless transparency. The Seventh (1924), in which *Valse triste* is quoted with a combination of chords (A flat major and D major seventh chord) and rhythm, is also popular. When Jalas asked about the *Valse triste* quotation and its significance, Sibelius responded with a pregnant silence.[5]

The Fifth is a tragic work, in terms of the composer's biography. He is said to have passed away in his home in Ainola on 20 September 1957 at 9.15 pm, at the time of a performance of the said work in Helsinki under Malcolm Sargent.[6] As a representative selection for both experts and lovers of his music, and also appropriate

[1] JS quoted in Legge 1998, p. 203. For more detail on JS, Karajan and the Fourth Symphony, see Pickett 2003, and Krones 2003a, p. 63: JS to Rudolf Gamsjäger (a Viennese music manager), 13 October 1955: 'I recently received his [Karajan's] recordings of my Fourth and Fifth Symphonies, which are outstanding.'

[2] See Erik W. Tawaststjerna 1997b, pp. 187 and 269.

[3] Copy of the original in the Åbo Akademie, supplemented by Adolf Paul to JS, 10 November 1921. See also Chap. 3.1 (pp. 156–7 above) for an extended version of this quotation.

[4] Hepokoski 1993.

[5] Jalas 1981, pp. 69–70.

[6] Salmenhaara 1996c, p. 156.

for the event, the pieces played at his funeral were the slow movement of the Fourth Symphony (Il tempo largo), three movements from the *Tempest* Suite (1925), *Swan of Tuonela* and *In Memoriam: Funeral March* (1909). The last of these may have been written in memory of the Finnish resistance fighter and patriotic assassin Eugen Schauman. At least the main themes that have been said to have come to Sibelius' mind in a dream may have originally been associated with Schauman's fate. After assassinating the Russian nationalist governor general, Nikolay Ivanovich Bobrikov, Schauman committed suicide while Bobrikov was treated in vain in hospital. This makes *In memoriam* a work of national relevance and appropriateness.[1]

Certain music lovers who cautiously probe beyond the 'Alla marcia' from the *Karelia* Suite, *Valse triste* from *Kuolema* and *Finlandia* considered the first two symphonies, which Sibelius himself suspected of Rydbergian 'gosselynne' (boyish spirits),[2] to be the essence of his art. They are not bothered by the fact that these two 'late Romantic' symphonies have been criticised 'for a somewhat schematic use of an existing tradition and for the still all-too-hesitant manifestation of new efforts' and for the composer's lack of originality.[3] They turn the criticism around and see the Romantic tendencies being attacked as an aesthetic that Sibelius unfortunately later abandoned. Familiar echoes, without the dubious flair of quotations, complete the impression: for example, a slow clarinet melody at the beginning of the First Symphony of 1899–1900 (E minor, but first B minor and G major) and in Tchaikovsky's Fifth (E minor) of 1888, which also employs the strategy of a slow beginning with strings in the finale; or a motif (*G–F♯–D*) often used by Grieg in the rapid main theme of the First and a Scherzo in an ambiguous 3/4 time as in Beethoven's Third Symphony ('Eroica', also with a Fugato). By contrast, many of the experts who believe in the modernity of Sibelius try to ignore *Finlandia* and *Valse triste* and deal only with *Luonnotar*, the late symphonies and *Tapiola*. Even Gray, who otherwise advocated the symphonies, said of *Tapiola* that this one work is 'the culminating point of his entire creative activity' and 'a consummate masterpiece'.[4]

When his publisher (probably in the 1940s) in Leipzig planned a study score of *Finlandia*, Sibelius expressed profound reservations: 'I still find that the miniature is a mistake, because this very clear work offers nothing of interest to study. Would you be so kind as to attempt it with my Sym. 4. You will be astonished how young musicians today will buy the score – not only here in the North but in England and America.'[5] But in the end, Sibelius was pragmatic: 'If Finlandia is published as a miniature score, I would like to write MM. ♩ = 104 for the melody in the middle, since the melody is always played too slowly.' He is referring to the tempo of the hymn, which

[1] See Erik W. Tawaststjerna 1986, p. p. 147.

[2] Jalas 1988, p. 31.

[3] See Salmenhaara 1996b, p. 149.

[4] Cecil Gray 1931, p. 88.

[5] National Archive Box 44; JS to Breitkopf & Härtel (undated draft).

FIG. 31. *Tapiola*, score, p. 17 (bars 175 ff.). This work contains passages reminiscent not only of Impressionism but also of micro-polyphony and Minimalism. For example, the transition in the exposition is Minimalist, while the fifty-five-bar build-up in the coda, partially illustrated here, is micro-polyphonic.

with a text by V. A. Koskenniemi (1940) added is a secret national anthem for many Finns. It obtains patriotic dignity by being performed slowly – contrary to Sibelius' intention and the character of the music. Originally the passage was part of a brilliant and entertaining piece of instrumental music with a wide spectrum of meanings beyond nationalism.

> Serious doubts about the piano pieces. By contrast, today I have big things in mind. As it should be, magnificent ego! If you spend too much time with trivial things, the weapons rust! An ancient truth! But how is one supposed to make money?![1]

4.2 Concertos and Chamber Music

The Violin Concerto and the Humoresques: 'Dreadful and Boring'?

The Concerto for Violin and Large Orchestra in D minor of 1903–4 (rev. 1905) has no immediate precursor in Liszt or Wagner, but the gesture — especially in its first version, which became accessible in 1990[2] — is the result of the same reformist stance. Sibelius explicitly considered Brahms's Violin Concerto 'too symphonic'.[3] This fundamental distinction was also felt by Joseph Joachim, who had helped Brahms compose his concerto. He considered Sibelius' virtuoso concerto 'scheusslich und langweilig' (dreadful and boring) and advised his students in Berlin to ignore it.[4] This is quite remarkable since all the violinists who were responsible for the premieres of the two versions of the concerto or otherwise candidates for its dedication — Willy Burmester, Franz (Ferenc) von Vecsey, Viktor Nováček and Carl Halir (Karel Halíř) — were Joachim's students. Fritz Struss, Sibelius' last violin teacher in Berlin, had been a student of Leopold von Auer, an early student of Joachim, and even of Joachim himself. The relative modernity and post-Wagnerian dissonances of the work can hardly be what disturbed the grand old Berlin maestro, since it represents the direct continuation of the Romantic tradition of the genre and by no means a revolution. The problem was rather its rhapsodic, fantastic progression, which Joachim (unlike many of his students) simply detested. It is reasonable to view Joachim as one source of the enduring animosity, or at least reservation, towards Sibelius felt by some German musicians even today.

Salmenhaara summarises comments on the piece as 'modern, strange, and difficult'.[5] It may superficially seem 'dreadful' and 'strange' next to Brahms, but its style results all the more directly from the innovations of Liszt and Wagner, albeit in the context of an ultra-conservative genre. Neither its formal frame nor its tonality deviates from classical models to a degree abnormal for its time, yet the totality of its gestures, orchestral texture and the nature of its motifs is expressive at the expense of classicist balance. The traditional harmony is made to sound unfamiliar by the

[1] Diary, 6 June 1912.

[2] For a recording, see BIS CD 500 (1990–91); Leonidas Kavakos with the Lahti Symphony Orchestra under Osmo Vänskä.

[3] JS to Aino, 26 January 1905.

[4] Quoted from Robert Lienau to JS, 20 October 1905; cf. Erik W. Tawaststjerna 1976, p. 278.

[5] Cf. Salmenhaara 1996a, p. 9.

orchestra's use of dissonances and their resolution from which Sibelius extracted a maximum of melodic tension within the framework of functional tonality with modal details in the formation of scales. The transitions are rough — especially in the first version. The independence of the layers of sound is also emphasised more in the first version as a result of the greater heterogeneity of the motifs. That explains both the approach of critics and Sibelius' own desire to 'forge' a balanced, more likable version from the same material.

Of the critics, Karl Flodin is the most important; he referred to the problems of the genre and did not see any solution to them in Sibelius' concerto. Salmenhaara reminds us of Flodin's significance and believes that, as a Swedish-speaking intellectual in Helsinki, he has gone almost unnoticed by generations of leading Sibelius scholars.[1] In his reviews in *Euterpe* and daily papers Flodin often addressed problems of which the apologists were not aware and even later could not contextualise. Despite his competence in the field, in the literature he is often suspected of having had personal reasons for rejecting the concerto;[2] rarely is much thought given to the similarly personal reasons others have for admiring a composition. In 1908 Flodin moved to Buenos Aires and returned to Finland in 1921 only for the last years of his life. His commitment to Sibelius is documented in a 78 rpm gramophone recording from 1904 on which he accompanied on the piano his wife, the soprano Adée Leander-Flodin, including a performance of 'Den första kyssen', op. 37.

The art of symphonic form, even in a solo concerto, lies in the ability to treat inconsistent material as a unity of timbre and texture. In Sibelius' case, this does not result from a compelling chain but unfolds instead like the unity of a dream or a complex vision. When Robert Layton wrote that Felix Mendelssohn Bartholdy's Violin Concerto in E minor is superior to Sibelius' concerto in 'symmetry, perfect homogeneity and a stylistic purity that make it a better work of art',[3] he exposed a flank to younger analysts whose arguments are influenced by postmodernism and thus respond critically to such categories. Sibelius did not, however, cling to his natural qualities of open conflict and imaginative unity but rather made the new version more homogeneous and more symmetrical in its syntax, rather than working out the original controversies and creating a new piece without compromises. The inconsistencies in the first version were, after all, not unintended mistakes — as can be shown, at least indirectly, by comparing the two, similarly divergent versions of the Fifth Symphony[4] as well as the history of the concerto's creation.

It is possible that the concerto essentially builds on Sibelius' own violin playing.

[1] Salmenhaara 1996a, pp. 18–20 (quoting Flodin's critics in *Helsingfors-Posten*, 9 and 11 February 1904, and *Euterpe*, 13 October 1904), and Salmenhaara 1996b, pp. 157–8.

[2] Salmenhaara 1996a, p. 26.

[3] Layton [1965] 1978, p. 103.

[4] For a recording, see BIS CD 863, featuring both versions played by the Lahti Symphony Orchestra under Osmo Vänskä.

Thus as a project it was 'only natural',[1] since even Tawaststjerna argues that 'he composed neither for Burmester nor any other violinist but for himself, or rather the kind of virtuoso he had dreamt of being'.[2] That Freudian line of argument is supported by the relative neglect in his oeuvre of chamber music for strings, since in that *métier* there were no unfulfilled ambitions to provide the basis for the composer's phantasmagoria. As a chamber musician, he was active early and successfully, both in piano trios with his siblings (his sister usually played the piano, and his younger brother, Christian, the cello) and as second violin in quasi-professional string quartets and in Busoni's piano quintet in Helsinki. His experiences as a violinist were important at least insofar as his Violin Concerto is a bravura virtuoso concerto more clearly than that of Brahms, precisely not 'too symphonic', but rather characteristically structured.

The concerto's virtuosity is unconventional. The influence of bravura works from his youth is too imprecise to offer any meaningful approach to the work. Parallels to Brahms, Bruch, Tchaikovsky and Mendelssohn can be found,[3] but only abstractly, as a symptom of a peculiar inter-textuality in this genre (perhaps one reason for its conservatism). They reveal that Sibelius essentially started out from the Classical-Romantic schema but treated all the details in his own way. The significance of Louis Spohr's concertos deserves closer study. Sibelius' collection of scores includes Spohr's best-known minor-key concertos, of which the Second (in D minor) — as well as the Twelfth (in A minor), albeit in a more moderate tempo — has a final movement, Alla polacca, with a rhythm in the main theme that belongs to precisely the same genre of polonaise as his own theme. Likewise, the final movement, Moderato–Allegretto, of Karl Goldmark's Concerto in A minor, op. 28 (1878) is also based on a rhythm 'alla polacca' and contains several passing idioms (in particular with respect to the violin part) that recall Sibelius' movement.

Comparing Sibelius and Mendelssohn point by point helps to demonstrate what is new in Sibelius. Mendelssohn begins his concerto with circling chords in the orchestra. After a measure and a half, the violin enters with the theme in the middle range. Much as in the piano concertos by Mozart (D minor, K 466) and Sergey Rachmaninoff (no. 3 in D minor), the accompanying chords in the orchestra are clarified by means of accents in the bass line. In Mendelssohn's concerto, the beginning is clear in terms of metre. Despite the syncopation from the very beginning, that is also true in the case of Mozart, who, unlike his successor, retrospectively legitimises the accompanying chords as a component of the theme, thereby showing his genuine sophistication.[4] Sibelius, by contrast, leaves the metre open. It is not only the lack of pulses but also the rhythmic form of the theme that causes the metre to remain ambiguous for a long time. Coming from Mozart, this is the other extreme. It gives the

[1] Salmenhaara 1996a, p. 14.

[2] Erik W. Tawaststjerna 1976, p. 279.

[3] Cf. Mäkelä 1995b.

[4] On Mozart, see, for example, Mäkelä 1993.

violin maximum space to unfold its fundamental qualities in expressive intonation (Sibelius writes 'dolce e espressivo') of single tones. While the solo violin establishes a rhythmically regular 2/2 time (which corresponds to the metre as notated), the metre initially emerges only as syncopation. Only from measure 9 onwards does the phrasing gradually shift to the beats that are suggested by the time signature. A comparably extensive disguising of the metre at the beginning can be found only in the Second and Fourth Symphonies. In general, one central factor Sibelius employs to make his music stand out from the traditions of older and academic styles is a creative approach to metre.

On 18 September 1902 Sibelius reported on having 'wonderful themes for a violin concerto'.[1] A thematic inspiration specific to the violin — and possibly the concerto's first theme — was evidently the occasion to begin work. While writing the work he was in contact with the former leader of the Helsinki Philharmonic Orchestra, Willy Burmester, who had become an internationally active soloist and lived in Halensee, near Berlin. Burmester responded enthusiastically to the piano score of the first version. It is said that he had congratulated the composer of a violin concerto so heartily only once before Sibelius, when Tchaikovsky showed him his violin concerto.[2] It is not known whether Sibelius was able to appreciate that comparison. Burmester was supposed to be the soloist for the premiere, but that plan did not come to fruition because of delays completing the work even in its first version. That also led to the removal of the original dedication of the concerto (later it was dedicated to the young talent Ferenc von Vecsey, whose mother, Marguerite von Vecsey, was a friend of Sibelius),[3] which had, unfortunately, already been announced in the Berlin press.[4] As late as October 1903, Sibelius wrote to Burmester: 'The concerto is dedicated to you and can only be played by you. When it gets printed, it's something else; then it is nice when it is played. Did not think of anyone else but you.'[5] This *faux pas* made it more difficult to disseminate the work internationally, especially since the premiere of the first version with Burmester in Berlin — rather than the largely unnoticed performance with the Romanian violinist Viktor Nováček in Helsinki on 8 February 1904 — would have been possible in March 1904. Burmester was interested in the concerto

[1] JS to Aino, 18 September 1902.

[2] Mäkelä 1995b, p. 15, and Erik W. Tawaststjerna 1976, p. 275.

[3] For her correspondence with JS, see National Library Coll. 206: 39.

[4] National Archive Box 23; a postcard from Alfons Leonard to JS, 11 November 1903, to which he pasted a clipping from the *Berliner Börsen-Courier* with news of the dedication of the concerto to Burmester.

[5] National Archive: copy in the Tawaststjerna Collection; undated letter, which was received in Berlin on 10 October 1903, with the following address on the envelope: 'Herrn Willy Burmester, virtuoso of God's grace, Halensee, near Berlin'. Halensee is now part of the Charlottenburg-Wilmersdorf district of Berlin.

even after losing the world premiere. He only distanced himself from it after he was passed over a second time for — in his view — a lesser talent.[1]

Sibelius' decision to have the first version performed not by Burmester in Berlin but by a virtuoso available in Helsinki may also be an indication that he did not yet consider the work potentially successful. Similarly, the first versions of the symphonies often had their premieres in Helsinki, whereas only later versions were heard abroad. Certainly the influential composer Max von Schillings, who on 2 January 1904 — just ten days after the world premiere of the first version — had requested the score for possible performance at the Allgemeiner deutscher Musikverein's Tonkünstlerfest, a distinguished composers' festival in Frankfurt, was unsparing when he sent the work back to Burmester:

> Sibelius' Violin Concerto — I cannot conceal this from you — disappointed me deeply after working on it thoroughly. Artistically and personally, I have the greatest sympathy for Sibelius and I have advocated to the best of my ability for his [*Lemminkäinen*] Legends, but I cannot do the same for the concerto. Without a doubt, it offers the solo instrument a fine, interesting task, which you in particular will presumably master like no one else. But its invention has little effect on me, and some passages seem to me unstylish, sweet and shallow. Where Sibelius strikes his Nordic, rhapsodic tone, my feelings follow, but the Chopinesque, Lisztian phraseology, which occupies long passages in all three movements, has such a disagreeable effect on me that the work's merits vanish completely. The other member of our music commission assessed the concerto much as I did, and so I fear we will not be able to decide in favour of a performance in Frankfurt. Would that decision deprive us of any hope of counting on your participation? Two other concertos (by [Hermann] Zilcher and [Otto] Neitzel) have been proposed. Would you perhaps be interested in one of those? Please don't be angry at me, the miserable criticaster — how gladly I would have done everything for Sibelius.[2]

Burmester passed Schillings's position on to Sibelius unfiltered. It can no longer be determined whether that openness (or cruelty) may even have cost him the premiere of the final version in Berlin. The final version was premiered at the Berliner Philharmonie by Carl Halir and the Königlich-Preussische Hofkapelle under Richard Strauss on 19 October 1905. Halir was the leader of the Berlin orchestra and an active chamber musician. The reactions were not effusive but still quite positive.[3]

Another critic was Heinrich Strobel, who can therefore be included on the list of influential German-speaking grumblers about Sibelius — chronologically right after Joachim and before Adorno. On 20 March 1928 he wrote in the *Berliner Börsen-*

[1] For more detail, see Salmenhaara 1996a, pp. 15–16 and 22 ff.

[2] National Archive Box 23; a copy that was forwarded to JS.

[3] On the reviews, Salmenhaara 1996a, pp. 23–4.

Courier about a collection of pieces from a 'long-lost period of overly refined musical taste': 'A completely insipid piece, creeping along in shapeless monotony without a plastic theme (not even in the relatively lively movement), without genuine violin virtuosity, boring Nordic desolateness. Inconceivable that Furtwängler featured this anaemic concert at all.'[1] But of course there are 'plastic themes' and 'genuine violin virtuosity'! It might be that by 'plastic' (*plastisch*) Strobel meant the symphonic quality of the themes of Beethoven and Brahms – that is, their penchant for transparent motivic work – not the sub-thematic quality. By 'genuine violin virtuosity' he need not have meant artistic difficulty but rather effective, transcendental brilliance à la Paganini or the modern, innovative violin techniques to be found in Debussy and Ravel and of course in Paul Hindemith and Alban Berg.

Alfred Einstein's review completes the picture: he wrote cogently of that same performance in Berlin that the first movement 'does not know whether it wants to become *concertante* or symphonic'.[2] The 'virtuoso element', in turn, was 'conventional' in the tradition from Mendelssohn to Bruch. Possibly, these prominent critics (Strobel, Einstein) were both – despite otherwise considerable differences in taste and cultural-political orientation – criticising Sibelius' concerto from the perspective of 1928 as not being a promising basis for the future of the genre in the twentieth century but characterising it instead, despite the innovations in its details, as the last work in the tradition from Mendelssohn to Bruch. As so often with Sibelius, it is difficult here to make a favourable professional judgement about the work as long as one clings to the historical and aesthetic maxims of the apologists of Schoenberg or even Hindemith, which in 1928 certainly represented one of the normal approaches, alongside conservative and nationalist perspectives. Only much later did several critics begin to accept 'Nordic desolateness' as an artistic resource. The same is true of such other ideologically encumbered categories as 'symmetry', 'homogeneity' and 'stylistic purity' (Layton, as quoted above).

Despite the encouraging success of the second version, and despite various concerto ideas recorded only in sketches, no solo concerto followed, for the violin or any other instrument. Only in the preparatory work for the Sixth Symphony is there a note about a 'Violin Concerto II/Concerto lirico'. On 13 April 1915 Sibelius offered Breitkopf & Härtel the plan for a concerto, but the publishing house did not feel it was in a position to pay an advance and thus pin Sibelius down. He wanted 5,000 Reichsmarks for an edition of 10,000 copies.[3] This unusually businesslike approach, especially since no preparatory works are known, is explained by the dire financial situation of his family. Several years later, in 1922, he was explicitly asked to write a piano concerto for the Hansen publishing house. At first he responded with interest, though he suspected that 'the world wants a piano concerto à la Tchaikovffsky [*sic*] or

[1] Erik W. Tawaststjerna 1997a, pp. 274–5.

[2] Salmenhaara 1996a, p. 56, quoting the *Berliner Tageblatt* of 20 March 1928.

[3] Erik W. Tawaststjerna 1997b, p. 48.

Grieg' but he felt he was not in a position to write one. A few days later he remarked that 'I can no longer write what I want, but what I must'.[1] So the Violin Concerto in D minor remained his only solo concerto.

The six *Humoresques* for violin and orchestra from 1917 and 1918 do have concerto-like qualities. Thanks to the tonal arrangement, they can even be performed as a cycle: they progress from D minor by way of D major to G minor, which is established as the main key – with a digression into the sixth degree in the fifth *Humoresque* (E flat major). Much as he did in many character pieces for piano and even in concert suites from incidental music, Sibelius recorded ideas here that provide insight into his generously overflowing tonal imagination. The generic title he also considered using, 'Lyric Dances', clarifies the character of these compositions.[2] There are also *Two Serenades* (1912 and 1913) and *Two Serious Melodies*, op. 77: *Cantique: Laetare anima mea* (1914) and *Devotion: Ab imo pectore* (1915) for viola or cello with orchestra. As important as the latter two are for a complete picture of Sibelius – demonstrating that he was capable of highly differentiated expression even in small, concentrated forms of limited length – their position in the repertoire is marginal. Although piano versions exist, the sound of the orchestra is of irreplaceable value to these works.

One of the innovations of the Violin Concerto is the central position of the solo cadenza. The first, brief cadenza occurs before the orchestra's second theme in the exposition; another one comes before the extraordinarily clearly designed third theme (concealed in the reprise by a contrasting voice that is very idiomatic on the violin). In the first version, there was also a historicist cadenza à la Bach, whose considerable length (sixty-four measures) in the first version extends the first movement – or, more specifically, the reprise of the second group of themes. Jukka Tiilikainen, whose essay also explains in detail and illustrates the sketches for the concerto, has pointed out that Burmester had made a name for himself primarily as an interpreter of Bach and Spohr, which may explain why the original cadenza was at least in part in the style of Bach.[3] That would mean a rare (but perfectly possible) musical dedication – comparable with Schumann writing 'Chiarina' (*Carnaval*, op. 9, no. 9) for Clara Wieck in the style of Chopin, underlining the fact that Clara was already one of the foremost Chopin interpreters of her age. The long cadenza of the final version of the Violin Concerto is also the development and continuation of the reprise. Yet another motif is developed at the end. The symmetrical rounding off of the frame is called into question many times, and the sonata form is confirmed as a form based solely on development. The many cadenzas, the abrupt beginning with the main theme in the violin and the striking third theme loosen up the classical layout but do not reject it or replace it with another strategy. Moreover, the beginning of the development is remarkable insofar as the third theme stagnates melodically, and the music loses its

[1] JS to Wilhelm Hansen, 18 and 22 March 1922; quoted in Erik W. Tawaststjerna 1997b, p. 216.

[2] Diary, 1 May 1917.

[3] Tiilikainen 2004, p. 79.

momentum, so that the development with the solo violin begins as if out of nowhere. The sonata form develops its original bipartite structure. This strategy is supported tonally by the delayed return to the main key in the major-key variation (D major). Only later does D minor follow. Following the cadenza a kind of feigned reprise in G minor begins, which is, in fact – quite originally – the actual reprise in the wrong key (à la Beethoven). In the second movement, too, the redesign of the final version was primarily – almost exclusively – concerned with energetic ornaments and explosive cadenzas. Five measures before the conclusion, Sibelius had worked into the first version a brilliant solo cadenza, which he eliminated in favour of sentimental cantabile virtuosity in the style of Henryk Wieniawski and Henri Vieuxtemps. In general, in the second movement he continued the rhapsodic, fantastic shape of the tripartite song form. Already at the beginning he drew attention to the fragmented syntax. The sonorous, imploring melody on the violin's lowest string (G) in B major is slowed down by means of tonally flexible woodwind motifs. These characteristic motifs unfold as elements of the middle section. The overall shape of the movement represents a symphonic and dramatic extension of the simple 'Preghiera' *topos*. Wieniawski created the foundation for it with the second movement (in A major) of his Violin Concerto in F sharp minor, op. 14.[1] In both concertos, the main melody of the violin is harmonised by the winds in the style of Romantic church organ music on a small scale (music for small and even private chapels).

The comparison to Wieniawski also suggests itself in the third movement. For Donald Francis Tovey, the finale was a 'polonaise for polar bears'[2] – a catchy alliteration (but at the same time based on the typical climatic and zoological error that there are polar bears in Finland;[3] on the other hand, Finns too sometimes used the polar bear as their icon, like the Fourteenth Infantry regiment of Turku, part of the Wehrmacht's AOK Norwegen in Lapland.) Much like in Tchaikovsky's Fourth Symphony, the polonaise in the Violin Concerto does not in any way serve to illustrate a picturesque dance scene. The expressive character of the dance rhythm is by no means 'Nordic', either, but rather a mixture of polonaise and tarantella. Tovey presumably thought of the polar region simply because he associated the composer with the north in general. The polonaise was a nineteenth-century *topos* – inspired by nationalist, enlightened intellectuals' awareness of Poland's fate – that was often an expression of the 'human'.[4] Olin Downes described the movement by negation: 'This finale is not at all picturesque in the customary virtuoso manner, and many a violinist has found

[1] Cf. Mäkelä 2001b.

[2] Salmenhaara 1996a, p. 33; cf. Tovey [1936] 1989, p. 215.

[3] See the illustration of the Paris World's Fair of 1900 from *Journal des débats*, in Erik T. Tawaststjerna's one-volume edition of his father's works: Erik T. Tawaststjerna 1997, p. 109. It shows the Finnish Pavilion with a group of polar bear hunters. There are brown bears in Finland, and they appear in other illustrations and in the design of the pavilion.

[4] Taruskin 1997, p. 290.

little or no meaning in it.'[1] He was commenting on a performance with the Leopold von Auer student Efrem Zimbalist as soloist, who 'felt' the significance of the movement: 'his imagination was deeply stirred by it'. But the mere fact that the rhythm can be seen as a small gesture of acknowledgement to Spohr as a composer of important violin concertos and as a teacher of 'the father of Finnish music', Fredrik Pacius, does not encourage one to call the movement significant.

Salmenhaara decidedly rejects the notion of a 'national' concerto. Flodin had hoped to find such a tradition in Sibelius.[2] Édouard Lalo's *Symphonie espagnole* could perhaps be said to be programmatically national. Moreover there is a number of solo concertos with national, populist themes, especially in their final movement. Some of them are labelled accordingly, such as Wieniawski's op. 22, Allegro moderato (à la Zingara); Busoni's Piano Concerto, op. 39, whose fourth movement is titled All'italiana (Tarantella); or the Alla polacca typical of Spohr. On the one hand, there are finales with national features, and at least since Mozart's Piano Sonata, K 331, with its Rondo alla turca, they are not a feature limited to solo concertos but one found in multiple-movement sonatas for all sorts of instruments. On the other hand, there are composers, such as Grieg, who reveal their own nationality in their final movements. Flodin felt that Sibelius lacked a strong enough approach to the musical culture and national future of Finland. The same criterion was the reproach concealed in Tovey's 'polonaise for polar bears': Sibelius was thought to have interpreted the polonaise in a very Nordic fashion. Seen in this way, his final movement belongs between those of Wieniawski and Grieg. Flodin, in any case, was concerned with a question similar to those of Walter Niemann and Adorno: is it possible to create out of nationally specific material new art forms that expand the traditional palette of forms?[3] What matters here is not old repertoire (Grieg, Wieniawski) but rather the future of the genre. Sibelius did not write a national concerto but rather an individual one, especially since he defined what the national would be in Finnish music. The idea of the national is, of course, not disreputable: in the late twentieth century, composers looked in all directions – as far as Central and South-west Africa, as György Ligeti did in his Piano Concerto – to find new ways to structure that old racehorse the 'concerto' and even make it entertaining. In contrast to many of his colleagues and friends, Sibelius did not believe that he was in a position to make such extended expeditions – neither musically nor actually.

Voces intimae, Malinconia, and the Chamber Music for Strings

Whereas in his orchestral music Sibelius repeatedly strove to expand and question the formal framework of large-scale genres, the Fourth String Quartet in D minor of 1909

1 Salmenhaara 1996a, p. 58, citing the *New York Times*, 7 December 1930.

2 Salmenhaara 1996a, p. 21.

3 Discussed in detail in chapters 5.1 and 5.2 of this volume.

(*Voces intimae*, op. 56) remained an isolated attempt at a modern gesture – preceded by three conventional quartets from his youth – in E flat major from 1885, in A minor from 1889 and in B flat major from 1889–90 (op. 4) – as well as fragments and single movements. In contrast to the excursions into chamber music by other orchestral composers of the period – one need only think of Bruckner, Strauss or even Verdi – his op. 56 is an ambitious work. Here too its originality is connected to the New German aesthetic of the particular rather than the classical, although the exponents of the string quartet genre since Haydn were in the vanguard of thoroughgoing motivic and thematic structure in sonata form. *Voces intimae* was written immediately before such historical milestones as Ravel's, Schoenberg's and Hindemith's string quartets. Sibelius, too, distanced himself from Brahms, the leading composer of chamber music of the older generation, and created a style that sounds orchestral despite polyphonic voice leading. Thus he moved close to Schoenberg's programmatic sextet *Transfigured Night*, and not only because of the shared key, D minor, but also because of the articulation of sound. Sibelius himself regarded this orchestral quality of his string quartet with critical eyes (Diary, 24 April 1910): 'The melodic material is good, but the sound could be "lighter" and why not more "quartet"? Take this "cum grano salis"!' He did not venture another attempt, and he did not revise it either, for he knew that the project was a success. He wrote in his diary on 27 April 1910 – with understatement, but full of the implicit pride of a 45-year-old: 'I believe I have passed my journeyman's examination. Seek your path on the open sea! You can already do "something"!' The quartet is an interesting synthesis of the tradition shared by both Haydn and Brahms, with the stylistic characteristics of the successors to Liszt. The influence of Brahms is heard in the rhythm and in the shaping of the lines most clearly in the fourth movement (Allegretto ma pesante), whereas the first and third movements move in the direction of Schoenberg's early sextet. The final movement, however, is no Rondo alla zingaresca à la Brahms but rather an ecstatic dance with motifs resembling Scandinavian minstrel music.

Because of a handwritten date on a clipping from a Berlin newspaper in the Sibelius Museum in Turku, for a long time there was confusion about the date of the premiere. It was commonly thought that the quartet had been premiered in Berlin on 6 January 1910.[1] Sibelius, the likely author of the handwritten date, had probably forgotten the year had changed and meant 6 January 1911. It is likely that the work was actually premiered before that in Helsinki in April 1910. The Berlin performance on 6 January 1911 immediately preceded one in Leipzig. Sibelius wrote on 26 May 1910, from Helsinki: 'Several weeks ago, Voces intimae was premiered here by the local string quartet [...]. By the way, the work met with very great success. It is generally

[1] See, for example, Dahlström 1987, p. 40: 'First performance: Berlin, 6 January 1910. Cecilquartett (Prague).' The error 'Cecilquartett' was most likely caused by the Fraktur typeface and a typo in the newspaper *Germania*, 29 December 1910, which in fact had 'Secik-Quartett'.

thought to be my best work. I don't agree with that, but it is one of my best.'[1] His reservation is reasonable, since by 1910 he had already written three symphonies and *Kullervo* as well as the Violin Concerto and magnificent songs — not to mention *The Swan of Tuonela*, *Valse triste* and other successful works. On 14 January 1911 Lienau wrote from Berlin to inform Sibelius about what were apparently the first performances in Germany, to which the newspaper review mentioned above was referring: 'Several days ago I heard your string quartet here for the first time, performed in the Tonkünstlerverein by the Ševčik-Quartett. The performance was quite outstanding. [...] Though something quite different from all other string quartets. On the eighth was the first performance in Leipzig.'[2] Other notable performances of the quartet include one by the Amar-Quartett, with Hindemith, at the Nordisches Musikfest that took place in Heidelberg in 1924.[3]

Voces intimae has no programme, and nothing is known about any programmatic ideas Sibelius might have had in the preparatory phase. The famous title, which translates as 'intimate voices', is semantically striking; it first occurs in a note by Sibelius on 12 June 1909, in the context of correcting the proofs.[4] One possibility for making the musical meaning of this metaphor more precise is concealed in the printed score in an identical note by the composer concerning the tonally Janus-faced *pp* chords in the central third movement: three simple E minor triads are heard within expressive, chromatic F minor surroundings (più Adagio). Later in the course of the movement, they become comparable in gesture to C sharp minor chords, which in turn contrast tonally with F major. Even in the first movement (Andante), static chords occur in the chromatic, polyphonic context, albeit less prominently: for example, E major following C sharp minor in measure 38 or the C major seventh chord with a ninth following A major in measure 42, and so on. It is impossible to miss the interruption of the polyphonic flow by a chord twenty-two measures before the end (here with an A major seventh chord with a ninth, after F sharp minor) and five measures later (F major seventh with an added ninth, after D minor). Without the harmonic dimension, the idea of the chordal interruption of the flow of motion is also important in the second movement. There are unexpected gaps in the polyphonic fabric — a capricious form of expression in the Scherzo, which is repeated in altered form at the conclusion. Immediately before the section in F sharp minor and forty measures before the conclusion, Sibelius includes two pizzicato chords in a way that may not be harmonically spectacular but is unique in the context of this work. The name 'intimate voices' is plausible, especially as it is appropriate not only for the presentation of the E minor triads but also for the intimate dialogue between violin and cello at the

[1] National Archive Box 46; draft letter to Robert Lienau. Dahlström 2003a, p. 258, has 25 April 1910. There may have been private performances even earlier.

[2] National Archive Box 46.

[3] Gleissner 2002, pp. 71–2.

[4] National Archive; copy in the Tawaststjerna Collection.

beginning of the first movement. The effect is related to Janáček's distorted voices in the first movement of his quartet *Intimate Letters* (1928).

The title *Voces intimae* may originally be connected to the fear of dying recorded in the diary Sibelius had just begun in London. The work was written in London, Paris and Berlin. In February 1909, he completed the third movement, despite alarming health problems – later a growth was removed from his throat.[1] On 1 April, however, he wrote: 'Why am I running away from the quartet?' On 15 April 1909 his diary reads: 'The quartet is finished. Yes – my heart bleeds – why this sense of pain in life. O! O! O! That I even exist! My God!' These sighs of relief were perhaps primarily about financial problems and the conflict between earning money for the family and composing great works of art. He also reported to his wife that same day about his composition project: 'My quartet was finished some time ago but I withheld it. Today I have sent it to Lienau. It's a wonderful feeling, the sort of thing that prompts a smile to cross the lips at the moment of death. I say no more.'[2] He wrote to Aino more analytically both about death and about the problems of completing a work definitively than he did in his secret diary – probably considering more carefully, because of the quasi-public forum, the usual ambivalence of different stages of so-called completion. The reference to smiling 'at the moment of death' is peculiar, since many experience the quartet is rather elegiac. Melancholy is, however, always an ambivalent feeling, so Sibelius was smiling here as Schubert also did in *Death and the Maiden* (1824) in D minor.

Tawaststjerna mentioned Beethoven's String Quartet, op. 59, no. 1, as a significant model for Sibelius' op. 56.[3] Equally interesting are parallels to several prominent string quartets of the period. According to his diary, Sibelius first heard the Debussy quartet of 1893 on 21 October 1910 in London, even though it had been performed in Helsinki in February 1907 by the legendary Brussels String Quartet.[4] It is reasonable to assume that he attended this performance, since he had enjoyed other concerts by the same ensemble, as documented in correspondence with a member of the ensemble.[5] He was not travelling in February 1907, and such a concert was a major event in Helsinki for a violin player like Sibelius and moreover in the middle of winter. He could not, however, be familiar with Ravel's String Quartet of 1903–10, which built on Debussy's model. Reger, in turn, composed his String Quartet in E flat major, op. 109, at almost the same time as *Voces intimae*. Sibelius began composing in December 1908, as demonstrated by a sketch at the start of a letter dated 15 December 1908.[6]

Schoenberg's First String Quartet, op. 7 (also in D minor) dates from 1905 and was premiered in 1907. Sibelius' quartet bears comparison to such standard works

[1] Erik W. Tawaststjerna 1986, p. 117.

[2] Ibid., p. 113.

[3] Ibid., p. 118.

[4] Salmenhaara 1996c, p. 54.

[5] Cf. Hans Daucher to JS, 5 March 1955, National Library Coll. 206: 9.

[6] Ekman 1946, p. 198.

of modernism because it is original in its stylistic gestures, seems harmonically advanced and yet its sequence of movements conforms to the cyclical model of Debussy, Ravel, Schoenberg and Reger (first movement moderate, then fast, slow and fast). The originality of Sibelius' work comes in part from elements that, similarly to those found later in Janáček and Stravinsky, interrupt the traditional syntax, the 'flow', and produce surprising turns. Reger's String Quartet in E flat major is particularly closely related to Sibelius in this respect, although it cannot have been a model for him. In both works, the metre is constantly undermined. For example, the harmonic turn in the 'intimate' chords is, in its extended tonality on the margins of the functional, also typical of Reger and an example of Liszt's forward-looking maxim, which Reger pointedly cited on 17 July 1902: 'I rigorously follow the Lisztian principle: "Any chord can be followed by any chord."'[1] Sibelius employed his 'intimate' chords according to this same principle. The comparison between Sibelius and Reger draws attention to the stylistic position of the diverse modern artists who were the successors to Brahms and Wagner. What Eugen d'Albert was for Reger,[2] Karl Goldmark was for Sibelius for a time: a role model who prepared the way for the alternative synthesis that Schoenberg — consciously building on Reger — achieved more rigorously than his older colleagues.

Sibelius was demonstrably on Reger's trail in autumn 1910, when he experienced this multitalented artist playing the piano with the Bohemian String Quartet and went backstage at the Beethoven-Saal after the performance: 'I like Max Reger. He had no success whatsoever. But he is a great artist. For a work of chamber music, he receives 15,000 RM! So presumably I can raise my prices soon as well.'[3] And he tried to do so. Apparently a sympathetic discussion between experts on the deeper meaning of contemporary music had taken place.[4] In his diary on 15 October 1910, Sibelius was merciless in his opinion of Reger's music: 'Nationalist, German, ornate, and boring, but good precisely because of the German part.' This is not just about Reger but about the so-called German idiom, which Reger himself derived from Bach: 'Should I, the most ardent admirer of Johann Sebastian Bach, Beethoven, and Brahms preach their overthrow? All I want is just to continue to develop this style!'[5] There is no evidence that Sibelius encountered Reger's music before 1910. Only Busoni could have arranged any contact earlier. Busoni, who had known Reger personally since the 1880s, referred to Reger when presenting a concert on 3 January 1905[6] — just two days before Sibelius' arrival in Berlin[7] — as the 'greatest living' and, moreover, 'ur-German'

1 Max Reger to Constantin Sander, 17 July 1902, in Hase-Koehler 1928, p. 94.

2 See, for example, Mäkelä 2000e, pp. 39–40.

3 JS to Aino, 16 October 1910.

4 Schreiber 1981 mentions the concert of 15 October 1910. The programme consisted of Dvořák's op. 61, Reger's op. 113 and Schubert's op. 125; Schreiber 1981, p. 358.

5 Adalbert Lindner to Max Reger, 10 April 1897, in Hase-Koehler 1928, p. 56.

6 Schreiber 1981, p. 280.

7 Erik W. Tawaststjerna 1986, p. 23.

composer.[1] It is therefore conceivable that Busoni introduced his friend to Reger's music in January 1905. After all, Busoni numbered both Sibelius and Reger among the modernist elite. He supposedly said that the slow movement from Sibelius' Second Symphony, which was performed under Weingartner in Berlin in January 1905, was the 'best music there is'.[2] That movement, with its dramatic complexity, does indeed represent one of many high points in Sibelius' work. That fact that the composer quoted Busoni's statement to Aino without irony suggests that he considered the view plausible.

The cello, the instrument played by Sibelius' younger brother, Christian, plays only a minor role in Sibelius' oeuvre. It appears with violin in the early duet *Waterdrops* (before 1881), then as a solo instrument in the gesturally ambitious but at the same time problematic concert piece *Malinconia* of 1900. *Malinconia* is a virtuoso ballad for cello and piano that lasts thirteen minutes and is artistically very demanding but can very easily seem superficial. The thematic material is thin – probably intentionally, to give its expressive effects as much room to develop as possible. The piece presents completely unexpected hurdles for the inexperienced interpreter, as soon as he or she notices that the cascades of the piano by no means signify empty brilliance but are rather supposed to be expressive – in the style of Bach's *Chromatic Fantasy* (BWV 903). Tawaststjerna's association of Magnus Enckell's painting *Melancholy* (1895) with Sibelius' *Malinconia* is arbitrary. Tawaststjerna proposed the death of Sibelius' daughter Kirsti as the cause of the unusual work.[3] It can be argued against this conjecture that Sibelius reported to his wife in a businesslike fashion about his success with his 'Fantasy'. Kirsti had just died on 2 March. The melodic emptiness, which contrasts with the mannered expression, may articulate profound speechlessness in the face of a catastrophe. It is in keeping with this view that Sibelius supposedly never mentioned the name of his daughter after her death. Madetoja was the source of a rare, undated anecdote about a visit together to her grave, at which Sibelius allegedly said: 'Here rests my daughter. She was an angel.'[4]

His chamber music for violin solo is similarly enigmatic and inconsistent. Given his ambitions to be a violinist, it is surprising that his solo works for violin are so insignificant – they are among his shortest compositions – and that there are no large-scale fantasies or sonatas whatsoever. His motivic brilliance and masterly handling of character pieces for violin and piano are nevertheless testimony to the high level of his violin playing. They are a testament to the influence of Wieniawski at a time when Sibelius' major works were already far removed from the salon music of the nineteenth century. Unlike his works for piano, the compositions for violin are concentrated in his late years. *Danses champêtres* of 1925 and Four Pieces and Three Pieces, both from

1 Cadenbach 1991, p. 38.
2 JS to Aino, 9 January 1905.
3 Erik W. Tawaststjerna 1976, p. 224.
4 Quoted in Salmenhaara 1987, p. 90.

1929, are among his very last works. There are, however, progressive elements to be found much earlier – in op. 78, for example: in *Romance* in F major (no. 2; 1915), and especially in *Religioso* in G minor (no. 3; 1917), dedicated to his brother, 'Prof. C. Sibelius', and explicitly intended to be performed on cello as well. This piece, which was conceived as a 'Preghiera', achieves a sound that recalls César Franck's chorales, particularly for piano (i.e., in *Prélude, Choral et Fugue*). Nevertheless, there is little to be heard of the aesthetic problems that he was resolving in his orchestral works of this period. Many violin pieces demonstrate rather the composer's inner schism and raise the question of how desperate his situation must have been at times if he published this or that work while destroying the Eighth Symphony and delaying the publication of other orchestral works by making corrections.

On 25 July 1939 he wrote to the conductor and musicologist Toivo Haapanen (who was preparing a book on Finnish music) about his chamber music: 'As far as the Trio [Suite] in A major is concerned, I have decided to withdraw from the public as far as possible such juvenilia, which I no longer accept entirely.'[1] Similar issues were discussed in his correspondence with Otto Andersson, who was working on a Sibelius biography. In general, Sibelius was critical of his early works (all chamber music). On 28 February Andersson inquired about the existence of music for a Sonata for Violin and Piano in F major, the Piano Quintet in G minor and the 'so-called Korpo Trio' (1886).[2] On 8 May 1945 Sibelius wrote unequivocally: 'The main thing is that the compositions are not published under any conditions, not even after my death, and I want to take this opportunity to ensure you take my wish to heart.'[3] The quintet has now been available on a commercial recording for years, and all the juvenilia and fragments are being prepared for release on CD. They include three piano quartets (in C major, G minor and D minor)[4] and various trios from the 1880s. However, there has yet to be an adequately critical debate about the ethics of dealing with the composer's quite clear position – particularly because such productions are an unexpected blessing not only for Sibelius scholars but also for the owners of the copyrights.

Because the Piano 'Cannot Sing': The Sonatinas and Other Rough Pearls

Since the Glenn Gould recordings, the Sonatinas for Piano of 1912 (in F sharp minor, E major, and B flat minor) have been considered by connoisseurs to number among the finest works in the early twentieth-century repertoire for piano. They stand out for showing the courage to employ unusual voice progression, technical solutions and refined periodicity. Much as in the case of the symphonies, the title 'Sonatina' is not arbitrary but neither should it be regarded as the sole key to interpreting the character

[1] National Archive Box 34.

[2] Åbo Akademi.

[3] Ibid.

[4] Cf. Revers 1999, pp. 337–53. On the juvenilia for piano, see also Gräsbeck 2003 (commentary with catalogue of works).

FIG. 32. *Religioso*, op. 78, no. 3 (first page).

of the pieces. It merely shows that the pieces, dedicated to the piano teacher of his talented nine-year-old daughter, Katarina, are stylistically and gesturally anchored in the best classical tradition. They begin where Beethoven left off in his middle period piano sonatas (e.g., op. 31): they are grand sonatas in miniature. The spirit of Beethoven in these three-movement bagatelles can be traced here: for example, in the conclusion of the first movement in the Sonatina in F sharp minor, and similarly the conclusion of the second movement (apart from the last three measures); the type of polyphony in bars 9 ff. and similar passages in the first movement of the Sonatina in

E major; the rhythmic introduction of the final turn in the third movement of that Sonatina; or the recitative on the basis of continuous pedalling in the first movement of the Sonatina in B flat minor, which is similarly to the 'piano assai' or '*pp* sempre' in the second movement of Beethoven's Piano Sonata no. 17, op. 31, no. 2. Then there is the idiosyncratically Sibelian mixture of monophony, polyphony and harmony; the use of register; and the deliberately employed, although rare pedal effects.

The challenge for the interpreter lies in bringing out the aura that distinguishes an aesthetically successfully miniature from artefacts of just any length — of which Sibelius composed not a few, especially for piano — for example, by making use in performance of rhythmic freedom and timbral imagination. A differentiated approach to agogic accents is encouraged, measure by measure, by the innovative, chromatically accented harmony from this experimental, Expressionistic period around 1910, although here there is already a clear parallel tendency to classicism.

The wonderful cycle *Kyllikki*, op. 41 (1904), has been somewhat overshadowed by the Sonatinas. The title is the name of a female character in the *Kalevala*, in the stories about the 'Don Juan' Lemminkäinen. Because Sibelius' titles are so often interchangeable — both in so-called programme music and, apparently, even with titles such as 'Sonatina' or 'Symphony' in absolute music — there is no reason to believe that the name Kyllikki offers an important clue to the source of his inspiration. Sibelius wrote to the American pianist Helen Levin on 8 May 1936: 'but I have no folkloristic intentions in the music so you must approach it quite abstractly like a sonata and only closely follow the musical signs'.[1] This communication was not only to deny the seemingly obvious (the programme that should not do any harm even if it was interchangeable) but more importantly, far beyond this, to point to the dominant classicist processes of the composition *quasi una sonata*. The subtitle, 'Three Lyric Pieces for Piano', which can lead to misunderstandings in light of another work, the *Pensées lyriques*, op. 40, suggests that the three movements can be regarded outside of the context of the cycle. The second movement, Andantino, is particularly interesting. Here we encounter a master of heterogeneity. The piece contains many unprepared transitions and fleeting melodic gestures that remain undeveloped, like loose bricks. Right at the beginning, Sibelius plays with metrical ambiguity in the context of a motif that has absorbed the sadness and ponderousness of the intonation of the songs of Volga bargemen (though the similarity is not enough to suspect a conscious quotation or *topos*) — though in the appropriate tempo (Andantino, definitely not Grave), it sounds more graceful. Although the technical difficulties of the entire cycle call for great professionalism, the peculiar syntax of the characters represents, as it does in the Sonatinas, the real hurdle to a sensitive interpretation. The main difficulty for the pianist is giving time to the scattered ideas. Briskly running through the music is as little suited to its art as exaggerated melancholy. As always in Sibelius' piano

[1] Draft letter; National Archive Box 35.

music, every note and every gesture — not just the obvious ones — has to be weighed individually.

Although the *Kyllikki* Suite is one of the few bravura pieces idiomatic to the piano in Sibelius' oeuvre, the reaction of the pianist Edward Weiss of Berlin, who continued to correspond with Sibelius even after emigrating to the United States, is easy to understand: Weiss wanted to propose some pianistic changes, which his Finnish student Leea Isotalo could implement. She was not permitted to take her sheet music with her when she left Germany during the war, so that it was lost, along with her letters from Sibelius. As she recalls, however, the changes were bass doublings — that is, just details. Nevertheless, on 26 November 1941 she cautiously asked Sibelius for his opinion, and he drafted a reply: 'Because I have no idea what sort of changes you mean, I cannot say anything about that. However, I doubt that Mr Weiss can understand the style of *Kyllikki* in general. Nevertheless, I suspect that the changes do not contain anything that violates the style. I am, by the way, grateful and pleased that you are performing my compositions and please give my best regards to Mr Weiss.'[1] This draft letter is a revealing document of the nature of his correspondence and proof that he tolerated revisions — at least in piano music.

Other works for piano, such as the Sonata in F major of 1893 (which was certainly influenced by the summery atmosphere of the period in Ruovesi when he wrote it), the numerous lyric pieces and the character pieces fill out our picture of Sibelius, especially as a composer with a more light-hearted muse. This is particularly true of the two *Rondinos*, op. 68: the first in the style of a nocturne, the second as a quick pendant, quasi impromptu, which has parallels to the gestures of Wieniawski's best character polonaises and is perfect for performance as a rarity at the end of an ambitious piano recital. The pieces were written because the Viennese publisher Emil Hertzka of Universal Edition was unwilling in 1912 to publish two old violin pieces — which were ultimately published with the appropriate numbering as op. 2: *Romance* in B minor and *Epilogue* — with a higher opus number that would make them seem more recent but the correct date (1888) unless he was offered something new at the same time.[2] Hertzka did not want to harm the young Universal Edition's reputation for supporting contemporary expression (Schoenberg, Milhaud, and so on). In August 1913, Sibelius sent Hertzka (as well as other publishers, such as Zimmermann) his tone poem *The Bard*; in the 1930s, Universal was interested in the *Lemminkäinen Legends*, which had not yet been published. But neither project was ultimately published in Vienna.

Many of his piano pieces make it clear the composer was able to compose music by improvising. The six *Impromptus*, op. 5 (1890–3), represent fascinating experiments with gestures, with reminiscences of the unpublished juvenilia. *Polonaise* and

[1] National Library Coll. 206: 17, draft letter, 20 December 1941.

[2] National Archive Box 47; Emil Hertzka to JS, 27 September 1912. JS' letters to the publishing house are published in Krones 2003a, pp. 52 ff. The autograph copies in the archives of the publishing house are also illustrated ibid., pp. 35 ff.

Rondoletto from *Pensées lyriques*, op. 40 (1912–16), come across as entertainingly pianistic, both featuring carefree tonal and rhythmic turns. The play with harmony in *Pensée mélodique* from the same cycle is even more exalted. *The Spruce*, op. 75, no. 5 (1914–19), is a timeless salon piece as well as an extraordinary example of Sibelius' clever approach to the *topos* of the waltz. *The Spruce* demonstrates, even more convincingly than *Valse triste*, the opportunities Sibelius would have had as a popular composer if he had not 'had it in him' to 'do something bigger' as well.[1] A stylistically and melodically interesting bridge between *Finlandia* (1900) and the Sonatina in B flat minor (1912) is the brief, pianistically effective *Romance*, op. 24, no. 9 (1901). If that was indeed the year it was written, it cannot have been a preparatory work for the *Finlandia Hymn* (or rather the A flat major section in *Finlandia*, op. 26, of 1900). Hepokoski believes that this motif was derived from Arvid and Emil Genetz's choral work *Herää, Suomi!* of 1882 (especially bars 36 ff.) — with a further reference to Robert Schumann's op. 46[2] — which is possible, but not compelling, given the simple melody. Whereas Genetz's patriotic choral work is little known today, the *Finlandia Hymn* became, with a text by Veikko Antero Koskenniemi added in 1940, the unofficial national anthem (even though it was written as the finale of an orchestral work), with its vision of 'näytit maailmalle' (you showed it to the world). This kind of sideswipe is lacking in Zachris Topelius' and Fredrik Pacius' love of landscape and homeland of 1848, as manifested in the national anthem *Vårt land* (or *Maamme* in Finnish).

Despite interesting details and numerous motifs cross-referencing the orchestral works, there is a risk that the works for piano create the impression of being the result of writing too much and of arbitrary melodic invention. That is in part because in his small compositions Sibelius revealed himself as a composer who was extraordinarily talented musically but did not always undertake the final revisions and formation. Evaluating the smaller compositions, without being held up by the fine polish of compositional abstraction, provides a profound look into the creative soul of a composer who brilliantly juggled the means of Romanticism and late nineteenth-century modernity. It is therefore all the more surprising that he was almost never prepared to strike folkloristic notes. Despite numerous requests from patrons and publishers, he would not even provide characteristic sounds of his homeland even when he was in financial straits. One exception — though it is not really an exception — is the six folksong arrangements for piano: *Finnish Folksongs* (1902–3), which are some of the most advanced modern piano arrangements of folksongs immediately before and in part in parallel with Béla Bartók and have scarcely a trace of true folklore. The originality of the cycle is best demonstrated by *Fratricide* (no. 5, Andante con moto), which is also a setting of a painting of that name by Akseli Gallen-Kallela (1898). The three points of reference — the *Kalevala*, Gallen-Kallela and a folksong — probably sparked Sibelius' imagination in equal measure in this case. Sibelius places the simple

[1] JS to Martin Wegelius, 11 January 1891.

[2] Hepokoski 2001b, p. 328, and Hepokoski 2003.

Romance

FIG. 33. *Romance*, op. 24, no. 9 (opening).

melody, which would be harmonised in C sharp minor (the only notes that occur are $c\sharp^1$, $d\sharp^1$, e^1, $f\sharp^1$ and $g\sharp^1$), above the pedal point $F\sharp_1$ (moreover, a flexible middle voice results in a diminution of the tritone: *f♯–c–a–g♯–f♯*). He leaves this pedal point only briefly, when he shifts the melody to E minor (with *A* in the bass). This is probably where he comes closest to the ambitious level of the construction of his Sonatinas.

For the interpretation of his lyrics Sibelius always desired the *bel canto* style rather than *l'art de dire.*[1]

4.3 Vocal Music

Songs also 'without Words' in the Context of the Period

Sibelius' songs for solo voice and piano represent 'his innermost self', not '*pièces d'occasion*',[2] whereas there was often a specific occasion for the choral works. Nevertheless, even choral music is a treasure in the composer's oeuvre that receives far too little attention. One of the highlights among the choral songs is *Ej med klagan*, 'Till minnet av Albert Edelfelt 24. 8. 1905' (Not with lamentation), written in memory of the great painter. It was not just solemn occasions that inspired him to compose choral music, however, but also brilliant poems. The choral music on texts from the *Kalevala* and *Kanteletar*, including the *Rakastava* (The lover) cycle and *Saarella palaa* (Fire on the island), are truly genuine in style. Somewhat more conventional, but all the more artful, is his choral music with Swedish texts for Svenska Folkskolans Vänner (Friends of the Swedish Elementary School), especially *Män från slätten och havet* (People of land and sea), op. 65, no. 1, written at the request of the Sängarfest (the choir festival of the Svenska Folkskolans Vänner) of 1912 in Vaasa, and *Drömmarna* (Dreams; 1917). The latter was published by the organisation but not performed.

Aino Ackté and Ida Ekman encouraged Sibelius to write songs. Between 1903 and 1915, Ackté, the greatest Finnish opera diva of the era, inspired him to write expressive melodies with a wide range.[3] Her art is well represented by the tone poem *Luonnotar* of 1913 and the brilliant soprano part in the Graduation Cantata of 1894; the songs with piano accompaniment 'Jubal', op. 35, no. 1; 'Teodora', op. 35, no. 2; 'Höstkväll' (Autumn evening), op. 38, no. 1; 'Fåfäng önskan' (Idle wishes), op. 61, no. 7, 'Kyssen' (The kiss), op. 72, no. 3; and 'Kaiutar' (The echo nymph), op. 72, no. 4. Sibelius wrote of Ida Ekman in his diary on 17 January 1916: 'This wonderful singer is bearable even in her private life. Natural and conversational as she is. I cannot bear the chitchat addiction of my other singers.' On 2 August 1924, by contrast, he wrote of Ackté and her husband, General Bruno Jalander: 'The Acktés here; day now *aus* ['over' in German]. Terrible emptiness in their hearts and heads! They are friendly people, but they talk only of themselves.' In the 1890s Ackté was considered to be in the international avant-garde in her field. In 1900 she was a soloist at the Grand Opéra de Paris. As Marguerite, Elsa and Salome (she was probably a little too lyrical for this last role, but she was also one of the very first singers to dance in the role as well), she enjoyed great success especially in Paris but also in New York, London and Leipzig. But her

[1] Newmarch 1939, p. 55.

[2] Levas 1960b, p. 85.

[3] Karlson 1993, p. 19, describes her voice.

character was (as far as we can judge from the documents) problematic. In December 1910 she irritated Sibelius with an advertising campaign intended to put him in a secondary role: as 'producer of commercial goods', as he wrote to Axel Carpelan. This disgruntlement put an end to a promising plan based on Edgar Allan Poe's 'The Raven'.[1] Sibelius' explanation, which helps to correct the common view that his work on the Fourth Symphony was the reason, demonstrated his cautious way of arguing in public (here in a letter to Rosa Newmarch): 'concerning Madame Ackté [...]. The matter took a very different turn from what was initially presented to me. The advertisements above all. Because the advertisements described in detail precisely what the composition is, what direction it takes, etc., even though the work is not finished, it made the whole composition process impossible for me. Moreover, they wanted to present me as a completely unknown composer — in Munich! Etc.'[2] The tone between them did not improve again until 1912, but then, the very next year, Sibelius wrote the ideally matched masterpiece *Luonnotar* for Ackté.

Ida Ekman's lyrical art, which Sibelius put to use many times from 1890 to 1917, was shown to best advantage in the songs on flowers, op. 88.[3] Her dramatic abilities are revealed in 'Svarta rosor' (Black roses), op. 36, no. 1, her refinement in 'På verandan vid havet' (On a balcony by the sea), op. 38, no. 2. The latter was Sibelius' favourite song.[4] Both Ackté and Ekman were active internationally. The songs performed in a semi-public context of salons contributed worldwide to a better understanding of the composer's musical language at a time when large orchestras were not yet ready to risk a Sibelius symphony. The evening at Otto Lessmann's home in Berlin in 1900 when Sibelius established contact with prominent figures in the Allgemeiner Deutscher Musikverein, at which Ekman and her husband performed, or the well-meaning but apparently unsuccessful attempt to present Sibelius by performing his songs at the Music Club in London, which was connected to Queen's Hall and the conductor Henry Wood, initiator of the Proms, clarifies the role played by his songs.[5] Sibelius composed few songs after Ackté and Ekman had ended their careers.[6] The pianists were important as well, for the special quality of Sibelius' songs lies, to no trivial extent, in the piano part. In Finland, Ackté performed with Oskar Merikanto; Ekman with her husband, Karl, the father of the Sibelius-author Karl Ekman (junior). Both Merikanto and Ekman (senior) were leading authorities on musical life in Finland. Ekman was the first prominent pianist to dedicate himself to Sibelius' works for piano.

[1] In her direct way, Ackté reported on the events to her mother, Emmy Ackté, for example, on 13 October 1910. Cf. Vainio and Salolainen 2002, 315 ff. JS, in turn, wrote to Axel Carpelan on 12 December 1910; cf. Dahlström 2010, p. 295.

[2] National Archive Box 121; JS to Rosa Newmarch, 1 January 1911 (in German).

[3] Levas 1960b, p. 85. See also Gornaya 2003.

[4] Levas 1960b, p. 86. On the sketches, see Tiilikainen 2003.

[5] See Bax 1943, pp. 61–2; quoted in Rickards 1997, 106; see also Erik W. Tawaststjerna 1986, 106 ff.

[6] See Tiilikainen 2000, p. ix.

The poets set by Sibelius could not be more different. Newmarch – who translated some of the poems into English herself, by the laboriously roundabout way of the composer's own rough translations into German – made that clear with two examples:

> On the whole we can see two sides of Sibelius' mind most clearly reflected in his songs. […] settings of Runeberg's clear-cut, luminous and classic lyrics […] fit like a glove; but his art as a songwriter touches its highest achievement in his music to the mystical and visionary poetry of his friend Rydberg. […] For the interpretation of his lyrics Sibelius always desired the *bel canto* style rather than *l'art de dire*. Anything of the nature of point-making or tricks to overemphasize the significance of the text displeased him. He often makes great demands upon the singer by his austerity of accompaniment.[1]

Sibelius supposedly said that his songs could also 'be sung without words', or expressed more judiciously: 'They are not so dependent on poetry as the songs of many other composers.'[2] On the other hand, Sibelius noted in his diary on 3 December 1910, still working on Viktor Rydberg's translation of Poe's 'The Raven': 'Doubts about the text. "Words" are always the onus in my art.' In general, he took texts seriously; he understood 'onus' to mean an obligation, not just a burden. His statement about songs 'without words' did not in any way mean that the poems were interchangeable. He was, however, convinced – in the spirit of Symbolism – that music made the text almost superfluous, but that means a particularly close reading of the text. Occasionally he had doubts about his point of view: 'Possibly I have understood the poet incorrectly, but that doesn't matter, since the new idea is supposed to illustrate the impression the poem made on me.'[3] This comprehensive stance was not always his point of departure when composing a song, but it was at least possible and could relieve the 'onus'.

One reason why his songs in Swedish and several of the six songs in Finnish are often more experimental than his songs in German is the text. Swedish and Finnish literature were enjoying a heyday toward the end of the nineteenth century. Avant-garde authors such as August Strindberg and Henrik Ibsen were active in Scandinavia, and in Finland writers also benefited from the equally advanced Russian literature of the period. Aleksis Kivi, Juhani Aho and Eino Leino in particular not only created the basis for Finnish poetry but at the same time defined with the pathos of their first flourishing a modern classicism that holds its own even today. They created a Finnish sound for literature. Sibelius' enormous respect for Kivi was expressed in the slightly grotesque, all too human but modest concern that if he also were buried in Tuusula, where Kivi was, and which was close to Ainola, a larger tombstone would be erected for him. Hence he did not wish to be buried in the same cemetery

1 Newmarch 1939, p. 55.
2 Levas 1960b, p. 85.
3 JS to Aino, 27 January 1891.

but instead on private ground, as was eventually done.[1] Although his songs function 'without words', the language represents a hurdle outside those circles familiar with Swedish if one wishes to avoid translations. Not even in Finland is Sibelius recognised by the majority of citizens as a composer of art songs, since only six of his songs are in Finnish, and one of these is a Christmas song. Only sixteen of his songs are not in Swedish. Unfortunately, only a single, not especially significant song was written in English: *Hymn to Thaïs*.[2] Nine songs set German texts, six of them in op. 50 (1906). They represent an entertaining concession to the German public: well composed but superficial. Another German text stands isolated in op. 72 as no. 5, a collection reduced by adverse circumstances: its first two songs disappeared at the very beginning of the First World War en route from Leipzig to London, on their way from the headquarters of Breitkopf & Härtel to its English office.[3] 'Der Wanderer und der Bach' (The wanderer and the stream) by Martin Greif (Friedrich Hermann Frey) is a brief aphoristic poem that marks the parallels between a wanderer and a stream without any original depth of thought.

Op. 50, no. 1, a setting of Arthur Fitger's 'Lenzgesang' (A song of spring),[4] belongs to the genre of cheerful spring songs, along with 'Maj' (May), op. 57, no. 4; 'Vårtagen' (The spell of springtide), op. 61; 'Vårförnimmelser' (The coming of spring), op. 86, no. 1; and two of the 'flower songs' of op. 88: 'Blåsippan' (The anemone) and 'Sippan' (The primrose). 'Lenzgesang' seems more masculine, in part because of the bass-heavy piano part but also because of the content of the poem. The poet described spring in the woods from the perspective of a forester with a harmless romantic tone (not unlike that in Karl August Tavaststjerna's 'Vårförnimmelser'), without philosophical symbolism and metaphysics and especially without using spring as a political metaphor in the manner of the German Romantics. Ambiguity and metaphor are completely foreign to the poem. In its distance from the urban intellectualism and decadence of the time, 'Lenzgesang' is already almost advanced postmodernism.

Sibelius gives a distinctive rhythm to the diction of the poem. He emphasises with melodic accents the sequences of short, hard syllables that are common in German. If it were not for its unambiguous tonality, the song could be equated with Darius Milhaud's *Machines agricoles*, op. 56 (especially with 'La Fouilleuse-Draineuse'), as its rhythmic verve is so progressive. It is also plausible to compare it to Mahler's 'Der Trunkene im Frühling' (The drunkard in spring) from the cycle *Das Lied von der Erde* of 1907, though Sibelius avoids the pathos of the successors to Wagner and creates a more homogeneous construct without the implicit drama. The poem 'Sehnsucht' ('Yearning'; set as op. 50, no. 2) by Emil Rudolf Weiss, who is primarily known as a typographer, reveals Sibelius' potential as a composer of entertaining operetta melo-

[1] Salmenhaara 1984, p. 428.

[2] Text by Arthur H. Travers Borgström. See Borgström's letters to JS: National Library Coll. 206: 39.

[3] Erik W. Tawaststjerna 1996, p. 102.

[4] From the collection *Fahrendes Volk* (Oldenburg: Schulze, 1875). Several songs from op. 50 are from Hans Bethge's popular anthology *Deutsche Lyrik seit Liliencron* (Leipzig: Hesse, 1905).

FIG. 34. 'Sehnsucht' (Longing), op. 50, no. 2 (opening).

dies. Here too the accompaniment moves in the bass register. The piano writing is ambitious, with unusual rhythms and chromatic, closely set, low chords, whereas the text suggests associations with somewhat later hit tunes: 'Oft am langen Tage, seufz ich, ach! nach dir, fühl ich dich mir nahe, sprech ich so mit dir' (Often during the long day, I sigh, alas! for you, I feel close to you, I speak to you). Weiss's trivial rhymes often include 'mir' (to me) and 'dir' (to you). The 6/8 time ('comodo', 'poco passionate' and 'pesante ma dolce') is not only ambiguous in phrasing (3+3 or 2+2+2 with frequent notations of accelerando and ritardando), but also permits various dance characters, especially the fashionable waltz character with heroic accents à la polonaise.

The low literary rank of the text of Sibelius' Schumannesque setting of Margarete Susman's 'Im Feld ein Mädchen singt' (In the field a girl is singing), op. 50, no. 3, is beyond doubt, as is the indirectly projected elegy she is intending. The lyrical self experiences an evening mood, hears a sad song and suspects the girl singing is experiencing a similar mood: 'Ich möchte zu ihr gehen. Wir müßten uns wohl verstehen, da sie so traurig singt.' (I would like to go to her. We would surely understand each other, since she sings so mournfully.) One of the unusual qualities of the song is a metrical ambiguity: the piano part begins syncopated on the second beat, and the voice enters on the upbeat with regular crotchet notes, which causes a temporary metrical fluctuation. This transcends the popular song character that the text alone would legitimate. Also grounded in the tradition of the German Lied is Sibelius' approach to Richard Dehmel's 'Aus banger Brust' ('O, Wert Thou Here'), op. 50, no. 4. Much as in the first song of this cycle, the rhythms are varied, while the piano accompaniment ensures a lively *perpetuum mobile* (Con moto). The establishment of the key at the beginning is also polyvalent harmonically, since the clear D minor scale of the vocal part is only hesitantly confirmed by the piano. By way of F minor and B flat 7^0 (diminished), the piece modulates to G sharp minor – not functionally but chromatically. Later similar bridges lead from G sharp minor to D major (G sharp major triad, G sharp major seventh chord with diminished fifth ($7+/5^0$), G sharp diminished major chord, D major 6/4). Because of the added minor and major seconds, all of the chords sound dissonant in context. The harmony and the restless gestures of the piano sum up the Dehmel poem musically without going into the details of the natural elements mentioned in the text. Only in the melody of the voice part did Sibelius take up Dehmel's erotic elements. His naturalisms are not reflected in the piano part.

Sibelius also realised Dehmel's 'Die stille Stadt' (The silent city), op. 50, no. 5, using atmospheric chords that do not call the tonality into question but move within a floating sound field. It invites being programmed with Richard Strauss's and Alma Mahler's settings in a concert. The latter are not only modern and Impressionistic like Debussy's piano piece *La cathédrale engloutie* but also accompany the monotonous upper part with traditional chords. Sibelius concentrated on the final lines – 'Doch als den Wandrer graute, / da ging ein Lichtlein auf im Grund; / und durch den Rauch und Nebel / begann ein leiser Lobgesang / aus Kindermund' (Yet as the wanderer shuddered, / a small light began to shine below; and through the smoke and fog, / a quiet song of praise began to rise / from a child's mouth) – rather than underscoring the gloomy, foggy atmosphere of the beginning. The accompanying chords strongly emphasise the treble register. Sibelius emphasises Dehmel's asymmetrical metre with prolonged notes on the word 'Kindermund' (B major, F major, G minor).

After initial reminiscences of Debussy in 'Rosenlied' (Rose song; text by Anna Ritter), op. 50, no. 6, he composed in a style close to Mahler's — and yet unmistakably Sibelian. By means of dissonances, shifts in key and an independent piano texture, he designed a miniature that from the outset brings out the ambiguity of the rich metaphor of the text — a lyric description of a flower, but one that strives to be more than that. For example, he sharply accentuates the line 'Von Liebe gebrochen, zu Liebe gebracht' (Broken by love, made to love) by means of sevenths in the bass and likewise the lines 'er senkt unsre Schönheit verwelkt in die Gruft' (it lowers our beauty into the grave) and 'Der Lenz strich vorüber und küsste uns leis, / der Tag ward so still und die Nächte so heiss' (Spring swept past and kissed us quietly; / the day grew so still and the nights so hot). On the whole, op. 50 is a collection of sensitively worked-out songs in German, which bring to light unfamiliar sides of the composer. In comparison to his most ambitious songs, such as op. 57 (Josephson), op. 50 does not seem experimental at all, but its details are elaborated more carefully; the songs work well. After all, most of the texts are very popular in style. The Dehmel poems, the only ones that can be called significant poetry, are the exception, accounting for the stylistic variety in a collection without the cohesion of a cycle.

Sibelius' closeness to the bourgeois romance of Scandinavian origin, which was a result of his biography as a physician's son from Hämeenlinna, is clear in many of the songs. Educated Finns in the nineteenth century were particularly fond of the poems of Johan Ludvig Runeberg — and not just 'Vårt land' (Our country), Fredrik Pacius' setting of which had been the national anthem since 13 May 1848. Whereas the Finnish elements were made manifest by Kivi's plays and novels — *Kullervo*, *Nummisuutari* (Heath cobblers), and *Seitsemän veljestä* (translated as *Seven Brothers*) — and led to a radicalisation of realism and idealism, in *Fänrik Ståls sägner* (translated originally as *The Songs of Ensign Stål*, later more correctly as his *Tales*) of 1860, the year of Kivi's *Kullervo*, Runeberg created a masterpiece that heroically integrated Finnish culture into Western European history.

Runeberg had been Sibelius' father's Latin teacher.[1] The art historian Walter von Konow, one of Sibelius' most faithful and oldest friends, was the nephew of Colonel Carl Johan von Konow, whom Runeberg memorialised in *Fänrik Ståls sägner*. These are tales of the semi-Napoleonic war between Russia and Sweden 1808–9 after which Finland became part of the Russian Empire — a sort of collective psychotherapy for the depressive Finnish people by means of narrative literature. Such connections like that between the families Runeberg, Sibelius and Konow made Sibelius' identification with the great poet easier. Tawaststjerna even wrote of the Runeberg 'cult' of the composer's father, Christian Sibelius, and at the age of six, after the death of his father, the composer was permitted to visit Runeberg in Borgå (Porvoo), not far from Lovisa. As late as 1912, Sibelius defended Runeberg's status as 'national writer', even though he wrote in Swedish, which led to conflicts with Finnish nationalist idealists such as

[1] See Erik W. Tawaststjerna 1976, pp. 8 and 19.

Heikki Klemetti. Klemetti's letter to Sibelius on 4 February 1912 shows that Sibelius did not approve of Klemetti's refusal, based on his aggressively anti-Swedish attitudes, to conduct the choir of the University of Helsinki at the Runeberg statue in order to honour the poet.[1] Here too Sibelius found himself between the two fronts – though he allowed himself to be appropriated by both.

Runeberg's poems – such as 'Till Frigga' (To Frigga), 'Norden' (The North), 'Under strandens granar' ('Neath the Fir Trees'), 'Sippan' (The primrose), and of course 'Serenad' (1888; Sibelius' first published work, though in a collection called *Det sjungande Finland* and edited by Sibelius' teacher Martin Wegelius[2]), and the orchestral song *Arioso*, op. 3 (1911) – are by far the best represented among Sibelius' solo songs, with twenty-seven settings altogether. Runeberg was also the author of the texts for Sibelius' first separately published work, Seven Songs, op. 13 (1892). Alongside Runeberg, Zachris Topelius, the librettist of the first Finnish (albeit Swedish-language), eclectically loyalist opera *Kung Karls Jakt* (The hunt of King Charles; 1852) by Pacius, was another representative of the conservative, educated bourgeoisie of the mid-nineteenth century. This brilliant poet and author (unjustly remembered today primarily as a writer of fairy tales) also earned the status of national poet, especially since his intellectual and political achievements did much to unify a culturally divided region in terms of one striving towards nationality. Sibelius wrote to Mauri Noro on 22 February 1952: 'Topelius has been so important to me since childhood that it is impossible for me to say how I was influenced by him. One can probably say that an entire era in Finland was permeated by the spirit of Topelius.'[3] But as an advocate of multicultural pragmatism Topelius never became an icon of any of the strong parties, neither of the Finnish- nor Swedish-orientated cultural nationalists, unlike Runeberg and Eino Leino (just to name two). And even Sibelius was only inspired by him to write five brief songs. Sibelius' closer friends among poets included the naturalist Karl August Tavaststjerna, who like him primarily spoke Swedish but was inclined, albeit in a nonconformist way, to the Fennoman movement;[4] the *Euterpe* circle member Bertel Gripenberg (e.g., 'Teodora'); Mikael Lybeck[5] ('I systrar, I bröder, I älskande par!' (Ye sisters, ye brothers, ye loving couples), op. 86, no. 6); and Hjalmar Procopé ('Små flickorna' (Young ladies), 1920). This last song testifies to Sibelius' feeling for modern, metropolitan themes and wit – typewriters, telephones and snack machines are all mentioned: 'De gå med käcka miner / och morgonyra luggar / till surr av skrivmaskiner/ och telefonhallå. // […] Vår frihet vi ej sälja, / om ock bland symamseller / vår middag vi få svälja / på första automat.'

[1] National Archive Box 22.

[2] See Tiilikainen 2000, p. x.

[3] National Archive; copy in the Tawaststjerna Collection.

[4] Erik W. Tawaststjerna 1986, p. 136. His other settings of poems by Karl A. Tavaststjerna (no relation to the author Erik Tawaststjerna) include 'Dolce far niente', 'När jag drömmer', 'Långsamt som kvällskyn', 'Och finns det en tanke'.

[5] Even more important is Lybeck's Symbolistist play *Ödlan* (The lizard), for which JS composed the music in 1909; see Erik W. Tawaststjerna 1986, pp. 129 and 149 ff.

Procopé is more important as the author of the play *Belshazzar's Feast*, whose setting (op. 51, 1906–7), especially as a concert suite, established Sibelius' reputation as an expert on the Orient (frequently used in early film music). Of Swedish poets, Ernst Josephson, whom Sibelius had read as a youth,[1] is represented by eleven major poems, including 'Svarta rosor', 'Jubal' and 'Näcken' (The elf king , a male freshwater spirit), op. 57, no. 8; and Viktor Rydberg by seven: 'I natten' (In the night), op. 38, no. 3; 'Vattenplask' (Lapping waters), op. 61, no. 2; 'Kyssen', 'Höstkväll' and his 'favourite song': 'På verandan vid havet', op. 38, no. 2; an eighth song is thought to be lost. Rydberg was also the author of 'Skogsrået' (The Wood Nymph). The melodrama *Skogsrået* was premiered in April 1895. There is also an early song of the same title (1888–9). Rydberg had also written the text for Sibelius' *War Song of Tyrtaeus* for male choir (1899, one of the strongest nationalist gestures according to the Finnish interpretation during the decades of Russian oppression) and, like Gripenberg as well, for several important works for choir. The only poems in Finnish that Sibelius set for voice and piano were by August V. Forsman ('Souda, souda sinisorsa' (no op. no.) and 'Illalle', op. 17, no. 6), 'Ilmari Calamnius' ('Lastu lainehilla', op. 17, no. 7) and 'Larin-Kyösti'[2] ('Kaiutar', op. 72, no. 4).

Sibelius' sole significant contribution to the orchestral song — a fashionable genre at the turn of the century, prominently represented by Gustav Mahler — was *Luonnotar*. A setting of Erik Johan Stagnelius' 'Serenad' for baritone and orchestra (1895) was his first effort with orchestra and voice after *Kullervo* and the Graduation Cantatas of the 1890s. It was followed by *The Rapid-Rider's Brides*, op. 33 (1897) and Runeberg's *Arioso* op. 3 (1911), as well as several arrangements of songs with piano accompaniment: 'Se'n har jag ej frågat mera' (Then I questioned no further), op. 17, no. 1, 1903; 'Höstkväll' (1904); 'På verandan vid havet' (1903); and 'Hertig Magnus' (Duke Magnus) op. 57, no. 6, 1909), and so on.[3] By contrast, the 'tone poem for soprano and orchestra' *Luonnotar* (1913) is a genuine masterpiece about the creation of the world.[4] The main character of the scene set to music in it is Ilmatar or Luonnotar, a Janus-faced goddess, the nymph of nature and the air, freely adapted from the 'Genesis' (Canto 1, lines 111–242) of the *Kalevala*. The vocal part, written for Ackté, is for a range a semitone wider than even his most ambitious songs for soprano and piano: the highest note is a magnificent $C\flat^3$; the lowest is a *b*. This tone poem is occasionally listed simply as a '*Kalevala* setting',[5] but it is one example for the composer's specific, by no means uncritical relationship to the epic collection of poetry. The theme had

[1] Erik W. Tawaststjerna 1976, p. 20; Tawaststjerna lists Topelius, Runeberg, Tavaststjerna, Rydberg, Gustaf Fröding, Josephson, Gripenberg and Erik Axel Karlfeld as poets Sibelius read as a youth.

[2] Larin-Kyösti was the pseudonym of Kyösti Larson, a childhood friend of JS.

[3] This repertoire was published in the *Jean Sibelius Complete Works*, vol. 8.1 (ed. Timo Virtanen).

[4] Not to be confused with a 'Luonnotar' sketch from 1905, one of the unspecified preparations for the Third Symphony; see Salmenhaara 1984, p. 210, but also ibid., p. 221. For more detail, see Hepokoski 1996.

[5] Cf. Altenburg 1998, p. 166. *En saga* and *Finlandia* are mentioned there as being based on the *Kalevala*, though clearly they are not.

* See the Critical Remarks.

FIG. 35. *Luonnotar*, bars 47–58. The passage illustrated here depicts a gust of wind ('tuulenpuuska') and a crown of foam ('meren kuohuille'), where the sound is intensified by two harps. With Tranquillo assai begins a lament by Ilmatar (goddess of the air, parallel to Luonnotar, the goddess of nature), who loses her virginity and thus contributes to the creation of the world as 'luonnotar' and 've'en emonen' – in essence, goddess of nature and water.

occupied him earlier in 1894 in connection with plans for an opera, as he wrote to Aino from Germany on 28 July: 'I am thinking about my opera. The first act has the problem that the melodic motif of Luonnotar is in a minor key and is rhythmically weak, so there is no contrast to the first recitative. Strange that I have recognised this only now. The motif has to be at once dreamy and lyrical. I let the wind blow through the entire first act.' We even find the wind in the orchestral song *Luonnotar*, just about twenty years later. The minor key has now developed into a complex mixture of tonal, chromatic, modal and octatonic structures. Just three years before completing the 'tone poem', he wrote in his diary on 3 December 1910: 'Took up the *Kalevala* and it stunned me — how much I have grown out of this naive poetry.' This feeling is manifest in *Luonnotar* as a free '*Kalevala* setting'.

This attitude makes it clear how thoroughly he had to intervene in the form of the text.[1] His interventions are 'authentic' insofar as traditional *runo* singers present their own interpretation of the stories, sagas, myths and legends. Elias Lönnrot, the editor of the *Kalevala*, also saw himself as just a 'singer' who transcribed the works and gave a name to the tradition.[2] Most likely he did even more by writing a substantial number of lines himself. Because Sibelius had direct contact with the tradition not only through the *Kalevala* but also in the homes of musicians in Karelia and in the home of Larin Paraske, at least in Helsinki and possibly also in Porvoo, he could claim for himself a similar role. It argues against this model, however, that he deviated from the trochaic tetrameter otherwise well established in the tradition. The beginning of his setting is faithful to its model, but then it becomes freer, though retaining the rhythm, and ultimately treats the number of syllables per line independently of the trochees. It follows neither the old version of 1835, which lacks the section on Ilmatar and Luonnotar, nor the abridged school version of *Kalevala* of 1862, the latest of the editions by Lönnrot. His starting point was the so-called new, most refined edition of 1849.[3] He treats the text of the first Canto (lines 111 ff.), which is a supplementary insertion into the structure of the *Kalevala* of 1835 (a more excursive explanation of the brief reference to Ilmatar as the mother of the world and the air and of the birth of Väinämöinen; lines 79 ff. in the 1835 version) in such a way that the *Kalevala*'s semantically extending doublings of lines (in the style and perhaps under the influence of the Psalms) are limited while particularly effective, spectacular lines are emphasised. Especially for listeners familiar with the original text, his version is an inventive summary.

The solid status of the original Finnish language in performances of *Luonnotar* was not so much the work of Sibelius as it was of Ackté. On 28 May 1913 he mentioned the composition project for the first time. On 17 July 1913 he wrote to Ackté that the

[1] See also Hepokoski 1996, pp. 121–2 and 125.

[2] Honko 1999, pp. viiff., and Salminen's preface to the abridged *Kalevala* in Salminen 2001, pp. 7 ff.

[3] On the versions, earlier work by others and their reception in the nineteenth century, see Honko 1999, pp. vii–viii.

text was taken 'extremely freely' from the first poem of the *Kalevala*. He proposed that the work be sung in French when performed abroad. She responded on 20 August that, as enthusiastic as she was about the finished composition, she rejected the idea decisively: 'It would be a shame to translate the text.' He had already made preparations for a translation, marking every line with the corresponding passage in the *Kalevala* that was its basis. His idea was that someone would find the passages in an existing translation of the *Kalevala* into English or French and set them poetically; he remarked that it was important to find 'good vowels'.[1] Ackté performed *Luonnotar* in Finnish on 10 September 1913 in Gloucester. Sibelius thoroughly reworked the score following the premiere – 'My mind has been preoccupied with it recently', as he wrote in his diary on 10 September 1913 – before sending it to Ackté and his publisher in Leipzig on 23 October, according to his diary.

From Runeberg's Salon Romance to Magical Modernity

Among the roots of Sibelius' more than one hundred songs, which makes them about one fifth of his oeuvre in sheer number, Valerie Sirén includes the German Lied from Schubert to Strauss, the Scandinavian romance, the songs of the French Impressionists and archaic song – the *runos*.[2] She believes *runos* to have been especially significant. In particular, she believes Larin Paraske's singing represented a stage of ancient popular culture that would have been unknown to Central European composers for centuries – or which, after Erich von Hornbostel's recordings, they were hoping to learn again. It was a living culture of singing in the nineteenth century that had nothing to do with the bourgeois salons in which the art song was at home, and hence it seemed to embody the cultural 'other'. The confrontation with such a tradition could have had fundamental consequences for Sibelius, giving birth to his most original and expressive style. Yet the importance of intoning *runos* à la Larin Paraske can be exaggerated. The art of the extroverted concert songs of Richard Strauss and Sergey Rachmaninoff – a diary entry on 29 June 1910 confirms he studied both composers – and Finnish, Russian and Swedish folksongs, Christmas songs and more were at least equally important as a foundation for his style. Moreover, Sibelius explicitly distanced himself from the overtly expressive, as a striking note following a performance reveals on 4 May 1918: 'A. Ackté's voice too emotive in "Maj" [op. 57, no. 4]. It has to be sung brighter and lighter, and in rhythm. It – our choir – "makes too much" out of every phrase. The absolute music I write is so exclusively musical and, strictly speaking, "independent" of the word that reciting it is out of place. Ida Ekman understood this, hence her superiority!' This is an almost Mozartian approach.

The diary entry reflects the change from the dramatic texts evoking nature in his early work to the Impressionist, aphoristic and intimate poems of the later songs. The

[1] JS to Aino Ackté, 14 August 1913; National Archive Box 16.

[2] Sirén 1996, p. 172.

Josephson songs (1909) mark the transition. The diary entry also calls attention to the individuality of his songs rather than a unified style. His admonition of 4 May 1918 is about just one song — 'Maj' — and by no means about 'Norden', 'Kaiutar' and a few other melodically lavish compositions (like *Luonnotar*) that refine the magic power of the archaic lament, a Karelian *itkuvirsi* (a sort of folkloric Requiem, performed only by women).

Valerie Sirén identified as other possible sources of influence the cantabile instrumental genres as well as arias from operas and Singspiels that Sibelius had known since youth. At the same time, Paraske's Karelian influence may have extended far beyond the song: from 'Kullervon valitus' (the final section of the third movement of the *Kullervo* symphony, which also exists as a concert aria with piano accompaniment) to the Violin Concerto and the late symphonies. Another model for the songs was the melodrama, which Sibelius had also encountered as an improvisational practice. Even *Kullervo* of 1892 was intended, until just a few months prior to completion, to contain melodramatic elements.[1] 'Teodora' is on the margins of that tradition. Long before he set it, Sibelius had accompanied a melodramatic improvisation of Bertel Gripenberg's poem by the Norwegian actress Johanne Dybwad.[2] One early melodrama is Rydberg's *Skogsrået* (1894), which also exists as an orchestral ballad with no vocal part; the history of its composition was complicated, and the existence of alternate versions gives it multiple meanings. It was preceded by a setting of Ellen Hackzell's *O, om du sett* (Oh, if you had seen; 1888[?]) for reciter and piano as well as of Runeberg's *Svartsjukans nätter* (Nights of jealousy; 1888) for reciter, violin, cello and piano. Melodramatic recitation is also found, along with choir and orchestra as a soloistic element, in *Snöfrid* (Rydberg, 1900), in Topelius' patriotic metaphor *Islossingen i Uleå älv* (The melting of the ice on the Uleå River; 1899) — which Erik Tawaststjerna suspected, based primarily on the patriotic context, was groundwork for *Finlandia*[3] — and in *Grevinnans konterfej* (The countess's portrait; 1906). One late work documents Sibelius' continued interest in the dramatic art form of the turn of the century: Gripenberg's *Ett ensamt skidspår* (The lonely ski trail; 1925) for orchestra and reciter. There are also several songs in his incidental music, such as 'Sången om Korsspindeln' (Fool's song of the spider, originally with harp) from *Kung Kristian II*, op. 27 (1898; text by Adolf Paul), and two Shakespearean songs from *Twelfth Night*, op. 60 (1909).

Even the later Runeberg cycle, op. 90, has been seen by Jukka Tiilikainen, the editor of the songs in the *Complete Edition*, as an expression of national nostalgia and a need for harmony in times of 'anarchy'.[4] Once again, notes in his diary are striking: 'Anarchy is increasing. My unhappy country. [...] Misery and lack of culture' (Diary,

1 See Salmenhaara 1984, p. 84.

2 Erik W. Tawaststjerna 1986, p. 99.

3 Erik W. Tawaststjerna 1976, pp. 219 ff.

4 Tiilikainen 2000, p. ix.

18 December 1917), 'Excesses of anarchy dreadful' (22 December 1917), 'Red Guard underway. […] Nature is jubilant and people are worse than animals' (29 January 1918). This is a rare note that may be read as criticism of the cruelty of nature (in contrast to culture and civilisation). But even in this context, Sibelius was concerned not least about his own work, as is clear from an entry on 3 January 1919: 'Politics more dismal than ever. And I believe that my livelihood as a composer is now impossible, since everything is about bolshevism, pro and con.' In such a thoroughly political environment he could not see any future for his art, and things soon got even worse.

With Runeberg's help, Sibelius constructed the romantic picture of the Finnish people in an age of national crisis. The music is – in the context of his new style after the Fourth Symphony – no longer late romantic (post-Wagnerian) but inward-looking in a classicist context. One of the most effective songs, and at the same time simplest in terms of the piano accompaniment, is 'Norden', op. 90, no. 1, 1917, a fascinating synthesis of vocalisation and consideration of Ida Ekman's vocal qualities. In changing metre and with 'Liberamente' melismas, the effect is evocative and the interpretation of the poem unconventional. Certainly the text is also an expression of a global vision – entirely free of regional connection and emphatically metaphysical: 'Den som från södern längtar, hans längtan söker en himmel.' (The man from the South who is yearning [for the North]; his yearning is for the sky.) It builds a broad formal arc. Harmonically, too, the resolution occurs only at the end, in the piano alone.

Sibelius' personal favourite, 'På verandan vid havet',[1] begins with a line that touches on the composer's relationship to nature: 'Minns du de skymnande böljornas suck, att vid målet de hunnit / endast en jordisk kust, icke det evigas strand?' (Do you remember the sigh of the roaring waves when at their destination they reach only an earthly coast, not the eternal shore?) The symbols (heavens, stars) are magnificent and the individual phrases expressive (invocations of melancholy, ephemerality, infinity, the idea of God), yet Sibelius interprets this opulently spiritual poem lyrically by separating the reciting voice from the piano. The piano's active role is by no means limited to the prelude and interlude; it creates a foundation that provides space for the recitative-like melody of the vocal part. The piano strings vibrate sympathetically after a chord is sounded. This may recall Sibelius' doubts (Diary, 4 May 1918): 'I rely too much on the long echoing sounds of the piano, which do not work well with singing. My piano style is too ascetic in my older things.' The harmonies of the song demonstrated that Sibelius had completely mastered the technical means of Expressionism long before the change in his style in 1901. The song is notated in C minor and concludes in A flat major (on 'God'). The first inversion of the A flat major chord is prepared by the second inversion of C minor. The third strophe consists of a recitation whose melody uses the C minor scale (with F sharp as secondary dominant) and is supported by a floating C minor as a kind of tonal carpet and a bass trill on *G–F♯*

[1] Op. 38, no. 2 (Rydberg, September 1903; 'Auf dem Balkon [Söller] am Meer', trans. F. Tilgmann).

as a sort of secondary dominant. The second part of the second strophe is based on a similar design, though instead of C minor it is B minor (on 'ephemerality'). The first strophe is based on B minor.

Ecstatic episodes, which according to mood and symbolism are shifted to a new, tonally very distant yet chromatically closely related key (B flat, B and C minor) and yet still sound like reminiscences, are framed by chromatic passages in the piano and, in the case of the second strophe, of the voice as well. Only at the end is chromaticism lacking, so that 'idea of God' becomes the conclusion in A flat major. The three chromatic passages belong to a cadential process, as the lowered sixth degree (for example, the first is $g\flat^7$ with the enharmonic minor seventh E in the bass), the cadence remains stuck at the subsequent first degree in the second inversion ($B\flat^6$). The resolution into the root position of the first degree (B flat, B or C minor) occurs only after the chord has sounded – and also without the relevant dominant. Moreover, the melodic resolution of the lowered sixth degree violates the rules and blurs the harmonic functionality. In addition to the chromatic voice leading, it is above all the building block-like construction of tonally remote passages that constitutes the distinctive feature of the song's harmony. The harmony supports the sense of space and the lack of a centre. Because no key is established, there is no structural key change. The chords float next to one another without regard to the functional harmony of cadences – a method that later became famous in Stravinsky's work. The music accentuates the unreality, the surreal quality of dreams and the Symbolist visions of waves pounding on the shore.

Also reminiscent of Stravinsky are the building blocks that Tiilikainen isolates in 'Dolce far niente', op. 61, no. 6, 1910. The author uses the word 'puzzle' ('palapeli'),[1] which admittedly presumes a *telos* – as if the very means needed to assemble the building were there from the start. Sibelius combines them skilfully – not exactly a rare method in more recent music, though in Stravinsky it is considerably easier to follow in the end result.[2] One of the first building blocks Sibelius conceived was the initial motif, with which both the prelude and the vocal part begin.[3] This gesture establishes the expressive character and thus offers an important clue to interpreting Karl August Tavaststjerna's light-hearted poem (1897): Allegretto, *mp*, marked rhythm, vague tonality (D minor). The building block was not complete in its complexity from the outset, however, but rather the result of a series of detailed sketches that even in their earliest stages had motifs that are also found in the finished version. The sketches document Sibelius' attempts to treat the building block as a polyphonically articulated element that is nuanced from the beginning and is an effective musical gesture. The fundamental significance of the basic structural elements, which need not seem smooth in their syntax, is also unmistakable in the second strophe: 'Jag

1 Tiilikainen 1998c and Tiilikainen, 1998b. See also Tiilikainen 2003.

2 Mäkelä 2004a.

3 Tiilikainen 1998b, pp. 315 ff.

älskar på nytt och jag hoppas' (I love anew and I hope), which in the first sketch was conceived without accompaniment, *con recitativo*. The accompaniment was not supposed to enter until 'hoppas'. This idea was abandoned in favour of rhythmically and harmonically continuous accompaniment. Continuity and flow replaced originality and clear caesuras. This principle — which distinguishes Sibelius from Stravinsky, who began with simple ideas and made them more complex, whereas Sibelius tended rather to simplify (polish) his ideas — is also evident to the listener where two versions are available in commercial recordings: in the Violin Concerto or the Fifth Symphony. The first versions are less subtly smoothed out in terms of their caesuras. The final versions sacrifice originality for organic flow or even classical symmetry.

Tiilikainen even identifies key changes in the sketches. This is something else that in Stravinsky's case occurs only in a later stage of composition. The most important change in terms of the work's expressive character is that in a series of revisions Sibelius dispensed with brief eruptions in the piano (arpeggios, often based on augmented triads) and instead employed broken chords in duplets and triplets as a continuum. Tiilikainen interprets the '"life-and-death" struggle' (as a metaphor for work, as documented in Sibelius' diary on 25 July 1910) as a struggle against the erratic and chaotic nature (the 'anarchy', as Sibelius wrote in connection with the civil war of 1918) of the original in favour of abstract order and consistency, which could only be achieved by Sibelius smoothing out spontaneous outbursts and replacing them with more refined material. Nevertheless, from the perspective of modernist critics, he did not achieve the ideals of abstract order and consistency. From the sketches for 'Dolce far niente' — and similarly from the known early versions of the Violin Concerto and the Fifth Symphony — it is clear that Sibelius repeatedly took that path. In the spirit of the nineteenth century, he regarded the very path that from our present perspective seems progressive for his time as a consequence of a 'lack of talent'.

Opus 88 (1917) is a fascinating collection of Scandinavian romances on poems about flowers by Runeberg and Frans Mikael Franzén. It is the only work for which Sibelius himself used the term 'cycle'.[1] As in several songs from other collections — 'En blomma stod vid vägen' (A flower in the path), op. 57, no. 2; 'Jag är ett träd' (The tree), op. 57, no. 5; 'Svarta rosor', op. 36, no. 1; and 'Rosenlied' (Rose song), op. 50, no. 6 — it is entirely about plants. Not unlike Milhaud's *Catalogue de fleurs*, op. 57 (1920), several of these songs about flowers are simply realistic descriptions and have nothing to do with Art Nouveau. Others tell of flowers in a functional context. Formally, most of the works never move outside the framework of a miniature. One exception is 'Törnet' (The thorn) from Runeberg's *Lyriska dikter* (1852). Its effect benefits from the range of the melody, which within a single measure rises several times from $e\flat^1$ to $a\flat^2$. The song 'Svarta rosor' is comparable, climbing first from e^1 to e^2 and then from e^1 to g^2 and finally to $g\sharp^2$.

The high note $g\sharp^2$ (in the original version) is reached in other songs as well, such as

[1] Tiilikainen 2000, p. ix; ibid., n. 13: 'sång cyckel' (title page of MS).

'Den första kyssen' (The first kiss), op. 37, no. 1; 'Var det en dröm?' (Was it a dream?), op. 37, no. 4, 1902 (whose lowest note is *b*) and the moralistic – but nonetheless effectively set – Runeberg scene 'Flickan kom ifrån sin älsklings möte' (The girl returned from meeting her lover), op. 37, no. 5.[1] This song is one of the many 'also without words' whose verses do not always motivate the grand gestures of the music. The music goes far beyond the text in terms of expression and significance. Despite some high notes ($a\flat^2$), 'Fåfäng önskan', op. 61, no. 7, is rather restrained melodically, but it makes a virtuoso impression thanks to its accompaniment à la Chopin (the Étude, op. 10, no. 8, in particular). In his setting of Rydberg's 'Kyssen' (as op. 72, no. 3), too, Sibelius used nearly the entire soprano range, keeping also within the range of a mezzo-soprano. The melodic range of *b* to g^2 is well chosen. In his diary on 28 July 1910 he admitted to occasional elements in the piano part reminiscent of Chopin but added: 'Are such arpeggiated chords and traditional modulations anyone's property? It is easy to distort something beyond recognition, especially when it comes to "similarity to Chopin". But is it not more respectable to admit without resorting to roundabout ways how one thought and felt about the thing, with inspiration rather than reflection?'

The colossal work 'Kaiutar' (text by Larin-Kyösti; op. 72, no. 4), with its ballad-like elements and mythological figures, lives essentially from its melodies. The drama of the poem is overdrawn in the musical setting. It reaches its climax with 'huhuilevi, kuuntelevi, kirkuvi, kimahuitellen' ('listened, screamed', etc. – the original words are unusual even in a Finnish context and onomatopoetically effective), rather than at the end of the song, which is permeated by profound melancholy. Not only the high notes as such but also the way they are expressed – the $g\flat^2$ occurs immediately after a pause in *piano* – transforms this song into a grand concert etude.

The Josephson song 'Jubal', op. 35, no. 1 (1908), which presents in vocalisations the Symbolist vision of a biblical scene – 'Jubal såg en svana fly över vattnet högt mot sky' (Jubal saw a swan flying over the water up towards the sky) – exceeds all the other songs in its effect. The recitative and the heterogeneous stylistic means are also more ambitious in the piano part than in the other songs. The vocal part reaches the high note $b\flat^2$ directly from f^1 just a few measures after the lowest note, $c\flat^1$, has faded. The text for this impressive passage reads: 'Sjöng så Jubal: "svana vit, varje kväll jag vänder hit att din död besjunga"' (Jubal sang thus: 'white swan, every evening I come here to sing of your death'). The theme of the swan song is the myth of the origin of all expressive music. Jubal, the inventor of song, has shot a swan and listened, deeply moved, to its dying song. Now Jubal imitates the song every evening.

Although the poem has literary and musical-lyrical qualities, 'Jubal' as a composition is not dependent on understanding the text. The Impressionist-seeming but more Surrealist gesture is full of mysteries. The vocal style is derived from opera recitatives,

[1] On feminine subjects (op. 13, no. 6; op. 35, no. 2; op. 37, nos. 4–5, and op. 50, no. 4), see Kallberg 2004.

FIG. 36. 'Jubal', op. 35, no. 1, bars 88 ff. In *Gula rosor* (Yellow Roses) of 1896, the Swedish Symbolist Ernst Josephson published a scene with Jubal (cf. Genesis 4.17–21), in which Jubal is portrayed as a carefree hunter who is enchanted by the beauty of the swan's song and inspired to create music.

which Sibelius maintains, even including the at times sparse accompaniment, which resembles Gustav Holst's miniature opera *Savitri* (1907–8). There is a prototype of this style, which is also found in 'Kaiutar', in Sibelius' own earlier work, in addition to a brief passage of this kind in *Kullervo* (in his sister's narrative monologue, in which she tells what she had done: 'Elä huua hullu tyttö' (Do not scream, mad girl)) in 'En slända' (A dragonfly), op. 17, no. 5 (1894, text by Oscar Levertin), with long vocalisations on *a*, unaccompanied passages and high notes (a^2 and b^2). The text accounts for the unusual setting only in part. On the whole, the seven songs of op. 17 represent a heterogeneous collection of effective single songs. Some of them date from the early 1890s and had been published separately before they were collected to form op. 17. 'Illalle' (To evening), op. 17, no. 6, is a characteristic concert piece sung predominately on the middle note c^2. All these songs derive their power from expressive vocalisation and harmonically intense, tonally flexible writing for the piano. In the most original songs, which are dramatic in their lyrical brevity, Sibelius employs means that had already been proven effective in recitatives.

The Josephson Songs: Between Cultural Criticism and Experiment

There are three cycles dedicated to a single poet, which results in a great deal more cohesion in comparison to Sibelius' other cycles: Seven Songs, op. 13 (1890s), and Six Songs, op. 90 (1917–18), both on texts by Runeberg, and Eight Songs, op. 57 (1909), on texts by Josephson. One song on a text by Josephson, 'Svarta rosor', op. 36, no. 1, exists outside this series. Whereas Runeberg was the Swedish-language national poet of the older generation and even today has the reputation of having been the 'inventor of Finnish identity',[1] Josephson belongs to the second rank of the Scandinavian avant-garde. His poems are rich in symbolism and passionate expression, and these settings are among Sibelius' boldest experiments. That was due to the inspired haste in which they were written. The entire cycle was composed in April and May, in the weeks immediately prior to the significant and enigmatic diary entry of 21 May 1909: 'I have to go home. I can no longer work here [in Berlin]. A change in style?!' On 3 May he had written: 'The songs are turning out well. I fell so very connected to them, and in general my work here is going so well.' This mood is also palpable in a letter to the architect Eliel Saarinen: 'my work here has been a joy!'[2] (In the original Swedish, Sibelius places strong emphasis on being 'out here'.) The contract with Robert Lienau in which Sibelius had agreed to produce work regularly – albeit with quite favourable financial terms – was putting pressure on him: '8 Songs, Opus 57, finished. Contract with Lienau met. Went to bed at 9 o'clock, dead tired.'[3] Not the quality but the number

[1] See Klinge 2004, pp. 403 ff.

[2] JS to Eliel Saarinen, undated (*c.* April–May 1909); quoted in Erik W. Tawaststjerna 1986, p. 114.

[3] JS to Aino, 24 February 1908. Cf. also Diary, 18 May 1909.

of pieces was what counted *de jure*, but in general the publisher proved to be understanding and for the most part received masterpieces in return.

The Josephson Songs, op. 57, whose texts Sibelius took from various publications, are the results of the Expressionist phase around 1910 that culminated in the Fourth Symphony in 1911. Wagnerian *Tristan* harmonies have been replaced by a use of chords whose functionality is largely qualified, which is closely connected to the second essential feature: the shaping of the sound and the Impressionist writing for the piano. By contrast, the melodies are not very distinctive. The unwieldy character of the cycle corresponds to the Symbolistically ambiguous poetry. For example, 'Älven och snigeln' (The river and the snail), op. 57, no. 1, is not a depiction of nature but a vision of power and spirit, force and soul, as well as of ideas and physicality. The river symbolises society with its norms, whereas the forest through which the river makes its way represents the universe. By means of austere dissonances on a vaguely sad C minor foundation and asymmetrical accents, Sibelius illustrates defiance and force, whereas the second strophe, in which the snail is introduced, is accompanied by a moving piano part in quintuplets. The metaphors become more complex in the third strophe, in which the music of the first strophe is initially repeated, when a barefoot boy enters and finds a pearl in a freshwater oyster. The boy is the idealist who is in a position to discover the crystallisation of the mind and the soul. As soon as he spots the pearl, the river freezes over, but the pearl nevertheless adorns 'day and night / the breast of the most beautiful queen'. This phrase does not signify any glorification of the cognitive powers of an idealist in contrast to the appropriation of beautiful nature. Rather, the boy has destroyed the natural order and ignored the power that limits the freedom of the mind but also produces a balance.

The old idea that the emancipation of thinking poses a threat to nature becomes manifest here. Sibelius supports this interpretation by accentuating the contrast between the discovery of the pearl – three lines without accompaniment are followed by a splendidly polyphonic measure to the words 'den skönsta pärlan som fanns' (the most beautiful pearl there was) in A flat major – and the freezing of the river and carries out this transformation without delay. The song ends with C major chords. A piano part that does not accompany a melodramatic-seeming singing line but instead moves in parallel with it considerably intensifies the expression of the first song. Artfully harmonic accompaniment occurs only at the end of the song, after the description of the pearl, if only in terms of the tonal linking of all the parts. The simplicity of the tonal rules has a striking effect at the end thanks to the polytonality and the tonal ambiguity of the previous lines. Without a doubt, the musical setting glorifies the final state hinted at in the poem. It should not be overlooked, however, that the final strophe (C major/winter) is restrained in its gestures in comparison to the description that immediately precedes it (A flat major/pearl). That supports the thesis that Sibelius wanted to emphasise the ambiguity. All in all, the first song is a delicate, anything but easy-going piece that sets high ethical standards. This reading critical of modern civilisation is confirmed by the other songs.

In the second song, 'En blomma stod vid vägen' (A flower in the path), a girl contradicts the natural order. She picks a flower, liberating it from the kisses of a butterfly, and places the butterfly in a birdcage and gives it a bird as its 'spouse'. In the end, the flower dries out alone in its glass, 'since all its friends are friends of others'. The bird cannot act instinctively in the artificial world. Next to the cage stands the glass with the flower, which comments on the 'wedding'. The refrain recalls the natural order: 'Since all my friends are also yours.' The challenge is to see through the elegiac fragility of the harmoniously naive depiction. The symmetry becomes interesting when Sibelius takes the repeating line of the refrain ('Since all my friends are also yours') on its first occurrence as the occasion to radically change the rhythmic structure and the accompanying figuration of the piano and retains this configuration until just before the beginning of the final strophe, where a reprise of the beginning is introduced. The complex form of the poem as the result of the refrain is smoothed out musically. This poem is not an allegory of love either but rather a symbolic depiction of the destructive power of human beings and their often unnatural idea of justice. The marriage of a butterfly and a bird in a cage produces a surreal image of a hermetically sealed world of unhappiness.

The third song, 'Kvarnhjulet' (The millwheel), which concludes the first section, which features a consistent world view, is an allegory of industrialisation, symbolised by an old, discarded millwheel and a new, tarred one, as well as by doves playing in the spray. In Sibelius' interpretation, the focus is on the old wheel observing the world. The change in scene (spray versus wheel) is emphasised in the harmony by shifts from F major to E flat minor and G flat major. Finally, the F major movement of the beginning is suggested (much as it had been throughout) but the new tonal environment remains intact nevertheless.

'Maj' (May), the fourth song in op. 57, which Sibelius wrote should not be performed too 'emotively', begins a new section. The individual is now the focus. The oddly idyllic spring atmosphere initially sketched in detail in the poem 'Maj' with realistic means (air, waves, birds, rivers, flowers, etc.) represents in the end a stirring of the soul. The subject's mood is projected on to his environment as an object-orientated introspection. Because of the lightness of expression and the superficiality of the text, this song is an intermezzo. The fifth song, 'Jag är ett träd', is a monument to symbolic thought. Here too the soul is the context for the ideas, but it is a scene from Job. The tree is sad; the autumn storm has destroyed its leaves, but its surroundings still have their late summer colours. The tree (standing for a human being) asks God for a winter that will make everything equal. The song differs from the poem 'Maj' in that the man projects his happiness into nature — but in the process connects to the theme of death in the first songs. In the fourth and fifth songs, the lyrical self feels separated from his surroundings, which in the final song gives rise to jealousy, aggression and despair. Sibelius accentuates these *topoi* of expression by means of the piano part (Grave e pesante), which is subordinated to the singing and the lyrical expression of the self.

The ballad 'Hertig Magnus', op. 57, no. 6, tells of the desire to be united with nature and its elements, in this case water and the nymph living in it — whose gender is unspecified in the original language, by the way. The duke (based on Magnus Vasa, the mad Duke of Östergötland and Prince of Sweden, 1542–95) has been confused by horrible events at the Stockholm court. From the height of his castle, protected by solid walls, the nobleman wishes he were down amid the elements, far from all intrigues. He finds his bliss in the embrace of a 'friendly water spirit'. It remains unclear whether that means his death. The final line — 'oskadd, slumrande på stranden' — means he was found 'unharmed, sleeping on the beach'. That could be a romantic metaphor for a peaceful death as the fulfilment of his yearning. At the same time, it reflects a well-known legend of the real Magnus Vasa based on events that may have occurred in 1563. 'Hertig Magnus' is a showpiece of ballad composition and represents a mixture of styles with aspects from the older, programmatic and historicising Sibelius and the new, experimental one. The piano writing remains independent of the melody throughout, with only the extent of its subordination changing. There is also flexible parallel leading of the voices. Elements familiar from Sibelius' older works, such as ornaments (trills and triplets) and harmonic turns like the melodically employed sequence of D minor, A minor and F major, are used effectively here too. Sibelius exploits the expressive power of the harmony on several levels: first, to clarify subtle differences between individual lines and, secondly, to establish a formal demarcation of the middle section (G flat major instead of the initial melancholy D minor and F major) in which the water spirit speaks to the duke. One unusual feature is that the melodic material remains the same, despite the suggestion of conflict. Certainly it would be possible to compose it dramatically in accordance with the text. In that sense, it is not really a narrative ('ballad') but a vision explained by the text.

A song of friendship, 'Vänskapens blomma' (The flower of friendship), continues the cycle. The function of this seventh song is, much like that of 'Maj', that of a musical, melodic (and incidentally also popular) intermezzo — this time followed by the ambitious finale, 'Näcken' (The elf king). At first glance, the flower seems egocentric. It promises the dying man bliss and alleviates the experience of death as a 'balsam of friendship'. By using rondo form and alternating between D major and a modulating D minor couplet, Sibelius clarifies the ambiguity between friendship and death. In Scandinavian mythology, the *näcke* (neck, a male water spirit) lies in wait in the stream for people. The alternation of fantasy and reality, vision and actuality is dynamic. The conclusion is unusual; its theme is the separation of these two dimensions of consciousness: 'Gossen var blott min egen fantasi, / näcken var forsen, som brusade förbi / och stänkte sitt skumm på min kind' (The boy was merely my imagination / the neck was a rapid that rushed past / and sprayed its foam on my cheek). As the conclusion of the cycle, this homoerotic turn, which the piano part (Lento assai, pesante) underscores, takes on an overarching meaning, though one that weakens the critique of civilisation. The melancholic mood of the final lines is made clearer by the music than it is in the poem, which is important considering that the cycle

FIG. 37. Ernst Josephson, *Näcken.*

was compiled from various publications by Josephson. Harmonically, Sibelius goes his own way by using Impressionist elements, a writing style based on original scales, chromaticism and adding symbolic chords — such as the rush of E major accompanying the line 'i skummande silver och gull' (in frothing silver and gold). As in the first song, the expressive focus is on the piano part, which gives material form to a vision of the fleeting scenes suggested in the poem. This detail gives the attentive listener an idea of what Sibelius meant by 'pure cold water' as a metaphor for his style,[1] and how profound his musical symbolism could be nevertheless. Those who are not scared off by the Swedish (and in a few cases Finnish) texts will find in Sibelius an original, moving contribution to the art of the song.

Josephson produced paintings not only on the theme of 'Näcken' but also of 'Jubal' and 'Hertig Magnus', though Sibelius only saw *Näcken* — and possibly even that only in 1915 in Gothenburg (Diary, 28 March 1915): 'Art museum with its "Josefsons" etc.' Josephson's interpretation of the mythological theme in a sensuously modern (even erotic) drawing does not seem to have influenced Sibelius' own reading.

[1] Furuhjelm, quoting JS, cited in Cecil Gray 1931, p. 11.

> Will the truth about the originality of my motifs ever come out? – No!! So only one side of your art will become apparent.[1]

5 ARTIST, NATURE, HOMELAND
From Insight to Intention

5.1 Walter Niemann and 'Heimatkunst'

Between Chauvinism and Exoticism

According to a long-established assumption, Sibelius, as the personification of the authentically Finnish will to style, made it possible to look into the souls of the Finnish people and Finland's 'landscape'. The question arises whether the thesis that 'landscapes are culture before they are nature; constructs of the imagination projected onto wood and water and rock'[2] is also valid. Sibelius' popularity abroad depends on how much an individual wishes to come to terms with or even identify with Finland and the so-called North. This is not just about the culture (including landscape as a manifestation of culture) but also about the extent to which the 'natural' is seen as 'genuine'.

This mode of reception bypasses Sibelius the individual, since the artist is interpreted within a folkloric and/or existential framework and in a narrow regional context. Even today, he represents for many 'classical northern music'.[3] This emphasis easily becomes a limitation. Because it is seen in only one aspect, his music is forced into a pigeonhole that the German composer, music educator and poet Hermann Freiherr von Waltershausen defended and Paul Bekker attacked all the more furiously.[4] 'New music will only be written when we once again have German, French, Italian, Slavic and ... Jewish composers. The enormous talent that is available everywhere here has been placed in terrible danger by today's cosmopolitan education. Perhaps we have to undergo a complete breakdown before a path to the new can be paved', agitated von Waltershausen in 1920. By promoting the regionally specific and *völkisch* (ethnic-populist, tribalist) movement – by blatantly stumbling over the word 'Jewish' – he provoked opposing positions. (At least von Waltershausen, unlike Richard Wagner, professed that Jews had their 'own' art.[5]) Unfortunately, it is clear which side Sibelius was thought to be on.

The effect was similar to that of the German composer and conservative author

1 Diary, 19 June 1910.

2 Schama 1995, p. 61.

3 Bünning 2001, p. 45.

4 See Waltershausen 1920, and Bekker 1921, p. 327, with the 1920 essay 'Die Rückkehr zur Natur'.

5 Wagner [1850] 1982, p. 182.

Hans Pfitzner, who, unlike Sibelius, made a pre-emptive strike in the form of his polemical essay 'Futuristengefahr' (Danger of Futurists; 1917), which poisoned the climate. Sibelius' friend Ferruccio Busoni's *Entwurf einer neuen Ästhetik der Tonkunst* (two versions: 1907 and 1916; translated as *Sketch of a New Esthetic of Music* in 1911), whom Pfitzner made the target of his bitter critique of modernism, lacked 'the objectivity of thought indispensable for an object of discussion', as a faithful sympathiser put it.[1] The impossibility of positioning Sibelius on this chequerboard of appreciation makes it clear how much he suffered under the listening habits of his day, when the history of contemporary music was radically divided (once again by Pfitzner) into 'impotence' and 'potence'.[2] Sibelius would only have had a real chance to be understood beyond clichés by critics who could have worked independently of this trend to polarisation at the time – in art criticism no less than in politics.

From a domestic perspective, the Finnish and even generally Nordic aspects of Sibelius divided opinion. Already in the 1920s, the majority of Finns considered him less 'Finnish' than the legendary Olympic athlete Paavo Nurmi, who won nine gold medals and three silver between 1920 and 1928. This brave man embodied 'sisu' – a Sisyphean unyieldingness and strength inherent in every true Finn. Sibelius, by contrast, was too 'universal' to remain an unqualified symbol for the entire nation after 1918, whereas the long-distance runner Nurmi represented in pure form the Finno-Ugric 'race' that some Finns thought existed genetically.[3] Nurmi became a national hero, a titan related to the 'genuine natives', whereas Sibelius was seen as elitist, Swedish-speaking and cosmopolitan and hence for the majority of Finns offered only limited opportunity for national identification.

Authors who call the universal validity of ideas and international modernism into question on the basis of regionalism want to show that Sibelius was not one of many, much less an ordinary representative of a civilisation whose crisis around 1900 was obvious but rather a laudably courageous loner. The most famous of the early authors on Sibelius in this mould is the German composer, pianist and musicologist Walter Niemann,[4] the 'reliable guide to Scandinavian music, typical of the state of mind and the picturesque moods of nature in the land of a thousand lakes'.[5] Niemann was interested in the search for an alternative to the cosmopolitan and universally valid trends of his time. Nevertheless, his position has for generations been misunderstood as constituting an exceptionally malevolent criticism of Sibelius. Even Tawaststjerna

[1] Bekker, 'Futuristengefahr?' (1917), in Bekker 1921, p. 267.

[2] Bekker, 'Impotenz oder Potenz?' (1920), in ibid., pp. 310 ff., a response to Hans Pfitzner's *Die neue Ästhetik der musikalischen Impotenz? Ein Verwesungssymptom?* (1919; 2nd edition Munich: Verlag der Süddeutschen Monatshefte, 1920).

[3] Meinander 1999, p. 128.

[4] Niemann belonged to a generation of authors easy to attack today. Cf. Painter 1995, pp. 236 ff., and Niemann 1913a, pp. 136 ff. Niemann's picture of Mahler is, admittedly, problematic and less reflective than his attitude towards JS.

[5] *Neue Freie Presse*, 3 December 1935, p. 8.

admitted that he considered the decision of the Breitkopf & Härtel publishing house in Leipzig to give Niemann the contract for the first German-language monograph on Sibelius a mistake with grave consequences, since Niemann's previous writings had supposedly demonstrated how wrong his new contribution would necessarily be.[1] Breitkopf & Härtel, which published Niemann's book as well as a lot of Sibelius' music, was accused of carelessness – that is how critically Niemann's interpretation of Sibelius was regarded in Finland.

Niemann's renown as an author spoke in his favour. Alongside studies on the history of notation and the Western repertoire, Nordic culture – including Johannes Brahms the 'Hamburger', as Niemann called him (which can be called either canonic limitation or specification) – was his focus. As a composer, Niemann was concerned with a close 'connection to nature, the folksong and folk dance' and with 'poetry, saga and fairy tales of the fatherland' all this 'on a neo-Romantic, modern, beautiful-sounding, but above all spiritual and imaginative foundation'.[2] He composed works with titles such as *Alt-China* (Old China), *Pharaonenland* (Land of the pharaohs), *Die lustigen Chinesen* (The happy Chinese), and *Bunte Lampions* (Colourful Chinese lamps). As an active composer of the generation following Louis Moreau Gottschalk's then popular and exotic character pieces for piano (so-called souvenirs), Russian subjects (his op. 189 uses a Pushkin text) and entertainment (*Der gelbe Tango* (The yellow tango) etc.) were not foreign to him either. His own north-west German identity – he called himself 'Hamburgensis holsatus' and felt uneasy even in central Germany and Saxony[3] – was important to Niemann. Nevertheless, he was no ordinary chauvinist but a critical professional. He recognised that taking Robert Schumann and Brahms as models would not permit an evolution of piano music, which he thus sought in Impressionist and exotic sounds, though without abandoning the functional framework of domestic music. By dedicating his Sibelius book to his uncle Gustav Niemann, who had been active as leader of the theatre orchestra in Helsinki from 1864 to 1881, he made clear what he associated with the far North. His uncle – who had taken master classes with the great Ferdinand David, the most prominent of Louis Spohr's numerous students and a teacher of Joseph Joachim – had taught Robert Kajanus the violin, and even Sibelius' duet partner, Anna Tigerstedt, was allowed to perform before 'Niemand' ('Nobody', as Sibelius parodied his name in a letter);[4] poking fun at teachers and other authorities was one of Sibelius' favourite exercises.

Even Tawaststjerna made use of Niemann's translations from Finnish newspapers (rather than quoting books in the original), which leads to distortions and inaccuracies.[5] Much like Sibelius himself in Adorno's hands, Niemann became a victim of the turbulent climate of reception in the twentieth century. In Finland, his attempt to

[1] Erik W. Tawaststjerna 1997b, pp. 244–5.

[2] Sietz 1961, col. 1520.

[3] Ibid., cols. 1519 ff.

[4] See Goss 1997, pp. 21 and 53.

[5] Erik W. Tawaststjerna 1986, p. 245.

interpret Sibelius in the context of contemporary *Heimatkunst* (regionalist art) was immediately interpreted as an insult. Erik Furuhjelm, Toivo Haapanen and Leevi Madetoja defended Sibelius with furious essays addressed to a national and international public,[1] and Sibelius himself rejected the 1917 monograph, as can be seen in an isolated diary entry of 1919: 'Then this book by Niemann that crippled me for a long time.'[2] Sibelius did not react with such vehemence even to Karl Ekman's biography (or many other irritating essays on him), even though he would have had good reason to do so. He did it only in private. One of his final diary entries, on 14 January 1944, does address Ekman: 'Since Karl Ekman's book about me was published in 1935, it has made my life bitter and grey, and I cannot count how many sleepless nights Aino and I have had.' Ekman supposedly misquoted him and in general wrote polemically, although his attitude towards the composer seems extraordinarily favourable and respectful. He wrote that he permitted publication of the book in 1935 only as a favour to Karl's mother, Ida, and to save young Karl 'from ruin'.[3] Nevertheless, the book was reprinted in English as recently as 1976, whereas Niemann has become *persona non grata*. Even Ernst Tanzberger described Ekman as an 'authentic source', and Newmarch recommended him for his supposed accuracy.[4] Out of consideration to the Ekman family, Sibelius did nothing to discredit the book – neither publicly nor in his correspondence.

On the final page of his diary, on (or a little after) 14 January 1944, he wrote in Finnish his last completed thought recorded in this valuable document – and at the same time the only one in this language (with a tiny yet atypical misspelling or grammatical error): 'Olen saanut kylliksi maalitaulun[a] olemisesta' (I have had enough of being a target). He was probably not referring to Niemann but rather Karl Ekman junior, but Niemann was still one reason for his annoyance. In an undated draft letter from this period, he wrote in German: 'Niemann's book is incorrect in many cases and has done me a great deal of harm. Please ignore that work.'[5] In this draft Sibelius recommended Furuhjelm's book, since it 'primarily treats my childhood and youth. Everything there is correct. I just find the book somewhat naive.' Yet because on Sibelius' own account Niemann had written 'with sympathy',[6] the question remains what (apart from lapses) supposedly triggered nevertheless 'incorrect' and dangerous views. Circumstances contributed to the small mistakes. Niemann had used a recent Swedish source – Carl Göran Nyblom's eighteen-page brochure *Jean Sibelius*, which

[1] Cf. Erik W. Tawaststjerna 1997b, pp. 144–5.

[2] Diary, 17 February 1919. Cf. also JS to Breitkopf & Härtel, 10 April 1919; quoted in Erik W. Tawaststjerna 1996, p. 296.

[3] See JS to an unknown recipient, 3 May 1936; National Archive Box 36, JS to 'Käre Herr Kapellmästare', draft letter.

[4] Preface to Tanzberger 1962; Newmarch 1939, p. 36.

[5] National Archive Box 36, draft letter from JS to 'My dear Sir' (possibly Cecil Gray).

[6] JS to Breitkopf & Härtel, 22 August 1918 and 10 April 1919; quoted in Erik W. Tawaststjerna 1997b, p. 145.

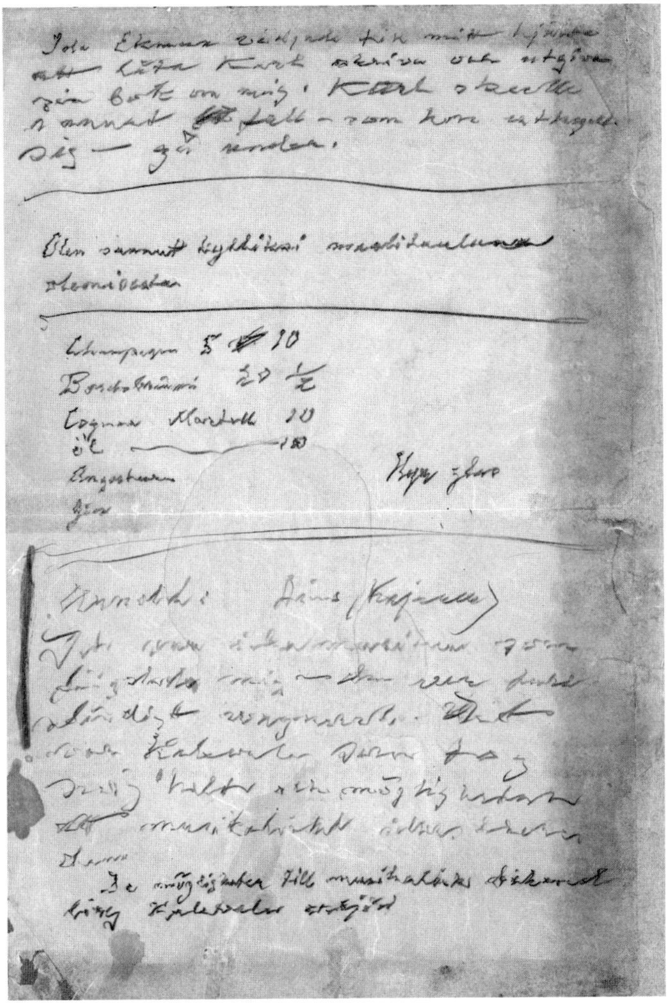

FIG. 38. Final page of Sibelius' diary. The complex text of the diary can be demonstrated on the basis of its final page. In addition to a shopping list for alcohol, there are sketches concerning his professional stance on the *Kalevala* (all undated) and before them an outburst of desperation over his inadequate reception in general and Karl Ekman's biography in particular (dated 14 January 1944, but starting on the previous page).

Sibelius also knew.[1] During the First World War, Niemann was unable to contact Sibelius, but the book had to be written.[2]

From the outset, Niemann was stigmatised as an enemy. One reason might be that as a composer and generally well-trained musician (his teachers were Hugo Riemann,

[1] See Diary, 12 January 1917.

[2] See Breitkopf & Härtel to JS, 29 April 1919; National Archive Box 42.

Engelbert Humperdinck and Carl Reinecke) Niemann was expected to have influence beyond his essays. There is an embittered note in Sibelius' diary on 10 September 1926: 'B & H have received the composition [*Tapiola*] – but they are hesitating – by chance I happen to know that my biographer W. Niemann sits on the "advisory board". Can't this know-it-all, who has done me more harm than anyone else, be eliminated[?]' But in fact Niemann was not scheming against Sibelius at all, and the engraving of the score was completed on 17 September 1926.[1] Niemann certainly did not harm Sibelius more than many others did.

Sibelius was frequently confronted with a trivialised version of the premises of the aestheticising *Heimat* movement. The movement originated from Schleswig-Holstein (the rural districts north of Hamburg), where Niemann also felt at home, and bore artistic fruit not only in regional history and ethnology but also in painting and literature. Journals such as *Die Heimat: Monatsschrift des Vereins zur Pflege der Natur- und Landeskunde in Schleswig-Holstein, Hamburg und Lübeck* (founded in 1890) attacked urban modernity and promoted natural history and regional studies. 'Rediscovering the provinces' and 'tribal characteristics' served as a means to resist 'urbanisation'.[2] Politically, it attacked both the socialist workers' movement and 'dehumanisation' by big capitalism. Its primary supporters consisted of pedagogues and teachers at primary and secondary schools. Ideas about popular education mixed with post-Romantic utopias. They reflected on Moritz Lazarus' and Heymann (Hajim) Steinthal's *Völkerpsychologie*: the idea of the people as 'psychological unity', which was to be demonstrated and passed on through education by collecting expressions of the 'soul of the people'. At the same time, it provided fruitful soil for cultural racism and militant chauvinism. Sibelius may have associated this with Niemann's work, without discerning the undertone of cultural criticism and the antimodernist details of Niemann's argument that he might have understood under other circumstances.

One example of the fruits of an enduring trivialisation of the *Heimat* movement is a letter from Bernd Haag in Berlin to Sibelius on 18 September 1948: 'I experienced Finland even though I have never seen the country. From the first sounds from the violins, I saw the broad, lonely, snow-covered Finnish landscape with its herds of reindeer; I experienced the awakening of nature in the Adagio, and rode on a sledge through forests by snow-covered lakes in the final movement.'[3] Sibelius and Finland were idealised as an alternative to the destroyed civilisation of Central Europe, such as Berlin. Sibelius was Finland and Finland Sibelius. In the *Heimat* movement organ *Der Kunstwart* – published from 1887, initially as the journal of the garden city and *Heimatschutz* (homeland protection/preservation) movement, an important segment of the *Heimat* movement – Karl Georg Göhler, a friend of Breitkopf & Härtel publisher Oskar von Hase, was already drawing the obvious conclusions from these

[1] See also Erik W. Tawaststjerna 1997b, p. 270.

[2] Christiansen 1980, pp. 9 and 16.

[3] National Library Coll. 206: 14.

ideas in 1908: 'Sibelius can, of course, be understood completely only by Finns, not because of his music but because of the world of ideas from which his emotional life has grown.'[1] The Austrian critic and poet Richard Batka wrote in the same journal in 1907: 'Anyone who wants to understand the tone poet has to travel to the tone poet's country. It is not difficult to recognise the connection between Sibelius' music and the land of a thousand lakes, with its dreadful winters and incomparable springs, its wonderfully bright starry nights.'[2] These views, which are still common today and not necessarily incorrect, belong in the same ideological context as Niemann. Largely influenced by theorists who never denied their Jewish identity,[3] the northern German *Heimat* movement developed the idea of a 'German folk soul'. By around 1905, the racist, exclusive attitude may have been dominant in the *Heimat* movement,[4] but many who identified with the movement, without belonging to it in the strict sense, still embraced the utopia of an ideal world, whose realisation the *Heimat* movement seemed to promise as a necessary correction to the urbanised present. Finland's reputation was boosted by such concepts, and not just Germany's.

Poetry was particularly important within the *Heimat* movement. It verbalised the love of homeland and built a bridge to essays critical of civilisation and cultural politics. Some of these poems were by *Heimat* poets of merely local relevance, but authors known beyond the region, such as the Alsatian Friedrich Lienhard, contributed to the movement as well. Lienhard was a leading advocate of *Heimatkunst* and was provocatively defended against the 'usual, repeated, thoughtless bracketing with the representatives of "*Heimatkunst*"' by Paul Bülow[5] – who ten years later would himself write *Adolf Hitler und der Bayreuther Kulturkreis* (Hitler and the cultural circle of Bayreuth). The same Paul Bülow corresponded with Sibelius in 1954,[6] when he was planning a sequel to Houston Stewart Chamberlain's essay 'Mein Weg nach Bayreuth' (My path to Bayreuth, originally a chapter in his *Lebenswege meines Denkens* of 1919), for which Bülow had written an introduction in 1937. The book Lienhard wrote to criticise metropolitan modernity, *Die Vorherrschaft Berlins* (1900), sheds light on the context of Sibelius' reception during this period: 'Many a harsh word has been said about the nationalism of the Berlin spirit, about Slavic interbreeding, about the influence of Berlin's Jews, about the effects of the café *literati* on our poetry, about Prussian bureaucracy, and so on. I do not even want to go into this side of the question in my brief proposals. That easily turns into unproductive theories, does only harm, and fosters nothing.'[7] In an age in which racist argumentation was considered

[1] Göhler 1908, p. 262; cf. Erik W. Tawaststjerna 1986, p. 98 (though he quotes a translation from a Finnish newspaper).

[2] Batka 1907, pp. 457–9.

[3] Belke 1971, p. xxvii

[4] Christiansen 1980, pp. 68.

[5] Bülow 1923, p. 8.

[6] National Library Coll. 206: 7: Bülow to JS, 28 March 1954.

[7] Lienhard 1900, p. 29.

rational by many, and the transition from cultural and religious anti-Judaism to racist anti-Semitism (as a kind of 'rational' variation on the somewhat nebulous prototype) was just being made (in the wake of the increasing importance of ethnic rather than linguistic or even cultural aspects as the basis of national identities),[1] Lienhard's distancing himself from a fashionable argument deserves respect. Even where he speaks of the 'German essence' or the 'spirit of the German people', he does so without misusing the category of race (even though an anti-Jewish undertone may be detectable, since in his view the main players in cosmopolitanism and world capitalism were Jewish). This distinction explains why not a single work by Lienhard, who died in 1929, was reprinted in Germany after 1933. By contrast, Niemann used concepts such as 'race', 'race question' and 'race standpoint'[2] without apparently recognising how dangerous they had become – this was so as early as 1879, in the context of the debate over anti-Semitism triggered by the imperial court chaplain Adolf Stoecker in Berlin.[3] The difference from such authors as Adolf Bartels, who in *Weshalb ich die Juden bekämpfe: Eine deutliche Auskunft* (Why I fight the Jews: clear information) of 1919 clearly articulated his old standpoint, was clear in his case as well: Lienhard, Niemann, Bülow and Bartels personified separate areas in the *Heimat* movement that more or less clearly anticipated the ideology of National Socialism but were not fully absorbed by it. A more discerning, not generalising study of these phenomena is a desideratum of the cultural history of the turn of the century, and it is one of the contexts that may help to explain some of the odd paths Sibelius' reception took over the years. The early *Heimat* movement, for which nature and landscape were more important than the shared ethnic traits of any 'people', should not be confused with Bartel's Deutschvölkischer Schutz- und Trutz-Bund (German nationalist protection and shelter union), but the latter is still one of the facets of the *Heimat* movement. Racist individuals like Bartels make it difficult to defend the others – even Niemann with his profound interest in Sibelius.

According to Lienhard, the social rise of the north-eastern German industrial metropolis Berlin as the capital of the empire and a general commercialisation 'raped' the 'spirit of our literature'.[4] He hoped to derive the strength to escape this decadence from a new 'German idealism'.[5] He accused French artists and their followers of formalism and banality. Although he was not himself a Wagnerian, he felt that a profound literary reception of Wagner was lacking (as opposed to focusing on his leitmotifs). He expected that 'modern *Heimatkunst*' would separate itself from 'intellectual, local and temporal particularism'[6] and reflect on the models of Lope de Vega, Shakespeare and Homer and especially on the second act of Wagner's *Siegfried* ('Waldwe-

[1] Hobsbawm 1990, pp. 101–10.

[2] Niemann 1913a, p. 270

[3] Belke 1971, pp. lxiff.

[4] Lienhard 1900, p. 3.

[5] Ibid., p. 37

[6] Ibid., pp. 11 ff. and 45.

ben' [Forest Murmurs] and the perception of nature) — as von Waltershausen would do twenty years later — and the Nibelungen saga in general. Unlike Émile Zola, Henrik Ibsen, Richard Dehmel, Gerhart Hauptmann and Maurice Maeterlinck, who employed refined narrative techniques to engage naturalistically and socially with the 'little problem of the immediate present' and upheld the fashionable category of the 'interesting',[1] Lienhard postulated an art that would re-establish the connection to the 'will' along with the 'idea' (Schopenhauer) and, freed of sentimentalism, *Nervenkunst* (neurotic art), *Verstandesdichtung* (literature of reason) and other trends, would find themes that speak to the 'people' as such or in Johann Gottfried von Herder's sense of *Volk*. By '*Volk* (*natio, populus*)', Herder meant an abstraction that 'is in all of us' and should by no means be confused with the 'fourth estate (*plebs*)'.[2]

Nationalism was also put on trial. The possibility of making a distinction in the history of ideas that would take into account an objective interpretation of Lienhard and of *Heimat* theory (and hence of Niemann as well) got lost in the wake of the accelerating process of modernisation and art's connection to metropolises. Consequently, in 1923 Paul Bülow no longer even attempted to defend *Heimatkunst* as an idea to be taken seriously,[3] particularly as he soon belonged to those who were eager to move towards National Socialism. Around 1900 contemporary literary culture was already offering occasional warnings against a one-sidedly chauvinistic interpretation of the *Zeitgeist* around the *Heimat* movement: the idea of *Heimat* in its original form was closely related both to a supra-regional, romanticising ruralism and to exoticism (which accounts for the exotic themes in Niemann's musical oeuvre) and exotic adventure novels were bestsellers in Germany, above all Karl May (*Winnetou*, etc.) and Friedrich Gerstäcker (*Germelshausen*, etc.) but also Rudyard Kipling. Anyone who reads early *Heimat* literature and exotic novels distances himself first of all from urbanism and mercantilism and plunges, in whatever direction, into the illusion of an intact naturalness. One of the possible directions, it cannot be denied, was the supranational facet of National Socialism. Before anyone could tell which path would lead to a dead end, an age of merciless polarisation dawned.

The radical nationalists of the 1920s to 1940s wilfully misused Lienhard's reformist ideas by deriving from them — on the trail of Wagner, who euphorically wrote of the 'healthy tribe', 'natural soil' and 'source of the people'[4] — their primitive blood-and-soil particularism and thus tried to bring their radical ideology close to nationalist, conservative forces on the one hand, and the uneducated population on the other, for whom the original arguments of the *Heimat* movement or the race theorists would have been far too complex.

Not the landscape at home or elsewhere but rather the landscape as idea was the

[1] Ibid., p. 30.

[2] Ibid., pp. 32–3.

[3] Bülow 1923, p. 8.

[4] Wagner [1850] 1982, pp. 181ff.

object of the yearnings of a society marked by millennial fears and structural change. For the *Heimat* movement and the culture of thought it came from, nature was not only a localisable 'natural monument' of their own region but also a global alternative to the city. Paul Gauguin's nativity scene transferred to a South Pacific backdrop, *The Birth* (1896), illustrates this using modern stylistic means: Gauguin effectively called into question topographically defined reality and did so in a place where European culture was sensitive. Landscape and the colour of people's skin represent a symbolic foundation of the depiction. Stanisław Przybyszewski, who was part of Sibelius' circle in Berlin and a friend of Strindberg, wrote of Gauguin: 'He carries his own Tahiti within himself, and so he proceeds with the unerring sense of a sleepwalker through our confusing cultural life, never straying from his path, in full command of his utterly cultureless Parsifalian nature.'[1] This kind of utopian and in part also romantically reactionary transcendentalism was an echo of the early nineteenth-century aesthetic of nature, which had survived despite realism and indeed even within the aesthetic of realism. Sibelius was heard in that context. Axel Carpelan, whom Sibelius included in the innermost circle of his creative process,[2] can be called as a witness for the accused. In a long letter, he wrote in 1914 – attacking Niemann but unwittingly supporting his premises: 'If someone like Niemann and the others had known the history and nature of Finland thoroughly, your style and some details of your particular nature would have seemed clearer.'[3]

Carpelan was an important witness. He had provided Sibelius with early indirect impulses for *Finlandia*, the Violin Concerto, *Voces intimae* and *Tapiola* (as 'forest symphony') in his prophetic letters and thus demonstrated his empathy. For example, he wrote of *Finlandia* in a letter to Sibelius on 13 March 1900: 'Your overture will be called "Finlandia" – won't it?' When Carpelan died, Sibelius wrote in his diary on 29 March 1919: 'For whom shall I compose now?' Even the fact that Sibelius never wrote a full-scale opera but instead many songs, brief salon pieces and choral works could be linked to Carpelan's idea of national art, as expressed in a long letter to Sibelius on 7 June 1900: 'Opera is a luxury for a small people, an expensive luxury, which at best claims the entire interest of the musical upper class and thus makes its taste superficial. There are countless examples. Sweden and Denmark are monitory examples for us. Operas are often just expensive playthings for the semi- or unmusical masses. What a small people like ours needs are not operas, not even national operas, but presumably primarily soulful "songs for one voice", mixed choirs (performances by male choirs are a disaster!).' Carpelan may have been one reason why Sibelius abandoned his plans for an opera on, say, a theme from the *Kalevala*.

Carpelan, the intimate connoisseur for whom Sibelius' music was the most impor-

[1] Przybyszewski, *Das Werk des Edvard Munch: Vier Beiträge* (Berlin: S. Fischer, 1894), p. 37; quoted in Asendorf 2003, p. 83.

[2] Cf. Diary, 1 May 1912.

[3] On Carpelan, see National Archive Box 18; Axel Carpelan to JS, 12 January 1914.

tant thing in his life, was certainly convinced that the right approach to the Finnish artist was via nature and history, presuming one had a 'thorough' knowledge of them – and in his view Niemann lacked that. The Finnish literary scholar and nationalist Eliel Aspelin-Haapkylä expressed himself in the same tone in a letter to Sibelius in 1915:

> Permit me to thank you for the beautiful world you have derived from the simple sounds of Finland's nature and the soul of its people. Before you opened the hiding place of our emotions [...], no one suspected they were so rich and magnificent. [...] Finland's future is dismal, but as long as ever new representatives of the healthy power of artistic creation rise up from the depths of the spirit of the people, it will never be condemned to disappear among the nations.[1]

Against that backdrop, the question arises how Niemann's position could ever have been successfully portrayed as an insulting attack as Sibelius' closest contemporaries in Finland used identical categories. Clearly, the problem with Niemann was not so much what he said and why but that he said it with a German accent.

'Nation, People and Tribe' in Contemporary Music

Paradigms of the *Heimat* movement influenced Niemann's magnum opus, *Die Musik der Gegenwart*, which classifies Sibelius as a 'national' artist. In comparison to his short, oft-cited Sibelius monograph of 1917, the image of Sibelius is discussed in detail with corresponding subtlety and at least a tendency to the scholarly. The first version was published in 1913 under the title *Die Musik seit Richard Wagner* (Music since Richard Wagner). As *Die Musik der Gegenwart*, it was published in numerous printings between 1918 and 1925. Both versions of the text, which was essentially unchanged, conclude with a section titled 'Nation, Volk und Stamm' (Nation, people and tribe). *Literaturgeschichte der deutschen Stämme und Landschaften* (A literary history of German tribes and landscapes) by the August Sauer pupil Josef Nadler,[2] published in three volumes at nearly the same time as Niemann's books (the first printing between 1912 and 1918), influenced these categories and thus even determined the academic *Zeitgeist*. Niemann actually drew the reader's attention to the core final section 'Nation, Volk und Stamm' in his foreword. The second part of the final section was called 'Gibt es eine deutsche musikalische Heimatkunst?' (Is there a German musical *Heimatkunst*?) in 1913.[3] The post-war edition was radically abridged here; there is only an 'Ausklang' (Final notes) of three pages. Niemann's scepticism (he did not believe music could become true *Heimatkunst*, and the closest

[1] National Library Coll. 206: 2, Eliel Aspelin-Haapkylä to JS, 7 December 1915.

[2] Nadler 1912. See Adam 2001.

[3] Niemann 1913a, pp. 270 ff.

to that he could imagine was Sibelius' 'national' idiom) was out of place after the war. In both versions, the guilty party behind the poverty of Occidental culture is identified in the tradition of Lienhard: the 'Americanising and equalising super-culture'[1] or 'Americanising business culture'.[2] Niemann's weakness lies in this polemic; that is where he makes himself vulnerable.

The history of music alone is not what interested Niemann but rather, as was usual in the *Heimat* movement, the political confrontation with urbanism, cosmopolitanism and industrialism, which were certainly very advanced in several regions of North America in 1913. This discourse can be traced up to the present. The importance to music of race, tribe, climate, homeland, national character and nature is emphasised even in the preface.[3] In 1913 the author wanted to unpick these concepts 'down to the last detail', but in 1918 and 1925 only 'where it is necessary'. The euphoria of 1913 was somewhat muted after the war. Both versions begin with a verse dedication to the author's father, Rudolph Niemann, a student of Ignaz Moscheles who had received a Premier Prix for piano from the Conservatoire de Paris in 1858. 'Was Du ihm wecktest, ist die innre Stimme, / Die ihm Natur und Heimat heilig sang' (What you awoke in him [Walter] is the inner voice, / Which piously sang nature and homeland to him). As well as: 'Was Du ihn lehrtest, ist der Geist des Deutschen, / Der täglich ihm aus Deinem Spiele klang' (What you taught him is the spirit of the German, / Which he heard daily in your playing). The ideals of nature, homeland, 'spirit of the German' and family (in this case both the son's love for his father and the binding alliance of family, which Niemann liked to emphasise) comprise the elements of originality.

In the 1913 version, he claimed that not even Brahms, who was 'the purest embodiment of the Low German idea and character in music',[4] could be considered a *Heimat* composer, whereas other arts in Germany had numerous representatives of this movement to show. There is no mention of Sibelius in this section, since '*Heimatkunst* in our sense, as a special value and undercurrent of the national within a boundary defined by landscape and the people, is unknown in foreign lands.'[5] But: 'Their *Heimatkunst* is the national.' In the section 'Nationale Musik', Sibelius is discussed at length and given full recognition. The reason why *Heimatkunst* could not develop fully in music lies in the 'mass breeding of musicians in conservatories'.[6] Little wonder then that Sibelius, who was not ruined by the urban conservatories under the guidance of international artists, and who himself had very similar thoughts about 'mass breeding' in 'hothouses', corresponded to Niemann's ideals. He did not treat Sibelius as a composer of 'modernity', along with Richard Strauss, Max Reger and Claude Debussy, or even of musical 'exoticism', which he discussed in detail as 'music of the

[1] Niemann 1913a, p. 287.

[2] Niemann [1918] 1925, p. 295.

[3] Niemann 1913a, p. ix.

[4] Ibid., p. 277.

[5] Ibid., p. 270.

[6] Ibid., p. 274.

future' and a constructive source of inspiration. For him, Sibelius was one of the 'great national composers' such as Frédéric Chopin, Mikhail Glinka, Niels Wilhelm Gade, Edvard Grieg, Piotr Tchaikovsky, Bedřich Smetana and Antonín Dvořák.[1]

Unfortunately, Niemann did not fail to speculate that 'the incredible growth of Jewry in musical creation and imitation' supported 'cosmopolitanism and [intellectual] homelessness'.[2] Because he did not idealise the specifically 'German' quality of *Heimatkunst*, he did not define the *Heimatkunst* movement in the regional and cultural sense. It is, however, possible that Niemann considered the 'expression of racial emotion, of belonging to a race and a landscape', which he despised ('without by any means belonging to the faithfully Teutonic enthusiasts of race', as he added), to be something typically German, although his discussion of the 'national' (of the *Heimatkunst* of foreign lands) was not less emphatic. In the 1918 and later versions it concludes the book; the 1913 section on the German struggle with the 'national' idiom and music's problem with *Heimatkunst* is omitted.

It is difficult to agree when Niemann writes of Johann Sebastian Bach, Georg Friderick Handel, Christoph Willibald Gluck and Wolfgang Amadeus Mozart that their art is 'deeply rooted in the primal ground of their own German popular tradition', is 'conditioned by the national' and is 'national in the broader sense'. 'Restrictedly national'[3] or 'national in the stricter sense', in turn, are terms he applies to any art that could not be adequately understood outside of its own context. Not everyone is in a position to assess such manifestations of the national: he writes that it is a common mistake to consider Brahms 'restrictedly national', when he is rather 'conditioned by the national'. Such an error in perspective, particularly in France, is associated with a 'restrictedly national' premise. By contrast, a composition that contains culturally specific allusions in the form of folksong quotations should be regarded as 'restrictedly national' and seems 'national in the stricter sense'. For Niemann, every form of the national has its legitimacy, even though they are all rooted in different contexts. Niemann accounted for the special position of German musical culture (clearly he had the New German School in mind) as the origin of an awareness of national tendencies in other peoples, even if it has a pronounced quality of the national 'in the broader sense', as in Bach and Brahms. Niemann pointed out that the German nation, despite its own heterogeneity and (consequently) relatively limited tendency to the national 'in the stricter sense', had become the 'heir to Italy's centuries-long dominant position in music':

> The most important masters of all non-German nations since Richard Wagner are not only the only ones who have truly penetrated into the musical life of the

[1] See table of contents. Grieg's reputation as a *Heimatkünstler* has a tradition in German texts, for example, La Mara [Marie Lipsius], *Edvard Grieg* (Leipzig: Breitkopf & Härtel, 1898), p. 2; quoted in Schwab 1992, p. 210.

[2] Niemann 1913a, p. 275.

[3] Ibid., p. 251.

> rest of Europe but especially of Germany but also those who were undeniably influenced by the musical culture of Germany. [...] For all the masters of more recent national music passed though, if not Bach, Beethoven or the Romantics, at least through Wagner and Liszt.[1]

Regardless of how many counterexamples there may be in the history of music, this description no doubt applies to Sibelius. The German model of the national 'in the broader sense' can be explained by the fact that it reveals itself as a 'national note' in the 'spiritual expression, qualities of character and differences in temperament' and by no means signifies the use of one's own national folk music.[2] Here Niemann rashly assumes that readers, even those outside the *Heimat* circle of the like-minded, will agree: 'Everyone knows how that is intended.'[3] The positive influence of Liszt and Wagner lay, in his view, in questioning principles of the Classical and Romantic aesthetic that were intended to be universally valid. Not coincidentally, exemplary national music should be sought in regions that 'stood outside all the great cultural work in music until the onset of Romanticism but were therefore able, as a consequence of this greater isolation, to preserve a wealth of melodically, rhythmically, and harmonically unique folk music and now not only put these elements into the service of music they consciously perceived as national but also sought to derive new aesthetic rules of art from the results.'[4] The fact that the 'northern Germanics' (among whom, as he specifically states, the Finno-Ugric tribes should not be included, though those, like Sibelius, with a Scandinavian family background should be) clung most tenaciously to national elements (in comparison to the Romance and Slavic peoples) lay in turn in the 'very slow mental and physical development, the healthy emotion that tends more to the robust than to decadence in any form, the unfavourable geographical position and lack of musical organisation.'[5] The critical undertone is unmistakable here, although the category of what is still original is defined positively.

The specific development of the national required not only 'subject matter and material' but also 'new aesthetic rules of art.'[6] Whether as operatic subject matter, themes, rhythms or tonal systems, there were 'popular' alternatives to the established and traditional (quasi-international) qualities cultivated all over the world as teaching material in the conservatories Niemann so harshly attacked.[7] The elegiac national note was especially typical of Finland and Norway, as a feature of the abstract soul of the people (à la Herder) and as the basis for a fruitful authenticity, 'the deep feeling

[1] Niemann 1913a, p. 253.

[2] Cf. Schoenberg 1984.

[3] Niemann 1913a, p. 254.

[4] Ibid., p. 256.

[5] Ibid., p. 265.

[6] Cf. Adorno's category of the 'extra-territorial', discussed in detail in chapter 5.2 in the present volume.

[7] For Bekker's critique of Waltershausen's *Das Siegfried-Idyll*, see Bekker 1921.

for nature', which in comparison to Sweden and Denmark 'intensified more into deep melancholy' (rather than muted into idyll).[1] In a letter from Vienna to Aino on 8 January 1891, Sibelius had observed: 'This sonorous, strangely melancholic monotony of all Finnish melodies is indeed characteristic, although it is a defect.' Distinguishing between beautiful and characteristic was typical of the time. In one of the most important letters to Aino, on 15 April 1891 he wrote: 'We Northerners tend more to the "contemplative". But when we manage to get free of our philosophising, we too can produce talents.'

From Gade to Sibelius, Niemann recorded popular versions of the myth of nature.[2] Apart from the *Kalevala*, which many non-Finns first encountered in the art of Sibelius and Gallen-Kallela, Niemann believed national music enabled one to get closer to the pure nature of the North: often they are musical 'landscape paintings' that have 'made us familiar with the nature of non-German countries'. Moreover, music can convey a feeling of homeland, which in the context of the *Heimat* movement was a value that could not be overestimated: 'Who does not feel at home in Norway once he has settled in with Grieg, or in Denmark with Gade and Hartmann, in Finland with Sibelius or in Russia with Tchaikovsky? [...] What we know of Finland's nature through painters such as Gallén and Järnefelt, but how much through Sibelius' music!' This is certainly not about a German sense of superiority in the spirit of Wilhelmianism but rather about awareness of Germany's own geographically determined limitations. Regardless of how correct the 'familiar' impressions are, his argument shows that as an independent representative of the *Heimat* movement he hoped the national music of the North could provide genuine access to the aspects of a feeling of homeland that were so important from his perspective. His own homeland was not enough, since it already represented a modern, depraved civilisation. According to this author, unfortunately the ur-homeland of humanity existed only in distant, foreign lands (which should not be too hastily equated with exoticism).

The German conductor and antimodernist composer Karl Georg Göhler identified the problem more specifically in the same ideological context: 'Is there not perhaps more alive in this foreign art [Sibelius] of that which is equally characteristic of all human emotion, perhaps much that is more valuable and stronger than some of what our own contemporary art presently grants us?'[3] Göhler had at least absorbed as an ideal the category of the global soul from the later Moritz Lazarus, and he was full of humility with regard to Sibelius' art. Sibelius' position in Niemann's work can be explained by noting that the author considered the ability to create complex forms to be something untypical of national artists. In literature, he felt that 'dramatists' were lacking there (he found plenty of poets, idyllists and elegists); great musical dramatists and genuine symphonists were also rare, in his view. To his own horror,

[1] Niemann 1913a, p. 254.

[2] Ibid., p. 259.

[3] Göhler 1908, p. 263.

he thought he had discovered an exception to the validity of national art – a situation that urgently needed to be remedied.[1] Moreover, he observed that characteristic 'genre-like movements form the climax of nearly all national symphonies'.[2] He explained the tendency to characteristic sound rather than intellectual and emotional depiction by reference to the 'lack of technical training of so many national composers' in countries that 'for generations offered dilettantes as national composers and still do'.[3] The declared ideal is the 'artful' treatment of the 'naively popular' (as compared with one's own characteristic 'rule of art'). Niemann believed in the dialectic of art and nature but without being able to identify such a utopian synthesis in the work of any composer. The objective was clear, namely, the realisation of three criteria: nature, genuine popularity and, in the spirit of the *Heimat* movement, 'healthiness'. 'Without these three things, art dies.'[4]

Was Sibelius in a position to save anything of the validity of the national in music beyond his own region and beyond the turn of the era?[5] 'In England, with its sharp eye for musical characters, it might seem so; in Germany, probably not.' Niemann observed: 'Despite great propaganda, perhaps not the dissemination but certainly not the inner understanding of genuine Finnish national music of the likes of Sibelius will not increase among us in this way.'[6] Germany remained sceptical, in his view, because Sibelius – the 'purest' and 'most noble' of the national composers of the modern era – was intellectually neither 'rich' nor 'flexible' but rather, in contrast to Chopin and Grieg, rather one-sided, appearing 'grey in grey, all too foreign and locally limited', albeit 'personal through and through, national through and through, evolved through and through from great nature'.[7] But Niemann hoped for Sibelius' success, since the national element he was defending needed a guiding figure in the modern era.[8] Sibelius' lead was still considerable: Johan Hartmann, Gade, Johan Peter Selmer, Johan Svendsen, Christian Sinding, Ludvig Norman, Albert Rubenson and Kajanus were 'either already dead to general European concert life or have [...] essentially retreated into their homes'; only Sibelius was still 'with increasing success and lastingly' present, and Carl Nielsen at least 'for a time'.[9] In the post-war editions (1918 and 1925), Niemann attacked the Nordic, denationalised neo-Romanticism in Sweden and Norway (Andreas Hallén, Wilhelm Peterson-Berger, Sinding) for its stylistic dependence on Germany and France. Thus he raised the question from 1913 – updated but with the same intention – of the extent to which Sibelius was different and could have an

1 Niemann 1913a, p. 261.
2 Ibid., p. 262.
3 Ibid., pp. 263–4.
4 Ibid., p. 288.
5 Ibid., p. 266.
6 Ibid., p. 264.
7 Ibid., p. 267.
8 Ibid., p. 269.
9 Ibid., p. 261.

enduring influence at all beyond the borders of his own country — without distorting the essence and significance of his art.[1]

How Finnish is Sibelius?

Niemann argued for 'conservation of nature and maintenance of the homeland' and attacked head-on international musical culture, the world bourgeoisie, 'levelling', the 'swallowing up of everything national and particular', the rejection of everything popular, the destruction of naivety, alienation from nature, 'musical super-culture', intellectualism and the power of money, all of which threatened the development of national art.[2] Even Mahler's 'Neo-Romanticism' and Strauss's 'Modernism' contributed to that, in his view, because they were working their way 'in every respect towards the world bourgeoisie, towards internationalism and cosmopolitanism'. In his 1917 monograph he wrote about Sibelius in more detail but his argument was more superficial in terms of worldview than that of *Die Musik der Gegenwart*. His attitude was far from 'phobic'.[3] The beginning of the small book reads like a defence of the *Heimat* aesthetic and places Sibelius in the context familiar from *Die Musik der Gegenwart*: 'Speaking of Jean Sibelius means grappling with the innermost essence of Finnish music.'[4]

The question relevant today — whether Sibelius and his generation of the first national idealists did not in fact create the Finnish essence and the innermost essence of Finnish music in the first place — is one Niemann answered in the negative. He already detected a 'Finnish tone' — 'slightly veiled by Spohrian influence'[5] — in Fredrik Pacius, a student of Louis Spohr and Moritz Hauptmann, resigned and gently melancholic:

> As if it [Finnish music] wanted to make up for its lateness, its young branch sprouted in the present age, with and alongside Sibelius, a wealth of leaves and blossoms. To us Germans in particular, their creations seem slightly personally Sibelian where in essence — probably very often in Sibelius' case as well — they reflect something universally Finnish, popular and national. For that very reason, we do not wish to and probably cannot speak of a Sibelian school.

Yet Niemann knew Finland and hence knew that Sibelius was celebrated there as the 'reviver of the national Finnish tone'.[6]

His point concerns Sibelius' reception — first in Germany and then in Finland. It was not the superficialities (above all rhythm and folksongs) but rather the 'original emotional tone that the reflective and serious northern German — Pacius was born in

1 Niemann [1918] 1925, p. 290.
2 Niemann 1913a, p. 266.
3 Hepokoski 1993, p. 4.
4 Niemann 1917, p. 5.
5 Ibid., p. 60.
6 Ibid., p. 61.

Hamburg – developed from the soil of his second homeland that was at the time immediately and gratefully recognised as "Finnish" in the sense of the lyrical elements of the national character'. He correctly emphasised the direct connection of many Finnish composers with Germany and dealt in detail with the history of music as 'musical soil'. In Sibelius' case too he recognised the influence of Romantic and Neo-Romantic music. His discussion of Kajanus, who was also published by Breitkopf & Härtel and had studied the violin with the author's uncle, Gustav Niemann, is notably detailed.[1]

Astonishingly, Niemann characterised Sibelius as an almost pure Finn: 'It is therefore not very probable that Jean Sibelius had Scandinavian-Swedish blood.'[2] Sibelius merely took from his mother the 'culture' of an educated minister's home. Precisely thanks to Swedish influence, Finland could 'with complete justification look down on its Russian neighbour, which was far superior to it in terms of immediate artistic temperament, artistic receptivity and talent but infinitely inferior in terms of culture'.[3] With regard to Berlin, the name of the composer Woldemar Bargiel is mentioned in the wrong context – as Sibelius' teacher.[4] He is also mistaken in his notion that Sibelius was continuously active as a composition teacher; this activity was in fact always only sporadic, albeit at times well paid, and he abandoned it entirely in 1901. Not least because of these errors in details, Niemann's book is a good example of the common approach to Sibelius' music in the first half of the twentieth century, and not only in Germany. It is also representative in terms of its general stance: 'It speaks for the ur-Finnish nature of the musical soil in which Jean Sibelius' art sprouted that one still has to dig deep, deep into the purely musical soil to get to its roots.'

This approach leads to regarding nature and people as 'determining forces of life and creation' alongside the subject matter and world of ideas of the saga, the myth and the history of the country. The basic tone of Finland's nature and people is 'inwardness', 'seriousness', 'gloominess' and 'melancholy'. 'The Finn lives in constant struggle with his nature.' Sibelius' music, in turn, is the 'Finnish nature become sound', which Niemann initially seeks in naively melancholic, elegiac, dreamy, longing, unworldly character pieces,[5] which no longer keep their distance from 'the mysterious pantheistic mysticism of the Nordic spirit'. His point of departure was works he could compare to the lyric pieces of Grieg and Peterson-Berger, yet Grieg's pathos of nature transformed into idyll in Sibelius' work. He identifies the 'elemental and charming poetry of nature' as a characteristic feature of the 'classicising Nordic idyll of nature'

[1] Niemann 1917, p. 7.

[2] Ibid., p. 8.

[3] Ibid., p. 11. The idea of Germanic cultural nations (*Kulturnationen*), in contrast to Slavic and Finno-Ugric peoples, was also familiar in Finland; on this, see Knapas 2001, p. 32; and even today essays elaborating this dichotomy are published (also in relation to JS). In an academic form, the dichotomy can be seen behind the dynamics of the 'Finnish barbarian' in contrast to Swedish 'culture' as described in Hepokoski 2001b, p. 326.

[4] Niemann 1917, p. 9.

[5] Ibid., pp. 14–15.

during the age of the reception of antiquity in Central Europe. The word 'elementary', which simply means 'concerning the elements' and is not at all pejorative here, deserves attention. Nevertheless, Sibelius' art is 'the musical expression of the soul of the Finnish people',[1] which in his work is explicitly not manifested in quoted folksongs and rhythms. Niemann explains alleged 'deficiencies', such as the irrational and illogical and the naturalistic quality of some expressions, by reference to the character of the people,[2] which is why these nationally limited details are celebrated in Finland while elsewhere — 'out of ignorance of the character of the Finnish people' — they are disdained. He believed he was relatively close to the Finnish soul as a northern German. For 'us', most Finnish music would still not mean a lot, because of its national limitation. Only in Sibelius' work are the 'personal, human and artistic' qualities so characteristic and significant 'that we can get past the initially alienating and limiting qualities of his art and appreciate and feel a significant portion of Finnish music'.[3]

Niemann's concentration on programmatic and lyrical genres at the expense of the symphonies can be explained by reference to his aesthetic and ideological concepts. Niemann declared his remarks on the programmatic and theatrical compositions — one need only think of his intuitively correct characterisation of *En saga* — to be the basis for a proper understanding of the absolute quality of the symphonies and other works.[4] In his view, even the symphonies reflect the soul of the Finnish people; their 'subject matter is the same from the first to the last: Finland's soul in nature and the people'.[5] The First Symphony (1899–1900), which even in 1917 he still considered the most significant one, was 'the deepest and most rooted piece of the maestro's symphonic *Heimatkunst*', whereas the Second and Third Symphonies were already approaching 'Western symphonic modernism' (the 'universal' in the pejorative sense).[6] The Fourth Symphony of 1911, in turn, was nearly 'on the same level as most modern Debussyan Impressionism and Schoenbergian Naturalism and Expressionism in music'. If this assessment is correct, it raises the question which other composer of his generation achieved such a synthesis. The Fifth was not yet finished in 1917.

When it came to potential 'symphonic' material, this enthusiast for northern lands, who was anything but a neoclassical apologist for the symphonic and felt all national art lacked only large forms (and drama), had doubts not only about Sibelius' invention but also about Nordic themes in general, because they were supposedly 'short-winded'. In Sibelius he saw 'impressionistically disposed talent' and the lack of the "Western" basic requirements of genuine symphonic creativity' ('monumentality, self-contained form, organic and logical inner development and design').[7] He praised

1 Ibid., p. 21.
2 Ibid., p. 22.
3 Ibid., p. 61.
4 Ibid., p. 47.
5 Ibid., p. 49.
6 Ibid., p. 50.
7 Ibid., pp. 47–8.

the 'juxtaposed insights'[1] of 'mostly wonderful melodic beauty and harmonic originality', the 'intensive and noble warmth of feeling', 'the fire of the choleric and wild temperament in the Finnish manner', 'the magic of his profound melancholy' and the 'bold success of the whole'. He attributes the general 'homogeneity and monotony' to the rhythmical and harmonic structure of Finnish folk melodies, regardless of the fact that Sibelius was an 'eminent connoisseur of symphonic, polyphonic textures':

> Thus in Sibelius' symphonies, now rhapsodic and episodic, now recitative, now balladic and epic ideas in loose combination await the harmonious elaboration and integration into the whole, often in vain. This entails a somewhat torn and choppy overall impression, placing one after the other and side by side according to a programme that is obvious yet kept hidden, a frequent breaking off and breaking though by means of fugatos and interpolations of recitative, imperfect cadence and strong contrasts, a struggling with imitation of, for example, Tchaikovsky's 'Pathétique' in a Finnish dialect, a more or less naturalistically characterised grey-in-grey painting beneath ghostly faces and burdensome psychological pressure that no coarse folk pleasure in the scherzos, no flight to nature in the all quite magnificent slow movements, no Goldmarkian dazzling orchestral apparel full of highly original and surprising instrumental effects can truly brighten and disguise. All the more splendid are the details, the manly steely power and freshness, the genuine, serious, massive and heavy pathos, the quick-witted and accurate naturalistic characteristics, the deeply and fully penetrating natural tone, the saturated melancholy.[2]

Nevertheless, Niemann has not only been accused of an aesthetic love–hate relationship but also of rejecting the object of his own research, even though his sentences are in no way characterised by a 'priestlike gesture within the cultic institution intended to keep pure the sacred space of Germanic symphonism'.[3]

All the qualities he lists are only pejorative for readers who themselves cling rigidly to the modernist foundations of the 'Western' — an adjective that is used pejoratively in Niemann's writings — classical symphony. Niemann, by contrast, was a cultural critic who concentrated on music and was enthusiastic about the rural *Heimat* idea of Schleswig-Holstein origin, for whom the classicistic, preferably entirely homogeneous and stringently constructed symphony — the precise counterpart to the ideal type influenced by Beethoven — was by no means self-evidently the most sublime genre. But he worried about the future of national art in light of its obvious problems with the development of large genres. In the spirit of *Die Musik seit Richard Wagner*, he portrayed the contradiction between the 'Western' civilisation of the symphony as

[1] Cf. Hanslick's critique of Liszt, quoted and interpreted in Dömling 1998, p. 123. Hanslick formulated it more elegantly than JS' critics, but his idea of a 'refined juxtaposition of the most disparate elements' is reflected in their writings.

[2] Niemann 1917, pp. 48–9.

[3] Hepokoski 1993, p. 4.

thesis, and the antithesis of an original based on *Heimat* and nature as a kind of negative dialectic — that is, he regarded a meaningful synthesis as impossible. Although not the only successor to Beethoven, Sibelius was at the very least the only composer of his day who was able to create great orchestral music from the basic ideas of so-called *Heimat* art and culture; from Niemann's 'sympathetic' perspective, Sibelius was not just a *primus inter pares* but an unrivalled contemporary.

Rejected professorship in Vienna by telegraph.
I cannot enslave myself again *pour l'honneur*.[1]

5.2 Voices from Exile

Between 'Extra-Territoriality' and 'La lumière de la spiritualité'

When the German composer Wolfgang Rihm declared that Adorno's 'Glosse', which was written in exile in 1938, was responsible for problems in Sibelius' reception in German-speaking countries, Reinhold Brinkmann of Harvard University was sceptical. Brinkmann not only had a less favourable opinion of Sibelius but another vision of Adorno's influence. Rihm numbered Sibelius among his colleagues who 'as a result of several statements by very prominent authors were in effect excluded from artistic activity'.[2] Even apart from the fact that Sibelius had almost entirely 'excluded' himself from public activity, long before Adorno's critique, there is a tendency in the Sibelius literature to blame Adorno for phenomena whose roots lie in the polemics of the 1920s and even earlier, while aspects of Adorno's aesthetic that in fact represent a sine qua non for a contemporary assessment of Sibelius are often overlooked.

Even Arthur Rubinstein, who was hardly likely to have been influenced by Adorno, contributed to the fact that his many devotees may have had a negative image of Sibelius. In *My Many Years*, he wrote: 'Musical life in the United States was not very stimulating during the war. True enough, every city had an orchestra, many of them fully professional, but the musical menus remained the same. [...] There were a few years of imposed Sibelius which finally caused a touch of indigestion.'[3] Such puns (and there are plenty of them about Sibelius) have been enormously influential.

The earliest evidence of Adorno's disapproval was 'Fussnote', which continued a debate, initiated by the essay 'Knut Hamsun: Zur Vorgeschichte der autoritären Ideologie' (Knut Hamsun: On the pre-history of authoritarian ideology) by the literary sociologist Leo Löwenthal and published in the *Zeitschrift für Sozialforschung*, on the 'epic greatness' of Knut Hamsun, the Norwegian inventor of new narrative techniques and a friend of the Nazis.[4] According to Löwenthal in the German original of 1937, anyone who saw in the Nobel Prize winner of 1920 signs of 'particular chastity, mature austerity and shyness enraptured with life' or of epic greatness in the 'sparseness of the cultural inventory' and 'shadowiness of the people he depicted' offered an example of 'weary resignation and social defeatism'. In his 'Fussnote', Adorno publicly agreed with Löwenthal but added to its argument critical of society, whose legitimacy

[1] Diary, 1 March 1912.

[2] Brinkmann and Rihm 2001, pp. 139–40.

[3] Rubinstein 1980, p. 497.

[4] Editor's note in Adorno 1986, p. 804. Cf. Löwenthal 1937, and Kittang 1994. A later version of Löwenthal's article in English was published as chapter 7 of Löwenthal, *Literature and the Image of Man: Sociological Studies of the European Drama and Novel, 1600–1900* (Boston: Beacon, 1953).

was completely beyond question in the cultural and political situation of the late 1930s, an example from the history of music: Sibelius.

As a footnote to the 'Fussnote', it is useful to read Adorno's letter of 1937 on the subject to his fellow scholar and mentor Max Horkheimer, as it expresses reservations similar to objections to Adorno raised by Sibelius connoisseurs (who are rarely Adorno connoisseurs): 'In my view, the basic error lies in a lack of experience with things that are under discussion; he [Löwenthal] applies finished categories to them rather than entering into a real process with the matter. In any case, I would advise great caution in the enormously difficult case of Hamsun. It is childishly easy to show that H. is fascist but correspondingly difficult to make this insight fruitful, and most difficult of all to save Hamsun from himself.'[1] Here Adorno touches on the core of all biographical research, which is (like Adorno) more interested in the history of art than in the life story of a single human being.

More significant than the oft-cited 'Glosse' or compact 'Footnote' to Löwenthal – both from the immediate biographical context of the essays 'Fragmente über Wagner' and 'Über den Fetischcharacter der Musik und die Regression des Hörens' (translated as 'On the Fetish-Character in Music and the Regression of Listening'), which were more important yet remarkably similar in their cultural criticism, is the fact that Sibelius was one of the few composers Adorno continuously used – even in the posthumously published *Ästhetische Theorie* (translated as *Aesthetic Theory*) – as a negative example of a worldview he despised. Adorno articulated a general criticism of Symbolism that concerned not objectives but implementation, using the example of Sibelius, as Löwenthal before him had used Hamsun. He did not believe in the truthfulness of Symbolist 'all nature' but rather saw in it proto-fascist and bourgeois commercial elements. The actual object, nature itself, indeed constitutes a central value in his thinking, which explains his agitation. He considered a cheap approach to be presumptuousness.

He addresses the concept of nature in his 'Fragmente über Wagner' (1937–8), which unlike his Sibelius essays is one of his most important works:

> If we were to summarize the 'idea' of the *Ring* in simple words we would say that man emancipates himself from the blind identity with nature from which he springs; he then acquires power over nature only to succumb to her in the long run. The allegory of the *Ring* asserts that dominion over nature and subjugation by nature are one and the same. The division of the world into nature and individuation is parallel to the split between authority and rebels. [...] The parable of the man who dominates nature only to relapse into a state of natural bondage gains an historical dimension in the action of the *Ring*: with the victory of the bourgeoisie, the idea that society is like a natural process, something 'fated', is reaffirmed, despite the conquest of particular aspects of nature. The

[1] Adorno and Horkheimer 1997, p. 346.

catastrophe arises at the moment when this much-vaunted 'natural process' is revealed to be the mere product and stigma of an undirected social process and the lackey of an all-knowing authority.[1]

In Sibelius, Adorno recognised not the 'life-giving' integration of 'Naturzusammenhang' (identity with nature) and 'Naturbeherrschung' (dominion over nature) that compels one to cultural optimism but rather criticised him, pessimistic and negative as usual, as a specimen 'of the remnants of traditional bourgeois art' – that is, as a stolid product of decadence without a 'protesting subjectivity'. Although Adorno's interpretation in his 'Fussnote' is hasty, his question touches on an important problem of Sibelius' work.[2] The 'darkness' of the sound – subsequent to his Symbolist visions of dream worlds, Odilon Redon would have spoken of 'la lumière de la spiritualité'[3] – is in Sibelius just a 'product of technical ineptness' that feigns spiritual 'depth'. Whether or not Adorno can appreciate this quality in Redon, he considers it a stylising of the bourgeois in Sibelius. Many of the details he lists (no development, too much colourism, trivial motifs, no coherence, etc.) now constitute legitimate subjects of a dispute over musical analysis. For example, Hepokoski analyses the subtlety of 'rotational form' and 'circular patterns' that result from repetition and the breaking of temporary linearity.[4] Such studies in effect respond to Adorno's challenge, though without mentioning his name.

In Adorno's view, the irreversibility of the historical process that determines the tendency of the musical material to evolve calls for compositional techniques to transform progressively and critically and to relate to the current social context in an oppositional relationship, thus supporting the morally valuable aspects of Western civilisation as it develops. Adorno did not see that effect at all in Sibelius. He regarded elements of folk music and traditional techniques (triads, etc.) that were in his view typical of Sibelius as reactionary and regressive in the context of the twentieth century. When he reflected on an exception – the 'extra-territorial music' of Janáček and Bartók[5] – in *Philosophie der Neuen Musik* (translated as *Philosophy of Modern Music*) of 1949, he did not think of Sibelius. Adorno wrote about Bartók in a brief essay from 1925 that already seems to anticipate the ideas of extra-territoriality.[6] In *Einleitung in die Musiksoziologie* (translated as *Introduction to the Sociology of Music*), Adorno repeated the approach without speaking of extra-territoriality.[7] As new examples of this phenomenon he added quotations of Bavarian folk art by the Blauer Reiter artists

[1] Adorno 1991, p. 137; the essay was originally published in German in the *Zeitschrift für Sozialforschung* in 1939.

[2] Adorno 1986, p. 804. For the expression 'life-giving', see Marquery Stoddard to JS, January 11, 1938, National Library Coll. 206: 37; see also chapter 2.1 in the present volume.

[3] Hofstätter 1972, p. 56.

[4] See Hepokoski 1993, pp. 23 ff. and 62 ff., and Hepokoski 1996.

[5] Adorno 1985, pp. 35–6 n. 5.

[6] Adorno 1984b, pp. 282–3.

[7] Adorno 1976, p. 166.

and parallels between Pablo Picasso and his friend Carl Einstein's ideas of African art, articulated for instance in his book *Negerplastik* (African sculpture) of 1915. The Austrian composer Franz Schreker, by contrast, whose music Adorno still regarded favourably as late as 1959 in terms of extra-territoriality, 'denies both cause and effect' and the 'actual determinant of composition.' He failed 'to construct an ego', but his music stands 'outside the demands of culture' ('exterritorial zu den Forderungen der Kultur'). 'But because it springs from a compulsion which is more potent than shame and testifies to the truth of things that culture proscribes, it gives expression to doubts about the value of culture as such. Schreker consciously deserts to the realm which culture has distanced itself from and consigned to the vulgar.'[1]

As late as 1960 Adorno praised Mahler, whose music he also heard as 'extra-territorial', for his ability to liberate himself from norms of alienation and overcome established techniques and genres. In his commentary on Paul Bekker's assessment of Mahler, Adorno emphasised the fundamental difference: Mahler distanced himself from the German art song and followed Mussorgsky and Janáček — in contrast to Schubert, Schoenberg and Webern: 'In that respect he is an outsider in the history of the German song.'[2] Adorno defined difference positively in Mahler's case, arguing that he was in a position to observe relicts of a pre-bourgeois society and an authentic mental state. He was said to have been able to overcome the outdated individuality and subjectivity of the German Lied. These central ideas in his monograph on Mahler, the footnote on Bartók and Janáček in *Philosophie der Neuen Musik* and his broadcast on Schreker make clear that Adorno was not thinking in a stereotypically Germano-centric way. Rather, his argument is a general critique of culture and ideology. He operates with the contrast between decadent alienation and genuine naturalness — not with topographical or universally political, much less naively racist, categories.

Adorno might have been able to appreciate Sibelius much as he did Schreker, Mahler and others if he had not already employed him as an example of something else within the framework of his overall critical theory, which is functionally superordinate to his musicology — a hierarchy that must be respected, even if it pains one to do so. In 'many agrarian regions in southeast Europe', in his view, the 'developmental tendency of Occidental music has not been purely developed', and thus the use of tonal material even into the recent past is 'not a matter of disgrace'. According to Adorno, both Janáček and Bartók profit from this, but not Sibelius — since, for whatever reason, Adorno does not suppose there was anything similar in north-eastern Europe. Because Adorno determined the historical adequacy of a given compositional technique with an eye to the valid form of society, a primarily agrarian society can have a different state of artistic technique from an urban industrial one like Vienna or Berlin. His interest was not, however, in the music of the peasants and village chapels of Transylvania but rather in two renowned artists (Janáček and Bartók)

[1] Adorno 1992, pp. 134 and 143. See also Kienzle 1998.

[2] See Adorno 1996, p. 75.

who were conscious of their connection to the rural folk culture of their environment (and beyond) even though they belonged to the urban European sphere.

When Adorno evaluates the music of Janáček historically and socially as 'magnificent in its consequences', the emphasis is discretely placed on 'consequence'. Bartók's compositions in particular (and, to be sure, no less magnificent in their 'consequences'), 'in spite of his folkloristic inclinations, are nonetheless among the most progressive in European musical art'. The fusion of folkloristic elements (equally typical of Janáček) and modern techniques is thus possible as well. In the work of Janáček and Bartók, the idea of fusion is unproblematic since the folkloristic avant-garde in their respective countries could not be reconciled even superficially with the aesthetic, totalitarian ideas of National Socialism, fascism or Stalinism and was not appropriated by them either: Janáček and Bartók practised 'external' cultural criticism, while Schoenberg's New Music did the same thing from within.[1] Bartók was at once Occidental and 'extra-territorial' and not someone whose artistic orientation was regionally limited. Although Adorno wrote of the 'legitimation of such music on the periphery' of an essentially central European culture and believed it 'lies foremost in its ability to formulate a technical canon which is in itself both correct and selective', it would be much too simple to understand 'extra-territoriality' with regard to a region as having the status of an outsider. Rather, it is about an alternative world that cannot be defined by reference to a dichotomy of inside and outside (or by 'we' and 'others').

The 'extra-territorial' not only stands outside a topographically defined core territory but also outside territoriality itself; correspondingly, the inside and outside of its cultural criticism refer not to Germany or Austria, on the one hand, and to 'others', on the other, but to the existence or lack of belonging to a modern cultural elite à la Paul Bekker.[2] He notes that Bartók and Janáček were active on the periphery of Central Europe's core regions around 1900, yet their unique quality as artists lay in the ability to develop their extra-territoriality with an eye to the 'Occidental' (rationalisation, logical consequence of development) modernism without abandoning their regionalism. Bartók and Janáček were, however (more clearly than Sibelius), politically aware nationalists who were interested both in the 'soil' of their region and the 'blood' of their people and thus resisted the supra-national music culture of Central Europe. Did Adorno not know that, or did he consciously ignore the social reality? It is difficult to believe, and impossible to prove, that Adorno made his judgement solely on the basis of his supposition that Sibelius *nolen volens* belonged to fascist or National Socialist circles. Nevertheless, it seems necessary to distinguish between actual and intended extra-territoriality. Because the efforts of Bartók and Janáček with regard to folk music were directed at finding its 'essence' within the framework of their own development, their intention was not 'extra-territorial' but rather concerned with their artistic identity. They were, however, 'extra-territorial' by Adorno's criteria: their

[1] This distinction corresponds to the position of Haffner 1983, pp. 59–60; cf. Splitt 1987, p. 214.

[2] See, for example, Bekker 1921, pp. 330–31.

music has qualities that are valid far beyond their integrative and synthetic way of approaching regional art and far beyond exoticism. The 'extra-territorial' explains the fascination with Bartók and Janáček of representatives of the more recent avant-garde.

According to Adorno, the splendour of the 'extra-territorial' in the work of Janáček and Bartók lay in their technical 'consequences'. Any value judgements must be related to the theoretical efforts of these composers that began with folklore studies but went far beyond them; and to the intellectually articulated, enlightened rather than irrational consciousness of both artists,[1] who worked analytically with their regional connection. Much like the modernist representatives of the 'Occidental' tradition, Janáček and Bartók studied the technical details of popular culture to find new methods and deliberately sought to develop artistically the musical material of their environment. They broke radically with the tradition of conventional local art. The academic stance was replaced by a non-academic one without dispensing with the logical and consequential. The new construct did not continue any tradition uncritically. Janáček and Bartók exchanged the more popular musical idiom of Josef Suk and others in their region for an enlightened avant-garde critical of Occidental culture, and traditional folk music for true art. But honestly, all of this applies to Sibelius as well. Adorno strove to distinguish sharply between archaic 'extra-territorial' art and 'blood-and-soil' ideology or 'nationalistic reaction'. Both directions are rooted in the regional, but only the 'extra-territorial' organises common musical material (triads and simple rhythmic gestures) differently from the common 'Occidental' tradition. The avant-garde and the 'extra-territorial' alone had the power of alienation, which fundamentally distinguish them from any 'nationalistic reaction' that seeks both the 'soil' and the 'blood' of a people. This alienation from the common musical material rooted in agrarian culture was 'external' criticism, and the 'inner-musical' criticism of the Schoenberg circle came to its aid. Both types of criticism rejected the relationship to the traditions of both 'blood-and-soil music' and folk music. Because Janáček created his 'diction' by means of language, he suspended the tradition of the belated, ideologically permeated and no longer 'true' triad even when he employed it himself.

From today's perspective, it seems plausible to characterise Sibelius as 'extra-territorial' as well. Even more clearly than Bartók or Janáček, he was from the periphery of the Occident, from a country that was 'agrarian' apart from its capital, Helsinki. He did not even grow up in the regional capital, though as a young adult he did become urban and metropolitan in orientation; through his family he came into contact with pan-European idealism and the educational goals of 'Occidental' high culture. His interest in Germany was connected neither with Wilhelminian pomp nor with the extremes of the Weimar Republic nor with the Third Reich but rather with the widespread idea that the elements of a sophisticated culture à la Goethe and

[1] In the case of Bartók, one thinks above all of the oft-cited theory of the three possibilities of folk music's influence on art music; cf., for example, Suchoff 1976, pp. 301–98. See also Bartók [1937] 1976a and Bartók [1942] 1976c on the categories of 'blood' and 'soil', in Suchoff 1976, pp. 25–8 and 29–32.

Alexander von Humboldt that were still most present in Germany and Austria — having already become rarer elsewhere — represented an elevated state in the history of humanity. This assessment is important, because it implies the international validity of his symphonic writing as a form of expression. Sibelius never imitated or created variations on Finnish folk music in his major works but instead let it inspire him to create 'extra-territorial' structures with elements of at times folkloristic flavour. Like Janáček, he delved more deeply into the structures of regional typical creativity than did artists, especially of the older generation, who cultivated the national in the form of citations of melodies.

In Sibelius' case, these processes were largely intuitive. The beginnings of a rational engagement were present only occasionally: in 1896 he postulated the spontaneous quality of folk culture as a role model, in contrast to what he saw as the exaggeratedly complicated, not very effective compositional techniques of his colleagues who employed noncommittal references to pre-modern styles of the late Middle Ages.[1] Ideas of 'personal' and 'national style', on the harmonisation of the folksong, on the significance of 'personality' for an artist, on the status of tonal systems and their reform and on rhythmic asymmetry were introduced but not worked out. His musical practice also lacked any effort to establish a new system of external cultural criticism (or anything like that) based on regional culture. In that sense, he did not fulfil two of Adorno's central conditions of the 'extra-territorial': the formation of a 'canon which is in itself both correct and selective' and the 'consequence' of technique. The draft lecture of 1896, written in the spirit of Felipe Pedrell's essay *Por nuestra música* (1891), gives hints that even Sibelius recognised in the regional an opportunity to protect himself against the threat of constructivism and the outdated 'Occidental'. The lack of a well-thought-out theory cannot have been Adorno's reason for excluding him. Rather, he must have suspected that Sibelius had developed the beginnings of an 'extra-territorial' approach in his music without a critical stance, affirmative with regard to Western culture. Adorno's mistake, however, was that he clung to intellectual forms of social criticism, not sensing the implied utopian in Sibelius (despite his closeness to Rousseau[2]), and did not know the anything but sentimental, highly academic context of Finnish idealism and national modernity prior to 1917.

One possibility for unconventional comparisons between Adorno and Niemann — two authors whose complex thinking appears to offer an inexhaustible source of critical engagement with the history of Sibelius' reception — is opened up by Wolfgang Welsch's modern/postmodern interpretation of Adorno. The concepts of the 'sublime' and of 'nature' are key categories in modern/postmodern philosophy (albeit with a slightly different meaning from that found in Immanuel Kant and Edmund

[1] Sibelius [1896] 1980, pp. 86 ff. For a few more details on this, see chapter 2.2 in the present volume.

[2] Welsch 1990, pp. 114 ff. See also Jauss 1989, p. 69, on Lyotard: 'in the aesthetic of the sublime, modern art finds its driving force and the logic of the avant-garde finds its axioms'; cf. Lyotard 1984; and on Adorno, see Jauss 1989, p. 74: 'Adorno, who could have called Rousseau as the chief witness of his theory of modernism, mentions him [...] virtually not at all.'

Burke), and they are certainly central to the reception of Sibelius as well. Adorno's own distinction between the pompous and the modern sublime (i.e., in the structure as 'matrix') itself deviates from Kant's idea of the sublime as it is used in elevated everyday language. Following Welsch, we observe that the trivial forms of the pompously beautiful in the art of Wilhelmianism are fundamentally different from manifestations of the modern sublime in Sibelius, for example, as well as in the *Heimat* movement (despite its programmatic, almost pathetic fidelity to the German Emperor, William II[1]). The programmatically sublime of idealist realism shores up the dominance of the power of capitals and the tradition of rulers against which the 'new idealism' of the nature enthusiasts rebelled. The regional and nature were also used as programmatic *topoi* in idealist realism, but they were inessential to the core of that aesthetic. The structurally sublime, by contrast, was closely connected to so-called nature and naturalness. Genuine or imagined landscapes were not glorified; rather, the utopian and mythical relationship between nature and the thinking and feeling 'I' was made problematic. The integration of people into nature that Nietzsche called for as the source of unlimited sovereignty and power was a similar utopia; this is the reason why Zarathustra speaks: 'Behold, I teach you the Superman. The Superman is the meaning of the earth. Let your will say: The Superman *shall be* the meaning of the earth! I entreat you, my brothers, *remain true to the earth*, and do not believe those who speak to you of superterrestrial hopes!'[2] From Adorno's point of view, which was not so much individual and transcendental as social and enlightened, but nonetheless pessimistic, harmony was *a priori* impossible, so that sublime art took on the task of depicting the dilemma as graphically as possible rather than, as conventionally, veiling with charming beauty. It should not simulate harmony, which in modern society would be deceptive, or reconcile human beings with their environment, as can certainly happen as a result of superficial blindness and immanent acceptance of socially predetermined forms.

Both Adorno and Lyotard as well as Niemann and Lienhard combated the rationalism of intellectualism and alienation by an urban, mechanistic and monetary society in which industrial effectiveness and the abstract logic of finance are considered the highest values. Whereas Adorno and Lyotard viewed the category of the sublime as an instrument of enlightenment in a situation that is hopeless anyway, Niemann still tried to organise the future of art and society. The ideal possible integration of human beings into nature was supposed to eliminate alienation, refute the 'fine taste' of the decadent tradition, liberate art from pre-existing models and prepare the way for a progressive anti-ideological and anti-commercial practice. According to Adorno, true nature showed the way around exaggerated rationalism as well – which accounts for his reserve toward dodecaphony and serialism[3] – even to unfolding

[1] Christiansen 1980, p. 68.

[2] Nietzsche 1976b, p. 42.

[3] See, for example, Adorno 2002.

diversity and the justified incompleteness of the fragment. To follow Welsch further, nature and the dynamic of the 'sublime' liberate art from the obligation to produce works as the ultimate reason for art. The not-yet-completed and never-to-be-finished become the representatives of the genuine. In Adorno's *Philosophy of Modern Music* one finds the simple but effective: 'Today the only works which really count are those which are no longer works at all.'[1] Unity is rejected as an attempt to reconcile and as an instrument of affirmation. This maxim prepares the paradigmatic advent of a natural diversity of postmodernism in art theory.

For Niemann and for Adorno, the 'law of art' sets the direction in connection with regionally characteristic music: in Niemann's case Sibelius and in Adorno's Bartók and Janáček. Both authors presume that 'extra-territorial' and modern 'popular' art can be 'capable of art' without losing their originality. Whereas the 'blood-and-soil' aesthetic, in Adorno's view, wanted to call established tradition into question — in contrast to the 'nationalistic reaction' — it was not, in contrast to forward-looking 'extra-territorial' art and the rest of the avant-garde, in a position to be 'art' in the emphatic sense and to strive for authentic naturalness or at least to enable the so-called experience of inability to do so. Niemann and Adorno describe this utopian art in a way that is nonbinding. Niemann in particular is uncertain whether his *primus inter pares* (Sibelius) was yet up to the epochal task or whether it is not perhaps better to wait longer for the Messiah. Adorno's examples are also exemplary, since in the work of all four of the composers he mentions (including Mahler and Schreker), extra-territoriality exists only in individual works. Adorno associates Sibelius with the province of blood and soil — or at least that is what is always claimed.[2] This fateful position cannot even be proved by reference to his 'Glosse', which states in simple sentences:

> The wrong triads: Stravinsky composed with them in all their consequences. By adding wrong notes, he demonstrated how the wrong had become right. In Sibelius, the pure ones sound wrong. He is Stravinsky against his will. Except he has less talent.
>
> His supporters do not want to know anything of that. Their song answers to the refrain: ''Tis all nature, 'Tis all nature.' The great Pan, depending on his need for blood and soil, promptly turns up. The trivial is taken for the original, the unarticulated for the sound of unconscious creation.[3]

The first paragraph is about the wrong 'material' ('triads', etc.), and the second is about its dubious reception by 'his supporters' and their concepts ('the great Pan' as symbol, blood and soil, myth of originality, etc.). But criticism of the behaviour of unqualified 'supporters' should not be equated totally with statements about the material. Adorno

[1] Adorno 1985, p. 30.

[2] Jackson and Murtomäki 2001, p. xii.

[3] Adorno 1982, p. 249.

associated without reserve proto-fascist ideas not with Sibelius but with the ideology of 'his supporters'. Sibelius simply had 'less talent'.

If one compares the stylistic typologies of Niemann and Adorno, the concept of *Heimat* music turns out to be composed of elements of the 'extra-territorial' and of early blood-and-soil ideology. Characterising *Heimat* music as 'nationalistic reaction' would be one-sided. This reaction included 'German neo-Romanticism' (Pfitzner *et al.*[1]) and in part 'German modernism' (Strauss, Ludwig Thuille, *et al.*[2]). The utopia of a contemporary *Heimat* music and nationalist modernism had some of the same roots as the later blood-and-soil madness — both can be derived from the Romantic aesthetic of nature and Rousseau's ideal of nature — but they became reality in 'extra-territorial' modernism.

Adorno is, of course, not an author who is easy to understand. The central categories of his thinking are generally 'more implicitly than explicitly directive'.[3] The same is true of Niemann: the naive, popular substance, which is accessible only to true *Heimat* artists, is not supposed to suffer from the effort to become 'capable of art' that is necessary to communicate or from the effort to achieve larger, symphonic constructions. Plurality should not be lost in the process of unifying the material but, in the interest of complete artistic validity and effect, it should not be left in an unregulated state either but should be formed according to an original 'artistic law'. The intimate experience of nature and naturalness — as opposed to its aesthetic subjugation or distanced observation — is from both perspectives at once a prerequisite of the design and the goal of the reception. Niemann believed in the utopian eventuality of *Heimatkunst* in large formats (symphonies, operas, etc.) and accused Sibelius of inconsequence in this regard — that is to say, that even in his symphonies the utopian goals were not achieved, of which Sibelius was also aware. It may be that Sibelius' irritation with Niemann was based on a sense that Niemann had precisely grasped the core of his tragedy as an artist. Adorno rejected both the idea of unity and the affirmation of the character of the work. He expected of art that it 'expose itself to [...] the irreconcilable'.[4] In his view, that was the only way to imagine the 'experience of possible participation in nature and a shared freedom with it'[5] — that is to say, the idea of a long-vanished natural splendour.

Adorno modified Niemann's figure of thought and showed the way out of the post-Romantic *Heimat* utopia into modern, sublime extra-territoriality. Much like Schoenberg in Adorno's writings, Niemann's Sibelius is an imperfect but nevertheless solitary, outstanding composer on the path to realising an old utopia. Yet Adorno, without suspecting it, shared important maxims with Sibelius as well. They felt a deep aversion both for Stravinsky and for the artistic mediocrity of the 'hothouses',

[1] Niemann 1913a, pp. 107 ff.

[2] Ibid., pp. 182 ff.

[3] Welsch 1990, p. 116.

[4] Adorno 1999, p. 249.

[5] Welsch 1990, p. 119.

contrasting with a vital interest in Schoenberg and the culture of the Central European metropolises of the turn of the century. Sibelius and Adorno were also linked by a utopian quality (mixed with cultural pessimism) as well as the conviction that radical art can be created in an extra-territorial context. They shared the view that it is 'necessary for the artistic production' that the artists thoroughly and critically analyse their own 'relationship to the [artistic] production of the present',[1] to the trends in the development of the musical material. Sibelius too toyed with the idea of an alternative path to the critically unconventional modernism that Adorno as theorist sensed alongside the avant-garde of Schoenberg and his students. There was only one thing that Sibelius resisted more stubbornly than his philosophically versed, more concept-conscious colleagues: taking a strict stance against the 'irreconcilable'.

A Close-Up in Adorno's Eyes

It was not Sibelius himself, whose thinking was inaccessible to Adorno, but Bengt de Törne's book *Sibelius: A Close-Up*, one of Faber and Faber's major publications of 1937, that was the occasion for Adorno's 'Glosse'. A review in the *Zeitschrift für Sozialforschung*, a journal that was important for the survival of critical theory during the Second World War but not widely read outside specialist circles,[2] was justified because the theme seemed symptomatic of the time from the perspective of social criticism. Törne's study shows how a well-meaning but poorly prepared attempt to provide a 'close-up' of Sibelius caused prejudices — at least more so than Niemann did, who has nevertheless been said to have 'armed the enemy'. In Törne's case, most authors on Sibelius regard not his popular essay but Adorno's reaction to it as the true enemy.

The beginning of the book is worth mentioning with regard to Adorno's other projects around 1938: Törne writes a lot about Sibelius' popularity as such.[3] That is followed by sections intended to convince the reader that Törne is indeed a reliable reporter. That is precisely what he was not. Törne was, however, an imaginative aesthetician and mediocre composer who was, it seems, treated with respect by Sibelius. This is apparently demonstrated by a document that survives only as a copy in Törne's handwriting: On 25 November 1947 Sibelius seems to have written in his polite and encouraging manner (but a few words make it clear that Sibelius was honestly interested): 'Dear Mr Bengt de Törne, Congratulations on your Ballad. I find it especially enjoyable. Your charm lies in mastering the pathos that you poured into the work.'[4] In keeping with the friendship between the artists, the book is rich in anecdotes. Törne tried to meet with Sibelius while working on the book, which gave occasion to a long

[1] Diary, 20 April 1912.

[2] Adorno mentions Törne's *Close-Up* only in an afterword, which is, unfortunately, not included in his *Gesammelte Schriften*.

[3] Törne 1937, p. 11.

[4] Åbo Akademi, copy in Törne's hand. Clearly, this is not the most reliable of sources.

letter as late as March 1937: 'Nevertheless, I would have liked to meet with the professor over the course of the summer.' He assured him that the book would contain nothing biographical and that it would be exclusively his own views of the music — although on the basis of direct experiences of his contact with Sibelius since 1916.[1] Later letters in the correspondence between Sibelius and Törne contain only a single reference to the book, after Tovey reviewed it positively in 1938.[2] There is no indication that Törne or Sibelius ever read Adorno's review.

However, Sibelius rejected at least Törne's central statements about Sibelius' contempt for Wagner. In a draft letter of 1946 he noted: 'Törne wrote his book about me without giving me an opportunity to look through it. That accounts for the many inaccuracies, concerning Wagner, for example, whom I have always admired.'[3] Georg Boldemann remarked to the composer in a similar tone in a letter of 16 February 1940: 'I very much regretted the recollections of your student. I have known you for nearly fifty years now and have heard you speak about Wagner, for example, so often that I cannot understand at all how the man came to such inaccurate elaborations. But one always grows smarter and more experienced; in other words, one never stops learning.'[4]

Three passages in Törne are striking: (1) 'Wagner's music has meant practically nothing to Sibelius; the influence of his orchestral idiom, even less.'[5] To be precise, Törne did not assert that these were Sibelius' words, and the general rejection of influence is followed by a list of concrete parallels between Wagner and Sibelius. As an artist and connoisseur of Wagner, Törne thus wanted to emphasise how different the aesthetic premises were, despite obvious parallels. (2) In a later passage, Sibelius asks the author about his opinion of Wagner and confirms that he too did not like several things 'in his personality, and consequently in his music.'[6] Sibelius supposedly characterised Wagner in general to Törne as 'brutal' and 'vulgar'. In fact, however, he merely considered a fortissimo declaration of love in Wagner to be 'brutal' and 'vulgar'. The third passage (3) is more complicated, not because of Wagner but because of its statements about the musical avant-garde, which has at most temporary 'moral and historical value':

> Sibelius as a musician and composer is decidedly opposed to the creator of the German musical drama. He told me how strongly he objected to the heaviness and rhetorical exaggeration of Wagner's musical style. Indeed, there is in the art of music nothing more alien to the mind of Sibelius than the overloaded baroque of Wagner. As we have seen, Sibelius never abandoned his own

1 See National Archive Box 31; Bengt de Törne to JS, 3 March 1937.

2 Ibid.; Bengt de Törne to JS, 17 December 1938.

3 National Archive Box 34; draft letter by JS, 14 February 1946.

4 National Archive Box 17; Georg Boldemann to JS, 16 February 1940.

5 Törne 1937, p. 36.

6 Ibid., pp. 58–9.

> convictions for the experiments of the modernistic schools; to his mind these deviations were episodes merely, and he was never greatly disturbed by them. He even grants them a certain moral and historical value, since in some cases they have helped to abolish old-fashioned conventionalism. With Wagner it is different. Sibelius' personal dislike of him is further increased by the conviction that the influence of that master and his whole school has been disastrous to the evolution of music.[1]

Although Törne's book is written like an aesthetic treatise only in passages – the author gave lectures on aesthetics in London for which studying with Sibelius was an enormous help[2] – the extent of the quotations makes one ask what could have caused Törne to invent them – other than, perhaps, lack of material. At the end of the chapter on Wagner, he points out that the conversation ran unusually long that day, which may account for the specific, not necessarily representative atmosphere.[3] Perhaps Törne took a late-night remark for a definitive statement. This conjecture receives support from a letter of autumn 1913 that Newmarch cites: 'It strikes me more particularly that musicians are still writing in the post-Wagnerian style – with the same laughable pose and the still more laughable would-be profundity. But that sort of thing does not easily die out.'[4] Newmarch had also experienced Sibelius in an anti-Wagnerian mood – and she emphasised this in her own anti-German mood. Another, less reliable author, Ekman, suggests that Sibelius reflected critically on Wagner: 'My decided antagonism to Wagner in my youth was, I fancy, dictated to some extent by the fear of being subjected to an influence I had seen taking possession of so many of my friends, both young and old. And yet I still place Verdi higher than Wagner.'[5] However, Sibelius' early commentaries on Wagner in letters to Wegelius from Berlin in 1889 were already critical,[6] as were letters to Aino from Munich and Bayreuth in summer 1894. But the context of this criticism was the overwhelming Wagnerism of others.

Adorno must also have been perplexed by Törne's statements about Brahms: 'he refused out of pure conservatism to believe in any further evolution of musical language'.[7] Törne the composer wrote, clearly provocatively, of Debussy: 'Enthusiasts, writing of Debussy, have tried to proclaim him the sovereign creator of all the music of the future; and many anecdotes would seem to indicate that he was by no means lacking in self-reliance. [...] But confronted by Sibelius, his usual self-confidence may

[1] Törne 1937, p. 59.

[2] Cf. Müller-Doohm 2005, esp. pp. 236 ff., on Adorno's simultaneous difficulties finding his feet in the United Kingdom.

[3] Ibid., p. 70.

[4] Newmarch 1939, p. 34.

[5] Ekman 1946, p. 263.

[6] National Archive Box 121.

[7] Törne 1937, p. 61.

have shrunk. The volcanic temperament of the great Northern symphonist perhaps made him realize temporarily what nature had refused him.'[1] Adorno argues precisely the opposite when he defends Debussy: 'To hear Debussy correctly one must hear how those miniature formats which arrogant Germans tend to confuse with genre pieces pass judgment on the metaphysical claims of German music.'[2] Törne quoted a statement that Sibelius had met Debussy and therefore knew precisely how to assess him: 'I know because I have met him.'[3] Törne's approach to Mahler is even more arrogant: in his typology of symphonic styles, he calls Mahler 'one of the most pathetic cases in the history of music', an uninspired symphonist of the 'epic' type (along with Haydn, Mozart, Brahms and Bruckner).[4] The 'dramatic and lyric character' with 'power of the themes and images' of the other type ('symphonic in spirit, if not in form') is represented, in his view, by Schubert, Berlioz and Tchaikovsky, who in contrast to Mahler are 'sure to fascinate future generations'. The third type unites the best qualities of the other two. Beethoven alone was in his view a model of equal rank for 'the greatest composer now living'[5] and 'meridian of contemporary music'[6] — i.e., Sibelius.

If we try to imagine how Adorno must have felt reading Törne, we are particularly struck by another passage: 'In our conversations he would never admit the claims of the more popular aesthetic currents. His own music is essentially esoteric. But such is the magic of his inspiration, he has found friends and admirers everywhere. Like all great art Sibelius' music can be enjoyed by everybody, although it will perhaps be reserved for comparatively few to reach a higher degree of comprehension of his greater symphonic works.'[7] Here Törne flourishes as an aesthetician and offers his younger colleague Adorno a wide target that has little to do with Sibelius but rather with an idea that circled the world in the first half of the twentieth century. Törne's position that 'all great art [...] can be enjoyed by everybody' was not one Adorno shared. The category of pleasure in particular leads one to suppose that Törne was an apologist for the emotional approach to great art in the old manner. That is not balanced out by the fact that in his aesthetics he accepted the importance of understanding and the deliberately elitist. Aesthetic greatness could, rather, be understood by everyone. Adorno would have had even less of an idea what to do with the 'essentially esoteric'.

1 Ibid., pp. 68–9.

2 Adorno 1976, p. 155.

3 Törne 1937, p. 69. JS did in fact talk about this encounter in February 1909 to others (Ekman 1946, p. 198, and Newmarch 1939, pp. 14–15). In a letter to Axel Carpelan of 27 March 1909 from London (cf. Dahlström 2010, p. 234, and Erik W. Tawaststjerna 1986, pp. 108–9), he wrote of Debussy's works that they are interesting; all of the compositions he heard in London — including Elgar and Bantock — 'confirmed my thoughts about the path I have taken, take and have to take[!]'.

4 Törne 1937, pp. 74 ff.

5 Ibid., p. 88.

6 Ibid., p. 103.

7 Ibid., p. 30.

In the Symbolist context and in light of the significance of the soul for Sibelius, however, this category is important. For Adorno, such concepts were the cheap remnants of bourgeois illusion.

Törne's vision of a 'magic of his inspiration', which may have won Sibelius many sympathisers, is also a touchy issue for many readers. Later in the book he wrote, with reference to the first two symphonies, of a 'magic spell of the North with a particular power and intensity'.[1] Of the suite for string orchestra *Rakastava*, op. 14, he wrote: 'An ethereal atmosphere is here evoked with an unusual magic. The writing for muted strings [...] seems to bring us a message from a distant world.'[2] A magician from Ainola had no place in Adorno's pantheon, and the possibility that Sibelius considered himself one intensified the conflict. After Törne observed that Sibelius, despite his Northern nature, possessed 'the magic of evoking quite different atmospheres' in *Pelléas et Mélisande* and *Belshazzar's Feast*, he continued his interpretation: 'Sibelius' art is formed principally on the life, the past and the landscape of his country, the subtle colours, heroic strength and endless melancholy of which he has conquered for the patrimony of music. Not only has he invoked the vast forests, innumerable lakes and islands; he also has an intense feeling for the archipelago fringing the Gulf of Finland.'[3] He supported this idea with quotations as well: 'and when we see those granite rocks we know why we are able to treat the orchestra as we do!'[4] Sibelius was using the royal 'we' here. Törne remarks insightfully on that: 'These words were spoken by the man who has himself created the Northern style of orchestration.'

Törne contrasts Sibelius' distance from traditional compositional practices[5] with modernism by doubting the complete transformations in art history and asserting[6] that 'the heart of man has not changed in two thousand years, his sorrows and joys, disillusions and exultations have remained the same for twenty centuries'. He reported: 'he had never stopped to ask whether he infringed the orthodox rules of good orchestration. On the other hand, he had not abandoned the main road expressly, to create sensation, but only when it had suited his purpose. This statement expresses his entire artistic creed: innovation must come from within and not be aimed at deliberately. [...] "You know, I am not legitimately married to the orchestra; I am its lover."'[7] Although that last sentence sounds unmistakably ironic, it is important that the word 'lover' signifies intuition and instinct, while 'legitimately married' suggests the nor-

[1] Törne 1937, p. 51.

[2] Ibid., p. 59.

[3] Ibid., p. 96.

[4] Ibid., p. 97.

[5] JS often spoke of the technical, engineering knowledge of composition, constructions, 'hothouse *Erzeugnisse* [products]', and so on, which suggests he had such an attitude; see, for example, JS to Axel Carpelan, 26 January 1914; quoted in Erik W. Tawaststjerna 1986, p. 161 (translation modified); Swedish original in Dahlström 2010, pp. 347–8.

[6] Törne 1937, p. 72.

[7] Ibid., p. 30.

mative. Adorno was always mistrustful when anyone claimed to have intuition that would make it possible to find the right path even without intellectual enlightenment.

Adorno also had to reject the ideal of orchestral sound postulated here: according to Törne's report, Sibelius believed the orchestra would be a perfect instrument if it had a 'pedal' like the piano. If one did not take the trouble to arrange a 'pedal', there would be holes in the texture. A note on the Fourth Symphony points in the same direction: '"Epic" in instrumentation. The "narrative". The colour should not be interrupted before it becomes necessary. In the instrumentation one has to take care that the "texture" [*Satz*] is not left without strings, in principle. The sound [otherwise becomes] "split".'[1] Sibelius continued on to say that the sound was essentially dependent on the 'purely musical "texture"' ('polyphony etc.'). Then he went into the current situation in bad orchestras (problems with oboes, etc.). In contrast to the Schoenbergian tradition, Sibelius created continuity in no small measure by means of organ (pedal) points, which is why he was occasionally (as a joke) called the *Hoforgelpunktist* (Court organ pointer).[2] According to Sibelius, Liszt's scores in turn suffered from the fact that he composed at the piano and forgot the necessary consequences (the instrumental pedal): 'While he was writing his scores he sat at the piano, pressing the pedal, and everything sounded perfect.' According to Törne, Sibelius said of the importance of musical themes: 'Themes are the most precious property of a composer, and I personally don't see how a work could be built up without them.'[3] Adorno and his predecessors were aware of the outstanding importance of melodic themes, yet they considered motifs and their elaboration more important than themes as such. But that is precisely what Sibelius believed as well, making this another typical example of Törne's fateful oversimplification. There are, or course, differences between the specific way Sibelius and, say, Anton Webern worked with motifs, and certainly when composing Sibelius relied more on fluent melodic inspiration than on a motivic cell, but the similarities would suffice if one were to analyse the shared artistic position.

Certainly Sibelius' creative process was less analytical than Adorno's ideal. Consequently, the original definition of the symphonic in Törne must have astonished Adorno, since Törne speaks of the symphonic in connection with orchestral sound: 'The great unity and homogeneity of colour thus obtained, in spite of the infinite variety of timbre, derive from a symphonic, that is to say, epic conception of life.'[4] Although Schoenberg discussed the problem of timbre towards the end of his *Harmonielehre* (translated as *Theory of Harmony*),[5] Adorno did not see any reason on his own, without Törne's guidance, to put Sibelius under the microscope with respect to

[1] Diary, 9 June 1910.

[2] Adolf Paul to JS, 8 September 1918; quoted in Erik W. Tawaststjerna 1996, p. 273: 'Hoforgelpunktist Exzellenz och Geheimeråd'. His ideal was related to Schreker's technique of orchestration; cf. Schreker, 'Meine musikdramatische Idee', pp. 6–7, in which the orchestra is viewed as an instrument.

[3] Törne 1937, p. 95.

[4] Ibid., p. 32.

[5] Schoenberg 1978, pp. 423–4.

that category in particular. For Sibelius, the model of a symphonic movement was the Mozartian Allegro: 'Think of its wonderful unity and homogeneity! It is like an uninterrupted flowing, where nothing stands out and nothing encroaches upon the rest.'[1] Adorno may have misunderstood this idea too, which was based on a holistic vision of the process of composition, as well as Sibelius' idea – recorded during work on the Sixth Symphony – that Mozart and Mendelssohn Bartholdy were his role models for orchestration, but Busoni also numbered Mozart, Carl Maria von Weber, Berlioz and Wagner among the composers in whose work instrumentation went hand in hand with exemplary invention. Sibelius' teacher Goldmark – like one of his own mentors, in turn, Anton Rubinstein – was, according to Törne, firmly convinced that Mozart was a vivid example and model.[2] Even Sibelius' supposed pragmatism was presumably suspect for Adorno: Törne reported that Sibelius compared orchestrating with a struggle for existence in which you had to forget 'your absolute idealism'; there could be no talk of the 'miserable fiddle' (Beethoven to the Austrian conductor and violinist Ignaz Schuppanzigh), the composer had to adapt to the abilities of the virtuoso (rather than divine inspiration, to paraphrase the Schuppanzigh anecdote). According to Törne, conducting also served to ensure he did not grow 'too idealistic'.[3] He said of Mahler that he was 'spoilt by "too good" orchestras' and notated ideas that only 'four or five orchestras in the whole world' could perform.[4] But Adorno knew that the orchestra of the Viennese court opera had only been elevated to that level in the first place by the challenge, which had been Mahler's achievement (from which Sibelius had, of course, rarely benefited).

Sibelius supposedly said of the young modernists in Paris: 'These people seem to be afraid of anything that is immediately given to us; their interest is practically confined to the recherché.'[5] Adorno did not object to originality, but he objected all the more so to such an anti-intellectual argument. Törne challenged him with this attitude when he wrote of *Rakastava*, which Sibelius considered one of his 'best works', according to a diary entry on 18 December 1911: 'As a matter of fact, it is sure to find admirers everywhere, except perhaps among the more ferocious intellectuals.'[6] Törne's other references to the significance of categories such as 'creative imagination', the 'spiritual independence' of the artist, 'individuality' and the 'true expression of ideas suggested to the author by his inspiration' aim pretentiously high: 'Sibelius certainly did not think of creating something new; he simply listened to his irresistible, volcanic inspiration and accepted its direction. The personal colour of the orchestral

[1] Törne 1937, p. 49.

[2] Ibid., p. 47; cf. Busoni 1957, p. 35.

[3] Törne 1937, p. 54.

[4] Ibid., pp. 91–2. Törne also calls attention to passages in the work of JS that are written ruthlessly and 'prophetic' (ibid., pp. 55–6).

[5] Ibid., p. 96.

[6] Törne 1937, p. 59.

FIG. 39. *Rakastava*, op. 14, first movement ('The Lover', opening). The titles of the three movements of *Rakastava* as well as the texts of the original versions for strings, chorus and soloists were taken, with minor changes, from *Kanteletar*, Elias Lönnrot's anthology of Finnish folk poetry (1840).

language is not intellectually thought out, but spontaneously created and entirely conditioned by the individual character and atmosphere of the music.'[1]

Törne's prose is always fascinating, even if we cannot be sure how much of it is by Sibelius. But there are also authentic statements by Sibelius on these problems that are more subtle and unpretentious. In a letter to Newmarch on 5 February 1927 he wrote: 'I still go on composing but I feel very much alone. There is so much in the music of the present day that I cannot accept. For example, that one should be able

[1] For example, ibid., pp. 65–6.

to make for oneself an ideal by reflexion (a reflected ideal). Also it seems to me that modern music does not progress, that it marks time without getting a step further. It is the urgent need for progress which lacks when the architectural form is neglected.'[1] Architecture and progress, yes; reflected, category-heavy concepts, no. Törne and Newmarch could have constructed a very different image of Sibelius from such statements, especially as they were able to speak to the composer. But they did not. Adorno could not, and given the introduction by Törne, supposedly the composer's favourite student, he did not have an opportunity to take a profound interest in the maestro himself – beyond socio-critical remarks and a narrow selection of works. When writing his 'Glosse', Adorno could not have suspected that Törne was one of the worst examples in the history of music of a 'student' taking advantage of his status, especially during his teacher's lifetime. It was not Niemann but Törne who 'armed the enemies' of Sibelius by provoking them to arm themselves.

Ernst Krenek and Viennese Modernism

Adorno was by no means an isolated guiding force in the critical interpretation of Sibelius, though he was probably the most distinguished spokesman for an important group of modernists. He accentuated what was thought, said and occasionally even published about Sibelius among the Viennese avant-garde and even earlier by the modernists in Berlin and Munich (Joseph Joachim, Max von Schillings, *et al.*). The pro-Mahler and anti-Sibelius mood is particularly well illustrated by Ernst Krenek's 'Biographical Essay' in the 1941 American edition of Bruno Walter's book on Mahler, so just a few years after Törne's *Close-Up* and Adorno's 'Fussnote' on Hamsun and 'Glosse' on Sibelius. This text is difficult to find today, since Walter did not accept Krenek's afterword, and later editions did not include it.[2]

The correspondence between Krenek and the commissioning editor Arne Ekstrom in the publishing house Greystone Press, New York, reveals how stubbornly Krenek defended his approach. The publishing house would have liked more 'facts' and fewer 'value judgments' (e.g., about the important question 'whether Sibelius can compose').[3] Krenek's remarks document parameters of the reception of Sibelius from the perspective of a very influential representative of New Music who was outside Schoenberg's immediate circle. In his posthumously published *Im Atem der Zeit: Erinnerungen an die Moderne* (In the breath of time: memories of the modern age), Krenek forgot Sibelius and his fierce debate with Walter and wrote: 'My impression

[1] Newmarch 1939, pp. 45–6.

[2] Krenek 1970, pp. 157–220, esp. pp. 211 ff. See Mäkelä 2000 f, pp. 103–6. A more detailed analysis of this text is found in Scheit and Svoboda 2002, pp. 92 ff. However, the authors use the German fair copy, not the final English version.

[3] His lengthy correspondence with Arne Ekstrom from the summer of 1941 is found among the Ernst Krenek Papers; University of California San Diego, Mandeville Department of Special Collections, today in the Ernst Krenek Institut at Krems, Austria.

is that whenever I had something personal to do with Walter everything went well on the simple basis of mutual professional respect.' Apparently because of another incident, Krenek noted cryptically: 'Unfortunately, in later cases I had no opportunity to talk things through with him, and so annoying misunderstandings spoiled our relationship, which I sincerely regret.'[1] Perhaps it was indeed about Sibelius?

Krenek introduced Sibelius in the context of asking why the enthusiasm for Mahler that began in Amsterdam, Vienna and Berlin in 1920 was hardly felt at all in the United States: the cause, in his view, was the 'peculiar interest exerted here by Jan [*sic*] Sibelius, Mahler's junior by only five years.'[2] Sibelius has barely been mentioned in the literature on Mahler in recent decades, but Krenek emphasised Sibelius dialectically – as if in response to Törne's trite criticism of Mahler ('one of the most pathetic cases') – as an opposite pole to Mahler, both in the history of their reception (concerning the 'peculiar interest') and in the history of composition ('present situation of music'): 'If one wants to ascertain the exact position of Mahler's work and to sound out its significance in the present situation of music, it is worthwhile to pause here for a moment and to examine his relation to Sibelius.' The first question concerns the themes, which in Mahler's case are largely compiled from familiar material but did not lead to popularity because of their context. Krenek calls them Mahler's 'surrealistic devices', whereas Sibelius is merely 'moderately modern': 'It lacks Mahler's dialectical relation to a lost musical world and, on the other hand, does not imply the forward pointing conclusions to be drawn from such dialectics.'[3] This key sentence – which of course also testifies to the friendship between Adorno and Krenek – exposes Krenek's weakness: the imbalance between his profound knowledge of Mahler, which permits innovative insights (also with regard to Surrealism, which is important for Sibelius as well), and his perfunctory image of Sibelius. Whereas as an artist he intended to follow Mahler's path (the 'forward pointing conclusions'), Sibelius clearly remained alien to him.

He believed Sibelius, like Bruckner (another arbitrary comparison), was 'a man of great natural simplicity of mind, endowed with profound poetic sensitivity' – which may be true to a degree but the comparison does not do justice to either of them:

> He also is a thinking musician, and the various original ways in which he approached the symphonic form show clearly that he has been mindful of the artistic problems involved. However, despite the relative merits of his accomplishments, these efforts seem historically somewhat belated in view of the more progressive solutions offered by Mahler. Sibelius is a legitimate heir of the symphonic tradition in that he exhibits some of the magnitude of gesture so characteristic of the old symphony. He does so, however, by renouncing almost

[1] See Krenek 1998, p. 1088.

[2] Krenek 1970, p. 214. In the German original, as quoted in Scheit and Svoboda 2002, p. 104, his first name is correctly given as Jean.

[3] Krenek 1970, p. 215.

> completely the contrapuntal pithiness of texture which was Mahler's fateful contribution to the problem of the symphonic form. Absence of textural complication and of straightforward thematic statements lend Sibelius' style a sort of bleakish, faint luster appealing to listeners who understand by symphonic style a distinguished musical display of soft-pedalled emotionalism (the factor of dignified distinction having been ushered in especially by Brahms, Cesar Franck and related composers). The great respect in which everything national is nowadays held has enhanced Sibelius' popularity, since the idiosyncrasies of his music have been rationalized as being particularly expressive of the character of the Finnish people and landscape. If that means provincialism (as opposed to the all-embracing universalism which animated the classical symphony), it can more conclusively be explained by the limitations of Sibelius' musical outlook than by arbitrary associations with extra-musical elements, race, landscape, and the like. Just appreciation of Mahler would by no means imply belittling Sibelius. Passing judgment on the magnitude of talent possessed by great artists and playing one up to the detriment of another is a futile entertainment of immature minds.[1]

Just like Adorno in his monograph on Mahler of 1960, Krenek in 1941 shows that Mahler found rigorously modern solutions to the problems of his generation by presenting the familiar and current (folksong quotations, dance rhythms, imitation of natural sounds, etc.) shockingly and surreally in an 'alarming context', which Sibelius was supposedly unable to do. Krenek finds Sibelius lacks 'counterpoint', which is plausible insofar as Sibelius himself had planned additional studies of it and undertook them on his own: 'Must begin with polyphonic studies. At first as little as it might be — ten minutes. Don't think about your forty-four years.'[2] Certainly the merits of his texture differ from those in Mahler but he certainly does not lack 'textural complication'. Krenek's notion that Sibelius' solutions for old problems in symphonic form are old-fashioned — the symphonies could not have been written earlier but even so they were not up to date — seems trivially modernist from today's perspective. The public, which expects symphonic writing to be 'soft-pedalled emotionalism', found Sibelius — who did indeed esteem the *una corda* sound — easily accessible, in Krenek's view. Moreover, national characteristics and extra-musical associations (race, landscape, the Finnish element) — that is, the fact that Sibelius belonged to a 'Nordic' people — were promoted in North America especially by Olin Downes, Lucien Price, Alf Klingenberg and many others. Krenek believed, not entirely without reason, that Sibelius profited from his background, whereas Mahler suffered as a result of worldwide anti-Semitism. All this is hard to prove, but both Sibelius and Mahler are indeed often seen in the context of their respective regional and cultural backgrounds.

[1] Krenek 1970 pp. 215–16. The details of the Bruckner analogy are skipped by Scheit and Svoboda 2002, p. 105.

[2] For example, Diary, 18 June 1910. Cf. Krenek 1970, p. 214.

The irony becomes quite clear when Krenek speaks of 'provincialism'. He found the attitude of younger musicians was changing: 'Prospects of a re-birth in America of thinking and feeling on a world scale rather than in terms of narrow nationalistic concepts coincide with the hope for a more adequate evaluation of Mahler's significance than he has hitherto enjoyed. The attitude of some younger musicians in this country seems to hold promises in this direction.'[1] His optimism was not justified, as Sibelius is a model for many young musicians even today.[2] Mahler's own words about Sibelius – which were based on knowledge of popular works such as *Valse triste*, although he never retracted them even though he became familiar with other works as well – were comparably devastating: 'The first composition was a standard piece of kitsch spiced with a national sauce prepared from those "Nordic" harmonies we know all too well.'[3] Mahler must have started to study the Violin Concerto, although Theodor Spiering, a friend of Sibelius since his time in Berlin in 1889–90,[4] had to take over for Mahler when Mahler was forced to cancel the season in New York in 1911. Artists who had an exposed position in their own national context could have been a thorn in Mahler's side in 1907 in particular, since that sort of position, especially in Vienna, did not seem easily achievable to him. In the literature one finds the assumption that Sibelius had expected Mahler to conduct his symphonies,[5] which is most likely incorrect as it contradicts Sibelius' style in general and his own detailed report of the meeting.[6] It is, however, fair to speculate whether, given Mahler's importance as a conductor, he secretly wished for him to conduct a performance. But he would have been too proud to express such a wish.

Schoenberg, who knew at least the Fifth Symphony and *Scaramouche* from the scores, mentioned Sibelius in his correspondence and notes only in passing (and always objectively) a 'more famous colleague'.[7] Another note referring to a letter to him from the Jewish Club in 1933 that did not use his first name is typical: 'Jews have not yet acknowledged that my first name is Arnold. But they certainly know the first name: Paul [Hindemith], Béla [Bartók], Igor [Stravinsky] and Jan.'[8] Sibelius' name is not mentioned in Schoenberg's writings in the context of the debate in Vienna about

[1] Krenek 1970, p. 220.

[2] Cf. Anderson 2004. The focus of that essay is on French, Scandinavian and Anglo-American composers.

[3] Gustav Mahler to Alma Mahler, 30 October 1907, in La Grange and Weiss 2004, p. 290.

[4] Erik W. Tawaststjerna 1976, p. 59.

[5] Gustav Mahler to Alma Mahler, 30 October 1907, in La Grange and Weiss 2004, p. 290: the commentary in that edition, with no source given, reads (ibid., p. 291): 'A certain tension must have been palpable during these meetings, for Sibelius was hoping that Mahler would offer to perform his music in New York.'

[6] Ekman 1946, pp. 190 ff.

[7] Krones 2003a, p. 47. Schoenberg's unpublished letters are in the Arnold Schönberg Center in Vienna: Collection of Unpublished Letters.

[8] Cf. Stuckenschmidt 1978, p. 448. Schoenberg's mistake – 'Jan', which Krenek also made (see above) – may be harmless but it is revealing in this context.

who would succeed Robert Fuchs at the music academy in 1912. In a letter from October 1934, by contrast, he lists Sibelius, clearly proud that he was named along with him – and Alexandre Tansman, Roger Sessions, George Gershwin, Aaron Copland and Stravinsky – as one of the most important composers in North America.[1] The other passing mentions are relatively neutral; only once does he mention 'monster symphonies'[2] à la Strauss, Mahler and Sibelius in reference to royalties for radio broadcasts. Alban Berg's letters to Schoenberg have only brief references to concerts in Vienna where he includes Sibelius among the composers who are performed with striking frequency there.[3]

Schoenberg apparently never conducted a polemic against Sibelius, at least not in writing, which should not be confused with recognition of his competence or spontaneous esteem. Lois Lautner, Schoenberg's first American student, described her teacher's tolerant attitude, who when teaching composition demanded only technical ability and 'new beauty' – independently of the stylistic idiom. 'Sibelius had created new beauty with old materials; there was no reason to suppose that new beauty could not emerge from any idiom.'[4] Another student of Schoenberg's, Dika Newlin, offered a quite critical report – without mentioning the significance of the date, Sibelius' birthday – of how Schoenberg on 8 December 1939 placed Sibelius in the music history department along with Berlioz, Mendelssohn, Liszt and Bruckner and classified all five of them as 'tone-poets' – and explicitly not symphonists: 'Take Sibelius, for example: he starts out with a very interesting idea, but pretty soon he begins to go astray. Then he stops, and then he gets a new idea, also very good, and repeats the same process, without an apparent reason for the stops or the starts. This method is characteristic of all five composers, as is also a tendency to be longwinded. That they are all great personalities, he [Schoenberg] recognizes; but he would certainly never put them in the first rank.'[5]

Newlin authored a parody that suggests a complex antithesis of Schoenberg's and Sibelius' concept of art and makes the latter part of a 'Garden of Earthly Delights' in the style of Hieronymus Bosch's altarpiece. The idea of having to study with Schoenberg drives the narrator of this parody to suicide – with a postlude in heaven:

> But winged spirits rescued him,
> And bore him to the skies,
> Where angels all day long on harps
> Played Schoenberg lullabies.
> In great dismay he ran away,

[1] Stein 1987, p. 192.

[2] On Schoenberg's unpublished letters from 28 February 1939 and 22 January 1951, see Krones 2003a, p. 47.

[3] Brand, Hailey and Harris 1987, pp. 23, 115, and 454.

[4] Lautner 1962, p. 23.

[5] Newlin 1980, pp. 152–3.

And straight to Hell went down;
There they were playing Sibelius,
Ah, what a lovely sound!
But as he revelled in these strains,
He heard a voice to say,
'No! No! Zey cannot practise here!
Please make zem go avay!'
And when he looked to see what 'twas,
He saw a little man,
Whose face was of the saffron hue,
His legs a dirty tan.[1]

[1] Ibid., pp. 160–61. Dated 29 December 1939. Her heartfelt relationship to her teacher is clear from her affectionate parody of the small man with an Austrian accent.

> Sibelius was Finnish to the depths of his heart. His music is national in the best sense of the word. But it is more than national: it has become international, the joint property of all humanity. We Finns can be pleased that the particular character of our nation is understood and esteemed thanks to Sibelius' music. The essence of the Finnish mentality through the centuries has never revealed anyone more full-blooded than Sibelius. [...] He had the privilege of living long enough to see his message made reality by a free Finnish people.[1]

5.3 Brief Encounters

From 'Citoyen' to 'Bourgeois'

Sibelius' music and personality had a very special fascination for authors writing in German – despite such critics as Joseph Joachim, Heinrich Strobel and Alfred Einstein as well as Adorno – which went far beyond any bourgeois or pseudo-academic pedagogical obligation to write about important foreign contemporaries. Usually Sibelius remained distant, although he could communicate with them in German with remarkable ease. For example, he wrote to the Viennese composer and music journalist Karl Franz Müller that 'unfortunately', in view of his 'advanced age', he was unable to help him,[2] even though he was pleased to learn 'that you wish to write about me'.[3] Heinrich Pudor, pioneer of naturism and pro-Nordic racism, did not receive any support either when he wanted to write about Sibelius for the *Berliner Tageblatt* and a 'German music magazine' in March 1900. Pudor published a survey article on Finnish music (with a very brief section on Sibelius) in the *Sammelbände der internationalen Musikgesellschaft* in November of that year. His article begins with the statement that all music produced in Finland has 'the scent of earth' ('Erdgeruch') and springs 'out of the people's blood' ('fliesst aus dem Blute des Volkes').[4] That is the kind of reception Sibelius did not need.

One author with whom Sibelius had close contact was Günther Thaer, who visited Ainola in the summer of 1935 and was touched by his warm reception.[5] The Berlin journalist wrote numerous articles for the *Nationalsozialistische Monatshefte* in 1936

[1] Yrjö Kilpinen, a Finnish composer and member of the Finnish Academy, in a speech on Finnish radio on the occasion of Sibelius' funeral on 30 September 1957.

[2] National Library Coll. 206: 62; JS to Karl Franz Müller, 17 March 1951. On JS' letters to Müller in the Vienna's municipal archive, see Krones 2003a, pp. 47 ff. and 57 ff.

[3] National Library Coll. 206: 62; JS to Karl Franz Müller, 3 February 1951.

[4] National Library Coll. 206: 30; Heinrich Pudor to JS, 5 March 1900 in Vaasa, Finland. On Pudor, see Linse 1997, p. 399. See also Pudor, 'Zur Geschichte der Musik in Finland', *Sammelbände der Internationalen Musikgesellschaft* 2, no. 1 (November 1900), pp. 147–57.

[5] National Library Coll. 206: 38; Günther Thaer to JS, 23 January 1936.

and for the *Völkischer Beobachter* in 1935, the year Sibelius turned seventy and received the silver Goethe Medal for Art and Science. He wrote in greater detail on 6 August 1938:

> It was three years ago I was granted an opportunity to call on you at the Hotel Karelia to have a discussion, and subsequently wrote, among other things, the anniversary essay in the Völkischer Beobachter for your seventieth birthday[,] for which, to my great pleasure, I received an approving letter from you. [...] [In Helsinki about a year and a half earlier] you did not feel in the mood [...] [so] the matter was postponed [...] Now chance and opportunity in the form of a government assignment have brought me to Helsinki for several days [...] [to work on] my book about Finland.

In 1936 he reported how Sibelius, who 'sat there listening with attention and resolve' and preferred to talk not about his music or himself but only about 'that strangely exciting ringing sound that runs through the bright, Nordic summer nights' or about 'the dark, mystical rustling that the wind brings out of the wild forests and of the singing play of the swarms of mosquitoes in the evening silence above the forest and marsh', and about this 'atmospheric sound that has since prehistoric times wafted around his Finnish people up there between the lakes and forests'.[1] Because we are aware of the cultural and political context in which these lines were written, we find it easy to categorise their subject matter. In light of the atmospheric sound of the 'swarms of mosquitoes [...] above the forest and marsh', the expression 'blood and soil', which quite accurately defines the context in which Thaer was working, seems strangely apt here.

Sibelius' post-war reception in German-speaking countries was largely dominated by two authors: Ernst Tanzberger and Erich Brüll. Tanzberger wrote for Breitkopf & Härtel in the West; Brüll promoted Sibelius' work in the German Democratic Republic as a contributor to the journal *Musik und Gesellschaft* and later as the author of a book. His slender volume *Jean Sibelius* was first published in Leipzig in 1986, the result of a personal interest of the author, who over the course of his occupation with the artist and his northern environment raised a series of central questions. The plan had been to translate Erik Tawaststjerna's biography, but the publisher decided instead on a new study, for which Brüll provided the 'outline' and a local justification: thirty concerts per season with music by Sibelius in the GDR alone made him a larger presence in the repertoire than any other composer, Brüll argued; moreover, around 1980 there was no current literature on him in German. Brüll was enthusiastic about Scandinavia and was able to communicate with Tawaststjerna in Swedish. On 23 January 1974 he wrote to his publisher:

> If the Deutscher Verlag für Musik nevertheless has compelling reason to make do with a tailor-made Sibelius book of around 250 printed pages, the author

[1] Thaer 1936, p. 62.

will be in an awkward situation if he wishes to proceed responsibly. On the one hand, he cannot get around Tawaststjerna's work; on the other hand, he will be reluctant to make use of the results of its research to produce a comparatively reductive presentation of his life and work, whose problems are all too obvious. [...] It is therefore necessary to base it on a conception with objectives differently accentuated from Tawaststjerna's, taking its own paths when bringing out certain focuses of examination, thus avoiding from the outset pointless summary (or at best interpretation) of existing material and hence any awkward comparisons.[1]

On 17 September 1974 Brüll told Tawaststjerna that he had been commissioned to write a short book for which he wished to conduct independent research. But a serious illness prevented him from doing so.

His outline did not lack declarations of intent to explain the social tensions in Finland, oppressed by the 'Russian tsarism' under which the bourgeois composer had to work: 'from this perspective Sibelius' path, to express it in a highly exaggerated manner, appears to have been the path from *citoyen* to *bourgeois*.' Brüll intended to treat Carl Nielsen in his Sibelius book as the 'only contemporary of equal rank among the northern European symphonists', which would certainly have been a profitable approach, especially as Nielsen was of 'rural proletarian' origin. Brüll was apparently unaware of the rural proletarian portion (however small) of Sibelius' heritage as he did not mention it.[2] He intended to interpret (correctly) Sibelius' salon music as a 'symptom of crisis in the bourgeois production of music' and treat Sibelius as one of the 'great musicians of the North', a region that was always admired in the GDR – until the very end of that state.[3] In the spirit of a *Heimat* movement for state socialism, he noted that Sibelius 'stood for an entire people. Listening to his music, one was reminded of the fate of the Finns. Thinking of Finland and its struggle for freedom, one saw it embodied in his work.' Only then followed the indispensable sentence: 'His music had a direct political effect.' Right after that Brüll discusses Sibelius as a national monument, whose image was fixed unusually early in regional media – that is to say, a discussion about the effect on society of his personality as an artist.

But Brüll rejected the image of the 'poet of the melancholic Finnish landscape; the tone poet of archaic Nordic myths; the singer of the ardent Finnish will to freedom'. That image – one of the last shoots of the ancient hypothesis of cultural geography that climate determined not only people's skin colour and physical build but also their customs and culture – existed long before the artist had completely developed his identity. Brüll found equally problematic Sibelius' later, second image as 'patriarch of Finnish music', the 'last great Romantic, elevated by the admiration of an entire nation', a 'national monument' with the 'bald pate of an old man' and 'scepti-

[1] National Archive: Tawaststjerna Collection, which also has a carbon copy of the 'outline'.

[2] For more detail on Otto Andersson and others from 1915 onwards, see chapter 1.

[3] Brüll 1986, p. 5.

cally piercing gaze'. 'In the blinding light of his fame, Sibelius has remained a largely misunderstood composer.' He may have been thinking of Jürgen Howitz's survey article of 1967, 'Jean Sibelius', which contains a great deal of inaccurate information and concludes with the sentence: 'He created the national music of Finland, which he heard from his people, and thus brought Finland's name to the entire world.' With above-average boldness, Brüll battled such exaggerations even in his own regional environment of the GDR.

In the historical context of the book's writing in 1974, Brüll's sketch of the cultural history of Germany and Austria in the nineteenth century was remarkably enlightened. 'That which came from "outside" was acknowledged rather disdainfully. That was especially true of the symphony.' Brüll turned a blind eye to the critical attitude towards German culture in Germany under the Weimar Republic, clearly in the interests of glorifying the enlightened point of view that was, to his mind, conceivable only in the GDR. Similarly problematic is Brüll's assessment of the premises of Sibelius' earlier reception in Germany: 'That an essential contribution to the continuation of the symphonic tradition would come from there [Finland], and that thanks not only to a talented composer but also by virtue of a specific social situation that lent political relevance to the concert life that was evolving at the time – this idea would have seemed paradoxical to the understanding of culture then current.'[1] On the contrary, there were certain prominent authors – one need think only of Niemann – who expected new impulses from the less industrialised regions outside the core zone of the West and from Sibelius in that context. Brüll too sought a path to Sibelius by way of an introduction to Finnish culture and history that included the usual clichés – but also many correct views. In his commentaries on the life and work, Brüll proves to have been well informed.

Ernst Tanzberger's legitimation was Sibelius, who on 6 March 1943 even authorised Tanzberger's finished dissertation, which was strikingly contemporary in its structure. Other letters from Ainola followed on 15 December 1942, after the book was printed, criticising only the analysis of *The Bard*, and on 15 January 1944, again with corrections concerning only *The Bard* and Robert Kajanus' *Aino*. Enthusiastic about this reaction, the doctoral student in Jena wrote back on 7 April 1943: 'The assessment you have offered of my thesis made me profoundly happy; it is the finest reward for my work and will be an incentive to champion your brilliant works in the future as well.'[2] And he did just that. Immediately after the war Tanzberger began thinking about a new book – in lieu of a planned second edition of his dissertation – as is documented in a letter from 30 August 1946. He tried to convince Sibelius that the symphony is 'not programme music', and on 15 February 1948, confronted him

[1] Ibid., p. 6.

[2] National Archive Box 31. Tanzberger as a student of music pedagogy in Weimar is discussed by Bruno Hinze-Reinhold, director of the Staatliche Franz-Liszt-Hochschule and one of Tanzberger's teachers, in a letter to JS from 22 June 1951 (National Library Coll. 206: 16). On Tanzberger, see also National Archive Box 35.

with the Walter Legge and Sibelius quotation on this subject from *Hufvudstadtsbladet* in 1934.[1] The long path to a new monograph included a testimonial in 1949 from Tanzberger's former doctoral adviser and editor of his dissertation, Otto zur Nedden, who was now living temporarily a little outside of university affiliations in Duisburg: 'The speedy publishing of Dr Tanzberger's work, which is written in a good, clear, easily comprehensible style [...] seems urgently needed!' Thereafter Tanzberger, who had since moved from Jena to Hanover and was teaching at a secondary school, maintained a lively correspondence with Sibelius.[2] As late as 12 August 1957 Tanzberger contacted Sibelius: 'In order to know whether I am "on the right track" I take the liberty of sending you an enclosed sample. It is the discussion of your Third Symphony. I have "analysed" your other symphonies in the same way. Would you [...] kindly send me your unreserved opinion and judgment [...]?' The letter in the Sibelius archive has Levas's customary remark: 'Vast. [replied] 8/28', just three weeks before the composer's death. Tanzberger himself indicated that he received a reply dated 19 September, just one day before the composer's death.[3] The Sibelius Museum has only an undated draft response, written by the composer's son-in-law, the conductor Jussi Jalas, to Tanzberger's letter of 12 August:

> Dear Dr Tanzberger, I am very pleased that you continue to be interested in my work and that with your study you wish to clarify the structure of my symphonies to the German public, as several others have already done in German. I am especially pleased that the weight given to classical symphonic form in my work is once again explicitly demonstrated and that the very misleading speculations about depictions of nature and folklore are done away with. // It was kind of you to send me the excerpt from your manuscript. Because my relationship to my music is instead synthetic and in any case subjective, I will leave it to you to decide how and where you want to present to the public your work as an analyst and writer. // I see in your forthcoming book a sign that my music is now better understood in Germany – as is also demonstrated by the founding of the Sibelius-Gesellschaft [Sibelius society] – and hope that you have great success with your new work.

The wording scarcely differs from that given by Tanzberger, who quoted it as saying it should be 'explicitly emphasised that the weight of my symphonies is given to classical [i.e., instead of classical symphonic] form.' It is, however, not at all the case that Tanzberger did away with 'the very misleading speculations about depictions of nature and folklore' in either of the two books.

The Deutsche Sibelius-Gesellschaft referred to in this correspondence is not the

[1] Quoted in Ringbom 1954, p. 58. Discussed in detail in chapter 3.4 in the present volume.

[2] National Archive Box 31.

[3] Tanzberger 1962, p. 253. The German draft by JS in the Åbo Akademi (Sibelius museum) has some minor corrections that are not reproduced in the following translation.

one founded in Berlin in April 1942 but the one founded in Wiesbaden in 1957; a third was founded in 1991.[1] The idea of publishing a monograph had been proposed by Hellmuth von Hase of Breitkopf & Härtel as early as 1942. The writers Herbert Gerigk and Günter Hausswald, who had experience and were faithful to the National Socialist party line, were considered as authors.[2] No correspondence with Sibelius seems to have survived (if it ever existed). A less famous author, Müller-Brockhausen (his first name is unclear), who on 11 June 1942 asked Sibelius for help with a popular alternative to Gerigk's 'scholarly' publication, was supposed to be involved as well. Especially interesting here are the critical footnote on Niemann and the reference to Sibelius' idea of an ideal biographer:[3]

> During a brief overnight stay in Stockholm, I observed with astonishment the miracle of a large city without its lights off and not affected by the war in any respect. [...] Dr Sibelius gave me a score of the Fourth Symphony with precise corrections. [...] In a few days, Dr H. Gerigk will arrive here to get into close contact with Sibelius about the biography of him to be written. I did not speak to Gerigk before my departure, and there is no agreement yet that he should actually submit the biography to B&H as publisher – but that is what the Deutsche Sibelius-Gesellschaft is striving to do. [...] I discussed now with Dr Sibelius the idea of a <u>short</u> biography (for one Reichsmark) and the intention to entrust Dr Hausswald with that. Sibelius firmly resists any biography whose author has not spent a significant amount of time with him in Finland and whose MS he has not reviewed <u>before</u> printing.* // * He railed at length about W. Niemann's biography! // [...] But I admit that even a <u>short</u> biography can only be written by someone who has met Sibelius himself and knows the Finnish mentality and land + people from personal experience. Now, <u>after</u> visiting Dr S, I had the idea of asking Dr Gerigk. [...] The weather is magnificent, and I believe my trip is worthwhile, because the Finns appreciate it <u>very</u> much when someone shows an interest in them.

Hase also wrote to Sibelius himself from Helsinki on 11 August 1942: 'With regard to the short biography, I have been thinking that perhaps the best thing would be to ask Dr Gerigk to abridge a short, popular biography from his <u>long</u> biography. If you find this idea sympathetic, I would ask you to discuss it with Mr Gerigk. Then we do not need to get a separate author moving on the short biography.'[4] One reason for the failure of the plan was that Gerigk fell ill in the autumn of 1942, which prevented a planned trip to Finland.[5] In the meanwhile, Niemann had also begun to think about

[1] Cf. Gleissner 2002, pp. 181 ff., 474 ff. and 493 ff.

[2] National Archive Box 23.

[3] Åbo Akademi, copy; original in Wiesbaden; Hellmuth von Hase to Breitkopf & Härtel on 11 August 1942.

[4] National Archive Box 20.

[5] Åbo Akademi; Breitkopf & Härtel to Gerigk, October 7, 1942; Gleissner was referring to another

a new biography. This is documented by a letter from Ernst Gerhard Welckes, a Kapellmeister in Leipzig and husband of the Finnish soprano Lea Piltti, to Sibelius on 22 August 1933:[1] 'From Dr Niemann I must convey his most devoted wishes and his assurance that he will work to see that he — or someone else! — can write a new and good biography. Then it is up to Breitkopf & Härtel to print the work.' Sibelius was probably all the more cooperative because it was Tanzberger, rather than Niemann, who could not be controlled, who began work.

Tanzberger's dissertation was published as the fourth volume in Otto zur Nedden's series *Musik und Nation*. The foreword was written by Heinz Drewes, president of the Deutsche Sibelius-Gesellschaft and initiator of the project. He too was like a character from a picture book: a conductor and musicologist with barely average training whose career had made a great leap as a member of the National Socialist Party. The book was explicitly intended as a greeting 'across the sea to our Finnish friends and comrades-in-arms'. Drewes drew the reader's attention to the fact that the study 'represented the first of several planned efforts' to offer 'an artistic recommendation of Jean Sibelius' genius' and to correct 'many an omission in contemporary German writing on music'. In the preface by the editor of the series, there was a clearly defined sketch of the manner of the Sibelius reception in Weimar and Jena. The names of conductors such as Ernst Nobbe and Paul Sixt were emphasised. That Sibelius was described in this context as an artist associated with 'the people and culture of Finland' — as Nobbe remarked in a talk during a concert in Weimar on 8 November 1935 — was inescapable, since categories such as 'music' and 'nation' seemed to Nedden to 'exist in a unique way' in Sibelius' work, especially in *The Swan of Tuonela*, *Finlandia*, the first two symphonies and the Violin Concerto. His empathetic remark of 8 December 1940 warrants intense reflection: 'In Strauss, there is an effective, quite brilliant tone painting; in Sibelius, an almost religiously tinged tone painting, or at least one that comes from deep inside.'[2]

Nedden did not forget Sibelius after the war, either. From Duisburg on 17 December 1949 he thanked Sibelius for sending a photograph and referred both to his student Tanzberger and his first experiences with Sibelius' music (the Violin Concerto and *Finlandia*). He summed it up thus: 'I see in your work of art the final fulfillment of Western symphonic writing and in your personality the greatest living composer of our time.' Until November 1950, Nedden continued to report on his uninterrupted

essay in *Musik im Kriege* 1, nos. 7–8 (October–November 1943), p. 156, in which it is reported that Gerigk's work has been nearly finished 'since early 1942' (cf. Gleissner 2000, 210); this was surely purely propagandistic exaggeration as no traces of this work are known. Gerigk was one of the leading musicologists of the National Socialist regime. Considering his other urgent projects, it would be surprising to hear that he had made progress with a book on JS.

[1] National Library Coll. 206: 40.

[2] Tanzberger 1962, p. 258, quoting the article 'Jean Sibelius: "Finnlands ungekrönter König",' *Jenaische Zeitung*, 8 December 1940.

work on Sibelius.[1] A nostalgia for National Socialism was in play here that Sibelius never rejected clearly enough.

Tanzberger confirmed the political context of his dissertation by quoting Drewes's speech on 10 April 1942, on the occasion of the founding of the Deutsche Sibelius-Gesellschaft in Berlin. Following several references to the Finnish people's joyful awareness of their 'ancient proximity to the Germanic world' and an introduction to Finnish mythology, which 'clearly runs parallel to the "Edda"', Drewes says: 'This and the serious, barren, yet also mysteriously beautiful landscape have become the true sources of Sibelius' creativity. [...] Thus the symphonic poem becomes his most distinguished form of expression.' This is followed in Tanzberger by citations of authorities that were not routine in the most advanced studies in the humanities in this period: above all Alfred Rosenberg's speech at the cultural conference at the 'Parteitag der Freiheit' (party conference of freedom) in Nuremberg in 1935. Rosenberg was not only the chief ideologue of the Nazi Party for many years, and one of the nastiest figures of his day in many other aspects as well, but apparently a genuine Sibelian, as documented in a file of the Finnish foreign ministry dated 30 December 1940 (long before the Anti-Comintern Pact between Germany and Finland of November 1941): 'The official Sibelius celebration has been postponed until January. The reason given was that Reichsleiter Rosenberg was not able to be present on the actual day.'[2] The birthday celebration with the Fifth Symphony and compositions by Richard Wagner and Piotr Tchaikovsky on the programme was delayed for more than a month so that the Reichsleiter (Reich leader) could participate. In his speech in Nuremberg, Rosenberg had emphasised – in the style of Drewes and the *Heimat* movement – the landscape qualities of all 'great' art, which moreover had been shaped 'by a specific blood-bound soul of the people'. Tanzberger too actively contributed to the effect to develop a specifically National Socialist aesthetic:

> The Finnish landscape and the soul of the Finnish people are the breeding ground from which Sibelius drew his strength. The path to Sibelius' music leads via the soul of the northern landscape. Correctly understanding and valuing the master means engaging with nature in Finland, the Finnish people and their cultural assets. These components form the basis on which Sibelius' work could emerge and fully develop.[3]

Tanzberger is interesting with regard to political issues even beyond the era of Rosenberg and Goebbels, given the similarity between the introductory lines of his dissertation in Jena and the introduction to his later monograph. Although Drewes and Rosenberg were no longer quoted directly in Tanzberger's new book of 1962, the essential ideas at the beginning were the same as those of 1943. The categories

[1] National Library Coll. 206: 42; Otto zur Nedden to JS, 17 December 1949 and 28 November 1950.

[2] National Archive Box 33.

[3] Tanzberger 1943, p. 1.

'landscape', 'soul of the people', 'breeding ground', 'nature', 'history' and 'cultural assets' followed in the original order. Tanzberger defined 'landscape' as a 'collective term for nature, people and climate'. Typical features of Finland include its 'infinite expanses and monotony' and 'deep melancholy and great loneliness': 'In the twilight of the pallid summer nights, the inscrutable forests whisper sagas from a grey prehistory.' This accounts for the 'serious spiritual attitude' of the people and their 'tendency to melancholy': 'Melancholy is a dominant quality of the soul of the Finnish people. [...] Many events that offer Germanic people an occasion to rejoice tend to evoke in Finns instead the emotion of infinite sadness.' As proof he cited a 'typical' Finnish poem. As the point of departure for his new analyses, Tanzberger provided a longer introduction to Elias Lönnrot's *Kalevala* than he had in 1943. Whereas Niemann in his 1917 *Jean Sibelius* only hinted at the *Kalevala* in the context of the *Heimat* aesthetic, in 1962 Tanzberger introduced the essence of the composer by means of Väinämöinen's magic spells, even though he also cited Sibelius' letter that explicitly emphasised the distance between the culture of his childhood and the *Kalevala*. Tanzberger called Busoni as a contemporary witness: 'Sibelius evolved quickly and confidently on the solid ground of Finnish folk music — ground he never left, except when he was forced into a detour by a Tchaikovskian wave. He overcame the influence in order to — now purified and more mature — re-enter his most intimate home and assert it from now on.'[1]

Even in 1962, there are still clear traces of the 'blood and soil' maxim in Tanzberger, although it would not have been at all difficult to modify the structure of the introduction and distance himself from his own old thoughts and the authors he once cited. His idea in 1946 for a new work indirectly draws attention to the necessity to expand his perspectives, which he presumably recognised himself. Over the course of the 1950s, he apparently recognised — *horribile dictu* — that all too many modifications would not have been 'in keeping with the times'. Even in 1962, Tanzberger did not hesitate to cite without comment literature closely connected to the National Socialist context. Nevertheless, he is taken seriously as an author on Sibelius even today, while Niemann, for example, is scorned.

Tanzberger was not writing for readers from Adorno's circle. The leftist theorist is not even mentioned. Granted, his first big public success was *Dissonanzen* in 1957, in which Sibelius is not mentioned (fortunately). Probably Tanzberger did not even know Adorno's texts, which was certainly possible in Hanover in the 1960s. In comparison to Tanzberger's superficiality, the GDR author Brüll was almost exemplary in his ability to analyse the paths to reception in the context of the 1980s and at least suggest an original, fruitful path: 'Only slowly did his true form emerge from the shadows of death; the human being with all his limitations. Again we are encounter-

[1] Busoni, review in *Zürcher Theater-, Konzert- und Fremdenblatt* (March 1916), quoted in Tanzberger 1962, pp. 17–18; on 15 March 1916, Busoni conducted the Second Symphony in Zurich; cf. Erik W. Tawaststjerna 1997b, p. 85.

ing his work: free of inhibition, daring, testing. Questioning what of that has faded with time and what has survived.'[1]

Tanzberger does do a service by documenting an interview with the composer and conductor René Leibowitz, the prominent author of 'Sibelius, le plus mauvais compositeur du monde' (1955), who in the nationalist Finnish scholarship on Sibelius is cited one-dimensionally as a representative of the colonialist 'Other' almost as often as Adorno. The transcript of a discussion in 1961 reveals a lot about Leibowitz's approach to the politics of music:

> Leibowitz: Sibelius risked symphonic forms that he could not come to master inwardly. His themes are not important and powerful enough to permit good 'development'. His thematic material is worn out and not new.
>
> Tanzberger: Beethoven and Bruckner did not always offer new material either, just like the composers of contemporary, modern music. Beethoven is just as unimaginable without Haydn and Mozart as the twelve-tone composers without Schoenberg and Webern.
>
> Leibowitz: That is correct. But I make no distinction between old and new music; for me, there is only music.
>
> Tanzberger: You know that Sibelius' symphonies have been performed by prominent conductors such as Toscanini, Beecham, Wood, Karajan and Furtwängler. It is scarcely reasonable to assume that these artists would have championed worthless music.
>
> Leibowitz: I did not say that Sibelius' music was worthless.
>
> Tanzberger: But that follows from your article.
>
> Leibowitz: The remark that Sibelius was the worst composer in the world was to a certain extent just a joke. At the time there was a survey going around in France about who was the best composer. Sibelius was mentioned. In response to this exaggerated glorification, I said he was the worst — as a joke.
>
> Tanzberger: In your article, as Johnson reported, you accused Sibelius of incompetence and ignorance.
>
> Leibowitz: That's not true!
>
> Tanzberger: Mr Leibowitz, do you know Sibelius' work well?
>
> Leibowitz: Really only the Fifth Symphony and the Violin Concerto; I have conducted those two myself. Of the other symphonies, I know — and only from hearing them — the Fourth and the First; not the others.

[1] Brüll 1986, p. 5.

Tanzberger: Do you like the Violin Concerto?

Leibowitz: It has very charming passages; the symphonies too have beautiful passages. But when I have the choice between Bruckner, Mahler and Sibelius, I prefer to 'do' Mahler and Bruckner. I find, by the way, that Mahler is performed far too infrequently.[1]

German Musicians

Helmut Thierfelder was an enthusiastic conductor of Sibelius who maintained active contact with the press.[2] From 1922 onwards, he was a truly pioneering Sibelian in Leipzig,[3] Wiesbaden and Hanover and the prominent director of the orchestra of the Kampfbund für deutsche Kultur (Militant league for German culture).[4] On 22 October 1929 he wrote:[5] 'Today we performed your "Autumn Evening" in Berlin with the Blüthner-Orchester of Berlin.' On 25 October 1933 he wrote from the south Karelian Vyborg about a performance of the Seventh Symphony in Helsinki, where Sibelius had supposedly been present. *Uusi Suomi* even published an interview in which Thierfelder attributed an important role to Finnish music after the 'death of the atonal movement': 'Although we value our own national efforts, we can also acknowledge national emotion when it appears on foreign soil.'[6] On 18 January 1938 he reported to Sibelius about his concerts in Sweden: 'In Stockholm and Gothenburg I conducted three concerts and was able to win over the Swedes with "Pohjola's Daughter" in particular; the press was, by the way, completely unfriendly and even before I appeared in Gothenburg had published an article warning about the "German" conductor.' As director of the Niedersächsisches Symphonie-Orchester, he wrote on 8 February 1942:

> My homeland is beginning to show more and more understanding of and love for your work. In the end, a kindly providence did indeed ordain that the hour of need should bring our two countries closer together than ever before and that the ground should be well prepared for musical understanding for that reason alone. [...] When you said to me several years ago 'in Germany it will take twenty years before I can point to a truly broad audience', I believe I can

1 Tanzberger 1962, p. 65.

2 A draft letter to Thierfelder is found in National Archive Box 35.

3 Among other things he conducted the German premiere of the Fifth Symphony.

4 Prieberg 1982, pp. 40 ff.

5 Postcard; it was signed by Kilpinen among others; National Archive Box 35. On Thierfelder's Nazi contacts, see also the chapter 'Die Sorgen eines Reichsmusikkammerpräsidenten' in Feuersenger 1982, pp. 41 ff., which discusses the meeting with Paul Graener, composer, National Socialist politician and student of Albert Becker, and the prominent Finnish pro-Nazi composer Kilpinen.

6 'Suomalaisia taiteilijoita kutsutaan Saksaan vierailemaan', *Uusi Suomi*, 17 October 1933; Finnish artists were invited to Germany. The author is grateful to Helena Tyrväinen for this detail.

assure you today that it will not take that long. There are other plans in the making of which you will certainly have more and welcome news soon.

On 6 June 1942 — in direct response to Sibelius' letter — he addressed problems with statements supposedly made to the press: 'Famously, press people are rarely bearable people. I have never spoken nonsense such as that Prof. Kajanus, whom we all admire, had been your mentor [...] that I can offer the best possible presentation of the symphonist Sibelius I so deeply admire. [...] The success of the concert had a positive effect on the press throughout the Reich. And it should continue that way.'[1] In the newspaper article to which Thierfelder referred, Sibelius crossed out the phrase 'my mentor, Prof. Kajanos' [*sic*] but not other phrases that are problematic from today's perspective, for example: 'Now life is worthwhile! Certainly we Finns have difficult years behind us [...]. But who would wish to complain when a shining goal stands before us: that of ultimate liberation. We Finns are happy and proud that our brave soldiers have been permitted to fight alongside the magnificent Germany army. We do not doubt for a moment that the war will end in a European spirit.' Or: 'His musical language is popular in the best sense and reflects the spirit, character and essence of the Finnish people. National pride and embodiment in the natural qualities of his homeland, the immediate connection to the landscape of a thousand lakes and its people is also what strikes a visitor to Järvenpää at the home of the great Finnish tone poet as the basic feature of the essence of the head of the house.' The reference to Kajanus upset Sibelius far more than the political constellation.

There is a draft of a reply dated 7 July 1942 with a characteristic handwritten correction: 'Journalists are and always will be journalists. I was very pleased that the success of the concert had a good effect on the press of the Reich. ~~I am convinced that you are the right man to make my music known in Germany, and in general~~ I am also happy when you conduct my works.' As so often, both in his correspondence and in his compositions, Sibelius wanted to modify this spontaneous, unpolished, unconventional statement and retreat behind the security of 'conventional lies'.[2] The 'press person' in question was Hanns Meseke, who admitted his misunderstanding to Levas.[3]

The spectrum of the many letters from Germany and Austria extends to Wieland Wagner's 11 January 1951 invitation to Bayreuth as a guest of honour, with an opportunity to stay in the Haus Wahnfried — fifty-seven years after Sibelius' pilgrimage to Bayreuth.[4] Klaus Kessler, in turn, reported from the eastern front on 10 July 1944 that

[1] For information on this incident, see Levas 1992, p. 456 n. 413.

[2] The phrase is from JS to Aino (from Vienna) 6 January 1891.

[3] The newspaper clipping is in National Archive Box 31: 'Bei Meister Sibelius auf Järvenpää: Ein deutscher Dirigent bei dem finnischen Komponisten', *Der Mitteldeutsche*, archived as an enclosure with Helmuth Thierfelder to JS, 19 May 1942.

[4] National Library Coll. 206: 44.

at his post at night he thought he heard the first notes of *Finlandia* in the silence.[1] One old acquaintance was Peter Raabe, who dramatically commentated on a performance of the Second Symphony under Fritz Zaun the previous day in Berlin: 'It was a great success with the audience, which was quite numerous despite the blackout.'[2] The connection many Germans felt to his music could scarcely be expressed more impressively. Perhaps Raabe's familiar tone is exaggerated but in 1901 he had reviewed the ADM concert programme for the *Allgemeine Musikzeitung*,[3] so that one cannot rule out that they were old acquaintances. He became president of the Reichsmusikkammer (Reich music chamber) when Richard Strauss was removed from that office in 1935. There was also official correspondence with people such as Paul Hanisch, senior inspector in Potsdam-Babelsberg, who wrote to Sibelius on 13 November 1941:

> In light of the renewed comradeship-in-arms of the brave Finnish people with the German people [...] [I have] arranged soldiers' marches as music for the Germany army [...] [such as] your March of the Finnish Jaeger Battalion [...]. Your March of the Finnish Jaeger Battalion was considered a symbol, much as the Horst-Wessel-Lied became later for us. [...] But in the end my arrangement was approved by the regimental aide-de-camp Werner von Bülow (a conductor at the court in his civilian profession) and by the young Mr Fazer. [...] [I would like] to express the wish that you approve my work, which will be sent to you shortly. (From the fact that records of my arrangement have been produced for radio broadcast one may conclude that it met with the approval of the artistic director of German radio.)[4]

This letter too was answered, on 29 December 1941, which was, as usual, marked on the document. Breitkopf & Härtel had to get involved in this tiresome matter as well, as a letter from Leipzig to Deutschlandsender Berlin makes clear: 'Mr Paul Hanisch [...] [has] submitted performance material to you for an arrangement of Jean Sibelius' "March of the Finnish Jaeger Battalion". [...] [We are obliged to inform you that] this arrangement [...] represents a violation of our copyright. [...] [The work has] been published for military band and in all sorts of other arrangements [...].'[5]

Among younger friends was the great German pianist Wilhelm Kempff, who reported from his adopted homeland, Italy, on 14 August 1956:

> [I have] played your Sonatina [...] in the Basilica Constantini. It was a special experience for me. The brief work, which has grown very dear to me, makes a big and profound impression. For me, it was as if the Nordic spirit were once

[1] National Library Coll. 206: 19.

[2] National Library Coll. 206: 30; Peter Raabe to JS, 5 November 1939.

[3] *Allgemeine Musikzeitung* 28, nos. 22–3 (31 May and 7 June 1901), pp. 279–80.

[4] National Library Coll. 206: 14. The reference to 'young Mr Fazer' is unclear. It may refer to Roger Lindberg, son of Georg Fazer's daughter and director of the Fazer publishing house since 1940.

[5] Åbo Akademi, Original in Wiesbaden: 24 January 1942.

Fig. 40. Sonatina in F-Sharp Minor, op. 67, third movement (excerpt).

again conquering Eternal Rome, but in a peaceful way. [...] The first movement caused the always somewhat distracted Romans to prick up their ears; by the second a reverent silence dominated, whereas the third — for me one of the most brilliant movements in all the literature for piano — seemed to reach the listeners less. Over the course of the winter I will play the Sonatina frequently,

> in Paris in April, for example. […] A Sibelius is needed here [in Capri and Amalfi] to turn the classicism of this Homeric landscape into music.[1]

Kempff, whom Aino called 'Wille the heroic' – he had to play Beethoven's op. 106, the 'Hammerklavier' Sonata, for Sibelius several times a day[2] – visited Ainola as early as 1922.[3] Kempff performed in Finland for the first time in January 1920 and spontaneously improvised on a theme by Sibelius on that occasion. Busoni had earlier delighted Sibelius with Beethoven's op. 106, as Sibelius wrote in his diary on 28 October 1912. On 19 February of that year, Busoni played Bach 'unforgettably'.[4] Kempff was a family friend from 1922 onwards, and he expressed that by dedicating his Violin Concerto to Sibelius in 1932. Kempff showed an extraordinary understanding of Sibelius. In a letter on 12 December 1923 he remarked of the new incidental music to *Scaramouche*: 'That is also so peculiar and yet so natural; it has to be that way.'

Julius Lindner, obviously an old acquaintance of Sibelius, wrote from Vienna on 25 September 1949 about a very special interpreter:

> The performance of your Seventh Symphony by the Wiener Symphoniker, led by Antonia [Brico], was simply perfect and left a profound impression on all my friends who heard it. It is a shame that we hear your works so rarely here in Austria. You are, after all, the last great living maestro. There is probably no better interpreter of your music than Antonia, because she has the great fortune of having been personally initiated by you into the secrets of reproducing your works.[5]

Antonia Brico, who had become famous in the 1930s as the conductor of an orchestra of a hundred women, addressed the Sibeliuses as 'papa and mama'.[6] That form of address must have been preceded by intimate encounters. In 1949 Sibelius received a letter from Frances Page in Denver stating that Brico 'seems to have an amazing insight into the meaning of your music, and must somehow be a true daughter of the North'.[7] Both Lindner and Page belong to a large group of people who do not seem to have left other traces in music history but who interacted with Sibelius with a familiar ease that suggests they knew him well. In Brico's case, both were exaggerating considerably.

Sibelius was also performed by the Kulturbund Deutscher Juden (Cultural league of German Jews),[8] so that the statement by Lea Piltti on 5 December 1935 that his

1 National Archive Box 22.
2 Erik W. Tawaststjerna 1997b, p. 240.
3 Ibid., p. 215.
4 Diary, 21 February 1922.
5 National Library Coll. 206: 23.
6 National Library Coll. 206: 6: postcards to JS, for example, on 2 September 1937.
7 National Library Coll. 206: 28: Frances Page to JS, 16 May 1949 (from Denver).
8 Goldsmith 2000, p. 251.

music is 'increasingly better understood and more frequently performed here in Germany, especially in Germany today'[1] by no means referred only to Kampfbund circles. Piltti sang in Weimar under Ernst Nobbe. Nobbe was soon dismissed by the party and moved from the Nationaltheater to Altenburg. He wrote to Sibelius from Weimar on 8 December 1945, reporting on the birthday performances of the First Symphony, *The Swan of Tuonela* and *Finlandia*.[2] Tanzberger first encountered Sibelius' music in this concert. By contrast, Sibelius' contacts with exiled musicians and emigrants were rare. One of these figures between worlds was the Berlin pianist Edward Weiss, who in 1941, when he lived on Knesebeckstrasse in Berlin-Charlottenburg, had contact with Sibelius. In 1945 he was already writing in English from New York, where after the destruction of his Berlin apartment he was counting on a happier future. He wanted to perform Sibelius' piano music in the United States and build a career as a Sibelius specialist.[3]

The conductor and composer Klaus Pringsheim, twin brother of Thomas Mann's wife Katia, wrote to Sibelius on 9 March 1937, in a context that presumably had nothing to do with Finnish foreign policy. Pringsheim thanked Sibelius for a letter commenting on his score and reported on performances of *The Swan of Tuonela* in Munich and Tokyo, where he was then living: 'The impression I had when I heard this wonderful piece for the first time (in Munich, it must be about thirty years ago) remains unforgettable to me, and it is a special pleasure for me to be able to report to you of the profound effect that it had on the Japanese audience here.' In his letter on 28 March 1936 Pringsheim noted to Sibelius: 'I believe firmly that the Japanese musical world will be very significant in the future and that with this work you are entering into a fruitful terrain.'[4] The context of that letter becomes clear in the context of a letter from Sibelius to Minister Ichikawa from 2 January 1936, which was probably not formulated entirely spontaneously: 'It has been exceedingly interesting for me to study Japanese music perusing the wonderful collection you kindly sent me. I know that a great future awaits the Japanese music. I can see in my mind how it builds on the foundation of a great past history.'[5] Similar ideas are found in an undated draft (*nota bene* in another hand): 'I feel as if the splendour of the millennia and the depths of life are reflected in Indian music.'[6] No formulation that could generate performances was too cheap for Sibelius and his assistants in Ainola. Here, as with Sibelius' letters

[1] National Library Coll. 206: 29. On her career in Germany, see Nivanka 1992; on Nobbe, ibid., p. 81.

[2] National Library Coll. 206: 27.

[3] National Library Coll. 206: 40; Edward Weiss to JS, 14 June 1941 (from Berlin) and 8 April 1945 (from New York); there are other letters from Weiss in the United States, documenting his successes with the music of JS and Busoni from 1948 to 1953.

[4] National Archive Box 35; draft.

[5] National Archive Box 34. The reference is probably to Hikotaro Ichikawa, who from October 1936 worked as a counsellor in the embassy in Helsinki.

[6] National Archive Box 36.

in general, it must be remembered that he was not always responsible for the written and unwritten, even when he signed it; a stamp with his signature was often used.

One person who was important to Sibelius, however, was the composer Günter Raphael, Albert Becker's grandson, one of the victims of National Socialist despotism. He contacted Sibelius from Leipzig on 7 November 1931, hoping for work in Finland.[1] Other relatives of Becker were also in contact with Sibelius, such as Gerhard Becker, who from 1949 to 1953 wrote from Brunswick and also received several replies, and Theo A. Becker, who was active as a cellist in Turku in 1920.[2] On 7 April 1932 Raphael announced he would be arriving in Helsinki: 'You were so kind as to arrange the position at Radio Helsingfors for me.'[3] A visit to Sibelius was on the agenda for his first month in Helsinki. On 18 May 1934, now back in Leipzig teaching composition, he wrote about ambitious plans for the centennial of Albert Becker's birth and asked Sibelius, as well as another prominent student of Becker, Karl Straube, for assessments of their studies in Berlin. An essay was planned to be published in the *Allgemeine Musikzeitung* for the anniversary. Sibelius declined, as he always did in such cases, which Raphael very much regretted, since: 'In the coming days the fate of my future will be decided. My position as composition teacher has been terminated, because I am not of pure Aryan origin, and it is very uncertain whether my lifework thus far and the name of my grandfather Albert Becker will ensure an opportunity to continue living in Germany as a working musician.'[4] On 16 August 1934 a letter from Denmark followed with a request for a letter of support formulated in apolitical terms, since he had indeed been dismissed: 'Furtwängler thinks that I will still be able to be performed in Germany.' Other letters followed in 1935 and 1936. On 17 October 1946, Raphael wrote to Sibelius that he had survived in a hospital; the letter has the customary remark 'Vast. [replied] 10/11/1946' and hence was at least answered by Santeri Levas the secretary.

The correspondence between Sibelius and Jehoshua Aberbach in Palestine immediately after the war is interesting with regard to Sibelius' Jewish reception.[5] Aberbach, who had been born in Germany and in his first letters described himself as a student of law, reported in detail on Sibelius' standing in his adopted homeland and observed, among other things, that only the Fifth had thus far (prior to 1947) been performed several times but that Sibelius' music was rather well known thanks to the music broadcasts of the BBC (General Overseas Programme), which were popular in Israel, but also thanks to concerts at the Army Centre. Aberbach became an advocate of Sibelius in Israel. His letters mention no antipathies towards the artist as a result

[1] National Archive Box 26. For an excellent documentation of the correspondence, albeit with controversial conclusions, see Timothy L. Jackson 2010.

[2] National Library Coll. 206: 3.

[3] National Library Coll. 206: 31.

[4] Ibid.; Günter Raphael to JS, 6 June 1934.

[5] National Library Coll. 206: 1; without exception, the letters from Jehoshua Aberbach to JS between 21 May 1947, and 1 December 1953, are marked 'Vast.' and hence were at least answered by Levas.

of the enthusiasm of National Socialist activists for Sibelius' music. Apparently there were none, which suggests that those involved were capable of making distinctions.

'... the light flooding my country these days'

Sibelius never sympathised with National Socialist Germany out of political conviction or even interest. When dealing with its government, corrections he made to draft letters placed before him, and even in the fair copies, tended to moderate enthusiastic formulations suggested by others. His thank-you letter to the German ambassador to Helsinki, Wipert von Blüchner, of 14 December 1940 is enlightening in that respect and is an extraordinarily valuable document:

> Your Excellency, your great kindness in offering congratulations on my seventy-fifth birthday pleased me greatly, and I do not wish to neglect to thank you sincerely for that.
>
> ~~It would please me from the depths of my heart if my music has succeeded in bringing my fatherland closer to the great German people.~~[1]

The final euphoric sentence was crossed out by him, even though it must really have been in accordance with his own outlook, since he was so concerned to have '*Erfolg*' in Germany especially and not just to be understood but also recognised by the German public. Nevertheless, Sibelius even changed the complimentary close: 'Ihr sehr ergebener' (Yours very faithfully) was changed to 'In vorzüglicher Verehrung' (With exquisite admiration). The new formulation was more elegant and underscored the equal rank of the correspondents. Sibelius' feel for subtleties of idiom is impressive. Unfortunately, he did not always have time (or energy) to monitor his assistants' work in that respect.

He even blamed the political *Zeitgeist* for his creative crisis, that is, for the enduring silence of Ainola: 'Dictatorship and war disgust me. The mere idea of tyranny and oppression, slave camps and the persecution of human beings, destruction and mass murder makes me mentally and physically sick. That is one of the reasons why I have not created anything in more than twenty years that I could have offered the public with an easy heart.'[2] A comment by one of Aino's cousins about a press photograph showing Sibelius at a speech before a meeting of Finnish right-wing extremists in 1930 tells the whole story. The inclination of his head suggests, however, he was sleeping. Aili Järnefelt wrote: 'I was thinking: "now Janne has probably got some inspiration."'[3] Apparently she knew that he urgently needed it. Törne summarised: 'like Dante

[1] National Archive Box 34.

[2] E. Michael Salzer, 'Letzter Besuch bei Jean Sibelius', *Frankfurter Allgemeine Zeitung*, 23 September 1957; quoted in Gleissner 2002, pp. 39–40. The thought could be authentic; apparently Adorno did not read Salzer's article.

[3] Aili Järnefelt to Aino, 12 July 1930 with newspaper photograph; quoted in Erik T. Tawaststjerna 1997, p. 288.

he is a revolutionary by temperament although a conservative by opinion'.[1] The revolutionary conservative attitude, however, would have been suited to fascism as well, but Törne did not think that subtly. Sibelius' acquaintances, probably without exception, sympathised with the political right, as did Aino, who characterised the strongest man of the right-wing movement, Pehr E. Svinhufvud, as a 'ray from the heavens that are watching over us' and gave the highest praise to his radio addresses.[2] Tawaststjerna explains this willingness to be associated even with the fascist movement — which is how the press photo has to be interpreted — with some embarrassment by reference to Sibelius' experiences with wartime communist patrols in 1918 near Ainola and generally in the vicinity of Helsinki.[3] By contrast, Aino's enthusiasm for Svinhufvud is not especially peculiar since he merely belonged to the nationalist conservative Kokoomus Party (National Coalition Party) with its royalist core. At the time, however, Svinhufvud systematically maintained close contact with the Finnish Suojeluskunta (White guard) movement, the patriotic militia.

Whereas Joseph Wulf duly spared Sibelius, other authors, such as Fred K. Prieberg, Michael Meyer, Robert Schlesinger and most recently Timothy L. Jackson, have offered hints of connections between Sibelius and the 'Reich'.[4] Pamela M. Potter even wrote of a plan in the Ministry of Propaganda to commission Herbert Gerigk, chief of the Hauptstelle Musik (Head office for music) in the 'Rosenberg office', to write a book about Sibelius for the series Unsterbliche Tonkunst (Immortal art of music).[5] These historians are not wrong to be concerned, and when Sibelius wrote to the politically instrumentalised Deutsch-Finnische Gesellschaft in Helsinki on 12 April 1943 that in his view the work of the society was 'great as the protector of ancient connections between Finnish and German culture',[6] he certainly meant that seriously. As with many other Finns active in this regard, he did not mean the present government but historical Germany. One proof of this was that ongoing contact between Sibelius and Germany did not become more intense during the National Socialist period, as it did for several other Finnish composers such as Yrjö Kilpinen. In addition to honours awarded in absentia, from the silver Goethe Medal in 1935 on his seventieth birthday[7] to his early membership in the academy in Berlin in January 1921,[8] which was

[1] Törne 1937, p. 53.

[2] Aino to Saimi Järnefelt, March 7, 1932, in Talas 2000, pp. 311–12.

[3] Erik W. Tawaststjerna 1997b, pp. 119 ff.

[4] Prieberg 1982, pp. 139, 141 and 374; Michael Meyer 1991, pp. 162–3; Schlesinger 1997, p. 122.

[5] Potter 1998, pp. 230 and 334. On Gerigk and his projects, see Vries 2001, pp. 173 ff, and other essays in the same volume. This plan is also discussed above.

[6] National Archive Box 35; draft letter in Finnish.

[7] Discussed in detail in Gleissner 2002, pp. 158 ff.

[8] JS sent his thanks for membership, already confirmed on 25 February 1921, in a letter dated 28 April 1921 in the Stiftungsarchiv der Akademie der Künste. In a draft letter dated 25 April 1921 (National Archive Box 34, in German), JS first mistakenly wrote 'ordinary member' and then corrected it to 'foreign member'. His membership had been proposed by Friedrich E. Koch, who informed JS of this on

renewed in 1956,[1] he received frequent invitations, such as the one to the Nordische Musikwoche in Heidelberg in October 1923, 'assuming that the circumstances in our fatherland have not become completely hopeless by that time'.[2]

The Nordische Gesellschaft in Lübeck, which since 1933 had been one of the party's discreetly veiled instruments of propaganda, had no more luck with its invitation in 1935, even though Sibelius would have had an opportunity to experience Furtwängler conducting the Seventh Symphony, something he greatly esteemed. He wrote to Gunnar Hauch, who was not involved in the matter, about it on 16 June 1935:[3] 'In my long life, I have rarely felt more joy than when learning that Wilhelm Furtwängler will perform my work in Germany.' In 1934 the society had ordered a memorial plaque for Sibelius in Lübeck, for which he expressed reserved thanks.[4] On 25 July 1939 the Germans began to apply pressure and pointed out (in vain) that the Nordische Gesellschaft was now all the more the 'expression of the close cultural connections between the lands of the North and Germany'. They wanted Sibelius to at least submit a short text for the planned volume *Zwiegespräch zwischen den Völkern: Deutschland und der Norden* (Dialogue between the peoples: Germany and the North), published in Lübeck in 1940. But here again he remained faithful to his habit and rejected the invitations. Fortunately, texts of this sort, unlike letters, were never written for him in his name in Ainola.

Given the constellation of world politics, it was only consistent with his character that Sibelius – or, more precisely, the correspondence office he set up in 1938 (in the person of Santeri Levas) – did not respond when Prince Hubertus von Löwenstein asked him by telegram on 28 January 1939 to take part in a fund-raising campaign to benefit exiles and emigrants, especially refugees from Germany.[5] It did not even help to mention Richard Strauss, whom Sibelius deeply admired as a colleague for all their profound stylistic differences, as an active supporter of the campaign in the year of his seventy-fifth birthday – a fact that deserves careful attention in biographies of Strauss. And when the National Guild of Jewish Women asked him for similar support, no one lifted a finger in Ainola.[6] In the case of Löwenstein's initiative, there is a highly revealing copy with a typewritten note, probably by Levas: '[Bank] Director

21 July 1921, justifying it for the 'genuineness' of JS' music, among other reasons (National Library Coll. 206: 20).

[1] National Library Coll. 206: 43; Hans Scharoun, president of the Akademie der Künste in Berlin-Dahlem (and famous as architect of the new Berlin Philharmonie building of 1963), to JS, 9 February 1956: JS was elected an extraordinary member of the music division at the second procedural meeting of members on 3–4 February 1956.

[2] National Library Coll. 206: 47; Hermann Poppen, music director of the university, to JS, 30 July 1923.

[3] National Library Coll. 206: 61.

[4] National Library Coll. 206: 63; draft letter to Dr Timm, 24 September 1934.

[5] National Library Coll. 206: 23.

[6] National Library Coll. 206: 27.

Ilves [the composer's son-in-law] believes it would be too risky to respond because a polite rejection could be interpreted in different ways.'[1] This assessment must be regretted very much today, especially as the consequences would certainly not have been serious, at most financial, if his work had been performed less frequently in Germany, for example.

Another event that should be understood in the context of correspondence he did not write himself occurred when he responded via the Finnish ambassador Hjalmar Procopé on the occasion of a Sibelius festival at Suomi College in the United States on 24 June 1941: 'I send my best wishes for the celebration and hope that the light flooding my country these days, with its eternal power, will shed light on the path of the Finnish tribe and drive away the clouds that once again threaten on the horizon. But no new storm, if it should strike us, can, I believe, overcome the friendship that exists between free America and freedom-loving Finland.'[2] Members of his family in particular — several of whom performed responsible functions — were well aware of the perspectives of *realpolitik* and Sibelius' role as a monument to the nation in the 1940s. Sibelius was apparently prepared to tolerate being used as an instrument in the interests of the nation's foreign policy and autonomy, which was threatened during the Second World War, and to sign documents — or at least to have them signed with a stamp of his signature — even if they cannot have corresponded to his own thinking. His creativity did not profit from this constellation.

That something like that could happen to him so easily is well documented in another case in his diary on 14 April and 6 May 1913: 'someone' had urged him to sign a recommendation for Kajanus, which distressed him considerably. Yet he had signed it — this time in his own hand, not with a stamp. The draft of a letter to Dmitry Kabalevsky on 7 May 1945 may be another such remote-controlled document: 'I wish the art of music in Soviet Russia continuing, glorious success.'[3] The political circumstances had changed, and now he had to bow towards the East. He was, however, genuinely interested in musical developments in the Soviet Union, if less so in Kabalevsky. Thanks to radio broadcasts from Moscow and Leningrad he was familiar with the outstanding significance of the classical symphony to Socialist Realism. Previously he had had only sporadic contacts with Russian composers — such as with the 'people's artist' Alexander Glazunov, who wrote in German from France on 4 December 1935, on the occasion of Sibelius' seventy-fifth birthday: 'Hail the creator of the national spirit in music, hail Finland's great maestro, Sibelius!'[4] The formulation 'creator of the national spirit in music' was deliberately chosen.

Courageous gestures of resistance, such as Franz Emil Sillanpää's 'Joulukirje diktaattoreille' (Christmas letter to dictators, 1938), with which the 1939 Nobel Prize

[1] National Archive Box 23.

[2] National Library Coll. 206: 63.

[3] National Archive Box 34.

[4] National Library Coll. 206: 13.

winner provoked an immediate ban on his work in Germany, were not possible for Sibelius for a variety of reasons but neither was he up to small gestures of resistance. Prior to his action, *Silja, die Magd* (1932), the German translation of Sillanpää's *Nuorena nukkunut* (1931; translated as *The Maid Silja* in 1933), had gone through eight printings. His success was comparable to Sibelius' own. Sillanpää's convincing glorification of 'Nordic' qualities of life had pleased the ideologues of the Third Reich, but his aggressive critique of Hitler — in an open comparison to representatives of humanist values such as Goethe, Bach and Beethoven — could not be excused; it was interpreted as fouling his own nest.

Possibly, Sibelius, like many others, did not recognise the fateful developments in Germany as clearly as Sillanpää. He and his family enjoyed the intense reception of his music in Germany. It included the founding of the Sibelius-Gesellschaft in 1942, which Sibelius judged optimistically from the perspective of a musician:[1] supposedly it was primarily about proper metronome indications and correcting wrong notions of tempo, comparable to the projects of the Sibelius Society in London and his publishers, W. Hansen and Breitkopf & Härtel. Sibelius was supposed to be celebrated as a Finnish composer who now possessed a 'right to homeland' in Germany, even though he was not even of pure 'Aryan' origin and belonged to the Freemasons, an organisation banned in Germany. The central idea of 'right to homeland' is also manifested in a telegram from Joseph Goebbels's office on 10 April 1942:

> It is a great pleasure for me to be able to inform you that today [9 April 1942] at my directive a German Sibelius Society was founded. Its task is to ensure that your work, which has long since acquired the right to homeland in Germany, will find increasingly deeper understanding, broader dissemination and recognition in German musical life. With best wishes for your continued well-being, Reichsminister Dr Goebbels.[2]

Sibelius' reaction was broadcast on radio in front of an audience at the Philharmonie in Berlin for a concert by the Städtisches Orchester (also known as the Volksorchester, formerly the Blüthner-Orchester and later the Kampfbundorchester) under Fritz Zaun, featuring *Finlandia*, the *Karelia* Suite and the First Symphony — a multimedia event with an extraordinary effect. Present in Berlin, representing her father, was his daughter Katarina Ilves, the bank director's wife.[3] Zaun and his orchestra had fostered Sibelius' music before, for example, performing the Fifth Symphony on 8 December 1940, at the Schiller-Theater on Bismarckstrasse, and the Second Symphony in 1939.[4]

On 12 March 1942 Goebbels did not conceal from his diary the primary foreign policy reason for the society's founding: 'The Finns are asking us to do somewhat

[1] Åbo Akademi (copy). See also Breitkopf & Härtel to Reichsfunk Berlin, 3 June 1942, in which JS' letter of 15 May 1942 concerning the recording was quoted and commented on.

[2] Original orthography of the actual telegram in Helsinki (National Library Coll. 206: 13).

[3] Gleissner 2000, p. 206.

[4] National Library Coll. 206: 42; Fritz Zaun to JS, 11 December 1940.

more for Sibelius. I approved the founding of a Sibelius society.'[1] 'The Finns' were presumably the secretary of the legation, Hans R. Martola, and the composer Yrjö Kilpinen, accompanied by Thierfelder.[2] Until that point, Sibelius had been a concern only of the Nordische Gesellschaft and its patron, Rosenberg. The latter remarked cynically on the founding of the society and the takeover of the German representation for Sibelius by Goebbels's Ministry of Propaganda, which did not please him and his co-workers (such as Gerigk):[3] 'It is the first case of which I am aware where a society for a composer is founded directly by the Ministry of Propaganda.' Hence the cultivation of Sibelius' music in the National Socialist state was supported at an unusually high administrative level. This raises the question of how broad an effect this exaggeratedly elevated level of influence had on people and how it influenced the acceptance of Sibelius specifically among professional musicians, who were often secretly critical of the government. The Kampfbundorchester was not regarded highly by all Germans, although the Berlin Philharmonic was.

In his speech, which is preserved in the archives of Finnish Radio, Sibelius expresses himself in a way that shows that the political dimension of the founding of the society was indeed well understood in Ainola: 'The great sympathy for my fatherland in these times of a shared fate and the great interest in my music expressed by the founding of the Deutsche Sibelius-Gesellschaft make me proud and happy. From the Finnish forests, I send my greeting to Germany, the radiant land of music.' The speech did not have an easy birth. In the National Archive in Helsinki, there is a handwritten version, which Tanzberger cited as well, albeit without the anti-Soviet phrase 'in these times of a shared fate'.[4] From this sketch is it evident that Sibelius initially intended to speak only of the 'land of music' and not the 'radiant land of music'. Moreover, the sketches have symbols that presumably indicate articulation and pauses for breath. A somewhat earlier sketch in another hand has a very different (and wooden) text: 'It is a great pleasure for me to express my deeply felt thanks for the interest evident from the Deutsche Sibelius-Gesellschaft. I send from the Finnish forests a sincere greeting to Germany, the land of music.'[5] This sketch raises the question who was the author of the speech. It makes use of clichés that seem in their obsequiousness ('from the Finnish forests') at once romantic and ironic and *de facto* make fun of the clichés of others by exaggerating them. The bell of the misunderstood *Heimat* aesthetic rings loud, and the universal quality of primal nature is directly addressed. The ironic ex-

[1] Fröhlich 1994, p. 460.

[2] Cf. Gleissner 2000, p. 202

[3] Bundesarchiv NS 15/98, fol. 1, quoted in Gleissner 2000, p. 200; for Gerigk's stance, see file note from 21 February 1942, quoted ibid., p. 203.

[4] Tanzberger 1962, p. 61.

[5] National Archive Box 34, in German.

pression 'from the forests' would be typical of Sibelius but that neither makes it easier to understand nor necessarily authentic.[1]

Just as incriminating for him as the events of the founding of the Sibelius-Gesellschaft in 1942 was his correspondence with Thilo von Trotha, the personal adjutant of Reichsleiter Rosenberg. On 21 September 1936 Trotha invited Sibelius in the name of the Hitler Youth to the Braunschweiger Musiktage: 'You can see from this invitation how much your work has moved to the foreground again in Germany, after all the influences have been shaken off that prevented not only our genuine German music but also your work from being heard. What you see from this invitation is that the musical youth of Germany is close to your work.'[2] Trotha visited Sibelius in March 1936, accompanied by the song composer Yrjö Kilpinen. He was in a position to cite Sibelius credibly, who was said to have interrupted the discussion between his visitors with a Solomonic remark: 'One cannot debate about who is better, Bach or Beethoven, just as one cannot debate about whether a Burgundy or a Bordeaux is better. Burgundy remains Burgundy and Bordeaux remains Bordeaux.' A draft of a response to this letter survives, with small grammatical errors to testify to its authenticity, in which Sibelius thanks him formally for the 'honour of an invitation from the Hitler Youth' and wishes 'the Braunschweiger Musiktage a splendid success'.

His draft response on 15 April 1941, replying to a request from the Berliner Philharmonisches Orchester that he supply a greeting to the orchestra and Wilhelm Furtwängler, was more emphatic. On 17 May he noted enthusiastically, albeit uncertainly struggling for suitable adjectives: 'To the B. Phil.Orch, ~~which is among~~ one of the best in the world / the best in the world, [illegible] and to Dr Wilhelm Furtwängler, who achieved true miracles, I send my best wishes, J.S.' In this case he had more reason for genuine gratitude than he could have known, since just a few months earlier Furtwängler had declared him to be the only composer outside Germany (apart from Tchaikovsky) who worked 'genuinely symphonically'.[3] Either Furtwängler's concept of the symphonic differed from that of Schoenberg, who questioned Sibelius' quality specifically as a 'symphonist',[4] or he knew the oeuvre better.

From Sympathy to Enthusiasm in the United Kingdom and the United States of America

The English-language literature on Sibelius, from reviews to essays and monographs, might at first glance appear to be an inexhaustible store of positively inclined Sibelius

[1] See also Diary, 13 May 1910 and JS to Busoni, 21 November 1921 (Berlin Staatsbibliothek, Mus. ep. J. Sibelius 6).

[2] National Library Coll. 206: 39.

[3] Gleissner 2002, p. 141, quoting Wilhelm Furtwängler, *Aufzeichnungen, 1924–1954*, ed. Elisabeth Furtwängler and Günter Birkner (Wiesbaden: Brockhaus, 1980), p. 213: statement from 1940.

[4] Schoenberg's statement of 8 December 1939, quoted in Newlin 1980, pp. 152–3; see chapter 5.2 in the present volume.

promotion. Michael Mäckelmann summarised the situation by saying that the phenomenon of seeing him as 'controversial' is 'essentially confined to the European continent'; the '*Sibelius "Problem"*' is, according to Mäckelmann, confined to certain 'latitudes'.[1] Whereas German authors such as Niemann crippled Sibelius with their sometimes complicated formulations, which were more dialectic and speculative than logical and pragmatic, the 'sympathy with which my ~~art~~ music has been received in England' at the beginning of the twentieth century was considerable in Sibelius' eyes. He conquered the United Kingdom and the United States with ease in the first years of a restructuring or commercialisation of musical life that had already taken place there.[2] He was able to do so with the essential support of branches of Breitkopf & Härtel in London and New York, which remained active until 1914. For the first time in history, the 'New World' took the lead, and aggressively commercial forms of concert life made it easy for new styles and artists to gain acceptance. While his life in the Finnish context overlapped auspiciously with Karelianism and the cult of the *Kalevala*, the reform of musical life in other countries stimulated the international dissemination of his music. So he had reason to assume that 'my music will never set roots in Germany'.[3]

Aaron Copland's scorn demonstrates that it was not only narrow-minded Central Europeans, emigrants and Schoenbergians who called Sibelius' standing into question – perhaps provoked by an overdose in the media, which in those days offered few alternatives. It should be said that Copland's remarks were directed more at American colleagues and specifically at Samuel Barber: 'They are composers who feel lost in the mazes of the contemporary idiom. Sibelius is a refuge to them.'[4] Here again it is important to distinguish between criticism of Sibelius' music and that of his devotees and of his presence in the media. Whereas in Germany only a few more recent composers have declared an interest in him – Manfred Trojahn and Wolfgang Rihm are among the prominent exceptions[5] – in the United States and the United Kingdom he is one of the role models who are always considered. According to Laura Gray, early on he was 'a kind of saviour who [...] seemed to lead the way out of the modern musical predicament'.[6] As a representative of the establishment and a mouthpiece of the *Zeitgeist* (and certainly also as a professional composer), Ralph Vaughan Williams, who dedicated his Fifth Symphony to Sibelius (1938–43, rev. 1951) and had indeed studied the latter's style while working on it,[7] emphatically confirmed his unconditional admiration as late as 1955: 'I do not count as civilized those mid-

[1] Mäckelmann 1983, p. 121.

[2] On this subject, see, for example, McVeigh and Ehrlich 2002, pp. 96 ff.

[3] National Library Coll. 206: 61; JS to Gunnar Hauch, 11 May 1924.

[4] Copland 1941, p. 45.

[5] Trojahn 1987, pp. 424–6, and Brinkmann and Rihm 2001, pp. 90 ff.

[6] Laura Gray 1996, p. 28.

[7] Corroborated by a letter to Gerald Finzi, quoted in Banfield 1988, p. 212.

Europeans who ignore Sibelius.'[1] In many cases, such enthusiasm was shored up by criticism of Schoenberg, as was the case with Ernest Newman, who somewhat cryptically but insightfully remarked that Schoenberg was attempting to do the same thing as Sibelius, but unsuccessfully.[2] Radical Sibelians considered Schoenberg's innovations flashes in the pan and held up Sibelius as an absolutely universally valid role model.[3] Granville Bantock wrote in that tone in 1946: 'I very doubt whether a lot of foreign music will last long – Schönberg and Honegger, for instance.'[4] Schoenberg's greatness was reduced to the – from an Anglo-American perspective – typically Teutonic, as in this open letter to Schoenberg from 1928: 'You are the Big Brain of music. But in music as in women we have always preferred beauty to brains.'[5] Few would laugh at such jokes today.

Characteristic of the attitude in the first half of the twentieth century was the stylistic and geopolitical dichotomy that Kaikhosru Sorabji articulated in his book *Mi contra Fa* of 1947. He criticised 'German pedantry' as leading to observations in a vacuum and to senseless forms. He credited non-academics such as Berlioz, Delius and Sibelius with the ability of creating a 'significant form'.[6] But why was Sibelius of all people a role model for so many British composers? Jürgen Schaarwächter explains Sibelius' success in terms of the rediscovery of Eastern Europe and Russia. He also believed that Rosa Newmarch's knowledge of Russian 'considerably smoothed the path for Sibelius in Great Britain'.[7] But Sibelius hardly spoke Russian at all. Newmarch was indeed an influential advocate of Eastern European and other undiscovered repertoires. The way she characterises Sibelius, however, does not support Schaarwächter's thesis: 'a striking and characteristic example of a man from the North – a Viking type'.[8] Schaarwächter accuses Sibelius and the Eastern Europeans of contributing with their 'late Romantic influence' to the 'dilution of the real intentions of British (and also French) composers',[9] but he does not define what their 'real intentions' were. Several British composers did indeed contribute to the Sibelius cult and the abandonment of their own identity to such an extent that it was easy for critics to play the popular game of role models and influences. For example, Edmund Rubbra's Second Symphony, op. 45 (1937), was greeted in the press as follows: 'Sibelius' long awaited Eighth Symphony was performed by the BBC Orchestra last night – but the composer was an Englishman, Edmund Rubbra.'[10] Rubbra was in Helsinki in January

[1] Kennedy 1964, pp. 333, 381 and 262.

[2] Erik W. Tawaststjerna 1986, pp. 284–5, quoting Newman's review in the *Birmingham Post*.

[3] Vaughan Williams [1963] 1986, p. 263.

[4] Brook 1946, p. 14.

[5] Coulter 1928, p. 115.

[6] Sorabji 1947, pp. 49 ff.

[7] Schaarwächter 1995, pp. 204 and 206.

[8] Newmarch 1939, p. 8.

[9] Schaarwächter 1995, p. 205.

[10] Foreman 1997, jacket copy.

1951, but he cannot have met Sibelius.[1] On 23 March 1952 he sent Sibelius in Ainola a recording of his Fifth Symphony 'as a token of my respect and admiration'.

Olin Downes of the *New York Times* was the leading apostle of Sibelius in the United States. In a draft letter, Sibelius wrote about him in way that it sounds as if it may have been some kind of letter of recommendation: 'He has penetrated the innermost depths of my art, and my fame in America is his work.'[2] After their first encounter, he had expressed himself more ambiguously, but in the privacy of his diary he observed: 'Olin Downes was here with us. A strange critic.'[3] Long before Downes, Newmarch had begun to work to build Sibelius' popularity in London. She was not only the legendary author of the programme essays for Henry Wood, the originator of the Proms, but also the author of two small books on Sibelius. Her career as a writer on Sibelius began in 1906 with *Jean Sibelius: A Finnish Composer*, right after completing her English translation of Tchaikovsky's letters. The American edition of her second book on Sibelius in 1939 had the apt title *A Short History of a Long Friendship* and constituted a milestone in the popular genre of brief biographies of friends. Sibelius had written her as early as 1913: 'How can I thank you enough for all that you have done for us in Finland? Your dear name is inscribed for ever in letters of gold in the history of our culture.'[4]

Her first book also emphasises the private side: she begins with a statement on her great Sibelius experience, of which the small book (actually just the publication of a lecture at the Music Club) was the fruit.[5] The text became the model for all later authors who would first explain in detail his 'race' and the *Kalevala*, then venture a gallop through the history of Finnish music and finally identify Sibelius as a representative of the 'spirit of the people' – all aspects that are almost irrelevant to Sibelius. Only the reception of the category of nature, which Newmarch also clearly accentuates, holds up to critical evaluation. Quoting Andrew Lang, Newmarch compares Sibelius' closeness to nature to common characteristics of the Celts and Finns: 'the expression of early humanity prevails among races isolated, remote, abiding in the solitude of hills and forests, culling their songs 'from the plumes of pine-trees', the winds in the woods, the music of many waters'.[6] Much like some of the Germans, Anglo-American authors believed that Sibelius and his music were closely integrated into the nature and naturalness of the North. He became the symbol of nature and a game piece in the battle between the cultural metropolis and the primal forest, civilisation and closeness to nature. Wilfrid Mellers spoke of a 'Delian desire to relinquish

[1] Cf. the response, JS to Edmund Rubbra, 15 March 1951; National Library Coll. 206: 32.

[2] National Archive Box 35; undated draft.

[3] Diary, 12 September 1926 (actually 1927, when Downes was in Helsinki). On this subject, see Goss 1995.

[4] JS to Newmarch, 1 July 1913; quoted in Newmarch 1939, pp. 33–4.

[5] Newmarch 1906, p. 3.

[6] Ibid., p. 23.

his personality in nature' and Robert Layton of the antithesis to the 'urbanization of music'.[1] That is by no means inaccurate.

The biographies of friendships triggered a contemporary interest in intimacies. It is one of those rare cases when an anecdote is corroborated – rather than disproven – by an authentic document: Granville Bantock in his foreword to Newmarch's book reports on a student in Birmingham who received 'a pound sterling' from Sibelius for the journey to London, where the Fifth Symphony was to be performed (it was in fact the Fourth Symphony, not the Fifth).[2] The student was the American composer Laurence Powell, who later reminded Sibelius of this event from 1921 (Bantock had not mentioned the date) to explain why he wanted to dedicate his First Symphony to Sibelius: 'I shall never as long as I live forget that Reception – when you so kindly offered to give me a pound sterling, so that I could go to London to hear your Symphony IV. I did so and sat with Miss Newmarch during the symphony. [...] I have composed my Symphony I. [...] I want to dedicate this symphony to you.'[3] Sibelius reported to his wife from Birmingham, mentioning the reception and the concert in London 'on Saturday', 26 February 1921. Busoni performed in the same concert.[4] Bantock's confusion is understandable, since Sibelius had conducted his Fifth Symphony two weeks earlier.[5] There was, however, no reception in Birmingham before that concert.

Sibelius became a composing 'media star', and thus one need have no scruples about writing about him, since he was an unconditionally public person. The eyewitness reports began in Newmarch's 1939 book, in the foreword by Bantock, who had invited Sibelius to join the Liverpool Orchestral Society in 1905; Bantock is thus claimed to have 'discovered' Sibelius' for England.[6] His report on Sibelius' arrival contributed to some enduring confusion in the history of his reception: 'as the great man then could speak little English, and my knowledge of Finnish was nil, our conversation was limited to a polyglot combination of French and German words. Knowing that Rosa Newmarch was a fluent Russian linguist and an accomplished translator I sought her aid, happily not in vain.'[7] The impression that she communicated with Sibelius in Russian is thus incorrect, since in fact his Russian was far more rudimentary than his English. He used Russian expressions in letters only rarely, for example 'ochen dobra' (very good) on 29 April 1884.[8] Newmarch's function was to translate from all languages for Bantock:

> I was put next to him at dinner with a vague idea that, as nobody knew the language he spoke, a little Russian might come in handy. I had been long enough

[1] Mellers 1957, p. 133; Layton 1993, p. 4.

[2] Newmarch 1906, pp. 6–7.

[3] National Library Coll. 206: 30; Laurence Powell to JS, 15 May 1929; written when Powell was a professor in Fayetteville, Arkansas.

[4] Erik W. Tawaststjerna 1997b, p. 200.

[5] Ibid., p. 197.

[6] Newmarch 1939, p. 8.

[7] Ibid., p. 5.

[8] Cf. Goss 1997, p. 65, and also Erik W. Tawaststjerna 1986, p. 80.

> in Russia and over the Finnish borders to know that the Finns were not too keen to speak the language of their big neighbour, but we soon effected a compromise: a sort of sandwich between French and German, to which, looking over our correspondence which has lasted over thirty years, I found to my amusement we always adhered.[1]

Even her translations of Sibelius' songs were made via German: 'he would walk up and down the room and declaim the words in a rough but vivid translation, generally into German. I, catching their meaning, in breathless haste would put them down in English in a sort of impromptu shorthand to be worked up later.'[2] In general Newmarch preferred French to German. That explains the remark in a letter Sibelius wrote her on 1 January 1911: 'Please forgive me for writing you in "German". *Mais que faire!* At the moment I do not have time to write in French.'[3] 'When I write in French, you know that I am nothing but a real Tommy Atkins', wrote Sibelius idiomatically.[4] He had studied French in school from 1881 onwards, and German from 1879, making it probably his first so-called foreign language – counting Finnish as the other local language of his youth.[5] On 3 January 1911 he wrote to Newmarch in English so fluent that she assumed (probably correctly) that Aino had helped him.[6] That gives a sense of the impression she had of his knowledge of English. All of Newmarch's letters to him from 1906 to 1939 were in French, as were some of his to her.

Newmarch's introduction is a little sarcastic, claiming the public had 'understood' Sibelius more quickly than the specialists:

> This insistence on the gloom and greyness of Sibelius' music is linked with our superficial ideas of the Finnish character, and our exaggerated conception of the composer as an exclusively national poet. It is true that his music reveals some salient features of the Finnish temperament; the Pantheism, the close intimacy with Nature, the aspirations of a people at once old and vigorous, and much of that deep-rooted indignation that was the outcome of age-long conflicts with man and climate. But this applies most appropriately to his early works based on episodes from the epic 'Kalevala'. Self-conscious nationalism began to disappear from his art with the appearance of the symphonic poem 'Night Ride and Sunrise' (Op. 55). Sibelius' spirit is too restless and complex to dwell content within geographical boundaries, even those which enclose the land and his heart.[7]

1 Newmarch 1939, p. 8.
2 Ibid., p. 22.
3 National Archive Box 121.
4 JS to Rosa Newmarch, undated; quoted in Newmarch 1939, p. 37
5 JS to Pehr Sibelius, 21 September 1881, in Goss 1997, p. 49.
6 Newmarch 1939, p. 39.
7 Ibid., pp. 52 ff.

The love of ideal beauty, which could of course also seem old-fashioned, she compared to John Keats, who had also been born with 'a clear pre-natal Hellenic strain in him'. Sibelius' negative attitude towards the sciences and philosophy was certainly also in keeping with Keats: 'Do not all charms fly / At the mere touch of cold philosophy?' and 'In the dull catalogue of common things / Philosophy will clip an Angel's wings.'[1] At the same time, she emphasised the dimension of depth: 'those who know Sibelius well realize that in him art and religion are one'.[2] This one-sided observation corresponds to a remark about him 'as a Finn': 'Sibelius as a Finn shows now and again a strong mystical tendency. In his music we come upon sudden flashes of religious feeling.'[3] She combined this with a report on Sibelius and inspiration: 'Musical inspiration is like the children's game of *Word-taking and Word-making*. A spiritual force (call it God) throws down to one a handful of letters — a message — and a voice says: "make what you can of this". Alas, we cannot always make the best of it.'[4] Newmarch too does not so much disagree with the accusation that the themes are not developed symphonically as consider it misguided. She quotes Ernest Newman, who described Sibelius with the sentence: 'To satisfy him the "art of transition" [...] had to be subjectively, not mechanically, solved.' She is equally aware that Sibelius was no iconoclast: to get to particular places in a park, Sibelius would not step on the grass. One could add: nor in other places.

With regard to Adorno's sideswipe, it is interesting how Newmarch doubts the genuineness of Newman's enthusiasm for Sibelius: 'I do not think that this perspicuous and open-minded concert-manager fully appreciated all the complex qualities of the Finnish composer's art, but he did recognize his striking originality, and welcomed the opportunity of his reappearance in London.'[5] Sibelius was in any case the first foreign composer the artistic director Newman invited after the First World War to conduct at Queen's Hall. Adorno writes of Newman, the supposed 'initiator of Sibelius' fame' (which is not true, given Bantock):

> More than thirty years ago I once asked Ernest Newman, the initiator of Sibelius' fame, about the qualities of the Finnish composer. After all, I said, he had adopted none of the advances in compositorial technique that had been made throughout Europe; his symphonies combined meaningless and trivial elements with alogical and profoundly unintelligible ones; he mistook esthetic formlessness for the voice of nature. Newman, from whose urbane all-round skepticism someone bred in the German tradition had much to learn, replied with a smile that the qualities I had criticized — and which he was not denying — were just what appealed to the British. Newman's humble view of music

1 John Keats, 'Lamia', quoted in Wind 1985, p. 47.

2 Newmarch 1939, p. 54.

3 Ibid., p. 55.

4 Ibid., p. 56.

5 Ibid., pp. 39–40.

> criticism, of which he was the Anglo-Saxon matador, corresponded with that attitude.[1]

Ignoring the fact that Adorno was provoking connoisseurs here, since of course Sibelius had adopted 'advances in compositorial technique that had been made throughout Europe' – though, to be fair to Adorno in some degree, one would have to ask what he means by 'adopted' (*rezipiert*) – Newman's reaction should certainly not be understood as mere politeness or 'all-round skepticism'. This shows that Adorno used categories that, if treated less partially, certainly could become the point of departure for an objective debate. British musical culture has, after all, been known for centuries for having welcomed such outstanding artists as Handel, Haydn, Muzio Clementi and Beethoven. For Newman, for more than thirty years before his encounter with Adorno, Sibelius was, among other things, a representative of a 'new civilization' and hence a way of accessing an interesting alternative to degenerate 'Western life'.[2]

One of the first attempts to provide an empirical foundation for a picture of Sibelius was launched by the Phi Beta Kappa member Lucien Price on 23 October 1910 with a questionnaire that Sibelius was supposed to fill in.[3] The occasion was performances of the First and Second Symphonies, *En saga* and *Finlandia* in Boston and at Harvard University, which had aroused in Price an 'interest in Finland itself'. Consequently he asked questions on the subject of nationality in music. Their complexity far exceeded Sibelius' ability to communicate in English in 1910, which Price had presumably not anticipated at all:

> Nationality in music: – The relation of race to its expression in musical form. / The historical element in music: – How far can legendary, patriotic or historical matters be expressed in music. / The relations of landscape to music: – Can mood, emotions or actual scene of a landscape be reproduced in sound? / The expression of color by an orchestra: – What sort of colors, for instance, can be best expressed. Were, for example, the moors and forests of Finland in your mind when composing the 'Saga' or the second of your symphonies? / Devices of instrumentation: – Are your own methods of producing the effects of weirdness, savagery, and the like, the result of deliberate planning or do they occur to you as inspirations? / The question of form: – Do you find yourself adhering with the strictness to classical form or do you incline to the so-called 'modern' school, as represented by Dr. Richard Strauss and others? / Have the tone-poems of Richard Strauss had any influence on your own compositions? / By what composers have you been influenced, if by any? / Is the strong 'national' element or tone which all critics appear to find in your works the result

[1] Adorno 1976, pp. 172–3.

[2] Newman's essay in *Manchester Guardian*, 4 December 1905; quoted in Erik W. Tawaststjerna 1986, p. 42.

[3] National Library Coll. 206: 30.

> of accident or of deliberate design. Is it the unconscious expression of beliefs, environment and tradition, or a conscious effort to express Finland in music? / What are your views of the compositions of the following Russian composers: Tschaikowsky, Rimsky-Korsakoff, Rubinstein, Scriabin, Rachmaninoff, Arensky and Glazunoff? / Is it true that your works have been directly inspired or influenced by the climatic, historical, the racial and scenic conditions in Finland? [...] it is likely that your works will add a national dignity to Finland which it has never had before in the eyes of the world. You have already begun to interpret your nation to the ears of the western continent, and we have heard, and, I believe, understood, even here in America.

The cover letter was addressed to 'Professor Jean Sibelius, Principal of the Conservatorium, Helsingfors, Finland'. In spring 1933, when Price wanted to travel to Finland, Downes wrote a letter of introduction, which shows that Sibelius had not responded to the 1910 questionnaire and had not even met Price during his trip to America in 1914: Downes introduced him as a colleague from Boston who was completely unknown to Sibelius.[1]

The year 1910 was early for American enthusiasm.[2] Performances of the first two symphonies under Wilhelm Gericke (1904) and Karl Muck (1907) had not yet convinced audiences and critics on the East Coast. Olin Downes compared Muck's performance of the First Symphony with reading Walt Whitman, which in the American context was supposed to suggest a familiarity with Sibelius (like Keats for Newmarch), but there were also other views. The Second Symphony, which had been a flop for Gericke, would provoke even less unanimously positive reviews in 1910. It is therefore all the more remarkable that Price mentioned the Second Symphony right alongside the First in his questionnaire of 1910. Price was apparently following directly Downes's shift in position, who was the first to understand the performance of the Second Symphony under Max Fiedler in 1909.

It is astonishing how direct Price's questions are, apparently not suspecting how reticent Sibelius was in such matters. It is hardly surprising that no reply from Sibelius has survived. In early November Sibelius had just returned from a trip to Berlin, and his diaries reveal how hard he was working on his Fourth Symphony and a work commissioned for Aino Ackté's tour of Germany, the song 'The Raven' (Poe). He had no time for elevated journalism à la Price. The diaries also show that at this very time he was struggling with strange difficulties concentrating. Moreover, he was far too often irritated by public references to the national: 'Am I really nothing other than a "nationalist" peculiarity?'[3] Price's 'interest in Finland itself' could not have made Sibelius feel better. But perhaps the probingly analytical questionnaire even indirectly encouraged Sibelius in his search for an unsparingly original style that was neither

1 Goss 1995, pp. 198–9.

2 Cf. ibid., pp. 32 ff.

3 Diary, 14 November 1910.

Russian modernism nor showed any trace of 'Dr Richard Strauss' — but was not explicitly 'expressionistic' either.

Price finally did meet Sibelius during a trip to Finland in 1933, as is documented by a handwritten excerpt from *En saga* that illustrates Price's novel *The Furies*: it shows a characteristic sequence of chords from *En saga* (twenty measures from the Lento assai) with a dedication to Price (signed in Järvenpää on 26 August 1933: 'To Mr Lucien Price ab imo pectore'),[1] and Price wrote a 'Portrait of Sibelius at Järvenpää', which was published in 1936 in *We Northmen*, an essay that seemed to document the relative closeness of American cultural history to contemporary movements in Germany. *We Northmen* is a kind of stylised travel journal, which contains, among other things, a summary of Price's conversations with Romain Rolland. Sibelius was said to be the 'saga man' of the symphony. 'The voice was one that seemed to know us better than we knew ourselves. It was of the North' and 'one of our own'.[2] A little later Price added: 'Beginning as saga man of the symphony, he ends by becoming saga man of the Northern spirit.'[3] Only Sibelius' music would pass the test of being confronted with nature, because it was 'close to the realities of the elemental nature'.[4] It is astonishing to see how cogently and perceptively Price argued.

The Nordic, nature, the national and the feeling of homeland were defined, not least in the United States, in Sibelius' favour.[5] For example, Walter Damrosch, who commissioned *Tapiola*, wrote to Sibelius: 'The variety of expression that you give to one theme in the various episodes, the closely-knit musical structure, the highly original orchestration, and, above all, the poetic imagery of the entire work, are truly marvellous. No one but a Norseman could have written this work.'[6] Price's argumentation was ideologically clearer: 'It is manliness, loyalty, courage, and a certain rough honesty, salted with humor.'[7] And: 'In Sibelius the symphony has reached its farthest north.'[8] In Price's assessment, Sibelius' work is not even connected to Christianity but more with the Edda and sagas; 'thus in Finland our pagan subsoil of the North is centuries nearer the surface.'[9] The enthusiasm of the writer and journalist for the archaic history of the culture of the North, long before the confrontation with 'Oriental', 'Mediterranean' and 'Hebraic' elements, is unmistakable, but that only makes his reticence in defining Sibelius' position all the more astonishing:

> I was startled to find this territory of thought by no means unfamiliar to Sibe-

[1] Price 1988, p. 19. One chapter in Price's book is titled 'Saga'. It is the name of a ship, a 'humble coastwise vessel'; ibid., p. 45.

[2] Price 1936, p. 352.

[3] Ibid., p. 366.

[4] Ibid., pp. 353–4.

[5] Pollack 2002, p. 182.

[6] Walter Damrosch to JS, 3 January 1927; quoted in Erik W. Tawaststjerna 1997b, p. 275.

[7] Price 1936, p. 355.

[8] Ibid., p. 363.

[9] Ibid., pp. 355–6.

lius. It was discussed repeatedly and with more frankness than I feel justified in reporting fully: not only by him but by Madame Sibelius, a most remarkable woman, and so in harmony with him intellectually that one finds himself involuntarily speaking to and thinking of them as one.[1]

Probably Price, like so many others, misinterpreted Sibelius' need for harmony in conversation and also spoke more often to Aino Sibelius (or with the two of them together), who was much more fluent in English. (The problems Sibelius had with English might also explain why he was less annoyed by Price than by Niemann.) No doubt the hints ('more frankness', etc.) are more striking today than any possible specific reportage — in agreement with other sources, particularly as far as Aino Sibelius is concerned[2] — that unfortunately Price chose not to offer.

On 20 April 1913, a few years after Price's first letter and his questionnaire of 1910, Sibelius responded to a questionnaire from Gunnar Hauch.[3] Hauch, the Danish editor of Grieg's letters, published a long essay on Sibelius based on their correspondence. According to his diary on 24 August 1915, Sibelius admired it very much: 'Monograph is extraordinary.' Sibelius now dated the beginning of his public career to 1892, when *Kullervo* was premiered — ignoring early chamber music performances such as the String Quartet in A minor at Wegelius' music institute, but also ignoring *Scène de ballet* premiered in April 1891 — and added promisingly: 'Soon I will publish this work.' Unfortunately, he never did so. Apparently he also wanted to publish a new version of *Scène de ballet* of 1891, which has yet to be published. The notes he wrote when expressing himself about the problem of a will to subjective expression and the occasion of his art proved more binding: *Valse triste*, for example, was related to Arvid Järnefelt's play *Kuolema*, he wrote, but the piece was, 'like everything else I have composed', purely musical in its motivation: 'Nothing literary has ever inspired me to a musical motif.' Although the titles of his works often suggest his works have a programme and are connected to a poem or even a dramatic scene, he followed Paul Valéry in defending his 'pure poetry', which presumes that the listener should pay attention to the 'sequence of the song', not the 'sequence of the thought'.[4] The calculation of semantic expression, especially with regard to a text by someone else, ran counter to his idea of the 'pure' work. In the context of his music, Sibelius strove to achieve a synthesis of 'extroverted semiosis' and 'being overcome by the subject matter of the interior'.[5] Freely adapting Johann Wolfgang von Goethe and Friedrich von Hausegger, he spoke of declarations of faith and 'Prayers',[6] which, in contrast to

[1] Ibid., pp. 363–4.

[2] See, for instance, Aino to Elli Järnefelt, 12 December 1900, in Talas 2000, p. 198, and discussed in chapter 3.5 in the present volume (p. 242 n. 3). Cf. also p. 391 n. 3 in the present chapter.

[3] National Library Coll. 206: 61.

[4] Cf. Valéry, Bremond and others, according to Wind 1985, p. 128.

[5] Cf. Bürger 2000, p. 204 (Mallarmé); Agawu 1991; and Jacobi [1940] 1978, p. 33.

[6] Cf. chapter 4.1 in the present volume.

Stéphane Mallarmé's and Valéry's Modernism, suggests a strong, Classical-Romantic author as subject. When Sibelius wrote 'Prayer' in an undated diary entry around 21 November 1914, he added 'Preghiera', which clarifies the object character of what he intended ('Preghiera' as *topos*). His creative process was indeed original and egocentric in Carl Gustav Jung's sense, and his artistic 'fantasy', but not his conventional and socialised 'persona',[1] consistently opened outwards – including the phylogenetic external.[2] The strength of his concept of the work, the demonstrative intellectual separation of the work and its genesis, made possible for him the modern detachment of the work from its author and the 'disappearance of the author in the expression',[3] leaving the initiative to the sounds themselves.

[1] On the concept of the persona, see Jacobi [1940] 1978, pp. 36–7: 'The persona is a compromise between individual and society about how one appears.'

[2] For Jung, a 'tree', consisting of family, tribe, nation, ethnic group, primitive human ancestors and primitive non-human ancestors (ibid., pp. 42 ff.).

[3] Bürger 2000, p. 204; he also quotes Stéphane Mallarmé's 'Crise de vers' (*Divagations*, 1897): 'L'œuvre pure implique la disparition élocutoire du poëte, qui cède l'initiative aux mots.'

In keeping with his Northern homeland, he has come to maturity later than usual, but in return he has remained unusually pure and unspoiled for his age.[1]

6 EPILOGUE

When Ferruccio Busoni was teaching at Martin Wegelius' music institute from the autumn of 1888 to the summer of 1890, he became friends with Jean Sibelius, a student his own age. Busoni's main subject was piano but he was also listed for music theory.[2] The Sibelius Academy, which has borne the composer's name since 1939, is still proud of this early golden age, whose fruits included the violinist and composer Sibelius. The presence of a talent such as Busoni was an inspiration well beyond his field, and he was just one of many.

The ambitious but small and fluctuating guild of cosmopolitan artists and academics in Helsinki fostered interdisciplinary contacts even outside the walls of the music institute. Nor was there an unbridgeable moat between talented students and the younger teachers. Given the lack of alternatives for socialising, there was no fear of contact among the teachers of different institutions, including the university. Busoni in particular, who had wide-ranging interests, was without exception willing to accept any opportunities for high-quality, stimulating conversation. In Helsinki, moreover, he met his future wife, Gerda Sjöstrand, the daughter of the renowned Swedish sculptor Carl Eneas Sjöstrand. Busoni was not always satisfied with his working conditions and the circumstances of his life there, but Helsinki was his first job, and despite his young age he was able to learn the role of a prominent teacher and department head thoroughly. Busoni is a mirror that helps us understand Sibelius far beyond his genuine Finnishness.

Although his near contemporary, the violinist and composition student Sibelius came from a 'Northern' homeland, and presumably for that reason had, in comparison to Busoni, achieved his artistic 'maturity' later.[3] Busoni recognised his extraordinary talent. Nor was there any superciliousness on Busoni's part, even though he came from the cultural luxury of Tuscany and had learned music very early from his parents. Busoni's oft-cited characterisation is one of the many surprisingly successful summaries of the early reception of Sibelius – one need only think of Adolf Paul's

[1] National Archive Box 121; Ferruccio Busoni to Heinrich Freiherr von Herzogenberg, September 1890. See chapter 3.1 in the present volume.

[2] Karvonen 1957, p. 276, lists Busoni both as an assistant teacher of music theory and also (on p. 280) as primary piano teacher. The information here on the teachers of the institute is based on teachers' lists from 1882 to 1957, ibid, pp. 272–93.

[3] Words from Ferruccio Busoni to Heinrich Freiherr von Herzogenberg (see n. 1 above).

FIG. 41. Boulevarde 2, the address of the music institute in Helsinki in 1882–8 (unknown photographer, prior to 1880). Ferruccio Busoni worked in this corner building and in the new rooms of the institute at Union Street 17 for two full academic years from 1888 to 1890 and met the student Jean Sibelius there.

early writings and Karl Flodin's extensive reviews. Only later did the construction of monuments and other forms of apologia distort the picture of the belated but original talent. Essential aspects of Sibelius' artistic being were already recognisable to those close to him in the 1880s and 1890s.

Busoni's early statement about Sibelius' delayed maturation is also a good example of the fate of certain central documents and strange (ideological) distortions in their interpretation. For example, the oral tradition about a remark in an extensive letter of recommendation (supposedly for Johannes Brahms in Vienna but in fact for Heinrich Freiherr von Herzogenberg in Berlin) only began in the 1930s in conversations between Karl Ekman Jr and Sibelius and was then circulated in Ekman's and Erik Tawaststjerna's biographies.[1] Not only did they distort the historical context of Busoni's statement, but they did not correctly represent the precise choice of words ('Northern' and 'maturity' rather than 'Nordic' and 'development'). Every link in the chain of reception from Busoni by way of Sibelius to Ekman and Tawaststjerna (and from there all over the place) contributed to a gradual distortion. Sibelius — by no means with Busoni's support but rather in the manner of the 1930s — was turned

[1] Ekman 1946, p. 93, and Erik W. Tawaststjerna 1976, p. 72. For more detail on this, see chapter 3.1 in the present volume.

into a 'Nordic' composer whose works should be listened to as the tone poetry of the imaginary North.

Topographically, it is undisputed that Sibelius (unlike Busoni) was born in northeastern Europe (61° N, 24° 27′ E), where he also lived and died (60° 24′ N, 25° 2′ E), but intellectually and artistically, he was orientated towards the south. In the process he 'developed' only in terms of technique, while his essence remained the same, and he did indeed 'mature.' Because both these geographical and cultural poles, the North as well as the South, are mainly imagined and are primarily manifested in stories such as the *Kalevala* and the *Iliad*, what emerged was an artful synthesis of visions and identities, which did not lead to a contradiction and was not a dialectical result of a crisis of diverging identities. More essential than cultural geography was Sibelius' elementary approach to nature and every other environment: city and country, water and forest. Whether one calls that the result of 'Heimatkunst' or 'universality' is a matter of taste (and perhaps a little of ideology), since both are accurate.

Anyone who, for whatever reason — whether ignorance of the sources or out of conviction — renders homage to the 'Nordic' or the nationalist in Sibelius and in the process presumes a gradual 'development', without acknowledging the complexity of aesthetic and philosophical processes around 1900 and the problem of artistic 'development' — which is by no means comparable to rational systems or even industrial production — limits the validity of his art. It risks turning one of the most interesting modernists, in the eyes of the public, into either a hollow victory — that is to say, an artist who achieved a certain mastery despite his origins — or a Finnish chauvinist whose music is suited to accompanying national celebrations and political announcements.

The latter happened in a particularly volatile way in Dresden on 13 February 2005, when an anti-American neo-Nazi organisation known as the Junge Landsmannschaft Ostpreussen (Youth national association of East Prussia), under the motto 'Stop the lies about the past and present', marched through Dresden on the anniversary of the bombing of that city on 13 and 14 February 1945 to the sounds of *Finlandia* (as well as Smetana, Orff and Wagner). It is not so much the organisers' interest in the work that is frightening as the possibility that there might have been people who did not experience *Finlandia* as especially out of place. In the context of his time, Sibelius composed strikingly little clearly political or ideological music, and nor are there any patriotic or even popular cantatas or the like from the euphoric period of national independence or the Second World War — only from the ideological and cultural 'twilight' (Hobsbawm) of the *fin de siècle*. Sibelius' feelings about politics were mostly ambivalent — even if he composed political music when commissioned to do so. His political compositions in the years of the Grand Duchy seem to have supported the Fennoman political movement (the radical Finnish-speakers), but in his diary (on 30 July 1914, in particular) we read about his doubts regarding 'our Finns' and his respect for the leadership of the 'Swedish element'. Using the metaphor of 'fallows' (Swedish or rather Danish — as often in Sibelius' notes — 'brackor'), caused by a flood that breaks a dam and left isolated behind the dam as the flood settles (in standard

Swedish the word rather means 'philistines', but the Danish–Low German influence on the Swedish spoken in Finland is strong), Sibelius worried that Finland would get lost in the wartime chaos. But he suffered from the fact that he realised how his worldviews were becoming increasingly old-fashioned, as he wrote in his diary of 19 September 1914, at a time when many in Finland were starting to wonder how to use the war for nationalist goals: 'My worldview is based, comfortably enough, on very old-fashioned and less well thought-out foundations. For instance, heritage and other costume jewellery of that sort.'

Sibelius' lifestyle and his oeuvre hardly corresponded to the 'Nordic virtues' claimed even today by so many from the wrong quarters, and not just in German-speaking countries. Sibelius, like many others born in the North, had characteristics of the South such as the vital impulsiveness, the passion, the hedonism and the searching impatience found in the likes of Don Juan and Leonardo da Vinci, Horace and Ovid. As the tone poet of the *Kalevala*, he was a Finnish Homer, whose Northernness consisted primarily of the fascination that the Mediterranean and antiquity had for him.

Because the imitation of Mediterranean cultures and the recognition of the Mediterranean south as a historical role model (Johann Joachim Winckelmann's, Goethe's and Nietzsche's *imitatio mediterranensis*) was a widespread *topos* north of the Alps, Sibelius can be characterised as a typically 'Nordic' artist precisely because he admired the south. He knew Nordic melancholy, the yearning for the south idealised from a distance. Neither Finland's contemporary artists in general nor Sibelius were responding to specifically Finnish problems but rather – much like Johann Sebastian Bach, Ludwig van Beethoven, Gustav Mahler, Paul Dukas, Benjamin Britten and Krzysztof Penderecki, each in his own specific regional and historical context – to problems that pertained to all of humanity, which, of course, took their own specific form in *fin-de-siècle* Finland and could be accentuated excellently by that country's situation in cultural history.

To the generation of modernity, *imitatio mediterranensis* meant both connection to the southern and central European tradition as well as a framework for a critical interpretation of the present. Whereas some of the metropolises battered by industrialism were seeking to find a solid basis for the Western civilisation of the future, Finnish cultural nationalists were still establishing their own national identity and culture of achievement, neither of which existed. Antiquity was always important as a point of reference. The Finnish identity of the *fin de siècle* drew on both Western and Eastern traditions, but at the same time it was distinct from both as a specific synthesis of the two, striving to suggest a kind of culture of Pindaric 'Hyperboreans' – happy behind the North wind, under the blessing of the warm Gulf Stream. 'We have discovered happiness, we know the way, we have found the exit out of the labyrinth of thousands of years', rails the spokesman of the Hyperboreans in Nietzsche's *The Antichrist*.[1] The similarity of their own efforts to those of Central Europeans must have

[1] Nietzsche 1986, p. 569.

struck the activists in Finland as well. In any case, neither Sibelius nor other Finnish artists were forging the *sampo* in fashionable Helsinki solely for their own 'people'; their art was supposed to be valid for the entire world. In that sense, Juhani Aho wrote in 1890: 'The *sampo* is a symbol for the great work of art and the tale of its making and at the same time a symbol of artistic creativity.'[1] This authentic vision is not limited to one nation. Regional elements were merely intended to help overcome decadence – Nietzsche's 'labyrinth'.

Both his independent choice of the Austrian capital – rather than Berlin with its almost 'Baltic' climate – as the site of his second year of study and wandering and his contemporary interest in the 'Southern' in musical theatre (Wolfgang Amadeus Mozart's *Don Giovanni*, Georges Bizet's *Carmen*, Karl Goldmark's *Die Königin von Saba* and Pietro Mascagni's *Cavalleria rusticana*) and subjects such as William Shakespeare's *The Tempest* already testified to his Mediterranean orientation. Paris as well as Rome and Venice fascinated him, as would Berlin and London later, respecting them all the more from a professional standpoint – apart from the music critics there and their academic traditionalism. Regarding the latter, he wrote to Aino from Vienna on 6 January 1891: 'They probably regard as barbarians all those who aren't tied to the conventional lies.' He left to avoid those lies.

Although he never travelled to Giovanni Verga's and Pietro Mascagni's scenic villages ('La Cunziria') close to Vizzini in central Sicily, he did at least visit Capri, the 'magic island',[2] where he wrote *Tapiola*, the tone poem about the forest god from Elias Lönnrot's *Kalevala*. Whereas the radius of Akseli Gallen-Kallela's travels ranged from Paanajärvi at the Polar Circle to Nairobi and from San Francisco to Nizhny Novgorod, the Island of Capri was the southernmost place Sibelius encountered.[3] Nor did he ever really know the truly Arctic North. Only in the warm season, when waterways and comfortable steamships on the inland seas were available did he spend time in the central Finnish cultural landscape north of Hämeenlinna (in Vaania and Kuhmoinen, for example), never in the distant provinces of the north-east beyond Savo and Karelia, much less in Lapland. Only once did he travel by train via southern Lapland (Tornio, famous as Baudelaire's 'Tornéo' in *Le Spleen de Paris*) to Stockholm,[4] though he must have taken a night train, as no reports have survived. In North America, too, he did not venture much beyond Niagara Falls. And although his walks are legendary, they would not even stand up to a romantic wanderer's need to move. For the most part, his walks were limited to his own property, though it was admittedly large. There is no evidence for any literary, art historical or scientific (geographic or biological) interest in northern Finland. But his strolls in the cities of the South were all the more substantial for that, whether literally or in the imagination with Homer.

[1] Quoted in Konttinen 2001, p. 15. On Aho around 1890, see also Nummi 2002.

[2] Werner Helwig, *Capri: Magische Insel* (Frankfurt am Main: Insel, 1979), p. 13, quoted in Asendorf 2003, p. 86.

[3] See Gallen-Kallela-Sirén 2001, pp. 159 ff., 344 ff. and 420 ff.

[4] Baudelaire (1867) 1963, p. 152. On Sibelius' travels, see www.sibelius.fi.

Neither use of castanets in *Scène de ballet* nor titles such as *Belshazzar's Feast* are the sole proof of the composer's cultural and geographic orientation towards the South. Just as important are the classicist tendencies, which account for both the dominance of the genres of Viennese Classicism and his interest in antiquity (*The Oceanides*, etc.). Such leanings show that Sibelius was no 'Nordic' outsider 'from the woods' but a strong advocate of Secessionist modernism. Around 1890, in the first development phase of his artistic personality, one found everywhere in Europe a mixture of Southern and 'Northern' *topoi* (including mountains). Extremes were fascinating. Critical debates over civilisation, which seemed to anticipate the catastrophes of the twentieth century, were, in the style of the Saint-Simonists, projected onto the Mediterranean Orient and Occident. One popular and influential case was Nietzsche, who in his 1872 study *The Birth of Tragedy from the Spirit of Music* used Greek antiquity to respond to Rousseau's questions about nature and civilisation.[1] Progress in archaeology and the scholarly reception of antiquity gave wing to the transcendental and Symbolist tendencies of the time. In northern Europe especially, and even in the bourgeois nationalist movement, in the wake of increasing social and cultural individuation, subjects and role models from antiquity provided meaning. Sibelius belonged to the *Euterpe* group, one of whose members, Emil Zilliacus, published a brilliant dissertation on modern French poetry and the reception of antiquity, *Den nyare franska poesin och antiken* (Modern French poetry and antiquity).[2] In addition to French-style neo-Hellenism, we can assume he was particularly familiar with the German reception of antiquity from Winckelmann to Nietzsche.

Despite the category of a 'development', which in the Sibelius literature is attributed to Busoni (even though Busoni spoke of 'maturity'), the present study shows that the 1890s were crucial, both ethically and aesthetically, to Sibelius' entire oeuvre. The core of what over the course of subsequent decades took on other, perhaps even more mature forms was already there. And that represented a national awakening only to a minor degree; it was in fact a European project that Northern artists (including Strindberg and Munch) shaped. If we consider that in 1895 Sibelius was already thirty, this is not surprising – regardless of the fact that he had only just written a few works of lasting value. There was later a 'development' with regard to technical know-how and routine, but the concepts that were the focus of his interest around 1890 provide a solid foundation for an interpretation of Sibelius' entire oeuvre. Even later his work is primarily about the dynamic of Symbolism and modernism.

Whereas the musicological debate over the terms 'Symbolism' and 'the Modern' has since 1978 been shaped by Carl Dahlhaus's critical position, in 1987 Matei Calinescu published a literary history of 'modernity' in the art and culture of the nineteenth century. According to Calinescu, aesthetic modernity covered four dec-

[1] Nietzsche 1967, pp. 43–4.

[2] See Riikonen 2000, pp. 267 ff.

ades (from 1890 to 1930).[1] In 1978, the same year Dahlhaus introduced his argument against the concept of Symbolism in favour of modernism when referring to the 1890s and the turn of the century, the dating of the beginning of aesthetic modernism that Dahlhaus had also assumed became established elsewhere: Malcolm Bradbury and James McFarlane discussed the years 1890 to 1930 as 'Modernism'.[2] Without getting into the question of how 'modernity' differs from 'Modernism', it seems relatively unproblematic to categorise stylistically Sibelius' entire work between the Piano Quintet in G minor (1890) and his op. 116 (1929), or in the orchestral domain between *Scène de ballet* (1891) and *Tapiola*, op. 112, as belonging to the age of aesthetic modernity. The disadvantage of such terminological economy (based on Dahlhaus's critique of the term 'Symbolism') is, of course, the loss of ways to differentiate between Symbolism, Expressionism, Surrealism, Vitalism, Neoclassicism and the avant-garde. These competing 'Modern' movements from 1890 to 1930 are relevant in various combinations to the interpretation of specific works by Sibelius and not just fashionable words of the turbulent art criticism of the period.

The feminine is a special theme whose relevance results from accentuating Symbolism, and until now it has been studied either with an eye to Sibelius' biography or, based on that, programmatically but not in terms of the history of ideas. This theme, too, can only be approached from the perspective of the cultural and geographical question of the artist's Northern versus Southern orientation. Around 1894, Edvard Munch spoke openly of the 'age of Carmen'.[3] A female creature of Southern character (a kind of sphinx) is the focus of attention for Gallen-Kallela, Robert Kajanus and Sibelius in Gallen-Kallela's *Symposium* (1894). Nordic women such as Kullervo's sister, the virgins of the island (Lemminkäinen's lovers and Kyllikki too), *Pohjola's Daughter* and *Luonnotar* dominate Sibelius' interpretation of the *Kalevala*. The Oceanides are a geographically unspecified female species. Without sharing the originally implicit limitation of Munch's note on the social emancipation of women (since *Carmen*, too, is about more than that), his vision can be expanded in the spirit of Symbolism. It is really about the age of Salammbô, in whose wake one breathes 'as it were the odour of a temple'; 'her whole being emitted something that was sweeter than wine and more terrible than death'.[4] Salammbô represents the late nineteenth-century attitude towards life more aptly than Carmen does. More concretely than Carmen or even than Oscar Wilde's Salomé, Salammbô, Hannibal's sister, is the 'symbol for "wild", undomesticated humanity' and the embodiment 'pure and simple of paradoxes of alienation'.[5] Despite his more Southern origins, Flaubert of all people shows the way to the centre of Sibelius' enigma as anything but a restrictedly 'Nordic' art.

The virgins in Sibelius' *Kalevala* are by no means specifically Nordic and often

[1] See Dahlhaus 1978 and Calinescu 1987.

[2] Bradbury and McFarlane 1978.

[3] See Müller-Westermann 2003, p. 71.

[4] Flaubert [1862] 2006, p. 22.

[5] Bosse and Stoll 1979, p. 427.

are objects of male desire, especially Kyllikki, 'Saaren kukka kaunokainen', 'Saaren kukka kuuluisinna'[1] and Kullervo's sister. The most thorough objectification of young women is in the third canto of the *Kalevala*, when Joukahainen offers his sister Aino to Väinämöinen as compensation for losing a singing contest.[2] Sibelius did not set this passage — his older rival Kajanus had done so, and with a lot of relish. The young woman who appears as a subject, Luonnotar ('kave korea', splendid woman),[3] is a mythological figure from the time of the creation of the world, a kind of mother of the world. Her most important achievement is to make Väinämöinen's birth possible. Whereas Kullervo in the *Kalevala* is praised for his handsomeness,[4] the attributes of the women are strikingly sparse. Even in the case of Aino, all Lönnrot describes is her beautiful hair.[5] Kullervo's sister is repeatedly referred to as 'tinarinta' (tin breast),[6] though that refers primarily to the characteristics of her voice. The description of the clothing of the beautiful 'Pohjan tytti' or 'Pohjan neiti' is a little more detailed: 'Tuop' on kaunis Pohjan tyttö.'[7]

More radically than the Finnish painters and writers who remained unmistakably 'Nordic', as a composer Sibelius managed to deprive the specifically 'Nordic spirit' (the Nordicness) of its power by invigorating the genius of the Southern with his own Central European, Symbolist and classicistic orientation. That benefited not least his approach to the figures of the *Kalevala*, which he drew as anything but restrictedly 'Nordic' (as Lönnrot had done before him but in contrast to Gallen-Kallela). In countless masterpieces, Sibelius demonstrated his ability to handle Southern subjects with similar subtlety. Decidedly Northern topics are rare. *Topoi* that could have been located in the geographic North as well retain their connection to Greek antiquity or Central European mythology in Sibelius' work. Moreover, they have no distinctly Finnish features musically either. Even the so-called Nordic orchestra sound of brass chords, modal sequences and timpani rolls[8] was developed by Sibelius himself. These sounds have no direct models in the *Kalevala* or in Finnish folk music — rather in Wagner, Bruckner and Tchaikovsky.

Only one orchestral work has the word 'North' in its title: *Pohjola's Daughter* (literally 'Daughter of the North', 1906). But Sibelius had proposed a French title: 'L'Aventure d'un héros'.[9] His publisher, Robert Lienau, had insisted on using the word 'North' in Finnish. 'Pohjola' suited the already established image of Sibelius as Finnish. The case of *Dance Intermezzo*, op. 45, no. 2, was different: the composition

1 *Kalevala* 11.161 ff. and pp. 195–6.
2 Ibid., 3.450 ff.
3 Ibid., 1.111 ff.
4 Ibid., 35.71 f.; on Lemminkäinen, see ibid., 11.164 and 26.363 ff.
5 Ibid., 2.552–4.
6 Ibid., 35.134 ff.
7 1835 version; 3.1 ff; in *Kalevala* 8.1 ff. and 10.439 ff.
8 On this topic, see Mäkelä 1992c and Mäkelä 1992a. See also Grimley 2004b, p. 237.
9 See chapter 3.4 in the present volume.

was originally called 'Music for a Scene' (1904) and had the motto 'A spruce tree … dreams of a palm' from Heinrich Heine's poem 'Fichtenbaum', which was illustrated by music and addresses the North–South problem but from a Romantic, German-French perspective. 'Norden', op. 90, no. 1, on a text by Runeberg, reflects a gloomy vision of the North from the perspective of a palm tree watching, filled with empathy, swans on their way north. Sibelius himself yearningly watched these wild birds on their way south. Much like them, he was only partly the 'son of the North' or even of the 'Finnish people'.[1]

Sibelius embodied the Oriental South just much as he did the biggest metropolises and the natural elements of the North. Such a heterogeneous image was increasingly undesirable in a musical world that was becoming ever more commercial and in an age of likewise increasingly uncompromising ideologies. The master of Nordic 'magic' or even 'prophet of the North'[2] fulfilled the expectations of many authors, interpreters and listeners. The result was a market-orientated image of Sibelius whose sharp distinctions went far beyond the biographical evidence.

Sibelius succeeded in recovering the specifically Nordic qualities from the spirit of Mediterranean antiquity within the framework of a subtle critique of civilisation that even around 1900 was still fundamentally organised around late Romantic Orientalism and exoticism. At the same time, he brilliantly attacked conventional symphonic practices with their epic character, without ever exposing himself to being dismissed as a radical reformer. Whereas the academic tradition of his time expected symphonic music to reflect the noble gesture of harmonic structure and countless minute causal interconnections, he was already taking risks, in anticipation of postmodernism, ruptures and synaesthesia. The meaning of a series is not always immediately recognisable, either for an unpractised or a prejudiced listener, and the inter-medial associations are rarely compelling. The composer often seems to change perspective and conceal the common objective of what is said behind turns that point in a diametrically opposed direction.

The reception of Sibelius' work is made difficult not by the innovation of such measures — which had recently been introduced in literature, at least (Flaubert *et al.*) — but rather by the paradoxical bracketing of external criteria from the line of Felix Mendelssohn Bartholdy, Robert Schumann and Johannes Brahms as well as from the poetic, programmatic tradition of Hector Berlioz, Franz Liszt, Richard Strauss and others. What is original and new in his work, even in terms of the histories of the various genres, is given more clearly concrete form in the cryptic formulations of his diary than it is in his compositions. Although his point of departure was clearly an all-embracing impression independent of the separation of the senses, Sibelius was concerned with architectonics and a 'heavenly' (not earthly) primal logic of sounds,

[1] On this common formulation, see, for example, the memorial plaque for the Vienna Philharmonic illustrated in Krones 2003a, p. 24.

[2] Törne 1937, p. 59, and Sjöblom 1944.

which enables us to establish the connection to Brahms, Schumann and Schubert, and the symphonists of his era. The quintessence of his formal language is, however, not the psychological, narrative logic of the classical epic. The Flaubertian 'illusion of the epic'[1] – which in the Romantic, classicistic framework adopted elements of a more recent Modernism and could only have such great success as a result of fateful misunderstandings by those who are in fact openly criticised in the text – finds striking parallels in Sibelius, both structurally and in the history of his reception, and in the modern narrative techniques of Knut Hamsun and others.

The trivial misunderstandings that led to the success of his art under fascism and National Socialism as well as among British and North American writers and in the German Democratic Republic are a thing of the past. The National Socialists knowingly overlooked the fact that Sibelius was no Aryan.[2] It is possible they did not know he was a Freemason, and hence a member of a group persecuted by the National Socialists and banned in the Third Reich. The Stalinists, in turn, closed their eyes to the fact that the population of Finland did not consist entirely of workers and peasants.

Not the North as such and nature, but rather Sibelius' original, subjective approach to the elements of his environment provided the foundation for associations that are at least equally useful for the interpretation of his music as detailed knowledge of the complex architecture of his works, which is inspired by Beethoven and Classicism. Sibelius was no autarkic Expressionist but rather an 'extroverted' creator.[3] His art represented a contemporary attempt to draw, within the realm of music, energetic 'lines' à la Henry van de Velde – drawn, in Munch's sense, not 'from nature' but 'from its kingdom'.[4] His organic, Dionysian vitality was also deeply innate and by no means limited to dance scenes such as *Valse triste* and by symphonic illustration of the act of love as found in *Kullervo* and *Lemminkäinen and the Maidens of the Island* (especially with Kyllikki, the 'most famous blossom of the island'). Not nationalism, pantheism, provincial salon romanticism, the *Kalevala* or even the 'Nordic' but rather the cosmos of Carl Gustav Jung, Munch, Nietzsche and van de Velde constituted his mental context.

Sibelius' 'heteronomy' identified by Michael Mäckelmann[5] is, even today, despite postmodernism, one of many causes of misunderstanding. Add to that the utopian quality of his lifework, which is manifested to only a small degree as an audible surface in his best-known compositions (perhaps more clearly in the projects he destroyed). Whereas Munch demonstrated his closeness to nature by deliberately subjecting his paintings to organic corrosion by storing them unprotected in an open barn (the executors of his estate got involved and arranged for the decaying paintings

1 Bosse and Stoll 1979, pp. 416 ff. The discussion concerns *Salammbô*.

2 See Gleissner 2002, pp. 89 ff. and 155 ff.

3 See Jacobi [1940] 1978, p. 33.

4 Munch quoted in Buchhart 2003, p. 25.

5 Mäckelmann 1983, p. 129. See chapter 2.3 in the present volume.

to be conserved),[1] in Sibelius' case the original ideas were recognisable to some extent but only partially realised. He too could not liberate himself as an artist from the traditional antagonism of composing and giving concerts, of planning and realising. The aesthetically ineffable, especially the unfinished Eighth Symphony, he destroyed within the framework of compositional abstraction and materialisation. He too failed to achieve the state of complete freedom from the 'conventional lies' that he dared to attack so bluntly in 1891.

Sibelius developed remarkably early an awareness of the problematic relationship between ideas and their realisation. This dilemma remained an essential aspect of his creative process – and that includes the Eighth Symphony, on which he was still working during the Second World War. While still conceiving *Kullervo*, he wrote to Aino Järnefelt on 12 October 1891: 'I have wonderfully beautiful (in my opinion) musical ideas, etc.; most of them are almost impossible to realise, or at least very difficult.' Apparently he could have used those words around 1940 as well, when he was working on the *Lemminkäinen Legends*, he noted, again to Aino, on 2 September 1894: 'If only I could realise my ideas in music now.'

For outsiders, his goals are an object of study outside the scope of aesthetic judgement. They document the cause of his aesthetic effect. Self-critical artists such as Sibelius, who not only think idealistically but also reflect on the effect of their art, may be dissatisfied with their own inability to transfer what they think and want into sensory materiality, also in respect of their public image, and perhaps they even fail just because of their self-critical attitude. Sibelius worried about that in the summer of 1910, when, while working on his Fourth Symphony, he wrote: 'Will the truth concerning the originality of my motifs ever come out? No!! So only one side of your art will become apparent' (Diary, 19 June 1910). It is true that hardly anyone is capable of seeing the other side of his art – except with the help of scholarly interpretation.

Again and again, he was disturbed by the difficulty of transferring, within the framework of tradition and the ordinary means of expression, the language of nature and the 'poetry in the art',[2] which he believed he understood in his way, into performable scores. The site of his creativity, his 'extra-territoriality', was not limited to the rural environment of Finland or to the Island of Capri, but rather touched on existential segments of Western culture of which Rousseau and Nietzsche dreamed. In the process, he made use of common compositional means. He left the explanation of the logic of his art, which remained original in its handling of old material, to students and acquaintances (in particular to Törne but also to Ekman), whose own motives do not stand up to critical examination and who apparently did not understand his motives either. He himself clung to his anti-intellectual, anti-philosophical and anti-verbal attitude. Even the quite useful and certainly timely modern, and at times

[1] See Buchhart 2003, pp. 25–6.

[2] Diary, 4 June 1911.

untimely, postmodern approaches of an author writing 'with sympathy' like Walter Niemann he wanted to disregard entirely.[1]

It was not Adorno or Niemann but Sibelius himself and his companions who covered up the clues to the secret of his art. They contributed to the creation of an aura that even today can scarcely be demystified. This aura hampers the immediate effect of his music, unprejudiced listening to his modern 'poetry in the air'. The degree to which the Berlin poet Gottfried Benn succeeded in doing that when he wrote his monumental *Valse Triste*[2] in 1936 – with its astonishing cross-references to Giuseppe Verdi's *Aida* – is his secret. The poem was written at the beginning of the critical phase in which the poet was forced to reflect on his relationship to National Socialism. What is clear is that Benn leads his readers into an intellectual world in which Classicism, Symbolism, exoticism, Vitalism, the phantasmagoria of the North and the dreamy South form a synthesis. This ecstatic mixture of stylistic impulses is also typical of Sibelius. Benn's poem is clearly more than evidence of the popularity of Sibelius' *Valse triste*. Benn's vision is a successful approach to Sibelius, especially if one is inclined to associate his music not only with the 'rage of nature' in the North but also with pharaohs and the gods of the Parthenon.

Benn's way of looking at things builds bridges to Central European Symbolism without distancing itself from the decentralised 'movimento modernista' of Sibelius' contemporary Rubén Darío, which emphasised the contribution of regions far from the geopolitical centre. Darío's 'modernismo', one of the earliest forms of aesthetic modernity,[3] represents the South American perspective of the cultural emancipation of the 'periphery' around 1890, which also claimed for itself a leadership position. Just as the Nicaraguan Dario become the leading modernist of Spanish-language literature, the Northern European 'periphery' – Hamsun, Munch, Ibsen, August Strindberg, Sibelius, Gallen-Kallela *et al.* – represented an avant-garde within modernism in general. Even today, these artists deserve to be protected from the attempt to destroy their historical validity by scorning or worshipping their original form of expression as merely a regional idiosyncrasy. Winckelmann's *imitatio mediterranensis* was by no means the condition of a progressive culture around 1890. The opportunity to serve humanity as an artist from the North consisted much more – and this is precisely what Sibelius did – of calling into question aspects of the Mediterranean tradition of the West and coming to the aid, from inside as well as from outside, of the aesthetic critique of culture that in the radical modern art of Central Europe and the American metropolises was articulated even in the work of artists who took their lead from the civilisation of the large Western cities of the late nineteenth century (Vienna, Paris, Berlin).[4]

[1] See JS to Breitkopf & Härtel, 22 August 1918 and 10 April 1919; quoted in Erik W. Tawaststjerna 1997b, p. 145. For more details, see chapter 5.1 in the present volume.

[2] Benn 1965, pp. 104–5.

[3] Calinescu 1987, pp. 69–70.

[4] This passage is paraphrasing the footnote on 'extra-territorial music' in Adorno 1985, pp. 35–6 n. 5.

In a letter of 21 February 1936 to the prominent poet Ina Seidel (one of the few women on Hitler's list of the *Gottbegnadeten*, the artists 'graced by God'),[1] Gottfried Benn wrote of the first strophe in *Valse Triste*:

> Prologue, not without its risks. The momentary 'Benn state'. / Rhymed world-view. [...] *Aida* was meant, did you realise that? / Six such verses, very rejecting, individualistic, tragically absolute and inwards. / But who other than me can still defend, articulate, depict all that in Germany? Answer![2]

The cultural and political context is clearer in a tragic-comic letter (almost *en résistance*) to Seidel on 27 August 1943: 'Terrible tragedy! The whole thing is gradually beginning to look like a backwater theatre that is constantly announcing *Faust* but the cast is only adequate for *Husarenfieber*. As great as it began, so dirty it looks today. But this is far from the end.'[3] Spoken like a true contemporary of Sibelius.

Incorporating Sibelius into poetry is not the exclusive province of German post-Symbolism. In English, too, he has occupied a prominent position — from bestselling detective stories like Vera Caspary's *Laura* of 1942 through collections of tales like Julian Barnes's *The Lemon Table* of 2005 (whose final tale, 'The Silence', is about Sibelius) to poetry like Michael Hartnett's *Sibelius in Silence* of 1992. Here, however, Sibelius seldom frees himself of the remnants of northernness, nor does he become free of simple associations with his home country. In Hartnett we read:[4]

> To have intricacies of lakes and forests,
> harbours, hills and inlets given —
> and none of these with a name;
> then to have posited nomads straggling
> from the barricading Urals,
> bearing on their backs and horses
> children, languages, and utensils,
> gods and legends;
> then to have brought all these together,
> yeast to have thawing mud —
> this was to make the Green Gold of the North
> an ethnic and enduring bread.

This is the conventional picture of Sibelius in 'the land of thousand lakes' that transcends both topographical and cultural ambiguity to avoid questions one might not want to answer.

1 See Rathkolb 1991, p. 176.

2 Quoted in Benn 1965, p. 51.

3 Ibid., p. 50. Benn was referring to Gustav Kadelburg's and Richard Skowronnek's comedy of 1907, widely known from Georg Jacoby's film of 1925.

4 From Michael Harnett, *Collected Poems* (Oldcastle, Co. Meath: Gallery Books, 2001), by kind permission of the Estate of Michael Hartnett and the Gallery Press.

Benn's bridge from the Nile to the Finnish inlets may be less conventional, but it is typical of the Winckelmannian synthesis. Benn's point of view is in keeping with the style of Sibelius – despite some ideological irritations (Benn's 'rhymed worldview'). In Sibelius' case one can concentrate on the non-political overtones as a fruit of the 'twilight' rather than of what followed. The last premiere of Sibelius was long before the fatal dance 'off the Finnish skerries' (to quote Benn) began. In the 1930s and 1940s, Sibelius danced his *Valse triste* in 'the silence of Ainola'. His friend Busoni was allowed to die soon after the horrors of the First World War, whereas Sibelius was made to see how much worse things could still be.

Gottfried Benn, *Valse Triste* (1936) [translated by Steven Lindberg][1]

Verfeinerung, Abstieg, Trauer –	Refinement, descent, sorrow –
dem Wüten der Natur,	the rage of nature,
der Völker, der Siegesschauer	of peoples, of victory's frissons
folgt eine andere Spur:	is followed by another trace:
Verwerfen von Siegen und Thronen,	Rejection of victories and thrones,
die große Szene am Nil,	the great scene on the Nile,
wo der Feldherr der Pharaonen	where the Pharaohs' general
den Liedern der Sklavin verfiel.	succumbed to the songs of the female slave.
Durch den Isthmus, griechisch, die Wachen,	Through the isthmus, Greek, the sentries,
Schleuder, Schilde und Stein	catapults, shields, and stone
treibt im Zephir ein Nachen	drifts a barque in the zephyr
tieferen Meeren ein:	into deeper seas:
die Parthenongötter, die weißen,	the Parthenon gods, the white ones,
ihre Zeiten, ihr Entstehn,	their eras, their creation,
die schon Verfall geheißen	who have already called for decay
und den Hermenfrevel gesehn.	and seen the mutilation of the herms.
Verfeinerte Rinden, Blöße.	Refined bark, nakedness.
Rauschnah und todverfärbt	Near rapture and discoloured by death,
das Fremde, das Steile, die Größe,	the alien, the steep, the greatness
die das Jahrhundert erbt,	that the century inherits,
getanzt aus Tempeln und Toren	danced from temples and gates
schweigenden Einsamseins,	of silent isolation,
Erben und Ahnen verloren:	heirs and ancestors lost
Niemandes –: Deins!	No one's –: yours!

[1] From Gottfried Benn, *Sämtliche Gedichte* (Stuttgart: Klett-Cotta, 1998).

Getanzt vor den finnischen Schären –
Valse triste, der Träume Schoß,
Valse triste, nur Klänge gewähren
dies eine menschliche Los:
Rosen, die blühten und hatten,
und die Farben fließen ins Meer,
blau, tiefblau atmen die Schatten,
und die Nacht verzögert so sehr.

Getanzt dem einen, dem selten
blutenden Zaubergerät,
das sich am Saume der Welten
öffnet: Identität –:
einmal in Versen beschworen,
einmal im Marmor des Steins,
einmal zu Klängen erkoren:
Niemandes –: seins!

Niemandes –: beuge, beuge
dein Haupt in Dorn und Schlehn,
in Blut und Wunden zeuge
die Form, das Auferstehn,
gehüllt in Tücher, als Labe
den Schwamm mit Essig am Rohr,
so tritt aus den Steinen, dem Grabe
Auferstehung hervor.

Dancing off the Finnish skerries –
Valse triste, bosom of dreams,
Valse triste, only sounds grant
this one human fate:
roses that bloomed and possessed,
and the colours flow into the sea,
blue, deep blue the shadows breathe,
and the night delays so much.

Danced to the one, to the rare
bleeding magic tool
that opens on the seam
of worlds: identity –:
evoked once in verses
once in the marble of stone,
once chosen for sounds:
No one's –: his!

No one's –: bend, bend
your head into thorn and sloe,
in blood and wounds beget
the form, the resurrecting,
wrapped in shrouds, the only refreshment
the vinegar-soaked sponge on a pole,
thus resurrection steps forth
from the stones, from the grave.

Systematic Catalogue of the Works of Jean Sibelius

by Fabian Dahlström

This catalogue contains works with and without opus numbers, but no minor sketches, drafts or fragments. The list includes some lost projects that are known to have existed as scores, such as the Eighth Symphony. First the works with opus numbers are listed numerically, followed by the works without opus numbers listed by JS number. The group 'K. Incidental Music' represents an exception to that (see below). The English translations of titles used in this list are based on Fabian Dahlström, *Jean Sibelius: Thematisch-bibliographisches Verzeichnis seiner Werke* (Wiesbaden: Breitkopf & Härtel, 2003). For some titles, other authors have suggested different translations, often based on the original title. The suggestions given by Dahlström are historical translations, often used in early English editions or programme notes. The original English titles are usually used, for good reason, in recordings and performances even today.

A. Orchestral Works

op. 6 Cassazione

op. 7 Kullervo (with vocal parts and male choir)

op. 9 En saga [A Legend / A Saga]

op. 10 Karelia Overture

op. 11 Karelia Suite: 1. Intermezzo; 2. Ballade; 3. Alla Marcia

[op. 15] Skogsrået [The Wood Nymph]

op. 16 Vårsång [Spring Song]

op. 22 Lemminkäinen Suite: 1. Lemminkäinen ja saaren neidot [Lemminkäinen and the Maidens on the Island]; 2. Tuonelan joutsen [The Swan of Tuonela]; 3. Lemminkäinen Tuonelassa [Lemminkäinen in Tuonela]; 4. Lemminkäinen palaa kotitienoille [Lemminkäinen's Return]

op. 25 Scènes historiques [I]: 1. All'Ouvertura; 2. Scena; 3. Festivo

op. 26 Finlandia

op. 27 Suite from Kung Kristian II [King Christian II]: Nocturne; Élégie et Musette; Serenade; Ballade

op. 39 Symphony no. 1 in E minor

op. 43 Symphony no. 2 in D major

op. 44 Two Pieces from Kuolema [Death]: 1. Valse triste; 2. Kurkikohtaus [Scene with Cranes]

op. 45 Two Pieces for Orchestra: 1. Die Dryade [The Dryad]; 2. Tanz-Intermezzo [Dance Intermezzo]

op. 46 Suite from Pelléas et Mélisande [Pelléas and Mélisande]: 1. Am Schlosstor [At the Castle Gate]; 2. Mélisande; 2a. Am Meer [At the Seashore]; 3. Am Wunderborn im Park [A Spring in the Park]; 4. Die drei blinden Schwestern

[The Three Blind Sisters]; 5. Pastorale; 6. Mélisande am Rocken [Mélisande at the Spinning Wheel]; 7. Zwischenaktmusik [Entr'acte]; 8. Mélisandes Tod [The Death of Mélisande]
op. 49 Pohjolan tytär [Pohjola's Daughter]
op. 51 Suite from Belsazars gästabud [Belshazzar's Feast]: 1. Einzug [Oriental Procession]; 2. Einsames Lied [Solitude]; 3. Nachtmusik; [Nocturne] 4. Khadras Tanz [Khadra's Dance]
op. 52 Symphony no. 3 in C major
op. 53a Pan und Echo [Pan and Echo]
op. 54 Suite from Svanevit [Swanwhite]: 1. Der Pfau [The Peacock]; 2. Harfenspiel [The Harp]; 3. Die Mädchen mit den Rosen [The Maiden with the Roses]; 4. Horch, das Rotkehlchen singt [Listen, the Robin Sings]; 5. Der Prinz alleine [The Prince Alone]; 6. Schwanenweiss und der Prinz [Svanevit and the Prince]; 7. Lobgesang [Song of Praise]
op. 55 Nächtlicher Ritt und Sonnenaufgang [Night Ride and Sunrise]
op. 59 In memoriam
op. 62b Valse romantique
op. 63 Symphony no. 4 in A minor
op. 64 Barden [The Bard]
op. 66 Scènes historiques II: 1. Die Jagd [The Chase. Overture]; 2. Minnelied [Love-Song]; 3. An der Zugbrücke [At the Draw-Bridge]
op. 73 Aallottaret [The Oceanides]
op. 82 Symphony no. 5 in E flat major
op. 91a Jääkärien marssi [March of the Finnish Jaeger Battalion]
op. 96 Three Pieces: a. Valse lyrique; b. Autrefois (with 2 sopranos); c. Valse chevaleresque
op. 98a Suite mignonne
op. 104 Symphony no. 6 in D minor
op. 105 Symphony no. 7 in C major
op. 109 From the Music for Stormen [The Tempest]: no. 1. Overture; no. 2. First Suite: 1. Der Eichbaum [The Oak Tree]; 2. Humoresque; 3. Calibans Lied [Caliban's Song]; 4. Die Herbstmänner [The Harvesters]; 5. Canon; 6. Scène; 7. Intrada. Berceuse; 8. Zwischenspiel. Ariels Lied [Entr'acte. Ariel's Song]; 9. Der Sturm; [The Storm] no. 3. Second Suite: 1. Chor der Winde; [Chorus of the Winds]; 2. Intermezzo; 3. Tanz der Nymphen [Dance of the Nymphs]; 4. Prospero; 5. Song I; 6. Song II; 7. Miranda; 8. Die Najaden [The Naiads]; 9. Tanz-Episode [Dance Episode]
op. 112 Tapiola
JS 54 Cortège
JS 62 Die Sprache der Vögel [The Language of the Birds] (Wedding March)
JS 80 Fechtmusik [Fencing Music] (lost)
from: JS 104 Coronation March
JS 127 Minuet
JS 135a Morceau romantique
JS 144 Overture in A minor
JS 145 Overture in E major
JS 151 Porilaisten marssi [I] [March of the Björneborgers] (lost)
JS 152 Porilaisten marssi [II] [March of the Björneborgers]
JS 155 Promootiomarssi [Academic March]
JS 163 Scène de ballet
JS 190 Symphony no. 8 (lost)
JS 223 Zirkus-Marsch (lost) [Circus March]

B. Works for Solo Instrument and Orchestra

op. 47 Violin Concerto in D minor
op. 69 Two Serenades. vn, orch
op. 77 Two Serious Melodies. vn or vc, orch: 1. Cantique (Laetare anima mea); 2. Devotion (Ab imo pectore)
op. 87 Two Humoresques. vn, orch

op. 89 Four Humoresques. vn, orch

JS 185 (op. 117) Suite. vn, str orch

C. Works for String Orchestra

from: op. 4 Scherzo [Presto]

from: op. 5 Impromptu

op. 14 Rakastava [The Lover]

op. 42 Romance in C

op. 62a Canzonetta

op. 98b Suite champêtre

op. 100 Suite caractéristique (str, hrp)

JS 34b Andante festivo

JS 88 Grevinnans konterfej [The Countess's Portrait]

D. Works for Wind Instruments

JS 25 Allegro

JS 45 Andantino and Minuet

JS 83 Prelude

JS 146 Overture in F minor

JS 200 Tiera

E. Chamber Music with Piano

JS 27 Allegro in D major. vn, vc, cl

JS 31 Andante – Allegro. str qt, cl

JS 43 Andantino in G minor. vn, vc, cl

JS 126 Minuet. 2 vn, cl

JS 156 Quartet in C major. 2 vn, vc, cl

JS 157 Quartet in D minor. 2 vn, vc, cl

JS 158 Quartet in G minor. vn, vc, harm, cl

JS 159 Quintet in G minor. str qt, cl

JS 165 Scherzo. vn, vc, cl (four-hands)

JS 205 Trio. 2 vn, cl

JS 206 Trio in A minor [I]. vn, vc, cl

JS 207 Trio in A minor [II]. vn, vc, cl (Havträsk)

JS 208 Trio in C major. vn, vc, cl (Lovisa)

JS 209 Trio in D major. vn, vc, cl (Korpo)

F. Chamber Music without Piano

op. 4 String Quartet in B major

op. 56 String Quartet in D minor (Voces intimae)

JS 12 Adagio in D minor. str qt

JS 14 Adagio in F minor. str qt

JS 16 Alla marcia. str qt

JS 17 Allegretto in A major. str qt

JS 20 Allegretto in D major. str qt

JS 28 Allegro in E minor. str qt

JS 32 Andante – Allegro molto. str qt

JS 34a Andante festivo. str qt

JS 37 Andante molto sostenuto. str qt

JS 38 Andantino in A major. vn, va, vc

JS 39 Andantino in C major. str qt

JS 50 Canon. vn, vc

JS 65 Duo. 2 va

JS 66 Duo. vn, va

JS 68 [E minor]. vn, vc

JS 85 Fugue for Martin Wegelius. str qt

JS 116 La pompeuse Marche d'Asis (lost)

JS 128 Minuet and Allegro. 2 vn, vc

JS 131 Moderato – Allegro appassionato. str qt

JS 134 Molto moderato – Scherzo. str qt

JS 149 Più lento. str qt

JS 154 Presto. str qt

JS 169 Serenata. 2 vn, vc

JS 183 String Quartet in A minor

JS 184 String Quartet in E flat major

JS 186 Suite in A major. vn, va, vc

JS 195 Theme and Variations in C sharp minor. str qt (fragment)
JS 197 Theme and Variations in G minor. str qt
JS 210 Trio in G minor. vn, va, vc
JS 216 Vattendroppar [Waterdrops]. vn, vc
JS 222 [Waltzes.] vn, *kantele*

G. Works for Solo Instruments and Piano

op. 2 Two Pieces. vn, pf: 1. Romance in B minor; 2. Epilogue
op. 20 Malinconia. vc, cl
from: op. 71 Scène d'amour. vn, cl
op. 77 Two Serious Melodies. vn or vc, pf: 1. Cantique (Laetare anima mea); 2. Devotion (Ab imo pectore)
op. 78 Four Pieces. vn or vc, pf: 1. Impromptu; 2. Romance; 3. Religioso; 4. Rigaudon
op. 79 Six Morceaux. vn, pf: 1. Souvenir; 2. Tempo di Menuetto; 3. Danse caractéristique; 4. Sérénade; 5. Dance Idyll; 6. Berceuse
op. 80 Sonatina in E major. vn, cl
op. 81 Five Pieces. vn, pf: 1. Mazurka; 2. Rondino; 3. Valse; 4. Aubade; 5. Menuetto
op. 102 Novellette. vn, cl
op. 106 Five Danses Champêtres. vn, cl
op. 115 Four Pieces. vn, pf: 1. Auf der Heide [On the Heath]; 2. Ballade; 3. Humoresque; 4. Die Glocken [The Bells] (Capriccietto)
op. 116 Three Pieces. vn, pf: 1. Scène de danse; 2. Danse caractéristique; 3. Rondeau romantique
JS 3 [A major I]. vn, cl
JS 4 [A major II]. vn, cl
JS 7 [A minor I]. vn, cl
JS 8 [A minor II]. vn, cl
JS 15 Adagio in F sharp minor. vc, cl
JS 19 Allegretto in C major. vn, cl
JS 22 Allegretto in E flat major. vn, cl
JS 26 Allegro in A minor. vn, cl
JS 33 Andante cantabile. vn, cl
JS 35 Andante grazioso. vn, cl
JS 36 Andante molto. vc, cl
JS 40 Andantino in C major. vc, cl
JS 49 [C major]. vn, cl
JS 67 [E minor]. vn, cl
JS 76 [E flat minor]. vn or vc, cl
JS 78 [F major]. vn, cl
JS 79 Fantasie. vc, cl
JS 86 [G major]. vn, cl
JS 89 [B minor I]. vn, cl
JS 90 [B minor II]. vn, cl
JS 91 [B minor I]. vc, cl
JS 92 [B minor II]. vc, cl
JS 132 Moderato — Maestoso. vn, cl
JS 162 Rondo. va, cl
JS 177 Sonata in A minor. vn, cl
JS 178 Sonata in F major. vn, cl
JS 187 Suite in D minor. vn, cl
JS 188 Suite in E major. vn, cl
JS 193 Tempo di valse [I]. vc, cl
JS 194 Tempo di valse [II]. vc, cl

H. Works for Violin or Violoncello Solo

JS 55 [D major]. vn
JS 70 En glad musikant [A Happy Musician] (Rangström). vn with text
JS 196 Theme and Variations in D minor. Vc

I. Works for Piano

op. 5 Six Impromptus
from: op. 11 Intermezzo and Ballad
op. 12 Sonata in F major
from: op. 15 Ur Skogsrået [From: The Wood Nymph]
op. 24 Ten Pieces: 1. Impromptu; 2. Romance (in A major); 3. Caprice; 4. Romance (D minor); 5. Valse; 6. Idyll; 7. Andantino; 8. Nocturno; 9. Romance (D flat major); 10. Barcarola
op. 26 Finlandia
op. 27 from: Kung Kristian II [King Christian II]: Elegy; Minuet; Musette; Fool's Song of the Spider (with added text)
op. 31, no. 2 Har du mod? [Have You Courage?] (with added text)
op. 31, no. 3 Athenarnes sång [War Song of Tyrtaeus] (with added text)
op. 34 Bagatelles: 1. Valse; 2. Air de danse; 3. Mazurka; 4. Couplet; 5. Boutade; 6. Rêverie; 7. Danse pastorale; 8. Joueur de harpe; 9. Reconnaisance; 10. Souvenir
op. 40 Pensées lyriques: 1. Valsette; 2. Chant sans paroles; 3. Humoresque; 4. Menuetto; 5. Berceuse; 6. Pensée mélodique; 7. Rondoletto; 8. Scherzando; 9. Petite sérénade; 10. Polonaise
op. 41 Kyllikki
op. 44, no. 1 Valse triste
op. 45 Two Pieces: 1. Die Dryade [The Dryad]; 2. Tanz-Intermezo [Dance Intermezzo]
op. 46 Suite from Pelléas et Mélisande [Pelléas and Mélisande]: 1. Am Schlosstor [At the Castle Gate]; 2. Mélisande; 2a. Am Meer [At the Seashore]; 3. Am Wunderborn im Park [A Spring in the Park]; 4. Die drei blinden Schwestern [The Three Blind Sisters]; 5. Pastorale; 6. Mélisande am Rocken [Mélisande at the Spinning Wheel]; 7. Zwischenaktmusik [Entr'acte]; 8. Mélisandes Tod [The Death of Mélisande]
op. 51 Suite From Belsazars gästabud [Belshazzar's Feast]: 1. Einzug [Oriental Procession]; 2. Einsames Lied [Solitude]; 3. Nachtmusik [Nocturne]; 4. Khadras Tanz [Khadra's Dance]
op. 53a Pan und Echo [Pan and Echo]
op. 58 Ten Pieces for Pianoforte: 1. Rêverie; 2. Scherzino; 3. Air varié; 4. Der Hirt [The Shepherd]; 5. Des Abends [The Evening]; 6. Dialogue; 7. Tempo di minuetto; 8. Fischerlied [Fisher Song]; 9. Ständchen [Serenade]; 10. Sommerlied [Summer Song]
op. 65b Die Glockenmelodie in der Kirche zu Berghäll [The Bells of Kallio Church]
op. 67 Three Sonatinas
op. 68 Two Rondinos
from: op. 71 Danse élégiaque; Scène d'amour
op. 74 Lyric Pieces: 1. Ekloge [Eglogue]; 2. Sanfter Westwind [Soft West Wind]; 3. Auf dem Tanzvergnügen [At the Dance]; 4. Im alten Heim [In the Old Home]
op. 75 Cinq Morceaux: 1. När rönnen blommar [Faded Blossoms / When the Roan Tree Flowers / When the Mountain Ash is Blooming]; 2. Den ensamma furan [The Solitary Fir Tree]; 3. Aspen [The Aspen]; 4. Björken [The Birch Tree]; 5. Granen [The Spruce]
op. 76 Treize Morceaux: 1. Esquisse; 2. Etude; 3. Carillon; 4. Humoresque; 5. Consolation; 6. Romanzetta; 7. Affettuoso; 8. Pièce enfantine [Children's Piece]; 9. Arabesque; 10. Elegiaco; 11. Linnaea; 12. Capriccietto; 13. Harlequinade
from: op. 83 Episodio; Scena; Canzone
op. 85 Cinq Morceaux: 1. Bellis [Bluebells]; 2. Œillet [The Carnation]; 3. Iris; [The Iris]; 4. Aquileja [Columbine]; 5. Campanula [The Campanula]
op. 91b Partiolaisten marssi [Scout March] (with added text)

op. 94 Six Pieces: 1. Danse [Dance]; 2. Nouvellette; 3. Sonnette; 4. Berger et bergerette [The Shepherd and the Shepherdess]; 5. Mélodie; 6. Gavotte
op. 96 Three Pieces: a. Valse lyrique; b. Autrefois; c. Valse chevaleresque
op. 97 Six Bagatelles: 1. Humoresque I; 2. Song; 3. Kleiner Walzer [Little Waltz]; 4. Humoristischer Marsch [Humorous March]; 5. Impromptu; 6. Humoresque II
op. 98 Two Suites: a. Suite mignonne; b. Suite champêtre
op. 99 Huit petits Morceaux: 1. Pièce humoristique; 2. Esquisse; 3. Souvenir; 4. Impromptu; 5. Couplet; 6. Animoso; 7. Moment de valse; 8. Petite Marche
op. 100 Suite caractéristique
op. 101 Five Romantic Compositions: 1. Romance; 2. Chant du soir; [Evening Song] 3. Scène lyrique; 4. Humoresque; 5. Scène romantique
op. 103 Five Characteristic Impressions: 1. The Village Church; 2. The Fiddler; 3. The Oarsman; 4. The Storm; 5. In Mournful Mood
from: op. 109 Episode (Miranda); Tanz der Nymphen [Dance of the Nymphs]; Scène
op. 114 Five Sketches [Five Esquisses]: 1. Maisema [Landscape]; 2. Talvikuva [Winter Scene]; 3. Metsälampi [Forest Lake]; 4. Metsälaulu [Song in the Forest]; 5. Kevätnäky [Spring Vision]
JS 1 À Betsy Lerche
JS 2 [A major]
JS 5 [A minor I]
JS 6 [A minor II]
JS 11 Adagio in D major
JS 13 Adagio in E major
JS 18 Allegretto in B minor
JS 21 Allegretto in E major
JS 23 Allegretto in F major
JS 24 Allegretto in G minor
JS 30a Andante in E flat major
JS 30b Andante cantabile. cl, harm
JS 41 Andantino in E major
JS 44 Andantino in B major
JS 46 [A flat major]
JS 47 Au crépuscule
JS 52 Con moto, sempre una corda
JS 53 Con passione
JS 74 [E flat major I]
JS 75 [E flat major II]
JS 81 Finnish Folksongs Arranged for Piano: 1. Minun kultani [My Beloved]; 2. Sydämestäni rakastan [I Love You with All My Heart]; 3. Ilta tulee, ehtoo joutuu [Evening Comes]; 4. Tuopa tyttö, kaunis tyttö [That Beautiful Girl]; 5. Velisurmaaja [The Fratricide]; 6. Häämuistelma [Wedding Memory]
JS 82 Florestan
JS 109 Kavaljeren [The Cavalier]
JS 117 Largo in A major
JS 119 Lento in E major
JS 123 Mandolinato
JS 124 Marche triste
JS 133 Moderato – Presto
JS 135b Morceau romantique
JS 148 Piano Works for Children (sketches)
JS 150 Più lento – Tempo di valse
JS 161 Rakkaalle Ainolle [To My Beloved Aino] (four-hands)
from: JS 134 Scherzo in E major
JS 164 Scherzo
JS 179 Sonatas (fragments)
JS 181 Spagnuolo
JS 198 Theme and Seven Variations (lost)
JS 201 To O. Parviainen
JS 202 Till trånaden [To Longing]
JS 221 Vivace
JS 225 18 19/XII 97

J. Works for Other Solo Instruments

op. 111 Two Pieces. org: 1. Intrada; 2. Surusoitto [Funeral Music]

from: op. 113 harm/org: 1. Avaushymni [Opening Hymn]; 10. Marche funèbre [Funeral March]

JS 63 Dolcissimo. *kantele*

JS 102 Kallion kirkon kellosävel. [The Bells of Kallio Church], see op. 65b

JS 130 Moderato. *kantele*

JS 153 Prelude and Postlude. org

K. Theatre Music

Through-composed Works (in chronological order)

JS 101 Jungfrun i tornet [The Maid in the Tower] (Hertzberg). Opera

op. 71 Scaramouche (Knudsen). Pantomime

Incidental Music (in chronological order)

op. 27 Kung Kristian II [King Christian II] (Paul)

JS 113 Kuolema [Death] (Järnefelt), see op. 44

JS 147 Pelléas och Mélisande [Pelléas et Mélisande] (Maeterlinck, trans. Gripenberg), see op. 46

JS 48 Belsazars gästabud [Belshazzar's Feast] (Procopé), see op. 51

op. 8 Ödlan [The Lizard] (Lybeck)

JS 189 Svanevit [Swanwhite] (Strindberg), see op. 54

op. 60 Trettondagsafton [Twelfth Night] (Shakespeare, trans. Hagberg)

JS 62 Die Sprache der Vögel [The Language of the Birds] (Paul)

op. 62 Kuolema [Death] (Järnefelt), addition to JS 113

op. 83 Jokamies [Everyman] (Hofmannsthal, trans. Jalkanen)

JS 182 Stormen [The Tempest] (Shakespeare, trans. Lembcke), see op. 109

Tableau Music (in chronological order)

JS 138 Näcken [The Watersprite] (Wennerberg)

JS 115 Kuvaelmamusiikkia/Tablåmusik [Incidental Music for the Viipuri Student Association], see op. 10, 11

JS 137 Musik zu den Pressefeiern [Music for the Press Celebration Days], see op. 25, 26

[op. 45, no. 2/1904]

JS 54 Cortège

op. 53a Pan und Echo [Pan and Echo]

JS 88 Grevinnans konterfej [The Countess's Portrait] (Topelius)

L. Works for Choir with Accompaniment

op. 7 Kullervo (Kalevala)

op. 19 Impromptu (Rydberg)

op. 28 Sandels (Runeberg)

op. 29 Snöfrid (Rydberg)

op. 30 Islossningen i Uleå älv [The Breaking of Ice on the Oulu River] (Topelius)

op. 31 Three Songs: 1. Laulu Lemminkäiselle [A Song for Lemminkäinen] (Weijola); 2. Har du mod? [Have You Courage?] (Wecksell); 3. Athenarnes sång [War Song of Tyrtaeus] (Rydberg)

op. 32 Tulen synty [Origin of Fire] (Kalevala)

op. 33 Koskenlaskijan morsiamet [The Rapid-Rider's Brides or The Ferryman's Brides] (Oksanen)

op. 48 Vapautettu kuningatar [The Captive Queen] (Cajander)

op. 91 Zwei Märsche: a. Jääkärien marssi [March of the Finnish Jaeger Battalion] (Nurmio); b. Partiolaisten marssi [Scout March] (Finne)

op. 92 Oma maa [My Own Land] (Kallio)
op. 93 Jordens sång [Song of the Earth] (Hemmer)
op. 95 Maan virsi [Hymn of the Earth] (Leino)
op. 110 Väinön virsi [Väinämöinen's Song] (Kalevala)
from: op. 113 Onward, Ye Brethren!
JS 51 Carminalia
JS 58b Suur' olet, Herra! [You are Mighty, O Lord] (Korpela)
JS 99 Italian Folksongs
JS 108 Karjalan osa [Karelia's Fate] (Nurminen)
JS 104 Cantata for the Coronation of Nicholas II (Cajander)
JS 105 Cantata for the University Graduation Ceremonies of 1894 (Lönnbohm)
JS 106 Cantata for the University Graduation Ceremonies of 1897 (Forsman), see op. 23
JS 160b Rakastava [The Lover] (Kanteletar), see op. 14
JS 213 Upp genom luften [Up through the Air] (Atterbom)
JS 218 Vi kysser du fader min fästmö här? [Why Kiss You, Father, My Sweetheart Here?] (Runeberg)

M. Works for A Cappella Choir

Mixed Choir

op. 18 from: Six Songs for Male Choir, arr.: 1. Sortunut ääni [The Broken Voice] (Kanteletar); 3. Venematka [The Boat Journey] (Kalevala); 4. Saarella palaa [Fire on the Island] (Kanteletar); 6. Sydämeni laulu [Song of My Heart] (Kivi)
op. 23 Cantata for the University Graduation Ceremonies of 1897 (Forsman): 1. Me nuoriso Suomen [We the Youth of Finland]; 2. Tuuli tuudittele [The Wind Rocks]; 3. Oi toivo, toivo sä lietomieli [Oh Hope, Hope, You Dreamer]; 4. Montapa elon merellä [Many on the Sea of Life]; 5. Sammuva sainio maan [The Fading Thoughts of the Earth]; 6a. Soi kiitokseksi Luojan [We Praise Thee, Our Creator]; 6b. Tuule, tuuli, leppeämmin [Blow, Wind, More Gently]; 7. Oi Lempi, sun valtas ääretön on [O Love, Your Realm is Limitless]; 8. Kun virta vuolas [As the Swift Current]; 9. Oi kallis Suomi, äiti verraton [Oh Precious Finland, Incomparable Mother]
from: op. 26 [Finlandia Hymn] (Koskenniemi)
op. 65 Two Songs: 1. Män från slätten och havet [People of Land and Sea] (Knape); 2. Kellosävel Kallion kirkossa [The Bells of Kallio Church] (Klemetti)
JS 9a Aamusumussa [In the Morning Mist] (Erkko)
JS 10 Ack, hör du fröken Gyllenborg [Ah, Do You Hear, Miss Gyllenborg] (Ballade aus Pernå)
JS 58a Den höga himlen och den vida jorden [The Lofty Heav'n] (Tegengren)
JS 60 Den 25 oktober 1902 [I] (Wasastjerna)
JS 61 Den 25 oktober 1902 [II] (Wasastjerna)
JS 64 Drömmarna [Dreams] (Reuter)
JS 69 Ej med klagan [Not with Lamentation] (Runeberg)
JS 72 Ensam i dunkla skogarnas famn [Alone in the Depths of the Forests] (von Qvanten)
JS 96 Hur blekt är allt [How Pale is All] (Runeberg)
JS 98a Isänmaalle [To the Fatherland] (Cajander)
from: JS 105 Juhlamarssi [Festival March] (Lönnbohm)
JS 122 Listen to the Water Mill (Anonymous) (fragment)
JS 129 Min rastas raataa [The Thrush's Toiling] (Kanteletar)

JS 139 När sig våren åter föder [When Spring Once More Comes to Life] (Runeberg)
JS 142 On lapsonen syntynyt meille [Christmas Song] (Jaakkola)
JS 160c Rakastava [The Lover] (Kanteletar), see op. 14
JS 176 Soitapas sorea neito [Play, Pretty Maiden] (Kanteletar)
JS 191 Tanke, se, hur fågeln svingar [Imagine, See how the Bird Swoops] (Runeberg)
JS 212 Työkansan marssi [Worker's March] (Erkko)
JS 214a Uusmaalaisten laulu [Song for the People of Uusimaa] (Terhi)

Male Choir

op. 1, no. 4 Jouluvirsi [Christmas Song or We Ask for Nothing, Rich or Rare]
op. 18 Six Songs: 1. Sortunut ääni [The Broken Voice] (Kanteletar); 2. Terve kuu (Kalevala) [Hail O Moon!]; 3. Venematka [The Boat Journey] (Kalevala); 4. Saarella palaa [Fire on the Island] (Kanteletar); 5. Metsämiehen laulu (Kivi) [The Woodsman's Song]; 6. Sydämeni laulu [Song of my Heart] (Kivi)
op. 21 Hymn (Gustafsson)
from: op. 26 [Finlandia Hymn] (Koskenniemi)
op. 84 Five Songs: 1. Herr Lager och Skön fager [Mr Lager and the Fair One] (Fröding); 2. På berget [On the Mountain] (Gripenberg); 3. Ett drömackord [A Dream Chord] (Fröding); 4. Evige Eros [Eternal Eros] (Gripenberg); 5. Till havs [At Sea] (Reuter)
op. 108 Two Songs (Larin Kyösti): 1. Humoresque; 2. Ne pitkän matkan kulkijat aus [Wanderers on the Long Way]
op. 113 Finlandia-Hymne (Sola)
JS 84 Fridolins dårskap [Fridolin's Folly] (Karlfeldt)
JS 93 Har du mod? [Have You Courage?] (Wecksell)
JS 94 Heitä, koski, kuohuminen [Leave off Foaming, Cataract] (Kalevala)
JS 98b Isänmaalle [To the Fatherland] (Cajander)
JS 100 Jone havsfärd [Jonah's Voyage] (Karlfeldt)
JS 114 Kuutamolla [In the Moonlight] (Suonio)
JS 118 Laulun mahti [The Power of Song], arr. (Auseklis, trans. Mikkola)
JS 121 Likhet [Resemblance] (Runeberg)
JS 160a Rakastava [The Lover] (Kanteletar), see op. 14
JS 170a Siltavahti [The Guard of the Bridge] (Sola)
JS 173 Skyddskårsmarsch [Skyddskår's March] (N. Runeberg)
JS 214b Uusmaalaisten laulu [Song for the People of Uusimaa] (Terhi)
JS 217 Veljeni vierailla mailla [Song of Exile] (Aho)
JS 219 Viipurin Laulu-Veikkojen (W. S. B:n) kunniamarssi [Honor March of the Singing Brothers of Viipuri (W.S.B.)] (Eerola)
JS 220 Viipurin Laulu-Veikkojen kunniamarssi [Honor March of the Singing Brothers of Viipuri] (Eerola)
JS 224 Two Songs (Schybergson): 1. Ute hörs stormen [One Hears the Storm Outside]; 2. Brusande rusar en våg [The Roaring of a Wave]

Female Choir

op. 1, no. 4 Joululaulu [Christmas Song or We Ask for Nothing, Rich or Rare]
from: op. 23 Soi kiitokseksi Luojan [We Praise Thee, Our Creator]

Children's Choir, Youth Choir, School Choir

op. 1, no. 4 Julvisa (Topelius) [Christmas Song] or [We Ask for Nothing, Rich or Rare]

from: op. 30 Nejden andas (Topelius)

JS 9b Aamusumussa [In the Morning Mist] (Erkko)

JS 51 Carminalia

JS 103 Kansakoululaisten marssi [Primary School Children's March] (Onnen Pekka)

JS 107 Cantata (von Konow)

JS 111 Kotikaipaus [Nostalgia] (von Konow)

JS 112 Koulutie [The Way to School] (Koskenniemi)

JS 172 Skolsång [School Song] (N. Runeberg)

from: JS 104 Terve Ruhtinatar! [Hail Princess!] (Cajander)

JS 199 Three Songs for American Schools: 1. Autumn Song (Dixon); 2. The Sun upon the Lake is Low (Scott); 3. A Cavalry Catch (Macleod)

N. *Solo Voice with Orchestra*

op. 3 Arioso (Runeberg)

from: op. 7 Kullervon valitus [Kullervo's Lament] (Kalevala)

op. 13, no. 4 Våren flyktar hastigt [Spring is Flying] (Runeberg)

op. 17, no. 1 Se'n har jag ej frågat mera [Then I Ceased to Ask Those Questions] (Runeberg)

op. 33 Koskenlaskijan morsiamet [The Rapid-Rider's Brides or The Ferryman's Brides] (Oksanen)

op. 36, no. 6 Demanten på marssnön [The Diamond on the March Snow] (Wecksell)

op. 37, no. 3 Soluppgång [Sunrise] (Hedberg)

op. 38 from: Five Songs: 1. Höstkväll [Autumn Night] (Rydberg); 2. På verandan vid havet [On a Balcony by the Sea] (Rydberg); 3. I natten [In the Night] (Rydberg)

op. 57, no. 6 Hertig Magnus [Baron Magnus] (Josephson)

op. 60, no. 1 Kom nu hit, död [Come Away, Death!] (Shakespeare, trans. Hagberg)

op. 70 Luonnotar (Kalevala)

op. 96b Autrefois (Procopé) (2 sopranos)

JS 168 Serenade (Stagnelius)

O. *Solo Songs with Piano*

op. 1 Five Christmas Songs: 1. Nu står jul vid snöig port [Now Stands Yule at the Snowy Gate] (Topelius); 2. Nu så kommer julen [Now is Christmas Coming] (Topelius); 3. Det mörknar ute [Christmas Carol] or [O'er Hill and Dale] (Topelius); 4. Julvisa [Christmas Song] or [We Ask for Nothing, Rich or Rare] (Topelius); 5. On hanget korkeat, nietokset [The Shining Snows are Driven High] (Joukahainen)

op. 3 Arioso (Runeberg)

from: op. 7 Kullervon valitus [Kullervo's Lament] (Kalevala)

op. 13 Seven Songs (Runeberg): 1. Under strandens granar ['Neath the Fir-Trees]; 2. Kyssens hopp [Kiss's Hope]; 3. Hjärtats morgon [The Heart's Morning]; 4. Våren flyktar hastigt [Spring is Flying]; 5. Drömmen [The Dream]; 6. Till Frigga [To Fricka]; 7. Jägargossen [The Young Sportsman] op. 17 Seven Songs: 1. Se'n har jag ej frågat mera [Then I Ceased to Ask Those Questions] (Runeberg); 2. Sov in! [Go to Sleep!] (Tavaststjerna); 3. Fågellek [Enticement] (Tavaststjerna); 4. Vilse [Astray] (Tavaststjerna); 5. En slända [A Dragonfly] (Levertin); 6. Illalle [To Evening] (Forsman); 7. Lastu lainehilla [Driftwood] (Calamnius)

op. 27, no. 4 Sången om korsspindeln [Fool's Song of the Spider] (Paul)

op. 33 Koskenlaskijan morsiamet [The Rapid-Rider's Brides or The Ferryman's Brides] (Oksanen)

op. 35 Two Songs: 1. Jubal (Josephson); 2. Teodora (Gripenberg)

op. 36 Six Songs: 1. Svarta rosor [Black Roses] (Josephson); 2. Men min fågel märks dock icke [But My Bird is Long in Homing] (Runeberg); 3. Bollspelet vid Trianon [Tennis at Trianon] (Fröding); 4. Säv, säv, susa [Reed, Reed, Rustle] (Fröding); 5. Marssnön [March Snow] (Wecksell); 6. Demanten på marssnön [The Diamond on the March Snow] (Wecksell)

op. 37 Five Songs: 1. Den första kyssen [The First Kiss] (Runeberg); 2. Lasse liten [Little Lasse] (Topelius); 3. Soluppgång [Sunrise] (Hedberg); 4. Var det en dröm? [Was It a Dream?] (Wecksell); 5. Flickan kom ifrån sin älsklings möte [The Tryst] (Runeberg)

op. 38 Five Songs: 1. Höstkväll [Autumn Night] (Rydberg); 2. På verandan vid havet [On a Balcony by the Sea] (Rydberg); 3. I natten [In the Night] (Rydberg); 4. Harpolekaren och hans son [The Harper and his Son] (Rydberg); 5. Jag ville, jag vore [I Would I Were Dwelling] (Fröding)

from: op. 46 De trenne blinda systrar [The Three Blind Sisters] (Maeterlinck, trans. Gripenberg)

op. 50 Six Songs: 1. Lenzgesang [A Song of Spring] (Fitger); 2. Sehnsucht [Longing] (Weiss); 3. Im Feld ein Mädchen singt [A Maiden Yonder Sings] (Susman); 4. Aus banger Brust [O, Wert Thou Here] (Dehmel); 5. Die stille Stadt [The Silent Town] (Dehmel); 6. Rosenlied [The Song of the Roses] (Ritter)

from: op. 51 Judeflickans sång / Solitude [The Jewish Girl's Song] (Procopé)

op. 57 Eight Songs (Josephson): 1. Älven och snigeln [The Snail]; 2. En blomma stod vid vägen [The Wild Flower]; 3. Kvarnhjulet [The Millwheel]; 4. Maj [May]; 5. Jag är ett träd [The Tree]; 6. Hertig Magnus [Baron Magnus]; 7. Vänskapens blomma [Friendship]; 8. Näcken [The Elfking]

op. 60 Two Songs from Trettondagsafton [Twelfth Night] (Shakespeare, trans. Hagberg): 1. Kom nu hit, död [Come Away, Death!]; 2. Hållilå, uti storm och i regn [Hey ho, the Wind and the Rain]

op. 61 Eight Songs: 1. Långsamt som kvällskyn [Shall I Forget Thee?] (Tavaststjerna); 2. Vattenplask [Lapping Waters] (Rydberg); 3. När jag drömmer [When I Dream] (Tavaststjerna); 4. Romeo (Tavaststjerna); 5. Romans [Romance] (Tavaststjerna); 6. Dolce far niente (Tavaststjerna); 7. Fåfäng önskan [Idle Wishes] (Runeberg); 8. Vårtagen [The Spell of Springtide] (Gripenberg)

op. 70 Luonnotar (Kalevala)

op. 72 Six Songs: 1. Vi ses igen [Farewell] (Rydberg) (lost); 2. Orions bälte [Orion's Belt] (Topelius) (lost); 3. Kyssen [The Kiss] (Rydberg); 4. Kaiutar [The Echo Nymph] (Larin Kyösti); 5. Der Wanderer und der Bach [The Wanderer and the Brook] (Greif); 6. Hundra vägar [A Hundred Ways] (Runeberg)

op. 86 Six Songs: 1. Vårförnimmelser [The Coming of Spring] (Tavaststjerna); 2. Längtan heter min arvedel [Longings Vain are my Heritage] (Karlfeldt); 3. Dold förening [Hidden Union] (Snoilsky); 4. Och finns det en tanke [And is There a Thought] (Tavaststjerna); 5. Sångarlön [The Singer's Reward] (Snoilsky); 6. I systrar, I bröder, I älskande par! [O Sisters, O Brothers, O Loving Couples!] (Lybeck)

op. 88 Six Songs: 1. Blåsippan [The Blue Anemone] (Franzén); 2. De bägge rosorna [The Two Roses] (Franzén); 3. Vitsippan [The Wood Anemone] (Franzén); 4. Sippan [The Primrose] (Runeberg); 5. Törnet [The Thorn] (Runeberg); 6. Blommans öde [The Flower's Destiny] (Runeberg)

op. 90 Six Songs (Runeberg): 1. Norden [The North]; 2. Hennes budskap [Her Message]; 3. Morgonen [The Morning]; 4. Fågelfängarn [The Bird Catcher]; 5. Sommarnatten [Summer Night]; 6. Vem styrde hit din väg? [Who Led Your Flight This Way?]

op. 96b Autrefois (Procopé) (2 sopranos)

JS 29 The American Millers' Song (lost)

JS 42 Andantino in E flat minor [Fröding]

JS 56 Då världar ännu skapade ej voro [When Worlds Still Uncreated Were] (Anonymous)

JS 57 Den första kyssen [The First Kiss] (Runeberg) (fragment)

JS 71 En visa [A Song] (Baeckman)

JS 73 Erloschen [Burn Out] (Busse-Palma)

JS 87 [G major] [Hedberg]

JS 97 Hymn to Thaïs, the Unforgettable (Borgström)

JS 120 Likhet [Resemblance] (Runeberg)

JS 136 Mummon syntymäpäivänä [Birthday Song to Grandmother]

JS 138 Song from Näcken [The Watersprite] (Wennerberg) (with vn, vc)

JS 140 Narciss [Narcissus] (Gripenberg)

JS 143 Orgier [Orgies] (Stenbäck)

JS 166 Segelfahrt [Sailing] (Öhquist)

JS 167 Serenade (Runeberg)

JS 170b Siltavahti [The Guard of the Bridge] (Sola)

JS 171 Skogsrået [The Wood Nymph] (Rydberg)

JS 174 Små flickorna [Young Girls] (Procopé)

JS 180 Souda, souda, sinisorsa [Row, Row Blue Duck] (Forsman)

JS 192 Tanken [The Thought] (Runeberg) (2 sopranos)

JS 204 Tre trallande jäntor [Three Warbling Maidens] (Fröding) (lost)

JS 211 Tule, tule kultani [Come, Come, My Sweetheart] (Volkslied)

JS 215 Vänskapens blomma [Friendship] (Josephson)

P. Melodramas

op. 15 Skogsrået [The Wood Nymph] (Rydberg)

JS 59 Den lilla sjöjungfrun [The Little Mermaid] (Andersen)

JS 77a, b Ett ensamt skidspår [The Lonely Ski Trail] (Gripenberg)

JS 88 Grevinnans konterfej [The Countess's Portrait] (Topelius)

JS 125 Melodram ur Svartsjukans nätter [Melodrama from 'Nights of Jealousy'] (Runeberg)

JS 141 O, om du sett [Oh! If You Had Seen] (Hackzell)

JS 203 Trånaden [Yearning] (Stagnelius)

Q. Musique religieuse

op. 113 Musique religieuse [Masonic Ritual Music] 1. Avaushymni [Opening Hymn]; 2. Suloinen aate [Thoughts Be Our Comfort] (von Schober, trans.

Leino); 3. Kulkue ja hymni: Näätkö kuinka hennon yrtin [Procession and Hymn: Though Young Leaves Be Green] (Pao Chao, trans. Tikkanen); 4. Kulkue ja hymni: Ken kyynelin [Procession and Hymn: Who Ne'er Hath Blent His Bread with Tears] (Goethe, trans. Leino); 5. On kaunis maa [How Fair Are Earth and Living!] (Simelius); 6. Salem (Rydberg); 7. Varje själ som längtan bränner [Whosoever Hath a Love] (Rydberg); 8. Veljesvirsi [Ode to Fraternity] (Sario); 9. Ylistyshymni [Hymn] (Sario); 10. Marche funèbre [Funeral March]; 11. Suur' olet, Herra [Ode] (Korpela); 12. Finlandia-hymni (Sola)

R. Liturgical Music

JS 58a Den höga himlen och den vida jorden [The Lofty Heav'n] (Tegengren)

JS 95 Herran siunaus [God's Blessing]

JS 110 Kolme johdantovuorolaulua [Three Introductory Antiphons]

Bibliography

1. *Archives and Collections Consulted (for details, see footnotes)*

Åbo Akademi University, The Sibelius Museum archive, Turku: collection of press clippings, general collections of correspondence and other research material
Archive of the Akademie der Künste, Berlin
Arnold Schönberg Center, Vienna: collection of unpublished letters
Breitkopf & Härtel KG, Wiesbaden: collection of correspondence
City of Helsinki, City Museum: collection of old photographs
Gesellschaft der Musikfreunde Vienna: 'Gottfried von Einem Papers'
National Archive of Finland, Helsinki: 'Jean Sibelius Collection', 'Erik Tawaststjerna Collection'
National Library of Finland (former University of Helsinki Library, Department of Special Collections and Rare Books), Helsinki: Collection 206 (Sibelius papers), 'Sibelius Sketches', and scores in Sibelius' possession
National Museum of Finland: Ainola, Tuusula: the library of Jean and Aino Sibelius
Stiftung Preussischer Kulturbesitz, Staatsbibliothek zu Berlin
Universität für Musik und darstellende Kunst Vienna: archives
University of California San Diego, Mandeville Department of Special Collections: 'Ernst Krenek Papers' (now at the Ernst Krenek Institut Krems, Austria)
Wiener Stadt- und Landesarchiv, Vienna

2. *Literature*

ABENDROTH, Walter. [1937] 1943. *Deutsche Musik der Zeitwende: Eine kulturphilosophische Persönlichkeitsstudie über Anton Bruckner und Hans Pfitzner*. Hamburg: Hanseatische Verlagsanstalt.

ADAM, Wolfgang. 2001. 'Literaturgeschichte als Gemeinschaftsprojekt: Neue Quellen zur Fachgeschichte der Germanistik in der ersten Halfte des 20. Jahrhunderts'. *Euphorion*, 95, 4, pp. 357–422.

ADAMS, Paul C., Steven HOELSCHER and Karen E. TILL, eds. 2001. *Textures of Place: Exploring Humanist Geographies*. Minneapolis: University of Minnesota Press.

ADORNO, Theodor W. 1976. *Introduction to the Sociology of Music*. Trans. E. B. Ashton. New York: Seabury. *Einleitung in die Musiksoziologie*. Frankfurt am Main: Suhrkamp, 1975.

——. 1982. 'Glosse über Sibelius'. In *Musikalische Schriften IV*, pp. 247–52. Vol. 17 of *Gesammelte Schriften*. Ed. Rolf Tiedemann. Frankfurt am Main: Suhrkamp.

Adorno, Theodor W. 1984a. 'Reflexionen über Musikkritik'. In *Musikalische Schriften VI*, pp. 573–91. Vol. 19 of *Gesammelte Schriften*. Ed. Rolf Tiedemann. Frankfurt am Main: Suhrkamp.

——. 1984b. 'Über einige Werke von Béla Bartók' (1925). In *Musikalische Schriften V*, pp. 282–6. Vol. 18 of *Gesammelte Schriften*. Ed. Rolf Tiedemann. Frankfurt am Main: Suhrkamp.

——. 1985. *Philosophy of Modern Music*. Trans. Anne G. Mitchell and Wesley V. Blomster. New York: Continuum. *Philosophie der Neuen Musik*. Frankfurt am Main: Suhrkamp, 1976.

——. 1986. 'Fussnote zu Sibelius und Hamsun'. In *Vermischte Schriften II*, p. 804. Vol. 20, bk. 2 of *Gesammelte Schriften*. Ed. Rolf Tiedemann. Frankfurt am Main: Suhrkamp.

——. 1991. *In Search of Wagner*. Trans. Rodney Livingstone. London: Verso. *Versuch über Wagner*. Berlin: Suhrkamp, 1952.

——. 1992. 'Schreker'. In *Quasi una fantasia: Essays on Modern Music*. Trans. Rodney Livingstone, pp. 130–44. London: Verso, 1978 'Quasi una fantasia'. In *Musikalische Schriften, I–III*, pp. 249–50. Vol. 16 of *Gesammelte Schriften*. Ed. Rolf Tiedemann. Frankfurt am Main: Suhrkamp.

——. 1996. *Mahler: A Musical Physiognomy*. Trans. Edmund Jephcott. Chicago: University of Chicago Press. *Mahler*. In *Die musikalischen Monographien*. Frankfurt am Main: Suhrkamp, 1972.

——. 1999. *Aesthetic Theory*. Trans. Robert Hullot-Kentor. Minneapolis: University of Minnesota Press. *Ästhetische Theorie*. Frankfurt am Main: Suhrkamp, 1970.

——. 2002. 'The Aging of the New Music'. Trans. Susan H. Gillespie. In *Essays on Music*. Ed. Richard Leppert, pp. 181–202. Berkeley: University of California Press. 'Das Altern der Neuen Musik'. In *Dissonanzen: Musik in der verwalteten Welt*, pp. 36–59. Göttingen: Vandenhoeck & Ruprecht, 1956.

Adorno, Theodor W., and Hanns Eisler. 1947. *Composing for the Films*. New York: Oxford University Press.

Adorno, Theodor W., and Max Horkheimer. 1997. *Briefwechsel*. Vol 1. Ed. Henri Lonitz. Frankfurt am Main: Suhrkamp.

Agawu, Kofi. 1991. *Playing with Signs: A Semiotic Interpretation of Classical Music*. Princeton: Princeton University Press.

Aho, Juhani. 1890. *Yksin*. Helsinki: Werner Söderström.

Aho, Kalevi. 1998. 'Sibelius suomalaisen metsän sävelrunoilijana'. In Vierimaa, Kilpeläinen and Sivuoja-Gunaratnam 1998, pp. 58–66.

Ahtola-Moorhouse, Leena, ed. 2004. *Albert Edelfelt, 1854–1905: Jubilee Book*. Helsinki: Ateneum.

Albrecht-Schröder, Klaus, and Antonia Hoerschelmann, eds. 2003. *Edvard Munch: Theme and Variation*. Vienna: Albertina. *Edvard Munch: Thema und Variation*. Vienna: Albertina, 2003.

Alesaro, Juhani. 2003. 'Sibelius and His "Free Moments" at the Piano'. In Huttunen, Kilpeläinen and Murtomäki 2003, pp. 293–8.

Almeida Cabrera, Pedro Juan. 1993. *Néstor: Tipismo y Regionalismo*. Las Palmas: Museo Néstor.

Altenburg, Detlef. 1997. 'Franz Liszt und das Erbe der Klassik'. In *Liszt und die Weimarer Klassik*. Ed. Detlef Altenburg, pp. 9–32. Weimarer Liszt-Studien 1. Laaber: Laaber.

——. 1998. 'Symphonische Dichtung'. In *Die Musik in Geschichte und Gegenwart*, Sachteil 9, 2nd edn. Ed. Ludwig Finscher, cols. 154–68. Kassel: Bärenreiter; Stuttgart: Metzler.

ANDERSON, Julian. 2004. 'Sibelius and Contemporary Music'. In Grimley 2004a, pp. 196–216.

ANDERSSON, Greger, ed. 2001. *Musikgeschichte Nordeuropas*. Stuttgart: Metzler.

ANDERSSON, Otto. 1955. *Jean Sibelius i Amerika*. Åbo: Bro.

APOLLINAIRE, Guillaume. 1966. *Œuvres complètes*. Vol. 4: *Les Peintres cubistes*. Ed. Michel Décaudin. Paris: Balland & Lecat.

ASENDORF, Christoph. 2003. 'Power, Instinct, Will: Munch's Energetic World; Theater in the Context of the Fin de Siècle'. In Albrecht-Schröder and Hoerschelmann 2003 (Eng. edn), pp. 83–90. 'Kraft, Trieb, Wille: Munchs energetisches Welttheater im Kontext des Fin de Siècle'. In Albrecht-Schröder and Hoerschelmann 2003 (Ger. edn), pp. 83–90.

ASPELIN, Eliel. 1904. *J. L. Runebergin suomalaisuus*. Helsinki: Suomalaisen Kirjallisuuden Seura.

BACHT, Nikolaus. 2001. 'Enlightment from Afar: The Structural Analogy of Myth and Music to Claude Lévi-Strauss.' *Acta Musicologica* 73, 1, pp. 1–20.

BANFIELD, Stephen. 1998. 'Vaughan Williams and Gerald Finzi'. In *Vaughan Williams in Perspective*. Ed. Lewis Foreman, pp. 202–21. [Somerset]: Albion Press.

BARANOVA, Irina. 2003. 'The Romantic Idiom of Sibelius's Waltzes'. In Huttunen, Kilpeläinen and Murtomäki 2003, pp. 299–302.

BARNETT, Andrew G. 2003. 'Oceanides: The Whole Story'. *Finnish Music Quarterly* 3, pp. 44–52.

BARRETT, Gregory. 2003. 'In Search of a Lost Chamber Work'. *Finnish Music Quarterly* 1, pp. 40–41.

BARTELS, Adolf. 1919. *Weshalb ich die Juden bekämpfe: Eine deutliche Auskunft*. Hammer-Schläge 8. Hamburg: Deutschvölkische Verlagsanstalt.

BARTELS, Klaus, ed. 1992. *Geflügelte Worte aus dem Griechischen und Lateinischen*. Darmstadt: Wissenschaftliche Buchgesellschaft.

BARTHES, Roland. 1957. *Mythologies*. Paris: Seuil.

BARTÓK, Béla. [1937] 1976a. 'Folk Song Research and Nationalism'. In Suchoff 1976, pp. 25–8.

——. [1920] 1976b. 'The Influence of Folk Music on the Art Music of Today'. In Suchoff 1976, pp. 316–19.

——. [1942] 1976c. 'Race Purity in Music'. In Suchoff 1976, pp. 29–32.

BATKA, Richard. 1907. 'Sibelius als Liederkomponist'. *Der Kunstwart: Rundschau über Dichtung, Theater, Musik, bildende und angewandte Künst* 20, 2 (July), pp. 457–9.

BAUDELAIRE, Charles. [1867] 1963. 'Any Where Out of the World' (*Le Spleen de Paris*, 1867). In *Flowers of Evil and Other Works*. Trans. Wallace Fowlie, pp. 150–53. New York: Bantam Books.

BAX, Arnold. 1943. *Farewell, My Youth*. London: Longmans & Green.

BEAUCAMP, Eduard. 2001a. 'Die Entgiftung der Toteninsel: Die Schweizer machen ihren Frieden mit Böcklin'. *Frankfurter Allgemeine Zeitung*, 22 May, p. 51.

——. 2001b. 'Maskeraden vor dem Fall'. *Frankfurter Allgemeine Zeitung*, 6 June, p. 53.

BEAUMONT, Antony, ed. and trans. 1987. *Ferruccio Busoni: Selected Letters*. New York: Columbia University Press.

BECKER, Ingeborg, and Sigrid MELCHIOR, eds. 2002. *Das Licht kommt jetzt von Norden: Jugendstil in Finnland*. Berlin: Bröhan-Museum.

BEKKER, Paul. 1921. *Kritische Zeitbilder*. Berlin: Schuster & Löffler.

——. 1932. *Beethoven*. Trans. M. M. Bozman. Rev. edn. London: Dent. *Beethoven*. Berlin: Schuster & Löffler, 1911.

Belke, Ingrid, ed. 1971. *Moritz Lazarus und Heymann Steinthal: Die Begründer der Völkerpsychologie in ihren Briefen*. Tübingen: J. C. B. Mohr.

Bell, Clive. 1914. *Art*. London: Chatto & Windus.

Benesch, Otto. 1962. 'Hodler, Klimt und Munch als Monumentalmaler'. In *Wallraff-Richartz-Jahrbuch: Westdeutsches Jahrbuch für Kunstgeschichte* 24 b, pp. 333–58.

Benestad, Finn. 2002. 'Edvard Grieg: Humor und Ernst, Natur und Geist; Skizze eines Persönlichkeitsprofils'. In Kreft 2002, pp. 183–94.

Benjamin, Walter. 1999. *The Arcades Project*. Trans. Howard Eiland and Kevin McLaughlin. Cambridge, Mass.: Belknap. *Das Passagen-Werk*. Vol. 5, bk. 1 of *Gesammelte Schriften*. Ed. Rolf Tiedemann. Frankfurt am Main: Suhrkamp, 1982.

Benn, Gottfried. 1965. *Leben ist Brückenschlagen: Lyrik und Prosa, Briefe und Dokumente*. Ed. Max Niedermayer. Munich: Droemer & Knaur.

Bergson, Henri. 1889. *Essai sur les données immédiates de la conscience*. Paris: Alcan.

——. [1896] 1910. *Matière et mémoire*. Paris: Alcan.

Bernaerts, Bruno, and Anna-Maria von Bonsdorff, eds. 2002. *Les Mondes intérieurs: Le Symbolisme finlandais*. Brussels: Marot/Tijdsbeeld.

Bertrand, Louis. 1968. *La Fin du classicisme et le retour à l'antique dans la seconde moitié du* xviii*e* *siècle et les premières anneés du* xix*e* *en France*. 2nd edn. Geneva: Slatkine.

Birgfeld, Rudolf. 1912. 'Siegmund von Hausegger's Natur-Symphonie'. *Signale für die musikalische Welt* 4 (24 January), pp. 107–8.

Bliss, Arthur. [1989] 1991. *As I Remember*. London: Thames.

Bloom, Harold. 1973. *The Anxiety of Influence*. New York: Oxford University Press.

——. 1975. *A Map of Misreading*. New York: Oxford University Press.

Bosse, Monika, and André Stoll. 1979. 'Die Agonie des archaischen Orients: Eine verschlüsselte Vision des Revolutionszeitalters'. In Flaubert [1862] 1979, pp. 401–8.

Botstein, Leon. 2003. 'Sozialgeschichte und die Politik des Ästhetischen: Juden und Musik in Wien 1870–1938'. In *Quasi una fantasia: Juden und die Musikstadt Wien*. Ed. Leon Botstein and Werner Hanak, pp. 43–63. Vienna: Wolke.

Bradbury, Malcolm, and James McFarlane, eds. 1978. *Modernism, 1890–1930*. Brighton: Harvester Press; Atlantic Highlands, N.J.: Humanities Press.

Brand, Juliane, Christopher Hailey and Donald Harris, eds. 1987. *The Berg–Schoenberg Correspondence: Selected Letters*. New York: Norton.

Braungart, Wolfgang. 1996. *Ritual und Literatur*. Tübingen: Niemeyer.

Brinkmann, Reinhold. 2004. 'Musikalische Lyrik im 19. Jahrhundert'. In *Musikalische Lyrik*. Ed. Hermann Danuser, pp. 9–124. Vol. 8, bk. 2 of Handbuch der musikalischen Gattungen. Laaber: Laaber.

Brinkmann, Reinhold, and Wolfgang Rihm. 2001. *Musik Nachdenken*. Regensburg: Con-Brio.

Brook, Donald. 1946. *Composers' Gallery*. London: Rockliff.

Brüll, Erich. 1971. 'Der Klassiker Sibelius: Einige Gesichtspunkte'. In *Musik und Gesellschaft* 9, pp. 582–8.

——. 1986. *Jean Sibelius: Für Sie porträtiert*. Leipzig: Deutscher Verlag für Musik.

Buchhart, Dieter. 2003. 'Disappearance: Experiments with Material and Motif'. In Albrecht-Schröder and Hoerschelmann 2003 (Eng. edn), pp. 23–39. 'Das Verschwinden: Experimente mit Material und Motiv'. In Albrecht-Schröder and Hoerschelmann 2003 (Ger. edn), pp. 23–40.

Bülow, Paul, 1923. *Friedrich Lienhard: Der Mensch und das Werk*. Leipzig: Koch.
Bünning, Eleonore. 2001. 'Die Finnen kommen: Esa-Pekka Salonen verteidigt Sibelius gegen seine Liebhaber'. *Frankfurter Allgemeine Zeitung*, 25 July, p. 45.
Bürger, Peter. 2000. *Das Verschwinden des Subjekts*. Frankfurt am Main: Suhrkamp.
Burmester, Willy. 1926. *Fünfzig Jahre Künstlerleben*, Berlin: Scherl.
Busoni, Ferruccio. 1911. *Sketch of a New Esthetic of Music*. Trans. T. Baker. New York: G. Schirmer, 1911. *Entwurf einer neuen Ästhetik der Tonkunst*. In Busoni, *Der mächtige Zauberer: Zwei Theaterdichtungen für Musik*. Trieste: Schmidt, 1907.
——. 1922. *Von der Einheit der Musik*. Berlin: Hesse.
——. 1957. 'The Theory of Orchestration'. In Busoni, *The Essence of Music, and Other Papers*. Trans. Rosamond Ley, pp. 34–7. London: Rockliff. 'Etwas über Instrumentationslehre'. In *Wesen und Einheit der Musik*. Ed. Joachim Herrmann, pp. 55–9. Berlin: Hesse, 1956.
Cadenbach, Rainer. 1991. *Max Reger und seine Zeit*. Laaber: Laaber.
Calinescu, Matei. 1987. *Five Faces of Modernity*. Durham, N.C.: Duke University Press.
Caspary, Vera. 1942. *Laura*. New York: Dell.
Chamberlain, Houston Stewart. 1937. *Mein Weg nach Bayreuth*. Introduction by Paul Bülow. Munich: Bruckmann.
Charbonnier, Georges. 1970. *Entretiens avec Edgard Varèse, suivis d'une étude de son œuvre par Harry Halbreich*. Paris: Belfond.
Chervìansky, David. [1947] 1952. 'Special Characteristics of Sibelius's Style'. In *Sibelius: A Symposium*. Ed. Gerald Abraham, p. 141–76. London: Oxford University Press.
Chipman, Abram. 2000. 'Janáček and Sibelius: The Antithetical Fates of Creativity in Late Adulthood'. *Psychoanalytic Review* 87, 3 (June), pp. 429–54.
Christiansen, Jörn. 1980. *'Die Heimat': Analyse einer regionalen Zeitschrift und ihres Umfeldes*. Neumünster: Wachholtz.
Cloot, Julia. 1999. 'Die Steigerung der theatralischen Illusion durch Musik: Anmerkungen zur Shakespeare-Rezeption der Romantiker'. In *Musik zu Shakespeare-Inszenierungen*, pp. 31–48. Kleine Schriften 40–41. Berlin: Gesellschaft für Theatergeschichte.
Cogniat, Raymond, and John Rewald. 1962. *Paul Gauguin: A Sketchbook*. Paris: Hammer Galleries (facsimile edn of the sketchbook of 1884–9, Armand Hammer Collection, UCLA Hammer Museum, Los Angeles).
Copland, Aaron. 1941. *Our New Music*. New York: McGraw Hill.
Coulter, George. 1928. 'An Open Letter to Schönberg and Company'. *Musical Mirror* (8 May), p. 115.
Dahlhaus, Carl. 1975. 'Wozu noch Biographie?' *Melos: Neue Zeitschrift für Musik* 1, 2, p. 82.
——. 1978. 'Schreker und die Moderne: Zur Dramaturgie des Fernen Klangs'. In Franz Schreker: Am Beginn der Neuen Musik. Studien zur Wertungsforschung 11. Ed. Otto Koleritsch. Vienna: Universal Edition, pp. 9–18. Reprinted in Vom Musikdrama zur Literaturoper. Munich: Katzbichler 1983, pp. 158–64.
——. 1980a. 'Cantabile und thematischer Prozess: Der Übergang zum Spätwerk in Beethovens Klaviersonaten'. *Archiv für Musikwissenschaft* 37, 2, pp. 81–98.
——. 1980b. *Die Musik des 19. Jahrhunderts*. Neues Handbuch der Musikwissenschaft 6. Laaber: Laaber; Wiesbaden: Akademische Verlagsgesellschaft Athenaion.
——. 1983. *Foundations of Music History*. Trans. J. B. Robinson. Cambridge: Cambridge University Press. Grundlagen der Musikgeschichte. Cologne: Gerig, 1977.
——. 1985. *Realism in Nineteenth-Century Music*. Trans. Mary Whittall. Cambridge: Cambridge

University Press. *Musikalischer Realismus: Zur Musikgeschichte des 19. Jahrhunderts*. Munich: Piper.

DAHLHAUS, Carl. 1989. *Nineteenth-Century Music*. Trans. J. Bradford Robinson. Berkeley: University of California Press, 1989. *Die Musik des 19. Jahrhunderts*. Neues Handbuch der Musikwissenschaft 6. Laaber: Laaber; Wiesbaden: Akademische Verlagsgesellschaft Athenaion, 1980.

——. 1991. *Ludwig van Beethoven: Approaches to His Music*. Trans. Mary Whittall. Oxford: Clarendon Press; New York: Oxford University Press. *Ludwig van Beethoven und seine Zeit*. Laaber: Laaber, 1987.

DAHLSTRÖM, Fabian. 1982. *Sibelius-Akatemia, 1882–1982*. Helsinki: Sibelius-Akatemia.

——. 1987. *The Works of Jean Sibelius*. Helsinki: Sibelius-Seura.

——. 1998. 'Otto Andersson och Jean Sibelius'. In Vierimaa, Kilpeläinen and Sivuoja-Gunaratnam 1998, pp. 67–81.

——. 2003a. *Jean Sibelius: Thematisch-bibliographisches Verzeichnis seiner Werke*. Wiesbaden: Breitkopf & Härtel.

——. 2003b. 'Sibelius's Diary'. In Huttunen, Kilpeläinen and Murtomäki 2003, pp. 12–19.

——, ed. 2005. *Jean Sibelius dagbok, 1909–1944*. Helsinki: Svenska Litteratursällskapet i Finland.

——, ed. 2010. *Högtärade Maestro! högtärade Herr Baron! Korrespondensen mellan Axel Carpelan och Jean Sibelius, 1900–1919*. Skrifter utgivna av Svenska Litteratursaellskapet i Finland 737. Helsinki: Svenska litteratursällskapet i Finland; Stockholm: Atlantis.

DAHLSTRÖM, Fabian, and Erkki SALMENHAARA. 1995. *Ruotsin vallan ajasta romantiikkaan: Keskiaika, 1899*. Suomen musiikin historia 1. Porvoo: Werner Söderström.

DANUSER, Hermann. 1977. 'Der Orchestergesang des Fin de siècle: Eine historische und ästhetische Skizze'. *Die Musikforschung* 30, pp. 425–52.

——. 1984. *Die Musik des 20. Jahrhunderts*. Neues Handbuch der Musikwissenschaft 7. Laaber: Laaber; Wiesbaden: Akademische Verlagsgesellschaft Athenaion.

——. 1991. *Gustav Mahler und seine Zeit*. Laaber: Laaber.

——, ed. 2004. *Musikalische Lyrik*. Handbuch der musikalischen Gattungen Vol. 8, bk. 2. Laaber: Laaber.

DANUSER, Hermann, and Herfried MÜNKLER, eds. 2001. *Deutsche Meister – böse Geister? Nationale Selbstfindung in der Musik*. Schliengen: Edition Argus.

DAVIDSON, Peter. 2005. *The Idea of North*. London: Reaktion.

DE CHIRICO, Giorgio. 1971. 'On Metaphysical Art'. In *Metaphysical Art*. Ed. Massimo Carrà, pp. 87–91. Trans. Caroline Tisdall. London: Thames and Hudson.

DINSLAGE, Patrick, 2001. 'Edvard Griegs Unterricht in Musiktheorie während seines Studiums am Leipziger Konservatorium, dargestellt an seinen Aufzeichnungen'. In Kreft 2001, pp. 94–105.

DJUPSJÖBACKA, Gustav. 2000. *Istumme ilokivelle: Sata suomalaista yksinlaulua*. Helsinki: Werner Söderström.

DOFLEIN, Erich. 1969. 'Schönbergs Opus 16 Nr 3: Der Mythos der Klangfarbenmelodie'. *Melos: Neue Zeitschrift für Musik* 36, 5 (May), pp. 203–6.

DÖMLING, Wolfgang. 1998. *Franz Liszt und seine Zeit*. 2nd edn. Laaber: Laaber.

DONINGTON, Robert. 1990. *Opera and Its Symbols: The Unity of Words, Music, and Staging*. New Haven: Yale University Press.

DOWNES, Olin. 1945. *Sibelius*. Ed. Paul Sjöblom and Jussi Jalas. Helsinki: Otava.

Downes, Stephen. 2004. 'Pastoral Idylls, Erotic Anxieties and Heroic Subjectivities in Sibelius's Lemminkäinen and the Maidens of the Island and First Two Symphonies'. In Grimley 2004a, pp. 35–48.

Draper, Joan E. 1987. 'Paris by the Lake: Sources of Burnham's Plan of Chicago'. In Zukowsky 1987, pp. 107–19.

Dreher, Martin. 1986. 'Markens Grøde'. In *Kindlers Literatur Lexikon*. Vol. 8, pp. 6049–50. Munich: Deutscher Taschenbuch Verlag.

Edinger, Edward F. 1973. *Ego and Archetype*. Baltimore: Penguin.

Edler, Arnfried. 1982. *Robert Schumann und seine Zeit*. Laaber: Laaber.

Eggebrecht, Hans Heinrich. 1975. 'Musikalisches Denken'. *Archiv für Musikwissenschaft* 32, pp. 228–9.

Ekman, Karl, Jr. 1935a. *Jean Sibelius: En konstnärs liv och personlighet*. Porvoo: Schildts.

——. 1935b. *Jean Sibelius: Taiteilijan elämä ja persoonallisuus*. Helsinki: Otava.

——. 1946. *Jean Sibelius: His Life and Personality*. Trans. Edward Birse. New York: Tudor.

Eliade, Mircea. 1962. *Aspects du mythe*. Paris: Gallimard.

Elkins, James. 1999. *The Domain of Images*. Ithaca, N.Y.: Cornell University Press.

Ellis, Katharine. 2000. 'Palestrina et la musique dite "palestrienne" en France au XIXe siècle: questions d'exécution et de réception'. In *La Renaissance et sa musique au XIXe siècle*. Ed. Philippe Vendrix, pp. 155–90. Paris: Klincksieck.

Englund, Einar. 1977. *Sibeliuksen varjossa: Katkelmia säveltäjän elämästä*. Trans. Riitta Kauko. Helsinki: Otava.

Engström, Albert. 1953. *En brevbok: Brev till Sigrid, 1892–1939*. Ed. Malin Engström and Helmer Lång. Stockholm: Bonniers.

Eydoux, Éric, Sophie Javel, Riitta Ojanperä and Anja Olavinen, eds. 2001. *Peintres du Nord en voyage dans l'Ouest: Modernité et impressionisme, 1860–1900*. Caen: Presses Universitaires de Caen; Musée des Beaux-Arts de Caen.

Fanselau, Rainer. 1992. 'Jean Sibelius: Pohjolas Tochter op. 49'. In *Programmusik: Analytische Untersuchungen und didaktische Empfehlungen für den Musikunterricht in der Sekundarstufe*. Ed. Albrecht Goebel, pp. 217–35. Mainz: Schott.

Fauser, Annegret, and Manuela Schwartz, eds. 1999. *Von Wagner zum Wagnérisme: Musik, Literatur, Kunst, Politik*. Leipzig: Leipziger Universitätsverlag.

Fechner-Smarsly, Thomas, ed. 1998. *August Strindberg: Verwirrte Sinneseindrücke; Schriften zu Malerei, Fotografie und Naturwissenschaften*. Amsterdam: Verlag der Kunst.

Ferguson, Robert. 1987. *Enigma: The Life of Knut Hamsun*. New York: Farrar, Straus and Giroux.

Feuersenger, Marianne. 1982. *Mein Kriegstagebuch: Zwischen Führerhauptquartier und Berliner Wirklichkeit*. Freiburg im Breisgau: Herder.

Finscher, Ludwig. 1998. 'Symphonie'. In *Die Musik in Geschichte und Gegenwart*, Sachteil 9, 2nd edn. Ed. Ludwig Finscher, cols. 16–153. Kassel: Bärenreiter; Stuttgart: Metzler.

——. 2004. 'Die neue MGG als internationales Lexikon'. In Mäkelä and Klein 2004, pp. 149–54.

Flaubert, Gustave. *Salammbô* (1862). Transl. Georg Brustgi. Frankfurt am Main: Insel 1979, pp. 401–48.

Floros, Constantin. 1978. *Beethoven's Eroica und Prometheus-Musik: Sujet-Studien*. Wilhelmshaven: Heinrichshofen.

——. 1992. *Alban Berg: Musik als Autobiographie*. Wiesbaden: Breitkopf & Härtel.

Foerster, Isolde von, Christoph Hust and Christoph-Hellmut Mahling, eds. 2001. *Musikforschung Faschismus Nationalsozialismus*. Mainz: Are.

Foreman, Lewis, ed. 1977. *Edmund Rubbra: Composer*. Rickmansworth: Triad Press.

——. 1987. *From Parry to Britten: British Music in Letters, 1900–1945*. London: Batsford.

Francis, Emerich. 1957. *Wissenschaftliche Grundlagen soziologischen Denkens*. Munich: Lehnen.

Frank, Manfred. 1988. 'Subjekt, Person, Individuum'. In *Die Frage nach dem Subjekt*. Ed. Manfred Frank, Gérard Raulet and Willem van Reijen, pp. 7–28. Frankfurt am Main: Suhrkamp.

Franklin, Peter. 2003. 'Reading the Profound Logic: Nature, Gender and Performed Narrative in Sibelius'. In Huttunen, Kilpeläinen and Murtomäki 2003, pp. 356–64.

Fredrikson, Erkki. 1994. *Finland Defined: A Nation Takes Shape on the Map*. Jyväskylä: Gummerus.

Frigyesi, Judith. 1998. *Béla Bartók and Turn-of-the-Century Budapest*. Berkeley: University of California Press.

Fröhlich, Elke, ed. 1994. *Die Tagebücher von Joseph Goebbels*. Vol. 2: *Diktate, 1941–1945*, part 3: January–March 1942. Munich: Saur.

Frosterus, Sigurd. 1935. *Stålålderns janusansikte och andra essäer*. Porvoo: Schildts.

Fuhrmann, Wolfgang. 2003. 'Trost und Zersetzung'. *Berliner Zeitung*, 7 November, p. 10.

Furuhjelm, Erik. 1916a. *Jean Sibelius: Hänen sävelrunoutensa ja piirteitä hänen elämästään*. Trans. Leevi Madetoja. Porvoo: Werner Söderström.

——. 1916b. *Jean Sibelius: Hans tondiktning och drag ur hans liv*. Porvoo: Schildts.

Gallego, Antonio, ed. [1891] 1985. *Por nuestra música: Algunas observaciones sobre la magna cuestión de una escuela lírica nacional motivadas par la Trilogía (tres cuadros y un prólogo) Los Pirineos expuestas por Felipe Pedrell*. Madrid: Música mundana.

Gallen-Kallela-Sirén, Janne. 2001. *Minä palaan jalanjäljilleni: Akseli Gallen-Kallelan elämä ja taide*. Helsinki: Otava.

——. 2002. 'Die Postulierung des finnischen Jugendstils: Akseli Gallen-Kallela und das Streben nach neuer Geschichte und neuer Kunst'. In Becker and Melchior 2002, pp. 42–50.

Gerhard, Anselm, ed. 2000. *Musikwissenschaft: Eine verspätete Disziplin; Die akademische Musikforschung zwischen Fortschrittsglauben und Modernitätsverweigerung*. Stuttgart: Metzler.

Gerigk, Herbert, and Theophil Stengel, eds. 1943. *Lexikon der Juden in der Musik*. 2nd edn. Berlin: Hahnefeld.

Gleissner, Ruth-Maria. 2000. 'Die deutschen Sibelius-Gesellschaften'. In Jäntti, Vogt and Holtkamp 2000, pp. 199–232.

——. 2002. *Der unpolitische Komponist als Politikum: Die Rezeption von Jean Sibelius im NS-Staat*. Frankfurt am Main: Lang.

Goethe, Johann Wolfgang von. 1901. *The Autobiography of Goethe: Truth and Fiction Relating to My Life*. Trans. John Oxenford. Vols. 1 and 2 of *The Works of Johann Wolfgang von Goethe*. Boston: Dana Estes, 1901. *Dichtung und Wahrheit*. Ed. Lieselotte Blumenthal and Erich Trunz. In *Werke*, Vol. 9, bk. 2.7, *Autobiographische Schriften*. Munich: C. H. Beck, 1981.

Göhler, Georg. 1908. 'Orchesterkompositionen von Jean Sibelius'. *Der Kunstwart: Monatshefte für Kunst, Literatur und Leben* 21, 23, 1 (September), pp. 261–9.

Goldsmith, Martin. 2000. *The Inextinguishable Symphony: A True Story of Music and Love in Nazi Germany*. New York: Wiley & Sons.

Gornaya, Irina. 2003. 'The Art of "Playing Garlands" and "Making up Bouquets" in Jean Sibelius's Song Cycle, Opus 88'. In Huttunen, Kilpeläinen and Murtomäki 2003, pp. 287–92.

Goss, Glenda Dawn. 1995. *Jean Sibelius and Olin Downes: Music, Friendship, Criticism*. Boston: Northeastern University Press.

——, ed. 1996. *The Sibelius Companion*. Westport, Ct.: Greenwood, pp. 281–96.

——, ed. 1997. *Jean Sibelius: The Hämeenlinna Letters; Scenes from a Musical Life, 1874–1895*. Esbo: Schildts.

——. 1998. *Jean Sibelius: A Guide to Research*. New York: Garland.

——. 2000. 'Sibelius's Kullervo after 1892'. In Goss, Kilpeläinen, Moisala and Murtomäki 2000, pp. 61–72.

——. 2003a. 'A Backdrop for Young Sibelius: The Intellectual Genesis of the Kullervo Symphony'. *19th-Century Music*, 27, 1, pp. 48–73.

——. 2004. 'Vienna and the Genesis of Kullervo: "Durchführung zum Teufel!"' In Grimley 2004a, pp. 22–31.

——. 2005. 'Introduction'. In *Kullervo op. 7*. Series 1, Vol 1.1–3 of *Jean Sibelius Complete Works*, p. xii. Wiesbaden: Breitkopf & Härtel.

Goss, Glenda Dawn, Kari Kilpeläinen, Pirkko Moisala and Veijo Murtomäki, eds. 2000. *Hundra vägar har min tanke: Festskrift till Fabian Dahlström*. Porvoo: Werner Söderström.

Grant, Michael, and John Hazel. [1973] 1980. *Lexikon der antiken Mythen und Gestalten*. Munich: Deutscher Taschenbuch Verlag.

Gräsbeck, Folke. 2003. 'Jean Sibelius: Youth Production for Piano, 1885–1891'. In Huttunen, Kilpeläinen and Murtomäki 2003, pp. 104–14.

Gray, Cecil. 1926. 'Sibelius'. *The Nation & Athenaeum* 40, 9 (4 December), pp. 336–7.

——. 1927. 'Sibelius; or, Music and the Future'. *The Nation & Athenaeum*, 42, 12 (24 December), pp. 483–4.

——. 1931. *Sibelius*. London: Oxford University Press.

——. 1935. *Sibelius: The Symphonies*. London: Oxford University Press.

Gray, Laura. 1996. 'Sibelius and England'. In Goss 1996, pp. 281–96.

Grimley, Daniel M. 2003. 'Landscape and Structural Perspective in *Nightride and Sunrise*'. In Huttunen, Kilpeläinen and Murtomäki 2003, pp. 248–58.

——, ed. 2004a. *The Cambridge Companion to Sibelius*. Cambridge: Cambridge University Press.

——. 2004b. 'Performing Sibelius: Sir Colin Davis and Osmo Vänskä in Conversation with Daniel M. Grimley'. In Grimley 2004a, pp. 229–42.

——, 2006. *Grieg: Music, Landscape and Norwegian Identity*. Woodbridge: Boydell.

Grimm, Jacob. 1835. *Deutsche Mythologie*. Göttingen: Dieterich.

Grofton, Ian, and Donald Fraser. 1985. *A Dictionary of Musical Quotations*. New York: Schirmer.

Grönhagen, Yrjö von. *Finnische Gespräche*. Berlin: Nordland, 1941.

Grote, Adalbert. 1994. *Robert Fuchs: Studien zu Person und Werk des Wiener Komponisten und Theorielehrers*. Munich: Katzbichler.

Grotenfelt, O[ssian]. 1903. 'Johan Ludvig Runeberg och landets finska talande befolkning'.

In *Förhandlingar och uppsatser 16, 1902–1903*, pp. 85–112. Skrifter utgivna af Svenska Litteratursällskapet i Finland 56. Helsinki: Tidnings & Tryckerieaktiebolaget.

Gülke, Peter. 1961. 'Niederländische Musik: Von Ciconia bis Dufay'. In *Die Musik in Geschichte und Gegenwart*. Ed. Friedrich Blume, cols. 1461–70. Kassel: Bärenreiter.

Haapala, Vesa. 2005. *Kaipaus ja kielto: Edith Södergranin Dikter-kokoelman poetiikkaa*. Helsinki: Suomalaisen Kirjallisuuden Seura.

Haas, David. 1996. 'Sibelius's Second Symphony and the Legacy of Symphonic Lyricism'. In Goss 1996, pp. 77–96.

Haffner, Sebastian. 1983. *The Meaning of Hitler*. Trans. Ewald Osers. Cambridge, Mass.: Harvard University Press. *Anmerkungen zu Hitler*. 15th edn. Munich: Kindler, 1978.

Häkli, Pekka. 1955. *Arvid Järnefelt ja hänen lähimaailmansa*. Porvoo: Werner Söderström.

Hall, Wendy. 1950. 'Sibelius and the Finnish Landscape'. *Geographical Magazine* (December). Reprint: London & Watford: Sun Printers, n.d.

Hämäläinen-Forslund, Pirjo. 1994. *Seitsemän tietä taiteeseen: Maalareiden kehityskertomuksia*. Helsinki: Söderström.

Hamsun, Knut. 1917. *Markens grøde*. Kristiania: Gyldendal.

Handschin, Jacques. 1933. *Igor Strawinski: Versuch einer Einführung*. Zurich: Hug in Komm.

Hanslick, Eduard. 1889. *Musikalisches und Literarisches: Kritiken und Schilderungen*. 2nd edn. Die Moderne Oper 5. Berlin: Allgemeiner Verein für Deutsche Literatur.

——. 1989. *Aus dem Tagebuch eines Rezensenten: Gesammelte Kritiken*. Ed. Peter Wapnewski. Kassel: Bärenreiter.

Harrington, Elaine. 1987. 'International Influences on Henry Hobson Richardson's Glessner House'. In Zukowsky 1987, pp. 189–207.

Hartikainen, Markku. 2003. 'The Letters: Interesting Sibelius Documents'. In Huttunen, Kilpeläinen and Murtomäki 2003, pp. 20–6.

Hase-Koehler, Else von, ed. 1928. *Max Reger: Briefe eines deutschen Meisters; Ein Lebensbild*. Leipzig: Koehler & Amelang.

Hauch, Gunnar. 1922. *Breve fra Grieg: Et udvalg*. Copenhagen: Gyldendalske.

Hausegger, Friedrich von. 1885. *Die Musik als Ausdruck*. Vienna: Carl Koneger.

——. 1903. *Gedanken eines Schauenden: Gesammelte Aufsätze*. Ed. Siegmund von Hausegger. Munich: Bruckmann.

Headington, Christopher. 1981. *Britten*. London: Methuen.

Hegel, G. W. F. 1974. *Aesthetics: Lectures on Fine Art*, 2 vols. Trans. T. M. Knox. Oxford: Clarendon Press.

Heil, Johannes. 1997. '"Antijudaismus" und "Antisemitismus": Begriffe als Bedeutungsträger'. In *Jahrbuch für Antisemitismusforschung* 6. Ed. Wolfgang Benz, pp. 92–114. Frankfurt am Main: Campus.

Heiniö, Mikko. 1977. 'Sibeliuksen instrumentaatiosta' (Master's thesis, University of Helsinki).

Heller, Lynne. 1994. *Geschichte der Hochschule für Musik und darstellende Kunst in Wien*. Vol. 1: *1909–1917* (unpublished final report of a research project of the Bundesministeriums für Wissenschaft und Forschung, Vienna).

Heller, Reinhold. 1970. 'The Iconography of Edvard Munch's Sphinx'. *Artforum* 9 (October), pp. 72–80.

Hepokoski, James. 1993. *Sibelius: Symphony No. 5*. Cambridge: Cambridge University Press.

——. 1996. 'The Essence of Sibelius: Creation Myths and Rotational Cycles in Luonnotar'. In Goss 1996, pp. 121–46.

——. 1997. 'Sibelius'. In *The Nineteenth-Century Symphony*. Ed. D. Kern Holoman, pp. 417–49. New York: Schirmer; London: Prentice Hall.
——. 2001a. 'Rotation, Sketches, and the Sixth Symphony'. In Jackson and Murtomäki 2001, pp. 322–51.
——. 2001b. 'Sibelius, Jean'. In *The New Grove Dictionary of Music and Musicians*. Ed. Stanley Sadie. 2nd edn. Vol. 23, pp. 319–47. London: Macmillan.
——. 2003. 'Finlandia Awakens'. In Huttunen, Kilpeläinen and Murtomäki 2003, pp. 401–11.
HEYWORTH, Peter. 1996. *Otto Klemperer: His Life and Times*, 2 vols. Cambridge: Cambridge University Press.
HILL, Ralph 1947. '*Sibelius the Man*'. In *Sibelius: A symposium*, Ed. Gerald Abraham. New York: Norrton 1947, pp. 9–13.
HIRSBRUNNER, Theo. 1981. *Debussy und seine Zeit*. Laaber: Laaber.
——. 1982. Igor Strawinsky in Paris. Laaber: Laaber.
HOBSBAWM, Eric J. 1987. *The Age of Empire, 1875–1914*. New York: Pantheon.
——. 1990. *Nations and Nationalism since 1780: Programme, Myth, Reality*. Cambridge: Cambridge University Press.
HOCK, Udo. 2000. *Das unbewusste Denken*. Frankfurt am Main: Fischer Taschenbuch Verlag.
HOERSCHELMANN, Antonia. 2003. '"… a Shedding of Skin …"' In Albrecht-Schröder and Hoerschelmann 2003 (Eng. edn), pp. 11–12. '"… ein Sich-Häuten …"' In Albrecht-Schröder and Hoerschelmann 2003 (Ger. edn), pp. 11–12.
HOFSTÄTTER, Hans H. [1965] 1978. *Symbolismus und die Kunst der Jahrhundertwende: Voraussetzungen, Erscheinungsformen, Bedeutungen*. Cologne: DuMont.
——. 1972. *Idealismus und Symbolismus*. Vienna: Anton Schroll.
HOLMES, Michael Stuart. 2003. 'Sibelius's Reception'. In Huttunen, Kilpeläinen and Murtomäki 2003, pp. 412–29.
HONKO, Lauri. 1999. 'Pitkän eepoksen laulaja'. In *Kalevala: 1835 julkaistun Kalevalan laitoksen uusi painos*, pp. vii–xx. Helsinki: Suomalaisen Kirjallisuuden Seura.
HOSIAISLUOMA, Yrjö. 2000. *Lauri Viljanen*. Helsinki: Suomalaisen Kirjallisuuden Seura.
HOWELL, Timothy. 1989. *Jean Sibelius: Progressive Techniques in the Symphonies and Tone Poems*. New York: Garland.
HOWITZ, Jürgen. 1967. 'Jean Sibelius'. In *Aus dem Leben und Schaffen grosser Musiker*, no. 6, Berlin: Volk und Wissen, Volkseigener Verlag.
HUTTUNEN, Matti, Kari KILPELÄINEN and Veijo MURTOMÄKI, eds. 2003. *Sibelius Forum II*. Helsinki: Sibelius Academy.
HUUSKO, Timo. 2001. 'Dekorativivisuus'. In Ojanperä 2001, pp. 44–59.
ILVAS, Juha. 1996. *Akseli Gallen-Kallela*. Exh. cat. Helsinki: Ateneum.
JAAKKOLA, Jutta and Aarne Toivonen, eds. 2005. *Inspired by Tradition: Kalevala Poetry in Finnish Music*. Jyväskylä: Gummerus.
JACKSON, Stanley W. 1986. *Melancholia and Depression: From Hippocratic Times to Modern Times*. New Haven: Yale University Press.
JACKSON, Timothy L. 2010. 'Sibelius the Political'. In Jackson, Murtomäki, Davis and Virtanen 2010, pp. 69–124.
JACKSON, Timothy L. and Veijo MURTOMÄKI, eds. 2001. *Sibelius Studies*. Cambridge: Cambridge University Press.
JACKSON, Timothy L., Veijo MURTOMÄKI, Colin DAVIS and Timo VIRTANEN, eds. 2010.

Sibelius in the Old and New World: Aspects of His Music, Its Interpretation, and Reception. Frankfurt am Main: Peter Lang.

JACOBI, Jolande. [1940] 1978. *Die Psychologie von C. G. Jung: Eine Einführung in das Gesamtwerk, mit einem Geleitwort von C. G. Jung.* Frankfurt am Main: Fischer.

JÄKER, Benedikt. 1998. 'Vom ungarischen Volkstanz zur "Ungarischen Rhapsodie": Zu den Frühfassungen der "Ungarischen Rhapsodie" von Franz Liszt'. In *Musik als Text: Bericht über den Internationalen Kongress der Gesellschaft für Musikforschung Freiburg im Breisgau 1993.* Vol. 2, pp. 108–12. Kassel: Bärenreiter.

JALAS, Jussi. 1981. *Elämäni teemat.* Helsinki: Tammi.

——. 1988. *Kirjoituksia Sibeliuksen sinfonioista: Sinfonian eettinen pakko.* Helsinki: Fazer.

——. n.d. 'Vorwort'. In *Kullervo und seine Schwester op. 7 Nr. 3.* Wiesbaden: Breitkopf & Härtel.

JAMES, Burnett. 1983. *The Music of Jean Sibelius.* Rutherford, N.J.: Fairleigh Dickinson University Press.

JANÁČEK, Leoš. 1989. *Janáček's Uncollected Essays on Music.* Ed. and trans. Mirka Zemanová. London: Marion Boyars.

JÄNTTI, Ahti, Annemarie VOGT and Marion HOLTKAMP, eds. 2000. *Sibelius und Deutschland.* Berlin: Spitz.

JÄRNEFELT, Arvid. 1894. *Heräämiseni.* Helsinki: Otava.

——. 1900. *Veljekset.* Helsinki: Otava.

——. 1944. *Vanhempieni romaani.* Porvoo: Werner Söderström.

JAROCINSKI, Stefan. 1976. *Debussy: Impressionism and Symbolism.* London: Eulenburg (orig. 'Debussy a impresjonizm i symbolizm', Ph.D. dissertation, Warsaw University, 1964).

JAUSS, Hans Robert. 1989. *Studien zum Epochenwandel der ästhetischen Moderne.* Frankfurt am Main: Suhrkamp.

JENSEN, Jørgen I. 1996. 'Zeiten des Umbruchs'. *Österreichische Musikzeitschrift* 51, 6–7, pp. 392–4.

JENSEN, Ludvig Irgens. 1935. 'Jean Sibelius: Urkraft, Ursprünglichkeit, Symbol eines Volkes. Verstanden von einer Welt?' *Der Norden* 12, 12 (Special issue 'Jean Sibelius zum 70. Geburtstag') (December), p. 377.

JEWANSKI, Jörg. 1999. *Ist C = rot? Eine Kultur- und Wissenschaftsgeschichte zum Problem der wechselseitigen Beziehung zwischen Ton und Farbe.* Sinzig: Studio.

JOHNSON, Harold E. 1959. *Jean Sibelius.* New York: Knopf.

JOSEPHSON, Nors S. 2004. 'On Some Apparent Sketches for Sibelius's Eighth Symphony'. *Archiv für Musikwissenschaft* 61, 1, pp. 54–67.

JUSSILA, Osmo. 2004. *Suomen Suuriruhtinaskunta, 1809–1917.* Helsinki: Söderström.

KAHL, Willi. 1989. 'Bungert'. In *Die Musik in Geschichte und Gegenwart.* Ed. Friedrich Blume, Vol. 2, cols. 465–6. Kassel: Bärenreiter.

KALLBERG, Jeffrey. 2003. 'Sibelius, *Skogsrået,* and the History of Sexuality'. In Huttunen, Kilpeläinen and Murtomäki 2003, pp. 430–37.

——. 2004. 'Finnish Modern: Love, Sex and Style in Sibelius's Songs'. In Grimley 2004a, pp. 117–36.

KALLIO, Rakel. 2001. 'Estetiikkaa ja tunteita'. In Ojanperä 2001, pp. 14–27.

KARLSON, Anu. 1993. 'Aino Ackté: Prima Donna and Nationalist'. *Finnish Music Quarterly* 1, pp. 14–19.

KARTTUNEN, Antero. 2002. *Radion sinfoniaorkesteri, 1927–2002.* Helsinki: Yleisradio.

KARVONEN, Arvi. 1957. *Sibelius-Akatemia 75 vuotta.* Helsinki: Otava.

KEIL, Charles. 1979. *Tiv Song.* Chicago: University of Chicago Press.

KENNEDY, Michael. 1964. *The Works of Ralph Vaughan Williams*. London: Oxford University Press.

KIENZLE, Ulrike. 1998. *Das Trauma hinter dem Traum: Franz Schrekers Oper 'Der ferne Klang' und die Wiener Moderne*. Schliengen: Argus.

KILPELÄINEN, Kari. 1992. *Tutkielmia Jean Sibeliuksen käsikirjoituksista*. Studia Musicologica Universitatis Helsingiensis 3. Helsinki: Helsingin yliopiston musiikkitieteen laitos.

——. 2001. 'Jean Sibeliuksen musiikillinen ympäristö ennen ensimmäistä ulkomaanmatkaa 1889'. In Tyrväinen, Lappalainen, Mäkelä and Vierimaa 2001, pp. 223–35.

KISLINGER, Peter. 2002. '"Details" oder "Saft": Dirigenten zeitgenössischer Sibelius-Interpretation'. *Österreichische Musikzeitung* 57, 3–4, pp. 4–6.

KITTANG, Atle. 1994. 'Knut Hamsun et le nazisme'. In *Présence de Knut Hamsun: Lettres inédites*. Ed. Régis Boyer and Jean-Marie Paul, pp. 165–80. Nancy: Presses Universitaires de Nancy.

KLEIN, Tobias Robert. 2001. 'Wartburg-Mythos und biblisches Mysterium: Nationale und Religiöse Identität im Werk von August Bungert'. In Danuser and Münkler 2001, pp. 343–66.

KLEIN, Tobias Robert, and Tomi MÄKELÄ. 2004. 'Von regionaler Mehrsprachigkeit zur globalen Heimat: Eine Einleitung'. In Mäkelä and Klein 2004, pp. 9–19.

KLINGE, Matti. 1997. *Keisarin Suomi*. Espoo: Schildt.

——. 2004. *Den politiske Runeberg*. Stockholm: Atlantis/Söderströms.

KLUGE, Rolf-Dieter. 1997. *Der Russische Symbolismus*. Tübingen: Universität Tübingen.

KNAPAS, Rainer. 2001. 'Aatteiden maidemat'. In Ojanperä 2001, pp. 28–43.

KNAPAS, Rainer, and Maria Vainio, eds. 2004. *Albert Edelfelt och Ryssland: Brev från åren 1875–1905*. Stockholm: Atlantis; Helsinki: Svenska Litteratursällskapet.

KNIAZEVA, Janna. 2004. 'Jacques Handschin in St. Petersburg'. In Mäkelä and Klein 2004, pp. 49–57.

KOHLHAAS, Ellen. 2002. 'Himmelsstücke, Höllenfahrten: Die Finnischen Radiosymphoniker unterwegs'. *Frankfurter Allgemeine Zeitung*, 15 March, p. 52.

KOLBUS, Anita. 2001. *Maeterlinck, Debussy, Schönberg und andere: Pelléas et Mélisande; Zur musikalischen Rezeption eines symbolistischen Dramas*. Marburg: Tectum.

KONTTINEN, Riitta. 2001. *Sammon takojat: Nuoren Suomen taiteilijat ja suomalaisuuden kuvat*. Helsinki: Otava.

——. 2002. '"Uskollinen Totuudelle ja ideaalille": Eero Järnefelt ihmisten kuvaajana'. In Lindqvist 2002, pp. 149–72.

KORTELAINEN, Anna. 2001. *Niin kutsuttu sydämeni: Albert Edelfeltin kirjeet äidilleen, 1873–1901*. Helsinki: Otava.

KORVENMAA, Pekka. 2004. 'Takaisin luontoon — mutta sivistyneesti'. In Suvikumpu 2004, pp. 27–45.

KOSELLECK, Reinhart. 1992. 'Volk, Nation, Nationalismus, Masse'. In *Geschichtliche Grundbegriffe: Historisches Lexikon zur politisch-sozialen Sprache in Deutschland*. Vol 7. Ed. Otto Brunner, Werner Conze and Reinhart Koselleck, pp. 389–98. Stuttgart: Klett-Cotta.

KOSKIMIES, Yrjö S. 1990. 'Hämeenlinnan poika Janne Sibelius ja hänen kotikaupunkinsa'. In *Sibeliuksen Hämeenlinna*. Hämeenlinnna: Sibelius-seura.

KREBS, Carl. 1905. 'Konzerte'. *Der Tag*, 21 January, p. 14.

KREFT, Ekkehard, ed. 2001. *Kongressbericht über den 3. Edvard-Grieg-Kongress*. Altenmedingen: Junker.

——, ed. 2002. *Kongressbericht über den 4. Edvard-Grieg-Kongress*. Altenmedingen: Junker.

——. 2003. *Harmonik im Umbruch: Akkordtypen und Formationen vom 18. bis in das 20. Jahrhundert.* Frankfurt am Main: Lang.

Krellmann, Hanspeter. 1970. 'Plädoyer für Sibelius'. *Musica* 24, pp. 442–4.

Krenek, Ernst. 1970. 'Gustav Mahler'. In Bruno Walter, *Gustav Mahler*, pp. 157–220. Trans. James Galston. New York: Da Capo.

——. 1998. *Im Atem der Zeit: Erinnerungen an die Moderne.* Hamburg: Hoffmann und Campe.

Krohn, Ilmari. 1945–6. *Der Stimmungsgehalt der Symphonien von Jean Sibelius.* Vols. 1–2. Helsinki: Suomalaisen Kirjallisuuden Seura.

Krones, Hartmut. 2002. 'Jean Sibelius und Wien, 1890–1955: Ergänzungen zu einem vernachlässigten Kapitel'. *Österreichische Musikzeitschrift* 57, 3–4, pp. 29–32.

——. 2003a. '"… das alte liebe Wien wiederzusehen …": Jean Sibelius und Wien, 1890–1956'. In Krones 2003b, pp. 23–64.

——. 2003b. *Jean Sibelius und Wien.* Cologne: Böhlau, 2003.

——, ed. 2003c. 'Round Table: "Jean Sibelius und Wien heute"'. In Krones 2003b, pp. 157–69.

——. 2003d. 'Traditionelle "Wiener" Semantik im Liedschaffen von Jean Sibelius'. In Krones 2003b, pp. 143–56.

Krueger, Karl. 1946. 'Listener as Critic: Sibelius and Tchaikovsky in the Hands of the Pundits'. *Musical Digest* (November), p. 42.

Kurki, Eija. 1997. *Satua, kuolemaa ja eksotiikkaa: Jean Sibeliuksen vuosisadanalun näyttämömusiikkiteokset.* Helsinki: HeSe Print.

Kuukka, Väinö, Raija Majamaa and Hannu Vepsä. 2002. *Elias Lönnrot: Taitaja, tarkkailija, tiedemies.* Helsinki: Suomalaisen Kirjallisuuden Seura.

Kuusi, Matti. 1974. 'Poplore'. In *Folklore tänään.* Ed. Hannu Launonen and Kirsti Mäkinen, pp. 11–23. Tietolipas 74. Helsinki: Suomalaisen Kirjallisuuden Seura.

Kuusi, Matti, and Senni Timonen, eds. 1997. *Suomen kansan vanhat runot* 15. Helsinki: Suomalaisen Kirjallisuuden Seura.

Lacan, Jacques. [1953] 1966. 'Fonction et champ de la parole et du langage en psychoanalyse'. In *Écrits 1*, pp. 111–208. Paris: Éditions du Seuil.

La Grange, Henry-Louis de, and Günther Weiss, eds. 2004. *Gustav Mahler: Letters to His Wife.* Trans. Antony Beaumont. Ithaca, N.Y.: Cornell University Press. *Ein Glück ohne Ruh'*: *Die Briefe Gustav Mahlers an Alma.* Berlin: Siedler, 1995.

Laitinen, Heikki. 1976. 'Kalevalan kommentaarin runosävelmäliite vuodelta 1895'. In *Paimensoittimista kisällilauluun* (Tutkielmia kansanmusiikista, 1). Ed. Heikki Laitinen and Simo Westerholm, pp. 157–92. Kaustinen: Kansanmusiikki-instituutti.

Lambert, Constant. 1934. *Music Ho! A Study of Music in Decline.* London: Faber and Faber.

Lappalainen, Seija. 1990. 'Kauppi, Emil', in *Suuri Musiikkitietosanakirja.* Vol. 3, p. 183. Keuruu: Otava.

——. 1994. *Tänä iltana yliopiston juhlasalissa: Musiikin tähtihetkiä Helsingissä, 1832–1971.* Helsinki: Yliopistopaino.

——. 1998. 'Martin Wegelius – musiikkipedagogi ja wagneriaani'. In Vierimaa, Kilpeläinen and Sivuoja-Gunaratnam 1998, pp. 143–55.

Latham, Alison, ed. 2002. 'Scotch Snap'. In *The Oxford Companion to Music*, p. 1131. Oxford: Oxford University Press.

Laurila, Aarme. 1958. *F. E. Sillanpää vuosina 1888–1958.* Helsinki: Otava.

LAUTNER, Lois. 1962. 'Arnold Schoenberg in Kammern'. *Michigan Quarterly Review* (Spring), pp. 21–7.

LAYTON, Robert. [1965] 1978. *Jean Sibelius*. London: Dent.

——. 1970. *Sibelius and His World*. New York: Viking.

——. 1993. *Sibelius*. New York: Schirmer Books.

——. 1995. 'Sibelius – Twenty-Five Years On'. In *Proceedings from the First International Jean Sibelius Conference in Helsinki 1990*. Ed. Eero Tarasti, pp. 106–12. Helsinki: Sibelius-Akatemia.

LE BON, Gustave. 1899. *Psychologie des foules*. 4th edn. Paris: Alcan.

LEGGE, Walter. 1935. 'Conversations with Sibelius'. *Musical Times* (March), pp. 218–20.

——. 1998. *Words and Music*. Ed. Alan Sanders. London: Duckworth.

LEIBOWITZ, René. 1955. *Sibelius, le plus mauvais compositeur du monde*. Liège: Dynamo.

LEISIÖ, Timo. 2005. 'Stylistic Elements of Runo Song'. In Jaakkola and Toivonen 2005, pp. 30–40.

LEPSIUS, M. Rainer. [1990] 1993. 'Nation und Nationalismus in Deutschland'. In *Grenzfälle: Über neuen und alten Nationalismus*. Ed. Michael Jeismann and Henning Ritter. Leipzig: Reclam.

LEVANTO, Marjatta. 1987. *Ateneum Opas: Isack Wacklinista Wäinö Aaltoseen*. Helsinki: Otava.

LEVAS, Santeri. 1960a. *Järvenpään mestari*. Vol. 2. Porvoo: Werner Söderström.

——. 1960b. *Jean Sibelius: A Personal Portrait*. Trans. Percy M. Young. London: Dent.

——. 1972. *Jean Sibelius: A Personal Portrait*. Trans. Percy M. Young. 2nd edn. London: Dent.

——. 1973. *Sibelius: A Personal Portrait*. Trans. Percy M. Young. Lewisburg, Pa.: Bucknell University Press.

——. 1992. *Jean Sibelius: Muistelma suuresta ihmisestä*. Porvoo: Werner Söderström.

LEVI, Erik. 1994. *Music in the Third Reich*. Basingstoke: Macmillan.

LIENHARD, Friedrich. 1900. *Die Vorherrschaft Berlins*. Leipzig: Heimatverlag.

LINDQVIST, Leena, ed. 2002. *Taiteilijan tiellä: Eero Järnefelt, 1863–1937*. Helsinki: Otava.

LINNEBACH, Andrea. 1991. *Arnold Böcklin und die Antike: Mythos, Geschichte, Gegenwart*. Munich: Hirmer.

LINSE, Ulrich. 1997. 'Nordisches in der deutschen Lebensreformbewegung'. In *Wahlverwandtschaft: Skandinavien und Deutschland, 1800–1914*. Exh. cat. Ed. Bernd Hennigsen, Janine Klein, Helmut Müssener and Solfrid Söderlind, pp. 397–400. Berlin: Deutsches Historisches Museum.

LOBE, Johann Christian. 1844. *Compositions-Lehre; oder, Umfassende Theorie von der thematischen Arbeit und den modernen Instrumentalformen*. Weimar: Voigt.

LOCKSPEISER, Edward. 1943. (Review). *Music & Letters* 24, p. 188.

——. 1942. 'Trends in Modern English Music'. *Musical Quarterly* 28, p. 13.

LÖNNROT, Elias. [1835a]. 1999. 'Esipuhe'. In *Kalevala taikka vanhoja Karjalan runoja Suomen kansan muinoisista ajoista*, pp. i–xxviii. Helsinki: Suomalaisen Kirjallisuuden Seura.

——. [1835b] 2001. *Kalevala taikka vanhoja Karjalan runoja Suomen kansan muinoisista ajoista*. Helsinki: Suomalaisen Kirjallisuuden Seura.

——. [1849] 2000. *Kalevala*. Helsinki: Suomalaisen Kirjallisuuden Seura.

LOESTI, Friedhelm. 2001. 'Dezentrierende Harmonik als Ausdrucksmittel in Edvard Griegs "Sommerabend" op. 71, Nr. 2'. In Kreft 2001, pp. 163–73.

Löwenthal, Leo. 1937. 'Knut Hamsun: Zur Vorgeschichte der autoritären Ideologie'. *Zeitschrift für Sozialforschung* 6, pp. 295–8.

Lukkarinen, Ville. 1989. *Classicism and History: Anachronistic Architectural Thinking in Finland at the Turn of the Century: Jac. Ahrenberg and Gustaf Nyström.* Suomen muinaismuistoyhdistyksen aikakauskirja 93. Helsinki: Suomen muinaismuistoyhdistys.

Lukkarinen, Ville. 2004. '"Paikan henki" puhuttelee maisemamaalaria'. In *Suomi-kuvasta mielenmaisemaan: Kansallismaisemat 1800- ja 1900-luvun vaihteen maalaustaiteessa.* Ed. Ville Lukkarinen and Annika Waenerberg, pp. 92–155. Helsinki: Suomalaisen Kirjallisuuden Seura.

Luyken, Lorenz. 1995. '*... aus dem Nichtigen eine Welt schaffen ...*': *Studien zur Dramaturgie im symphonischen Spätwerk von Jean Sibelius.* Kassel: Bosse.

Lyotard, Jean-François. 1984. 'Answering the Question: What Is Postmodern?' In *The Postmodern Condition: A Report on Knowledge.* Trans. Geoff Bennington and Brian Massumi. Minneapolis: University of Minnesota Press.

——. 1987. 'Le Nom et l'exception'. In Herta Nagl-Docekal and Helmuth Vetter, eds. *Tod des Subjekts?* pp. 43–53. Vienna: Oldenbourg.

MacDonald, Malcolm. 1997. 'Aspects of Scottish Musical Nationalism in the Twentieth Century, with Special Reference to the Music of F. G. Scott, Ronald Center and Ronald Stevenson'. In Mäkelä 1997a, pp. 111–32.

Mäckelmann, Michael. 1983. 'Sibelius und die Programmusik: Eine Studie zu seinen Tondichtungen und Symphonien'. In *Programmusik: Studien zu Begriff und Geschichte einer umstrittenen Gattung.* Ed. Constantin Floros, Hans-Joachim Marx and Peter Petersen. Hamburger Jahrbuch für Musikwissenschaft 6, pp. 121–68. Laaber: Laaber.

——. 1986. 'Integration und offene Gestaltung: Zu Jean Sibelius und Allan Pettersson'. In *Allan-Pettersson-Jahrbuch: Beiträge zur skandinavischen Symphonik,* pp. 5–22. Wuppertal: Allan-Pettersson-Gesellschaft.

Mahling, Christoph-Hellmut, and Sigrid Wiesmann, eds. 1983. *Bericht über den internationalen Musikwissenschaftlichen Kongress Bayreuth 1981.* No. 5, supplement to *Die Musikforschung* 36.

Mahnkopf, Claus-Steffen. 1998. *Kritik der neuen Musik: Entwurf einer Musik des 21. Jahrhunderts.* Kassel: Bärenreiter.

Maidt-Zinke, Kristina. 2002. 'Zurück zu Sibelius: Ein Gespräch mit Sakari Oramo, Rattles Nachfolger in Birmingham'. *Süddeutsche Zeitung,* 10 July, p. 14.

Majamaa, Raija, and Marjut Paulaharju. 2004. *J. L. Runeberg: Suomen runoilija.* Helsinki: Suomalaisen Kirjallisuuden Seura.

Mäkelä, Tomi. 1992a. 'The Orchestra: Encumbrance or Enthusiasm?' *Finnish Music Quarterly* 1, pp. 12–16.

——. 1992b. 'Sonaattimuoto ja 1900-luvun alun vääristynyt traditio'. *Musiikkitiede* 1–2, pp. 63–98.

——, ed. 1992c. 'Suomalainen säveltäjä ja orkesteri: Kartoitus suomalaissäveltäjien tavoista suhtautua kokoonpanoon ja orkestraation ongelmiin'. *Musiikki* 22, 2, pp. 16–79.

——. 1993. 'Kontrast und Entfaltung: Texturelle, thematische und stilistische Folgerichtigkeit des d-Moll-Konzertes'. In *Bericht über den Internationalen Mozart-Kongress in Baden bei Wien.* Ed. Ingrid Fuchs, pp. 759–74. Tutzing: Schneider.

——. 1994. 'Jean Sibelius contra Theodor W. Adorno: "Das Prinzip des Stars ist totalitär geworden"'. *Finnish Music Quarterly,* special issue in German, pp. 16–19.

——. 1995a. 'Arnold Schönberg – ein religiöser Modernist? Von der Jakobsleiter zum Überlebenden aus Warschau'. In *Musik und Religion*. Ed. Helga de la Motte-Haber, pp. 163–88. Laaber: Laaber.

——. 1995b. 'Jean Sibelius' Violin Concerto and Its Dramatic Virtuosity'. In *Proceedings of the First International Jean Sibelius Conference, Helsinki 1990*. Ed. Eero Tarasti, pp. 254–80. Helsinki: Sibelius Akademie.

——. 1995c. 'Zwischen Imitation und Inspiration: Reger-Rezeption bei Aarre Merikanto'. *Die Musikforschung*, 48, 4, pp. 369–94.

——. 1996. *Aarre Merikanto: Das Konzert für Geige, Klarinette, Horn und Streichsextett ('Schott-Konzert')*. Meisterwerke Nordischer Musik 2. Wilhelmshaven: Noetzel.

——, ed. 1997a. *Music and Nationalism in Twentieth-Century Great Britain and Finland*. Hamburg: Bockel.

——. 1997b. 'Towards a Theory of Internationalism, Europeanism, Nationalism and "Co-Nationalism" in Twentieth-Century Music'. In Mäkelä 1997a, pp. 9–16.

——. 2000a. 'Der andersartige Aussenseiter: Die moderne Tonsprache Leoš Janáčeks'. In *Oper aktuell: Die Bayerische Staatsoper 2000/2001*. Ed. Hannspeter Krellmann, pp. 35–42. Munich: Stiebere.

——. 2000b. 'Die Konfigurierung des Klanges: Die Angaben zur Instrumentation von Ragtime für 11 Instrumente und Pribaoutki in Igor Strawinskys Skizzen'. *Mitteilungen der Paul Sacher Stiftung* 13, pp. 26–32.

——, ed. 2000c. *Europa stellt sich vor: Regionalstil, Provinzialismus und musikalische Sozialisation*. Magdeburg: Otto-von-Guericke-Universität.

——. 2000d. 'Jean Sibelius, Kullervo'. In *Oratorienführer*. Ed. Silke Leopold and Ullrich Scheideler, pp. 675–7. Stuttgart: Metzler.

——. 2000e. '"Verunglückt auf der Reise": Das "Erste Concert" (Fragment) von Max Reger mit Blick auf sein Klavierkonzert opus 114'. In *Musikalische Moderne und Tradition*. Ed. Alexander Becker, Gabriela Gefäller and Susanne Popp, pp. 37–54. Reger-Studien 6. Wiesbaden: Breitkopf & Härtel.

——. 2000 f. 'Zwischen Inspiration und Irritation: Jean Sibelius und die frühe Neue Musik'. In *Sibelius in Deutschland*. Ed. Ahti Jäntti, Annemarie Vogt and Marion Holtkamp, pp. 90–116. Berlin: Spitz.

——. 2001a. 'Der "exterritoriale" Sibelius: Zur artifiziellen Volkstümlichkeit in der Nordischen Moderne'. In Kreft 2001, pp. 66–76.

——. 2001b. 'Die "leise, fromme Weise" von Henryk Wieniawski: Zur poetischen, dramatischen und religiösen Virtuosität der "Preghiera" im Violinkonzert opus 14'. In *Henry Wieniawski: Composer and Virtuoso in the Musical Culture of the Nineteenth and Twentieth Centuries*. Ed. Macej Jablonski and Danuta Jasinska, pp. 21–33. Poznan: Rhytmos.

——. 2001c. 'Jean Sibelius, politiikka ja Theodor W. Adorno – vastaväittäjän puheenvuoro, lausunto ja loppukaneetti'. *Musiikki* 31, 1, pp. 39–64.

——. 2001d. 'Nationalismus und Kontinentalismus, "Britizismus" und Modernismus: Zur stilistischen und nationalen Orientierung Britischer Komponisten nach 1914'. In *Französische und deutsche Musik im 20. Jahrhundert: Symposion der Hochschule für Musik Frankfurt und des Paul Hindemith Instituts am 27.–29.11.1997*. Ed. Giselher Schubert, pp. 84–93. Mainz: Schott.

——. 2002a. 'Between Classicism and Eclecticism: The Hunt of King Charles; A Piece of Loyalist Anti-Nationalism'. *Finnish Music Quarterly* 2, pp. 52–9.

Mäkelä, Tomi. 2002b. 'Von "'Allnatur' zu Phantasielandschaft": Edvard Grieg, Jean Sibelius und das nordische Milieu'. In Kreft 2002, pp. 145–58.
——. 2003a. 'The Comedy of Errors: Biographies and Collected Letters'. *Finnish Music Quarterly* 2, pp. 57–60.
——. 2003b. '"Mein Kopf ist voller Walzer": Jean Sibelius und der Umkreis Pauline Luccas in Wien'. In Krones 2003b, pp. 65–78.
——. 2003c. 'Natur und Heimat in der Sibelius-Rezeption: Walter Niemann, Theodor W. Adorno und die "postmoderne Moderne"'. In Huttunen, Kilpeläinen and Murtomäki 2003, pp. 365–82.
——. 2003d. 'Two Dinosaurs: Recent Publications Include a Biography of Conductor Robert Kajanus and a Collection of Letters by Aino Ackté'. *Finnish Music Quarterly* 3, pp. 53–6.
——. 2004a. 'Defining Compositional Process: Idea and Instrumentation in Igor Stravinsky's *Ragtime* (1918) and *Pripaoutki* (1915)'. In *A Handbook to Twentieth-Century Musical Sketches*. Ed. Patricia Hall and Friedemann Sallis, pp. 131–45. Cambridge: Cambridge University Press.
——. 2004b. 'Finland's National Anthem, Runeberg and Finnish Artistic Identity'. *Finnish Music Quarterly* 4, pp. 36–9.
——. 2004c. 'Konflikt der Sprachen und Stämme: Jean Sibelius und das zweisprachige Finnland'. In Mäkelä and Klein 2004, pp. 59–66.
——. 2004d. 'Menter, Sophie'. In *Die Musik in Geschichte und Gegenwart*. Vol. 11. Ed. Ludwig Finscher, cols. 1657–8. Kassel: Bärenreiter; Stuttgart: Metzler.
——. 2004e. 'Sibelius and Germany: Wahrhaftigkeit beyond Allnatur'. In Grimley 2004a, pp. 169–81.
——. 2005. 'Die unsichtbare Stimme der Frau: Von musikalischer Diegese zu immanenter Deutung in Otto Premingers Film noir Laura (1944)'. In Dirk Fritsch and Eva Schäfer. *Filmverstehen: Audiovisuelle Kommunikation am Beispiel von Filmgeschichte und Filmanalyse*, pp. 143–78. Cologne: Von Halem.
——. 2008. 'Gregorian Chant and Modal Modernism: On the Non-Finnish Sources of "Modality" in Jean Sibelius's Music'. *Musurgia* 15, 1–3, pp. 61–9.
——. 2009. 'Die "gedachte Ordnung" der Nationalstile: Georg Philipp Telemann und die französische Claviermusik'. In *Telemann und Frankreich – Frankreich und Telemann (Report on the International Scientific Conference, Magdeburg, 12–14 March 1998, 14th Magdeburg Telemann Festival)*. Ed. Carsten Lange, Brit Reipsch and Wolf Hobohm, pp. 119–42. Hildesheim: Olms.
——. 2010. 'The Nordic Landscape and "Extra-Territoriality": Jean Sibelius in the Context of Cultural Geography and Adorno's Reception'. In Jackson, Murtomäki, Davis and Virtanen 2010, pp. 335–70.
——. 2011. 'The Wings of a Butterfly: Sibelius and the Problem of Musical Modernity'. In *Jean Sibelius and His World*, pp. 89–124. Ed. Daniel M. Grimley. Princeton: Princeton University Press.
Mäkelä, Tomi, and Tobias Robert Klein, eds. 2004. *Mehrsprachigkeit und regionale Bindung in Musik und Literatur*. Interdisziplinäre Studien zur Musik 1. Frankfurt am Main: Lang.
Malinowski, Bronislaw. 1962. 'The Life of Myth'. In *Sex, Culture and Myth*, pp. 289–94. New York: Harcourt, Brace.
Malmberg, Ernst, ed. 1941. *Mest om Albert Engström*. Uppsala: Lindblad.
Marquard, Odo. 1968. 'Zur Bedeutung der Theorie des Unbewussten für eine Theorie der

nicht mehr schönen Kunst'. In *Die nicht mehr schönen Künste: Grenzphänomene des Ästhetischen*. Ed. Hans Robert Jauss, pp. 375–92. Poetik und Hermeneutik 3. Munich: Fink.

——. 1987. *Transzendentaler Idealismus, romantische Naturphilosophie, Psychoanalyse*. Cologne: Dinter.

MARTENS, Günter. 1971. *Vitalismus und Expressionismus: Ein Beitrag zur Genese und Deutung expressionistischer Stilstrukturen und Motive*. Studien zur Poetik und Geschichte der Literatur 22. Stuttgart: Kohlhammer.

MARVIA, Einari. 1955. 'Jean Sibeliuksen musikaalinen sukuperintö'. *Uusi Musiikkilehti* 9, pp. 47–81.

MARVIA, Einari, and Matti VAINIO. 1993. *Helsingin kaupungin orkesteri 1882–1982*. Porvoo: Werner Söderström.

MASON, Daniel Gregory. 1914. 'Romanticism and Realism in Music' *New Music Review and Church Music Review* 13, 153 (August), pp. 398–402.

MAUCLAIR, Camille. 1909. *La Religion de la musique*. Paris: Fischbacher.

MCMULLIN, Michael. 1985. 'Sibelius: An Essay on His Significance'. *Music Review* 46, 3 (August), pp. 199–211.

MCVEIGH, Simon, and Cyril EHRLICH. 2002. 'The Modernisation of London Concert Life around 1900'. In *The Business of Music*. Ed. Michael Talbot, pp. 96–120. Liverpool: Liverpool University Press.

MEINANDER, Henrik. 1999. *Tasavallan tiellä: Suomi kansallissodasta 2000-luvulle*. Espoo: Schildt.

MELLERS, Wilfrid. 1957. *Romanticism and the Twentieth Century*. Fairlawn, N.J.: Essential Books.

MEYER, Alfred H. 1936. 'Sibelius: Symphonist'. *Musical Quarterly* 22, pp. 68–86.

MEYER, Andreas. 2000. *Ensemblelieder in der frühen Nachfolge (1912–1917) von Arnold Schönbergs Pierrot lunaire op. 21 – eine Studie über Einfluss und 'Misreading'*. Munich: Fink.

MEYER, Michael. 1991. *The Politics of Music in the Third Reich*. Frankfurt am Main: Lang.

MEYER-BAER, Kathi. [1936] 1975. *Bedeutung und Wesen der Musik: Der Bedeutungswandel der Musik*. Collection d'études musicologiques 5. Baden-Baden: Koerner.

——. 1970. *Music of the Spheres and the Dance of Death: Studies in Musical Iconology*. Princeton, N.J.: Princeton University Press.

MONELLE, Raymond. 1997. 'Scottish Music, Real and Spurious'. In Mäkelä 1997a, pp. 87–110.

MONTAIGNE, Michel de. 1973. *The Complete Essays*. Trans. Donald M. Frame. Stanford: Stanford University Press.

MORGAN, Paul. 1991. *Twentieth Century Music: A History of Musical Style in Modern Europe and America*. New York: Norton.

MOSIG, Yozan Dirk. 2003. 'The Archetypal Power of Sibelius'. In Huttunen, Kilpeläinen and Murtomäki 2003, pp. 438–44.

MOTTE-HABER, Helga de la. 1983. 'Warum es keinen musikalischen Surrealismus geben konnte'. In Mahling and Wiesmann 1983, pp. 458–62.

MUELLER, John H. 1950. *The American Symphony Orchestra*. Bloomington: Indiana University Press.

MÜLLER-DOOHM, Stefan. 2005. *Adorno: A Biography*. Trans. Rodney Livingstone. Cambridge: Polity Press. *Adorno: Eine Biographie*. Frankfurt am Main: Suhrkamp, 2003.

MÜLLER-WESTERMANN, Iris. 2003. '"The Age of Carmen": Gender Relationships in the Art of Edvard Munch, 1890–1920'. In Albrecht-Schröder and Hoerschelmann 2003 (Eng. edn), pp. 67–82. '"Die Zeit von Carmen": Zum Verhältnis der Geschlechter im Werk Edvard Munchs, 1890–1920'. In Albrecht-Schröder and Hoerschelmann 2003 (Ger. edn), pp. 67–82.

MUNCH, Edvard. 2001. 'St. Cloud Manifesto'. In *Manifesto: A Century of Isms*. Ed. May Ann Cause, p. 249. Lincoln: University of Nebraska Press.

MURTOMÄKI, Veijo. 1990. *Sinfoninen ykseys: Muotoajattelun kehitys Sibeliuksen sinfonioissa*. Musiikin tutkimuslaitoksen julkaisusarja 4. Helsinki: Sibelius-Akatemia.

——. 1993. *Symphonic Unity: The Development of Formal Thinking in the Symphonies of Sibelius*. Studia Musicologica Universitatis Helsingiensis 5. Helsinki: University of Helsinki.

——. 1996. '"Symphonic Fantasy": A Synthesis of Symphonic Thinking in Sibelius's Seventh Symphony and Tapiola'. In Goss 1996, pp. 147–66.

——. 1998a. 'Metsänhaltijatar ja "Nuoren Don Sibeliuksen seikkailut" — balladilaji ja erotiikka myöhäisromantiikan musiikissa'. In Vierimaa, Kilpeläinen and Sivuoja-Gunaratnam 1998, pp. 92–106.

——. 1998b. 'Russian Influences on Sibelius'. In Murtomäki, Kilpeläinen and Väisänen 1998, pp. 153–61.

——. 2000. 'Sibelius ja valssi'. In Goss, Kilpeläinen, Moisala and Murtomäki 2000, pp. 73–87.

——. 2001a. 'Sibelius ja ranskalainen orkesterimusiikki saksalaisen sinfoniatradition valossa'. In Tyrväinen, Lappalainen, Mäkelä and Vierimaa 2001, pp. 247–57.

——. 2001b. 'Sibelius's Symphonic Ballad Skogsrået: Biographical and Programmatic Aspects of His Early Orchestral Music'. In Jackson and Murtomäki 2001, pp. 95–138.

——. 2002. 'Sibelius Caught in a Political Vortex'. *Finnish Music Quarterly* 4, pp. 38–45.

——. 2004. 'Sibelius and the Miniature'. In Grimley 2004a, pp. 137–53.

MURTOMÄKI, Veijo, Kari KILPELÄINEN and Risto VÄISÄNEN, eds. 1998. *Sibelius Forum: Proceedings from the Second International Jean Sibelius Conference in Helsinki 1995*. Helsinki: Sibelius-Akatemia.

MURTOMÄKI, Veijo, and Tomi MÄKELÄ. 1991. 'Keskustelua sinfonisesta ykseydestä ja muotoajattelun kehityksestä Sibeliuksen sinfonioissa'. *Musiikki* 21, 1–2, pp. 79–91.

NADLER, Josef. 1912. *Literaturgeschichte der deutschen Stämme und Landschaften*. Vol. 1. Regensburg: Habbel.

NÆSS, Haral, and James MCFARLANE, eds. 1998. *Knut Hamsun: Selected Letters*. Vol. 2: *1898–1952*. Norwich: Norvik Press.

NECTOUX, Jean-Michel. 1998. *Mallarmé: Un clair regard dans les ténèbres; Peinture, musique, poésie*. Paris: Adam Biro.

NEWCOMB, Anthony. 1981. 'The Birth of Music out of the Spirit of Drama: An Essay in Wagnerian Formal Analysis'. *Nineteenth-Century Music* 5, 1 (July), pp. 38–66.

——. 1984. 'Once More "between Absolute and Program Music": Schumann's Second Symphony'. *Nineteenth-Century Music* 7, 3 (April), pp. 233–50.

——. 1987. 'Schumann and Late Eighteenth-Century Narrative Strategies'. *Nineteenth-Century Music* 112 (November), pp. 164–71.

NEWLIN, Dika. 1980. *Schoenberg Remembered: Diaries and Recollections, 1938–76*. New York: Pendragon.

NEWMARCH, Rosa. 1906. *Jean Sibelius: A Finnish Composer*. Leipzig: Breitkopf & Härtel.

——. 1939. *Jean Sibelius: A Short Story of a Long Friendship*. Boston: Birchard.

NICKLAUS, Hans-Georg. 1989. 'Das Erhabene in der Musik; oder, Von der Unbegrenztheit des Klangs'. In *Das Erhabene. Zwischen Grenzerfahrung und Grössenwahn*. Ed. Christine Pries, pp. 217–32. Weinheim: Acta Humaniora.

Niemann, Walter. 1903. 'Jean Sibelius und die Finnische Musik'. *Signale für die Musikalische Welt* 62, pp. 185–91.
——. 1906. *Die Musik Skandinaviens: Ein Führer durch die Volks- und Kunstmusik von Dänemark, Norwegen, Schweden und Finnland bis zur Gegenwart*. Leipzig: Breitkopf & Härtel.
——. 1909. *Das Nordlandbuch: Eine Einführung in die gesamte nordische Natur und Kultur*. Berlin: Duncker.
——. 1913a. *Die Musik seit Richard Wagner*. Berlin: Schuster & Loeffler.
——. 1913b. 'Jean Sibelius und die Finnische Musik'. *Die Musik* 13 (2 November), pp. 195–206.
——. 1917. *Jean Sibelius*. Leipzig: Breitkopf & Härtel.
——. [1918] 1925. *Die Musik der Gegenwart und der letzten Vergangenheit bis zu den Romantikern, Klassizisten und Neudeutschen*. Berlin: Schuster & Loeffler.
——. 1922. *Brahms*. Stuttgart: Deutsche Verlagsanstalt.
Niemann, Walter, and Gerhard Schjelderup. 1908. *Edvard Grieg: Biographie und Würdigung seiner Werke*. Leipzig: Peters.
Nietzsche, Friedrich. 1967. *The Birth of Tragedy*. In *The Birth of Tragedy and The Case of Wagner*. Trans. Walter Kaufmann. New York: Vintage. *Die Geburt der Tragödie aus dem Geiste der Musik*. Stuttgart: Reclam, 1984.
——. 1976a. *The Antichrist*. In *The Portable Nietzsche*. Ed. and trans. Walter Kaufmann. New York: Penguin. *Der Antichrist: Fluch auf das Christentum*. In Nietzsche. *Sämtliche Werke: Kritische Studienausgabe*, Vol. 6. Ed. Giorgio Colli and Mazzino Montinari, pp. 165–254. Munich: Deutscher Taschenbuch Verlag; Berlin: de Gruyter, 1999.
——. 1976b. *Thus Spoke Zarathustra*. In *The Portable Nietzsche*. Ed. and trans. Walter Kaufmann. New York: Penguin. *Also sprach Zarathustra: Ein Buch für alle und keinen*. Stuttgart: Kröner, 1975.
Nivanka, Leena. 1992. *Lea Piltti*. Porvoo: Werner Söderström.
Nummi, Jyrki. 2002. *Aika Pariisissa: Juhani Ahon ranskalainen kausi, 1889–1890*. Helsinki: Suomalaisen Kirjallisuuden Seura.
Nyberg, Paul, and Olav Panelius, eds. 1970. *Brev: Samlade Skrifter av Johan Ludvig Runeberg* 9. Helsinki: Svenska Litteratursällskapet i Finland.
Oberkrome, Willi. 1993. *Volksgeschichte. Methodische Innovation und völkische Ideologisierung in der deutschen Geschichtswissenschaft 1918–1945*. Göttingen: Vandenhoeck & Ruprecht.
——. 1999. 'Historiker im "Dritten Reich". Zum Stellenwert volkshistorischer Ansätze zwischen klassischer Politik- und neuerer Sozialgeschichte'. *Geschichte in Wissenschaft und Unterricht* 50, pp. 74–98.
Oechslon, Werner. 2002. '"Unter dem griechischen Himmel ...": Wirklichkeit und — vor allem — Fiktion: Projektin und Strategien'. In *Die griechische Klassik, Idee oder Wirklichkeit*. Ed. Frank Zimmer, pp. 685–8. Mainz: Zabern.
Ojanperä, Riitta, ed. 2001. *Pinta ja syvyys: Varhainen modernismi Suomessa, 1890–1920*. Helsinki: Ateneumin taidemuseo.
Okkonen, Onni. 1961. *Akseli Gallen-Kallela: Elämä ja taide*. Porvoo: Werner Söderström.
Oksala, Teivas. 2004. *J. L. Runebergin Kreikka ja Rooma: Tutkielmia runoilijan suhteesta antiikin ja klassiseen perintöön*. Helsinki: Suomalaisen Kirjallisuuden Seura.
Oramo, Ilkka. 1983. 'Vom Einfluss der Volksmusik auf die Kunstmusik: Ein unbekannter Aufsatz von Sibelius aus dem Jahre 1896'. In Mahling and Wiesmann 1983, pp. 440–44.
——. 1995. 'The Symphonic Poems: Formal Strategies'. In *Proceedings from the First Inter-*

national Jean Sibelius Conference in Helsinki 1990. Ed. Eero Tarasti, pp. 150–57. Helsinki: Sibelius-Akatemia.

Oramo, Ilkka. 2003. 'Sibelius as a Problem of Musical Historiography'. In Huttunen, Kilpeläinen and Murtomäki 2003, pp. 69–80.

Ory, Pascal, and Jean-François Sirinelli. 1992. *Les Intellectuels en France de l'affaire Dreyfus à nos jours*. Paris: Colin.

Osborne, Richard. 1998. *Herbert von Karajan: A Life in Music*. London: Chatto & Windus.

Osten, Gert von der. 1962. 'Europäische Kunst 1912'. In *Europäische Kunst 1912: Zum 50. Jahrestag der Ausstellung des 'Sonderbundes westdeutscher Kunstfreunde' in Köln*. Exh. cat. Cologne: Wallraf-Richartz-Museum.

Ostrovsky, Ruwim. 1998. 'Some Remarks on Sibelius's Treatment of Genre and Cycle in His Piano Impromptus Op. 5'. In Murtomäki, Kilpeläinen and Väisänen 1998, pp. 293–6.

Ouellette, Fernand. 1968. *Edgard Varèse: A Musical Biography*. Trans. Derek Coltman. New York: Orion. *Edgard Varèse*. Paris: Seghers, 1966.

Painter, Karen. 1995. 'The Sensuality of Timbre: Responses to Mahler and Modernity at the *Fin de Siècle*.' *Nineteenth-Century Music* 18, 3 (Spring), pp. 236–56.

Pascal, Blaise. 1976. *Pensées*. Ed. Philippe Sellier. Paris: Mercure de France.

———. 2005. *Pensées*. Trans. Roger Ariew. Indianapolis, Ind.: Hackett.

Paul, Adolf. 1891. *En bok om en människa*, Stockholm: Bonniers.

——. 1914. 'Zwei Fennonenhäuptlinge: Sibelius / Gallén'. In *Deutsch-Nordisches Jahrbuch für Kulturaustausch und Volkskunde 1914*. Ed. Walter George, pp. 114–19 and 121. Jena: Diederichs.

——. 1938. 'Mein Freund Sibelius i–iii'. *Völkischer Beobachter*, 22–9 January, n.p.

Peltovuori, Risto. 2005. *Suomi saksalaisin silmin, 1933–1939: Lehdistön ja diplomatian näkökulmia*. Helsinki: Suomalaisen Kirjallisuuden Seura.

Petschnig, Emil. 1912. 'Die Oper der Zukunft'. *Signale für die Musikalische Welt* 70, 9–10 (28 February and 6 March), pp. 279–81, 315–17.

Pevsner, Nikolaus. 1991. *Pioneers of Modern Design: From William Morris to Walter Gropius*. London: Penguin.

Pfannkuch, Wilhelm. 1956. 'Goldmark, Karl'. In *Die Musik in Geschichte und Gegenwart*, Vol. 5. Ed. Friedrich Blume, cols. 481–4. Kassel: Bärenreiter.

Pickett, David. 2003. 'The Fourth Symphony: Ending and Beginning in Complete Disaster'. In Huttunen, Kilpeläinen and Murtomäki 2003, pp. 88–96.

Pinder, Brigitte. 2005. *Form und Inhalt der symphonischen Tondichtung von Sibelius*. Berlin: Wissenschaftlicher Verlag Berlin.

Politoske, Daniel. 1996. 'Choral Music'. In Goss 1996, pp. 201–20.

Pollack, Howard. 2000. 'Samuel Barber, Jean Sibelius, and the Making of an American Romantic'. *Musical Quarterly* 84, 2 (Summer), pp. 175–205.

Potter, Pamela M. 1998. *Most German of the Arts: Musicology and Society from the Weimar Republic to the End of Hitler's Reich*. New Haven: Yale University Press.

Praz, Mario. 1970. *The Romantic Agony*. Trans. Angust Davidson. 2nd edn. London: Oxford University Press. *La carne, la morte e il diavolo nella letteratura romantica*. Milan: La Cultura.

Price, Lucien. 1936. *We Northmen*. Boston: Little, Brown.

——. 1988. *The Furies*. All Souls 3. Boston: Nimrod Press.

Prieberg, Fred K. 1982. *Musik im NS-Staat*. Frankfurt am Main: Fischer.

Pries, Christine, ed. 1989. *Das Erhabene: Zwischen Grenzerfahrung und Grössenwahn.* Weinheim: Acta Humaniora.

Rahkonen, Margit. 2004. *Alie Lindberg: Suomalaisen pianistin taiteilijaura 1800-luvulla.* Helsinki: Sibelius-Akatemia.

Rajala, Panu. 1983. *F. E. Sillanpää vuosina 1888–1923.* Helsinki: Suomalaisen Kirjallisuuden Seura.

——. 1988. *Siljan synty: F. E. Sillanpää vuosina 1923–1931.* Helsinki: Suomalaisen Kirjallisuuden Seura.

——. 1993. *Korkea päivä ja ehtoo: F. E. Sillanpää vuosina 1931–1964.* Helsinki: Suomalaisen Kirjallisuuden Seura.

Ranta-Meyer, Tuire. 2003. 'Ei päivää ilman kynänpiirtoa: Erkki Melartinin säveltäjäntyön, teosten tyylin ja reseption tarkastelua vuosina 1896–1911' (Master's thesis, University of Jyväskylä).

Rapetti, Rodolphe. 2000. 'Ad Astra: Gallen-Kallela ja kansainvälinen symbolismi'. In *Tuntematon horisontti: Suomen taidetta, 1870–1920.* Ed. Riitta Ojanperä, pp. 48–59. Ateneumin julkaisut 20. Helsinki: Ateneum.

Rathkolb, Oliver. 1991. *Führertreu und gottbegnadet: Künstlereliten im Dritten Reich.* Vienna: Österreichischer Bundesverlag.

Reinisch, Frank. 2000. 'Wiederholte Annäherung: Jean Sibelius und Breitkopf & Härtel'. In Jäntti, Vogt and Holtkamp 2000, pp. 175–98.

Revers, Peter. 1996. 'Jean Sibelius and Vienna'. In Goss 1996, pp. 13–34.

——. 1999. 'Das Klavierquartett von Jean Sibelius im Kontext der Gattungsgeschichte'. In *50 Jahre Musikwissenschaftliches Institut in Hamburg: Bestandaufnahme, aktuelle Forschung, Ausblick.* Ed. Peter Petersen and Helmut Rösing, pp. 337–53. Frankfurt am Main: Lang.

Rickards, Guy. 1997. *Jean Sibelius.* London: Phaidon.

Rienäcker, Gerd. 1996. 'Die Kunst des feinsten Übergangs? Notate zur Orchesterdramaturgie der 4. Sinfonie von Jean Sibelius'. In *Musica Baltica: Interregionale musikkulturelle Beziehungen im Ostseeraum.* Ed. Ekkehard Ochs, Nico Schüler and Lutz Winkler, pp. 168–78. Deutsche Musik im Osten 8. Sankt Augustin: Academia.

Riethmüller, Albrecht. 1988. *Ferruccio Busonis Poetik.* Mainz: Schott.

Riikonen, Hannu K. 2000. 'Draaman ja lyriikan klassismia maailmansotien välisenä aikana'. In *Kivettyneet ihanteet? Klassismin nousu maailmansotien välisessä Euroopassa.* Ed. Marja Härmänmaa and Timo Vihavainen, pp. 254–77. Jyväskylä: Atena.

Rilke, Rainer Maria. 1986. *Rodin and Other Prose Pieces.* Trans. G. Craig Houston. London: Quartet.

Ringbom, Nils-Eric. 1954. *Jean Sibelius: A Master and His Work.* Trans. G. I. C. Ceurcy. Norman: University of Oklahoma Press. *Jean Sibelius: Ein Meister und sein Werk.* Olten: Walter, 1950.

Ronka, Ilmari. 1948. 'The Sibelius I Knew'. In *Music and Dance in California and the West.* Ed. Richard D. Saunders, p. 46. Pasadena: Bureau of Musical Research.

Rookmaaker, Hendrik Roelof. 1972. *Gauguin and Nineteenth-Century Art Theory.* Amsterdam: Swets & Zeitlinger.

Rösing, Helmuth. 1998. 'Synästhesie'. In *Die Musik in Geschichte und Gegenwart,* Sachteil 9, 2nd edn. Ed. Ludwig Finscher, cols. 168–85. Kassel: Bärenreiter; Stuttgart: Metzler.

Ross, Alex. 2007. *The Rest Is Noise: Listening to the Twentieth Century.* New York: Farrar, Straus and Giroux.

Rousseau, Jean-Jacques.1995. *Confessions*. In Rousseau, *Œuvres complètes*. Ed. B. Gagnebin *et al.* Paris: Gallimard.

Rouzaud, Daniel, Claude Beaud and Claude Brachet. 1994. *Saint-Germain-En-Laye*. N.p.: Images d'Antan.

Rubinstein, Arthur. 1980. *My Many Years*. New York: Knopf.

Rufer, Josef. 1959. *Das Werk Arnold Schönbergs*. Kassel: Bärenreiter.

Rummenhöller, Peter. 1989. *Romantik in der Musik: Analysen, Portraits, Reflexionen*. Munich: Deutscher Taschenbuch Verlag; Kassel: Bärenreiter.

Runeberg, Johan Ludvig. 1879. *Johan Ludvig Runebergs efterlemnade skrifter*. Vol. 2. Wiborg: Clouberg.

Salmenhaara, Erkki. 1969. *Das musikalische Material und seine Behandlung in den Werken 'Apparations', 'Atmosphères' und 'Requiem' von György Ligeti*. Regensburg: Bosse.

——. 1970. *Tapiola*. Helsinki: Suomen Musiikkitieteellinen Seura.

——. 1984. *Jean Sibelius*. Helsinki: Tammi.

——. 1985. 'Kalevala, Sibelius ja Suomen säveltaide'. *Musiikki* 15, 1–2, pp. 75–92.

——, ed. 1987. 'Leevi Madetoja: Kirjoituksia musiikista'. Special issue of *Musiikki* 17, 3–4, pp. 1–190.

——. 1996a. *Jean Sibelius: Violin Concerto*. Ed. Heinrich W. Schwab and Harald Herresthal. Meisterwerke Nordischer Musik 1. Wilhelmshaven: Noetzel.

——. 1996b. *Kansallisromantiikan valtavirta, 1885–1918*. Suomen musiikin historia 2. Porvoo: Werner Söderström.

——. 1996c. *Uuden musiikin kynnyksellä, 1907–1958*. Suomen musiikin historia 3. Porvoo: Werner Söderström.

——. 1998. 'Sibelius's "Imatra Symphony"'. In Murtomäki, Kilpeläinen and Väisänen 1998, pp. 15–26.

Salminen, Aarne, ed. 2001. *Lyhyt Kalevala: Elias Lönnrotin 1862 tekemän lyhennelmän mukaan*. Helsinki: Suomalaisen Kirjallisuuden Seura.

Sarajas-Korte, Salme. 1966. *Suomen varhaissymbolismi ja sen lähteet: Tutkielma Suomen maalaustaiteesta, 1891–1895*. Helsinki: Otava.

——. 1995. 'The Finnish View of Symbolist Painting: From Antinoüs Myth to Kalevala Mysticism'. In *Lost Paradise: Symbolist Europe*. Exh. cat., pp. 285–92. Montreal: Montreal Museum of Fine Arts.

Sariola, Helmriitta. 2001. 'Väri'. In Ojanperä 2001, pp. 192–231.

Sather, Martin. 1994. *Die Kunstpolitik Wilhelms II*. Konstanz: Hartung-Gorre.

Savolainen, Irma. 2004. 'Hopeamaljasta siniseen tuoliin: Ainolan irtaimistosta'. In Suvikumpu 2004, pp. 137–53.

Schaal, Susanne. 1998. 'Abschied vom Leben oder musikpolitisches Manifest? Die "Vier letzten Lieder" von Richard Strauss'. In *Musik als Text: Bericht über den Internationalen Kongress der Gesellschaft für Musikforschung Freiburg im Breisgau 1993*. Vol. 2, pp. 548–51. Kassel: Bärenreiter.

Schaarwächter, Jürgen. 1995. *Die britische Sinfonie, 1914–1945*. Cologne: Dohr.

Schama, Simon. 1995. *Landscape and Memory*. London: HarperCollins.

Scheit, Gerhard, and Walter Svoboda. 2002. *Feindbild Gustav Mahler: Zur antisemitischen Abwehr der Moderne in Österreich*. Vienna: Sonderzahl.

Scherliess, Volker. 1983. *Igor Strawinsky und seine Zeit*. Laaber: Laaber.

Schindler, Anton. [1840] 1977. *Biographie von Ludwig van Beethoven*. Ed. Eberhardt Klemm. 3rd edn. Leipzig: Reclam.

Schlesinger, Robert. 1997. *Gott sei mit unserm Führer*. Vienna: Löcker.

Schmalenbach, Werner. 2001. 'Frage nicht nach Namen! Wider den Unfug, in Schwarzafrika individuelle Künstler zu suchen'. *Frankfurter Allgemeine Zeitung*, 19 July, p. 43.

Schmied, Wieland. 1989. *De Chirico und sein Schatten: Metaphysische und surrealistische Tendenzen in der Kunst des 20. Jahrhunderts*. Munich: Prestel.

——. 2002. *Giorgio de Chirico: The Endless Journey*. Munich: Prestel. Giorgio de Chirico: Reise ohne Ende. Munich: Prestel, 2001.

Schmitz, Arnold. 1927. *Das romantische Beethovenbild: Darstellung und Kritik*. Berlin: Dümmler.

Schneider, Marcel. 1982. 'Symbolist Music'. In *The Symbolist Movement in the Literature of European Languages*. Ed. Anna Balakian, pp. 471–81. Budapest: Akadémiai Kiadó.

Schneider-Seidel, Kerstin Mira. 2002. *Antike Sujets und moderne Musik: Untersuchung zur französischen Musik um 1900*. Stuttgart: Metzler.

Schoenberg, Arnold. 1965. 'Analysis of the Four Orchestral Songs Opus 22'. Trans. Claudio Spies. *Perspectives of New Music* 3, 2 (Spring–Summer), 1–21.

——. 1978. *Theory of Harmony*. Trans. Roy E. Carter. Berkeley: University of California Press. *Harmonielehre*. Vienna: Universal Edition, 2001.

——. 1984. 'Folkloristic Symphonies'. In *Style and Idea*. Ed. Leonard Stein. Trans. Leo Black, pp. 161–6. Berkeley: University of California Press.

Schopenhauer, Arthur. 1977. *The World as Will and Idea*. Trans. R. B. Haldane and J. Kemp. New York: AMS Press. *Die Welt als Wille und Vorstellung*. Zurich: Diogenes, 1977.

Schreiber, Ingeborg. 1981. *Max Reger in seinen Konzerten*. Part 2: *Programme der Konzerte Regers*. Bonn: Dümmler.

Schreker, Franz. 1919. 'Meine musikdramatische Idee'. *Musikblätter des Anbruch* 1, 1 (November), pp. 6–7.

Schubert, Giselher, ed. 1997. *Biographische Konstellation und künstlerisches Handeln*. Mainz: Schott.

Schumann, Robert. 1946. *On Music and Musicians*. New York: Pantheon. *Gesammelte Schriften über Musik und Musiker*. Vol. 1. Ed. Martin Kreisig. 5th edn. Leipzig: Breitkopf & Härtel, 1914.

Schwab, Gabriele. 1987. *Entgrenzungen und Entgrenzungsmythen: Zur Anthropologie der Subjektivität im modernen angloamerikanischen Roman*. Stuttgart: Steiner.

Schwab, Heinrich W. 1982. 'Das Lyrische Klavierstück und der nordische Ton'. In *Gattung und Werk in der Musikgeschichte Norddeutschlands und Skandinaviens*. Ed. Friedhelm Krummacher and Heinrich W. Schwab, pp. 136–53. Kieler Schriften zur Musikwissenschaft 26. Kassel: Bärenreiter.

——. 1992. 'Zur Kontroverse um "Weltmusik und Nordischer Ton"'. In *Weltgeltung und Regionalität: Nordeuropa um 1900*. Ed. Robert Bohn and Michael Engelbrecht, pp. 197–212. Frankfurt am Main: Lang.

——. 2001a. 'Epilog: Musik und Landschaft'. In *Musikgeschichte Nordeuropas*. Ed. Greger Andersson. Stuttgart: Metzler.

——. 2001b. 'Mozarts Klaviersonate A-Dur (K 331): Gattungsnorm und Individualität'. In Tyrväinen, Lappalainen, Mäkelä and Vierimaa 2001, pp. 273–89.

Schwartz, Manuela. 1999. *Wagner-Rezeption und französische Oper des Fin de siècle: Untersuchungen zu Vincent d'Indys Fervaal.* Sinzig: Studio.
——. 2000. 'Visualisierung der Musik – Musikalisierung der Bilder: Zur konzeptionellen Wende in Oper, Schauspiel und Film des Fin de siècle'. In *Zeitenwenden – Wendezeiten: Von der Achsenzeit bis zum Fall der Mauer.* Ed. Peter Segl, pp. 151–67. Dettelbach: Röll.
——. 2002. '"Une union encore plus intime de la poésie et de la musique": Schauspielmusik am Ende des 19. Jahrhunderts in Frankreich'. In *Stimmen – Klänge – Töne: Synergien im szenischen Spiel.* Ed. Hans-Peter Bayerdörfer, pp. 253–64. Tübingen: Gunter Narr.
Schwarz, Joachim. 1998. 'Structural and Formal Principles in Sibelius's *Lemminkäinen Suite*'. In Murtomäki, Kilpeläinen and Väisänen 1998, pp. 303–10.
Schweitzer, Albert. 1966. *J. S. Bach.* Trans. Ernest Newman. New York: Dover.
Schwemmer, Oswald. 1987. *Über Natur: Philosophische Beiträge zum Naturverständnis.* Frankfurt am Main: Klostermann.
Seebohm, Reinhard. 1969. 'Pfitzner und sein Zeitgenosse Sibelius'. *Mitteilungen der Hans Pfitzner-Gesellschaft* 25 (October), pp. 1–10.
Sembach, Klaus-Jürgen. [1990] 1996. *Jugendstil: Die Utopie der Versöhnung.* Cologne: Taschen.
Severini, Gino. 1921. *Du cubisme au classicisme.* Paris: Povolozky.
Shlifstein, S., ed. 2000. *Sergei Prokofiev: Autobiography, Articles, Reminiscences.* Trans. Rose Prokofieva. Honolulu, HI: University Press of the Pacific, 2000.
Sibelius, Jean. [1896] 1980. 'Några synpunkter beträffande folkmusiken och dess inflytande på tonkonsten'. Ed. Ilkka Oramo. *Musiikki* 10, 2, pp. 106–22.
Sietz, Reinhold. 1961. 'Niemann'. In *Die Musik in Geschichte und Gegenwart. Allgemeine Enzyklopädie der Musik.* Ed. Friedrich Blume, cols. 1518–21. Kassel: Bärenreiter.
Sihvo, Hannes. 2002. *Elävä Kivi: Aleksis Kivi aikanansa.* Helsinki: Suomalaisen Kirjallisuuden Seura.
Siikala, Anna-Leena, Lauri Harvilahti and Senni Timonen, eds. 2004. *Kalevala ja laulettu runo.* Helsinki: Suomalaisen Kirjallisuuden Seura.
Sillanpää, Franz Emil. 1953. *Poika eli elämäänsä: Muistelua.* Helsinki: Otava.
Simpson, Robert. [1952] 1986. 'Sibelius, Nielsen and the Symphonic Problem'. In *Carl Nielsen: Symphonist.* Lonson: Kahn & Averill.
Sinisalo, Johdanto Soili. 2001a. 'Elämänvoimaa ja unelmia'. In Ojanperä 2001, pp. 8–13.
——. 2001b. 'Alkuperäisyyden kaipuu: Primitiivisyys'. In Ojanperä 2001, pp. 78–83.
Sirén, Valerie. 1996. 'The Songs'. In Goss 1996, pp. 171–200.
Sirén, Vesa. 1999. 'More Pathos, Please!' *Finnish Music Quarterly* 2, pp. 31–41.
——. 2000. *Aina poltti sikaria: Jean Sibelius aikalaisten silmin.* Helsinki: Otava.
——. 2002. 'Uusiko Sibelius Aallottaret turhaan?'. *Helsingin Sanomat,* 24 October, p. B9.
——. 2004. 'Sibeliuksen kirjeet Armas Järnefeltille löytyivät'. *Helsingin Sanomat,* 12 September, p. C1.
Sivuoja-Gunaratnam, Anne. 2003. 'Aino Acktén rooli Juhan Libretistinä'. In *Veisuin ylistäkää.* Ed. Jarmo Hakkarainen, Ville Kiiveri and Pekka Metso, pp. 175–94. Festschift Hilkka Seppälä, Publications of Orthodox Theology 32. Joensuu: University of Joensuu.
Sjöblom, Paul. 1944 'Sibelius – Pohjolan profeetta'. *Suomen Kuvalehti* 50, 16 December, pp. 1456–7.
——. 2000. *Finland from the Inside: Eyewitness Reports of a Finnish-American Journalist 1938–1997.* Ed. Glenda Dawn Goss. Helsinki: New Bridge Press.

Smeds, Kerstin. 1996. *Helsingfors – Paris: Finland på världsutställningarna, 1851–1900*. Helsinki: Svenska Litteratur Sällskapet i Finland and Finska historiska samfundet.

Sola, Wäinö. 1952. *Wäinö Sola kertoo II*. Porvoo: Werner Söderström.

Sorabji, Kaikhosru. 1947. *Mi contra Fa*. London: Porcupine.

Spanuth, August. 1912. 'Musikalischer Mammutismus'. *Signale für die musikalische Welt* 8 (21 February), pp. 243–5.

Splitt, Gerhard. 1987. *Richard Strauss, 1933–1935: Ästhetik und Musikpolitik zu Beginn der nationalsozialistischen Herrschaft*. Pfaffenweiler: Centaurus.

Stege, Fritz. 1936. 'Jean Sibelius und die nordische Tonwelt'. *Hochschule und Ausland* 14, pp. 44–50.

——. 1942. 'Musik der Wälder'. In *Das Antlitz Finnlands*. Ed. Herta von Grönhagen and Yrjö von Grönhagen, pp. 138–47. Berlin: Wiking.

Stein, Erwin. 1987. *Arnold Schoenberg: Letters*. Trans. Eithne Wilkins and Ernst Kaiser. Berkeley: University of California Press. *Ausgewählte Briefe*. Ed. Erwin Stein. Mainz: Schott, 1958.

Steiner, Stefanie. 2001. *Zwischen Kirche, Bühne und Konzertsaal: Vokalmusik von Haydns 'Schöpfung' bis zu Beethovens 'Neunter'*. Kassel: Bärenreiter.

Stephan, Rudolf. [1970] 1985. 'Gibt es ein Geheimnis der Form bei Richard Wagner?'. In *Vom musikalischen Denken: Gesammelte Vorträge*. Ed. Rainer Damm and Andreas Traub, pp. 63–9. Mainz: Schott.

Stewen, Riikka. 2000. 'Démasquée, 1888'. In *Tuntematon horisontti: Suomen taidetta, 1870–1920*. Ed. Riitta Ojanperä, pp. 100–103. Ateneumin julkaisut 20. Helsinki: Ateneum.

Straus, Joseph Nathan. 1990. *Remaking the Past*. Cambridge, Mass.: Harvard University Press.

Strauss, Botho. 2001. *Der Narr und seine Frau heute Abend in 'Pancomedia'*. Munich: Carl Hanser.

Stravinsky, Igor. 1947. *Poetics of Music: In the Form of Six Lessons*. Trans. Arthur Knodel and Ingolf Dahl. Cambridge, Mass.: Harvard University Press. *Poétique musicale sous forme de six leçons*. Cambridge, Mass.: Harvard University Press, 1942.

Streller, Friedbert. 2003. *Sergej Prokofjew und seine Zeit*. Laaber: Laaber.

Strömborg, J. E. 1928–1931. *Biografiska anteckningar om Johan Ludvig Runeberg* 1–4. Helsinki: Svenska Litteratursällskapet i Finland.

Stuckenschmidt, Hans Heinz. 1958. *Schöpfer der Neuen Musik*. Frankfurt am Main: Suhrkamp.

——. 1978. *Schoenberg: His Life, World, and Work*. Trans. Humphrey Searle. New York: Schirmer Books. *Schönberg: Leben, Umwelt, Werk*. Zurich: Atlantis, 1974.

——. 1979. *Zum Hören geboren: Ein Leben mit der Musik unserer Zeit*. Munich: Piper.

Suchoff, Benjamin, ed. 1976. *Béla Bartók: Essays*. Béla Bartók Archives: Studies in Musicology 8. New York: St. Martin's.

Sulkunen, Irma. 2004. *Suomalaisen Kirjallisuuden Seura, 1831–1892*. Helsinki: Suomalaisen Kirjallisuuden Seura.

Suomalainen, Yrjö. 1950. *Oskar Merikanto: Suomen kotien säveltäjä*. Helsinki: Otava.

——. 1952. *Robert Kajanus: Hänen elämänsä ja toimintansa*. Helsinki: Otava.

Suvikumpu, Liisa, ed. 2004. *Ainola: Jean ja Aino Sibeliuksen koti*. Helsinki: Suomalaisen Kirjallisuuden Seura.

Szabolcsi, Bence, ed. 1972. *Béla Bartók: Musiksprachen; Aufsätze und Vorträge*. Leipzig: Reclam.

TALAS, SuviSirkku, ed. 2000. *Aino Sibeliuksen kirjeitä Järnefeltin suvun jäsenille.* Helsinki: Suomalaisen Kirjallisuuden Seura.

TALAS, SuviSirkku. 2001. *Sydämen aamu: Aino Järnefeltin ja Jean Sibeliuksen kihlausajan kirjeitä.* Helsinki: Suomalaisen Kirjallisuuden Seura.

——. 2003. *Tulen synty: Aino ja Jean Sibeliuksen kirjeenvaihtoa, 1892–1904.* Helsinki: Suomalaisen Kirjallisuuden Seura.

——. 2004. '"Ja minun pitäisi olla välittäjänä sinun ja mailman välillä": Aino Sibeliuksen elämää maailmankuulun säveltäjän puolisona'. In Suvikumpu 2004, pp. 83–102.

TAMMARO, Ferruccio. 1984. *Jean Sibelius.* Turin: ERI-Edizioni RAI.

TANZBERGER, Ernst. 1943. *Die symphonischen Dichtungen von Jean Sibelius: Eine inhalts- und formanalytische Studie.* Ed. Otto C. A. zur Nedden. Musik und Nation 4. Würzburg: Triltsch.

——. 1962. *Jean Sibelius: Eine Monographie.* Wiesbaden: Breitkopf & Härtel.

TARUSKIN, Richard. 1997. *Defining Russia Musically: Historical and Hermeneutical Essays.* Princeton, N.J.: Princeton University Press.

TAUSCHER, Hildegard. 1940. 'Finnisches Volkslied'. *Allgemeine Musikzeitung* 67, pp. 37–41.

TAWASTSTJERNA, Erik T. 1997. *Sibelius.* Helsinki: Otava.

——. 2003. 'Die Wiener Klassik in den Klavierstücken von Jean Sibelius'. In Krones 2003b, pp. 93–101.

TAWASTSTJERNA, Erik W. 1957. *Ton och tolkning: Sibelius-studier.* Helsinki: Schildts.

——. 1976. *Sibelius.* Vol. 1: *1865–1905.* Ed. and trans. Robert Layton. London: Faber and Faber.

——. [1979a] 1987. *Jean Sibelius: The Complete Original Piano Music.* BIS 153, compact disc. Liner notes.

——. 1979b. 'Über Adornos Sibelius-Kritik'. In *Adorno und die Musik.* Ed. Otto Kolleritsch, pp. 112–24. Graz: Institut für Wertungsforschung.

——. 1986. *Sibelius.* Vol. 2: *1904–1914.* Ed. and trans. Robert Layton. London: Faber and Faber.

——. 1988. *Jean Sibelius 5.* Helsinki: Otava.

——. 1989. *Jean Sibelius 1–4.* 2nd edn. Helsinki: Otava.

——. 1991. *Jean Sibelius: Åren 1904–1914.* Ed. Gitta Henning. Helsinki: Söderströms.

——. 1992. *Jean Sibelius: Åren 1865–1893.* Ed. Gitta Henning. Helsinki: Söderströms.

——. 1994. *Jean Sibelius: Åren 1893–1904.* Ed. Gitta Henning. Helsinki: Söderströms.

——. 1996. *Jean Sibelius: Åren 1914–1920.* Ed. Gitta Henning. Helsinki: Söderströms.

——. 1997a. *Jean Sibelius: Åren 1920–1957.* Ed. Gitta Henning. Helsinki: Söderströms.

——. 1997b. *Sibelius.* Vol. 3: *1914–1957.* Ed. and trans. Robert Layton. London: Faber and Faber.

TAYLOR, Charles. 1989. *Sources of the Self: The Making of the Modern Identity.* Cambridge, Mass.: Harvard University Press.

TEUBER, Bernhard. 2003. 'Imaginatio borealis in einer Topographie der Kultur'. In *Ultima Thule: Bilder des Nordens von der Antike bis zur Gegenwart.* Ed. Annelore Engel-Braunschmidt, Gerhard Fouquet, Wiebke von Hinden and Inken Schmidt, pp. 173–201. Imaginatio borealis: Bilder des Nordens 1. Frankfurt am Main: Lang.

THAER, Günther. 1936. 'Jean Sibelius: Dem finnischen Meister als Gruss und Gedenken'. *Nationalsozialistische Monatshefte* 7, 1, pp. 62–5.

TIILIKAINEN, Jukka. 1998a. 'Introduction'. In *Jean Sibelius.Complete Works,* Series 8, vol. 2. Ed. Jukka Tiilikainen.Wiesbaden: Breitkopf & Härtel, pp. viii–ix.

——. 1998b. 'Palapelistä teokseksi: Jean Sibeliuksen laulun Dolce far niente synnystä musiikillisten lähteiden perusteella'. *Musiikki,* 28, 3, pp. 308–44.

——. 1998c. 'Uusi laitos Jean Sibeliuksen laulusta Höstkväll op. 38 nro 1'. *Musiikki* 28, 3, pp. 284–307.
——. 2000. 'Introduction'. In *Jean Sibelius: Complete Works*, Series 8, vol. 3. Ed. Jukka Tiilikainen. Wiesbaden: Breitkopf & Härtel, pp. viii–x.
——. 2003. 'The Evolution of Jean Sibelius's Songs as Seen in His Musical Manuscripts'. In Huttunen, Kilpeläinen and Murtomäki 2003, pp. 39–49.
——. 2004. 'The Genesis of the Violin Concerto'. In Grimley 2004a, pp. 66–80.
TÖRNE, Bengt de. 1937. *Sibelius: A Close-Up*. London: Faber and Faber.
TOUCHARD, Maurice. 1914. 'Un musicien finlandais: Sibelius'. *La Nouvelle Revue* 4, 11 (January), pp. 55–65.
TOVEY, Donald Francis. 1981. *Essays in Musical Analysis*. Vol. 1: *Symphonies and Other Orchestral Works*. London: Oxford University Press.
——. 1981. 'Sibelius: Violin Concerto Op. 47'. In *Essays in Musical Analysis*. Vol. 2: *Concertos and Choral Works*, pp. 206–10. London: Oxford University Press.
TROJAHN, Manfred. 1987. 'Ein verpasstes Jubiläum: Zum 30. Todestag von Jean Sibelius am 20. September 1987'. *Musica* 41, 5, pp. 424–6.
TUAN, Yi-Fu. [1974] 1990. *Topophilia: A Study of Environmental Perception, Attitudes, and Values*. New York: Columbia University Press.
TYRVÄINEN, Helena. 1998. 'Sibelius at the Paris Universal Exposition of 1900'. In Murtomäki, Kilpeläinen and Väisänen 1998, pp. 114–28.
——. 2003. 'Helsinki, Saint Petersburg, Paris'. Finnish Music Quarterly 1, pp. 52–9.
TYRVÄINEN, Helena, Seija Lappalainen, Tomi Mäkelä and Irma Vierimaa, eds. 2001. *Muualla, täällä: Kirjoituksia elämästä, kulttuurista, musiikista*. Jyväskylä: Atena.
VÄISÄNEN, Armas O. 1921. 'Jean Sibelius vaikutelmistaan'. *Kalevalaseuran vuosikirja* 1, pp. 77–81.
VAINIO, Matti. 2002. *'Nouskaa aatteet!' Robert Kajanus, elämä ja taide*. Porvoo: Werner Söderström.
VAINIO, Matti, and Pentti SALOLAINEN, eds. 2002. *Aino Ackté: Elämänkaari kirjeiden valossa*. Porvoo: Werner Söderström.
VARÈSE, Edgard. 1971. 'The Liberation of Sound (New Instruments and New Music, 1936)'. In *Perspectives on American Composers*. Ed. Benjamin Boretz and Edward T. Cone, pp. 25–33. New York: W. W. Norton.
VARGES, Kurt. 1940. 'Die geistige Kultur um Jean Sibelius'. *Universum* 57, 9 (28 November), p. 220.
VAUGHAN, William. 2000. 'Spiritual Landscapes'. In *Kingdom of the Soul: Symbolist Art in Germany, 1870–1920*. Ed. Ingrid Ehrhardt and Simon Reynolds, pp. 79–107. Munich: Prestel.
VAUGHAN WILLIAMS, Ralph. [1963] 1986. 'Sibelius (1865–1957): A Tribute Written on the Occasion of His Ninetieth Birthday'. In *National Music and Other Essays*. Ed. Michael Kennedy, pp. 261–4. Oxford: Oxford University Press.
VIDAL, Pierre. 1995. 'The Symphonic Poem of Jean Sibelius and the European Tradition of the Form'. In *Proceedings from the First International Jean Sibelius Conference in Helsinki 1990*. Ed. Eero Tarasti, pp. 203–7. Helsinki: Sibelius-Akatemia.
VIERIMAA, Irma, Kari KILPELÄINEN and Anne SIVUOJA-GUNARATNAM, eds. 1998. *Siltoja ja synteesejä: Esseitä semiotiikasta, kulttuurista ja taiteesta*. Helsinki: Gaudeamus.
VIGNAL, Marc. 2004. *Jean Sibelius*. Paris: Fayard.

VILJANEN, Lauri. 1950. *Taisteleva humanismi: Kulttuurikriitillisiä ääriviivoja Goethestänykypäivään*. Hämeenlinna: Karisto.

VIRTANEN, Timo. 1998. '"Pohjola's Daughter" in the Light of Sketch Studies'. In Murtomäki, Kilpeläinen and Väisänen 1998, pp. 315–24.

——. 1999. 'Sibeliuksen Pohjolan tytär: Käsikirjoitukset, syntyhistoria ja ohjelmallinen tausta'. *Musiikki* 29, 3, pp. 243–61.

——. 2003. 'The Third Symphony: A Sketch Study'. In Huttunen, Kilpeläinen and Murtomäki 2003, pp. 59–68.

——. 2005. *Jean Sibelius, Symphony No. 3: Manuscript Study and Analysis*. Studia Musica 26. Helsinki: Sibelius Academy.

VOLLSNES, Arvid O. 2002. 'Grieg und die Natur: Empfindung und Malerei'. In Kreft 2002, pp. 68–83.

VRIES, Willem de. 2001. 'Der Sonderstab Musik des Einsatzstabes Reichsleiter Rosenberg: Weitere Recherchen nach dem Schicksal von Beutemusik in Polen und Russland'. In Foerster, Hust and Mahling 2001, pp. 173–80.

WACZKAT, Andreas, ed. 2003. *Wozu Biographik? Zur Rolle biographischer Methoden in Vermittlungsprozessen und Musikanalyse*. Rostock: Universität Rostock.

WAENERBERG, Annika. 2002. 'Tunteesta ja havainnosta maisemaan: Eero Järnefeltin maisemakäsitys päiväkirjamerkintöjen valossa'. In Lindqvist 2002, pp. 203–21.

——. 2004a. 'Eero Järnefelt ja muita suomalaistaiteilijoita 1890-luvun Roomassa — kokemuksia ja kommentteja'. In *Rooman kävijät: Taiteen ja historian löytöretkiä*. Ed Annika Waenerberg, pp. 123–43. Jyväskylä: Atena.

——. 2004b. 'Syysmaisema vai kansallismaisema: Eero Järnefeltin Kolin kuvien tarkennetut kehykset'. In *Suomi-kuvasta mielenmaisemaan: Kansallismaisemat 1800- ja 1900-luvun vaihteen maalaustaiteessa*. Ed. Ville Lukkarinen and Annika Waenerberg, pp. 186–328. Helsinki: Suomalaisen Kirjallisuuden Seura.

WAGNER, Richard. [1850] 1982. 'Das Judentum in der Musik'. In *Mein Denken: Eine Auswahl der Schriften*. Ed. Martin Gregor-Dellin, pp. 173–90. Munich: Piper.

WALDMANN, Guido. 1958. 'Kalinnikow'. In *Die Musik in Geschichte und Gegenwart*. Vol. 7. Ed. Friedrich Blume, col. 442. Kassel: Bärenreiter.

WALLNER, Bo. 2001. 'Die symphonische Ära'. In *Musikgeschichte Nordeuropas*. Ed. Greger Andersson, pp. 281–306. Stuttgart: Metzler.

WALTERSHAUSEN, Hermann W. S. Freiherr von. 1920. *Siegfried-Idyll; oder, Die Rückkehr zur Natur*. Munich: Bruckmann.

WASSERMANN, Jakob. 1928. *Lebensdienst: Gesammelte Studien; Erfahrungen und Reden aus 3 Jahrzehnten*. Leipzig: Grethlein.

WEBER, Horst, and Manuela SCHWARTZ, eds. 2003. *Quellen zur Geschichte emigrierter Musiker, 1933–1950*. Vol. 1: *Kalifornien*. Munich: Saur.

WEIDBERG, Ron. 2003. 'Sonic Design in Jean Sibelius's Orchestral Music'. In Huttunen, Kilpeläinen and Murtomäki 2003, pp. 216–26.

WELSCH, Wolfgang. 1988. *Unsere postmoderne Moderne*. Weinheim: Acta Humaniora.

—— 1989. 'Adornos Ästhetik: Eine implizite Ästhetik des Erhabenen'. In Pries 1989, pp. 185–213.

——. 1990. *Ästhetisches Denken*. Stuttgart: Reclam.

WENNEWIRTA, Ludwig. 1950. *Eero Järnefelt*. Helsinki: Otava.

WERBECK, Walter. 1996. *Die Tondichtungen von Richard Strauss*. Documente und Studien zu Richard Strauss 2. Tutzing: Schneider.

WHITTALL, Arnold. 1997. 'Personal Style, Impersonal Structure? Music Analysis and Nationality'. In Mäkelä 1997a, pp. 17–25.
——. 1999. *Musical Composition in the Twentieth Century*. Oxford: Oxford University Press.
WIECHERT, Bernd. 1997. *Heinrich von Herzogenberg, 1843–1900: Studien zu Leben und Werk*. Göttingen: Vandenhoeck & Ruprecht.
WIEGANDT, Matthias. 1997. *Vergessene Symphonik? Studien zu Joachim Raff, Carl Reinecke und zum Problem der Epigonalität in der Musik*. Sinzig: Studio.
WIGGERSHAUS, Rolf. 1988. *Die Frankfurter Schule*. Frankfurt am Main: Suhrkamp.
WILLIAMS, Hermine Weigel. 1998. *Sibelius and His Masonic Music: Sounds in 'Silence'*. Studies in the History and Interpretation of Music 59. Lewiston, N.Y.: Edwin Mellen Press.
WINCKELMANN, Johann Joachim. 1756. *Gedanken über die Nachahmung der Griechischen Werke in der Malerey und der Bildhauerkunst*. Dresden/Leipzig: Walther.
WIND, Edgar. 1985. *Art and Anarchy*. 3rd edn. London: Duckworth, 1985.
WITESCHNIK, Alexander. 1940. 'Jean Sibelius. Zum 75. Geburtstag des finnischen Nationalmusikers'. *Der getreue Eckart* 18, p. xlii.
WOOD, Henry. 1938. *My Life of Music*. London: Gollancz.
WÖRNER, Karl Heinrich. 1949. *Die Musik der Gegenwart*. Mainz: Schott.
——. 1973. *Karlheinz Stockhausen: Life and Work*. Trans. Bill Hopkins. London: Faber and Faber. *Karlheinz Stockhausen: Werk und Wollen, 1950–1962*. Ed. Heinrich Lindlar. Kontrapunkte 6. Rodenkirchen: Tonger, 1963.
Wulf, Joseph. 1983. *Musik im Dritten Reich: Eine Dokumentation*. Frankfurt am Main: Ullstein.
WYZEWA, Théodore de. 1885. 'Peinture Wagnérienne, le Salon de 1885'. *Revue wagnérienne* 5 (8 June), pp. 154–6.
——. 1886. 'Notes sur la peinture Wagnérienne et le Salon de 1886'. *Revue wagnérienne* 12, pp. 100–103.
ZEITLER, Rudolf. 1990. *Skandinavische Kunst um 1900*. Leipzig: Seemann.
ZILLIACUS, Emil. 1905. *Den nyare franska poesin och antiken*. Helsinki: Handelstryckeriet.
ZUKOWSKY, John, ed. 1987. *Chicago Architecture, 1872–1922: Birth of a Metropolis*. Munich: Prestel-Verlag in association with the Art Institute of Chicago.
ZWEIG, Stefan. 1944. *Die Welt von Gestern: Erinnerungen eines Europäers*. Stockholm: Fischer.

Index of Works by Jean Sibelius

General Index